The Principle of Mutual Recognition in EU Law

OXFORD STUDIES IN EUROPEAN LAW

Series Editors: Paul Craig, Professor of English Law at St John's College, Oxford and Gráinne de Búrca Professor of Law at New York University School of Law

The aim of this series is to publish important and original research on EU law. The focus is on scholarly monographs, with a particular emphasis on those which are interdisciplinary in nature. Edited collections of essays will also be included where they are appropriate. The series is wide in scope and aims to cover studies of particular areas of substantive and of institutional law, historical works, theoretical studies, and analyses of current debates, as well as questions of perennial interest such as the relationship between national and EU law and the novel forms of governance emerging in and beyond Europe. The fact that many of the works are interdisciplinary will make the series of interest to all those concerned with the governance and operation of the EU.

OTHER TITLES IN THIS SERIES

The Coherence of EU Free Movement Law
Constitutional Responsibility and the Court of Justice
Niamh Nic Shuibhne

European Law and New Health Technologies
Edited by Mark L Flear, Anne-Maree Farrell, Tamara K Hervey, and Thérèse Murphy

The Legal Effect of EU Agreements
Mario Mendez

The Enforcement of EU Law
The Role of the European Commission
Stine Andersen

European Agencies
Law and Practice of Accountability
Madalina Busuioc

The Foundations of European Union Competition Law
The Objective and Principles of Article 102
Renato Nazzini

The Emergence of EU Contract Law
Exploring Europeanization
Lucinda Miller

Participation in EU Rule-making
A Rights-Based Approach
Joana Mendes

Regulating Cartels in Europe
Second Edition
Christopher Harding, Julian Joshua

Religion and the Public Order of the European Union
Ronan McCrea

Governing Social Inclusion
Europeanization through Policy Coordination
Kenneth A Armstrong

Judicial Control in the European Union
Reforming Jurisdiction in the Intergovernmental Pillars
Alicia Hinarejos

EU Counter-Terrorist Policies and Fundamental Rights
The Case of Individual Sanctions
Christina Eckes

From Dual to Cooperative Federalism
The Changing Structure of European Law
Robert Schütze

Conflicts of Rights in the European Union
A Theory of Supranational Adjudication
Aida Torres Pérez

Judicial Deliberations
A Comparative Analysis of Transparency and Legitimacy
Mitchel de S O l'E Lasser

Racism and Equality in the European Union
Mark Bell

Constitutional Principles of EU External Relations
Geert De Baere

Civil Procedure and EU Law
A Policy Area Uncovered
Eva Storskrubb

The Principle of Mutual Recognition in EU Law

CHRISTINE JANSSENS

OXFORD
UNIVERSITY PRESS

OXFORD
UNIVERSITY PRESS

Great Clarendon Street, Oxford, OX2 6DP,
United Kingdom

Oxford University Press is a department of the University of Oxford.
It furthers the University's objective of excellence in research, scholarship,
and education by publishing worldwide. Oxford is a registered trade mark of
Oxford University Press in the UK and in certain other countries

First Edition published in 2013

Impression: 1

Published in the United States of America by Oxford University Press
198 Madison Avenue, New York, NY 10016, United States of America

British Library Cataloguing in Publication Data
Data available

Library of Congress Control Number: 2013943833

Data available

ISBN 978–0–19–967303–2

Printed and bound in Great Britain by
CPI Group (UK) Ltd, Croydon, CR0 4YY

To mama and papa
To Iván, Laura, and Sarah
with love

Foreword

Christine Janssens successfully defended her doctoral thesis at the University of Antwerp, Belgium, on 3 October 2011. Her thesis, which was written under my supervision but whose merits were all hers, focused on the status of the principle of mutual recognition in the EU internal market and in the field of EU criminal justice. This book contains the results of her doctoral research and provides the reader with an excellent analysis of that most important topic.

Christine Janssens' work distinguishes itself through four major characteristics. First, she develops a true thesis throughout this book, holding that a cross-policy approach to the principle of mutual recognition is both feasible and desirable. This is an original thesis, and one that she arrives at following a complete and meticulous analysis of EU law. Secondly, she adopts a very systematic approach, carefully building her thesis upon an analysis of both internal market law (Part I) and the law on judicial cooperation in criminal matters (Part II). The two components of this analysis are united in Part III, in which she studies mutual recognition from a cross-policy perspective, discussing its workability before drawing general conclusions. The study is innovative in that the author systematically identifies links between internal market law and European criminal law. Thirdly, she undertakes a truly complete and in-depth study of a fascinating, though difficult subject. After explaining the structure and methodology of her research, she presents her research results alongside extensive references to international and European jurisprudence and case law. Finally, the book is written in a pleasant, accessible style which guides the reader smoothly through the EU's internal market and criminal law, even in spite of the extensive bibliographic references, detailed analyses, and numerous complex legal issues faced by the author in tackling this multi-faceted subject.

Unsurprisingly, Christine Janssens' doctoral jury, composed of internationally renowned, high-level experts from academic, judicial, and/or policy backgrounds, responded to her work with much enthusiasm and unanimous praise.

In view of the steadily increasing importance of judicial cooperation in both civil and criminal matters within the European Union, as recognized by the Treaty of Lisbon, I have no doubt that this book will become an enduring reference in the academic literature on EU law. It makes it absolutely clear that any complete study of mutual recognition in EU law must rest upon an analysis which should of course be in-depth, but also sufficiently broad to take the various pertinent angles into account.

I sincerely congratulate Christine Janssens on her thoughtful and stimulating book, unique in its kind, which will undoubtedly prove a must-read for all those interested in EU law on the internal market, criminal justice, and mutual recognition, be they academics, practitioners, administrators, or decision-makers. The reader will discover a book rich in well-founded opinions and ideas which is certain to become a generous source of inspiration for the future evolution of EU law in these domains.

Prof. Johan Meeusen LL.M.
Vice-Rector and Professor of EU Law and
Private International Law,
University of Antwerp
15 July 2012

Series Editors' Preface

This study addresses two of the most important areas of EU law and policy—the internal market and criminal justice—in its examination of the scope and application of the principle of mutual recognition within these two fields.

The aim of the book is to evaluate whether the principle of mutual recognition, which emerged and developed in the context of internal market law and policy, is suitable also for application to the more recent and constantly growing field of EU criminal justice.

To that end, the book begins with a careful definition of the principle of mutual recognition, followed in Part I by a systematic analysis of the way this principle emerged through the jurisprudence—and later in legislative developments—in the field of free movement of goods, persons, services and capital. Subsequent chapters look at the interaction between the principle of mutual recognition and other related principles of EU law such as the principles of mutual trust, sincere cooperation, proportionality and subsidiarity. The confusion created by the use of different names—the 'country of origin principle' and the 'principle of equivalence' for different aspects of mutual recognition is addressed and clarified, and the relationship between harmonization and mutual recognition is discussed. An important discussion on the limits to the applicability of the principle of mutual recognition – including the possible impact on human rights—is included. The practical workability of the principle of mutual recognition in the internal market field is discussed, with an emphasis on the complexity and uncertainty of its practical operation, together with and some suggestions for improving its functioning. Part II of the book then moves on to focus on the field of criminal justice, and conducts a similar analysis of the emergence, operation, workability, problems and limits of the principle of mutual recognition here, following closely the structure and logic of Part I.

The normative core of the book's thesis is contained in Part III, which addresses the question of the suitability of the principle of mutual recognition for 'cross-policy' application to the field of criminal justice just as to the internal market. On this question the author's response is clearly positive. She argues that the principle is suitable for application both to the area of the internal market and to that of criminal justice, despite the differences between these two fields, and despite the instinctive reaction many have had against the extension of such a principle from an economic context into the criminal justice context, with all the concerns about individual liberties and human rights that this seems to raise.

Overall, this book contains a rigorously argued, systematic and thorough analysis of an important principle, together with a clear argument in favour of its cross-applicability to these two different policy domains. The work should be of considerable interest to students, scholars and practitioners alike, across all fields of EU law and policy.

Gráinne de Búrca
Paul Craig

Acknowledgments

This book is the result of my PhD thesis, defended at the University of Antwerp on 3 October 2011. After several years of research, the book is finished and my work is done. Of course, the story does not end here. The principle of mutual recognition is still in development and will undoubtedly continue to raise new questions in the coming years. For now, however, the time has come to thank the many professionals, colleagues, friends, and family members who have all contributed in some way to the completion of this book.

I am especially indebted to my thesis supervisor, Johan Meeusen, for his infinite confidence, encouragement, and enthusiasm, for the space he gave me to think, for the many stimulating discussions we have had over the years, and for his pertinent suggestions and criticisms. I also owe an enormous debt to the other members of my jury, André Klip (Professor at Maastricht University), Chris Van den Wyngaert (Judge at the International Criminal Court, The Hague, and Professor at University of Antwerp), Daniel Flore (Director-General 'Legislation, Fundamental Rights and Freedoms' at the Belgian Ministry of Justice, and Professor at Université de Liège), Gert Straetmans (Professor at University of Antwerp), and Koen Lenaerts (Vice-President of the Court of Justice of the European Union, Luxembourg, and Professor at KU Leuven), who all took the time to read my manuscript carefully, despite their overloaded agendas, and who all provided me with so many valuable ideas. Their favourable comments and their enthusiastic support for the publication of this book have meant a lot to me.

The same applies to the others from whose comments and support I have greatly benefited. In particular, I would like to thank Peter Cullen, director of the European Public and Criminal Law Department at the Europäische Rechtsakademie Trier (ERA) at the time I was writing, and his successor, Laviero Bueno, for allowing me to sneak into a number of interesting annual conferences on 'Mutual recognition and the role of the national judge', which were in principle open only to national judges and prosecutors. Attending these conferences provided me with many invaluable insights into the daily practice of judicial cooperation in criminal matters and also with useful unedited information on the benefits and drawbacks of certain legal instruments. Moreover, such conferences allowed me to meet and exchange thoughts and views with national and EU practitioners, as well as with other young researchers working on related topics. Thank you Chiara Mancuso, Jannemieke Ouwerkerk, Karen Weis, Massimo Fichera, Stef De Decker, Valentina Covolo, Vanessa Franssen, and Wendy De Bondt for sharing so many interesting legal and non-legal discussions with me. I also owe a particular word of gratitude to Franky De Keijzer, Deputy to the Prosecutor-General at the Court of Appeal in Antwerp, Javier Gómez Bermúdez, president of the Sala de lo Penal (Audiencia Nacional, Madrid), Michel Rozie, President at the Court of Appeal in Antwerp, and Stefaan Guenter, Advocate-General at the Court of Appeal in Ghent, who granted me access to a number of interesting, unpublished judgments and provided me with interesting examples of their own experiences with mutual recognition instruments in day-to-day practice. Finally, I am also very grateful to Hans Ingels, Mauro Miranda, and Ana Rodríguez Pérez, administrators at the European Commission, who generously took the time to discuss several topics with me that were related to the principle of mutual recognition in an internal market context, and from whose experience and knowledge I have learnt a lot.

For generously supporting my retreat into academic liberty, I am very grateful to the University of Antwerp and to the Fund for Scientific Research–Flanders. Moreover, special thanks must go to my colleagues and friends, Melissa Vanmeenen and Stefan Rutten, for convincing me to switch from the private sector to the academic world. If in the summer of 2004 they had not drawn my attention to the job vacancy announcement for research assistant in EU law, I probably would never have written a PhD! The University of Antwerp has proven a warm, hospitable, and intellectually challenging environment in which to work. I am thankful to all my colleagues and friends at the Law Faculty for their friendship and support. I would like to single out some of my closest colleagues. Thank you, Angela Ortega Gonzalez, Britt Weyts, Emily Nordin, Emmanuelle De Bock, Jolande Prinssen, Julie Ryngaert, Lieve Hoornaert, Liselot Samyn, Marie Collard, Miroslawa Myszke, Siska Castelain, and Veronique Joosten for your invaluable friendship and for the numerous hours of endless discussion and chat about all topics imaginable (including some of this book). I deeply cherish the enjoyable lunches, well-deserved coffee breaks, relaxing movie nights, cosy dinners, the legendary ELMC experience, and so many other memorable moments that I have spent with you! You have all become so much more than just colleagues. Thank you also Cathérine Van de Heyning, Jeroen De Herdt, Sarah Verstraelen, and Werner Vandenbruwaene for your invaluable help while I was preparing my PhD defence. On 3 October 2011 I benefited greatly from all your tips and tricks ! A final word of thanks must go to my 'EU'-colleagues from the KU Leuven, Geert De Baere, Janek Nowak, Tim Corthaut, Timothy Roes, Tina Van den Sanden, and Vincent Vercauteren: I have learned a lot from you and working together with you was not only intellectually stimulating, but also great fun!

With regard to the publication, I am grateful to Alex Flach, Barath Rajasekaran, Catherine Cragg, Clare Kennedy, Robert Crossley, Natasha Flemming and their colleagues at OUP who have been very helpful and supportive throughout the different phases of the book's publication process. A particular word of gratitude is also due to the anonymous academic reviewer who read my book during the publication process and who made it so much better with his excellent comments and questions. Many thanks also to Karine Roobrouck and Samantha Brunt (Linguapolis, University of Antwerp) who have done a wonderful job of revising my English and who have made clear ideas that were previously expressed inadequately. I also owe an enormous debt to the University of Antwerp's Research Board for their generous financial support as far as the corresponding costs of the language check is concerned.

My final words must go to my family and friends. I am particular grateful to Montse Hervas Zurita and Linda García Delgado, with whom I undertook an LLM in EU law at the Carlos III University in Madrid, for their invaluable friendship and unconditional help, always. Thank you Sangita Bhatia, my former colleague at the European Commission's DG Justice and Home Affairs, where we both did a traineeship, for your very useful linguistic comments on some of my earliest drafts, and for being such a great friend. Many thanks also to Heidi Defrenne, Helga Coppen, Joyce Huybrechts, Julie Van duynslaeger, Liesbet Vermeiren, Sabine Janssens, Tina Verstraeten, and Veronique Broeckhoven—my lifelong friends—not just for giving me so much enthusiastic support on 3 October 2011, but, more importantly, for so many great moments that we have spent together and for always being there when I need you. My parents, my brother Mark, my aunt Lief, and my grandparents have inspired me in so many ways. Their love, wisdom, and strength have undoubtedly had an effect on this book. To my partner, Iván Blanco García, and to our little girls, Laura and Sarah, who came to join us during the writing of this book, I owe a lifetime of joy and intense happiness. This book is dedicated to them with love.

Christine Janssens
1 September 2012

Contents

III. MUTUAL RECOGNITION FROM A CROSS-POLICY PERSPECTIVE: INVESTIGATING THE VIABILITY OF THE INTERNAL MARKET ANALOGY

List of Abbreviations

Legal Journals

AA:	Ars Aequi
Am. Journal of Comp. Law:	American Journal of Comparative Law
B.T.S.Z.:	Belgisch Tijdschrift voor Sociale Zekerheid
CABG:	Cahiers Antwerpen Brussel Gent
C.D.E.:	Cahiers de droit européen
C.L.R.:	Criminal Law Review
CML Rev.:	Common Market Law Review
Col. J. Eur. L.:	Columbia Journal of European Law
Crim Law and Philos:	Criminal Law and Philosophy
CYELP:	Croatian Yearbook of European Law and Policy
CYELS:	Cambridge Yearbook of European Legal Studies
DD:	Delikt and Delinkwent
E.B.L.R.:	European Business Law Review
EHRLR:	European Human Rights Law Review
E.I.P.R.:	European Intellectual Property Review
E.L.J.:	European Law Journal
E.L.R.:	European Law Reporter
E.L.Rev.:	European Law Review
EPL:	European Public Law
EuConst:	European Constitutional Law Review
EuR:	Europarecht
Eur. Journ. Crime Cr.L.Cr.J.:	European Journal of Crime, Criminal Law and Criminal Justice
Eur. J. Migration and L.:	European Journal of Migration and Law
EuZW:	Europäische Zeitschrift für Wirtschaftsrecht
EWS:	Europäisches Wirtschafts- und Steuerrecht
Fordh. Int. L. J.:	Fordham International Law Journal
G.A.:	Goltdammer's Archiv für Strafrecht
G.J.:	Gaceta Juridica
G.R.U.R.Int.:	Gewerblicher Rechtsschutz und Urheberrecht—International
IBLJ:	International Business Law Journal
ICLQ:	International and Comparative Law Quarterly
IJCL:	International Journal of Constitutional Law
IJEL:	Irish Journal of European Law
IRPL:	International Review of Penal Law
J.C.M.S.:	Journal of Common Market Studies
J.D.E.:	Journal de droit européen
J.D.I.:	Journal du droit international
JECL:	Journal of European Criminal law
JEPP:	Journal of European Public Policy
JPP:	Journal of Public Policy
JTDE:	Journal des tribunaux–Droit européen
Law and Contemp. Probs.:	Law and Contemporary Problems
LIEI:	Legal Issues of Economic Integration

Loy. L.A. Int'l and Comp. L. Rev.:	Loyola Los Angeles International and Comparative Law Review
MJ:	Maastricht Journal
MLR:	The Modern Law Review
NJ:	Nederlandse Jurisprudentie
NJb:	Nederlands Juristenblad
NjW:	Nieuw Juridisch Weekblad
N.J.C.M.Bull.:	NJCM-Bulletin
NJECL:	New Journal of European Criminal Law
NTER:	Nederlands Tijdschrift voor Europees Recht
NTM:	Nederlands Tijdschrift voor de Mensenrechten
OJLS:	Oxford Journal of Legal Studies
Panopticon:	Panopticon tijdschrift voor strafrecht, criminologie en forensisch welzijnswerk
RAE:	Revue des Affaires Européennes
RBDI:	Revue belge de droit international
RDCE:	Revista de Derecho Comunitario Europeo
RDUE:	Revue du Droit de l'Union Européenne
R.D.P.:	Revista de Derecho Penal
Rec. Cours:	Recueil de cours
R.E.P.:	Revista de Estudios Políticos
Rev. dr. san. soc.:	Revue de droit sanitaire et social
Rev. Der. Com. Eur.:	Revista de Derecho Comunitario Europeo
Rev. Esp. Der. Eur.:	Revista Española de Derecho Europeo
Rev. Gen. Der. Eur.:	Revista General de Derecho Europeo
Rev. Sc. Crim.:	Revue des Sciences Criminelles
RMC:	Revue du Marché Commun
RMCUE:	Revue du Marché Commun et de l'Union Européenne
RMUE:	Revue du Marché Unique Européen
RTD. Eur.:	Revue trimestrielle de droit européen
RTDH:	Revue trimestrielle des droits de l'homme
R.W.:	Rechtskundig Weekblad
SEW:	Tijdschrift voor Europees en Economisch Recht
StV:	Strafverteidiger
SLR:	Statute Law Review
U.E.A.:	Unión Europea Aranzadi
Y.E.L.:	Yearbook European Law
ZaöRV:	Zeitschrift für ausländisches öffentliches Recht und Völkerrecht
ZEuS:	Zeitschrift für Europarechtliche Studien
ZRP:	Zeitschrift für Rechtspolitik
ZStW:	Zeitschrift für die gesamte Strafrechtswissenschaft

Other Abbreviations

AG:	Advocate General
Charter:	Charter of Fundamental Rights of the European Union
CISA:	Convention Implementing the Schengen Agreement
DIR:	Directive

ECHR:	European Convention on Human Rights
ECJ:	Court of Justice of the European Union
ECtHR:	European Court of Human Rights
EU:	European Union
FD:	Framework Decision
REG:	Regulation
TFEU:	Treaty on the Functioning of the European Union
TEU:	Treaty on the European Union

Table of Cases

ECtHR

ECJ

Table of Legislation

Treaties

Directives

Framework Decisions and Decisions

Table of Policy Documents

Policy Documents Related to the Internal Market

Policy Documents Related to Judicial Cooperation in Criminal Matters (and the Area of Freedom, Security, and Justice)

Introduction

> 'Perhaps the greatest irony today is that while questioned in the single market area, the spirit of Cassis thrives elsewhere. For one, we are witnessing a systematic extension of the principle of mutual recognition to the realm of justice and home affairs, in other words, the acceptance by judges and police forces throughout Europe of each other's procedures and judgments. To be sure, 'wanted in one EU country, wanted everywhere in the EU', does not sound as liberal as its Cassis forbear, and we do not yet have 'refugees admitted here, admitted everywhere.' But the time will come. In the meanwhile we must live with the 'rejected here, rejected everywhere'.[1]

I. Background and Motivation for a Study on the Principle of Mutual Recognition

This study concerns the principle of mutual recognition in the EU legal order, particularly in the EU internal market (four freedoms) and in the EU criminal justice context (judicial cooperation in criminal matters), and employs a cross-policy approach.

One of the main reasons for embarking on this study is that this principle has gained substantial importance in the EU legal order and in Member States' own legal orders during the last thirty years, first in the EU internal market area, and more recently in the area of judicial cooperation in criminal matters. This latter issue relates to the EU area of freedom, security, and justice, one of the most challenging projects on today's European agenda.

In 1997, the Treaty of Amsterdam formulated the ambitious aim of transforming the Union into an area of freedom, security, and justice. Shortly afterwards, in June 1998, the European Council recognized the need to enhance national legal systems' ability to work closely together and asked the Council to determine the scope for greater mutual recognition of judicial decisions. As part of the first Action Plan of the Commission and the Council on this topic,[2] the Council was asked to initiate a process that would facilitate the mutual recognition of decisions and the enforcement of judgments in criminal matters. Subsequently, at a meeting in Tampere on 15–16 October 1999, the European Council endorsed the principle of mutual recognition and declared that it should become the cornerstone of judicial cooperation within the Union.[3] Many policy documents followed in which the principle of mutual recognition maintained a central position.[4] Furthermore, within the scope of the former 'third pillar', a large number of legislative

[1] K. NICOLAÏDIS, 'Kir Forever. The Journey of a Political Scientist in the Landscape of Mutual Recognition', in M. POIARES MADURO and L. AZOULAI (eds.), *The Past and Future of EU Law. The Classics of EU Law Revisited on the 50th Anniversary of the Rome Treaty* (Oxford, Hart Publishing, 2010) 454.

[2] Action Plan of the Council and the Commission on how best to implement the provisions of the Treaty of Amsterdam on an area of freedom, security and justice—Text adopted by the Justice and Home Affairs Council of 3 December 1998, *O.J.* C-19, 23.01.1999, p. 1–15.

[3] Tampere European Council—Presidency Conclusions, 15 and 16 October 1999, retrievable at: <http://ue.eu.int/ueDocs/cms_Data/docs/pressData/en/ec/00200-r1.en9.htm>, § 33.

[4] See, for instance: The Hague Programme: strengthening freedom, security and justice in the European Union *O.J.* C-53, 03.05.2005, p. 12; The Stockholm Programme—An open and secure Europe serving and protecting citizens, *O.J.* C-115, 04.05.2010, p. 12.

instruments for mutual recognition were introduced and adopted,[5] though certain other proposals are currently still pending.[6] Even the case law of the ECJ, which until the Treaty of Amsterdam had been denied any competence in judicial cooperation in criminal matters, has repeatedly addressed the principle of mutual recognition during the past decade. With remarkable casualness, the ECJ referred in its first 'third pillar' judgment *Gözütok and Brügge* to the mutual trust that the Member States place in their respective criminal justice systems and stated that 'each of them should recognise the criminal law in force in the other Member States even in the event of a different outcome if its own national law were to be applied'.[7] Many other judgments followed in which the ECJ explained and further refined the contours of the principle of mutual recognition in different contexts.[8] These developments in policy, legislative law, and case law ultimately culminated in the Treaty of Lisbon, in which the core position of the principle of mutual recognition in the EU criminal justice area was firmly established.[9]

The launch of the principle of mutual recognition at the Tampere European Council and all its subsequent developments have had a major impact on the rapid development of the EU criminal justice area, but it has also raised many questions about the exact meaning and scope of the principle of mutual recognition. Some of these issues have been addressed recently in outstanding research publications on the principle of mutual recognition. Some investigate the showpiece of the mutual recognition programme, the FD EAW;[10] some address the concept of mutual recognition within the EU criminal justice policy area;[11] some examine the principle from an (external) comparative law perspective;[12] and some focus on the national implementation of certain mutual recognition instruments in national legal orders.[13] Other aspects related to the principle of mutual recognition, however, have not yet been exhaustively addressed by the research projects mentioned above and will be discussed in more detail in the current study.

Despite the recent developments in the principle of mutual recognition regarding judicial cooperation in criminal matters, it should not be forgotten that the principle of mutual recognition is a classic of EU law with roots in EU internal market law. It bears particular relation to the *Cassis de Dijon* judgment (on the free movement of goods), in which the ECJ stated, in terms similar to those it would use some 30 years later in *Gözütok and Brügge*, that 'there is no valid reason why, provided that they have been lawfully produced and marketed in one of the Member States, alcoholic beverages should not be introduced into any other Member State'.[14] This statement, which clearly incorporates the

[5] FD EAW; FD EOFPE; FD MRFP; FD MRCO; FD TIA; MRCS; FD ESO (post-trial); FD EEW; FD IAJ; FD ESO (pre-trial); DIR EPO.

[6] PROP DIR EIO.

[7] ECJ, Joined Cases C-187/01 and C-385/01 *Gözütok and Brügge* [2003] ECR I-1345, para 33.

[8] See: Part II, chs 1 and 2.

[9] Articles 67(3) and 82 TFEU.

[10] See, in particular: M. FICHERA, *The Implementation of the European Arrest Warrant in the European Union: Law, Policy and Practice* (Antwerp, Intersentia, 2011).

[11] See, in particular: P. NALEWAJKO, *Grundsatz der gegenseitigen Anerkennung. Eckstein der justiziellen Zusammenarbeit in Strafsachen in der Europäischen Union?* (Berlin, Duncker & Humblot, 2010).

[12] See, in particular: J. OUWERKERK, *Quid Pro Quo? A Comparative Law Perspective on the Mutual Recognition of Judicial Decisions in Criminal Matters* (Antwerp, Intersentia, 2011).

[13] See, in particular: G. ORMAZABAL SANCHEZ, *Espacio penal y mutuo reconocimiento. Perspectiva alemana y española* (Madrid, Marcial Pons, 2006); A. SUOMINEN, *The Principle of Mutual Recognition in Cooperation in Criminal Matters. A Study of the Principle in Four Framework Decisions and in the Implementation Legislation in the Nordic Member States* (Antwerp, Intersentia, 2011).

[14] ECJ, Case 120/78 *Rewe-Zentral AG (Cassis de Dijon)* [1979] ECR 649, para 14.

principle of mutual recognition, was also applied to the other economic free movement categories shortly afterwards.[15]

The 1985 White Paper on the completion of the internal market put the principle of mutual recognition firmly on the European agenda,[16] and even today, nearly three decades later, the principle remains, waiting for new developments and challenges.[17]

Three decades of applying the principle of mutual recognition to the internal market context have brought about a significant number of interesting case law developments, a host of legislative instruments, numerous policy documents, many evaluation reports, and an infinite list of publications in legal journals and books. This does not mean, however, that everything has been said or made clear where this subject is concerned; in fact, the opposite is true. The internal market is, like its cornerstone principle, not a static concept but one that evolves, and one that has undergone constant reconsideration and refinement over the years, both in the EU legislative acquis and in the ECJ's case law. This evolution has meant that the principle is seen as a somewhat 'mystic' or 'hybrid' concept, the exact contours of which are far from clear and in need of further exploration.[18]

It is precisely the combination of its past—a rich inheritance of case law and related legislative instruments—and future—its potential role in developments in the internal market and in judicial cooperation in criminal matters—that makes the principle of mutual recognition such a challenging subject of research in both contexts.

II. The Delineation of this Study's Subject of Research

The previous section has made two things clear: firstly, both the EU internal market and the EU criminal justice domain would benefit from further research on the role, scope, and function of the principle of mutual recognition, and secondly, any further research must take due account of the fact that the principle of mutual recognition originates from the internal market context.

While the link between the two areas of law is evident in the wording and reasoning used by the ECJ in the aforementioned *Cassis de Dijon* and *Gözütok and Brügge* judgments, it was also explicitly confirmed in a Communication of 2000 in which the European Commission stated that 'borrowing from concepts that have worked very well in the creation of the Single Market, the idea was born that judicial cooperation might also benefit from the concept of mutual recognition'.[19] The question of whether this latter statement, itself the subject of intense debate in academic writing,[20] is indeed correct will be the central subject of research in this book. In other words, the research

[15] See: Part I, Chapter 1, I. 'Mutual Recognition and the Four Freedoms'.

[16] White Paper from the Commission to the European Council—Completing the Internal Market, COM (1985) 310, p. 17.

[17] See, for instance: M. MONTI, *A New Strategy for the Single Market – At The Service of Europe's Economy and Society. Report to the President of the European Commission José Manuel Barroso*, 2010, p. 39, 50, and 58, retrievable at: <http://ec.europa.eu/bepa/pdf/monti_report_final_10_05_2010_en.pdf>.

[18] Pelkmans stated that 'mutual recognition is many things to many people': J. PELKMANS, 'Mutual Recognition: Economic and Regulatory Logic in Goods and Services. Bruges European Economic Research Papers 24/2012', 2012, retrievable at: <http://www.coleurope.eu/sites/default/files/research-paper/beer24.pdf>, 2.

[19] Communication from the Commission to the Council and the European Parliament on mutual recognition of final decisions in criminal matters, COM (2000) 495 final, p. 2.

[20] See, for instance: M. BAJO FERNÁNDEZ, 'Tiene futuro un derecho penal europeo?', in M. BAJO FERNÁNDEZ, S. BACIGALUPO, and C. GÓMEZ-JARA DÍEZ (eds.), *Constitución*

will address the question of whether the principle of mutual recognition, as developed in relation to the free movement provisions (internal market), can be applied to judicial cooperation in criminal matters (area of freedom, security, and justice) and if so to what extent, and is this cross-policy application desirable? Discussion of the feasibility and the desirability of a cross-policy approach has become even more relevant since the Lisbon Treaty came into force, since this abolished to a great extent the former pillar structure, which has in turn led to a further rapprochement of the former first and third pillars.

Before addressing the central question of this study, three preliminary issues need to be dealt with: first, the concept of 'principle of mutual recognition' that is used in this study (the desirability of a working definition); secondly, the parameters that are most suitable for performing the cross-policy test (the parameters of the study); and thirdly, how this study's subject of research will be delineated (the scope of the study).

A. A working definition of 'mutual recognition'

In both the internal market context and the criminal justice context, the EU institutions have been very reluctant to provide a clear and concise definition of mutual recognition. Instead, most documents focus either on specific elements that are deemed relevant for the principle of mutual recognition, such as, for instance, equivalence requirements, the role of the country of origin, trust, and harmonization. Admittedly, these latter elements are highly relevant when discussing the contours of the principle of mutual recognition but, when viewed separately, they are insufficient for providing a working definition of the principle of mutual recognition.

Fortunately, in both the internal market context and the area of criminal matters, some documents do go further than simply stating these preceding elements and do provide some kind of definition, or at least a description of the mechanism behind the principle of mutual recognition.

With regard to the internal market, particularly the free movement of goods, the European Commission has maintained that the principle means that '*notwithstanding technical differences between the various national rules that apply throughout the EU, the Member States of destination cannot forbid the sale on their territories of products which are not subject to Community harmonisation and which are lawfully marketed in another Member State*, even if they were manufactured according to technical and quality rules different from those that must be met by domestic products. The only *exceptions* to this principle are restrictions that are justified on the grounds described in [old] Article 30 EC or on the basis of overriding requirements of general public importance recognised by the case law of the Court of Justice, and are proportionate to the aim pursued'

europea y derecho penal económico. Mesas redondas derecho y economía (Madrid, Editorial universitaria Ramón Areces, 2006) 302 ff; D. FLORE, *Droit pénal européen. Les enjeux d'une justice pénale europénne* (Brussels, Larcier, 368–9); A. KLIP, *European Criminal Law* (Antwerp, Intersentia, 2009) 352; N. KEIJZER, 'The European Arrest Warrant Framework Decision between Past and Future', in E. GUILD (ed.), *Constitutional challenges to the European Arrest Warrant,* (Nijmegen, Wolf Legal Publishers, 2006) 69–70; M. MÖSTL, 'Preconditions and Limits of Mutual Recognition', *CML Rev.* 2010, 409; S. PEERS, 'Mutual Recognition and Criminal Law in the European Union: Has the Council got it Wrong?', *CML Rev.* 2004, 24; E. SPAVENTA, 'Remembrance of Principles Lost: On Fundamental Rights, the Third Pillar and the Scope of Union Law', *Y.E.L.* 2006, 175; J. SPENCER, 'An Academic Critique of the EU Acquis in Relation to Trans-Border Evidence-Gathering', *ERA Forum: Special Issue on European Evidence,* 2005, 37, who warns that 'Courts are not the same as supermarkets'; V. MITSILEGAS, *EU Criminal Law* (Oxford, Hart Publishing, 2009) 117–18.

(emphasis added).[21] Thus, according to the Commission, 'the mutual recognition principle in the non-harmonised area consists of a rule (notwithstanding differences in national legislations, products lawfully produced or marketed in a Member State enjoy a basic right to free movement) and an exception (Treaty-based exceptions or mandatory requirements developed in the ECJ's jurisprudence, subject to compliance with the principle of proportionality)'.[22] This definition can, *mutatis mutandis*, be applied to the other free movement provisions.

As regards the criminal justice context, the Commission maintains that 'mutual recognition is based on the thought that while *another state may not deal with a certain matter in the same or even a similar way* as one's own state, the results will be such that they are *accepted as equivalent to decisions by one's own state* [. . .]. Based on this idea of equivalence and the trust it is based on, the results the other state has reached are allowed to *take effect in one's own sphere of legal influence*. On this basis, a decision taken by an authority in one state could be accepted as such in another state, even though a comparable authority may not even exist in that state, or could not take such decisions, or would have taken an entirely different decision in a comparable case [. . .] Recognising a foreign decision in criminal matters could be understood as *giving it effect outside of the state in which it has been rendered*' (emphasis added).[23] Further refinements to the mutual recognition mechanism can be found in the 2001 'Programme of measures to implement the principle of mutual recognition of decisions in criminal matters'. This instrument underlines the broad scope of the principle (in that it applies to pre-trial, trial, and post-trial decisions, and that it includes duties not only to recognize and execute foreign decisions but also to take them into account) but also acknowledges that the principle is subject to limits (refusal grounds).[24]

On the basis of the preceding elements, the following cross-policy working definition of the principle of mutual recognition in the EU legal order can be formulated: 'the principle of mutual recognition requires that, notwithstanding differences between the various national rules that apply throughout the EU, objects, activities or decisions that are lawful in accordance with a Member State's legal framework must be accepted as equivalent to objects, activities or decisions carried out by one's own state, and must be allowed to take effect in one's own sphere of legal influence (either by granting them access to the national territory, or by taking them into account in any subsequent decisions, or by executing them), unless one of the available grounds for non-recognition applies'.

B. The parameters of this study

In order to develop relevant parameters for assessing the viability of a cross-policy application of the principle of mutual recognition, reference should first of all be made to the parameters that determine the principle of mutual recognition's effectiveness in each context.

[21] Commission staff working document, Free Movement of goods—Guide to the application of Treaty provisions governing Free Movement of Goods (Articles 28–30 EC), SEC (2009) 673 final, p. 19.

[22] Commission staff working document, Free Movement of goods—Guide to the application of Treaty provisions governing Free Movement of Goods (Articles 28–30 EC) (n 21).

[23] Communication from the Commission to the Council and the European Parliament on mutual recognition of final decisions in criminal matters, (n 19) p. 4.

[24] Programme of measures to implement the principle of mutual recognition of decisions in criminal matters, *O.J.* C-012, 15.01.2001, p. 10–12.

With regard to criminal matters, the aforementioned 2001 'Programme of measures' mentions several parameters: general or limited scope; the double criminality check; mechanisms for safeguarding rights (of third parties, victims, and suspects); the definition of common minimum standards; the definition and scope of (i) a validation procedure (if any), (ii) refusal grounds, and (iii) the Member States' responsibilities.[25]

As far as the internal market is concerned, the relevant parameters are not listed together in a single instrument but can be determined by checking all relevant policy documents and legislation. In particular, the following parameters are considered relevant: the scope of the instrument;[26] equivalence requirements;[27] safeguarding SHEC (safety, health, environmental, and consumer) interests;[28] the role of the country of origin;[29] trust;[30] harmonization;[31] and exceptions to mutual recognition.[32]

From a cross-policy approach, the two groups of parameters can be consolidated into and summarized as the following five elements: the scope of the mutual recognition mechanism; equivalence requirements (including any double criminality checks); the distribution of competences between home/issuing state and host/executing state; harmonization measures (common minimum standards); and limits to mutual recognition (in order to safeguard crucial interests).

[25] Programme of measures to implement the principle of mutual recognition of decisions in criminal matters (n 24).

[26] Compare, for instance, the more limited scope of mutual recognition in DIR 2006/48/EC with the very broad scope of mutual recognition in DIR 2006/123/EC. For more examples, see: Part I, ch 2, I, B, 2. 'A more in-depth approach: one principle, many forms'.

[27] See, for instance: First biennial report on application of the principle of mutual recognition in the market of goods and services, SEC (1999) 1106, 13.07.1999, p. 9–10; Commission interpretative communication—Facilitating the access of products to the markets of other Member States: the practical application of mutual recognition, *O.J.* C-265, 04.11.2003, p. 7–9.

[28] See, for instance: Report from the Commission to the Council and the European Parliament on the implementation of the Commission's White Paper on completing the internal market. 1993 Report, COM (1994) 55 final, p. 66; Communication from the Commission to the European Parliament and the Council—The impact and the effectiveness of the single market, COM (1996) 520 final, p. 16.

[29] See, for instance: Report from the Commission to the Council and the European Parliament on the implementation of the Commission's White Paper on completing the internal market. 1993 Report (n 28) p. 16, 54 and 93; Communication from the Commission to the European Parliament and the Council—The impact and the effectiveness of the single market (n 28) p. 13.

[30] See, for instance: Communication from the Commission to the European Parliament and the Council—Management of the Mutual Recognition of national rules after 1992. Operational conclusions in the light of the inventory drawn up pursuant to Article 100b of the EC Treaty, COM (1993) 669 final. Communication from the Commission to the European Parliament and the Council—The impact and the effectiveness of the single market (n 28) p. 17; Report from the Commission to the Council and the European Parliament on the state of the internal market for services presented under the first stage of the Internal Market Strategy for Services, COM (2002) 441 final, p. 53; Communication from the Commission to the Council, the European Parliament, the European Economic and Social Committee and the Committee of the Regions–Report on the implementation of the Internal Market Strategy Priorities 2003–2006, COM (2004) 22 final, p. 14.

[31] See, for instance: Fifth Report from the Commission to the Council and the European Parliament on the implementation of the Commission's White Paper on completing the internal market, COM (1990) 90 final, p. 16–19; Council Resolution of 28 October 1999 on mutual recognition, *O.J.* C-141, 19.05.2000, p. 5–6; Communication from the Commission to the Council, the European Parliament, the European Economic and Social Committee and the Committee of the Regions–Report on the implementation of the Internal Market Strategy Priorities 2003–2006 (n 30) p. 12.

[32] See, for instance: Communication from the Commission to the European Parliament and the Council—Reinforcing the Effectiveness of the Internal Market, COM (1993) 256 final, p. 21; First biennial report on application of the principle of mutual recognition in the market of goods and services (n 27) p. 10–12; Commission interpretative communication—Facilitating the access of products to the markets of other Member States: the practical application of mutual recognition (n 27) p. 3.

Besides the parameters mentioned in the previous point, four other parameters will also be taken into account when investigating the viability of a cross-policy application of the principle of mutual recognition during the course of this study, namely: the mutual recognition 'mechanism', including the characteristics of the principle of mutual recognition; the 'object' of the principle of mutual recognition; the 'actors' involved in the mutual recognition mechanism; and finally, the 'workability' of the principle of mutual recognition.

C. The scope of this study

This book examines the principle of mutual recognition in relation to the 'four freedoms' of the internal market (free movement of goods, persons, services, and capital) and in relation to judicial cooperation in criminal matters (as an element of the area of freedom, security, and justice). In principle, however, this study does not examine its relation to any other areas of law.[33]

Furthermore, the regulations, directives, and framework decisions selected will not be analysed in their entirety but only insofar as their provisions are considered relevant for the study of the principle of mutual recognition and in particular for this study's central research question.[34]

[33] Also in other fields of the area of freedom, security, and justice, the principle of mutual recognition has been introduced, see, for instance, in relation to *judicial cooperation in civil matters*: M. ANDENAS, 'National Paradigms of Civil Enforcement: Mutual Recognition or Harmonization in Europe?', in M. ANDENAS, B. HESS, and P. OBERHAMMER (eds.), *Enforcement Agency Practice in Europe* (London, BIICL, 2005) 7–25; T. ANDERSSON, 'Harmonization and Mutual Recognition: How to Handle Mutual Distrust', in *Enforcement Agency Practice in Europe* (this footnote) 245–53; M. TULIBACKA, 'Europeanization of Civil Procedures: in Search of a Coherent Approach', *CML Rev.* 2009, 1527–165; in relation to the EU's policy on (irregular) *immigration and asylum* policy, see, for instance: E. GUILD, *The Legal Elements of European Identity. EU Citizenship and Migration* (The Hague, Kluwer Law International, 2004) 172 ff.; I. STAFFANS, 'Convergence and Mutual Recognition in European Asylum Law', in J. KLABBERS and M. SELLERS. (eds.), *The Internationalization of Law and Legal Education* (Dordrecht, Springer Netherlands, 2008) 149 ff. In relation to *police cooperation in criminal matters*, which is characterized by a strong emphasis on the principle of availability, opinions diverge. Some authors suggest that there is no question at all of mutual recognition in this context: G. VERMEULEN, 'Mutual Recognition, Harmonisation and Fundamental (Procedural) Rights Protection', in M. MARTIN (ed.), *Crime, Rights and the EU: the Future of Police and Judicial Cooperation* (London, Justice, 2008) 94. Others argue, more convincingly, that there is a close connection between the principle of availability and the principle of mutual recognition. See, for instance: J. DE ZWAAN, and F.A.N.J. GOUDAPPEL, *Freedom, Security and Justice in the European Union. Implementation of the Hague Programme* (The Hague, TMC Asser Press, 2006), 223; M. FLETCHER, R. LOOF, and B. GILMORE, *EU Criminal Law and Justice* (Cheltenham, Edward Elgar, 2008) 94–5; MITSILEGAS, *EU Criminal Law* (n 20); A. WEYEMBERGH, 'L'espace pénale européen', in X. LEURQUIN, J.-F. BELLIS, M. FAVART, and A. WEYEMBERGH (eds.), *Actualités en droit européen et rappel de quelques principes* (Brussels, Bruylant, 2006) 83.

[34] With regard to the *criminal justice* context, I have examined: FD EAW; FD EOFPE; FD MRFP; FD MRCO; FD TIA; FD MRCS; FD ESO (post-trial); FD EEW; FD IAJ; FD ESO (pre-trial); and PROP DIR EIO. With regard to the *internal market* context, my final selection of relevant directives was determined by, on the one hand, a scrutiny of the EU's legislative framework, the ECJ's case law as well as the relevant doctrine on the mutual recognition principle and, on the other hand, interesting discussions with administrators at the European Commission, in particular, Hans Ingels (DG Enterprise and Industry); Mauro Miranda (DG Internal Market), and Ana Rodríguez Pérez (DG Internal Market).

III. The Structure of this Study

This study comprises three major parts, each of which will contribute to the central question of this book, namely whether a cross-policy approach to the principle of mutual recognition is feasible or desirable.

In Part I, I analyse the function of the principle of mutual recognition in the internal market context from three perspectives: the development of the principle of mutual recognition in the ECJ's case law on the free movement provisions (Chapter 1); the development of the principle of mutual recognition in the secondary legislation on the internal market (Chapter 2); and the workability of the principle of mutual recognition in the internal market context (Chapter 3). This last analysis gives rise to the formulation of certain interim conclusions (Chapter 4).

In Part II, I explore the function of the principle of mutual recognition in the context of judicial cooperation in criminal matters using a similar approach, as follows: first, the development of the principle of mutual recognition in the ECJ's *ne bis in idem* case law (Chapter 1); secondly, the development of the principle of mutual recognition in the secondary legislation (Chapter 2); thirdly, the workability of the principle of mutual recognition (Chapter 3); and finally I conclude with a number of interim conclusions (Chapter 4).

In Part III, I carry out the proper 'cross-policy test' by assessing whether (i) the pursued objectives in both areas of law (Chapter 1), (ii) the mechanism of the principle of mutual recognition, including its object, actors, and characteristics (Chapter 2), and (iii) its workability (Chapter 3) display signs of convergence or divergence in either context. On the basis of these findings, I will draw conclusions as to whether the internal market analogy is viable or not, and if it is, to what extent, and also whether (in the last hypothesis) any potential benefits and/or pitfalls arise from a cross-policy analysis. This final part will be concluded with a summary of the main findings (Chapter 4).

IV. The Study's Research Method

This study approaches the principle of mutual recognition from an EU perspective, namely that the principle of mutual recognition is a legal principle that has been developed in the EU legal order through the ECJ's case law and through (primary and secondary) EU legislation in two main areas of EU law: the internal market context and the criminal justice context. The study will therefore rely on an internal comparative law method, which compares the function of the principle of mutual recognition in the EU internal market and in EU judicial cooperation in criminal matters. Its main sources of law will comprise: primary and secondary EU law (including any relevant proposals); the case law of the ECJ (including the corresponding opinions of the AGs); policy documents and any other relevant documentation from EU institutions and/or EU bodies; and finally, a selection of relevant publications in books and legal periodicals.

The different ways in which the principle of mutual recognition is interpreted and applied in the Member States' legal systems bear little relation to how this principle is applied in the ECJ's case law and for this reason they will not be addressed systematically in this study. However, when assessing the workability of the principle of mutual recognition, national experiences of the mutual recognition instruments are of course highly relevant and I will therefore refer in this context to national comparative law-based research on a purely functional basis.

While this study aims at clarifying the meaning and contours of the principle of mutual recognition in the EU legal order, particularly in the internal market context and in the area of judicial cooperation in criminal matters, this study will occasionally—on a strictly functional basis—refer to legislative or case law developments in other areas of EU law in which the principle of mutual recognition has been introduced (e.g. judicial cooperation in civil matters) as well as to certain relevant aspects of the ECtHR case law that are related to the principle of mutual recognition.

I have endeavoured to state the law as of 1 June 2013.

PART I

FRAME OF REFERENCE

Mutual Recognition in the Internal Market Context

Part I of this book aims at tracing the essential characteristics of the principle of mutual recognition in the internal market context, from both the judicial and legislative perspectives. It is divided into four chapters. First, I analyse the legal reasoning adopted by the ECJ when the principle of mutual recognition was introduced and developed throughout its case law on the Treaty provisions on free movement (referred to as judicial mutual recognition, Chapter 1). Then, I investigate how this principle has been elaborated as a legislative tool in the secondary legislation of the EU internal market policy (called the regulatory or legislative mutual recognition, Chapter 2).[1] Next, I evaluate the workability of the principle of mutual recognition in a day-to-day context (Chapter 3). Finally, I conclude Part I with a summary of the main findings on the fundamental characteristics of the principle of mutual recognition in the internal market context (Chapter 4).

[1] On this division, see: J. PELKMANS, 'Mutual Recognition in Goods: On Promises and Disillusions', *JEPP* 2007, 700–3, and, more recently: J. PELKMANS, 'Mutual Recognition: Economic and Regulatory Logic in Goods and Services. Bruges European Economic Research Papers 24/2012', 9–11, retrievable at: <http://www.coleurope.eu/sites/default/files/research-paper/beer24.pdf>. It should be mentioned that The European Commission reserves the term mutual recognition for the judicially developed concept (interview with H. INGELS, administrator at the European Commission, DG Enterprises, Brussels, 9 February 2007) whereas legal doctrine suggests that the concept applies to both. Since much secondary legislation explicitly mentions the term mutual recognition and the TFEU refers to it in a legislative context (Art. 53 TFEU on the mutual recognition of diplomas, and former Art. 293 EC on the mutual recognition of companies, which was repealed under the Lisbon Treaty), I am inclined to support Pelkmans and to accept that it makes sense to speak of 'mutual recognition' in both contexts.

1

The Principle of Mutual Recognition as Judicial Impetus for the Free Movement Provisions

I. Mutual Recognition and the Four Freedoms

It is important to consider the launch of the principle of mutual recognition within its historical context: at a time when the internal market integration process was being hampered by a demanding unanimity requirement within the Council, and when a non-discriminatory approach to technicalities barring free movement provisions proved insufficient in tackling hindrances from divergent national legislations, the principle of mutual recognition was intended to breathe new life into the internal market project.[1]

A. Mutual recognition and the free movement of goods

(1) Cassis de Dijon: *the first unequivocal manifestation of a duty of mutual recognition*

The introduction of the principle of mutual recognition has often been linked to the *Cassis de Dijon* judgment. In this case, the ECJ was asked whether Germany was allowed to refuse the import of French Cassis de Dijon on the grounds that this liqueur did not correspond to the minimum alcohol percentage required by German law. The ECJ concluded that the German provision was prohibited under Article 34 TFEU and stated that there was no valid reason why, provided that 'they have been lawfully produced and marketed in one of the Member States, alcoholic beverages should not be introduced into any other Member State'.[2] It is generally acknowledged that with this famous statement the ECJ introduced into the free movement of goods area the principle of mutual recognition of goods[3] and of the underlying legislative provisions

[1] On this subject, see, in particular, the different contributions in: R. BIEBER, R. DEHOUSSE, J. PINDER, and J.H.H. WEILER, *1992: One European Market* (Baden-Baden, Nomos, 1988).

[2] ECJ, Case 120/78 *Rewe-Zentral AG (Cassis de Dijon)* [1979] ECR 649, para 14.

[3] See, for instance: C. BARNARD, *The Substantive Law of the EU. The Four Freedoms* (Oxford, Oxford University Press, 2010) 624; D. CHALMERS, G. DAVIES, and G. MONTI, *European Union Law* (Cambridge, Cambridge University Press, 2010) 745; C. HAMMER, *Handbuch zum freien Wahrenverkehr* (Vienna, Manzsche Verlags- und Universitätsbuchandlung, 1998) 27; P.J.G. KAPTEYN, A.M. McDONNELL, K.J.M. MORTELMANS, and C.W.A. TIMMERMANS (eds.), *The Law of the European Union and the European Communities with Reference to Changes Made by the Lisbon Treaty* (The Netherlands, Wolters Kluwer, 2008) 581; A. MATTERA, *Le marché unique européen: ses règles, son fonctionnement,* (Paris, Jupiter, 1990) 285; P. OLIVER and M. JARVIS, *Free Movement of Goods in the European Community under Articles 28 to 30 of the EC Treaty* (London, Sweet and Maxwell, 2003) 6.70; M. POIARES MADURO, *We, the Court. The European Court of Justice and the European Economic Constitution* (Oxford, Hart Publishing, 1998) 33; A. STONE SWEET, *The Judicial Construction of Europe* (Oxford, Oxford University Press, 2004) 135; L. WOODS, *Free Movement of Goods and Services within the European Community* (Hants, Ashgate Publishing, 2004) 69. See, however, U. BECKER, 'Kommentar zum Artikel 28 EGV', in J. SCHWARZE (ed.), *EU-Kommentar* (Baden-Baden, Nomos, 2009) 452, who argues that reading a principle of mutual recognition in *Cassis de Dijon* is a too far-reaching interpretation of the judgment. Furthermore, some authors underline that it was mainly the Commission's Communication concerning the consequences of this judgment (Communication

applicable to them, also known as the principle of equivalence,[4] and/or the principle of home state control (or country of origin).[5] The alternate use of these terms by legal commentators will be expanded on later.[6] However, at this stage, the diversity of terms can essentially be explained by two factors. First, we cannot ignore the ECJ's reluctance, until very recently,[7] to embrace the term 'principle of mutual recognition' unambiguously.[8] Neither in *Cassis de Dijon* nor any subsequent judgment in this area did the ECJ employ the term 'principle of mutual recognition' prior to *Commission v Italy*.[9] In fact, the only judgments in which the ECJ actually used this wording *expressis verbis* were judgments which referred to the mutual recognition concept in its capacity as a legislative instrument.[10] Secondly, we should be aware that the principle that is the subject of this research is flexible, with a variety of characteristics all focusing on different aspects of the free movement mechanism of Article 34 TFEU. Depending on the specific characteristic we wish to emphasize, different terms may be appropriate.[11]

A fundamental aspect of the mutual recognition reasoning, explicitly introduced by the ECJ in *Cassis de Dijon*, concerns the rule of reason, i.e. the mandatory requirements that Member States were thenceforth permitted to invoke in order to justify a national measure which would constitute a barrier to the free movement of goods. The Court introduced this rule of reason by stating that 'in the absence of common rules [...] it is for the Member States to regulate all matters relating to the production and

from the Commission concerning the consequences of the judgment given by the Court of Justice on 20 February 1979 in Case 120/78 ('Cassis de Dijon'), *O.J.* C-256, 03.10.1980, p. 2–3) which truly introduced the principle of mutual recognition, the *Cassis de Dijon* judgment merely laying down its foundations. See, for instance: P. CRAIG and G. DE BURCA, *EU Law. Text, Cases and Materials* (Oxford, Oxford University Press, 2011) 685; L. GORMLEY, *EU Law of Free Movement of Goods and Customs Union* (Oxford, Oxford University Press, 2009) 411–12.

[4] See, for instance: HAMMER, *Handbuch zum freien Wahrenverkehr* (n 3) 27; N. STOFFEL VALLOTTON, *La prohibición de restricciones a la libre circulación de mercancías en la Comunidad Europea* (Madrid, Dykinson, 2000) 420; OLIVER and JARVIS, *Free Movement of Goods in the European Community under Articles 28 to 30 of the EC Treaty* (n 3) 6.70.

[5] See, for instance: CHALMERS, DAVIES, and MONTI, *European Union Law* (n 3) 745; N. REICH, *Understanding EU Law. Objectives, Principles and Methods of Community Law* (Antwerp, Intersentia, 2005) 102.

[6] See: Part I, ch 1, III. 'Equivalence, Country of Origin, and Mutual Recognition: What's in a Name?'

[7] ECJ, Case C-110/05, *Commission v Italy* [2009] ECR I-519, para 34. In this judgment the ECJ explicitly states that Article 34 TFEU reflects the obligation to respect *the principle of mutual recognition* of products lawfully manufactured and marketed in other Member States. See also: ECJ, Case C-108/09 *Ker-Optica*, [2010] ECR I-12213, para 48; ECJ Case C-484/10 *Ascafor*, nyr, para 53 ECJ, Case C-385/10 *Elenca*, nyr, para 29.

[8] Apparently, the AGs seemed more eager to apply the term 'principle of mutual recognition' than the ECJ itself. See, for instance: Opinion of AG Van Gerven in Case C-340/89 *Vlassopoulou* [1991] ECR I-2357, § 12; Opinion of AG Elmer in Case C-189/95 *Franzén* [1997] ECR I-5905, § 53; Opinion of AG Cosmas in Case C-389/93 *Aher Waggon* [1998] ECR I-4473, § 18; Opinion of AG La Pergola in Case C-184/96 *Commission v France* [1998] ECR I-6197, § 28–31; Opinion of AG Geelhoed in Case C-212/03 *Commission v France* [2005] ECR I-4213, § 39. Other opinions spoke in rather vague terms of 'the conditions laid down in the *Cassis de Dijon* case'; see, for instance: Opinion of AG Darmon in Case C-17/90 *Pinaud Wieger* [1991] ECR I-5253, § 78.

[9] ECJ, Case C-110/05 *Commission v Italy* [2009] ECR I-519.

[10] Some authors believed that the ECJ had finally recognized the term 'principle of mutual recognition' in its *Foie Gras* judgment (ECJ, Case C-184/96 *Commission v France* [1998] ECR I-6197, paras 1, 3, 5, 13, and 28). See, in particular: A. MATTERA, 'L'arrêt *Foie Gras* du 22 octobre 1998: porteur d'une nouvelle impulsion pour le perfectionnement du Marché unique européen', *RMUE* 1998, 114. Such an interpretation is, however, in my view, a too optimistic reading of this judgment. In the judgment at hand the ECJ solely mentioned the wording 'mutual recognition' in relation to 'mutual recognition' clauses, but it had no intention to introduce the concept 'principle of mutual recognition' in its general capacity of judicially developed principle.

[11] See: Part I, ch 1, III. 'Equivalence, country of origin, and mutual recognition: what's in a name?'

marketing of [products] on their own territory' and 'that obstacles to movement within the Community resulting from disparities between the national laws relating to the marketing of products in question must be accepted in so far as those provisions may be recognized as being necessary in order to satisfy mandatory requirements'.[12] This paragraph is at least as relevant as the one cited at the beginning of this chapter, as it neutralizes to a considerable extent the potentially far-reaching consequences that the principle of mutual recognition could otherwise have had.[13] The classical test to which the ECJ has systematically submitted every non-discriminatory national measure since *Cassis de Dijon* that could present an obstacle to the free movement of goods highlights the conditional, unlimited nature of the principle. This is a three-step test, which checks first that there is no harmonized European measure on the matter that prevents the Member State from regulating, secondly, that the Member State has invoked an acceptable mandatory requirement, and thirdly, that this national measure is adequate and proportionate to satisfy the mandatory requirement.[14] The test does indeed guarantee that free movement and mutual recognition are counterbalanced with interests that are deemed worthy of protection from a Member State's perspective, and quite often also from an EU perspective.

(2) The outlines of the mutual recognition mechanism

Even assuming that the *Cassis de Dijon* judgment was a milestone in the ECJ's mutual recognition case law regarding the goods sector, we should not overlook the importance of certain previous rulings in this area, such as that of the *Dassonville* case.[15] Indeed, *Dassonville*'s broad definition of Article 34 TFEU, which resulted in the prohibition of every trading rule capable of hindering—directly or indirectly, actually or potentially—intra-community trade, had clearly paved the way for the launch of the principle of mutual recognition in *Cassis de Dijon*. Furthermore, one particular statement in the *Dassonville* judgment, specifically that a Member State is in principle allowed to take

[12] ECJ, Case 120/78 *Rewe-Zentral AG (Cassis de Dijon)* [1979] ECR 649, para 8.

[13] Opinions diverge in academic reading as to whether the ECJ has given the Member States little or much margin to act. Compare, in this regard, for instance: C. BARNARD, 'Derogations, Justifications and the Four Freedoms: Is State Interest Really Protected', in C. BARNARD and O. ODUDU (eds.), *The Outer Limits of European Union Law* (Oxford, Hart Publishing, 2009) 273 ff., who argues that in the 'give and take world' of *Cassis de Dijon* there has generally been little room for Member States to defend crucial national interests; with: N. BERNARD, 'On the Art of Not Mixing One's Drinks: *Dassonville* and *Cassis de Dijon* Revisited', in M. POIARES MADURO and L. AZOULAI (eds.), *The Past and Future of EU Law. The Classics of EU Law Revisted on the 50th Anniversary of the Rome Treaty* (Oxford: Oxford University Press, 2010) 460, who argues that the principle of mutual recognition was confined to marginal situations, where no significant regulatory objectives were at stake.

[14] On these conditions, see for instance: KAPTEYN, McDONNELL, MORTELMANS, and TIMMERMANS, *The Law of the European Union and the European Communities* (n 3) 645 ff; K. LENAERTS and P. VAN NUFFEL, *Europees recht* (Antwerp, Intersentia, 2011) 155–9. At least two different aspects can thus be distinguished in relation to the proportionality test: (i) the measure must be adequate to protect a particular interest and (ii) the measure must be necessary or indispensable, i.e. that no other, less intrusive, measures are available. These criteria have been the subject of much academic writing, see, for instance: KAPTEYN, McDONNELL, MORTELMANS, and TIMMERMANS (n 3) 649 and the authors mentioned therein. Some authors underline that in some, albeit limited number of ECJ judgments a third aspect of the proportionality test can be distinguished, namely a proportionality check *sensu stricto*, which implies a true balancing of the conflicting interests at stake: W.T. EIJSBOUTS, J.H. JANS, L.A.J. SENDEN, and A. PRECHAL, *Europees recht. Algemeen Deel. Sinds het Verdrag van Lissabon* (Groningen, Europa Law Publishing, 2010) 108–11; C. SEMMELMANN, 'The European Union's Economic Constitution under the Lisbon Treaty: Soul-Searching Shifts the Focus to Procedure', *E.L. Rev.* 2010, 534–9.

[15] ECJ, Case 8/74 *Dassonville* [1974] ECR 837, para 5.

measures to prevent unfair (commercial) practices subject to the condition that these measures should be reasonable,[16] could be seen as a forerunner of the rule of reason, as developed in *Cassis de Dijon* and subsequent case law. However, other judgments of the pre-*Cassis de Dijon* era also exemplified aspects which would later appear to be crucial elements of the ECJ's mutual recognition approach, such as the need for good cooperation between the Member States' authorities,[17] for instance, or the qualification of the free movement provisions as individual and enforceable rights.[18]

Certain important features of the mutual recognition mechanism, on the other hand, were developed in subsequent case law, such as the equivalence criterion together with the prohibition of double controls or dual burdens.[19] The post-*Cassis de Dijon* case law indicated, furthermore, that the nature of the mutual recognition duty could be either substantive (e.g. mutual recognition of fabrication rules)[20] or procedural (e.g. mutual recognition of testing/controlling procedures or the need for a procedural framework in order to make mutual recognition work).[21] Another crucial development in the case law on free movement of goods was the *Keck and Mithouard* judgment and its subsequent case law which, because of its focus on a market access test, restricted the scope of the principle of mutual recognition considerably.[22]

B. Mutual recognition and the free movement of services

The principle of mutual recognition has also gained primary status in the other free movement areas. In the area of the free movement of services, a first cautious move can be identified, even prior to *Cassis de Dijon*, in the *Choquet* and *Van Wesemael* judgments. In *Choquet*, the ECJ considered the insistence on a driving test that clearly duplicated a

[16] ECJ, Case 8/74 *Dassonville* [1974] ECR 837, para 6.

[17] See, for instance: ECJ, Case 104/75 *de Peijper* [1976] ECR 613, para 27.

[18] See, for instance: ECJ, Case 74/76 *Ianelli* [1977] ECR 557, para 13 (free movement of goods); ECJ, Case 48/75 *Royer* [1976] ECR 467, para 19 (free movement of workers); ECJ, Case 2/74 *Reyners* [1974] ECR 631, para 25 (freedom of establishment); ECJ, Case 33/74 *Van Binsbergen* [1974] ECR 1299, para 27 (freedom to provide services).

[19] See, for instance: ECJ, Case 251/78 *Denkavit* [1979] ECR 3369, paras 22–3; ECJ, Case 27/80 *Fietje* [1980] ECR 3839, para 12; ECJ, Case 132/80 *United Food* [1981] ECR 995, para 29; ECJ, Case 272/80 *Biologische Producten* [1981] ECR 3277, paras 14–15. Some reputed authors criticize the paramount weight that was attributed to the *Cassis de Dijon* judgment, as they believe that the principle of mutual recognition should be interpreted as a consequence of the equivalence test. Therefore, they suggest that the principle of mutual recognition rather starts with the *Biologische Producten* judgment. See: M. FALLON, *Droit matériel général de l'Union européenne* (Louvain-la-Neuve, Bruylant, 2002) 150–1; M. FALLON and J. MEEUSEN, 'Private International Law in the European Union and the Exception of Mutual Rrecognition', in P SARCEVIC and P. VOLKEN (eds.), *Yearbook of Private International Law. Volume IV* (The Hague, Kluwer Law International, 2002) 41–2. In the other free movement areas, namely the free movement of establishment and the free movement of services, the 'equivalence' criterion made its entry, albeit prudently, at an earlier stage: ECJ, Case 71/76 *Thieffry* [1977] ECR 765, para 27; ECJ, Case 11/77 *Patrick* [1977] ECR 1199, para 18; ECJ, Case 16/78 *Choquet* [1978] ECR 2293, para 8; ECJ, Joined Cases 110/78 and 111/78 *Van Wesemael* [1979] ECR 35, paras 28–30.

[20] Such as, for instance: ECJ, Case 53/80 *Kaasfabriek Eyssen* [1981] ECR 409 (as to the legal ingredient requirements of cheese); ECJ, Case 130/80 *Kelderman* [1981] ECR 527 (as to the legal ingredient requirements of bread).

[21] See, for instance, for the first category: ECJ, Case 251/78 *Denkavit* [1979] ECR 3369; ECJ, Case 27/80 *Fietje* [1980] ECR 3839, para 12; and for the second category: ECJ, Case 304/84 *Muller* [1986] ECR 1511, para 26; ECJ, Case 178/84 *Commission v Germany* [1987] ECR 1227, para 45, where the ECJ underlined the need to foresee, in case of a required market authorization, a procedure which is easily accessible to traders and which can be concluded within a reasonable time.

[22] See: Part I, Chapter 1, IV, A, 1. 'A prudent hands-off approach with an emphasis on a national perspective'.

test taken in another Member State for the classes of vehicle the person wished to drive to be incompatible with freedom of services (Art. 56 TFEU).[23] The ECJ thus introduced, albeit prudently, a ban on dual burdens and a duty to compare and, if necessary, take into account tests taken in another Member State. The *Van Wesemael* case produced a similar result. In the latter ruling, the ECJ was of the opinion that a licence requirement for entertainment activities may in principle be justified by the general good or by the need to protect the entertainer. However, it was decided that a licence could not be imposed by the Member State in which the service was provided when the entertainer already held a licence issued by the Member State in which he or she was established, and which was issued under conditions comparable to those required by the state in which the service was performed.[24] Both the basic ideas of equivalence and mutual recognition and the imperative requirements theory were thus clearly present already.[25]

Several other judgments followed in which the ECJ reiterated that an authorization or licence requirement could only be justified if it served an overriding purpose related to public interest which had not yet been safeguarded by the Member State of establishment.[26] In other words, the ECJ was clearly obliging the Member State in which the service was performed to take into account all requirements that had previously been complied with in the Member State of establishment, and to avoid unjustified duplications of equivalent statutory provisions.

It was not until the *Säger* judgment, however, that a definition of mutual recognition à la *Cassis de Dijon* was truly achieved. In *Säger*, the ECJ ordered the abolition of any restriction, even if it applied without distinction to national providers of services and to those of other Member States, if it was liable to prohibit or otherwise impede the activities of a provider of services established in another Member State where similar services had been provided lawfully.[27] In other words, this judgment definitively made it clear that, in the absence of any justification grounds, there was no valid reason why services that were lawfully performed in one Member State should not be permitted in another.

C. Mutual recognition and the free movement of persons

(1) Mutual recognition of diplomas

With regard to the free movement of persons, the principle of mutual recognition has gained significant attention from the very beginning, especially in relation to the mutual recognition of diplomas.[28] However, the specific backgrounds of these first judgments

[23] ECJ, Case 16/78 *Choquet* [1978] ECR 2293, para 8.

[24] ECJ, Joined Cases 110/78 and 111/78 *Van Wesemael* [1979] ECR 35, paras 28–30. See also: ECJ, Case 279/80 *Webb* [1981] ECR 3305, paras 17–20.

[25] The latter had already been previously recognized in the *Van Binsbergen* judgment: ECJ, Case 33/74 *Van Binsbergen* [1974] ECR 1299, para 12.

[26] Regarding insurance services, see, for instance: ECJ, Case 220/83 *Commission v France* [1986] ECR 3663, paras 17–18; ECJ, Case 252/83 *Commission v Denmark* [1986] ECR 3713, paras 17–18; ECJ, Case 205/84 *Commission v Germany* [1986] ECR 3755, para 47; ECJ, Case 206/84 *Commission v Ireland* [1986] ECR 3817, paras 17–18. Regarding services in the tourist sector: ECJ, Case C-154/89 *Commission v France* [1991] ECR I-659, paras 14–15; ECJ, Case C-180/89 *Commission v Italy* [1991] ECR I-709, paras 17–18; ECJ, Case C-198/89 *Commission v Greece* [1991] ECR I-72, paras 16–17.

[27] ECJ, Case C-76/90 *Säger* [1991] ECR I-4221, para 12. See also: ECJ, Case C-288/89 *Gouda* [1991] ECR I-4007, para 12; ECJ, Case C-353/89 *Commission v Netherlands* [1991] ECR I-727, para 12.

[28] ECJ, Case 71/76 *Thieffry* [1977] ECR 765; ECJ, Case 11/77 *Patrick* [1977] ECR 1199 (both on freedom of establishment) and ECJ, Case 222/86 *Heylens* [1987] ECR 4097 (on free movement of workers).

have dissuaded many authors from drawing far-reaching conclusions.[29] It was only in the early 1990s that the ECJ clarified and generalized the meaning of the duty of mutual recognition in this field,[30] a clarification that was urgently needed. The existence of a specific Treaty provision on the mutual recognition of diplomas (Art. 53 TFEU), which called for directives on mutual recognition and coordination to be issued in order to facilitate free movement, and which had no counterpart in the other free movement areas, had cast doubt on the possibility of applying the principle of mutual recognition in a similar way in this area in the absence of any coordinating directive.

Inspired by the objective of Article 49 TFEU[31] and—most likely—by the non-committal wording of Article 53 TFEU,[32] the ECJ imposed in *Vlassopoulou* a duty of mutual recognition under conditions that were very similar to those it had previously applied in the other free movement areas. The ECJ maintained, in particular, that 'a Member State which receives a request to admit a person to a profession [...] *must take into consideration* the diplomas, certificates and other evidence of qualifications which the person concerned has acquired in another Member State by making *a comparison* between the specialized knowledge and abilities certified by those diplomas and the knowledge and qualifications required by the national rules. If that comparative *examination procedure* results in the finding that the knowledge and qualifications certified by the foreign diploma correspond to those required by the national provisions, the Member State *must recognize* this diploma as fulfilling the requirements laid down by its national provisions' (emphasis added).[33]

By analogy with its case law in the area of goods and services, the ECJ thus focused in *Vlassopoulou* and its subsequent case law in this area[34] on (i) a duty to compare; (ii) a duty to ensure that qualifications and professional experience[35] obtained in another Member State were accorded their proper value and duly taken into account; and (iii) a duty to recognize, either fully or partially,[36] when equivalence was demonstrated.

[29] In fact, the duty of mutual recognition that was at stake in *Thieffry* and *Heylens* was based on a unilaterally developed recognition procedure that had been installed by one Member State and the ECJ did not (yet) address at that time the need of such a procedure from a European perspective. C.A. CRISHAM, 'Case Note Thieffry and Patrick', *CML Rev.* 1978, 370; J. WOUTERS, *Het Europees vestigingsrecht voor ondernemingen herbekeken. Een onderzoek naar de grondslagen, draagwijdte en begrenzing van de vrijheid van vestiging van ondernemingen in de Europese Unie* (Katholieke Universiteit Leuven, Faculteit der Rechtsgeleerdheid, 1996), Vol. I, 433.

[30] ECJ, Case C-340/89 *Vlassopoulou* [1991] ECR I-2357.

[31] ECJ, Case C-340/89 *Vlassopoulou* [1991] ECR I-2357, paras 13–15.

[32] Leaving aside medical and pharmaceutical professions (Art. 53(2) TFEU), Article 53 TFEU does not make the principle of recognition conditional upon the prior adoption of coordinating directives. It merely suggests that the free movement of persons will be facilitated by the adoption of coordinating directives.

[33] ECJ, Case C-340/89 *Vlassopoulou* [1991] ECR I-2357, paras 16 and 19.

[34] See, for instance: ECJ, Case C-104/91 *Aguirre Borrel* [1992] ECR I-3003, paras 11–14; ECJ, Case C-319/92 *Haim* [1994] ECR I-425, paras 26–8; ECJ, Case C-234/97 *Fernández de Bobadilla* [1999] ECR I-4773, paras 31–2; ECJ, Case C-313/01 *Morgenbesser* [2003] ECR I-13467, paras 57–70; ECJ, Case C-345/08 *Pesla* [2009] ECR I-11677, para 39; ECJ, Joined Cases C-372/09 and C-373/09 *Josep Peñarroja Fa,* [2011] ECR I-1785, para 58. See also, prior to *Vlassopoulou*: ECJ, Case 222/86 *Heylens* [1987] ECR 4097, para 13.

[35] See, for instance: ECJ, Case C-104/91 *Aguirre Borrel* [1992] ECR I-3003 (on real estate agents). Compare, however, with: ECJ, Case C-61/89 *Bouchoucha* [1990] ECR I-3551, in which the ECJ was far more reserved, probably owing to the higher degree of sensitivity surrounding medical and paramedical professions.

[36] The ECJ has underlined that the possibility of partial recognition should be more than merely notional: ECJ, Case C-345/08 *Pesla* [2009] ECR I-11677, para 58.

Three striking differences between *Vlassopoulou* and the other free movement judgments that dealt with mutual recognition can be detected: the focus in *Vlassopoulou* on the equivalence criterion (which was not always explicitly present in the other mutual recognition judgments); the absence in *Vlassopoulou* of any reference to imperative requirements (which was invariably present in the other mutual recognition judgments); and the focus on procedural requirements. We should not overestimate the significance of these findings, however. First, the equivalence criterion was undoubtedly relevant in the other domains but was simply not addressed in some judgments for a given reason, for instance because the proportionality test had already failed at a previous level.[37] Secondly, the fact that the ECJ paid little or no attention to imperative requirements[38] in many of its judgments on mutual recognition of diplomas should certainly not lead us to the conclusion that these justification grounds were irrelevant in the area of diplomas. Imperative requirements do actually play an important role in this area. The ECJ removed any remaining doubts on this matter in its *Kraus* judgment, in which it accepted that national measures may be invoked to pursue a legitimate objective, justified by pressing reasons of public interest insofar as they are appropriate for ensuring the achievement of this objective and do not go beyond what is necessary.[39] Thirdly, from a procedural perspective, the ECJ clearly went one step further in *Vlassopoulou* than in its previous case law on mutual recognition by imposing a duty on each Member State to install an *autonomous* procedure that would compare and verify, within a reasonable amount of time,[40] whether equivalence could be demonstrated as regards knowledge and qualifications.[41] Furthermore, any decision following such a procedure must be capable of being subject to judicial proceedings in which its legality under EU law can be reviewed, and the person concerned must be able to ascertain the reasons for the decision taken.[42] Although the ECJ has perhaps not always reiterated this obligation in the same vigorous wording in the other free movement areas as it did in *Vlassopoulou*, where it referred to an 'autonomous procedure', similar procedural requirements also apply, without any doubt, to the other free movement areas.[43]

[37] See: Part I, ch 1, III. 'Equivalence, Country of Origin, and Mutual Recognition: What's in a Name?'

[38] In *Thieffry* (ECJ, Case 71/76 *Thieffry* [1977] ECR 765, paras 12 and 15), the ECJ mentioned that the freedom of establishment 'is subject to observance of professional rules justified by the general good, particularly rules relating to organisation, qualifications, professional ethics, supervision and liability'. However, in the subsequent case law on mutual recognition of diplomas such reference to imperative requirements was no longer mentioned.

[39] ECJ, Case C-19/92 *Kraus* [1993] ECR I-1663, para 32. See aso: ECJ, Case C-108/96 *McQuen* [2001] ECR I-837, para 28; ECJ, Case C-294/00 *Gräbner* [2002] ECR I-6515, para 50; ECJ, Case C-330/03 *Colegio de Ingenieros de Camino* [2006] ECR I-801, para 39.

[40] The ECJ did not mention this requirement explicitly, but see: Opinion of AG Jacobs in Case C-104/91 *Aguirre Borrel* [1992] ECR I-3003, § 23, who seemed convinced that the requirement of 'a reasonable period' was implicitly present in the *Vlassopoulou* and *Heylens* judgments.

[41] ECJ, Case C-340/89 *Vlassopoulou* [1991] ECR I-2357, paras 17–21. If a Member State does not have such a procedure, the ECJ does not refrain from condemning the corresponding Member State: ECJ, Case C- 375/92 *Commission v Spain* [1994] ECR I-923, para 18.

[42] ECJ, Case 222/86 *Heylens* [1987] ECR 4097, para 17; ECJ, Case C-340/89 *Vlassopoulou* [1991] ECR I-2357, para 22; ECJ, Joined Cases C-372/09 and C-373/09 *Josep Penarroja Fa* [2011] ECR I-1785, paras 62–4, with explicit reference to the Charter.

[43] As far as the area of goods is concerned, see, for instance: ECJ, Case 304/84 *Muller* [1986] ECR 1511, para 26; ECJ, Case 178/84 *Commission v Germany* [1987] ECR 1227, para 45, where the ECJ underlined the need to foresee, in case of a required market authorization, a procedure which is easily accessible to traders and which can be concluded within a reasonable time. As far as services is concerned, the ECJ referred in *Unibet* (ECJ, Case C-432/05 *Unibet* [2007] ECR I-2271, para 61) to *Vlassopoulou* and *Heylens* in relation to the duty to provide a legal remedy securing effective judicial protection of the rights under EU law. But, contrary to *Vlassopoulou*, the ECJ did *not* require the national

(2) Gebhard *and the convergent approach of the ECJ*

The relevance of the principle of mutual recognition in the area of freedom of persons goes far beyond diploma-related issues, however, as illustrated for example by the *Gebhard* judgment[44] on the right to establishment, the *Bosman* judgment[45] on the free movement of workers, the *Sayn-Wittgenstein* and *Vardyn-Wardyn* judgments on the free movement of EU citizens,[46] or the *Cartesio*, *Sevic*, and *Vale* judgments on the transfer of company seats, cross-border mergers, and cross-border conversions.[47]

In the *Gebhard* judgment, the ECJ followed the trend of converging freedoms by ceasing to restrict its reasoning to one of the four freedoms and by addressing all freedoms in more general terms. At the same time, it also stated that national measures liable to hinder or make less attractive the exercise of fundamental freedoms guaranteed by the Treaty must fulfil four conditions: first, they must be applied in a non-discriminatory manner; secondly, they must be justified by imperative requirements in the general interest; thirdly, they must be suitable for securing the attainment of the objective which they pursue; and fourthly, they must not go beyond what is necessary in order to attain that objective.[48]

The duty to compare and take into account any equivalent diploma remains important,[49] though it is no longer the starting point of the ECJ's reasoning but rather a logical corollary to the ECJ's test and the proportionality requirement embodied therein. This test's similarity to the tests developed by the ECJ in *Cassis de Dijon* and *Säger* is striking. *Gebhard* can thus be read as the culmination of a gradual process towards an approach to all freedoms,[50] and as an implicitly cross-freedom approach to the principle of mutual recognition.

legal order of a Member State to provide for an autonomous procedure, i.e. a free-standing action for an examination of whether national provisions are compatible with Article 56 TFEU, provided that other effective legal remedies are available, which are no less favourable than those governing similar domestic actions (principle of equivalence) and which do not render virtually impossible or excessively difficult the exercise of rights conferred by Union law (principle of effectiveness) (ECJ, Case C-432/05 *Unibet* [2007] ECR I-2271, paras 43 and 65). Similarly: ECJ, Case C-524/04 *Test Claimants in the Thin Cap Group Litigation* [2007] ECR I-2107, para 111; ECJ, Joined Cases C-338/04, C-359/04 and C-360/04 *Placanica* [2007] ECR I-1891 para 63. See also, in the area of cross-border conversions of companies: ECJ, Case C-378/10 *Vale*, nyr, para 48. On the growing 'proceduralization' of the proportionality test in the free movement provisions in general and further examples of case law across the different free movement areas, see, for instance: C. BARNARD, 'Derogations, Justifications and the Four Freedoms: Is State Interest Really Protected', in C. BARNARD and O. ODUDU (eds.), *The Outer Limits of European Union Law* (Oxford, Hart Publishing, 2009) 286–7; S. PRECHAL, 'Free Movement and Procedural Requirements: Proportionality Reconsidered', *LIEI* 2008, 201–16.

[44] ECJ, Case C-55/94 *Gebhard* [1995] ECR I-4165.

[45] ECJ, Case C-415/93 *Bosman* [1995] ECR I-4921.

[46] ECJ, Case C-208/09 *Sayn-Wittgenstein* [2010] ECR I-13693; ECJ, Case C-391/09 *Vardyn-Wardyn* [2011] ECR I-3787. The issue of mutual recognition of surnames, had already previously been addressed by the ECJ in: ECJ, Case C-148/02 *Garcia Avello* [2003] I-11613; ECJ, Case C-353/06 *Grunkin Paul* [2008] I-7639.

[47] ECJ, Case C-210/06 *Cartesio* [2008] ECR I-9641; ECJ, Case C-411/03 *Sevic Systems* [2005] ECR I-10805; ECJ, Case C-378/10 *Vale*, nyr. See also the other case law mentioned in these judgments related to the mutual recognition of companies in a cross-border context.

[48] ECJ, Case C-55/94 *Gebhard* [1995] ECR I-4165, para 37.

[49] ECJ, Case C-55/94 *Gebhard* [1995] ECR I-4165, para 38.

[50] J. LONBAY, 'Case Note Gebhard', *CML Rev.* 1996, 1081–3; S. WEATHERILL, *Cases and Materials on EU Law* (Oxford, Oxford University Press, 2006) 320. See also, for a more prudent approach: E. BALLON, 'Case Note Gebhard', *Col. J. Eur. L.* 1997, 150; M. TISON, *De interne markt voor bank- en beleggingsdiensten. Een rechts-vergelijkende juridische analyse van de wederzijdse erkenning als techniek van marktunificatie in de Europese interne markt* (Antwerp, Intersentia, 1998) 80–2.

Notwithstanding the undisputable reference the ECJ made in the *Gebhard* test to all freedoms, many authors have remained hesitant to give voice to this issue and appear to believe that the principle of mutual recognition has a rather limited role to play in the area of freedom of establishment.[51] While they generally recognize that the principle of mutual recognition is essential in relation to diplomas or other aspects having to do with access to a profession, they heavily contest the idea that the same basic assumptions should be in place regarding rules that regulate an activity.[52]

It is, however, difficult to reconcile such a view with the ECJ's case law on the freedom of establishment, which has on repeated occasions imposed a duty to recognize national rules that go far beyond the acceptance of access-related aspects of establishment. In several judgments, the ECJ has applied mutual recognition reasoning to national rules that had repercussions for the economic attractiveness of pursuing certain activities rather than for access to an economic activity. In *Pfeiffer*, the ECJ ruled that forbidding a business to use a certain trade name, which would impede the business's application of a uniform advertising concept throughout the EU, was in principle contrary to free movement of establishment; in *Uberseering*, the same verdict condemned a national rule which had denied a business the legal capacity to defend its rights under a contract in court; and in *CaixaBank*, a national measure which prohibited the remuneration of sight accounts was said to constitute a breach of free movement of establishment.[53] These judgments all seem to indicate that the principle of mutual recognition, applied in the context of freedom of establishment, should not be restricted to purely access-related

[51] See, for instance: M. GARDEÑEZ SANTIAGO, *La aplicación de la regla del reconocimiento mutuo y su incidencia en el comercio de mercancías y servicios en el ámbito comunitario e internacional* (Madrid, Eurolex, 1999) 53–4; P.J.G. KAPTEYN and P. VERLOREN VAN THEMAAT, *Introduction to the Law of the European Communities. From Maastricht to Amsterdam* (The Hague, Wolters Kluwer, 1998) 738, where it was held that 'in the case of establishment, in the absence of specific provisions at Community level, the presumption is in favour of the permissibility of the national rule, whereas this is not the case for the free movement of goods and which is also much less the case for the freedom to provide services' (compare, however, with: KAPTEYN, McDONNELL, MORTELMANS, and TIMMERMANS, *The Law of the European Union and the European Communities* (n 3) 725–8, where the previous statement is no longer mentioned); P.J. SLOT, R. BARENTS, R.A. LAWSON, and J. MEEUSEN, *Inleiding Europees recht* (Groningen, Noordhoff, 2008) 137; TISON, *De interne markt voor bank- en beleggingsdiensten* (n 50) 80; WOUTERS, *Het Europees vestigingsrecht voor ondernemingen herbekeken* (n 29) 365, 489, and 655; Opinion of AG Van Gerven in Case *Vlassopoulou* [1991] ECR I-2357, § 12; Opinion of AG Tizzano in Case C-442/02 *Caixa Bank* [2004] ECR I-8961, § 29–75. This point of view is possibly inspired by the unequal progress that has characterized both freedoms over the years and, in particular, the fact that the ECJ did not seem to attribute the freedom of establishment the same scope as the free movement of goods and services. For an overview of the evolution in the ECJ's case law on this issue, see: P. BEHRENS, 'Die Konvergenz der wirtschaftlichen Freiheiten im europäischen Gemeinschaftsrecht', *EuR* 1992, 145–62; N. BERNARD, 'Discrimination and Free Movement in EC Law', *ICLQ* 1996, 82–108; G. STRAETMANS, *Consument en markt* (Deurne, Kluwer, 1998) 312–23.

[52] For an overview of some criteria that have been developed in legal doctrine, see TISON, *De interne markt voor bank- en beleggingsdiensten* (n 50) 77–80.

[53] See, for instance: ECJ, Case C-255/97 *Pfeiffer Großhandel* [1999] ECR I-2835, para 20; ECJ, Case C-208/00 *Uberseering* [2002] ECR I-9919, para 82; ECJ, Case C-442/02 *CaixaBank France* [2004] ECR I-8961, para 24. Even though the ECJ nowhere in *CaixaBank France* explicitly mentioned the more permissible Spanish legislation on this matter, it is evident that implicitly it is present. The outcome of the judgment is, indeed, governed by the principle of mutual recognition, since it forbids a national measure which precludes a French subsidiary of a Spanish company to apply the more permissible Spanish legislation to its activity regarding sight accounts. For some examples of judgments of the ECJ's case law prior to *Gebhard*, see for instance: ECJ, Case C-19/92 *Kraus* [1993] ECR I-1663, para 18; ECJ, Case C-106/91 *Ramrath* [1992] ECR I-3351, para 23.

rules[54] or, perhaps more correctly, that the concept of 'access to the market' should be interpreted very broadly.[55]

In these judgments, the broad scope of the principle of mutual recognition is also reflected by the fact that (all of) the free movement provisions (and the principle of mutual recognition enshrined therein) can be invoked not only by natural persons but also by legal persons. As far as the latter category is concerned, it has been argued by some authors that the contours of the principle of mutual recognition sometimes seem remarkably less restrictive than for natural persons. In this respect, reference is often made to the *Centros* and *Inspire Art* judgments, in which the ECJ imposed a quasi-automatic recognition duty when confronted with two diverging national legislations and the position of legal persons.[56] This approach is in sharp contrast with the ECJ's previously discussed case law on diplomas, which revealed an emphasis on thorough analysis and comparison of the qualification and experience acquired abroad, and which will only lead to a duty of recognition in the event of full equivalence.[57] The ECJ's more stringent mutual recognition test in the latter area would then potentially result in the lower mobility of natural persons than of legal persons or goods.[58] However, such an interpretation must be nuanced in the light of two arguments. First, in the ECJ's case law on EU citizenship, the final outcome of the judgments is rarely—if ever—detrimental to the natural persons concerned.[59] Secondly, the ECJ's more recent case law on cross-border company transfers clearly reveals that in that context free movement and mutual recognition duties are far from absolute, especially in view of the fact that—as EU law currently stands—Member States still possess considerable power with regard to the creation of companies and their subsequent use of the free movement rights.[60] In sum, given this analysis of the ECJ's case law it would be erroneous to conclude that either natural persons or legal persons enjoy preferential treatment vis-à-vis the other category.

[54] L. GONZÁLEZ VAQUÉ, 'L'arrêt *Caixa Bank France*: La Cour de Justice des Communautés Européennes confirme la convergence de sa jurisprudence relative à la libre circulation dans le marché intérieur', *Euredia* 2006, 170.

[55] E. SPAVENTA, 'From *Gebhard to Carpenter*: Towards a (Non-) Economic European Constitution', *CML Rev.* 2004, 763, who warns that an extremely broad construction of the market access test is capable of encompassing virtually any rule. In *CaixaBank* the ECJ seems indeed convinced that the national measure at stake makes the *access to the market* more difficult: ECJ, Case C-442/02 *CaixaBank France* [2004] ECR I-8961, para 14. Similarly, ECJ, Case C-400/08 *Commission v Spain* [2011] ECR I-1915, para 64, where the ECJ recalls that for the purposes of Article 49 TFEU the concept of restriction covers measures which affect *access* to the market, whereas with regard to Article 56 TFEU the ECJ has repeatedly forbidden 'any restriction which is liable to prohibit, to impede or to render less advantageous the *activities* of a provider of services established in another Member State in which he lawfully provides similar services': ECJ, Joined Cases C-372/09 and C-373/09 *Josep Peñarroja Fa* [2011] ECR I-1785, para 50.

[56] ECJ, Case C-212/97 *Centros* [1999] ECR I-1459; ECJ, Case C-167/01 *Inspire Art* [2003] ECR I-10155.

[57] See, for instance: ECJ, Case C-340/89 *Vlassopolou* [1991] ECR I-2357.

[58] A plea for a more convergent approach can be found in: Opinion of AG Lenz in Case C-1/93 *Halliburton Services* [1994] ECR I-1147, § 41–6, and, approving, WOUTERS, *Het Europees vestigingsrecht voor ondernemingen herbekeken* (n 29) 484–6. See also: P. CABRAL and P. CUNHA, 'Presumed Innocent: Companies and the Exercise of the Right of Establishment under Community Law', *E.L. Rev.* 2000, 162; M. POIARES MADURO, 'Harmony and Dissonance in Free Movement', in M. ANDENAS and W.-H. ROTH (eds.), *Services and Free Movement in EU Law* (Oxford, Oxford University Press, 2002) 67.

[59] See, for instance: ECJ, Case C-148/02 *Garcia Avello* [2003] ECR I-11613; ECJ, Case C-200/02 *Zhu and Chen* [2004] ECR I-9925.

[60] See, for instance: ECJ, Case C-210/06 *Cartesio* [2008] ECR I-9641, paras 104, 109–10, where the ECJ started by recalling that companies are creatures of national law; or: ECJ, Case C-378/10 *Vale*, nyr, paras 43–5 and 48, where the ECJ explained that a cross-border conversion requires the consecutive

D. Mutual recognition and the free movement of capital

With regard to the free movement of capital, any role for the principle of mutual recognition was entirely absent for a long time.[61] According to some authors, this delay was due to the fact that there was no need to introduce the principle of mutual recognition officially in this area, since capital movements are by their nature almost perfect.[62] A far more plausible explanation lies in the fact that the Treaty provisions on free movement of capital were initially far more limited than their counterparts in the other freedoms.[63]

It was only with the coming into force of the Treaty of Maastricht, which enshrined the freedom of capital (Art. 63 TFEU), albeit with potentially far-reaching restrictions (Art. 65 TFEU), that case law on free movement of capital was truly developed and began to show significant convergence with the other freedoms.[64] The ECJ not only granted Article 63 TFEU direct effect, which it had done much earlier for the other free movement provisions, but also adopted a wide understanding of what amounts to a restriction and limited the exceptions enshrined in Article 65 TFEU by applying its normal rule of reason test in combination with a proportionality check, in the same way that it had been doing until then with the other freedoms.[65] In light of this evolution, it was not surprising that the ECJ condemned on the basis of (both Article 56 TFEU and) Article 63 TFEU a national obligation to establish a financial guarantee in a given Member State where such a rule precluded the taking into account of obligations comparable to those the provider was already subjected to in the Member State of establishment.[66] The prohibition of such a 'dual burden' was perfectly in line with the mutual

application of two national laws. Admittedly, this national law cannot escape all review in light of the Treaty provisions on free movement. However, the equivalence and effectiveness tests that the ECJ applies do not impose an absolute regime of mutual recognition. In fact, in the present case it was the refusal to record in the commercial register the company of the Member State of origin (para 56, breach of the principle of equivalence) and the practice in the host Member State of refusing, *in a general manner*, to take account of documents obtained from the authorities of the Member State of origin (para 60, breach of the principle of effectiveness), that constituted a breach of the free movement provisions.

[61] A. BERNEL, *Le principe d'équivalence ou de reconnaissance mutuelle en droit communautaire* (Zürich, Schulthess Polygrafischer Verlag, 1996); D. CHALMERS, 'Repackaging the Internal Market—the Ramification of the Keck Judgment', *E.L. Rev.* 1994, 393.

[62] F.K. PADOA SCHIOPPA, 'Mutual Recognition, Unemployment and the Welfare State', in F.K. PADOA SCHIOPPA (ed.), *The Principle of Mutual Recognition in the European Integration Process* (New York, Palgrave, 2005) 217.

[63] For an analysis of the ECJ's modest *Casati* judgment (ECJ, Case 203/80 *Casati* [1981] ECR 2595) and some other judgments of the pre-Maastricht era, see, for instance: R. MURPHY, 'Free Movement of Capital: Directive 88/361', paper presented at Jean Monnet Workshop 'The Legislature, the Judiciary and the Completion of the Internal Market', 8–9 March 2010, University of Antwerp.

[64] M. AUDIT, 'Régulation du marché intérieur et libre circulation des lois', *J.D.I.* 2006, 12–14; L. FLYNN, 'Coming of Age: the Free Movement of Capital Case Law 1993-2002', *CML Rev.* 2002, 804.

[65] See, for instance, with regard to direct taxation: ECJ, Joined Cases C-163/94, C-165/94 and C-250/94 *Sanz de Lera* [1995] ECR I-04821, para 48; ECJ, Case C-35/98 *Verkooijen* [2000] ECR I-4071, para 43 (with reference to previous case law in the field of services and workers); ECJ, Case C-319/02 *Manninen* [2004] ECR I-7477, para 29. See, for instance, with regard to the acquisition of real estate and secondary residences: ECJ, Case C-302/97 *Konle* [1999] ECR I-3099, para 40; ECJ, Joined Cases C-515/99, C-519 to C-524/99 and C-526/99 to C-540/99, *Reisch* [2002] ECR I-2157, para 33. See, for instance, with regard to the *golden shares*: ECJ, Case C-367/98 *Commission v Portugal* [2002] ECR I-4731; ECJ, Case C-483/99 *Commission v France* [2002] ECR I-4781; ECJ, Case C-503/99 *Commission v Belgium* [2002] ECR I-4809; ECJ, Case C-463/00 *Commission v Spain* [2003] ECR I-4581. For an in-depth analysis of the relevant case law, see: J. SNELL, 'Free Movement of Capital: Evolution as a Non-Linear Process', paper presented at Jean Monnet Workshop 'The legislature, the judiciary and the completion of the internal market', 8-9 March 2010, University of Antwerp; J. USHER, 'The Evolution of the Free Movement of Capital', *Fordh. Int. L. J.* 2007–08, 1533 ff.

[66] ECJ, Case C-279/00 *Commission v Italy* [2002] ECR I-1425, paras 34 and 37.

recognition rationale developed in case law in relation to the other freedoms. By the same token, the ECJ condemned a national rule which did not grant a tax deduction to a charity body of another Member State that nonetheless fulfilled all of the criteria and all of the objectives that were required of charity bodies in that (non-granting) Member State (it therefore concerned 'equivalent' bodies).[67] Furthermore, it authorized (and, in fact, urged) the Member State to apply any measures necessary that would enable the authorities to ascertain in a clear and precise manner whether the charity body met the conditions imposed by national law in order to be entitled to the exemption (thus a duty of cooperation to assess the existence (or lack) of equivalence).[68] Finally, the ECJ has stated in a more recent judgment that equivalence checks must not be applied too formalistically.[69]

Despite the strong similarities that emerged between the four freedoms after the Treaty of Maastricht came into force, two features that set apart the Treaty provisions on the free movement of capital cannot be left unmentioned here as they have a potential impact on the scope of the principle of mutual recognition. These provisions are, paradoxically, both broader and more restricted than the other free movement provisions. First, they are broader in that they not only apply to the free movement of capital between Member States but also vis-à-vis third countries. This is highly relevant from a mutual recognition perspective, as it has been correctly argued that a world of difference exists between, on the one hand, a worldwide free movement regime between sovereign states with vastly different social, economic, and political conditions and, on the other, a single market among a relatively homogenous group of countries within the framework of a project of political integration where the Member States have, albeit within limited fields, agreed to limit their sovereign rights.[70] Such an interpretation was confirmed in the case law on free movement of capital where the ECJ held that 'restrictions on the exercise of the freedoms of movement within the EU cannot be transposed in its entirety to movements of capital between Member States and non-Member States, since such movements take place in a different legal context'.[71] Secondly, the Treaty provisions on the free movement of capital are more restricted than the other free movement provisions in that the restrictions enshrined in Article 65(1) TFEU reflect a remnant of sovereignty that relates to the Member States' competence in the area of tax law, which has no counterpart in the other free movement provisions. Although the ECJ interpreted this restriction narrowly in *Manninen*,[72] and in doing so gave more leeway to the principle of mutual recognition in one of the crown jewels of national sovereignty, namely direct taxes, other judgments in this same area of law, such as *Kerckhard*,[73] demonstrate that the ECJ's concerns for safeguarding and respecting national sovereignty in this particular field of law remain a key consideration.[74]

[67] ECJ, Case C-386/04 *Centro de Musicologia* [2006] ECR I-8203, para 40; ECJ, Case C-318/07 *Persche* [2009] ECR I-359, para 49.

[68] ECJ, Case C-386/04 *Centro de Musicologia* [2006] ECR I-8203, para 48; ECJ, Case C-318/07 *Persche* [2009] ECR I-359, paras 55–8.

[69] ECJ, Case C-262/09 *Meilicke,* nyr, para 46.

[70] BERNARD, 'On the Art of Not Mixing One's Drinks: *Dassonville* and *Cassis de Dijon* Revisited' (n 13) 464.

[71] See, for instance: ECJ, Case C-101/05 *A* [2007] ECR I-11531, paras 60 ff; ECJ, Case C-194/06 *Orange European Smallcap Fund* [2008] ECR I-3747, paras 87–90; ECJ, Joined Cases C-436/08 and 437/08 *Haribo* [2011] ECR I-305, paras 119–20; ECJ, Case C-72/09 *Rimbaut* [2010] ECR I-10659, para 40.

[72] ECJ, Case C-319/02 *Manninen* [2004] ECR I-7477.

[73] ECJ, Case C-513/04 *Kerckhaert* [2006] ECR I-10967.

[74] For a good understanding of the relevant distinction between both judgments, see, in partiuclar: K. LENAERTS and L. BERNARDEAU, 'L'encadrement communautaire de la fiscalité directe',

E. Four freedoms: one principle?

The question of whether and to what extent the ECJ's case law on the free movement provisions is characterized by either convergence or divergence is a matter of intense debate.[75] Although both the TFEU and the ECJ's case law have demonstrated signs of both tendencies throughout the years, it cannot be denied that the predominant trend in the ECJ's case law aims at merging its approach across the different free movement domains towards a joint understanding of the principle of mutual recognition. This common approach reveals itself in common actors (the principle of mutual recognition is, in principle, addressed to the Member States),[76] a common definition of the concept 'restriction to free movement', and a parallel application of the mandatory requirements and their corresponding proportionality tests, with an emphasis on dual burdens.[77]

While the ECJ is thus clearly willing to maintain the integrationist effects of intra-Union market penetration, we cannot deny that differences exist in how the freedoms of the internal market, and its underlying principle of mutual recognition, operate in practice.[78] In other words, in its case law on the free movement Treaty provisions, the ECJ embraced a convergent approach but resisted pressure from certain learned writers and AGs who argued for the development of a truly unified approach.

C.D.E. 2007, 59–63. See also: Part I, ch 1, IV, A, 1. 'A prudent hands-off approach with an emphasis on a national perspective'.

[75] See, for instance: M. ANDENAS and W.-H. ROTH, *Services and Free Movement in EU Law* (Oxford, Oxford University Press, 2002); S. ENCHELMAIER, 'Four Freedoms, How Many Principles', *OJLS* 2004, 155–72; V. HATZOPOULOS, 'Trente ans après les arrêts fondamentaux de 1974, les quatre libertés: quatre', in P. DEMARET, I. GOVAERE, and D. HANF (eds.), *30 Years of European Legal Studies at the College of Europe. Liber professorum 1973–74—2003–04* (Brussels, Peter Lang, 2005) 185–201; S. FEIDEN, *Die Bedeutung der 'Keck'-Rechtsprechung im System der Grundfreiheiten. Ein Beitrag zum Kovergenz der Freiheiten* (Berlin, Duncker & Humblot, 2003); KAPTEYN, McDONNELL, MORTELMANS, and TIMMERMANS, *The Law of the European Union and the European Communities* (n 3) 593–4; P. OLIVER and W.-H. ROTH, 'The Internal Market and the Four Freedoms', *CML Rev.* 2004, 407–41; S. PEERS, 'Free Movement of Capital: Learning Lessons or Slipping on Spilt Milk', in C. BARNARD and J. SCOTT (eds.), *The Law of the Single European Market* (Oxford, Hart Publishing, 2002) 334–49; J. SNELL, *Goods and Services in EC Law. A Study of the Relationship between the Freedoms* (Oxford, Oxford University Press, 2002); SNELL, 'Free Movement of Capital: Evolution as a Non-Linear Process' (n 65); A. TRYFONIDOU, 'Further Steps on the Road to Convergence among the Market Freedoms', *E.L. Rev.* 2010, 36–56.

[76] The often mentioned divide in academic writing between public entities (free movement of goods) and private entities (free movement of services), must be nuanced for two reasons. First, the ECJ upholds in its case law on the free movement of goods a broad interpretation of the concept 'Member State' or 'public entity'. Secondly, the entities of a non-public nature that have occasionally been present in the ECJ's case law on the free movement of persons are nearly all entities with close affinities to public entities (see, for instance: ECJ, Case C-415/93 *Bosman* [1995] ECR I-4921; ECJ, Case C-341/05 *Laval un Partneri* [2007] ECR I-11767; ECJ, Case C-318/05 *Commission v Germany* [2007] ECR I-6957).

[77] See, for instance: ECJ, Case C-55/94 *Gebhard* [1995] ECR I-4165, para 37; ECJ, Case C-390/99 *Canal Satélite Digital* [2002] ECR I-607, paras 33–7; ECJ, Case C-330/03 *Colegio de Ingenieros de camino* [2006] ECR I-801, para 30; ECJ, Case C-243/01 *Gambelli* [2003] ECR I-13031, paras 64–5; Opinion of AG Bot in Case C-110/05, *Commission v Italy* [2009] ECR I-519, § 118–19 and 131.

[78] See, for instance: the strong focus on the equivalence requirement in combination with a comparative examination procedure in the area of mutual recognition of diplomas (see: Part I, ch 1, I, C. 'Mutual recognition and the free movement of persons'), the influence of the *Keck* judgment on the development of the case law on the free movement of goods (see: Part I, ch 1, IV, A, 1. 'A prudent hands-off approach with an emphasis on a national perspective'), or the peculiarities of the free movement of capital (see: Part I, ch 1, I, D. 'Mutual recognition and the free movement of capital' and Part I, ch 1, IV, A, 1. 'A prudent hands-off approach with an emphasis on a national perspective'). See, moreover, the very restrictive interpretation of Article 35 TFEU on restrictions on export of goods (ECJ, Case 15/79 *Groenveld* [1979] ECR, 3409), which has no equivalent in the ECJ's case law on services, and the Opinion of AG Trstenjak, who suggested, in vain, a change of the *Groenveld* line of case law: Opinion of AG Trstenjak in Case C-205/07 *Gysbrechts* [2008] ECR I-9947, § 42–66.

This position deserves approval, as one-size-fits-all legal solutions tend not to work in practice, and are often inelegant in conception and even worse in implementation.[79]

In what follows, I will also demonstrate that the ECJ's application of a single test, albeit with distinguishing features, leads to results which will not only diverge in terms of the freedom at stake but also—thanks to a flexible proportionality test—in terms of the matter's political sensitivity and/or the specific circumstances of the case at hand.[80]

II. Legal Basis and Interrelation with Other General Principles of EU Law

Having situated the principle of mutual recognition in the framework of the four freedoms, the next question for this study concerns the legal basis on which this principle should be founded. Before discussing the legal bases that the ECJ and legal doctrine have put forward, it is useful to refer briefly to a number of internal market Treaty provisions in which the term mutual recognition is (or was) explicitly incorporated.

A. Explicit references to mutual recognition in the former EC Treaty

The term mutual recognition was mentioned twice in the former EC Treaty, first in relation to the mutual recognition of diplomas (former Art. 47 EC, currently Art. 53 TFEU) and secondly in terms of the mutual recognition of companies (former Art. 293 EC, abrogated by the Treaty of Lisbon).[81] However, in both of these clear-cut fields, the idea of mutual recognition was not presented as a general judicial principle of mutual recognition but rather as an incentive for the Council and the Member States to take the necessary (legislative) measures to facilitate the internal market process. These articles can therefore not be considered a sound legal basis for a judicially developed principle of mutual recognition.

Another old Treaty article, formerly Article 100 B EC, introduced by the Single European Act but abrogated by the Treaty of Amsterdam, cannot serve as a legal basis either, for obvious reasons, but is nevertheless worth mentioning. This former Treaty provision stipulated that the Council could decide that national provisions which had not been harmonized with former Article 100 A EC by the 1992 deadline should be recognized as equivalent to provisions applied in other Member States. Ultimately, the Council never applied former Article 100 B EC,[82] but it did come in for intense criticism and saw divergent interpretations of its true meaning and relation to the judicially developed

[79] L. GORMLEY, 'Silver Threads among the Gold... 50 Years on the Free Movement of Goods', *Fordh. Int. L. J.* 2008, 1691.

[80] See: Part I, ch 1, IV, A. 'The ECJ's evaluation of justification grounds'.

[81] Article 53(1) TFEU stipulates that 'in order to make it easier for persons to take up and pursue activities as self-employed persons, the European Parliament and the Council shall [...] issue directives for the mutual recognition of diplomas [...]'. Former Article 293 EC stipulated that 'Member States shall, so far as is necessary, enter into negotiations with each other with a view to securing for the benefit of their nationals [...] the mutual recognition of companies or firms [...]'.

[82] The Commission itself was apparently not inclined to promote an application of former Article 100 B EC. In the conclusions of the inventory which was drawn up pursuant to Article 100 B EC the Commission argued that 'it did not see the need for any specific measures for the recognition of equivalence at Community level'. The Commission did, however, believe that it was essential to ensure compliance with the principle of mutual recognition, by managing transparently, effectively, and consistently what must remain exceptions to the principle. See: Communication from the Commission to

principle of mutual recognition. Some authors expressed fears that this provision could have jeopardized the entire mutual recognition acquis that had been developed by the ECJ since *Cassis de Dijon*.[83] Yet, had it been interpreted differently, this article could plausibly have paved the way for automatic application of the principle of mutual recognition with regard to the measures the Council would have considered appropriate, i.e. without the need to verify the equivalence requirement or without the possibility of invoking mandatory justification grounds.[84]

Article 53 TFEU (former Art. 47 EC), former Article 293 EC, and former Article 100 B EC are mentioned here because they reflect the relevance and added value of the principle of mutual recognition for the internal market project, and also because they may have inspired the ECJ during the search for an adequate interpretation of the Treaty provisions on free movement.

B. The principle of proportionality[85]

Many authors are inclined to consider the principle of mutual recognition an application of the principle of proportionality, or at least an avenue to more frequent mutual recognition of other Member States' legal acts.[86] As I mentioned above, when discussing the rule of reason test in the free movement areas, the ECJ investigates whether a national measure serves a mandatory ground and—if so—whether that measure is necessary and proportionate. As a general rule, national measures that duplicate equivalent norms are considered disproportionate. If the objective that the national measure seeks to protect is already safeguarded by an equivalent rule in the Member State of origin, the principle

the European Parliament and the Council—Management of the Mutual Recognition of national rules after 1992. Operational conclusions in light of the inventory drawn up pursuant to Article 100b of the EC Treaty, COM (1993) 669 final, p. 14 and 17.

[83] See, in particular: P. PESCATORE, 'Observations critiques sur l'Acte Unique européen', in *L'Acte unique européen: journée d'études Bruxelles, 1er mars 1986* (Brussels, Institut d'Etudes Européennes, 1986) 39. *Contra,* defending a more moderate attitude: J. DE RUYT, *L'Acte Unique européen. Commentaire* (Brussels, Editions de l'Université de Bruxelles, 1989) 159–60; M. WAELBROECK, 'Le rôle de la Cour de justice dans la mise en oeuvre de l'Acte unique européen', *C.D.E.* 1989, 42 and 62, and the references mentioned therein.

[84] Moreover, such an interpretation finds support in the original Commission's proposal regarding the text of former Article 100 B EC. In the original Commission's proposal, which went clearly further, mutual recognition would apply even without the need of a Council's decision and would, furthermore, apply to all measures relating to the free movement of persons, goods, services, and capital, which had not been subject to harmonization measures by 1992. On this provision, see: M. LÓPEZ ESCUDERO, 'La aplicación del principio del reconocimiento mutuo en el derecho comunitario', *G. J.* 1993, D-19, 158–64; H. MATTHIES, 'Zur Anerkennung gleichwertiger Regelungen im Binnenmarkt der EG (Art. 100b EWG-Vertrag)', in J.F.BAUR and K.P. MAILANDER (eds.), *Festschrift für Ernst Steindorff zum 70. Geburtstag am 13. März 1990* (Berlin, De Gruyter, 1990) 1287–301; WAELBROECK, 'Le rôle de la Cour de justice dans la mise en oeuvre de l'Acte unique européen' (n 83) 61.

[85] Article 5(4) TEU and Protocol No 2 on the application of the principles of subsidiarity and proportionality.

[86] N. EMILIOU, *The Principle of Proportionality in European Law* (The Hague, Kluwer, 1996) 230–2; FALLON, *Droit matériel général de l'Union européenne* (n 19) 150–1; KAPTEYN, McDONNELL, MORTELMANS, and TIMMERMANS, *The Law of the European Union and the European Communities* (n 3) 145; K. LENAERTS and P. VAN NUFFEL, *European Union Law* (London, Sweet and Maxwell, 2011) 225; MATTERA, *Le Marché unique européen: ses règles, son fonctionnement* (n 3) 288; T. TRIDIMAS, *The General Principles of EU Law* (Oxford, Oxford University Press, 2006) 218–19; W. VAN GERVEN, 'Les principes de subsidiarité, proportionnalité et coopération en droit communautaire européen', in *Hacia un nuevo órden internacional y europeo. Estudios en homenaje al Profesor Don Manuel Díez de Velasco* (Madrid, Tecnos, 1993) 1287–8.

of mutual recognition must prevail. There is abundant case law to support this view.[87] From this perspective, the principle of mutual recognition could be seen as grounded in the principle of proportionality. Yet the finding that the principle of mutual recognition is predominantly present in the context of a proportionality test (which I would qualify as mutual recognition *sensu stricto*), i.e. mutual recognition as an equivalence test, does not necessarily exclude this principle's playing a more autonomous role.

In fact, it is my belief that certain arguments suggest that the scope of the principle of mutual recognition should not be limited simply to a proportionality test since it also plays a role at an earlier stage, namely as a point of departure when evaluating national measures which potentially constitute barriers to one of the four freedoms. This is what I would call mutual recognition *sensu lato*. From this perspective, mutual recognition not only prevails in cases where dual burdens or equivalent legislations are considered disproportionate to a specific imperative requirement but also in cases where, in the absence of any proportionality test, there is simply no valid imperative requirement to justify the non-application (or non-recognition) of a foreign national legislation or action. I will therefore argue that the principle of mutual recognition and the principle of equivalence should not be treated as synonyms, but rather that the latter, being part of the proportionality test, helps to determine the scope of the former. Seen from this broader perspective, the principle of proportionality certainly is relevant, albeit insufficiently, as a legal basis for the principle of mutual recognition.

C. The principle of subsidiarity[88]

Another general principle of EU law that has been linked to the principle of mutual recognition is the principle of subsidiarity.[89] Long before its introduction in the Maastricht Treaty and its reinforcement through a specific Protocol adhered to the Amsterdam Treaty,[90] the principle of subsidiarity had in fact manifested itself in what was called the New Approach of the Commission. The ECJ had paved the way for the Commission's New Approach firstly by declaring that, in the absence of harmonized rules relating to the production and marketing of products, it was for the Member States to regulate all these matters, and secondly by obliging these Member States to recognize in principle all products lawfully produced and marketed in another Member State.[91] As part of its new policy, the Commission announced that it would renounce an excessively detailed

[87] See, for instance: ECJ, Case 251/78 *Denkavit* [1979] ECR 3369, para 3; ECJ, Case 132/80 *United Food* [1981] ECR 995, para 29; ECJ, Case 272/80 *Biologisch Producten* [1981] ECR 3277, paras 14–15; ECJ, Case 188/84 *Type approval for woodworking machines* [1986] ECR 419, paras 16–17.

[88] Article 5(3) TEU and Protocol No 2 on the application of the principles of subsidiarity and proportionality.

[89] Report from the Commission to the Council and the European Parliament—The implementation of the Commission's White Paper on completing the internal market, COM (1994) 55 final, p. 35; K. LENAERTS, 'De Europese Unie: doel of middel', *R.W.* 1998-99, 705; A. MATTERA, 'Subsidiarité, reconnaissance mutuelle et hiérarchie des normes européennes', *RMUE* 1991, 8; S. VAN RAEPENBUSCH, *Droit institutionnel de l'Union et des Communautés européennes* (Paris, De Boeck, 1998) 134–5; J.S. WATSON, 'Wederzijdse erkenning binnen de interne markt: een nieuwe impuls', *NTER* 2000, 42.

[90] Protocol on the application of the principles of subsidiarity and proportionality, annexed to the Treaty establishing the European Community, *O.J.* 1997, C-340/1, para 8. See also: K. LENAERTS, 'De Europese Unie: doel of middel', *R.W.* 1998–99, 705, who connects the principle of mutual recognition with the Protocol and the principle of community loyalty that is mentioned therein, to conclude that the *Cassis de Dijon* judgment should be seen as an application *avant la lettre* of point 8 of this Protocol.

[91] ECJ, Case 120/78 *Rewe-Zentral AG (Cassis de Dijon)* [1979] ECR 649, paras 8 and 14.

harmonization policy. It subscribed to the principle of mutual recognition and declared that the Commission's work on harmonization would henceforth be directed mainly at national laws having an impact on the functioning of the common market where barriers to trade arose from national provisions admissible under the criteria set by the ECJ.[92] In other words, the New Approach clearly focused on harmonizing only those matters that could not be dealt with sufficiently by the Member States using the principle of mutual recognition. Seen in this light, the New Approach can be considered an early application of the principle of subsidiarity.

However, this conclusion should by no means imply that the principle of subsidiarity may be considered a legal basis for the principle of mutual recognition. In fact, the principle of mutual recognition as a judicially developed principle is applied by the ECJ in cases where no harmonized measures are present and only where the national legislations of two Member States govern the conflict. The principle of subsidiarity, as a guiding principle for dividing the exercise of competence between the EU and the Member States, may well be the starting point for the EU's legislative approach to the four freedoms, but it has little impact on the judicially developed principle of mutual recognition and is therefore inadequate as a legal basis.

D. The principle of sincere cooperation[93]

In only a small number of mutual recognition judgments has the ECJ's reasoning been supported by the principle of sincere cooperation in addition to the free movement provisions. These few judgments, furthermore, were almost exclusively situated in the area of the mutual recognition of diplomas. For example, in *Thieffry*, its first judgment on the mutual recognition of diplomas, the ECJ's reasoning was based both on Article 49 TFEU and on Article 4(3) TEU in order to conclude that a Member State had a duty to realize the objectives set out by the Treaty and to recognize a diploma if permitted by the national legislation (though European harmonization measures had not yet been adopted), as well as an obligation to set up a particular procedure.[94]

The ECJ has also referred occasionally to Article 4(3) TEU outside of the diploma context, however. For example, in *Hedley Lomas*, in the area of free movement of goods, the ECJ invoked Article 4(3) TEU in order to sustain that a given Member State, when unilaterally adopting on its own authority corrective or protective measures designed to obviate any other Member State's breach of the rules of EU law, was not taking all measures necessary to guarantee the application and effectiveness of EU law.[95] In other words, a breach of Article 4(3) TEU committed by taking unilateral measures would be seen as jeopardizing the mutual recognition process unjustifiably and was thus condemned. The ECJ's approach made it abundantly clear that the principle of

[92] Communication from the Commission concerning the consequences of the judgment given by the ECJ on 20 February 1979 in Case 120/78 ('Cassis de Dijon') (n 3) p. 3. White Paper from the Commission to the European Council—Completing the Internal Market, COM (1985) 310 final, p. 19–25. The New Approach was followed by the Council in: Resolution of the Council—A new approach to technical harmonization and standards, *O.J.* C-136, 04.06.1985, p. 1–9.

[93] Article 4(3) TEU.

[94] ECJ, Case 71/76 *Thieffry* [1977] ECR 765, paras 16–17. See also: ECJ, Case 222/86 *Heylens* [1987] ECR 4097, para 12; ECJ, Case C-340/89 *Vlassopoulou* [1991] ECR I-2357, paras 14–15; ECJ, Case C-104/91 *Aguirre Borrel* [1992] ECR I-3003, para 9 and ECJ, Case C-19/92 *Kraus* [1993] ECR I-1663, paras 31–2; Opinion of AG Stix-Hackl in Case C-231/03 *Consorzio Aziende Metano* [2005] ECR I-7287, § 52.

[95] ECJ, Case C-5/94 *Hedley Lomas* [1996] ECR I-2553, paras 19–20.

mutual recognition, read in light of the principle of sincere cooperation, implies a duty of solidarity and mutual respect between Member States.[96] Such duties of solidarity and respect, furthermore, must be distinguished from the principle of reciprocity or *pacta sunt servanda*, in force in international law.[97]

The ECJ's scant reference to Article 4(3) TEU outside of the diploma context has not prevented distinguished authors suggesting that the principle of mutual recognition can be read as an expression of Article 4(3) TEU.[98] In view of the broad wording of this provision, however, it would be less than convincing to propose that this principle alone could suffice as a legal basis for the principle of mutual recognition. At the most, it could play a role as a co-legal basis,[99] in combination with one of the specific free movement provisions that will be discussed hereinafter.

E. The principle of mutual trust

In the aforementioned *Hedley Lomas* judgment, the ECJ also insisted that Member States trust each other to carry out inspections on their respective territories.[100] This duty of mutual trust had already been recognized as a general principle in *Bouchara* some years earlier.[101] The ECJ underlined in the latter judgment that the prohibition of double controls and dual burdens, as established in its previous case law,[102] was in fact a particular application of the more general principle of mutual trust between Member States' authorities. There was no mention of the legal ground upon which this principle had been introduced in the EU legal order, but one provision that can surely qualify as a legal ground is the principle of sincere cooperation discussed above (Art. 4(3) TEU).[103] Indeed, the concept of trust, which from a more general socio-economic perspective is defined as a basic social mechanism for coping with system complexity and for sustaining long-term cooperation,[104] is particularly important for a system such as the EU, which

[96] An explicit reference to a duty of 'mutual respect' under the principle of sincere cooperation was explicitly incorporated in Article 4(3) TEU by the Treaty of Lisbon.

[97] V. CONSTANTINESCO, 'L'article 5 CEE, de la bonne foi à la loyauté communautiare', in *Du droit international au droit de l'intégration. Liber amicorum Pierre Pescatore* (Baden-Baden, Nomos, 1987) 101–2; R.-E. PAPADOPOULOU, *Principes généraux du droit et droit communautaire. Origine et Concrétisation* (Athens, Sakkoulas, 1996) 102.

[98] See, for instance: M. BLANQUET, *L'article 5 du traité CEE. Recherche sur les obligations de filélité des états members de la communauté* (Paris, L.G.D.J., 1994) 90–1; K. LENAERTS, 'Le devoir de loyauté communautaire', in J. VERHOEVEN (ed.), *La Loyauté. Mélanges offerts à Etienne Cerexhe* (Brussels, Larcier, 1997) 238–9; KAPTEYN, McDONNELL, MORTELMANS, and TIMMERMANS, *The Law of the European Union and the European Communities* (n 3), 155.

[99] J. TEMPLE LANG, 'The Principle of Legal Cooperation and the Role of the National Judge in Community, Union and EEA Law', *ERA Forum* 2006, 500.

[100] ECJ, Case C-5/94 *Hedley Lomas* [1996] ECR I-2553, paras 19–20, confirmed in: ECJ, Case C-11/95 *Commission v Belgium* [1996] ECR I-4115, para 88; ECJ, Case C-1/96 *Compassion in World Farming* [1998] ECR I-1251, para 47.

[101] ECJ, Case 25/88 *Bouchara* [1989] ECR 1105, para 18. The ECJ had mentioned the obligation of mutual trust, without referring to it as a general principle, years before in the context of a harmonized directive in: ECJ, Case 46/76 *Bauhuis* [1977] ECR 5, para 22.

[102] See, in particular: ECJ, Case 272/80 *Biologische Producten* [1981] ECR 3277, and the subsequent, related judgments.

[103] See, for instance: G. MAJONE, *Regulating Europe* (London, Routledge, 1996) 279; V. HATZOPOULOS, *Le principe communautaire d'équivalence et de reconnaissance mutuelle dans la libre prestation de services* (Brussels, Bruylant, 1999) 120.

[104] D. GAMBETTA, 'Can We Trust Trust' in D. GAMBETTA (ed.), *Trust: Making and Breaking Cooperative Relations* (Oxford, Basil Blackwell, 1988) 213–37; N. LUHMANN, *Vertrauen. Ein Mechanismus der Reduktion sozialer Komplexität* (Stuttgart, UTB/Lucius and Lucius, 2000) 27 ff.

depends on the loyal cooperation of its Member States and their administrations for the formulation and implementation of common rules.[105]

Trust is said to arise whenever a community shares a set of values in such a way as to create expectations of regular and honest behaviour.[106] In the EU's internal market context, two crucial questions are, first, whether, in the absence of harmonization and by converting the duty of mutual trust into a general principle, the ECJ simply took the assumption of legal equality between the different systems of the EU for granted, and, secondly, whether there is indeed a sufficient common ground available to make the principle of mutual trust (and mutual recognition) work effectively. A related question is whether such an absolute position (mutual trust *in abstracto*) might jeopardize the credibility and workability of mutual trust among the Member States (mutual trust *in concreto*) or whether it might in fact enhance European integration and help to overcome the prejudices, stereotypes, and lack of trust among them.[107] The truth probably lies somewhere in between. Encouraging a general climate of mutual trust may oblige Member States to do away with a certain amount of prejudice towards or ignorance of other Member States' systems, but the continuous success of mutual trust will nevertheless require this trust to be justified. Trust inevitably goes hand in hand with certain trust-building processes. It should not be seen as a static or invariable concept but rather as a soft and flexible concept, subject to permanent reconsideration under changing circumstances, and some room must be left for individual considerations.[108] Mutual trust should also be based on mutual knowledge (of the foreign system), which must be updated constantly.[109] The ECJ's internal market case law, as I will indicate later, does indeed incline in that direction. Instead of simply imposing a blind or naive duty of trust, the ECJ enables Member States with justified doubts to take a number of control measures, mainly through contact with the other Member State. If necessary, they are entitled not to apply the principle of mutual recognition.

F. The Treaty provisions on free movement as the most adequate legal basis

The observations made above serve to confirm the interrelationship of the principle of mutual recognition with a number of very significant principles, all of which help to better gauge the true meaning of the principle of mutual recognition.[110] In light of these observations, it is not easy to highlight one legal basis in particular.[111] However, taking

[105] MAJONE, *Regulating Europe* (n 103) 278.

[106] F. FUKUYAMA, *Trust. The Social Virtues and the Creation of Prosperity* (London, Penguin, 1995) 153.

[107] See, for a similar question in a different area of EU law: F. BLOBEL and P. SPATH, 'The Tale of Multilateral Trust and the European Law of Civil Procedure', *E.L. Rev.* 2005, 541–2.

[108] BLOBEL and SPATH, 'The Tale of Multilateral Trust and the European Law of Civil Procedure' (n 107) 536 and 544–7.

[109] K. NICOLAÏDIS, 'Globalisation with Human Faces: Managed Mutual Recognition and the Free Movement of Professionals', in F.K. PADOA SCHIOPPA. (ed.), *The Principle of Mutual Recognition in the European Integration Process* (New York, Palgrave, 2005) 139.

[110] P. PELLEGRINO, 'Réflexions autour du principe du pays d'origine', *RDUE* 2010, 555–8.

[111] Even the AGs based their reasoning, on repeated occasions, on a combination of several principles. See for instance: Opinion of AG Van Gerven in Case 205/89 *Commission v Greece* [1991] ECR I-1361, § 11 (who links the prohibition of a dual control to the principle of proportionality and the principle of mutual trust); Opinion of AG La Pergola in Case C-184/96 *Commission v France* [1998] ECR I-6197, § 28–31 (who relates the obligation of mutual recognition to the principle of mutual trust); Opinion of

into account the ECJ's internal market case law as a whole, I maintain that in the context of the internal market, it is preferable to consider the free movement provisions the most adequate legal basis for the principle of mutual recognition.

The ECJ's few references to the principle of sincere cooperation (Art. 4 (3) TEU) in the area of diplomas were made in the early years, when the ECJ likely relied on Article 4(3) TEU in combination with the free movement provisions in order to make the (judicial) principle of mutual recognition more acceptable in this context. Indeed, since the Treaty provisions demanded—in principle—legislative measures, the existence of a principle of sincere cooperation probably made accepting a judicial principle of mutual recognition more defensible, in the absence of harmonization measures. The ECJ's more recent case law in this area clearly indicates that an interpretation of the general obligations contained in Article 4(3) TEU is not necessary whenever the more specific EU obligations a Member State is bound to fulfil under Article 45 TFEU (free movement of workers) have not been fulfilled.[112]

This finding suggests that the free movement provisions alone should suffice as a legal basis for the principle of mutual recognition. It should not be forgotten that the ECJ's explicit goal when introducing the principle of mutual recognition in the four freedoms was to enhance the internal market's integration process. Having examined the ECJ's free movement judgments on mutual recognition, the ECJ's reasoning appears to rely mainly on an extensive interpretation of the relevant Treaty provisions, namely Article 34 TFEU (goods), Article 45 TFEU (persons), Article 49 TFEU (establishment), Article 56 TFEU (services), and Article 63 TFEU (capital). In fact, in each case where the ECJ decided explicitly or implicitly that the Member State had not (sufficiently) taken into account the (equivalent) rules to which a product, service, or person adhered in their country of origin (in other words, that a violation of the principle of mutual recognition had occurred), this was considered by the ECJ to be a breach of Article 34 TFEU, Article 45 TFEU, Article 49 TFEU, Article 56 TFEU, or Article 63 TFEU.[113] Similarly, duties closely related to the principle of mutual recognition, such as the requirement of an active approach and the obligation to cooperate with other Member States' bodies, can be linked to the free movement provisions.[114] Furthermore, in a number of recent judgments the ECJ has explicitly recognized that 'Article 34 TFEU reflects the obligation to respect [. . .] the principle of mutual recognition',[115] and, more generally, that the case law on the mutual recognition of diplomas 'is the expression of a principle which is inherent in the fundamental freedoms of the TFEU'.[116] In view of this case law and

AG Geelhoed in Case C-212/03 *Commission v France* [2005] ECR I-4213, § 39 (who treats the principle of mutual recognition and the principle of trust as synonyms); Opinion of AG Ruiz-Jarabo Colomer in Joined Cases C-338/04, C-359/04 and C-360/04 *Placanica and others* [2007] ECR I-1891, § 128 (who considers the refusal to take into consideration an investigation carried out in another Member State a breach of both Article 4(3) TEU and the principle of mutual trust).

112 See, for instance: ECJ, Case C-108/96 *McQuen* [2001] ECR I-837, para 20; ECJ, Case C-31/00 *Dreessen* [2002] ECR I-663, para 30; ECJ, Case C-464/02 *Commission v Denmark* [2005] ECR I-7929, para 84.

113 Even in cases where a party explicitly sustained that there had been a breach 'of the principle of mutual recognition', the ECJ remained silent on this issue and concluded that there had been a breach of one of the free movement Treaty provisions. See, for instance: ECJ, Case C-30/99 *Commission v Ireland* [2001] ECR I-4619, para 22; ECJ, Case C-243/01 *Gambelli* [2003] ECR I-13031, para 29.

114 See, for instance: ECJ, Case C-432/03 *Commission v Portugal* [2005] ECR I-9665, paras 47 and 52.

115 ECJ, Case C-110/05 *Commission v Italy* [2009] ECR I-519, para 34.

116 ECJ, Case C-345/08 *Pesla* [2009] ECR I-11677, para 38, with reference to previous case law in which this view was already expressed.

of the previous considerations, I maintain that from the ECJ's perspective, mutual recognition is essentially a principle inherent to the free movement Treaty provisions, with no independent existence or independent scope,[117] and I therefore conclude that the Treaty provisions on free movement must be considered the most adequate legal bases for the principle of mutual recognition in each of the respective domains.

III. Equivalence, Country of Origin, and Mutual Recognition: What's in a Name?

I mentioned earlier that the principle of mutual recognition is also referred to by two other names in academic writing, namely the principle of equivalence and the principle of the country of origin. The three names are—unfortunately[118]—often used as synonyms, though they in fact refer to different aspects crucial to the mutual recognition reasoning that has been applied by the ECJ since *Cassis de Dijon*. In what follows, I analyse each name individually in order to verify which term is more appropriate, i.e. which term best represents the reasoning reflected in the ECJ's case law in the internal market context.

A. Equivalence

(1) Arguments in favour

Adherents to the term 'principle of equivalence' emphasize that the mutual recognition mechanism is in fact a mere consequence of acknowledging a level of equivalence between two Member States' legal or administrative regimes.[119] The core of the ECJ's reasoning amounts to the question of whether goods, persons, or undertakings are already subject to obligations in one Member State that are comparable, with respect to their objective of safeguarding a particular interest, to those imposed by the destination Member State's legislation. If equivalent obligations have indeed been fulfilled, the destination Member State has a duty to recognize them and, consequently, not to impose similar requirements or at least to simplify such requirements. For example, a licence requirement, authorization, work permit, or duty to pay employer's contributions are contrary to the principle of equivalence and mutual recognition in that those conditions duplicate equivalent conditions which have already been satisfied in the Member State of establishment.[120] Likewise, Member States are not entitled to request additional

[117] See, for a similar view: A. MATTERA, 'L'arrêt Cassis de Dijon: une nouvelle approche pour la réalisation et le bon fonctionnement du marché intérieur', *RMC* 1980, 513, who stressed that the ECJ had given a mere interpretation of an existing legal provision and had certainly not created a new rule of law. However, more recently this same author mentioned the principle of mutual recognition as 'an innovative principle stemming from Cassis de Dijon': A. MATTERA, 'The Principle of Mutual Recognition and Respect for National, Regional and Local Identities and Traditions', in F.K. PADOA SCHIOPPA (ed.), *The Principle of Mutual Recognition in the European Integration Process* (New York, Palgrave, 2005) 9.

[118] For a critique on the 'mixing up' of the country of origin principle and the mutual recognition principle, see: M. RADEIDEH, *Fair Trading in EC Law. Information and Consumer Choice in the Internal Market* (Groningen, Europa Law Publishing, 2005) 103.

[119] BERNEL, *Le principe d'équivalence ou de reconnaissance mutuelle en droit communautaire* (n 61) 133–8; HAMMER *Handbuch zum freien Wahrenverkehr* (n 3) 27; STOFFEL VALLOTTON, *La prohibición de restricciones a la libre circulación de mercancías en la Comunidad Europea* (n 4) 420.

[120] ECJ, Joined Cases 110/78 and 111/78 *Van Wesemael* [1979] ECR 35, para 28; ECJ, Case 279/80 *Webb* [1981] ECR 3305, paras 17 and 20; ECJ, Case 205/84 *Commission v Germany* [1986] ECR 3755,

technical or chemical analyses or laboratory tests when similar tests and analyses have already been carried out in another Member State, the results of which satisfy the requirements of the importing Member State.[121] Furthermore, if a comparative examination of diplomas finds that the knowledge and qualifications certified by the foreign diploma correspond to those required by the national provisions, the Member State must recognize this diploma as fulfilling the requirements laid down by its national provisions.[122] Products can be manufactured and marketed according to widely divergent procedures and rules across Member States, but providing the product poses no threat to human life or health and providing consumers are informed about the specific characteristics of the product by means of equivalent labelling information, these products (and the underlying manufacturing and marketing rules) must in principle be recognized and accepted in other Member States.[123] Similarly, the ECJ has condemned in *Uberseering* and *Vale* situations in which a company properly incorporated in the Member State of origin was denied access to the legal proceedings in the host Member State,[124] and in which, during cross-border conversion, a host Member State refused to record a company formed in the Member State of origin as the converted company's 'predecessor in law' in the commercial register.[125]

In all cases in which specific national requirements have been complied with in an equivalent manner in another Member State, each Member State has the duty to recognize the foreign regulation, to refrain from enforcing its own rules and to provide the product, service, or person with access to the national market. The principle of equivalence and mutual recognition is, in this respect, strongly related to the principle of proportionality, since the refusal to recognize a good, person, or service because of non-compliance with national requirements already fulfilled equivalently in another Member State is according to the ECJ's case law a disproportionate measure, and therefore prohibited under the free movement provisions.[126]

para 47; ECJ, Case 220/83 *Commission v France* [1986] ECR 3663, para 17; ECJ, Case C-43/93 *Vander Elst* [1994] ECR I-3803, paras 15–16; ECJ, Case C-272/94 *Guiot* [1996] ECR I-1905, paras 16–19.

[121] The ECJ held on repeated occasions that national inspectors were required to ascertain whether the documents at their disposal raised a presumption of compliance with the national legislation—and thus equivalence—which should lead to a simplification or relaxation of any later controls. See, for instance: ECJ, Case 251/78 *Denkavit* [1979] ECR 3369, para 23; ECJ, Case 272/80 *Biologische Producten* [1981] ECR 3277, para 14; ECJ, Case 132/80 *United Food* [1981] ECR 995, para 29; ECJ, Case 124/81 *Commission v UK* [1983] ECR 203, paras 25–6 and para 30; ECJ, Case C-293/94 *Brandsma* [1996] ECR I-3159, para 12.

[122] See, for instance: ECJ, Case 71/76 *Thieffry* [1977] ECR 765, para 19; ECJ, Case 11/77 *Patrick* [1977] ECR 1199, para 18; ECJ, Case 222/86 *Heylens* [1987] ECR 4097, para 13; ECJ, Case C-340/89 *Vlassopoulou* [1991] ECR I-2357, para 19; ECJ, Case C-104/91 *Aguirre Borrel* [1992] ECR I-3003, para 14; ECJ, Case C-55/94 *Gebhard* [1995] ECR I-4165, para 38; ECJ, Case C-313/01 *Morgenbesser* [2003] ECR I-13467, para 70.

[123] See, for instance: ECJ Case 788/79 *Gilli and Andres* [1980] ECR 2071, para 7; ECJ, Case 27/80 *Fietje* [1980] ECR 3839, para 12; ECJ, Case 130/80 *Kelderman* [1981] ECR 527, para 12; ECJ, Case 220/81 *Robertson* [1982] ECR 2349, para 12; ECJ, Case 261/81 *Rau* [1982] ECR 3961, para 17; ECJ Case 182/84 *Miro* [1985] ECR 3731, para 15; ECJ, Case C-293/93 *Houtwipper* [1994] ECR I-4249, paras 16 and 19. However, there are limits to very diverse legislations: where a product offered for sale under a particular name is so different, in terms of its composition or production, from the products generally understood as falling within that description within the EU that it cannot be regarded as falling within the same category, Member States may require the persons concerned to alter the description of the foodstuff. See, for instance: ECJ, Case C-366/98 *Geffroy* [2000] ECR I-6579, paras 22–3.

[124] ECJ, Case C-208/00 *Uberseering* [2002] ECR I-9919, para 93.

[125] ECJ, Case C-378/10 *Vale*, nyr, para 56.

[126] See for instance: ECJ, Case 73/84 *Denkavit* [1985] ECR 1013, para 14; ECJ, Case C-165/98 *Mazzoleni* [2001] I-2189, paras 36 and 39; ECJ, Case C-281/98 *Angonese* [2000] ECR I-4139, para 44; ECJ, Case C-390/99 *Canal Satélite Digital* [2002] ECR I-607, para 36; ECJ, Case C-153/02 *Neri* [2003] ECR I-13555, paras 49–50.

On the basis of the above-mentioned examples, we can conclude that whenever a sufficient degree of equivalence exists between two regimes, a duty of mutual recognition arises. The equivalence element can thus be seen as crucial for applying the principle of mutual recognition. Consequently, a Member State would only be able to set aside the principle of mutual recognition when the interest its national legislation aims to protect is not safeguarded in an equivalent way by the foreign regulation. Such an approach would require a thorough comparison of both regulations in order to determine the regimes' (differences in) levels of protection. However, the ECJ, often limited by restrictions intrinsic to the preliminary ruling proceeding, has only occasionally ventured into a detailed analysis and comparison of the legislations of different Member States,[127] preferring mostly to delegate this difficult task to the national judge.[128]

(2) Arguments against

Many judgments, including *Cassis de Dijon*,[129] have been passed without any reference to an equivalence test, which raises doubts as to whether this criterion of equivalence is indeed indispensable for the application of the principle of mutual recognition. We might ask whether its hitherto assumed role as a *conditio sine qua non* for the application of the principle of mutual recognition should in fact be reconsidered.[130] Two subsequent questions are relevant in this respect. First, is the principle of mutual recognition limited to cases where a sufficient degree of equivalence has been established or can a duty of mutual recognition be imposed equally on a Member State in the absence of any equivalence test (section 2.1)? Secondly, vice versa, can the ECJ refrain from imposing a duty of mutual recognition even where there are arguments to suggest that the interests at stake were protected in an equivalent manner (section 2.2)?

[127] See, for instance, in the framework of infringement proceedings: ECJ, Case 124/81 *Commission v U.K.* [1983] ECR 203, paras 25–7, where the ECJ examined milk heat treatment proceedings in several Member States and concluded that there were no major differences which could justify the British system of prior individual licences. Or: ECJ, Case 188/84 *Type approval for woodworking machines* [1986] ECR 419, paras 16–22. And, in the framework of a preliminary ruling procedure: ECJ, Case 16/78 *Choquet* [1978] ECR 2293, para 7; ECJ, Case 193/94 *Skanavi* [1996] ECR I-929, para 24. Following a comparative study of the laws on woodworking machines (Case 188/84) and on the issues of driving licences (*Choquet* and *Skanavi*) in the different Member States, the ECJ concluded in these cases that the substantial differences prevented the application of the principle of mutual recognition.

[128] See, for instance: ECJ, Case 27/80 *Fietje* [1980] ECR 3839, para 15; ECJ, Case 272/80 *Biologische Producten* [1981] ECR 3277, paras 16–17; ECJ, Case C-340/89 *Vlassopoulou* [1991] ECR I-2357 para 23; ECJ, Case C-165/98 *Mazzoleni* [2001] ECR I-2189, paras 37–40.

[129] In *Cassis de Dijon* the German and French legislation on alcohol content in alcoholic beverages were clearly not equivalent, but perhaps the underlying interests on consumer protection or public health were protected in both legislations in an equivalent way? The ECJ chose *not* to address this issue. It mainly focused on the German legislation and on the question whether this German legislation, analysed on its own, could be justified on the basis of consumer protection or public health. The French legislation is briefly mentioned, but not to discuss the issue of its equivalence. By stating that goods that have been lawfully produced and marketed in one Member State must be recognized in other Member States, the ECJ thus seems to pass by any equivalence test. The fact that the German legislation was not adequate to protect human health and that less drastic measures could have been applied (e.g. adequate labelling) was sufficient to conclude that there was a breach of the freedom of goods (and, thus of the principle of mutual recognition).

[130] Similarly, Poiares Maduro argues that the ECJ's case law on consumer protection illustrates that it is indeed doubtful if mutual recognition is only applicable when there is equivalence between the different national policies: M. POIARES MADURO, 'So Close and Yet So Far: the Paradoxes of Mutual Recognition', *JEPP* 2007, 820–1. See also: PELKMANS, 'Mutual Recognition: Economic and Regulatory Logic in Goods and Services' (n 1) 12–14, who explains that restrictions are often declared illegal under EU law for many other reasons, which tend to be verified—in standard case law proceedings—*before* arriving at an equivalence test.

2.1. Mutual recognition without an equivalence test

With regard to the first question, a number of the ECJ's judgments reveal that—even in the absence of a system of equivalence—unjustified restrictions may arise as a result of applying national rules to a person who has already satisfied the requirements of the legislation of the Member State where he or she is established. This was suggested in *Gouda*, where the ECJ stated that a restriction on the freedom guaranteed by the Treaty may arise even in the absence of a system of equivalence.[131] Furthermore, this view was confirmed in *Säger*, where the ECJ ruled that by restricting the pursuit of certain activities to service providers in possession of a specific professional qualification, the Member State in question (Germany) went beyond what was necessary to protect the interest it aimed to protect, i.e. safeguarding service recipients from harm they could suffer as a result of taking legal advice given to them by persons who did not possess the necessary professional or personal qualifications.[132] The measure was thus found to be disproportionate not because equivalent requirements had been fulfilled in another Member State, but because the equivalent requirements were deemed to go beyond what was necessary to protect the interest at stake. In other areas, too, such as the food sector,[133] certificates of civil status,[134] diplomas,[135] and company law,[136] the absence of an equivalent level of protection does not necessarily preclude the ECJ from implementing the duty of mutual recognition. The ECJ has repeatedly maintained that the fact that one Member State imposes less strict rules than another Member State or has chosen a system of protection different from that adopted by another Member State does not mean that the latter's rules are disproportionate and thus incompatible with Union law.[137] A crucial element of the ECJ's mutual recognition reasoning therefore appears not to be the equivalence criterion itself, or any comparative exercise between two legal regimes, but rather the question of whether the national provision, analysed on its own, can be justified in order to avoid an insupportable risk which might jeopardize the interest at stake. The ECJ clearly requires some kind of benchmark against which to measure its reasoning but, as we will see later, this benchmark need not necessarily be limited to another Member State's legal framework.

131 ECJ, Case C-288/89 *Gouda* [1991] ECR I-4007, para 12.

132 ECJ, Case C-76/90 *Säger* [1991] ECR I-4221, paras 16–17. Some authors, who are convinced of the crucial role of the principle of equivalence, consider this judgment as an isolated incident, an exception to the general rule: LÓPEZ ESCUDERO, 'La aplicación del principio del reconocimiento mutuo en el derecho comunitario' (n 84) 142; A. MATTERA, 'Les principes de "proportionnalité" et de la "reconnaissance" mutuelle dans la jurisprudence de la Cour en matière de libre circulation des personnes et des services: de l'arrêt *Thieffry* aux arrêts *Vlassopoulou, Mediawet* et *Dennemeyer*', *RMUE* 1992, 200–1.

133 A significant difference in nutritional value between two products may suggest a different degree of human health protection (i.e. non-equivalence), but cannot be equated to an unjustified threat to human health, and, thus, must be accepted. See, for instance: ECJ, Case 274/87 *Commission v Germany* [1989] ECR 229, para 10. However, in cases where the ECJ has deep concerns as to whether a product causes a threat to human life and health, the ECJ will focus on the right of each individual Member State to enact and apply its own legislation to protect public health. See for instance: ECJ, Case 53/80 *Kaasfabriek Eyssen* [1981] ECR 409, para 13; ECJ, Case 174/82 *Sandoz* [1983] ECR 2445, para 16; ECJ, Case 97/83 *Melkunie* [1984] ECR 2367, para 14; ECJ, Case C-95/01 *Greenham and Abel* [2004] I-1333, paras 42–3.

134 See, for instance: ECJ, Case C-336/94 *Dafeki* [1997] ECR I-6761, paras 16–19.

135 See: Part I, ch 2, II, B, 2. 'Enhancing mutual trust and mutual recognition in the area of diplomas'.

136 See, for instance: ECJ, Case C-212/97 *Centros* [1999] ECR I-1459, para 27; ECJ, Case C-167/01 *Inspire Art* [2003] ECR I-10155, para 121.

137 See, for instance: ECJ, Case C-384/93 *Alpine Investments* [1995] ECR I-1141, para 51; ECJ, Case C-3/95 *Reisebüro Broede* [1996] ECR I-6511, para 42; ECJ, Case C-67/98 *Zenatti* [1999] ECR I-7289, para 34; ECJ, Case C-108/96 *MacQuen* [2001] ECR I-837, paras 33–4.

2.2. No mutual recognition, despite (possible) equivalence

With regard to the second question, there are also a number of factors in the ECJ's case law that seem to undermine the purportedly pivotal role of the principle of equivalence.

A first example that can be mentioned in this regard concerns the ECJ's case law on the free movement of services in the gambling sector. In particular, the early years of the ECJ's 'gambling saga' revealed ongoing tension between the AGs, who were insisting on the need for an equivalence test and suggesting there were reasons to conclude that the outcome of such a test might be positive,[138] and the ECJ, that was resolutely ignoring these hints and deciding cases largely[139] without referring to an equivalence test.[140] Instead of reminding the Member States of their duty to take into account any requirements already fulfilled in the Member State of origin, the ECJ emphasized from the very beginning, for reasons that are unclear,[141] that any assessment of the need for and proportionality of the provisions adopted had to be made '*solely* by reference to the objectives pursued by the competent authorities of the Member State concerned and the degree of protection which *they* seek to ensure' (emphasis added).[142] In *Liga Portuguesa*, a judgment concerning the online provision of games of chance, the ECJ went even further in minimizing the relevance of equivalence checks by ruling that—in this specific

[138] Opinion of AG Gulmann in Case C-275/92 *Schindler* [1994] ECR I-1039, § 94–7; Opinion of AG La Pergola in Case C-124/97 *Läärä* [1999] ECR I-6067, § 36; Opinion of AG Fennelly in Case C-67/98 *Zenatti* [1999] ECR I-7289, § 28; Opinion of AG Alber in Case C-243/01 *Gambelli* [2003] ECR I-13031, § 91. Opinion of AG Ruiz-Jarabo Colomer in Joined Cases C-338/04, C-359/04 and C-360/04 *Placanica and others* [2007] ECR I-1891, § 129–32. See, however, more recently and more reserved; Opinion of AG Mazák in Case C-176/11 *HIT hoteli*, nyr, § 24, who expresses his doubts as to the possibility of actually comparing the level of protection in different legal systems.

[139] For instance, in the *Gambelli* and *Placanica* judgments the ECJ paid some attention to the concept of equivalence in the gambling area, albeit in a far more modest way than what had been suggested by the respective AGs in both cases. By stating in *Gambelli* that the national court will also need to determine 'whether the measure is a restriction that goes beyond what is necessary to combat fraud, *especially where the supplier of the service is subject in his Member State of establishment to a regulation entailing controls and penalties*' (emphasis added) (ECJ, Case C-243/01 *Gambelli* [2003] ECR I-13031, para 73) and in *Placanica* that 'a blanket exclusion of companies quoted on the regulated markets goes beyond what is necessary' (ECJ, Joined Cases C-338/04, C-359/04 and C-360/04 *Placanica and others* [2007] ECR I-1891, para 62), the ECJ required that Member States took the possibility of double regulatory burdens, and hence, the principle of equivalence, seriously. A. LITTLER, 'Regulatory Perspectives on the Future of Interactive Gambling in the Internal Market', *E.L. Rev.* 2008, 218–20.

[140] ECJ, Case C-124/97 *Läärä* [1999] ECR I-6067, para 36; ECJ, Case C-67/98 *Zenatti* [1999] ECR I-7289, para 34; ECJ, Case C-6/01 *Anomar* [2003] ECR I-8621, para 80.

[141] The ECJ's reluctance to apply the equivalence test in this area can be explained by various plausible factors. Some suggested that the ECJ was confronted in these judgments with the practical limits of the principle of equivalence, as the wide public interest objectives which were invoked were not of such a nature as to permit an adequate assessment of equivalence (see, for instance: Opinion of AG La Pergola in Case C-124/97 *Läärä* [1999] ECR I-6067, § 36; L. GORMLEY, 'Pay Your Money and Take Your Chance', *E.L. Rev.* 1994, 652). Others claimed that the ECJ's silence was due to the fact that implicitly the ECJ assumed that other national measures of control could not reach a sufficient level of equivalence, compared to the absolute prohibition of gambling activities (see, for instance: Opinion of AG Fennelly in Case C-67/98 *Zenatti* [1999] ECR I-7289, § 28). And still others pointed out that by doing so the ECJ substituted its otherwise strict proportionality test for a very superficial control, a classic example of the ECJ's hands-off approach in areas which involve political choices in sensitive areas (see, for instance: Opinion of AG Tizzano in Case C-6/01 *Anomar* [2003] ECR I-8621, para 71; B. ALLEN, 'Ladies and Gentlemen, No More Bets Please', *LIEI* 2000, 204; G. STRAETMANS, 'Case Note *Läärä* and *Zenatti*', *CML Rev.* 2000, 1001).

[142] ECJ, Case C-42/07 *Liga Portuguesa* [2009] ECR I-7633, para 58; ECJ, Case C-46/08 *Carmen Media Group* [2010] ECR I-8149, paras 46 and 48; both with reference to its earlier *Läärä* (paras 35 and 36) and *Zenatti* (paras 33 and 34) judgments; ECJ, Joined Cases C-186/11 and C-209/11 *Stanleybet International Ltd and others*, nyr, para 28.

sector—a Member State was entitled to the view that the fact alone that an operator lawfully offers services in another Member State, in which it is established and where it is in principle already subject to statutory conditions and controls enforced by that State's authorities, is insufficient assurance that national consumers will be protected from the risks of fraud and crime.[143] This entitlement was granted in view of the difficulties likely to be encountered in such a context by the authorities of the Member State of establishment in assessing the professional qualities and integrity of operators.[144] The ECJ's view that a Member State was not required to perform any equivalence assessment,[145] along with its blunt acceptance that a Member State was entitled to presume that such equivalence was not fulfilled in another Member State, came as a surprise to many, particularly in light of the ECJ's traditional mutual recognition case law and its strong focus on duties of mutual trust and cooperation.[146]

A second example which clearly puts the relevance of the equivalence criterion into perspective relates to the ECJ's case law on the free movement of services in the area of public health care. In this area, instead of imposing a duty of mutual recognition in cases of equivalence, the ECJ appears to draw the opposite conclusion. A duty of mutual recognition, i.e. a duty to reimburse people for public health services accessed abroad, can only be imposed if a similar or equally effective (i.e. equivalent) treatment cannot be obtained without undue delay at an establishment that has a contractual arrangement with the person's insurance provider.[147] In order to safeguard an adequate, balanced, and permanent supply of hospital care, the ECJ accepts that Member States must not blindly recognize (and reimburse) services provided abroad. Instead, it entitles them to subject public health establishments and infrastructures to planning, and to adopt

[143] ECJ, Case C-42/07 *Liga Portuguesa* [2009] ECR I-7633, para 69; confirmed in ECJ, Case C-258/08 *Ladbrokes Betting and Gaming and Ladbrokes International* [2010] ECR I-4757, para 54; ECJ, Case C-347/09, *Dickinger*, nyr, para 96. The controversial paragraph 69 was, however, no longer mentioned in the ECJ's grand chamber judgment *Markus Stoß*, in which the ECJ explicitly confirmed that mutual recognition obligations did not apply in the area of games of chance at stake. Instead of addressing the equivalence issue, the ECJ argued—in a more convincing way—that whenever a public monopoly is held to be legitimate and proportionate in light of the ECJ's case law, any obligation to recognize foreign, private authorizations is to be excluded, simply by virtue of the existence of such a monopoly: ECJ, Joined Cases C-316/07, C-358/07 to C-360/07, C-409/07 and C-410/07 *Markus Stoß and others* [2010] ECR I-8069, para 109.

[144] ECJ, Case C-42/07 *Liga Portuguesa* [2009] ECR I-7633, para 69.

[145] In *Dickinger* the ECJ was asked to apply its traditional case law on equivalence requirements, but instead stated that the case law according to which it 'is not compatible with Article 49 EC to make a provider subject to restrictions for safeguarding the public interest *in so far as that interest is already safeguarded in the Member State where he is established* does not apply in the present state of development of European Union law [...]' (emphasis added): ECJ, Case C-347/09, *Dickinger*, nyr, para 99. See, in this regard also: Opinion of AG Bot in Case C-347/09, *Dickinger*, nyr, § 134–7.

[146] For a critical analysis of this judgment, and, in particular, paragraph 69, see, for instance: A. DAWES and K. STRUCKMANN, 'Rien ne va plus? Mutual Recognition and the Free Movement of Services in the Gambling Sector after the Santa Casa Judgment', *E.L. Rev.* 2010, 242–3; C. JANSSENS and L. HOORNAERT, 'Annotatie Liga Portuguesa', *SEW* 2010, 375–6; F. PICOD, 'L'appréciation de la proportionnalité des restrictions des jeux de hasard. Rien ne va plus à la Cour de Justice', *La Semaine Juridique.- Edition Générale* 2009, No 46, 14; S. PLANZER, 'Liga Portuguesa—the ECJ and its Mysterious Ways of Reasoning', *E.L.R.* 2009, 372.

[147] See, for instance: ECJ, Case C-157/99 *Smits and Peerbooms* [2001] ECR I-5473, para 103; ECJ, Case C-385/99 *Müller Fauré* [2003] ECR I-4509, para 89; ECJ, Case C-56/01 *Inizan* [2003] ECR I-12403, para 59. Opinion of AG Cruz Villalón in Case C-173/09 *Elchinov* [2010] ECR I-8889, § 77. The rationale behind the ECJ's approach is that citizens should not be encouraged to be treated in other Member States whenever equivalent treatments are available in their own Member State, as the consequent outflow of patients would jeopardize and imbalance the supply of hospital medical care and logistical and financial wastage.

measures that affect the extent and conditions of hospital treatment provision in its own territory. The aim of this is to control the number of authorizations issued for treatment in another Member State, and ultimately to develop a manageable mutual recognition mechanism.[148]

A final example can be found in the area of free movement of goods: in *Dynamic Medien*, which concerned the importation of DVDs and videos of Japanese cartoons from the United Kingdom to Germany, the ECJ barely addressed the equivalence criterion.[149] The principle of mutual recognition was in this case hampered by German law, which prohibited the sale by mail order of image storage media (DVDs and videos) that were not labelled as having been checked in Germany for their suitability for young people. The 'equivalence criterion'-argument was explicitly put forward by one party, who pointed out that the image storage media had already been examined and classified by the competent authority in the Member State of export with the aim of protecting young people and were labelled accordingly.[150] It was also pointed out that 'the examination criteria used for the protection of young people by the competent British and German authorities were *equivalent*, since both the United Kingdom and Germany had signed and ratified the Convention on the Rights of the Child adopted in New York on 20 November 1989' (emphasis added).[151] The AG rejected this argument, as the Convention had not laid down a common standard for the protection of young people with regard to the content of image storage media. Neither the AG nor the ECJ attempted to ascertain whether equivalence was indeed present despite the absence of harmonization measures. In fact, the equivalence test, though recognized as part of the proportionality test, was not even considered because of a lack of sufficient facts.[152] Both the AG and the ECJ focused instead on the fact that, in the absence of EU harmonization, it is for the Member States to determine the level at which they intend to protect the interest concerned, provided that their rules are suitable for securing the objective and do not go beyond what is necessary in order to attain it.[153] The ease with which the ECJ accepted the proportionality test is remarkable. As in the aforementioned case law on gambling, the ECJ recognized that 'the mere fact that a Member State has opted for a system of protection which differs from that adopted by another Member State cannot affect the assessment of the proportionality of the national provisions enacted to that end and that those provisions must be assessed *solely* by reference to the objective pursued and the level of protection which the Member State in question intends to provide' (emphasis added).[154]

In conclusion, the criterion of equivalence should be seen as a relevant though not indispensable element for consideration when evaluating hindrances to the free movement provisions.[155] It can be—and in many judgments often is—present in the ECJ's

[148] See, for instance: ECJ, Case C-372/04 *Watts* [2006] ECR I-4325, para 92; ECJ Joined Cases C-570/07 and C-571/07 *Blanco Pérez* [2010] ECR I-4629, paras 43 and 70; ECJ, Case C-211/08 *Commission v Spain* [2010] ECR I-5267, para 75; ECJ, Case C-173/09 *Elchinov* [2010] ECR I-8889, paras 40–3. In this judgment the ECJ explicitly recalled that it cannot be excluded that the possible risk of seriously undermining the financial balance of a social security system may constitute an overriding reason in the public interest, capable of justifying an obstacle to the freedom to provide services.

[149] ECJ, Case C-244/06 *Dynamic Medien* [2008] ECR I-505.

[150] Opinion of AG Mengozzi in Case C-244/06 *Dynamic Medien* [2008] ECR I-505, § 72.

[151] Opinion of AG Mengozzi in Case C-244/06 *Dynamic Medien* [2008] ECR I-505, § 73.

[152] Opinion of AG Mengozzi in Case C-244/06 *Dynamic Medien* [2008] ECR I-505, § 80 and § 86.

[153] Opinion of AG Mengozzi in Case C-244/06 *Dynamic Medien* [2008] ECR I-505, § 78–83. ECJ, Case C-244/06 *Dynamic Medien* [2008] ECR I-505, paras 45–6.

[154] ECJ, Case C-244/06 *Dynamic Medien* [2008] ECR I-505, para 49.

[155] Similarly: POIARES MADURO, 'So Close and Yet So Far : the Paradoxes of Mutual Recognition' (n 130) 820–1.

reasoning. It does not, however, warrant its *conditio sine qua non*. In judgments where equivalent requirements are clearly fulfilled, the ECJ will usually rely on the principle of proportionality to condemn the national regulation. In cases where equivalence between two national regimes is less pronounced, on the other hand, reference to the requirement of equivalence will often be minimal. Furthermore, in cases where no valid or proportionate justification grounds are presented, the legislation of the country of origin will usually be recognized and applied irrespective of any equivalence test.

B. Country of origin

In the literature, a number of authors of recognized competence have not shied away from interchanging the term 'principle of mutual recognition' with the expression 'home state' or 'country of origin' principle,[156] or even 'home state control' principle.[157]

Much attention was paid to this principle in the discussions surrounding the Directive on the free movement of services (DIR 2006/123/EC), which in turn provoked heavy debate on the exact meaning of this concept and its ambiguous relation to the principle of mutual recognition.[158] Even prior to DIR 2006/123/EC, however, the principle of the country of origin had frequently been used as a legislative harmonization tool in other directives related to the services sector.[159]

[156] See, for instance: M. FALLON, 'Variations sur le principe d'origine, entre droit communautaire et droit international privé', in *Nouveaux itinéraires en droit. Hommage à François Rigaux* (Brussels, Bruylant, 1993) 189–201; A. GRANDPIERRE, *Herkunftsprinzip kontra Marktortanknüpfung. Auswirkung des Gemeinschapftsrecht auf die Kollisionregeln im Wettbewerbsrecht* (Frankfurt am Main, Peter Lang, 1999) 57–60; HAMMER *Handbuch zum freien Wahrenverkehr* (n 3) 27; N. REICH, 'Rechtsprobleme grenzüberschreitender irreführender Werbung im Binnenmarkt', *RabelsZ.* 1992, 491–6; REICH, *Understanding EU Law* (n 5) 102.

[157] CHALMERS, DAVIES, and MONTI *European Union Law* (n 3) 745.

[158] Some authors are convinced that the principle of country of origin has been a fundament of EU law ever since *Cassis de Dijon* and that its implementation in the secondary legislation must be seen as a confirmation of this case law, see for instance: M.-D. GARABIOL-FURET, 'Plaidoyer pour le principe du pays d'origine', *RMCUE* 2006, 82; M.-D. GARABIOL FURET, 'Vrais et faux semblants de la directive services', *RMCUE* 2006, 219; D. KUGELMANN, 'Die Dienstleistungs-Richtlinie der EG zwischen der Liberalisierung von Wachstumsmärkten und europäischem Sozialmodell', *EuZW* 2005, 329. The mainstream of the legal doctrine is, however, of the opinion that the principle of country of origin is not just a mere confirmation of the ECJ's case law since *Cassis de Dijon*: see for instance: L. ALBATH and M. GIESLER, 'Das Herkunftslandprinzip in der Dienstleistungsrichtlinie—Eine Kodifizierung der Rechtsprechung', *EuZW* 2006, 42; E. BELHADJ, S. EVANS, and J.W. VAN DE GRONDEN, 'De dienstenrichtlijn: de gebreken van de deugden? Een eerste verkenning van de Dienstenrichtlijn', *SEW* 2007, 144; S. D'ACUNTO, 'La proposition de directive sur les services dans le marché intérieur', *RDUE* 2004, 220; T. UYEN DO, 'La proposition de directive relative aux services dans le marché intérieur…définitivement hors service', *RDUE* 2006, 118–19; O. DE SCHUTTER and S. FRANCQ, 'La proposition de directive relative aux services dans le marché intérieur: reconnaissance mutuelle, harmonization et conflits de loi dans l'Europe élargie', *CDE* 2005, 606; B.J. DRIJBER, 'De bezems van Bolkestein', *NTER* 2004, 116; B.J. DRIJBER, 'The Country of Origin Principle in the proposed Directive on Services in the Internal Market', *EuConst* 2005, 16; W. GEKIERE, 'Towards a European Directive on Services in the Internal Market: Analysing the Legal Repercussions of the Draft Services Directive and its Impact on National Services Regulation, 2004, retrievable at: <http://openbarediensten.acv-online.be/Images/2004-10%20EU%20Diensten%20-%20Impact%20Draft%20final1_tcm86-67173.pdf>; R. GRAHAM, 'Mutual Recognition and Country of Origin in the Case Law of the European Court of Justice', in *Freedom of Services in the European Union. Labour and Social Security Law: The Bolkestein Directive* (The Hague, Kluwer, 2006) 42; R.M. JENNAR, 'la proposition de directive Bolkestein', *Courrier hebdomadaire* 2005, No 1890-1, 38; P. MANKOWSKI, 'Wider ein Herkunftslandprinzip für Dienstleistungen im Binnenmarkt', *IPRax* 2004, 391.

[159] See: Part I, ch 2: 'The Development of the Principle of Mutual Recognition in the Secondary Legislation'.

In what follows, I will attempt to shed light on the meaning of the judicially developed home state principle in order to address the question of whether it is advisable to employ that term in a purely judicial context as a synonym for the term principle of mutual recognition.

In the past, the term 'home state control' or 'country of origin' principle has all too often conveyed the false impression that this principle pertained to rules on the distribution of competence among Member States, and attributed the relevant competences for regulating and controlling the application of regulations to the state of origin. Consequently, the home state principle has been considered a conflict rule.[160]

Such a view, however, is not reconcilable with the ECJ's case law. In accordance with the Treaty provisions, the ECJ's logical point of departure is that, in the absence of harmonization measures, each Member State is considered competent to conceive rules that will be valid in its own territory. However, this legislative competence should be nuanced in view of the TFEU provisions on the free movement of goods, services, persons, and capital. They prohibit all national measures that might render less attractive or hinder free movement, and therefore impose an obligation on each Member State to be 'other Member State'-regarding, i.e. open-minded towards the regulations of other Member States. The principle requires that any Member State take into account regulations and measures which have already been fulfilled in the state of origin.[161] In other words, it is a kind of *negative* obligation not to apply a Member State's regulation if its rule would constitute an unjustified hindrance of the free movement provisions, but it certainly does not imply a *positive* attribution of competence to the Member State of origin.[162]

Moreover, the term home state principle is misleading as it wrongfully suggests that in the absence of any acceptable justification ground, the home state's regulation would always prevail. In fact, it is perfectly conceivable that in certain cases where the home state's regulation presents an unjustified barrier to free movement, it will be this regulation that is set aside.[163] The underlying principle of the ECJ's reasoning, then, is less about recognizing the legislation of the Member State of origin, let alone seeing this legislation as the applicable law; instead, it is more about taking into account the rules of any relevant Member State in order to prevent the national rules of a Member State becoming an unjustifiable impediment to the access of goods, services, persons, or capital to another Member State's market. As I will show,[164] the mechanism of home

[160] For a thorough debate on this issue with references to an abundant literature on the matter, see: BERNEL *Le principe d'équivalence ou de reconnaissance mutuelle en droit communautaire* (n 61) 112–33; G. DE BAERE, 'Is this a Conflict Rule which I see Before Me? Looking for a Hidden Conflict Rule in the Principle of Origin as Implemented in Primary Community Law and in the Directive on Electronic Commerce', *MJ* 2004, 287–319; M. FALLON, and J. MEEUSEN, 'Private International Law in the European Union and the Exception of Mutual Recognition', in P. SARCEVIC and P. VOLKEN (eds.), *Yearbook of Private International Law. Volume IV* (The Hague, Kluwer Law International, 2002) 37–66; GARDEÑEZ SANTIAGO, *La aplicación de la regla del reconocimiento mutuo y su incidencia en el comercio de mercancías y servicios en el ámbito comunitario e internacional* (n 51) 177–238.

[161] The AG, unlike the ECJ, refers from to time to time to the concept 'home state principle'. See, for instance: Opinion of AG Alber in Case C-59/01 *Commission v Italy* [2003] ECR 1759, § 64; Opinion of AG Kokott in Case C-189/03 *Commission v the Netherlands* [2004] ECR I-9289, § 35–8.

[162] MANKOWSKI 'Wider ein Herkunftslandprinzip für Dienstleistungen im Binnenmarkt' (n 158) 392.

[163] See, for instance: ECJ, Case C-415/93 *Bosman* [1995] ECR I-4921; ECJ, Case C-148/02 *Garcia Avello* [2003] ECR I-11613; ECJ, Case C-446/03 *Marks and Spencer* [2005] ECR I-10837; ECJ, Case C-522/04 *Commission v Belgium* [2007] ECR I-5701; ECJ, Case C-210/06 *Cartesio* [2008] ECR I-9641; ECJ, Case C-371/10 *National Grid*, nyr.

[164] See: Part I, ch 2, I. 'A Conceptual Debate: Principle of Mutual Recognition or Country of Origin Principle?'

state control is above all an attractive tool for the EU legislator rather than a judicially developed principle detracted from the TFEU. This was confirmed by the ECJ in its judgment *Germany v European Parliament and Council*, in which Germany sought the annulment of a directive on deposit-guarantee schemes, one of the arguments being that the directive would infringe upon the principle of home Member State supervision. In less than one paragraph, the ECJ rejected Germany's argument by stating that, since the principle of home state supervision was not a principle laid down by the Treaty, the [EU] legislator was in principle entitled to depart from it.[165]

C. Principle of equivalence, principle of country of origin, or principle of mutual recognition?

Following the above analysis, it should now be decided which of these three terms is to be preferred. All of these principles certainly reflect aspects of the elements taken into consideration when the ECJ passes judgment on possible breaches of the free movement provisions.

The 'equivalence' aspect is undoubtedly an important, oft-invoked, relevant element that the ECJ has taken into account throughout its case law. However, it has been applied in a very flexible way: in some judgments equivalence was at the core of the ECJ's reasoning; in others it appeared at first glance to be absent, at most implicitly present; and in yet others, equivalence was indeed entirely absent. Similarly, in some judgments 'equivalence' meant truly equivalent, very similar or quasi-identical obligations; in others it referred to the protected interest at stake, which often did not require protection that was equivalent—taking into account the proportionality requirement and the specific interest at stake—but simply sufficient. From this perspective, it would seem incorrect to restrict the principle of mutual recognition to a principle of equivalence, since it would not cover those judgments in which recognition is imposed in the absence of equivalence.

The term 'home state' or 'country of origin' principle also seems inappropriate for describing the core principle of the four freedoms. Not only did the ECJ explicitly reject a Treaty-based home state control principle, it also clearly indicated that the regulations of both the country of origin and the country of destination could be challenged when assessing infringements of the free movement provisions. It would be misleading to speak of a home state principle in this context. Furthermore, confusion could arise as a result of the different meanings that the country of origin concept has undergone in both the judicial and legislative contexts.

Compared to the above two concepts, the term 'mutual recognition' has some obvious advantages. First, it is broader than an equivalence test. The duty to recognize other Member States' goods, services, people, and capital is a duty intrinsically related to and derived from the free movement provisions and can only be set aside if some kind of overriding public interest needs to be safeguarded. Not infrequently, a lack of equivalent protection for an overriding interest will cause a justified limitation to the principle of mutual recognition. On other occasions, however, the principle of mutual recognition goes beyond an equivalence check, as it appears that requiring an equivalent level of

[165] ECJ, Case C-233/94 *Commission v Germany* [1997] ECR I-2405, para 64; W.-H. ROTH, 'Case Note *Commission v Germany*', *CML Rev.* 1998, 471–2; J. WOUTERS, 'The Community Legislature's Role Regarding the Freedom of Establishment and the Freedom to Provide Services: Theory and Practice', *Euredia* 1999, 243–4. See, however, Opinion of AG Stix-Hackl in Case C-36/02 *Omega* [2003] ECR I-9609, § 37, who argues that the country of origin principle is inherent in Article 56 TFEU.

protection might sometimes be considered disproportionate to the protected interest in question. Secondly, mutual recognition is, from one perspective, broader than a country of origin principle (as it imposes a duty on all Member States to take into account the legislation of other Member States, and not necessarily only that of the Member State of origin). From another perspective, it is also less intrusive than a country of origin principle (since it does not imply that the country of origin's regulations are considered to be the applicable law but only that they must be taken into account when the application of another Member State's legislation might restrict the free movement principle).

In sum, despite some degree of overlap between the three concepts, the principle of mutual recognition seems to reflect the ECJ's case law on free movement in the internal market most successfully. Although the ECJ very rarely employs the wording 'duty to recognize' in this context, it is, as an inevitable counterpart to the free movement principle,[166] implicitly there. They are, in a way, two sides of the same coin.

IV. The Limits of the Judicial Principle of Mutual Recognition

Cassis de Dijon owes its fundamental status not only to the well-known mutual recognition passage but also to the intrinsically related rule of reason doctrine, with which the ECJ had experimented some years earlier in the *Dassonville* and *Van Binsbergen* judgments.[167] By creating an unlimited list of justification grounds, specifically for non-discriminatory measures, in addition to the limited list of justification grounds set out in the TFEU, the ECJ stressed from the very beginning the non-automatic or conditional nature of the principle of mutual recognition.

In the following section, I start by dealing with the question of how the ECJ evaluates the justification grounds that are invoked by the Member States as a barrier to the principle of mutual recognition (section IV, A). I then proceed to examine the margin of control that is left to a Member State when it is confronted with cases of (presumed) inaccuracy or misapplication of EU law by another Member State (section IV, B), or with cases of fraud or abuse of law (section IV, C).

A. The ECJ's evaluation of justification grounds

One of the reasons behind the application of a rule of reason (or a Treaty exception) is the recognition that at legislative level, EU law does not yet offer guarantees of certain interests or values.[168] The ECJ was prompted to introduce the rule of reason by two issues: first, the lack of a sufficient level of harmonization and the related lack of an equivalent level of protection for certain interests, and secondly, the limited list of exceptions laid out in the Treaty. From *Cassis de Dijon* onwards, the ECJ made it very clear that in the absence of harmonization measures, it is in principle up to each Member State to determine the level of protection required for the interest in question in accordance with

[166] Similarly, AG Stix-Hackl in Case C-231/03 *Consorzio Aziende Metano* [2005] ECR I-7287, § 49-50; AG Kokott in Case C-514/03 *Commission v Spain* [2006] ECR I-963, § 44; ECJ, Case C-110/05 *Commission v Italy* [2009] ECR I-519, para 34; ECJ, Case C-345/08 *Pesla* [2009] ECR I-11677, para 38, with reference to previous case law in which this view was already expressed.

[167] ECJ, Case 33/74 *Van Binsbergen* [1974] ECR 1299; ECJ, Case 8/74 *Dassonville* [1974] ECR 837.

[168] L. GORMLEY, 'The Genesis of the Rule of Reason in the Free Movement of Goods' in A. SCHRAUWEN (ed.), *Rule of Reason. Rethinking another Classic of European Legal Doctrine* (Groningen, Europa Law Publishing, 2005) 23–4.

its own scale of values. This statement should be nuanced, however, since neither the Treaty exceptions nor the rule of reason constitutes grounds for a *réserve de souverainité* in favour of the Member States, and the ECJ has constantly maintained that restrictions must be interpreted narrowly as they constitute exceptions to the general rule of free movement and mutual recognition.[169] Unilateral measures adopted on these justification grounds are required to satisfy the ECJ's proportionality test, which can be lenient or rigid.[170] This elastic application of the proportionality principle is an indication that the rigid or broad application of the principle of mutual recognition will often be influenced by the kind of national interest that is at stake. In some sensitive areas, the ECJ has proved unwilling to take up its role as constitutional adjudicator and has preferred an unequivocal hands-off approach (section A, 1); in a second category of judgments, the principle of mutual recognition was set aside because of a lack of equivalent or sufficient protection of the interest at stake in a particular Member State (section A, 2); in a third category of judgments, meanwhile, the ECJ entered into a delicate balancing act between the free movement rights and a very crucial element on the European agenda, namely the protection of fundamental rights (section A, 3).

(1) A prudent hands-off approach with an emphasis on a national perspective

In some areas, the ECJ has not hesitated to grant the Member States a considerable margin of discretion. As regards public morality, the ECJ stated in *Henn and Darby* that it is for each Member State to determine the requirements of public morality in its territory in accordance with its own set of values and in the form it has selected.[171] Without referring to any necessity or proportionality test, the ECJ excluded the application of the principle of mutual recognition by concluding that a Member State may lawfully impose prohibitions on the importation of goods which are of an indecent or obscene nature according to domestic law. However, a duty of mutual recognition would resume as soon as the ECJ became aware that a Member State had an unequivocally more lenient approach to similar national goods.[172] Ultimately, this was not the case in *Henn and Darby* where, despite some variation in the law in force in different parts of the United Kingdom, there was a clear unitary concept regarding the prohibition of pornographic films and magazines. The ECJ's finding that the Member State's approach genuinely reflected a concern to attain the objective of protecting public morality in a consistent

[169] Even justification grounds like health and life of humans which rank foremost among the interests that are safeguarded by the Treaty. See, for instance: ECJ, Case C-333/08 *Commission v France* [2010] ECR I-757, para 87.

[170] In the framework of a preliminary ruling procedure, the ECJ will leave the concrete evaluation—i.e. the difficult choice that has to be made about the balance between imperative market integration and the pursuit of other social objectives—generally in the hands of the national courts, especially where the available information is poor. In some preliminary rulings, where the available information was not poor, the ECJ has performed an assessment itself whereas in other preliminary rulings the ECJ has refrained from doing an assessment, despite the fact that it had sufficient elements at its disposal. See, for instance: KAPTEYN, McDONNELL, MORTELMANS, and TIMMERMANS, *The Law of the European Union and the European Communities* (n 3) 650.

[171] ECJ, Case 34/78 *Henn and Darby* [1979] ECR 3795, para 15.

[172] ECJ, Case 34/78 *Henn and Darby* [1979] ECR 3795, para 22. See, for instance, the *Conegate* judgment, another British case on the import of erotic articles, where no national prohibition existed on the manufacture or marketing of the same goods. Therefore, the Member State was not allowed to invoke the exception ground and had a duty to recognize and accept the erotic dolls and other articles: ECJ, Case 121/85 *Conegate* [1986] ECR 1007, para 20. Similarly, in the area of prostitution: ECJ, Case C-268/99 *Jany and others* [2001] ECR I-8615, paras 61–2.

and systematic manner[173] was thus decisive in granting the Member State in question a considerable margin of discretion and in eliminating any duty of mutual recognition in that particular case.

A similarly generous attitude on the part of the ECJ towards a Member State's margin to act can be found in the highly controversial and extensively discussed *Grogan* judgment, which concerned the Irish prohibition of distributing information on foreign abortion practices.[174] The ECJ classified the matter—on questionable grounds—as lying beyond the scope of EU law and avoided, in such a way, the thorny debate as to whether such a prohibition could be reconciled with the free movement provisions and/or with the fundamental right to freedom of expression.[175] The ECJ chose not to take sides, stating that it was not for the ECJ to substitute its assessment for that of the legislature in those Member States where an allegedly immoral activity was being practised legally.[176] The ECJ's extremely prudent approach, which contrasted sharply with the stronger opinion expressed by its AG,[177] was harshly criticized. The ECJ's attitude in this judgment, however, should be seen in its historical context. It is difficult to bring to mind a more controversial issue from that period around which moral and legal issues were so radically polarized than that of abortion. Furthermore, the European unification process had at that point barely touched upon the basic fundamental rights of the individual, such as the right to life. With these points in mind, the ECJ's uneasiness on the topic should not come as a surprise.[178]

The ECJ's distant or hesitant behaviour as far as fundamental rights issues are concerned has changed dramatically since then, and the hands-off approach which

[173] For a more recent reference to this 'consistency and coherence' test with reference to other judgments: ECJ, Case C-137/09 *Josemans* [2010] ECR I-13019, para 70. See also, for a good analysis of this test and its evolution in the ECJ's case law: G. MATHISEN, 'Consistency and Coherence as Conditions for Justification of Member State Measures restricting Free Movement', *CML Rev.* 2010, 1021–48.

[174] ECJ, Case C-159/90 *Grogan* [1991] ECR I-5253. For some of the many comments on this judgment, see: C. BARNARD, 'An Irish Solution', *New Law Journal* 1992, 526–33; C. COLVIN, 'Irish Abortion Law and the Free Movement of Services in the European Community', *Fordh. Int. L. J.* 1991–92, 476–526; L. DUBOUIS, 'L'interruption volontaire de grossesse au regard du droit communautaire', *Rev. dr. san. soc.* 1992, 52–7; C. LANGENFELD and A. ZIMMERMANN, 'Interdependenzen zwischen nationalem Verfassungsrecht, Europäischer Menschenrechtskonvention und Europäischem Gemeinschaftsrecht', *ZaöRV* 1992, 259–317; R. LAWSON, 'Miscarriage of Justice?', *NTM* 1992, 47–55; S. O'LEARY, 'The ECJ as a Reluctant Constitutional Adjudicator: An Examination of the Abortion Information Case', *E.L. Rev.* 1992, 138–57; D.R. PHELAN, 'Right to Life of The Unborn v. Promotion of Trade in Services: The European Court of Justice and the Normative Shaping of the European Union', *MLR* 1992, 670–89; F. RIGAUX, 'La diffusion d'informations relatives aux interruptions médicales de grossesse, une liberté économique selon le droit communautaire', *RTDH* 1992, 63–71.

[175] ECJ, Case C-159/90 *Grogan* [1991] ECR I-5253, paras 25–7.

[176] ECJ, Case C-159/90 *Grogan* [1991] ECR I-5253, para 20. Similarly: ECJ, Case C-268/99 *Jany and others* [2001] ECR I-8615, para 56 (concerning restrictions on free movement with regard to the work of window prostitutes).

[177] AG Van Gerven had suggested not to avoid the difficult task of balancing the two conflicting fundamental rights at stake: on the one hand, the freedom to distribute information and, on the other, the prohibition on the distribution of information, promoted by what was considered an imperative requirement of public interest, the protection of the unborn. The AG considered the latter objective to be a policy choice of a moral and philosophical nature which a Member State was entitled to make. Opinion of AG Van Gerven in Case C-159/90, *Grogan* [1991] ECR I-5253, § 25–38.

[178] Furthermore, one of the most difficult dilemmas for the ECJ was probably, as Curtin suggested, the unprecedented fact that a similar case was pending before the ECtHR at exactly the same time and that the ECJ would have to deliver its judgment first: D. CURTIN, 'Case Note *Grogan*', *CML Rev.* 1992, 598–9.

characterized *Grogan* has been replaced by a thorough exercise that attempts to balance the conflicting interests at stake.[179]

The famous *Sunday trading* judgments[180] constitute another area in which the ECJ appeared to struggle with the boundaries of a correctly applied mutual recognition approach. They also paved the way for the revolutionary *Keck and Mithouard* judgment. Unlike the *Grogan* judgment, the *Sunday trading* cases did not deal with a morally charged subject but nevertheless reveal, once again, the ECJ's determination not to accept an unlimited approach to the principle of mutual recognition. The ECJ emphasized in these judgments that national rules regarding shop opening hours on Sundays reflected certain choices relating to particular national or regional socio-cultural characteristics, which had to be decided upon by the Member States themselves.[181] Again, the proportionality test was barely mentioned; instead, the ECJ seemed to assume that it had been fulfilled. Following the *Sunday trading* judgments, increasing doubts arose as to whether a host state that simply exercised its power to regulate shop opening hours in a non-discriminatory way could ever be in breach of Article 34 TFEU. Would it not seem rather inappropriate and indeed excessive for the free movement provisions (and its underlying principle of mutual recognition) to apply to such issues as shop opening hours or other issues regarding selling arrangements which reflect internal economic and social policy choices of Member States and which do not concern—contrary to the *Cassis de Dijon* line of case law on product requirements—the problem of dual burdens?

The *Keck and Mithouard* judgment, which dealt with a far less delicate subject, namely resale at a loss, cut the knot by introducing the oft-criticized distinction between product rules and selling arrangements. Product norms would still be subject to a duty of mutual recognition, whereas certain rules on selling arrangements—which applied to all relevant traders operating within the national territory and which affected the marketing of domestic and foreign products in the same manner—would no longer fall within the scope of Article 34 TFEU. A duty of mutual recognition would thus no longer apply to the latter category of rules.[182] The selling arrangements that the ECJ had in mind in *Keck and Mithouard* neither prevented nor impeded access to the market any more than they impeded the access of domestic products,[183] and so the ECJ concluded that Article 34 TFEU and its underlying principle of mutual recognition had no role to

[179] See: Part I, ch 1, IV, A, 3. 'Balancing conflicting interests: free movement versus fundamental rights. In search of a European public order concept?'

[180] ECJ, Case C-145/88 *Torfaen Borough Council* [1989] ECR 3851; ECJ, Case C-312/89 *Conforama* [1991] ECR I-997; ECJ, Case C-332/89 *Marchandise* [1991] ECR I-1027; ECJ, Case C-169/91 *Council of the City of Stoke-on-Trent* [1992] ECR I-6653. A. ARNULL, 'Anyone for Tripe', *E.L. Rev.* 1993, 314–23; C. BARNARD, 'Sunday Trading: A Drama in Five Acts', *MLR* 1994, 449–60.

[181] ECJ, Case C-145/88 *Torfaen Borough Council* [1989] ECR 3851, para 13; ECJ, Case C-312/89 *Conforama* [1991] ECR I-997, para 11; ECJ, Case C-332/89 *Marchandise* [1991] ECR I-1027, para 12; ECJ, Case C-169/91 *Council of the City of Stoke-on-Trent* [1992] ECR I-6653, para 11.

[182] ECJ, Joined Cases C-267 and C-268/91 *Keck and Mithouard* [1993] ECR I-6097, paras 15–16. For some of the many comments on this judgment, see, for instance: CHALMERS, 'Repackaging the Internal Market' (n 61) 385–403; L. GORMLEY, 'Reasoning Renounced? The Remarkable Judgment in *Keck and Mithouard*', *E.B.L.R.* 1994, 63–7; R. JOLIET, 'La libre circulation des marchandises: L'arrêt *Keck et Mithouard* et les nouvelles orientations de la jurisprudence', *JT Dr Eur.* 1994, 145–51; A. MATTERA, 'De l'arrêt *Dassonville* à l'arrêt *Keck*: l'obscure clarté d'une jurisprudence riche en principes novateurs et en contradictions', *RMUE* 1994, 117–60; K.J.M. MORTELMANS, 'De interne markt en het facettenbeleid na het Keck-arrest: nationaal beleid, vrij verkeer en harmonisatie', *SEW* 1994, 236–50; J. STUYCK, 'L'arrêt *Keck et Mithouard* (vente à perte) et ses conséquences sur la libre circulation des marchandises', *C.D.E.* 1994, 435–58.

[183] ECJ, Joined Cases C-267 and C-268/91 *Keck and Mithouard* [1993] ECR I-6097, para 17.

play in those areas. In introducing these new criteria, the ECJ consciously aimed at putting a halt to traders' increasing tendency to invoke Article 34 TFEU and at cutting back unnecessary intrusions into the laws of the Member States. The *Keck and Mithouard* judgment therefore concerns the distribution of competences between the country of destination and the country of origin and rules out the operation of the principle of mutual recognition in areas which originate from the internal policy choices of Member States.[184] The non-absolute character of the principle of mutual recognition was thus confirmed once more, but the exact contours of its limits had not become much clearer since the pre-*Keck and Mithouard* era. The dichotomy between 'product rules' and 'selling arrangements' has often proven difficult to apply in practice,[185] and the ECJ, wisely rejecting any attempt to introduce a third category of measures which would fall outside the scope of Article 34 TFEU and its mutual recognition mechanism,[186] has recently shifted its case law towards another crucial element that has lain at the heart of the ECJ's reasoning when judging national trade barriers since *Keck and Mithouard*, namely the market access test.[187]

The specific social and cultural features of each Member State, which had prompted the ECJ's restrictive approach in the *Sunday trading* case law, came to the fore again some years later in relation to the services sector of gambling activities. The moral, religious, or cultural aspects of lotteries justified national authorities in maintaining a sufficient degree of freedom in determining what was required to protect players and more generally, to maintain order in society.[188] The quasi-unlimited power of assessment that had been recognized in the *Schindler* judgment was also granted in many subsequent gambling

[184] H. MUIR WATT, 'Aspects économiques du droit international privé (réflexions sur l'impact de la globalisation économique sur les fondements des conflits de lois et de juridictions), *Rec. Cours* 2004, 184–7.

[185] See, for instance: ECJ, Case C-358/95 *Morellato* [1997] ECR I-1431; ECJ, Case C-20/03 *Burmanjer* [2005] I-4133; ECJ, Case C-82/05 *Commission v Greece* [2006] ECR I-93; ECJ, Joined Cases C-158/04 and C-159/04 *Alfa Vita* [2006] ECR I-8135; ECJ, Case C-54/05 *Commission v Finland* [2007] ECR I-2473.

[186] See, in this regard, with regard to the 'rules on use': ECJ, Case C-110/05 *Commission v Italy* [2009] ECR I-519; ECJ, Case C-142/05 *Mickelsson and Roos* [2009] ECR I-4273, and the corresponding interesting, opposing opinions of the AGs. For a more in-depth analysis of these judgments and its implications on the *Keck*-line of case law, see also: W. ALBIN and F. VALENTIN, 'Dassonville oder doch Keck—Zwei anstehende Urteile des EuGH zur Anwendung des Art. 28 EG auf Verwendungsbeschränkungen', *EWS* 2007, 533–40; M. DERLEN and J. LINDHOLM, 'Article 28 EC and Rules on Use: a Step towards a Workable Doctrine on Measures Having Equivalent Effect to Quantitative Restrictions', *Col. J. Eur. L.* 2010, 191–231; N. DE SADELEER, 'L'examen, au regard de l'article 28 CE, des règles nationales régissant les modalités d'utilisation de certains produits', *J.D.E.* 2009, 247–50; N. FENGER, 'Article 28 EC and restrictions on use of a legally marketed product', *E.L.R.* 2009, 326–37; L. GONZÁLEZ VAQUÉ, 'La sentencia Mickelsson y Roos del TJCE: Good Bye, Keck y Mithouard!', *Rev. Esp. Der. Eur.* 2009, 389–406; E. SPAVENTA, 'Leaving Keck behind? The Free Movement of Goods after the Rulings in Commission v Italy and Mickelsson and Roos', *E.L. Rev.* 2009, 914–32.

[187] For an evaluation of the post-*Keck and Mithouard* case law and a discussion on the evolution of the criteria that were developed therein, see for instance: T. CONNOR, 'Accentuating the Positive: the Selling Arrangement, the First Decade, and Beyond', *ICLQ* 2005, 127–60; S. FEIDEN, *Die Bedeutung der 'Keck'-Rechtsprechung im System der Grundfreiheiten* (Berlin, Duncker & Humblot, 2003); L GORMLEY, 'The Definition of Measures Having Equivalent Effect', in A. ARNULL, P. EECKHOUT, and T. TRIDIMAS (eds.), *Continuity and Change in EU Law. Essays in Honour of Sir Francis Jacobs* (Oxford, Oxford University Press, 2008) 189–204; I. HIGGINS, 'The Free and Not so Free Movement of Goods since Keck', *I.J.E.L.* 1997, 166–80; K.J.M. MORTELMANS, 'De *Keck* check', *NTER* 2005, 247–61; G. STRAETMANS, 'Case Note *Gourmet*', *CML Rev.* 2002, 1407–21; S. WEATHERILL, 'After Keck: Some Thoughts on How to Clarify the Clarification', *CML Rev.* 1996, 885 ff.

[188] ECJ, Case C-275/92 *Schindler* [1994] ECR I-1039, paras 58–9 and para 61.

cases.[189] Only in cases where it was found that a Member State's authorities had not behaved consistently, for example by inciting and encouraging consumers to participate in lotteries or games of chance instead of genuinely contributing to the alleged objective (i.e. non-compliance with the consistency test), was that Member State's margin of discretion reduced to zero and the national rule in question not upheld.[190]

Unlike the *Sunday trading* cases and especially the *Grogan* case, in which the ECJ's hands-off approach reflected absolute neutrality, the ECJ's negative appreciation of gambling activities came to light when it emphasized the high risk of crime, particularly fraud, that is connected to lotteries in addition to the damaging individual and social consequences such activities might have.[191] This outspoken stance on the part of the ECJ could have been either a reaction to criticisms of its more reticent approach in previous case law or a response to the specific subject matter, which was less controversial than previously discussed matters, since 'the *general tendency* of the Member States is to restrict, or even prohibit, the practice of gambling' (emphasis added).[192] The ECJ thus expressed what could be considered the *majoritarian* view of the Member States on this matter.[193] The case law on gambling seems to have been concerned less with the protection of the public order of one Member State (as had been the case in *Grogan* or, for instance, the *Omega* case,[194] which is further discussed) and more with highlighting the existence of a kind of European public order concept, which subsequently granted the Member States leeway for a considerable margin of discretion.[195]

A similarly bold approach is found in the *Josemans* judgment,[196] which involved the Dutch policy of tolerance towards the sale and consumption of cannabis, and where the ECJ had to rule on the validity of a municipal regulation which, in an effort to reduce drug tourism, had prohibited the admission of persons other than residents to particular Maastricht coffee shops. Initially, the local authorities' ambivalent position vis-à-vis residents and non-residents seemed to conflict with the ECJ's aforementioned consistency test. Yet, the ECJ explicitly maintained that the discriminatory nature of the rules did not necessarily imply that the way in which the intended objective was

[189] See, for instance: ECJ, Joined Cases C-338/04, C-359/04 and C-360/04 *Placanica and others* [2007] ECR I-1891, para 47; ECJ, Case C-42/07 *Liga Portuguesa* [2009] I-7633, para 57; ECJ, Joined Cases C-316/07 C-409/07 and C-410/07 *Markus Stoß* [2010] ECR I-8069, para 76; ECJ, Case C-46/08 *Carmen Media Group* [2010] ECR I-8149, para 46; ECJ, Case C-212/08 *Zeturf*, nyr, paras 40–2; ECJ, Case C-470/11 *Garkalns SIA*, nyr, para 38.

[190] See, for instance: ECJ, Case C-243/01 *Gambelli* [2003] ECR I-13031, paras 62 and 69. On the relevance of the consistency test, which must be performed by the national judge, see also: ECJ, Case C-258/08 *Ladbrokes Betting and Gaming and Ladbrokes International* [2010] ECR I-4757, para 37; ECJ, Case C-212/08 *Zeturf*, nyr, para 62; ECJ, Case C-470/11 *Garkalns SIA*, nyr, paras 46–7; ECJ, Joined Cases C-186/11 and C-209/11 *Stanleybet International Ltd and others*, nyr, paras 31–6.

[191] ECJ, Case C-275/92, *Schindler* [1994] ECR I-1039, para 60.

[192] ECJ, Case C-275/92, *Schindler* [1994] ECR I-1039.

[193] Likewise, in *Jany* (on the allegedly immoral character of room prostitution) the ECJ's finding that 'prostitution, far from being prohibited in all Member States, is tolerated, even regulated, by most of them' (in other words, a majority view on non-prohibition of the conduct at stake), might have had an impact on the ECJ's decision not to accept the alleged threat to public order: ECJ, Case C-268/99 *Jany and others* [2001] ECR I-8615, para 57. For another example, see: Opinion of AG Bot in Case C-141/07 *Commission v Germany* [2008] I-6935, § 128. On the importance of the 'majoritarian' approach in the ECJ's case law, see, in particular: POIARES MADURO, *We, the Court* (n 3) 194; S. WEATHERILL, 'Recent Case Law Concerning the Free Movement of Goods: Mapping the Frontiers of Market Deregulation', *CML Rev.* 1999, 69.

[194] See: Part I, ch1, IV, 3. 'Balancing conflicting interests: free movement versus fundamental rights. In search of a European public order concept?'

[195] G. STRAETMANS, 'Case Note Läärä and Zenatti', *CML Rev.* 2000, 1002–5.

[196] ECJ, Case C-137/09 *Josemans* [2010] ECR I-13019.

pursued was inconsistent. Instead, the ECJ focused on the specific legal context of the case at hand.[197] The fact that the case concerned products which, by their very nature, were prohibited in all Member States (*majoritarian* view),[198] and more importantly that combatting drug tourism—as a means of combatting drugs—is written down as one of the objectives in various international conventions and in EU primary and secondary law,[199] implied that an unrestricted free movement (and mutual recognition) approach to the disputed goods would conflict with the European public order and was therefore rejected.[200]

The ECJ's prudent hands-off approach, however, is not limited to morally-charged areas of law, or fields in which social and cultural features play a decisive role, but can also be identified in judgments where elements are at stake that are closely related to a Member State's national identity,[201] and in other sensitive areas of law such as those which Member States have traditionally considered to be at the core of their national sovereignty.[202] The free movement of capital, particularly the area of (direct) taxes, with its broadly defined Treaty exception ground, is a good example of an area of law where the ECJ has always acted with great respect towards the Member States' sovereignty, which is reflected in the limited enforcement of the principle of mutual recognition. An illustration of this is the *Kerckhaert* judgment.[203] In light of the ECJ's case law on the free movement of capital, arguments based on the principle of mutual recognition (and on the elimination of its corresponding dual fiscal burdens) will only succeed when restrictions on the free movement of capital are due to a specific Member State's exercising its tax competences in a discriminatory manner.[204] They will not succeed, however, when these dual burdens are simply the consequence of disparities between the Member

[197] ECJ, Case C-137/09 *Josemans* [2010] ECR I-13019, para 76.

[198] ECJ, Case C-137/09 *Josemans* [2010] ECR I-13019, paras 41 and 78.

[199] ECJ, Case C-137/09 *Josemans* [2010] ECR I-13019, paras 37–40, 67–8, and 77.

[200] On the 'European public order' concept in this case, see, in particular: Opinion of AG Bot in Case C-137/09 *Josemans* [2010] ECR I-13019 § 113 ff. For an in-depth analysis of the 'European public order' concept, see: T. CORTHAUT, *EU Ordre Public* (The Hague, Kluwer Law International, 2012). For a similar 'European' approach vis-à-vis the public security exception, see: ECJ, Joined Cases, C-22/08 and C-23/08 *Vatsoeras and Koupatantze* [2009] ECR I-4585, para 46; ECJ, Case C-348/09 *P.I.*, nyr, paras 25–8, discussed by C. JANSSENS, 'Annotatie *P.I.*', *SEW* 2012, 479–82.

[201] See, for instance: ECJ, Case C-208/09 *Sayn-Wittgenstein* [2010] ECR I-13693, paras 92–3, where the ECJ underlined that 'in accordance with Article 4(2) TEU, the European Union is to respect the national identities of its Member States, which include the status of the State as a Republic', and concluded that 'by refusing to recognize the noble elements of a name such as that of the applicant in the main proceedings, the Austrian authorities responsible for civil status matters do not appear to have gone further than is necessary in order to ensure the attainment of the fundamental constitutional objective pursued by them'.

[202] See, for instance, with regard to criminal law and, more precisely, domestic violence, the margin of discretion granted to a Member State in: ECJ, Joined Cases C-483/09 and C-1/10 *Magatte Gueye and Valentín Salmerón Sánchez*, nyr, discussed by C. JANSSENS, 'Annotatie *Magatte Gueye and Valentín Salmerón Sánchez*', *SEW* 2012, 159–63.

[203] ECJ, Case C-513/04 *Kerckhaert* [2006] ECR I-10967. On the revolutionary or non-revolutionary nature of this judgment, in light of previous case law on free movement of capital, see, for instance: M. FABRA VALLS, 'Régimen fiscal aplicable a los dividendos entrantes percibidos por personas fisicas y relaciones entre el Derecho Comunitario y los Convenios de Doble Imposicion', *Noticias de la UE* 2009, 78–80; LENAERTS and BERNARDEAU, 'L'encadrement communautaire de la fiscalité directe' (n 74) 59–63; SNELL, 'Free Movement of Capital: Evolution as a Non-Linear Process' (n 66) 10 ff.; USHER, 'The Evolution of the Free Movement of Capital' (n 65) 1560.

[204] See, for instance: ECJ, Case C-319/02 *Manninen* [2004] ECR I-7477, para 39; ECJ, Case C-170/05 *Denkavit* [2006] ECR I-11949, para 29; ECJ, Case C-43/07 *Arens-Sikken* [2008] ECR I-6887, paras 52–3; ECJ, Case C-510/08 *Mattner* [2010] ECR I-3553, para 34; ECJ, Case C-233/09 *Dijkman* [2010] ECR I-6649, para 47.

States' tax legislation and their parallel exercise of fiscal sovereignty.[205] It follows from the ECJ's case law that mere disparities in (tax) legislation—which may or may not be to a citizen's or company's advantage, depending on the circumstances—must be accepted, as the TFEU offers no guarantee to either citizens or companies of the Union that cross-border transfers of capital will be neutral as regards taxation.[206]

Although the lack of common, harmonized rules also creates obstacles to smooth application of the principle of mutual recognition in other areas of law,[207] it cannot be denied that given the present EU acquis in the field of direct taxes and the corresponding fiscal sovereignty of the Member States in dividing taxing power, the ECJ can do very little regarding the dual burdens that arise from disparities in national tax legislation besides preventing a Member State exercising its tax competences in a discriminatory manner. Furthermore, there is a crucial difference between moves that address the possible risks of undermining the financial balance of a national tax system and the vast majority of mandatory requirements that are invoked in relation to the other free movement areas. Whereas the latter are usually protected to an equivalent or sufficient extent in the host and home states, this is not at all the case in the area of taxes, where revenue collection in one state by no means protects the fiscal interests of another.[208]

(2) Verifying equivalent and/or sufficient levels of protection

It is not only in cases where the ECJ adopts a non-interfering approach that limits to the principle of mutual recognition emerge. As I mentioned earlier, the rule of reason and the Treaty justification grounds essentially serve as compensatory measures for situations in which there is a lack of harmonization or compatibility between different Member States. The majority of the ECJ's case law, then, comes down to the question of whether the level of protection required by a Member State is considered to be proportionate, either compared to the level of protection in the Member State of origin (section 2.1) or to other standards (section 2.2).

2.1. Lack of equivalent protection in the country of origin

I have already mentioned that in an important part of the ECJ's case law, specifically the area of diplomas or inspection of goods, the ECJ does not refrain from insisting explicitly on an equivalence test. Another field in which the equivalence criterion plays a pivotal

205 See, for instance: ECJ, Case C-374/04 *Test Claimants in Class IV of the ACT Group Litigation* [2006] ECR I-11673, paras 55 and 61–2; ECJ, Case C-513/04 *Kerckhaert* [2006] ECR I-10967; ECJ, Case C-194/06 *Orange European Smallcap Fund* [2008] ECR I-3747, para 37; ECJ, Case C-128/08 *Damseaux* [2009] ECR I-6823, paras 27–31; ECJ, Case C-67/08 *Block* [2009] ECR I-883, para 28. See also: Opinion of AG Geelhoed in Case C-374/04 *Test Claimants in Class IV of the ACT Group Litigation* [2006] ECR I-11673, § 43–7; Opinion of AG Sharpston in Case C-250/08 *Commission v Belgium* [2010] ECR I-5267, § 46.

206 See, for instance: ECJ, Case C-67/08 *Block* [2009] ECR I-883, para 35; ECJ, Case C-240/10 *Schulz-Delzers*, nyr, para 42. Similarly, in the area of social security, see, for instance: ECJ, Case C-211/08 *Commission v Spain* [2010] ECR I-5267, para 61; ECJ, Joined Cases C-611/10 and C-612/10 *Hudzinski en Wawrzyniak*, nyr, para 43.

207 See, for instance, in the area of gambling services, where the ECJ held in *Stoß* and *Dickinger* that 'having regard to that margin of discretion *and the absence of any Community harmonization in the matter*, a duty mutually to recognize authorizations issued by the various Member States cannot exist having regard to the current state of EU law' (emphasis added): ECJ, Joined Cases C-316/07, C-358/07, C-359/07, C-360/07, C-409/07 and C-410/07 *Markus Stoß and others* [2010] ECR I-8069, para 112; ECJ, Case C-347/09 *Dickinger*, nyr, para 96. Or, in the area of public health services and social security: ECJ, Case C-211/08 *Commission v Spain* [2010] ECR I-5267, para 61; ECJ, Case C-562/10 *Commission v Germany*, nyr, para 57.

208 SNELL, 'Free Movement of Capital: Evolution as a Non-Linear Process' (n 65) 24. A similar reasoning holds true with regard to the area of social security.

role is the ECJ's case law on yet another area of great socio-political sensitivity, namely the protection of social rights.

From the very beginning, the ECJ's point of departure in this area has been that a Member State is in principle entitled to extend its legislation or collective labour agreements (relating to minimum wages) to any person who is employed, even temporarily, within its territory, regardless of the country in which the employer is established.[209] According to some authors, such a statement jeopardizes Article 45 TFEU and Article 56 TFEU and gives too much prevalence to the host state's labour market.[210] Some authors go even further and argue that it would be more correct to state that mutual recognition plays no role at all in this sector.[211]

In my opinion, the latter views ignore the basic characteristics of the principle of mutual recognition as developed since *Cassis de Dijon* for two reasons. Firstly, if no common, harmonized or equivalent rules exist, it is in principle for the Member States to decide upon the degree of protection they intend to assure and the extent to which they accept foreign products that lack an equivalent degree of protection (hence the prevalence of the host state's legislation). Secondly, this starting point was refined—some might say reversed, even—by introducing the mutual recognition reasoning, which reduced the dominance of the host state's legislation considerably and fortified the importance of the home state's legislation. This was done in order to reduce any additional costs or burdens which might constitute an unjustified barrier to the free movement provisions, albeit tempered by the rule of reason theory (in the event of an acceptable justification ground and insofar as the measure was both necessary and proportionate).

Contrary to what some authors have suggested,[212] such reasoning is equally present in the ECJ's case law on minimum wages and social law in general. The basic assumption that Member States can apply their social legislation is put into perspective by the principle of mutual recognition, according to which the host state's legislation can no longer be imposed when employees enjoy the same protection or very similar protection by virtue of the obligations to which the employer is already subject in the Member State of establishment, i.e. the equivalence criterion.[213] In other words, the application of the host state's national rules can only be imposed when they confer real additional

[209] In most of its older judgments in this area the ECJ limited the Member States' competences explicitly to issues related to minimum wages and/or matters of public policy, see: ECJ, Joined Cases 62/81 and 63/81 *Seco* [1982] ECR 233, para 14; ECJ, Case C-43/93 *Vander Elst* [1994] ECR I-3803, paras 23–5; ECJ, Case C-272/94 *Guiot* [1996] ECR I-1905, para 12; ECJ, Joined Cases C-369/96 and C-376/96 *Arblade* [1999] ECR I-8453, paras 41–2. However, in other, more recent judgments such nuances were no longer made by the ECJ, which seems to suggest that a Member State would basically be entitled to apply *all* aspects of its labour law to foreign service providers, see: ECJ, Case C-113/89 *Rush Portuguesa* [1990] ECR I-01417, para 18; ECJ, Case C-445/03 *Commission v Luxemburg* [2004] ECR I-10191, para 29; ECJ, Case C-244/04 *Commission v Germany* [2006] ECR I-885, para 44; ECJ, Case C-168/04 *Commission v Austria* [2006] ECR I-9041, para 47.

[210] D. MARTIN, 'Case Note Arblade', *Eur. J. Migration and L.* 2000, 105.

[211] PADOA SCHIOPPA, 'Mutual Recognition, Unemployment and the Welfare State' (n 62) 190, who implicitly relies on Article 45 TFEU where he states that 'the European Union endorses in this sector an opposite principle, named equal treatment'. It can, however, not be denied that in the context of posted workers the ECJ completely ruled out the application of Article 45 TFEU in *Finalarte*: ECJ, Joined Cases C-94/98, C-50/98, C-52/98, C-54/98 and C-68/98 to C-71/98 *Finalarte* [2001] ECR I-7831, paras 22–3.

[212] PADOA SCHIOPPA, 'Mutual Recognition, Unemployment and the Welfare State' (n 62) 190.

[213] See, for instance: ECJ, Case C-43/93 *Vander Elst* [1994] ECR I-3803, para 16 (regarding work permits); ECJ, Case C-272/94 *Guiot* [1996] ECR I-1905, para 18 (regarding the payment of social contributions); ECJ, Joined Cases C-369/96 and C-376/96 *Arblade* [1999] ECR I-8453, para 51 (regarding minimum wages, the payment of social contributions, and the drawing up of social or labour documents); ECJ, Case C-445/03 *Commission v Luxemburg* [2004] ECR I-10191, para 29 (regarding a work licensing system); ECJ, Case C-244/04 *Commission v Germany* [2006] ECR I-885, para 44

protection to posted workers, a genuine benefit which significantly enhances their social protection.[214] The required level of equivalence must be determined in context and must take all relevant criteria into account.[215]

Aside from this equivalence test, in *Finalarte* and in subsequent judgments the ECJ explicitly urged the national courts to balance the administrative and economic burdens that the rules impose on service providers with the increased social protection conferred on employees compared to that guaranteed by the law of the Member State where their employer is established.[216] This imposed balancing act, together with an equivalence test and a proportionality test that was introduced relatively late,[217] made three things clear. First, in this instance the ECJ disassociated itself from a hands-off approach in a very sensitive area. Secondly, the host Member State's labour legislation would not necessarily always prevail. Thirdly, the art of reconciling free movement provisions with social rights and social dumping concerns would henceforward be at the core of the ECJ's reasoning in the case law on this subject.[218]

The judgment on *Type approval for woodworking machines* is possibly the most clear-cut example of a case in which the lack of equivalence, thoroughly investigated by the ECJ,[219] ruled out any duty of mutual recognition. A crucial element in this judgment was the finding of a difference in focus between the French legislation (which focused on the idea that woodworking machine users ought to be protected from their own mistakes, and thus resulted in a clear preference for the complete automation of dangerous apparatus) and the German legislation (which focused on thorough and continuous training to ensure that the user was capable of responding correctly if a machine malfunctioned). Although it was perfectly conceivable that each system alone ensured an adequate level of protection in the respective Member State, the same could not necessarily be said for a combined approach in which the systems were mingled, for example where a German machine (built for skilled users) became available for French users (who were used to automated machines). It was exactly this difference in approach that highlighted the systems' incompatibility and led the ECJ to conclude that it had not been

(regarding controls *a priori* and a one-year employment condition); ECJ, Case C-168/04 *Commission v Austria* [2006] ECR I-9041, para 47 (regarding residence permits); ECJ, Case C-341/05 *Laval un Partneri* [2007] ECR I-11767, para 116 (regarding collective agreements).

[214] ECJ, Joined Cases C-94/98, C-50/98, C-52/98, C-54/98 and C-68/98 to C-71/98 *Finalarte* [2001] ECR I-7831, paras 45 and 53 (regarding paid leave fund schemes to finance holiday).

[215] Thus, for example, when considering the level of minimum wages, Member States must examine whether the workers concerned enjoy an equivalent position overall in relation to remuneration, taxation, and social security contributions in the host Member State and in the Member State of establishment: ECJ, Case C-165/98 *Mazzoleni* [2001] ECR I-2189, para 35.

[216] See, for instance: ECJ, Case C-515/08 *dos Santos Palhota and others* [2010] ECR I-9133, para 58 with reference to *Arblade* and *Finalarte*.

[217] Compare the rather blunt assumption 'that Member States may extend their legislation relating to minimum wages to any person who is employed, even temporally, within their territory' (in Joined Cases C-369/96 and C-376/96 *Arblade* [1999] ECR I-8453, para 41), with the *Mazzoleni* judgment in which the ECJ introduced the proportionality check by stating that 'there may be circumstances in which the application of rules on minimum remuneration would be neither necessary nor proportionate to the objective pursued, in casu the protection of workers' (ECJ, Case C-165/98 *Mazzoleni* [2001] ECR I-2189, para 30).

[218] Not only national provisions on minimum wages, but also national rules on other delicate social rights, such as the right to collective action (strike), can in certain circumstances jeopardize the free movement provisions. Here too the ECJ's case law imposes a duty to balance or reconcile both fundamental rights, see: Part I, ch 1, IV, A, 3. 'Balancing conflicting interests: free movement versus fundamental rights. In search of a European public order concept?', in particular, the *Laval* and *Viking Line* judgments that are discussed there.

[219] ECJ, Case 188/84 *Type approval for woodworking machines* [1986] ECR 419, paras 10–22.

established that the (German) machines would provide the same level of protection for (French) users. In other words, the ECJ concluded that there was a lack of equivalence.

In most cases, though, where the ECJ perceives potential problems with equivalence or does not have sufficient information to settle the case, a detailed assessment is left to the national judge. The judge's task of comparing two levels of protection or two types of control is a complex one, as technical difficulties may often arise which can only be resolved by reference to expert opinion.[220] A number of other cases have required no in-depth analysis whatsoever of the ECJ, such as when Member States had clearly ignored all equivalence criteria when setting up or applying their national legislation.[221]

An analysis of the ECJ's case law reveals that the mechanism of mutual recognition and the appreciation of the equivalence requirement is not an 'all or nothing' issue. In other words, where equivalence appears to be absent, the duty of mutual recognition is usually not set aside completely by the ECJ but rather refined. In order to prevent dual burdens, Member States have a duty to put themselves in contact with colleagues from other Member States in their pursuit of equivalence and to take into account corresponding certificates, tests, or legislation which might fully or partially cover the required level of protection.[222] Additional measures that top up the required level of protection may then be imposed,[223] whereas requirements that are even partially repetitive are forbidden outright.[224] Such an approach should encourage Member States to restrict hindrances to free movement as far as possible, though without jeopardizing legitimate interests unnecessarily.

2.2. Lack of sufficient protection

In a considerable portion of the ECJ's case law, the required level of protection in a given Member State is assessed without making any reference or comparison to the level of protection offered in the country of origin. This approach can also be found in the ECJ's case law where, for example, public health arguments arise as possible barriers to the principle of mutual recognition. In those judgments, the ECJ very rarely looks into the home state's legislation when examining national requirements but focuses instead on the host state's legislation. The latter is evaluated firstly in the light of international

[220] D. WYATT, 'National Safety Checks on Imported Goods Must Not Duplicate Identical Checks in Country of Origin—Denkavit Followed', *E.L. Rev.* 1982, 204.

[221] ECJ, Case C-444/05 *Stamatelaki* [2007] ECR I-3185, paras 36–8 (on the refusal to recognize private hospitals, without verifying whether they are able to provide appropriate—identical or equivalent—medical treatment); ECJ, Case C-318/05 *Commission v Germany* [2007] ECR I-6957, para 105 (on the refusal to recognize foreign private schools, without verifying whether their operating methods are largely identical).

[222] This duty of cooperation which rests on the Member States, is repeatedly mentioned in the ECJ's case law. See, for instance: ECJ, Case 104/75 *de Peijper* [1976] ECR 613, para 27; ECJ, Case 251/78 *Denkavit* [1979] ECR 3369, para 23; ECJ, Case C-124/81 *Commission v UK* [1983] ECR 203, para 30; ECJ, Case 97/83 *Melkunie* [1984] ECR 2367, para 14; ECJ, Case 406/85 *Gofette and Gilliard* [1987] ECR 2525, para 11; ECJ, Case C-228/91 *Commission v Italy* [1993] ECR I-2701, para 22; ECJ, Case C-496/01 *Commission v France* [2004] ECR I-2351, para 74. Admittedly, this duty of cooperation is not a blind or unconditional obligation to take into account whatever comes from another Member State, but it does not leave a great margin of discretion to the Member States either. See: Part I, ch 1, IV, B, 1. 'Presumed inaccuracies in controls, certificates or documents subject to mutual recognition'.

[223] ECJ, Case 272/80 *Biologische Producten* [1981] ECR 3277, para 14 or the abundant case law on mutual recognition of diplomas, cited under the heading: Part I, ch 1, I, C, 1. 'Mutual recognition of diplomas'.

[224] See, for instance, regarding driving licences: ECJ, Case 16/78 *Choquet* [1978] ECR 2293, para 8; or in relation to health inspection, for instance: ECJ, Case C-251/78 *Denkavit* [1979] ECR 3369, paras 22–3; ECJ, Case 132/80 *United Food* [1981] ECR 995, para 29.

research results and secondly with regard to national consumption habits in the host state.[225] Indeed, Member States may regulate, for instance, the presence of pesticide residues on foodstuffs in a way which varies from one country to another according to a range of conditions, such as climate, the normal diet of the population and their state of health, as long as no further information is available from scientific research.[226] The ECJ clearly refrains from applying any equivalence approach in this area and prefers to make use of (international) scientific research results as a yardstick, complemented by the national food habits in the host Member State.

The ECJ's approach to international research results is very cautious,[227] and was adopted together with a soft proportionality test in order to grant a considerable margin of appreciation to the Member States, who can themselves decide on the required level of protection whenever uncertainties about the present state of scientific research remain.[228] Member States' arguments are mostly accepted, particularly when the use of the product meets a real technical (or nutritional) need.[229] The appreciation of a technical need is one of the few instances in which the ECJ refers back to the home Member State: the technical need for a product must be assessed taking into account the raw materials that were used in its production and the assessment that was made by the authorities of the home Member State.[230]

[225] See, for instance: ECJ, Case 53/80 *Kaasfabriek Eyssen* [1981] ECR 409, para 13 and ECJ, Case C-42/90 *Bellon* [1990] I-4863, para 14 (in which the ECJ referred to research that had been performed by the Food and Agriculture Organization of the United Nations and the World Health Organization); ECJ, Case 94/83 *Heijn* [1984] ECR 3263, para 13 (in which the ECJ mentioned Council Directive 76/895 in relation to pesticides); ECJ, Case 304/84 *Muller* [1986] ECR 1511, para 24 and ECJ, Case 247/84 *Motte* [1985] ECR 3887, para 20 (where the ECJ mentioned the work of a competent EU scientific committee); ECJ, Case C-473/98 *Toolex* [2001] ECR I-5681, paras 42–4 (in which the ECJ relied on the International Cancer Research Agency, set up by the World Health Organization, as well as a German case study and an American epidemiological study). See, in relation to the latter judgment, the critical analysis of J.P Montfort who suggests that the ECJ accepted far too easily the so-called dangerous character of the substance, without thoroughly analysing the studies that were mentioned: J.P. MONTFORT, 'L'arrêt Trichloroethylene et la libre circulation des produits chimiques: un nouveau défi pour le marché intérieur', *C.D.E.* 2001, 335; ECJ, Case C-121/00 *Hahn* [2002] ECR I-9193, paras 41–5 (in which the ECJ referred to the research work of the Scientific Committee on Veterinary Measures); ECJ, Case C-333/08 *Commission v France* [2010] ECR I-757, para 87.

[226] ECJ, Case 54/85 *Mirepoix* [1986] ECR 1067, para 15.

[227] Although certain substances are not harmful in themselves, their consumption beyond a certain level may create a risk to human health. Since in the present stage of scientific research there is uncertainty as to the critical threshold of harmfulness—which depends to a large extent on eating habits in the different Member States—it is in principle for each Member State to decide upon what degree of protection they intend to assure: ECJ, Case 304/84 *Muller* [1986] ECR 1511, paras 20–1; ECJ, Case C-42/90, *Bellon* [1990] ECR I-4863, para 11.

[228] ECJ, Case 174/82 *Sandoz* [1983] ECR 2445, para 16; ECJ, Case 227/82 *Van Bennekom* [1983] ECR 3883, paras 36–7. The precautionary principle, which acquired an explicit Treaty basis following the Maastricht Treaty (former Article 174 EC, currently Article 191 TFEU) was explicitly mentioned in: ECJ, Case C-192/01 *Commission v Denmark* [2003] ECR I-9693, para 49; ECJ, Case C-95/01 *Greenham and Abel* [2004] ECR I-1333, para 48; ECJ, Case C-24/00 *Commission v France* [2004] ECR I-1277, para 56; ECJ Case C-41/02 *Commission v Netherlands* [2004] ECR I-11375, para 45. On the meaning and contours of this principle, see: Communication from the Commission on the Precautionary Principle, COM (2000) 1; G. BERENDS and I CARREÑO, 'Safeguards in Food Law—Ensuring Food Scares are Scarce', *E.L. Rev.* 2005, 386–405; D. CHALMERS, 'Food for Thought: Reconciling European Risks and Traditional Ways of Life', *MLR* 2003, 532–62; E. FISHER, 'Precaution, Precaution Everywhere: Developing a Common Understanding of the Precautionary Principle in the European Community', *MJ* 2002, 7–28.

[229] See, for instance: ECJ, Case 174/82 *Sandoz* [1983] ECR 2445, para 19; ECJ, Case 304/84 *Muller* [1986] ECR 1511, para 22; ECJ, Case C-42/90 *Bellon* [1990] ECR I-4863, para 14.

[230] ECJ, Case 178/84 *Commission v Germany* [1987] ECR 1227, para 52; C.A.W. TIMMERMANS, 'Annotatie *Commission v Germany*', *SEW* 1988, 126.

The burden of proof in this domain is therefore not a heavy one.[231] Public health arguments are rebutted only when no (detailed) risk assessment has been performed by the host state or when international research results exclude any doubts as to the possible risks to public health.[232] The ECJ finds itself in an extremely difficult position in that it has to weigh the economic values of the common market against public health concerns. When balancing these types of value using the proportionality test, there is always the risk that the ECJ might get it wrong and should, consequently, face the burden of responsibility for the citizens of the respective Member State.[233] The highly sensitive nature of the subject matter—the ECJ has repeatedly stated that public health and human life rank foremost among the assets and interests protected by the Treaties[234]—has likely pushed the ECJ towards this very lenient approach. As a result, though, the prominence of the principle of mutual recognition in this area has been reduced considerably.[235]

Another area in which the ECJ refrains from applying an equivalence test concerns the area of environmental justification grounds. Despite the great importance that the ECJ attaches to the protection of the environment as one of the essential objectives of the EU,[236] in principle the ECJ only checks whether the measure truly aims at protecting the environment and whether the measure is proportionate. If either of these checks

[231] See, for instance: ECJ, Case C-24/00 *Commission v France* [2004] ECR I-1277, para 70, with regard to energy drinks such as Red Bull, where the mere identification of studies showing that an excessive caffeine content and the presence of certain substances was harmful to human health, would seem sufficient to discharge the burden of proof. For a comment on this judgment, see: M. JARVIS, 'Case Note *Commission v France*', *CML Rev.* 2004, 1406. Moreover, according to AG Trstenjak, the ECJ's case law reveals that even though it is not necessary for a Member State to give an absolutely rigorous and scientific demonstration of the existence of a risk, the allegation of the existence of a risk must, in any event, be based on comprehensible and well-established arguments: Opinion of AG Trstenjak in Case C-319/05 *Commission v Germany* [2007] ECR I-9811, § 79.

[232] Public health arguments were, for instance, not accepted in ECJ, Joined Cases C-13/91 and C-113/91 *Debus* [1992] ECR I-3617, paras 24–5, where the ECJ acknowledged that the limits of the maximum doses as prescribed by the Food and Agriculture Organization and the World Health Organization would not be exceeded and so no real threat to human health was at stake. Furthermore, some protectionist intentions were present in this case as the same amount of the product was accepted in other alcoholic beverages whose consumption was much higher in the Member State concerned. See also: ECJ, Case 17/93 *Van der Veldt* [1994] ECR I-3537, para 18, where the Member State had neglected to produce any scientific data.

[233] M. AVBELJ, 'European Court of Justice and the Question of Value Choices. Fundamental human rights as an exception to the freedom of goods', Jean Monnet Working Paper 2004, 22, retrievable at: <http://centers.law.nyu.edu/jeanmonnet/archive/papers/04/040601.pdf>; J. WEILER, 'Mutual Recognition, Functional Equivalence and Harmonization in the Evolution of the European Common Market and the WTO', in F.K. PADOA SCHIOPPA (ed.), *The Principle of Mutual Recognition in the European Integration Process* (New York, Palgrave, 2005) 49, who argues that the success of mandatory requirements is a ticking time-bomb.

[234] See, for instance: ECJ, Joined Cases C-171/07 and C-172/07 *Apothekerkammer des Saarlandes and Others* [2009] ECR I-4171, para 19; ECJ, Joined Cases C-570/07 and 571/07 *Blanco Pérez* [2010] ECR I-4629, para 44; The reference to this crucial position of human health does not imply, however, that the outcome of the proportionality test will always be to the advantage of the Member State; see, for instance: ECJ, Case C-89/09 *Commission v France* [2010] ECR I-12941, para 42 (and the corresponding Opinion of AG Mengozzi, who underlined the very specific nature of medicaments which distinguishes itself from other goods and therefore needs particular protection, at § 117); ECJ, Case C-108/09 *Ker-Optica* [2010] ECR I-12213, paras 58 and 74; ECJ, Case C-421/09 *Humanplasma* [2010] ECR I-12869, paras 32 and 46.

[235] FISHER, 'Precaution, Precaution Everywhere: Developing a Common Understanding of the Precautionary Principle in the European Community' (n 228) 25, speaks of a burden of *reasoning* as opposed to a burden of *proof.*

[236] ECJ, Case C-28/09 *Commission v Austria*, nyr, paras 120–2.

produces a negative result, a duty of mutual recognition is imposed.[237] Here, too, recourse to international conventions is sometimes needed in order to evaluate whether the national measure can be justified.[238]

Consumer protection, often closely linked to public health arguments, is another field where equivalence checks are rarely performed. The ECJ prefers to consider the national measure from the perspective of an average consumer, who is thought to be reasonably well-informed and reasonably observant and circumspect.[239] In general, the ECJ has refrained from focusing on a comparison of average consumers in the home and host states and has instead appeared to pursue a more general, European consumer concept, i.e. the figure of a rather self-reliant, rational consumer who, when provided with adequate labelling, is expected to be capable of making a proper choice.[240] However, this concept of the *European* consumer is sometimes substituted for a more locally tinted concept, which takes into account social, linguistic, and cultural aspects.[241] The ECJ's analysis of 'consumer protection' exceptions tends to involve a remarkably strict proportionality test,[242] unless the case in question touches upon sensitive areas[243] or concerns vulnerable consumers.[244]

[237] See, for instance: ECJ, Case 302/86 *Commission v Denmark* [1988] ECR 4607, paras 20–1 (disproportionate measure); ECJ, Case C-209/98 *Sydhavnens Sten and Gruss* [2000] ECR I-3743, para 51 (absence of any indication of danger to the environment); ECJ, Case C-28/09 *Commission v Austria*, nyr, para 150 (disproportionate).

[238] See, for instance: ECJ, Case C-67/97 *Bluhme* [1998] ECR I-8033, para 36, where reference is made to the Rio Convention in relation to the protection of biodiversity.

[239] See, for instance: ECJ, Case 369/88 *Delattre* [1991] ECR I-1541, para 58; ECJ, Case C-470/93 *Mars* [1995] ECR I-1944, para 24; ECJ, Case C-358/01 *Commission v Spain* [2003] ECR I-13145, para 58. See also: ECJ, Case C-362/88 *GB Inno* [1990] ECR I-667, paras 14–16, where the ECJ resolved the mutual recognition conflict, arising from two opposite legislations in two different Member States, by evaluating the consumer protection in light of the instruments that had been adopted at that time by the Council.

[240] On the emerging 'European' notion of the consumer, see: STRAETMANS, *Consument en markt* (n 51), 390 and 416; S. WEATHERILL, *EU Consumer Law and Policy* (Cheltenham, Edward Elgar, 2005) 51–9.

[241] See, for instance: RADEIDEH, *Fair Trading in EC Law. Information and Consumer Choice in the Internal Market* (n 118) 64–8, who indicates that the traditional and general concept of the *European* consumer has developed to a consumer image which recognizes the *diversity* of consumers among Member States. See, in particular, *Graffione* and *Estée Lauder* in which the ECJ emphasized that 'linguistic, social and cultural differences must be taken into account when deciding upon the presumed expectations of an average consumer, who is reasonably well informed and reasonably observant and circumspect' (ECJ, Case C-313/94 *Graffione* [1996] ECR I-6039, para 22; ECJ, Case C-220/98 *Estée Lauder* [2000] ECR I-117, para 29). In these judgments, where the ECJ recognized different levels of 'necessary' protection of consumers, depending on the social, linguistic, and cultural background, equivalence seems to play some role, as precisely the lack of equivalence as to social, linguistic, or cultural aspects, can justify the setting aside of the mutual recognition principle. See also: C.C. VAN DAM, 'De gemiddelde Euroconsument—een pluriform fenomeen. Over de Richtlijn oneerlijke handelspraktijken en de rechtspraak van het Hof van Justitie', *SEW* 2009, 3 ff.

[242] An absolute prohibition is rarely considered to be proportionate, see, for instance: ECJ, Case 120/78 *Rewe-Zentral AG (Cassis de Dijon)* [1979] ECR 649, para 13; ECJ, Case 261/81 *Rau* [1982] ECR 3961, para 17; ECJ, Case 407/85 *Glocken* [1988] ECR 4233, para 16; ECJ Case C-126/91 *Y. Rocher* [1993] ECR I-2361, para 18; ECJ, Case C-315/92 *Clinique* [1994] ECR I-317, paras 21–2; ECJ Case C-470/93 *Mars* [1995] ECR I-1944, paras 23–4.

[243] As regards public health, see, for instance: ECJ, Case 97/83 *Melkunie* [1984] ECR 2367, para 20; ECJ, Case C-220/98 *Estée Lauder* [2000] ECR I-117, para 28; ECJ, Case C-358/01 *Commission v Spain* [2003] ECR I-13145, para 53. As regards alcohol-related or medicine-related advertising, see for instance: ECJ, Case C-405/98 *Gourmet* [2001] ECR I-1755, para 33; ECJ, Joined Cases C-1/90 and C-176/90 *Aragonesa* [1991] ECR I-4151, paras 17–18; ECJ, Case C-262/02 *Commission v France* [2004] ECR I-6569, para 36; ECJ, Case C-429/02 *Bacardi* [2004] ECR I-6613, para 38; ECJ, Case C-320/93 *Ortscheit* [1994] ECR I-5257, paras 19–20. As regards medicines: ECJ, Joined Cases 266/87 and 267/87 *Royal Pharmaceutical Society* [1989] ECR 1295, para 22, ECJ, Case C-322/01 *Deutscher Apothekerverband* [2003] ECR I-14887, paras 117–19.

[244] ECJ, Case 286/81 *Oosthoek* [1982] ECR 4575, para 18; ECJ Case C-382/87 *Buet* [1989] ECR 1235, para 13; ECJ, Case C-244/06 *Dynamic Medien* [2008] ECR I-505, para 39.

(3) *Balancing conflicting interests: free movement versus fundamental rights. In search of a European public order concept?*

In some judgments, the ECJ searches neither for a sufficient nor equivalent level of protection but chooses instead to develop a delicate balancing act between two conflicting interests, the result of which aims once again at a refined mutual recognition mechanism.

The area *par excellence* in which the ECJ has been performing such a delicate balancing act is its emerging free movement/fundamental rights case law. The protection of fundamental rights themselves or of their application when evaluating a free movement justification ground is not a recent phenomenon,[245] of course, but judgments in which fundamental rights are invoked as independent (or quasi-independent) barriers to a fundamental freedom, and therefore to the principle of mutual recognition, are clearly setting a new trend.[246]

3.1. The protection of fundamental rights: a rule of reason, or something more?

From a theoretical perspective, it is an interesting question whether 'the protection of fundamental rights' should be read as one of the existing Treaty-based or rule of reason-based justification grounds or whether it should be recognized as an independent category.[247] In my view, 'the protection of fundamental rights' should indeed be considered an independent category, a kind of upgraded rule of reason. Surely, the protection of fundamental rights shares some common ground with the traditional rule of reason in that the ECJ considers it as 'a legitimate interest which, in principle, justifies a restriction to one of the four freedoms', and in that the ECJ applies the traditional proportionality check ('suitability' and 'not go beyond what is necessary') to it. However, fundamental rights are not simply derivations from the economic freedoms. They are protected by EU law itself[248] and the balancing act is therefore not only about checking whether the fundamental right in question can justify the restriction of free movement, but also about verifying whether the free movement provisions are being applied in accordance with the fundamental right in question. A thorough analysis of the nature of the fundamental right will therefore be the logical starting point for the ECJ's analysis.

[245] As early as 1970 the ECJ recognized the protection of fundamental rights as general principle of EU law: ECJ, Case 11/70 *Internationale Handelsgesellschaft* [1970] ECR 1125, para 4. And in *ERT* and *Familiapress* the ECJ interpreted the justification grounds at stake in light of a fundamental right: ECJ, Case C-260/89 *ERT* [1991] ECR I-2925, para 43; ECJ, Case C-368/95 *Familiapress* [1997] ECR I-3689, para 24.

[246] Opinion of AG Jacobs in Case C-112/00 *Schmidberger* [2003] I-5659, § 89.

[247] Some authors have qualified the fundamental rights protection as part of the public policy concept, see for instance: T. ACKERMANN, 'Case Note Omega', *CML Rev.* 2005, 1115; F.G. JACOBS, 'Human Rights in the EU: the Role of the ECJ', *E.L. Rev.* 2001, 336–7. Other authors have considered it as an unwritten public interest ground in Article 36 TFEU and Article 52 TFEU; see for instance: J. MORIJN, 'Balancing Fundamental Rights and Common Market Freedoms in Union Law: Schmidberger and Omega in light of the European Constitution', *E.L.J.* 2006, 39. Another part of legal doctrine has categorized it under the mandatory requirements; see for instance: A. ALEMANNO, 'Libre circulation des personnes', *RDUE* 2003, 527; J. JANS, 'Annotatie *Omega*', *SEW* 2005, 186. A final group of authors suggests to consider it as a separate category, see for instance: AVBELJ, 'European Court of Justice and the Question of Value Choices' (n 233) 62; K.J.M. MORTELMANS, 'Botsende algemene belangen en de werking van de interne markt', *SEW* 2004, 245.

[248] See, in particular Article 6 TEU. According to the ECJ, the protection of fundamental rights forms part of the very foundations of the EU legal order: ECJ, Joined Cases C-402/05 P and C-415/05 P *Kadi and Al Barakaat International Foundation* [2008] ECR I-6351, paras 303–4.

Furthermore, the role of the protection of fundamental rights aims to be far broader than that of the Treaty-based or rule of reason-based justification grounds. The application of these latter two will necessarily lead to a restriction of the free movement provisions (and of the principle of mutual recognition) and they are therefore to be interpreted restrictively. Fundamental rights, on the other hand, can also be applied by the ECJ to reinforce the free movement provisions,[249] and should therefore not necessarily be interpreted restrictively.

3.2. The evaluation of the protection of fundamental rights from a combined national-EU perspective

In contrast to the previously discussed *Grogan* judgment, the ECJ has ceased to maintain a strictly hands-off approach in its recent case law, and chooses instead to verify whether the (national) fundamental right invoked is entitled to protection from an EU perspective. In *Schmidberger*, *Omega*, *Viking Line*, and *Laval un Partneri*, the ECJ aimed at reconciling fundamental freedoms with fundamental rights, without establishing any hierarchical relationship between them.[250] Depending on the type of fundamental right in question and on the particular application of the proportionality test to the case, the ECJ's analysis will lead either to the confirmation or to the rejection of the principle of mutual recognition.

The ECJ's approach in this matter is not based on a comparison of different levels of protection between the Member States involved in order to establish the degree of equivalence between them. Instead, the ECJ analyses the national public order concept or standard of fundamental rights protection in light of a European benchmark, i.e. the EU standard of fundamental rights protection. The national interpretation of a fundamental right can certainly be the starting point and the ECJ emphasizes, furthermore, that a Member State may choose a system of protection different from that adopted by another Member State,[251]

[249] Free movement provisions were, for instance, reinforced by fundamental rights in: ECJ, Case C-60/00 *Carpenter* [2002] ECR I-6279, paras 40–5; ECJ, Case C-109/01 *Akrich* [2003] ECR I-9607 paras 59–60; ECJ, Joined Cases C-482/01 and C-493/01 *Orfanopoulos and Oliveri* [2004] ECR I-5257, paras 97–9. See also: ECJ, Case C-391/09 *Vardyn-Wardyn* [2011] ECR I-3787, paras 86–91, in which fundamental rights were at stake that both limited the principle of mutual recognition (Art. 22 Charter, on the right to respect the cultural and linguistic diversity) and that reinforced it (Art. 7 Charter, on the right to private life).

[250] On the duty to reconcile, see for instance: ECJ, Case C-112/00 *Schmidberger* [2003] ECR I-5659, para 77; ECJ, Case C-36/02 *Omega* [2003] ECR I-9609, para 36; ECJ, Case C-341/05 *Laval un Partneri* [2007] ECR I-11767, para 94; ECJ, Case C-438/05 *Viking Line* [2007] ECR I-10779, para 46. On the absence of any hierarchy between both rights and the need to balance them, see, for instance: Opinion of AG Poiares Maduro in Case C-341/05 *Laval un Partneri* [2007] ECR I-11767, § 23–4; Opinion of AG Mengozzi in Case C-438/05 *Viking Line* [2007] ECR I-10779, § 62, § 84 and § 252 ff. See also: B. BERCUSSON, 'The Trade Union Movement and the European Union: Judgment Day', *E.L.J.* 2007, 296–305; R. NIELSEN, 'Free Movement and Fundamental Rights', *European Labour Law Journal* 2010, 29–30; N. REICH, 'Gemeinschafliche Verkehrsfreiheiten versus Nationales Arbeitskampfrecht', *EuZW* 2007, 392; SEMMELMANN, 'The European Union's Economic Constitution under the Lisbon Treaty: Soul-Searching Shifts the Focus to Procedure' (n 14) 534–9; V. SKOURIS, 'Fundamental Rights and Fundamental Freedoms: The Challenge of Striking a Delicate Balance', *E.B.L.R.* 2006, 237. Exceptionally, in some judgments, the ECJ did not perform any balancing act, see, for instance: ECJ, Case C-470/03 *AGM-COS.MET* [2007] ECR I-2749, para 72.

[251] ECJ Case C-36/02 *Omega* [2003] ECR I-9609, para 31 and paras 38–9; ECJ, Case C-244/06 *Dynamic Medien* [2008] ECR I-505, paras 44 and 49. Critical of the carte blanche given to the Member States: J. BROHMER, 'Zulässige Untersagung eines Tötungsspiels (Rs C-36/02 Omega Spielhallen-GmbH)', *EuZW* 2004, 756; G. CHU, 'Playing at Killing Freedom of Movement', *LIEI* 2006, 93–4; JANS, 'Annotatie *Omega*' (n 247) 186. Approving the carte blanche approach: ACKERMANN, 'Case Note *Omega*' (n 247) 1117; M.K. BULTERMAN and H.R. KRANENBORG, 'What if Rules on Free Movement and Human Rights Collide', *E.L. Rev.* 2006, 99.

but on no account may the national perspective suffice as the sole reference.[252] A Member State relying on a particular fundamental right that is recognized in its own national legal (or even constitutional) order may not always be pursuing an objective which must be regarded as legitimate as a matter of EU law.[253] As a result, the ECJ does not accept that the legitimate interest at stake should be determined unilaterally by each Member State without any supervision from the EU institutions. The ECJ will begin its analysis by placing the invoked fundamental right into both the EU context and into a broader international framework of the protection of fundamental rights, in order to check whether the value at stake does indeed require protection at European level.[254] However, as far as the specific interpretation of the right in question is concerned—in other words, the application *in concreto*—the ECJ often refers back to the national authorities.[255] The ECJ is thus attempting to reconcile European standards (European public order concept) with a national interpretation of these standards (margin of discretion) on an ad hoc basis. Logically, in areas where each Member State recognizes the specific fundamental right at hand, the ECJ can focus on a European standard.[256] In the event of divergent approaches among the Member States, though, often in sensitive areas, the ECJ's approach is remarkably more cautious.[257] In the latter scenarios, the ECJ confines itself to a rather superficial review of whether the national measure is acceptable from an EU perspective, without imposing a European fundamental rights standard. In this regard, *Omega* is a rather nice illustration, not of how a concept common to (all of) the Member States will triumph, but of how a concept unilaterally developed within one national constitutional framework might well be accepted if it is compatible with the EU framework. If, on the other hand, a national constitutional provision is not acceptable from an EU perspective, it will not be upheld.[258] This approach, which ultimately amounts to a compatibility check, should be welcomed as it is not the ECJ's task to participate actively in the (judicial) harmonization of national fundamental rights law by imposing an exclusively European public order concept.

[252] From the very beginning the ECJ made it clear that it would be inspired by the constitutional traditions *common* to the Member State: ECJ, Case 11/70 *Internationale Handelsgesellschaft* [1970] ECR 1125, para 4.

[253] Opinion of AG Jacobs in Case C-112/00 *Schmidberger* [2003] ECR I-5659, § 96–8, supported by G. FACENNA, 'Schmidberger: Freedom of Expression and Assembly vs. Free Movement of Goods', *EHRLR* 2004, 79.

[254] See, for instance: ECJ, Case C-112/00 *Schmidberger* [2003] ECR I-5659, para 79; ECJ, Case C-36/02 *Omega* [2003] ECR I-9609, paras 33-34; ECJ, Case C-438/05 *Viking Line* [2007] ECR I-10779, paras 43–4; ECJ, Case C-244/06 *Dynamic Medien* [2008] ECR I-505, para 39.

[255] See, for instance: ECJ, Case C-36/02 *Omega* [2003] ECR I-9609, para 31; ECJ, Case C-438/05 *Viking Line* [2007] ECR I-10779, para 87; ECJ, Case C-244/06 *Dynamic Medien* [2008] ECR I-505, para 44. A. ALEMANNO, 'A la recherché d'un juste équilibre entre libertés fondamentales et droits fondamentaux dans le cadre du marché intérieur', *RDUE* 2004, 751.

[256] In *Schmidberger* the fundamental right in question was not only incorporated in the Austrian Constitution, but also in the other Member States' constitutions and it is, furthermore, incorporated in the Charter: A. BIONDI, 'Free Trade, a Mountain Road and the Right to Protest: European Economic Freedoms and Fundamental Individual Rights', *EHRLR* 2004, 59.

[257] In *Omega*, human dignity was incorporated in the German Constitution, but not in several other Member States' constitutions. The ECJ and its AGs therefore checked whether human dignity could be considered in light of several international instruments as worthy of protection within the EU legal order: Opinion of AG Stix-Hackl in Case C-36/02 *Omega* [2003] ECR I-9609, § 82–91.

[258] See, for instance: Opinion of AG Bot in Case C-274/05 *Commission v Greece* [2008] ECR I-7969, § 16 and § 39–40, who considered the Greek Constitution's provision that reserves higher education solely to *public* establishments as irreconcilable with the principle of mutual recognition. The ECJ confirmed the Advocate General's opinion on this point of law: ECJ, Case C-274/05 *Commission v Greece* [2008] ECR I-7969, paras 18–41.

3.3. The influence of the ECtHR's case law

In areas where the interpretation of a specific right has already been developed within the case law of the ECtHR, the ECJ will refer to this development. In the area of fundamental rights, for example, which has been developed meticulously by the ECtHR, it is indeed desirable, not only for the sake of uniformity, but also because of the ECtHR's expertise in this field, that the latter's case law serves as a yardstick. An analysis of the ECJ's case law reveals that the ECJ's approach is certainly influenced by the ECtHR,[259] though without being simply a copy of it.[260] The ECJ's reasoning exposes a mixture of the classic Strasbourg style and the classic Luxembourg style, in which both free movement and fundamental rights have their place and in which mutual recognition will only be blocked when a fundamental right is acceptable from the EU perspective. The current relationship between the two courts is one of mutual respect, mutual influence, and dialogue, rather than of strict submission. This implies that if one case were to be brought before the two courts, the final outcome would not necessarily be the same.[261] Furthermore, it is perfectly feasible—and has already been the case—that one of the courts' lines of reasoning may lead to the other court's deciding to adapt its established line of reasoning on a specific matter.[262]

B. Margins of control left to the Member States when applying the principle of mutual recognition

With a particular view to ensuring the efficiency of the free movement provisions (and the principle of mutual recognition), the ECJ allows only a limited margin of control to the Member States. This approach can be deduced from the limited number and scope of the tools at the Member States' disposal for reacting to (presumed) inaccuracies (section B, 1), and from the ECJ's hesitant attitude towards accepting the extraterritorial application of justification grounds (section B, 2).

[259] In several internal market judgments where fundamental rights were involved, the ECJ did not refrain from referring to case law of the ECtHR. See, for instance: ECJ, Case C-112/00 *Schmidberger* [2003] ECR I-5659, para 79; ECJ, Case C-109/01 *Akrich* [2003] ECR I-9607, paras 59–60; ECJ, Joined Cases C-482/01 and C-493/01 *Orfanopoulos and Oliveri* [2004] ECR I-5257, paras 97–9; ECJ, Case C-438/05 *Viking Line* [2007] ECR I-10779, para 86.

[260] FACENNA, 'Schmidberger: Freedom of Expression and Assembly vs. Free Movement of Goods' (n 253) 80. With regard to the *ne bis in idem* principle included in Article 4(1) Protocol No 7 to the ECHR and Article 50 Charter and, in particular, the question regarding the application of the *ne bis in idem* principle to an administrative and a criminal penalty, compare: ECtHR, 10 February 2009, *Zolotukhin v Russia*, 14939/03, paras 120–2, with ECJ, Case C617/10 *Fransson*, para 37 (and the corresponding Opinion of AG Cruz Villalón at § 70–87).

[261] See, for instance, the *Gambazzi* case, where the ECtHR dismissed the claim as manifestly ill-founded, whereas the ECJ left a margin of discretion to the national judge to establish in light of a comprehensive assessment of all the circumstances as a whole whether the exclusion on the grounds of the non-compliance with a procedural order constituted manifest and disproportionate infringement of the right to be heard. According to Kuipers, cases like *Gambazzi* demonstrate that the EU affords in general higher protection of the right to a fair trial than the jurisprudence of the ECtHR: ECJ, Case C-394/07 *Gambazzi* [2009] ECR I-2563; J.J. KUIPERS, 'The Right to a Fair Trial and the Free Movement of Civil Judgments', *CYELP* 2010, 45–6.

[262] See, for instance, how the ECtHR's case law has been influenced by the ECJ's case law with regard to the *ne bis in idem* principle: ECtHR, 10 February 2009, *Zolotukhin v Russia*, 14939/03 (where the ECtHR aligned its case law with the criteria developed by the ECJ). For other examples where the ECtHR has adapted its line of case law to the ECJ's one, see: J. CALLEWAERT, 'Het EVRM en de Europese Unie: van Bosphorus naar Lissabon', *NTER* 2010, 102.

(1) *Presumed inaccuracies in controls, certificates, or documents subject to mutual recognition*

In its case law on the free movement provisions, the ECJ has urged Member States to facilitate cooperation and to simplify controls of products or documents that originate from other Member States. In light of this case law, it is feasible to deduce a number of basic guidelines as to how national authorities are required to deal with controls performed in other Member States and/or with documents issued in other Member States. In this regard, the questions to be addressed are, specifically, whether the country of destination is prevented from performing any new (product) controls; whether it is bound by a document issued in another Member State; whether and how it must proceed when serious doubts arise as to the validity or accuracy of a foreign control or document; and which type of shortcomings may justify an objection to a document or to a product analysis.

First of all, it follows from the ECJ's case law that a practice in which the authorities of a host Member State refuse, by default, to take account of documents issued by the authorities of the Member State of origin is not acceptable in light of the free movement provisions.[263] However, the new form of (simplified and facilitated) cooperation brought about by the free movement provisions does not preclude the Member States from carrying out inspections to ensure the observance of the standards in question. In the framework of product inspections, the ECJ has repeatedly maintained that, in principle, it is for the national authorities to ascertain whether the substantiating documents at hand provide some evidence that the imported goods comply with domestic legislation.[264] Yet, even an assumption of accuracy in favour of the relevant documents, or the finding that a certificate of analysis was issued by a properly authorized research institute in the Member State of origin, would not prevent a Member State from subjecting products to an appropriate control in order to test its conformity with EU law.[265] However, a Member State's margin of action is not unrestricted as they are required, first, to take into account the controls already carried out in the Member State of origin,[266] and secondly, their controls may not be performed systematically but by means of spot checks.[267]

With regard to the validity of a foreign document, the ECJ's point of departure is fully in line with the principle of trust and states that a Member State is bound by a duty to accept documents issued in the Member State of origin, i.e. a presumption of compliance. However, such a presumption of compliance can be set aside if the competent authority in the Member State of destination has ascertained that the accuracy of the document is seriously undermined by concrete evidence relating to the individual case in question.[268] Furthermore, not all irregularities are sufficient to justify an objection to a document and thus jeopardize the principle of mutual recognition. The ECJ, well aware that irregularities can vary significantly in nature and importance and from case to

[263] See, for instance: ECJ, Case C-378/10 *Vale*, nyr, para 60.

[264] See, for instance: ECJ, Case 104/75 *de Peijper* [1976] ECR 613, para 28; ECJ, Case 124/81 *Commission v United Kingdom* [1983] ECR 203, para 30.

[265] See, for instance: ECJ, Case 124/81 *Commission v United Kingdom* [1983] ECR 203, para 31; ECJ, Case C-105/94 *Celestini* [1997] ECR I-2971, para 37.

[266] See, for instance: ECJ, Case C-105/94 *Celestini* [1997] ECR I-2971, para 37.

[267] See, for instance: ECJ, Case 42/82 *Commission v France* [1983] ECR 1013, paras 54–7.

[268] See, for instance: ECJ, Case C-336/94 *Dafeki* [1997] ECR I-6761, para 19; ECJ, Case 42/82 *Commission v France* [1983] ECR 1013, para 32. Member States cannot rely on general suspitions: See, for instance: ECJ, Case 42/82 *Commission v France* [1983] ECR 1013, para 56.

case, is only willing to accept irregularities that are considered substantial, such as those capable of rendering a document useless for the fulfillment of its function.[269]

In cases where justified doubts exist with regard to the accuracy of a document, the field of action left to the Member State of destination is somewhat restricted. The competent authority will not be authorized to draw up a (new) certificate itself (as a substitute for the defective certificate issued in the country of origin); nor will it be entitled to define the conditions for issuing such a certificate; and nor will it be allowed simply to ignore the allegedly false certificate. Instead it is required to take steps to regularize the document by contacting the competent authority in the Member State of origin.[270] Having done so, the competent authority is first required to request that the competent body in the Member State of origin check the documents and entries in the record and then, if necessary, it must ask for any relevant information such as documents and other evidence to be forwarded. Upon receipt of this additional information, the presumption of compliance is again applied, as the Member State of destination is in principle bound by this new information unless objective factors reveal manifest inaccuracies.

(2) *The ECJ's hesitant attitude towards accepting Member States' arguments for protecting extraterritorial interests*

A Member State generally invokes a justification ground in order to protect a public interest which is in danger within its own territory. Nevertheless, in some cases a Member State has taken measures, based on the Treaty-based or rule of reason-based justification grounds, to protect a public interest under threat in another Member State. The crucial question is whether Member States are indeed entitled to invoke such justification grounds in extraterritorial contexts regarding the free movement of goods or services.[271]

The extraterritorial application of Article 36 TFEU has often been alluded to but the ECJ has seldom entered into the discussion, since the matter was regulated

[269] See, for instance: ECJ, Case 42/82 *Commission v France* [1983] ECR 1013, paras 26–8. The ECJ did not accept that a document was affected by a substantial irregularity where the document, in contravention of Regulation 1153/75, had not been completed in typescript or block capitals but was perfectly legible, or where the document had not been completed fully although it contained indirectly all the required information. On the other hand, the ECJ accepted that a document was affected by a substantial irregularity where the document failed to state the alcoholic strength or where the document did not state the Italian authority which had issued it or where documents contained illegible statements or where documents did not give any information, not even indirectly, enabling the country of origin to be identified.

[270] See, for instance: ECJ, Case 42/82 *Commission v France* [1983] ECR 1013, paras 30–2. The fact that the ECJ analysed these duties in light of Regulation 1153/75, does not impede me from drawing conclusions with regard to the non-harmonized area of EU law as the ECJ explicitly underlined in this judgment that these duties of cooperation are inherent in the EU system (at para 36) and, furthermore, that it condemned France on the basis of Article 34 TFEU (at para 45).

[271] See, in general, on the issue of an extraterritorial application of justification grounds: N. BERNARD, *Multilevel Governance in the European Union* (The Hague, Kluwer, 2002) 53–60; G. BETTLEM, 'Cross-border Private Enforcement of Community Law', in J. VERVAELE (ed.), *Compliance and Enforcement of European Community Law* (The Hague, Kluwer, 1999) 397–412; M. DOUGAN, 'Minimum Harmonization and the Internal Market', *CML Rev.* 2000, 866–78; Y. HOFHUIS, *Minimumharmonisatie* (Deventer, Kluwer, 2006) 136–9; KAPTEYN, McDONNELL, MORTELMANS, and TIMMERMANS, *The Law of the European Union and the European Communities* (n 3) 653; OLIVER and JARVIS, *Free Movement of Goods in the European Community under Articles 28 to 30 of the EC Treaty* (n 3) 230–3; H.G. SEVENSTER, *Eco-imperialisme binnen de Europese Unie; een juridisch probleemand* (Deventer, WEJ Tjeenk Willink, 1998) 15–33; P.J. SLOT and G. STRAETMANS, 'Harmonisatie van wetgeving in de EG', *Tijdschrift voor Privaatrecht* 2003, 740–2.

in a directive and thus dealt with in the corresponding harmonization framework.[272] Yet in relation to some judgments, the AGs have performed a thorough analysis of the extraterritoriality issue within the context of the free movement Treaty provisions, despite the presence of a harmonizing directive.[273] For instance, in *Hedley Lomas*, AG Léger was not convinced that a sufficient level of harmonization had been reached to rule out the application of Article 36 TFEU and performed an in-depth analysis of the question related to the extraterritorial application of Article 36 TFEU. He concluded this question firmly in the negative, providing a variety of arguments: the need to interpret Article 36 TFEU restrictively as an exception to a fundamental freedom; the principle of mutual trust; the fact that only the Member State on whose territory a protective measure was taken was capable of verifying whether the measure was strictly necessary; and, finally, the ECJ's previous case law, which did not appear to support the idea of any extraterritorial application of Article 36 TFEU.[274] In *Compassion in World Farming*, AG Léger was again opposed to the extraterritorial application of Article 36 TFEU, but also made an important point: Article 36 TFEU did not allow a Member State to restrict its export on account of any extraterritorial circumstances which did not affect the interest protected by this provision on *its own national territory*.[275] In other words, where the contested measure did produce (some) effect on the national territory, a justification ground could probably be invoked.

In the absence of any harmonizing directive, the ECJ was at one point obliged to adopt a stance on the issue of extraterritoriality in the services area in *Alpine Investments*, where it stated that although the protection of consumers in the other Member States was not in itself a matter for the Dutch authorities, the nature and extent of that protection would nonetheless have a direct effect on the Dutch financial service providers' reputation.[276]

In sum, we could conclude that while the ECJ does not reject the extraterritorial application of the justification ground outright, neither is it eager to recognize it officially.[277] The ECJ seems to allow it only to the extent that the (foreign) public interest can be linked to a public interest in the Member State of origin. The ECJ may well be correct in

272 In the following judgments the ECJ refused to analyse the case in light of the TFEU provisions arguing that the directive provided for (sufficient) harmonization: ECJ, Case C-169/89 *Gourmetterie Van den Burg* [1990] ECR I-2143, paras 6–9; ECJ, Case C-5/94 *Hedley Lomas* [1996] ECR I-2553, paras 18–19; ECJ, Case C-1/96 *Compassion in World Farming* [1998] ECR I-1251, paras 47, 56, 64–6. On the (often) difficult choice between a Treaty framework or a directive's framework, see: Part I, ch 2, III, A. 'Limits resulting from the chosen harmonization approach: the fine line between the Treaty's framework and the secondary legislation's framework'.

273 For an analysis of the ECJ's reasoning in *Hedley Lomas* and in *Compassion in World Farming*, see: Part I, ch 2, III, B. 'Limits linked to the level of control left to the host Member State'.

274 Opinion of AG Léger in Case C-5/94 *Hedley Lomas* [1996] ECR I-2553, § 31–8. As a matter of fact, some other AGs had previously reached the same conclusion, albeit in a less detailed way on this particular point of law, see: Opinion of AG Trabucchi in Case 8/74 *Dassonville* [1974] ECR 837, § 5; Opinion of Van Gerven in Case C-169/89 *Van den Burg* [1990] ECR I-2143, § 7.

275 Opinion of AG Léger in Case C-1/96 *Compassion in World Farming* 1998] ECR I-1251, § 113. AG Léger accepted that a Member State could in principle consider that harm caused to the life or health of animals through the use of a rearing system (in other Member States) was a matter of public morality (of the Member State of exportation). The ECJ did not follow its AG on this point as it believed that this justification ground did not constitute a separate justification, but was in fact intrinsically linked to the ground on animal health, which had constituted the objective of a harmonization measure: ECJ, Case C-1/96 *Compassion in World Farming* [1998] ECR I-1251, paras 66–8.

276 ECJ, Case C-384/93 *Alpine Investments* [1995] ECR I-1141, para 43. V. HATZOPOULOS, 'Case Note Alpine Investments', *CML Rev.* 1995, 1442–3; G. STRAETMANS, 'Case Note Alpine Investments', *Col. J. Eur. L.* 1995–96, 163.

277 The ECJ seems to have remarkably fewer problems in accepting an exclusive extraterritorial application of the economic activity. See, for instance: *Carmen Media Group* in which a gambling licence limited to 'offshore bookmaking' was present: ECJ, Case C-46/08 *Carmen Media Group* [2010] ECR

adopting this prudent approach, as it would be inconsistent with the EU framework and with the ECJ's case law to allow a Member State to impose its system of universal values on other Member States.

The ECJ showed a similarly reticent attitude when responding to the question of whether the national court could be permitted to decide whether the legislation of another Member State was in accordance with EU law. The ECJ has consistently maintained that special vigilance is required in such cases.[278] The ECJ thus seems reluctant to judge the validity of a Member State's legislation in a preliminary proceeding that involves another Member State. Neither does it seem willing to accept that a Member State could take certain measures following the assessment of another Member State's legislation. Such behaviour would amount to the taking of unilateral measures, which is prohibited under EU law. A Member State of the opinion that another Member State's legislation hampers the principle of mutual recognition appears to have no other course than to start proceedings under Article 259 TFEU, or to inform the Commission to start proceedings under Article 258 TFEU.

C. Forum shopping, abuse of law, and race to the bottom preoccupations

The TFEU provisions on the internal market and the principle of mutual recognition, which to a large extent promote the co-existence of Member States' disparate legislation, have long raised two main concerns. Firstly, it has been argued that the existence of divergent legislation inspires both natural persons and legal persons to evade the application of (less favourable) national legislation and to search instead for national legislation that would provide them with the most benefit. By intentionally creating a link to the territory of another Member State, private persons and companies could apply the (more favourable) provisions of that Member State to their situations (forum shopping). Secondly, the principle of mutual recognition has been criticized in that it could lead to a lowering of standards in the Member States, and eventually to the lowest common denominator (race to the bottom).[279]

I-8149, paras 42–3. In light of the ECJ's generally broad interpretation of the free movement provisions, this is hardly surprising. See, however, the more reluctant and very lengthy discussions of AG Mengozzi on this point of law (at § 28 to 47). He argued that 'extraterritorial licences of this kind could hardly be regarded as constituting conduct which fosters mutual trust between Member States'. For this reason, he argued that 'the possibility of relying on the freedom to provide services is subject to the essential requirement that the licence granted by the Member State of establishment authorizes the service provider to provide the service in question in that Member State where it is established'.

[278] ECJ, Case 244/80 *Foglia v Novello* [1981] ECR 3045, para 30; ECJ, Case C-318/00 *Bacardi* [2003] ECR I-905, para 45.

[279] On the (limited) role of regulatory competition in the EU and the 'race to the bottom' argument, see, for instance: F. ABRAHAM, *Building Blocks of the Single Market. The Case of Mutual Recognition, Home country Control and Essential Requirments*, International Economics Research Paper, Leuven, CES, 1991; L. GORMLEY, *Prohibiting Restrictions on Trade within the EEC* (Amsterdam, Elsevier, 1985) 50; W. KERBER and R. VAN DEN BERGH, 'Mutual Recognition: Misunderstandings, Inconsistencies and a Suggested Reinterpretation', *Kyklos* 2008, 451 and 457–9; C. RADAELLI, 'The Puzzle of Regulatory Competition', *JPP* 2004, 1–23 (and the authors mentioned therein); M. SEIDEL, 'Die sogenannte Cassis de Dijon-Rechtsprechung des Europäischen Gerichtshofs und der Schutz von Herkunftsabgaben in der Europäischen Gemeinschaft', *G.R.U.R. Int.* 1984, 87–8; P.J. SLOT, 'Commentaar op een opmerkelijke brief', *SEW* 1981, 181; J. SNELL, 'Who's Got the Power and Free Movement and Allocation of Competences in EC Law', *Y.E.L.* 2003, 334–5; H. SØNDERGÅRD BIRKMOSE, 'Regulatory Competition and the European Harmonization Process', *E.B.L.R.* 2006, 1075–97; STOFFEL VALLOTON, *La prohibición de restricciones a la libre circulación de mercancías en la Comunidad Europea* (n 4) 424.

Forum shopping has raised many doubts and concerns among Member States as to whether and to what extent a person is indeed allowed to circumvent national legislation by taking advantage of the free movement provisions, and also as to the measures a Member State is entitled to take in order to prevent or remedy such behaviour. The ECJ's case law on the matter, which is mostly referred to in legal doctrine as the ECJ's abuse of law theory,[280] has always begun from the premise that Member States are indeed entitled in principle to take measures to prevent citizens wrongfully evading the application of national legislation.[281] However, the subsequent case law has clarified that the ECJ adopts a very restrictive approach to what should be considered abuse (or evasion) of the law. Although legal doctrine tends to refer to an objective and a subjective element,[282] the ECJ itself very rarely focuses on these two elements explicitly[283] and instead concentrates on evaluating the behaviour of the person concerned in light of the EU right invoked.

An example is the highly controversial *Centros* judgment on freedom of establishment, in which a Danish couple wishing to circumvent Danish legislation on minimum capital registered their company in the UK and were consequently blocked from registering a branch in Denmark based on abuse of law arguments. In this case, the ECJ condemned this block, concluding that no objective evidence of abuse of law had been provided. The ECJ began its reasoning with an analysis of the Treaty provisions on freedom of establishment, which are intended specifically to enable companies formed in accordance with a Member State's law, and having their registered office, central administration, or principal place of business within the EU, to pursue activities in other Member States through an agency, branch, or subsidiary.[284] In other words, the couple's intention to form their company in a Member State whose legal system appeared least restrictive was a logical corollary of this right and could not be considered an abuse of rights. Thus far, the ECJ's reasoning was indeed logical and coherent with the TFEU. Less convincing, however, was the ECJ's statement in *Centros* and in a subsequent case, *Inspire Art*, that the fact alone that the company had not conducted any business in the

[280] ECJ, Case C-321/05 *Kofoed* [2007] ECR I-5795, para 38, where the ECJ refers in a harmonized context to a provision of a directive which 'reflects the *general Community law principle* that abuse of rights is prohibited' (emphasis added). For an extensive study on this subject and an overview of the relevant case law, see, in particular, the opinions of AG Poiares Maduro in Case C-255/02 *Halifax* [2006] ECR I-1609, § 60–101 and Case C-311/06 *Consiglio Nazionale degli Ingegneri* [2009] ECR I-415, § 38–64. For some relevant publications on this issue, see: R. DE LA FERIA and S. VOGENAUER, *Prohibition of Abuse of Law: A New General Principle of EU Law* (Oxford, Hart Publishing, 2011); R. DE LA FERIA, 'Prohibition of Abuse of (Community) Law: the Creation of a new General Principle of EC Law through Tax', *CML Rev.* 2008, 398–441; V. EDWARDS and P. FARMER, 'The Concept of Abuse in the Freedom of Establishment of Companies: a Case of Double Standards', in A. ARNULL, P. EECKHOUT, and T. TRIDIMAS (eds.), *Continuity and Change in EU Law. Essays in Honour of Sir Francis Jacobs* (Oxford, Oxford University Press, 2008) 206–27; K. ENGSIG SORENSEN, 'Abuse of Rights in Community Law: a Principle of Substance or Mere Rhetoric', *CML Rev.* 2006, 423–59; J. MEEUSEN, 'System Shopping in European Private International Law in Family Matters', in J. MEEUSEN, M. PERTEGAS, G. STRAETMANS, and F. SWENNEN (eds.), *International Family Law for the European Union* (Antwerp, Intersentia, 2007) 239–78; P. SCHAMMO, 'Arbitrage and Abuse of Rights in the EC Legal System', *E.L.J.* 2008, 351–76.

[281] See, for instance: ECJ, Case 33/74 *Van Binsbergen* [1974] ECR 1299, para 13; ECJ, Case 115/78 *Knoors* [1979] ECR 399, para 25; ECJ, Case C-61/89 *Bouchoucha* [1990] ECR I-3551, para 14; ECJ, Case C-148/91 *Veronica* [1993] ECR I-487, para 12; ECJ, Case C-23/93 *TV 10* [1994] ECR I-4795, para 20; ECJ, Case C-19/92 *Kraus* [1993] ECR I-1663, para 34; ECJ, Case C-212/97 *Centros* [1999] ECR I-1459, para 24.

[282] See, in particular: the authors mentioned in footnote 280.

[283] See, in particular: ECJ, Case C-110/99 *Emsländ Stärke* [2000] ECR I-1156, paras 52–3.

[284] ECJ, Case C-212/97 *Centros* [1999] ECR I-1459, para 26. For a similar reasoning, see: ECJ, Case C-167/01 *Inspire Art* [2003] ECR I-10155.

Member State where its registered office was located, and that it pursued its activities only in the Member State where its branch was established, was not sufficient evidence of abuse or fraudulent conduct.[285] The Member State's margin for proving abuse of law in this case seemed almost non-existent and it could be concluded that too wide a duty of mutual recognition had perhaps been imposed.

However, this radical position seems to have been nuanced somewhat in more recent judgments. In *Cadbury Schweppes*, the ECJ recognized that taxpayers may seek to arrange their (cross-border) tax affairs in the manner most advantageous to themselves but only to the extent that the arrangement is genuine, which is to say not a wholly artificial construct aimed at abusing and circumventing national tax legislation.[286] The concept of establishment in a Treaty provisions context presupposes the *actual* establishment of the company concerned in the host Member State in addition to the pursuit of a *genuine* economic activity there which can be verified using objective factors such as the physical existence of premises, staff, and equipment.[287] The criterion for defining an artificial manoeuvre, then, which had been present in a number of other abuse of law judgments[288] but apparently lacking in *Centros* and *Inspire Art*, is thus brought clearly to the fore. Although it should be borne in mind that, in contrast with *Centros* and *Inspire Art*, the *Cadbury Schweppes* judgment concerned secondary establishment (as opposed to primary establishment) and also touched upon a rather sensitive area of EU law, namely tax law, there are clear indications that the ECJ's ruling in *Cadbury Schweppes* should be considered a significant qualification of the rulings in *Centros* and *Inspire Art*.[289]

The ECJ followed a similar line of reasoning in another heavily contested judgment, this time on the free movement of persons, the *Chen* ruling.[290] Here, the ECJ decided that there had been no abuse of rights in a situation where a third-country national had gone deliberately to Northern Ireland to give birth to her child so that it would receive an Irish passport and thus become a EU citizen with all the rights pertaining to that status. A crucial element of the ECJ's reasoning was that the baby had acquired

[285] ECJ, Case C-212/97 *Centros* [1999] ECR I-1459, para 29, with reference to the older judgment: ECJ, Case 79/85 *Segers* [1986] ECR 2375, para 16; ECJ, Case C-167/01 *Inspire Art* [2003] ECR I-10155, para 139.

[286] ECJ, Case C-196/04 *Cadbury Schweppes* [2006] I-7995, para 51 and the case law mentioned therein.

[287] ECJ, Case C-196/04 *Cadbury Schweppes* [2006] I-7995, paras 53–4 and 66–7. See, on the requirement of a genuine activity, years earlier: Opinion of AG Darmon in Case 81/87 *Daily Mail* [1988] ECR 5483, para 3.

[288] See, for instance: ECJ, Case C-264/96 *Imperial Chemical Industries* [1998] ECR I-4695, para 26; ECJ Case C-110/99 *Emsländ Stärke* [2000] ECR I-1156, para 59; or—less explicitly—ECJ, Case 229/83 *Leclerc* [1985] ECR 1, para 27; confirmed in ECJ, Case C-322/01 *Deutscher Apothekerverband* [2003] ECR I-14887, para 129.

[289] It is significant, in my view, that the ECJ in *Cadbury Schweppes*—when developing its argument on the artificial construction—explicitly refers to non-fiscal judgments: ECJ, Case C-196/04 *Cadbury Schweppes* [2006] ECR I-7995, paras 51–5. See, furthermore: ECJ, Case C-286/06 *Commission v Spain* [2008] ECR I-8025, para 69 (where the ECJ refers—in the context of diplomas—to both *Centros* and *Cadbury Schweppes*); Opinion of AG Poiares Maduro in Case C-210/06 *Cartesio* [2008] I-9641 § 29; Opinion of Poiares Maduro in Case C-311/06 *Consiglio Nazionale degli Ingegneri* [2009] ECR I-415, § 43–4; Opinion of AG Bot in Case C-347/09 *Dickinger*, § 64–5. See also: DE LA FERIA, 'Prohibition of Abuse of (Community) Law: the Creation of a new General Principle of EC Law through Tax' (n 280) 405–8; EDWARDS and FARMER, 'The Concept of Abuse in the Freedom of Establishment of Companies: a Case of Double Standards' (n 280) 220; S. FRANCQ, 'Chronique de jurisprudence du Tribunal de la Cour de Justice des CE. Circulation de personnes et des services', *J.D.I.* 2007, 657–8. See, however, more cautious: SCHAMMO, 'Arbitrage and Abuse of Rights in the EC Legal System' (n 280) 372, who wondered whether *Cadbury Schweppes* would have practical significance outside the field of tax law.

[290] ECJ, Case C-200/02 *Chen* [2004] ECR I-9925.

Irish citizenship according to the provisions of Irish legislation, which were based on the granting of nationality *iure soli*. In other words, there had been no artificial construction, as the pair had simply benefited from the generous Irish legislation in combination with the TFEU provisions on European citizenship. The ECJ emphasized that the United Kingdom was not entitled to refuse residence to nationals of other Member States such as baby Chen.[291] The United Kingdom was thus obliged to recognize Irish nationality legislation (duty of mutual recognition), since the opposite conclusion would violate Article 20 TFEU.

In adhering to a generally restrictive approach to the abuse of rights and in allowing only a very restrictive margin of action to the Member States, the ECJ clearly wishes to emphasize that the principle of mutual recognition should in principle prevail, and that it should only be blocked in cases of conspicuous abuse or fraud. The ECJ and its AGs do not deny that, regrettably, competition may occur between Member States without restriction due to the (total) absence of harmonization and the existence of divergent legislation, but such a situation requires a political or legislative intervention rather than a judicial one.[292]

It must now be beyond doubt that the ECJ accepts and even encourages companies and individuals to move within the EU in order to take advantage of the fact that national laws differ by choosing the most attractive legislation; such an attitude does not constitute an abuse of rights in itself but is the logical corollary of the free movement provisions. Forum shopping is not a taboo but an attractive tool within the internal market that should only be curtailed in the event of material fraud (e.g. a counterfeit document or a marriage of convenience) or when the person concerned refuses to accept all of the legal consequences of the free movement provision in question (e.g. the absence of a genuine economic activity in *Cadbury Schweppes*).[293] If, on the other hand, no artificial construction can be detected and the individual or company fully accepts the rights and duties required by the free movement provision in question, any personal motive for invoking a free movement provision in combination with the (more attractive) national legislation of another Member State becomes irrelevant, and the principle of mutual recognition can in principle be applied in full. The evaluation of a person's behaviour using the abuse of law criteria, however, is only the first step in assessing a Member State's restrictive mutual recognition policy. The next step will consist in checking whether the national rule concerned, which limits the mutual recognition principle, is suitable for counteracting the abuse of law and that it does not go beyond what is necessary for that purpose.[294]

I now come to the other main concern that has often been voiced since the coming into force of the principle of mutual recognition and which is closely related to the issue of forum shopping, namely the dreaded race to the bottom effect. The reasoning runs that if market participants develop a tendency to seek out the country with the most permissive legislation (forum shopping),[295] Member States will eventually be

[291] ECJ, Case C-200/02 *Chen*, paras 39–40.

[292] ECJ, Case 115/78 *Knoors* [1979] ECR 399, para 27; ECJ, Case C-212/97 *Centros* [1999] ECR I-1459, para 28; Opinion of AG Léger in Case C-196/04 *Cadbury Schweppes* [2006] ECR I-7995, paras 55 and 60.

[293] MEEUSEN, 'System Shopping in European Private International Law in Family Matters' (n 280) 258–60.

[294] See, for instance: ECJ, Case C-196/04 *Cadbury Schweppes* [2006] ECR I-7995, para 122.

[295] However, market participants will not necessarily always fall back on forum shopping, but might stick to the (more severe) national legislative framework. For an evaluation of the various factors that

forced to deregulate and abolish higher standards (race to the bottom). Studies have indeed indicated that competition between rules may ultimately lead to convergence at the lowest possible standard.[296] However, a number of important counters to this process of downward harmonization are present. The crucial role of Treaty-based exceptions and mandatory requirements,[297] for example, along with that of reputation building[298] and other conditions,[299] have largely precluded the occurrence of a race to the bottom. Not infrequently, they have actually led to a process of 'bottom up' harmonization, either by means of formal harmonization or by national governments' copying of each other's regulatory innovations.[300]

might influence their choice, see: H. SØNDERGÅRD BIRKMOSE, 'A Race to the Bottom in the EU', *MJ* 2006, 35–80.

[296] See, for instance, the study of Van Cayseele and Heremans in which they indicate that downward harmonization is one possible outcome of regulation game, mentioned in: ABRAHAM, *Building Blocks of the Single Market* (n 279) 15.

[297] See, for instance: EMILIOU, *The Principle of Proportionality in European Law* (n 86) 235; PELKMANS, 'Mutual Recognitions in Goods: on Promises and Disillusions' (n 1) 708; SLOT, 'Commentaar op een opmerkelijke brief' (n 279) 191.

[298] See, for instance: ABRAHAM, *Building Blocks of the Single Market* (n 279) 16–21.

[299] See, for instance: SØNDERGÅRD BIRKMOSE, 'A Race to the Bottom in the EU' (n 295) 35–80, who identifies a number of circumstances that can act as barriers to competition such as language, the influence of legal advisors, harmonization, and the risk of political intervention.

[300] See, for instance: L. ENRIQUES, 'EC Company Law and the Fear of a European Delaware', *E.B.L.R.* 2004, 1266 ff.; SNELL, 'Who's Got the Power?' (n 279) 335, who gives some interesting examples of how high(er) standards can serve as a source of competitive advantage, although he recognizes that this may vary from sector to sector. Examples of both a race to the bottom and a race to the top are also given by: J. HÖRNLE, 'Country of Origin Regulation in Cross-border Media: One Step beyond the Freedom to Provide Services', *ICLQ* 2005, 124.

2

The Development of the Principle of Mutual Recognition in the Secondary Legislation

Inspired by the ECJ's *Cassis de Dijon* ruling and confronted with a lack of progress in the huge task that is the internal market's harmonization process, the Commission launched a new legislative strategy in the mid-1980s that was based on mutual recognition in combination with minimum harmonization.[1] Subsequently, in its legislative proposals for the four freedoms, the Commission would make a clear distinction between what needed to be harmonized and what could be left to the mutual recognition of national regulations and standards. The essence of the Commission's reasoning, by analogy with the ECJ's underlying reasoning in *Cassis de Dijon*, was that the objectives of national legislation which aimed at guaranteeing certain objectives worthy of protection—such as safety, health, environmental, and consumer (SHEC) interests—were very often identical or equivalent in each of the EU Member States. The Commission was therefore of the opinion that mutual recognition should be the rule and that harmonization should be left to aspects which could be justified by the criteria set out in the ECJ's case law on mandatory requirements.

Although the past had shown that an exclusively harmonizing approach would be over-regulatory, inflexible (thus stifling innovation), and above all time-consuming in its implementation,[2] the Commission was nevertheless aware that opting for the other extreme (i.e. a perspective of exclusive mutual recognition) could seriously jeopardize a number of fundamental interests.[3] Thus, with mutual recognition as a starting point,

[1] Communication from the Commission concerning the consequences of the judgment given by the ECJ on 20 February 1979 in Case 120/78 ('Cassis de Dijon'), *O.J.* C-256, 03.10.1980, p. 2–3; White Paper from the Commission to the European Council—Completing the Internal Market, COM (1985) 310, June 1985, p. 17–19. On the New Approach, see, for instance, the different contributions in R. BIEBER, R. DEHOUSSE, J. PINDER and J.H.H. WEILER, *1992: One European Market* (Baden-Baden, Nomos, 1988); M. LÓPEZ ESCUDERO, 'La aplicación del principio del reconocimiento mutuo en el derecho comunitario', *G. J.* 1993, D-19,146–52; M. MONTI, *De interne markt en het Europa van morgen. Een voortgangsverslag van de Europese Commissie* (Luxemburg, Publicatiebureau Europese Gemeenschappen, 1997) 28–39; D. VIGNES, 'Le rapprochement des législations mérite-t-il encore son nom', in *L'Europe et le droit. Mélanges en hommage à Jean Boulouis* (Paris, Ed. Dalloz, 1991) 533–46.

[2] See, for instance: General Programme of 28 May 1969 for the elimination of technical barriers to trade which result from disparities between the provisions laid down by law, regulation or administrative action in Member States, *O.J.* C-076, 17.06.1969, p. 1; R. BARENTS, 'Harmonisatie van wetgeving: moeilijk, moeizaam maar onvermijdelijk', in C.G. TROJAN, C.W.A. TIMMERMANS, R. BARENTS et al. (eds.), *Ondernemen in Europa. Bedrijfskundige opstellen over de Europese eenwording na 1992* (Zwolle, Tjeenk Willink, 1989), 19–20, who concluded that this ambitious programme would have implied the adoption of more than 600 directives and that, taking into account that under the old veto regime the average time for the adoption of a production directive was about ten years, such an approach could not have led to a satisfying result.

[3] See, for instance: Communication from the Commission to the European Parliament and the Council on Reinforcing the Effectiveness of the Internal Market, COM (1993) 256 final, p. 4 and 21, in which the Commission clearly recognized that some legislative intervention was required in order to meet the internal market programme's first objective, namely that 'the opening of the markets will lead to an improved level of social protection and of working conditions as well as of an increased level of protection of health, safety, environment and economic interests'. Furthermore, the Commission

accompanied by a policy of minimum harmonization, the Commission emphasized from the very beginning the complementary nature of the relationship between mutual recognition and harmonization.

This chapter aims to trace the contours of the legislative principle of mutual recognition by analysing certain legislative internal market instruments which can be considered representative of the free movement provisions, and which are above all relevant from the mutual recognition perspective. First, I focus on the range of terminology and on the various techniques for mutual recognition that have been put in place in these instruments (section I). Subsequently, I examine how the nature of the relationship between harmonization and mutual recognition has fluctuated through time and across domains in the internal market legislative acquis (section II). Finally, I discuss the as yet undiscussed legislative mechanisms which tend to limit the application of the principle of mutual recognition, in order to better define its scope (section III).

I. A Conceptual Debate: Principle of Mutual Recognition or Country of Origin Principle?

An overall analysis of the application of the principle of mutual recognition throughout divergent domains of the internal market and through time reveals a number of characteristics that relate to the conceptual debate on mutual recognition and the country of origin principle. I consider the term 'country of origin principle' inappropriate as a synonym for the judicially developed principle of mutual recognition, as discussed earlier.[4]

In what follows, I analyse the country of origin principle in the internal market's legislative context in order to ascertain whether, in a legislative context, the country of origin principle should be considered a synonym for the principle of mutual recognition as a more far-reaching principle (a characteristic which is often attributed to it in legal doctrine) or something else entirely. My analysis begins with the legislator's reluctance to refer explicitly either to a mutual recognition principle or to a country of origin principle (section I, A). I then proceed to analyse the features of the country of origin principle (section I, B), before drawing a conclusion on the meaning of the country of origin principle within the legislative internal market context (section I, C).

A. The legislator's preference for internal market or free movement clauses over country of origin clauses

The term 'principle of home country control' was first introduced in the 1985 White Paper as a new legislative strategy for the financial services sector in addition to the principle of mutual recognition,[5] and was later referred to as 'the principle of home Member State (prudential) supervision'[6] or 'the principle of home country authorisation, supervision

emphasized in this document that the mutual recognition principle is not automatic, but requires some kind of equivalence evaluation. See also: Opinion of AG Jääskinen in Case C-446/08 *Solgar* [2010] ECR I-3973, § 73, who underlined—with reference to a Communication from the Commission—'that food safety is not only of concern to the consumer, but is also at the very root of a proper functioning of the market'.

[4] See: Part I, ch 1, III. 'Equivalence, Country of Origin, and Mutual Recognition: What's in a Name?'

[5] White Paper from the Commission to the European Council—Completing the Internal Market (n 1) p. 29–30.

[6] See, for instance: § 7 and § 10 DIR 2006/48/EC; § 11 DIR 2009/138/EC; § 22 DIR 2004/39/EC.

and enforcement of obligations'[7] in the preambles of the most relevant directives accepted in this sector. In other preambles, the terminology changed slightly as a focus on supervision or authorization gave way to the more general 'principle that the law of the home Member State is to apply'[8] or simply 'the country of origin principle'. An explicit reference to the 'country of origin principle' can be found in the preamble to certain instruments of audiovisual media,[9] for instance, and in the financial services area.[10]

The absence of any explicit reference to the country of origin principle does not necessarily imply that no country of origin mechanism is at work. For example, the presence of an internal market clause which states that a service provider is, in relation to the coordinated field,[11] subject to the law of the Member State where the service provider is established bears close resemblance to a country of origin principle.[12] Such an implicit reference to the country of origin principle is, regrettably, far less obvious in other instruments, however.[13]

In some instruments, any explicit reference made to the country of origin or to the principle of mutual recognition in draft documents seems to have disappeared in the course of legislative proceedings. A first example of this is DIR 2005/29/EC, one of the draft versions of which made many references to the country of origin principle and had, like DIR 2000/31/EC, an internal market provision which made traders subject only to the law of the Member State in which they were established, in relation to the coordinated field. In the directive that was ultimately adopted, though, the preamble no longer mentioned the country of origin principle and the aforementioned provision was removed; the internal market clause was left in, but with a simple free movement of services provision.[14] A similar example can be found in DIR 2008/48/EC, the

[7] § 32 DIR 2004/39/EC. [8] § 23 DIR 2001/24/EC.

[9] § 33 DIR 2010/13/EU; § 18 DIR 93/83/EEC. [10] § 14 DIR 2003/71/EC.

[11] It can be observed that the European legislator when drafting internal market clauses is not always consistent in using the term 'coordinated' field. In fact, in some directives the legislator refers instead to the field 'covered' by the directive (for example, Art. 4 (1) DIR 1999/93/EC) or to the field 'approximated' by the directive (for example, Art. 4 DIR 2005/29/EC). Yet, these terms cannot be seen as mere synonyms as the 'coordinated field' does not necessarily refer to harmonized or approximated provisions. The European legislator, however, seems to ignore this difference and completely assimilates coordination and harmonization, converting by doing so coordination in a fictitious harmonization and imposing the legislative mutual recognition principle (with its restricted justification grounds). For a critique on this approach, see: O. CACHARD, 'The Field Coordinated by the Directive on e-Commerce and Private International Law', *IBLJ* 2004, 168–70; S. RODRIGUES, 'La proposition de directive relative aux services dans le marché intérie ur. Entre mythes et réalités', 2005, 10, retrievable at: <http://www.etudes-europeennes.fr>. See, on this issue, also: Part I, ch 2, III, A, 3. 'In pursuit of the correct framework for evaluating Member States' residual power in cases of minimum harmonization'.

[12] See, for instance: § 22 and Article 3 DIR 2000/31/EC, Article 4 DIR 1999/93/EC. For a legal analysis of the clause included in Article 3 DIR 2000/31/EC and its differentiation from a conflict-of-laws rule, see: ECJ, Joined Cases C-509/09 and C-161/10 *edate Advertising GmbH*, nyr, para 53 ff., and: J.J. KUIPERS, 'Case Note *edate Advertising GmbH*', *CML Rev.* 2012, 1224–31.

[13] See in this regard, for instance: DIR 2002/65/EC and the comment of E. LOMNICKA, 'The Financial Services Single Market and the Interface between Community Law and Domstic Law', in A. ARNULL (ed.), *Continuity and Change in EU Law. Essays in Honour of Sir Francis Jacobs* (Oxford, Oxford University Press, 2008) 280, who indicates that in the UK the view has been taken that this directive is intended to operate on a country of origin basis. See also: DIR 2009/110/EC, which, unlike its predecessor (§ 3 and Article 2(2) former Directive 2000/46/EC), does not refer explicitly to the principle of mutual recognition or the principle of a single licence system, neither in its preamble nor in its main provisions. The crucial position of the single licence system for this directive only reveals itself implicitly by means of the cross-reference included in Article 3(1) DIR 2009/10/EC, which refers back to Article 9(1) DIR 2007/64/EC and the single licence system that is enshrined therein.

[14] Compare in this regard: § 26–8, § 30, and Article 4 Proposal for a Directive of the European Parliament and of the Council concerning unfair business-to-consumer commercial practices in

final version of which omitted a previously incorporated mutual recognition clause.[15] Apparently, the European legislator was not yet willing to accept the explicit introduction of a country of origin principle or a principle of mutual recognition in the area of consumer law. Two key factors may have influenced this outcome. First, in the case of DIR 2008/48/EC, the Commission had aimed at imposing the law of the country of origin in relation to aspects which had not been subject to the full harmonization approach which underpins both directives. This is likely to have led to the Council's concluding that it would be too difficult for consumers to understand, and that it could lead to legal uncertainty owing to the application of different Member States' laws.[16] Similar arguments were far less convincing in the context of DIR 2005/29/EC, however, taking into account the full harmonization and the high level of consumer protection that this instrument achieved.[17] The second factor which may have led to the ultimate deletion of an explicit reference to the country of origin or mutual recognition principle in both instruments is the (originally) envisaged extension of the concept of country of origin/mutual recognition to the applicable law.[18] The extension from public law issues to private law issues (i.e. issues affecting contractual rights and obligations) has far-reaching consequences not only for public authorities but also for private persons (consumers), who will be faced with the application of a law they are unfamiliar with. A last example in this regard is DIR 2006/123/EC. Prior to the adoption of this instrument, heated discussions were carried out over the meaning of the country of origin principle, which had been mentioned explicitly in (old) Article 16 of the directive's proposal. Following fierce debates and lobbying activities, the final version left out any reference to the country of origin principle and replaced it with a free movement of services provision.[19]

the Internal Market and amending directives 84/450/EEC, 97/7/EC and 98/27/EC (the Unfair Commercial Practices Directive), COM (2003) 356 final, with Article 4 DIR 2005/29/EC.

[15] Compare in this regard: § 10–11 and Article 21 of the Modified proposal for a Directive of the European Parliament and of the Council on credit agreements for consumers amending Council Directive 93/13/EC (presented by the Commission pursuant to Article 250(2) of the EC Treaty), COM (2005) 483 final, with DIR 2008/48/EC.

[16] See, on this reasoning, the draft statement of the Council's reasons on the modified proposal for a Directive of the European Parliament and of the Council on credit agreements for consumers and repealing Council Directive 87/102/EEC, 14 September 2007, doc. 9948/07 ADD 1, p. 9, retrievable at: <http://www.consilium.europa.eu/documents/access-to-council-documents-public- register?lang = en>.

[17] Taking into account the fact that it concerned a full harmonization approach, concerns were not so much raised about the divergence of national legislations, which—in theory—should be identical, but rather about cases whereby the law is not effectively implemented. See, on this issue: Report of 18 March 2004 of the Committee on Legal Affairs and the Internal Market on the proposal for a European Parliament and Council directive concerning unfair business-to-consumer commercial practices in the Internal Market and amending Directives 84/450/EEC, 97/7/EC and 98/27/EC (the Unfair Commercial Practices Directive), COM (2003) 356–C5-0288/2003–2003/0134(COD), amendments suggested by the Committee on the Environment, Public Health and Consumer Policy on Art. 4. This illustrates that the practical application of mutual recognition can still be problematic, even after full harmonization.

[18] SER, 'Advies 2004/06. Oneerlijke handelspraktijken op consumententerrein in de EU', 48, retrievable at: <http://www.ser.nl/nl/publicaties/adviezen/2000-2007/2004/b22670.aspx>; HOUSE OF LORDS, EU COMMITTEE, Consumer Credit in the EU: Harmonization and Consumer Protection, 2005-06, 48, retrievable at: <http://www.publications.parliament.uk/pa/ld200506/ldselect/ldeucom/210/210i.pdf>. See also on this issue, in relation to the area of electronic commerce: SER, 'Advies 99/10. Oneerlijke handel in de interne markt', 27–30, retrievable at: <http://www.ser.nl/nl/publicaties/adviezen/1990-1999/1999/b17810.aspx>.

[19] Compare, in this respect, Article 16 of the original Commission's Proposal for a Directive of the European Parliament and of the Council on Services in the Internal Market, COM (2004) 2 final, with Article 16 of DIR 2006/123/EC.

The fear and sensitivity surrounding this term and its potential impact is clearly indicated by the fact that in all of the examples mentioned above, the term 'country of origin' appeared only in the preamble and was often explicitly absent from the main text owing to deliberate amendments during the course of the legislative proceedings. Is this fear or sensitivity justified, though? In other words, is a country of origin principle necessarily more intrusive than a free movement, internal market, or mutual recognition clause?[20] This brings me to the question of which features can be attributed to the country of origin principle.

B. The features of the country of origin principle

(1) The country of origin principle at first glance

The fundamental characteristics usually attributed to the country of origin principle in legal doctrine can be summarized as follows: a service provider will only be subject to those national provisions of the Member State of origin which fall within the coordinated field of the directive; the home state is under obligation to supervise cross-border services; and the justification grounds that can be invoked are usually more limited than the Treaty framework (Treaty-based exceptions and non-exhaustive rule of reason exceptions).[21]

A mechanism which leads to the quasi-automatic application of the country of origin's regulations and to which only a limited number of exceptions are available initially appears a more absolute and unconditional principle than, first, the principle of mutual recognition developed in the ECJ's case law; secondly, the legislatively developed principle of mutual recognition in the New Approach directives; and thirdly, the legislatively developed principle of mutual recognition in the directives on the mutual recognition of diplomas.

First, not only did the ECJ explicitly refuse to read a country of origin principle in the TFEU, it also created an unlimited group of justification grounds (rule of reason) for the judicially developed principle of mutual recognition which are able to block the principle if necessary.

Secondly, the New Approach directives make no reference in their preambles or in their main body texts to a country of origin principle. The directives provide for a free movement clause which, in principle, refers back to harmonized norms and thus not to the law of the home Member State. In the few texts that do refer to the national norms

[20] On the presumed distinctive nature of a country of origin principle in relation to the general services directive, see for instance: L. ALBATH and M. GIESLER, 'Das Herkunftslandprinzip in der Dienstleistungsrichtlinie—eine Kodifizierung der Rechtsprechung?' *EuZW* 2006, 41; M. AUDIT, 'Régulation du marché intérieur et libre circulation des lois', *J.D.I.* 2006, 22; C. BARNARD, 'Unravelling the Services Directive', *CML Rev.* 2008, 362–3; D'ACUNTO, 'La proposition de directive sur les services dans le marché intérieur', *RDUE* 2004, 202; O. DE SCHUTTER and S. FRANCQ, 'La proposition de directive relative aux services dans le marché intérieur: reconnaissance mutuelle, harmonisation et conflits de lois dans l'Europe élargie', *C.D.E.* 2006, 606; P. TIMMERMAN, 'Legislating amidst Public Controversy: The Services Directive', Egmont Paper 32, 2009, 36–40, retrievable at: <http://www.egmontinstitute.be/paperegm/sum/ep32.html>; M.W. GEKIERE, 'Towards a European Directive on Services in the Internal Market: Analysing the legal repercussions on the Draft Services Directive and its Impact on National Services Regulations. Research report commissioned by Anne Van Lancker. 24 September 2004', 15–16, retrievable at: <http://openbarediensten.acv-online.be/Images/2004-10%20 EU%20Diensten%20-%20Impact %20Draft%20final1_tcm86-67173.pdf>; R.M. JENNAR, 'La proposition de directive Bolkestein', *Courrier Hebdomadaire* 2005, 38 and 60–1.

[21] See, for instance: M. FALLON and J. MEEUSEN, 'Le commerce électronique, la directive 2000/31/CE et le droit international privé', *Revue critique de droit international privé* 2002, 435–90.

of the home Member State, the directive provides for specific procedures requiring an equivalence test or a comparison with international norms, clearly intended to avoid the straightforward application of the home Member State's rules.[22] Therefore, I believe it is more worthwhile to speak of a principle of mutual recognition in this context than of a country of origin principle. For the sake of thoroughness, however, it should be acknowledged that the boundaries between the two principles are sometimes difficult to define, since one of the characteristics of the country of origin principle, i.e. supervision by the home Member State, also appears in the majority of the New Approach directives where certification activities are entrusted to the authorities of the country of origin.

Thirdly, a similar conclusion can be drawn in the area of diplomas. The assumption that automatic mutual recognition is limited to those situations where the conditions for access to and exercise of a profession have been harmonized and the fact that supervision is entrusted to the host Member State can hardly be reconciled with a country of origin principle.[23] Here too, however, do the lines between mutual recognition and country of origin become somewhat blurred when we examine the services chapter of DIR 2005/36/EC. In no longer requiring the official establishment of a service provider's professional qualifications via an equivalence test, except in public health or public security-related sectors, and instead relying on a declaration from the service provider,[24] the (previous) focus on the host state shifts to a considerable focus on the country of origin in this area. The non-negligible position of the country of origin is also evident in the directive's provisions on administrative cooperation, in which it is clearly stated that 'the *home* Member State shall examine the veracity of the circumstances and *its authorities* shall decide on the nature and scope of the investigations which need to be carried out and shall inform the host Member State of the conclusions which it draws from the information available to it' (emphasis added).[25]

Furthermore, it should be pointed out that the ECJ's general focus in the area of diplomas lies on the mutual recognition mechanism itself and far less on the question of whose system should be recognized i.e. home state versus host state competence. This can be illustrated by a number of recent judgments in which a *host* Member State was obliged to recognize a degree awarded by a competent authority in another Member State but on completion of the education and training received, in whole or in part, in the *host* Member State, and which, under the legislation of that state, was not recognized as higher education.[26] The fact that a (competent) authority in one Member State had recognized a degree issued in the host state via a homologation agreement triggered the mutual recognition mechanism and resulted somewhat disturbingly in the host Member State's being forced to recognize a degree issued on its own territory but not recognized there as higher education.

[22] See, for instance: § 16 and Article 3 DIR 2001/95/EC.

[23] See, in particular: Articles 7, 14, and 21 DIR 2005/36/EC, and the comments of: L. DEFALQUE, J. PERTEK, P. STEINFELF, and P. VIGNERON, *Commentaire J. Mégret. Marché intérieur. Libre circulation des personnes et des capitaux. Rapprochement des législations* (Brussels, IEE, 2006) 265. For a focus on the host state's legal framework in the ECJ's case law on diplomas, see, for instance: ECJ, Case C-225/09 *Jakubowska* [2010] ECR I-12329, para 57; ECJ, Case C-359/09, *Ebert* [2011] ECR I-269, paras 39–40; ECJ Case C-424/09 *Toki* [2011] ECR I-2587, para 40.

[24] Article 7 DIR 2005/36/EC.

[25] Article 56 DIR 2005/36/EC.

[26] ECJ, Case C-274/05 *Commission v Greece* [2008] ECR I-7969, para 35; ECJ, Case C-286/06 *Commission v Spain* [2008] ECR I-8025, para 73.

(2) A more in-depth approach: one principle, many forms

The apparently more 'absolute' features of the country of origin principle, compared to the principle of mutual recognition, as discussed under the previous heading, should be put into perspective. An in-depth study of a number of directives reveals that the degree of absoluteness that this principle is often said to possess depends less on the terminology 'country of origin' and more on a combination of various factors, including: the scope of the directive (the 'coordinated field'); the level of harmonization achieved (exhaustive versus non-exhaustive); the harmonization method used; the justification grounds that can be invoked; and finally the distribution of supervisory competences between the country of origin and the country of destination. I will illustrate this now by looking at certain instruments in particular.

In the banking sector, a huge difference exists between, first, the 'softer' country of origin principle that is recorded in the directive on taking up and pursuing the business of credit institutions[27] and in the directive on the taking up, pursuit of, and prudential supervision of the business of electronic money institutions[28] and secondly, the more 'extreme' country of origin principle described in the directive on the reorganization and winding up of credit institutions. Whilst in the former two directives the country of origin principle[29] goes hand in hand with some harmonization of minimum (capital) requirements and prudential supervision measures,[30] the latter directive imposes a far-reaching country of origin[31] and mutual recognition[32] duty, without any previous harmonization.[33] Furthermore, in the former directives the host Member State can play a role of some importance through the application of justification grounds based on the general good,[34] or through the performance of inspections carried out in the framework of prudential supervisory duties,[35] whereas the latter directive determines a far more limited role for the host (or any other) Member State.[36]

In the insurance sector, too, the country of origin principle is characterized by a rather variable nature.[37] As in the banking directives, DIR 2009/138/EC is based on

[27] DIR 2006/48/EC. [28] DIR 2009/110/EC.

[29] Both directives subscribe to the basic principle of supervision by the home Member State (Art. 40 DIR 2006/48/EC and Art. 3(1) DIR 2009/110/EC *juncto* Art. 20 ff. DIR 2007/64/EC).

[30] Articles 6 to 12 and Article 14 DIR 2006/48/EC. Articles 3 to 8 DIR 2009/110/EC (with reference to the applicable provisions of DIR 2007/64/EC).

[31] § 6, Article 3, and Article 10 DIR 2001/24/EC.

[32] § 5, § 6, and Article 9 DIR 2001/24/EC.

[33] Only 'some coordination' of the roles of the competent authorities is required (§ 13 DIR 2001/24/EC).

[34] Article 31 DIR 2006/48/EC.

[35] Articles 30 and 41 DIR 2006/48/EC; Article 3(1) DIR 2009/110/EC *juncto* Articles 24 and 25 DIR 2007/64/EC.

[36] § 23, Article 20 and Article 32 DIR 2001/24/EC. Under this instrument the cooperation duties between the supervisory authorities of both Member States are limited to a duty to inform each other of a decision to open winding-up proceedings (Art. 4 and Art. 9(3)).

[37] Over the years, both the home and the host Member States have undergone significant changes in their respective competences owing to an increased level of harmonization following successive modifications to earlier versions of the directives that were adopted in this sector. See, for instance, the disappearance of old Article 18(1) Second Council Directive 88/357/EEC of 22 June 1988 on the coordination of laws, regulations, and administrative provisions relating to direct insurance other than life assurance and laying down provisions to facilitate the effective exercise of freedom to provide services and amending Directive 73/239/EEC, *O.J.* L-172, 04.07.1988, p. 1–14 (repealed), in more recent directives. See also: old Articles 11 and 19(6) Council Directive 93/22/EEC of 10 May 1993 on investment services in the securities field, *O.J.* L-197, 06.08.1993, p. 58 (repealed), according to which a host Member State was in charge of the implementation and supervision of compliance with the rules

a system of single authorization and supervision by the home Member State,[38] which is supported by the harmonization of minimum (capital) requirements and prudential supervision measures.[39] Although the directive clearly classifies the financial supervision of insurance and reinsurance companies as the sole responsibility of the home Member State,[40] several other provisions of this directive allocate far-reaching competences to the supervisory authorities of the host Member State.[41] With regard to the opening, conduct, and closure of winding-up proceedings, however, the country of origin maintains its central position.[42]

The main conclusion that can be drawn from the financial services directives as a whole is that the often attributed 'absolute' character of the country of original principle should be refined, since in light of the directives discussed above, this is largely determined by a clearly defined coordinated field. The attribution of competence to the home country does not go beyond this scope and justification grounds based on the general good in principle remain valid for the host Member States whenever harmonization is lacking.[43]

A similar pattern can also be identified in other services areas,[44] such as the audio-visual media services area[45] and the area of electronic commerce,[46] albeit with some distinctions. A crucial difference between these and the previous category of directives, for example, is that the country of origin principle is no longer limited to rules on access and supervision but also deals with rules on the exercise of an activity.[47] Compared to the previous category of directives, the coordinated field is often vaguely defined and

of conduct, and which were removed following subsequent harmonization on conduct rules, and was thus not taken over in DIR 2004/39/EC.

[38] § 5 and § 11 and Articles 14–15 DIR 2009/138/EC.

[39] Article 87 ff. DIR 2009/138/EC (on minimum capital requirements) and Article 27 ff. (on rules governing the prudential supervision).

[40] Article 10 DIR 2009/138/EC.

[41] See, in particular: Articles 155 and 158 DIR 2009/138/EC. The ECJ too has underlined, with regard to (former Article 9 of) the predecessor of DIR 2009/138/EC, that 'that provision cannot be interpreted as meaning that the Community legislature intended that the home Member State should have exclusive supervisory competence extending to the commercial conduct of insurance undertakings': ECJ, Case C-518/06 *Commission v Italy* [2009] ECR I-3491, para 116.

[42] § 123, § 125, and § 126, Article 273 ('only the competent authority of the home Member State shall be entitled to take a decision') and Article 274 (such a decision 'shall be recognized without further formality throughout the Community') DIR 2009/138/EC.

[43] V. HATZOPOULOS, *Le principe communautaire d'équivalence et de reconnaissance mutuelle dans la libre prestation de services* (Brussels, Bruylant, 1999) 448–9; M. TISON, *De interne markt voor bank- en beleggingsdiensten* (Antwerp, Intersentia, 1999) 922–93, who pleaded for more harmonization in order to remedy the incomplete character of the mutual recognition principle.

[44] In some sectors the Commission's intent to introduce mutual recognition failed as there was no political will to reach an agreement and only a soft mechanism of administrative cooperation was set into place. Compare, in this regard, for instance, in relation to the telecommunications sector: Proposal for a Council directive on the mutual recognition of licences and other national authorizations to operate telecommunications services, including the establishment of a Single Community Telecommunications Licence and the setting up of a Community Telecommunications Committee, COM (1992) 254 final, p. 4, with former Directive 97/13/EC of the European Parliament and of the Council of 10 April 1997 on a common framework for general authorizations and individual licences in the field of telecommunications services, *O.J.* L-117, 07.05.1997, p. 15–27, and with DIR 2002/21/EC, which repealed former Directive 97/13/EC.

[45] DIR 2010/13/EU. [46] DIR 2000/31/EC.

[47] V. HATZOPOULOS, 'Que reste-t- il de la directive sur les services', *C.D.E.* 2007, 305–6. Hatzopoulos calls the country of origin principle that is taken up in these directives the 'second generation' country of origin principle, compared to the 'first generation directives' (i.e. the passport directives in the insurance and banking sector) and the 'third generation directive' (the services directive).

goes hand in hand with a rather limited level of harmonization and a limited number of justification grounds. This has led a number of authors in the literature to conclude that the principle has reached its outer limits,[48] or that a new principle has emerged that is no longer based on mutual recognition after harmonization (i.e. mutual recognition of common rules) but rather on the mutual recognition of national rules.[49] The more absolute characteristics of this country of origin rule, however, have been attenuated to some extent by both the ECJ[50] and the European legislator, particularly with regard to the broadcasting area.[51]

It could be said that the country of origin principle took on its most heavily disputed form in the original proposal of DIR 2006/123/EC. The principle was not only mentioned obliquely in one of the many considerations of the preamble but also stood out as a point of interest in the chapter on the free movement of services. In comparison with the directives mentioned above, the proposal of DIR 2006/123/EC distinguished itself with a mixture of three elements, namely its very broad scope (being a horizontal directive); its extremely limited level of harmonization; and finally the relatively small number of justification grounds. The combination of these three factors amounted to an absolute representation of the country of origin principle that had seldom been seen previously.[52] As a result, it was heavily criticized and the final version of DIR 2006/123/

[48] See, for instance, with regard to DIR 2000/31/EC: FALLON and MEEUSEN, 'Le commerce électronique, la directive 2000/31/CE et le droit international privé' (n 21) 479; G. DE BAERE, 'Is this a Conflict Rule which I See before me?, *MJ* 2004, 310. See also: M. RADEIDEH, *Fair Trading in EC Law. Information and Consumer Choice in the Internal Market* (Groningen, Europa law Publishing, 2005) 104–5; and M. TISON, 'De Richtlijn electronische handel en financiële diensten: een brug te ver', in *Liber amicorum Yvette Merchiers* (Bruges, Die Keure, 2001) 605, who both argue that there is *no* absolute mutual recognition principle, rather on the contrary, the directive achieves, according to them, a good balance between free movement and consumer interests.

[49] V. DE SCHRYVER, 'Enige vragen bij de richtlijn electronische handel', *Financieel Forum. Bank en financieel recht* 2002, 70.

[50] In its case law on TV broadcasting, the ECJ has been applying the country of origin principle with caution, leaving the host Member State a remarkable margin of discretion. See for instance: ECJ, Joined Cases C-34/95, C-35/95 and C-36/95 *De Agostini* [1997] ECR I-3843, and the comments of A. CRISCUOLO, 'The 'TV Without Frontiers' and the Legal Regulation of Publicity in the European Community', *E.L. Rev.* 1998, 362–3; J. STUYCK, 'Case Note De Agostini', *CML Rev.* 1997, 1462–3; ECJ, Case C-429/02 *Bacardi France* [2004] I-6613 and the comment of J. STUYCK, 'Comment on Bacardi France', *CML Rev.* 2005, 801; ECJ, Case C-222/07 *Uteca* [2009] ECR I-1407, and the corresponding Opinion of AG Kokott, who underlined that 'the concept of 'more detailed or stricter rules' that Member States are permitted to adopt under this directive does conceivably encompass *a wide spectrum* of possible national measures' (emphasis added) (at § 38); ECJ, Case C-52/10 *Eleftheri tileorasi AE 'Alter Channel'*, nyr, para 35; ECJ, Case C-244/10 *Mesopotamia Broadcast*, nyr, para 37.

[51] See, for instance, Article 4 DIR 2010/13/EU and its system of 'mandatory cooperation' that insists on the need of finding mutually satisfactory solutions rather than focusing on the decisive power of one Member State. The concept originates from Sweden where it allows national regulatory authorities to mitigate any clashes between the rules of the country of origin and the country of destination, but was criticized, as it might lead to a watered-down version of the country of origin principle when compared to old directive 89/552/EEC: HOUSE OF LORDS, EU COMMITTEE, Television without Frontiers and Report with Evidence, 2007, 19–20, retrievable at: <http://www.publications.parliament.uk/pa/ld200607/ldselect/ldeucom/27/27.pdf>. On a Member State's margin of action under former directive 89/552/EEC and possible limits on the country of origin rule, see also: Opinion of AG Bot in Joined Cases C-244/10 and C-245/10, *Mesopotamia Broadcast*, nyr.

[52] For a critique on such an absolute principle, see, for instance: ALBATH and GIESLER 'Das Herkunftslandprinzip in der Dienstleistungsrichtlinie—eine Kodifizierung der Rechtsprechung?' (n 20) 38–42; B. DE WITTE, 'Setting the Scene: How did Services get to Bolkestein and Why', EUI Working Papers Law 2007/20, 8, retrievable at: <http://cadmus.iue.it/dspace/bitstream/1814/6929/1/LAW_2007_20.pdf>; M. FALLON and A.-C. SIMON, 'La directive "services": quelle contribution au marché intérieur', *JTDE* 2007, 38; GEKIERE, 'Towards a European Directive on Services in the Internal Market' (n 20) 15–16; DE SCHUTTER and FRANCQ, 'La proposition de directive

EC subsequently deleted all references to the term 'country of origin principle' and substituted it with 'the principle of freedom to provide services' (Art. 16(1)).[53]

C. The country of origin principle as a flexible tool for enhancing mutual recognition

The main conclusion of the previous overview is that the country of origin principle may have either an absolute or a more moderate character, depending on the subject matter. It has this in common with the principle of mutual recognition, whose level of automaticity can also diverge to a considerable extent from one instrument to another and even within one instrument.[54] Furthermore, neither the country of origin principle nor the principle of mutual recognition is a static concept, but both evolve and diverge through time and across domains, usually in terms of the achieved level of harmonization.[55]

The presence of a 'country of origin' provision, then, does not necessarily imply that the legislation of the country of origin will prevail absolutely or that the host country will be prevented from performing any supervision. The term 'country of origin' obviously refers to a relevant role for the country of origin but the exact contours can vary considerably from one instrument to another. Indeed, the specific duties of cooperation and the availability of justification grounds—two elements that are also typical of a mutual recognition approach—are mostly present in a 'country of origin' instrument and can

relative aux services dans le marché intérieur: reconnaissance mutuelle, harmonisation et conflits de lois dans l'Europe élargie' (n 20) 643; B.J. DRIJBER, 'De bezems van Bolkestein', *NTER* 2004, 116–17; RODRIGUES, 'La proposition de directive relative aux services dans le marché intérieur. Entre myths et réalités' (n 11) 9–10. For a more positive approach, tempering the absolute character of the country of origin principle, see for instance: SER, 'Advisory Report. The Directive on Services in the Internal Market' (July 2005), 89, retrievable at: <http://www.ser.nl/~/media/Files/Internet/Talen/Engels/2005/2005_07_volledig%20pdf.ashx>; HOUSE OF LORDS, EU COMMITTEE, Completing the Internal Market in Services, 2005-2006, 25–31, retrievable at <http://www.parliament.the-stationery-office.co.uk/pa/ld200506/ldselect/ldeucom/23/23.pdf>.

[53] This remarkable metamorphosis certainly smoothed the ruffled feathers of the *Bolkestein* directive—adversaries, but the impact of such a modification should not be overestimated either. Indeed, the list of justification grounds that a Member State is henceforward allowed to invoke under the new regime is still limited, which leads several authors—who, significantly, continue to use the term 'country of origin'— to conclude that such a provision makes the country of origin principle a step more absolute than the ECJ's regime on the matter. The country of origin principle would have been 'amended' rather than 'deleted', see, for instance: G. DAVIES, 'The Services Directive: Extending the Country of Origin Principle and Reforming Public Administration', *E.L. Rev.* 2007, 235 and Miranda, who suggests that the country of origin principle is still present, albeit with a different name: Interview with M. MIRANDA, administrator at the European Commission, DG Internal Market, Brussels, 23 April 23, 2007. Similarly: S. D'ACUNTO, 'Directive Services (2006/123/EC): radiographie juridique en dix points', *RDUE* 2007, 309. See also some of the views expressed in: HOUSE OF LORDS, EU COMMITTEE, The Services Directive Revisited, 16, retrievable at: <http://www.parliament.the-stationery-office.co.uk/pa/ld200506/ldselect/ldeucom/215/215.pdf>.

[54] See, for instance: DIR 2005/36/EC, discussed: Part I, ch 2, II, B, 2. 'Enhancing mutual trust and mutual recognition in the area of diplomas'.

[55] Compare, in this regard, in relation to the banking sector: ECJ, Case C-222/95 *Parodi* [1997] ECR I-3899, paras 24–6 and ECJ, Case C-222/02 *Peter Paul* [2004] I-9425, paras 36–7; in which the ECJ recalled that the 'first' banking directive (directive 77/780/EEC) was no more than a first step towards the mutual recognition by Member States of authorizations issued by each of them to credit institutions and that mutual recognition was made possible only by the entry into force of the 'second' banking directive (directive 89/646/EEC). Only rarely does a (quasi-) non-existing level of harmonization go hand in hand with a far-reaching country of origin principle and/or a mutual recognition principle, see, for instance: DIR 2001/24/EC.

seriously reduce the purportedly absolute character of the country of origin principle.[56] Moreover, in a number of specific internal market sectors, a clear shift away from home country control towards network control has taken place, in which the Commission or an EU agency has often acted as a network focal point.[57]

I therefore conclude that the two major currents developed in academic writing regarding the country of origin principle and its relation to the principle of mutual recognition should be nuanced. First, the country of origin principle is not simply a synonym for the principle of mutual recognition. Secondly, the principle of mutual recognition is not a 'light' version of the country of origin principle. The country of origin principle can perhaps best be defined as one of the tools at the European legislator's disposal for enhancing the free movement provisions and one that has manifested itself, like the principle of mutual recognition, not as a unique model but instead as a principle with considerably divergent forms. Both concepts are perfectly compatible and are often used together, particularly, as we have seen, in the free movement of services sector. However, in other legislative areas, namely the free movement of goods and the free movement of diplomas, the use of the term 'country of origin principle' is not at all common. It therefore seems more appropriate in a cross-freedom approach to use the more general term 'principle of mutual recognition', and to employ the term 'country of origin principle' only in the specific legislative context of the free movement of services and in relation to those services in which this principle has indeed been incorporated.

II. The Harmonization and Mutual Recognition Tandem under Scrutiny

A. A different technical approach: substantive or procedural harmonization and mutual recognition

Despite the considerable number of communications and reports that the Commission has issued on the principle of mutual recognition, little or no information has been released on the difference in approach between substantive and procedural mutual recognition. In the EU internal market acquis, however, both methods are clearly present.

(1) Substantive mutual recognition instruments

Under substantive mutual recognition, I include those instruments in which the duty of recognition applies to the substantive rules of a Member State, which have been harmonized at EU level.

The scope of substantive mutual recognition can differ widely, covering for example safety requirements for products and machinery,[58] health and consumer protection

[56] To put it differently, the difference between the country of origin and the freedoms established in the Treaty is foremost a conceptual one as Member States will make use of the derogations and the proportionality criterion will be interpreted along analogous lines to the proportionality test under the freedom of goods and services: J, HÖRNLE, 'Country of Origin Regulation in Cross-border Media: One Step beyond the Freedom to Provide Services?', *ICLQ* 2005, 125.

[57] For some examples, see: A.M. KEESSEN, *European Administrative Decisions. How the EU Regulates Products on the Internal Market* (Groningen, Europa Law Publishing, 2009) 87 ff.

[58] The New Approach directives, are retrievable at: <http://ec.europa.eu/enterprise/newapproach/standardization/harmstds/reflist.html>. See, for instance: DIR 2006/95/EC; DIR 2009/105/EC; DIR 2009/48/EC.

requirements relating to food products,[59] requirements for access to the taking up and pursuit of credit or insurance institutions,[60] content requirements for certain television broadcasting services,[61] requirements for the establishment and exercise of information society services,[62] requirements for the content of diplomas,[63] driving licences,[64] and aeronautical products.[65]

Mutual recognition in this context is always related to the recognition of decisions concerning harmonized[66] European norms originating either from national administrative authorities (single licence decision) or from EU authorities (EU decision). This is in contrast with the judicially developed principle of mutual recognition, which refers solely to the mutual recognition of decisions concerning national provisions that have not been harmonized and that stem from national administrative authorities (national decision).[67]

[59] See, for instance: DIR 89/108/EEC; DIR 2000/36/EC; DIR 2002/46/EC; REG 1925/2006; REG 1169/2011.

[60] DIR 2006/48/EC; DIR 2009/138/EC; DIR 2004/39/EC.

[61] DIR 2010/13/EU.

[62] DIR 2000/31/EC.

[63] See, in this regard the six sectoral directives adopted between 1975 and 1985 which have all been repealed by DIR 2005/36/EC. Former Council Directives 75/362/EEC and 75/363, 16/06/1975 concerning the mutual recognition of diplomas, certificates and other evidence of formal qualifications in medicine, including measures to facilitate the effective exercise of the right of establishment and freedom to provide services, *O.J.* L-167, 30.06.1975, p. 1–16 (codified by Directive 93/16/EEC, *O.J.* L-165, 07.07.1993); former Council Directive 77/452/EEC and 77/453 of 27 June 1977 concerning the mutual recognition of diplomas, certificates and other evidence of the formal qualifications of nurses responsible for general care, including measures to facilitate the effective exercise of this right of establishment and freedom to provide services, *O.J.* L-176, 15.07.1977, p. 1–10; former Council Directives 78/686/EEC and 78/687/EEC of 25 July 1978 concerning the mutual recognition of diplomas, certificates and other evidence of the formal qualifications of practitioners of dentistry, including measures to facilitate the effective exercise of the right of establishment and freedom to provide services, *O.J.* L-233, 24.08.1978, p. 1–4; former Council Directives 78/1026/EEC and 78/1027 of 18 December 1978 concerning the mutual recognition of diplomas, certificates and other evidence of formal qualifications in veterinary medicine, including measures to facilitate the effective exercise of the right of establishment and freedom to provide services, *O.J.* L-362, 23.12.1978, p. 1–9; former Council Directives 80/154/EEC and 80/155 of 21 January 1980 concerning the mutual recognition of diplomas, certificates and other evidence of formal qualifications in midwifery and including measures to facilitate the effective exercise of the right of establishment and freedom to provide services, *O.J.* L-033, 11.02.1980, p.1–12; former Council Directive 85/432/EEC of 16 September 1985 concerning the coordination of provisions laid down by Law, Regulation or Administrative Action in respect of certain activities in the field of pharmacy, *O.J.* L-253, 24.09.1985, p. 34–42.

[64] DIR 2006/126/EC.

[65] REG 216/2008.

[66] Legislative instruments will—by contrast—hardly ever prescribe the recognition of non-harmonized national standards. In fact, this would seem redundant as such an obligation follows directly from the TFEU and the judicially developed mutual recognition principle. However, in some legislative instruments there is a reference to mutual recognition of national norms, but, in the absence of any uniform standard, the presumption of equivalence will logically be less rigid than for harmonized norms and can more easily be put aside. See, for instance: Article 14 REG 178/2002, which refers, on the one hand, to the mutual recognition of (harmonized) *Community* provisions on food law (Art. 14 (7)), and, on the other hand, to the mutual recognition of provisions of *national* food law (Art. 14 (9)). In both provisions the directive states that the provisions 'shall be deemed to be safe', but in relation to the latter, explicit reference to former Article 30 EC (currently, Art. 36 TFEU) is mentioned. See, for instance, also: Article 7 DIR 2006/95/EC.

[67] KEESSEN, *European Administrative Decisions. How the EU Regulates Products on the Internal Market* (n 57) 27–81. This author distinguishes between four types of decisions (national, community, single licence, and mutual recognition decisions) whereas I consider that 'mutual recognition' decisions can apply to each of these categories.

Substantive harmonization under the New Approach will focus on the establishment of common (minimum) standards of essential requirements, which in the goods sector ultimately amounts to the following four interests: safety, health, environmental, and consumer requirements (hereafter SHEC requirements).[68] Harmonizing these interests raises the level of presumed equivalence—as it exists in the judicial approach—to an accomplished equivalence valid throughout the whole EU in the legislative approach.[69]

However, substantive harmonization does not necessarily imply that Member States ought to behave passively by applying mutual recognition quasi-automatically. The margin of discretion that is left to the Member States depends on various questions, such as: whether the directive has regulated the matter exhaustively; which harmonization technique has been used; whether the directive provides for any safeguard clauses or justification grounds; how much controlling power is granted to the host Member State; and to what extent Member States are entitled to take measures to combat fraud or forum shopping.[70]

(2) Procedural mutual recognition instruments

By procedural mutual recognition, I mean those instruments in which the European legislator emphasizes the harmonization and recognition of procedural rules which are necessary to make the principle of mutual recognition work. The intrinsic characteristics of goods, services, or diplomas are less the subject of harmonization and recognition than the national procedural elements of controlling and testing procedures, with the focus lying on the latter aspects in order to enhance the mutual recognition of the results of such procedures. Furthermore, uniform procedural frameworks have been developed in order to enhance the efficiency of the principle of mutual recognition. Several examples can be mentioned, for example in relation to the area of the free movement of goods[71] or services,[72] or more specifically in relation to food controls,[73] roadworthiness tests,[74] in the pharmaceutical sector, or in the area of diplomas.

[68] The 'SHEC' interests were crucial from the very beginning and are still relevant today. See, for instance: White Paper from the Commission to the European Council—Completing the Internal Market (n 1) p. 21–3; J. PELKMANS, 'Mutual Recognition in Goods and Services: An Economic Perspective', in F.K. PADO SCHIOPPA (ed.), *The Principle of Mutual Recognition in the European Integration Process* (New York, Palgrave Macmillan, 2005) 92. Many other, more specific interests can often be categorized under one of these general categories, such as, for instance, road safety (e.g. DIR 2006/126/EC) which can be considered as a subcategory of safety, the protection of minors (e.g. DIR 2010/13/EU) or the protection of savers (e.g. DIR 2006/48/EC) which can both be considered as examples of consumer protection.

[69] Producers who choose not to apply the EU certification system and who rely on mutual recognition of national norms generally face more difficulties in getting their products recognized: See, for instance: ECJ, Case C-254/05 *Commission v Belgium* [2007] ECR I-4269.

[70] See: Part I, ch 2, III. 'The Limits of the Legislative Principle of Mutual Recognition'.

[71] See, for instance: REG 764/2008.

[72] See, for instance: DIR 2006/123/EC.

[73] See, for instance: DIR 83/643/EEC; DIR 89/608/EEC; DIR 1999/93/EC; DIR 2004/41/EC; REG 882/2004. For an interpretation of some of these instruments (or their predecessors) in the ECJ's case law, with a focus on the need of a good cooperation and the prohibition of repetitive, systematic controls, see: ECJ, Joined Cases 2/82, 3/82 and 4/82 *Delhaize* [1983] ECR 2973, para 18; ECJ, Case 190/87 *Moorman* [1988] ECR 4689, para 17; ECJ, Case 186/88 *Commission v Germany* [1989] ECR 3997, para 17; ECJ, Joined Cases C-277/91, C-318/91 and C-319/91 *Ligur Carni* [1993] ECR I-6621, para 27; ECJ, Case C-105/94 *Celestini* [1997] ECR I-2971, para 37.

[74] DIR 2009/40/EC. For some judgments on its predecessor, former Directive 96/96/EC, see, for instance: ECJ, Case C-451/99 *Cura Anlagen* [2000] ECR I-3193, para 62; ECJ, Case C-170/07

In the pharmaceutical sector, the European legislator's main approach has always been to focus on harmonizing the procedures for market authorization and the mutual recognition of such authorizations.[75] One of the key ideas underpinning these directives is that once a product has been authorized in one Member State, it should in principle be allowed in the other Member States. Detailed procedures with specific time limits were introduced for the national authorization procedure, for the mutual recognition procedure of (previously attributed) national authorizations, and for the decentralized procedure (where no market authorization is yet available). The national authorization procedure, according to which a product can only be allowed access to a Member State's market when uniform testing procedures (as set out in Annex I of this directive) have been followed, is a clear example of how procedural rules should largely guarantee equivalent standards of the quality, safety,[76] and efficiency of a medicinal product, without in-depth harmonization of the specific product's substantive content. Uniform tests and criteria will help to avoid differences in evaluation[77] and should thus create trust in Member States' authorization decisions.[78]

In the area of diplomas, the general system of mutual recognition has caused a significant change from the previously adopted directives in this field,[79] since the general system indicates a shift away from the substantive harmonization of diploma requirements

Commission v Poland [2008] ECR I-87, para 39. For a restrictive interpretation of the mutual recognition principle due to a limited level of harmonization, see for instance: ECJ, Case C-55/93 *Van Schaik* [1994] ECR I-4837, para 22. Compare with: ECJ, Case C-393/05 *Commission v Austria* [2007] ECR I-10195, paras 47–9 and para 55.

[75] DIR 2001/82/EC; DIR 2001/83/EC. Apart from these instruments on decentralized mutual recognition procedures, reference should also be made to the centralized procedure, regulated by: REG 726/2004. This instrument was introduced with regard to a specific category of pharmaceuticals in order to overcome a number of problems that had been identified with the traditional mutual recognition procedure in the past.

[76] The ECJ has underlined that the safeguard of public health is one of the principal aims of DIR 2001/83/EC. See, for instance: ECJ, Case C-185/10 *Commission v Poland*, nyr, para 27. In this light, the ECJ has condemned a national practice which accepted the importation of equivalent medicinal products *without* a market authorization: ECJ, Case C-185/10 *Commission v Poland*, nyr, para 52.

[77] § 11 DIR 2001/83/EC.

[78] Despite some tangible results, the main problem with the mutual recognition procedure in this area is, first, that Member States—despite the directive's clear wording and objectives—re-evaluate cases and, secondly, that medicinal products that originate from other Member States and that are authorized in accordance with the directive's requirements are all too often not recognized. See, for instance: ECJ, Case C-452/06 *Synthon* [2008] ECR I-7681, para 32. European Commission, 'Review of Pharmaceutical Legislation—discussion document (final version), 22 January 2001, 4, retrievable at: <http://ec.europa.eu/enterprise/pharmaceuticals/review/doc/reviewrp_en.pdf>. One of the major problems that has been identified is the lack of clarity on the notion 'public health requirements' (i.e. the lack of substantive harmonization) which Member States are entitled to invoke under the mutual recognition procedure. Therefore, specific guidelines were developed on the definition of 'a potential serious risk to public health': Guideline on the definition of a potential serious risk to public health in the context of Articles 29(1) and 29(2) of Directive 2001/83/EC-March 2006, *O.J.* C-133, 08.06.2006, p. 5–7; Guideline on the definition of a potential serious risk to human or animal health or for the environment in the context of Articles 33(1) and 33(2) of Directive 2001/82/EC-March 2006, *O.J.* C-132, 07.06.2006, p. 32–5. The added value of these guidelines, which include an annex with specific examples, should, however, not be overestimated as the guidelines themselves recognize that these scientific guidelines give guidance for the evaluation of an application in general, but different interpretations cannot be excluded on a specific set of data.

[79] Former Council Directive 89/48/EEC of 21 December 1988 on a general system for the recognition of higher-education diplomas awarded on completion of professional education and training of at least three years' duration, *O.J.* L-19, 24.01.1989, p. 16–23; former Council Directive 92/51/EEC of 18 June 1992 on a second general system for the recognition of professional education and training to supplement Directive 89/48/EEC, *O.J.* L-209, 24.07.1992, p. 25–45, both repealed by DIR 2005/36/EC.

and instead a concentration on developing the methods and criteria a Member State is obliged to take into account when assessing and recognizing a diploma issued by another Member State. The lack of harmonization with regard to the content of the diploma requirements prevents the automatic application of the principle of mutual recognition, but the directive nevertheless facilitates the principle by creating a clear procedural framework: Member States are entitled to make the recognition conditional upon a number of clearly defined compensatory measures, but they are also required to take a reasoned decision within the fixed time limit.[80]

B. Harmonization measures and cooperation procedures for enhancing mutual trust and mutual recognition

The importance of mutual trust[81] for the success of the mutual recognition strategy, the internal market project, and the EU integration project as a whole was highlighted earlier when I described how the ECJ has elevated the principle of mutual trust to a general principle of the EU legal order.[82]

Since the very beginning, the European legislator has also heeded the central role that mutual trust must play in the overall internal market approach.[83] According to the European Commission, indeed, the single market stands or falls on trust.[84] In some policy documents, the Commission has referred in merely rhetorical phrases to the assumed level of trust existing among the Member States,[85] whereas in other documents the Commission and the European legislator have both shown more realism by emphasizing the need to develop specific trust-building measures in order to enhance the principle of mutual recognition.[86]

In what follows, I indicate that in the majority of legislative mutual recognition instruments, harmonization measures have been devised in order to enhance mutual trust and procedures have been put in place in order to smooth over any flaws in mutual trust

[80] See, in particular: Articles 14 and 51(2) Directive 2005/36/EC.

[81] In some document the term 'mutual confidence' (instead of 'mutual trust') is used. From an etymological point of view, trust and confidence refer to different aspects: F. BLOBEL and P. SPATH, 'The Tale of Multilateral Trust and the European Law of Civil Procedure', *E.L. Rev.* 2005, 536. For this study, however, I do not consider it necessary to enter at length into this difference; all the more since both the ECJ and the Commission tend to use both terms as synonyms. For the sake of consistency, I will, in what follows, only use the term 'mutual trust'.

[82] See: Part I, ch 1, II, E. 'The principle of mutual trust'.

[83] See, for instance: White Paper from the Commission to the European Council—Completing the Internal Market (n 1) p. 15 and 28; Communication from the Commission to the European Parliament and the Council—Management of the Mutual Recognition of national rules after 1992. Operational conclusions in light of the inventory drawn up pursuant to Article 100b of the EC Treaty, COM (1993) 669 final, p. 2.

[84] Communication from the Commission to the Council—Single Market Action Plan, p. 1, retrievable at: < http://ec.europa.eu/internal_market/strategy/docs/plan_en.pdf>.

[85] See, for instance, the previously mentioned 1985 White Paper in which the Commission argued that 'the objectives of national legislation are more often than not identical so that national rules should normally be accorded recognition in all Member States' or the Commission's frequent references to 'the common cultural heritage of European universities'. For a critique on such general statements, see, for instance: G. MAJONE, 'Mutual Recognition in Federal Type Systems', EUI Working Papers 1993, 15.

[86] See, for instance: Communication from the Commission to the European Parliament and the Council—Management of the Mutual Recognition of national rules after 1992. Operational conclusions in light of the inventory drawn up pursuant to Article 100b of the EC Treaty (n 83) p. 7; Communication from the Commission to the Council, the European Parliament, the European Economic and Social Committee and the Committee of the Regions—Report on the implementation of the Internal Market Strategy Priorities 2003–2006, COM (2004) 22 final, p. 12.

through dialogue and cooperation. I illustrate this with reference to various domains, namely the New Approach directives (section B, 1), the area of diplomas (section B, 2), the area of driving licences (section B, 3), and a number of other services areas (section B, 4). In some instruments, however, mutual trust is simply assumed to be present, in the absence of any common rules (section B, 5).

(1) Enhancing mutual trust and mutual recognition in the New Approach directives

Under the New Approach, a CE marking or a certificate of conformity guarantees in principle that a product is trustworthy as it means that it conforms to the (harmonized) SHEC objective(s) laid down in the corresponding directive, as well as to the specific standards that were further developed by one of the three private European Standards Organizations.[87] Provided that every link in this chain (manufacturer; conformity assessment procedure; role of the notified bodies; certification procedure) works well, the system of mutual trust and mutual recognition will be able to function smoothly. However, imported products carrying CE markings have in fact failed to comply with the safety requirements in the corresponding directive on a number of occasions,[88] sometimes resulting in severe injuries.[89] Of course, such incidents seriously jeopardize the image of reliability that the EC labelling is intended to stand for, as well as mutual trust among Member States in general.

In cases such as *Yonemoto*, *AGM-COS.MET*, and *Medipac*, the question was raised as to whether blind trust (and free movement) should dominate whenever a CE marking has been assigned or whether Member States should instead remain vigilant at all times. In other words, can the other side of the principle of mutual recognition be seen as a duty to refuse to apply this principle whenever there are signs that a product does not satisfy safety or security standards?[90]

Supported by the texts of the New Approach Directives, which systematically provide for safeguard clauses,[91] the ECJ clearly maintains that Member States are required to block a product's access to the market when a failure to meet a harmonized standard fully, or a failure to apply such a standard properly, is detected.[92] Safeguard clauses are,

[87] CEN (the European Committee for Standardization); CENELEC (the European Committee for Electrotechnical Standardization); and ETSI (the European Telecommunications Standards Institute). The basic element of the New Approach is that the directive will only define the objective, but that it will not indicate how to satisfy the objective at stake, any concrete specifications being performed by the standardized bodies. On the New Approach in the goods sector, see, for instance: G. GALLI and J. PELKMANS (eds.), *Regulatory Reform and Competitiveness in Europe I. Horizontal Issues* (Cheltenham, Edward Elgar, 2000) 245–56; LÓPEZ ESCUDERO, 'La aplicación del principio del reconocimiento mutuo en el derecho comunitario' (n 1) 143–58; J. McMILLAN, 'La certification, la reconnaissance mutuelle et le marché unique', *RMUE* 1991, 181–211; MONTI, *De interne markt en het Europa van morgen: een voortgangsrapport van de Europese Commissie* (n 1) 36–9.

[88] ECJ, Case C-470/03 *AGM-COS.MET* [2007] ECR I-2749; ECJ, Case C-6/05 *Medipac* [2007] ECR I-4557.

[89] ECJ, Case C-40/04 *Yonemoto* [2005] ECR I-7755.

[90] M. FALLON and F. MANIET, *Sécurité des produits et mécanismes du contrôle dans la communauté européenne* (Ghent, Story-Scientia, 1990) 282–3.

[91] See, for instance: Article 7 DIR 89/686/EEC; Article 8 DIR 97/23/EC; Article 9 DIR 99/5/EC; Article 9 DIR 2000/14/EC; Article 10 DIR 2004/108/EC; Article 9 DIR 2006/95/EC; Article 19 DIR 2004/22/EC. See, however, for some less explicit or more water-downed safeguard clauses: Article 9(4) DIR 94/62EC.

[92] ECJ, Case C-470/03 *AGM-COS.MET* [2007] ECR I-2749, para 62; ECJ, Case C-6/05 *Medipac* [2007] ECR I-4557, para 46.

in other words, an indication that Member States should remain vigilant rather than implementing an absolute or blind regime of trust towards other Member States. How far does this right or duty of market surveillance reach, however? Should market surveillance be considered a Member State's exclusive business? Or should it involve all market participants, such as a product's importer?

In *Yonemoto*, the ECJ struggled with this question and concluded that a Member State's duty to ensure that machinery or safety components covered by the directive are only placed on the market and put into service if they do not endanger users' health or safety cannot amount to an obligation on the importer's part to verify that the machine complies with the essential requirements laid down by the directive.[93] The free movement objective (and also, implicitly, the organized level of trust), which pervades the whole directive, would clearly be jeopardized if an importer could be held liable for the non-conformity of the machine.[94] *Yonemoto* thus clearly indicates that a market participant should, in principle, rely on and trust in the CE markings attached to the goods, in accordance with the directive. The only (*ex post*) obligation that might be imposed on the importer is a duty to cooperate with the authorities of that Member State by passing on information regarding accidents or risks, in order to ensure that similar accidents do not recur.[95]

With the likely objective of stimulating a climate of 'mutual trust', the ECJ does not in principle allow market participants to take their own measures in order to implement the safeguard clauses.[96] Such power lies, according to the safeguard procedure included in most directives, exclusively in the hands of the competent national authority. According to this procedure, the national authority is obliged to inform the Commission of the measures taken immediately so that a specific committee within the Commission can look into the case. This safeguard and cooperation procedure represents, as Reich so rightly puts it, both an active obligation on the part of the Member State concerned to protect the safety of its citizens (in accordance with this procedure) and a prohibition of action in cases where no measures from the directive's procedure have been taken.[97]

However, in some exceptional cases where strict adherence to the safeguard procedure would give rise to delays and thus seriously jeopardize public health, the ECJ seems to recognize that market participants can themselves take the interim measures required to safeguard the public health interest in light of the proportionality principle.[98]

(2) *Enhancing mutual trust and mutual recognition in the area of diplomas*

As far as the free movement of persons is concerned, the mutual recognition of diplomas is another area where both harmonization measures[99] and cooperation mechanisms have been developed in order to enhance mutual trust between Member States.

[93] ECJ, Case C-40/04 *Yonemoto* [2005] ECR I-7755, paras 46 and 53.

[94] ECJ, Case C-40/04 *Yonemoto* [2005] ECR I-7755, para 45.

[95] ECJ, Case C-40/04 *Yonemoto* [2005] ECR I-7755, para 52.

[96] See, in particular: ECJ, Case C-470/03 *AGM-COS.MET* [2007] ECR I-2749, para 70.

[97] N. REICH, 'AGM-COS.MET or: Who is Protected by EC Safety Regulation', *E.L. Rev.* 2008, 91. See, for instance, also: ECJ, Case C-132/08 *Lidl Magyarország* [2009] ECR, I-3841, para 44, where the ECJ held that: 'Where a Member State takes the view that the conformity with a harmonized standard does not guarantee compliance with the essential requirements laid down by that directive which that standard is supposed to cover, that Member State may, pursuant to Article 5 thereof, refer the matter to the committee. In the case of shortcomings of harmonized standards with respect to the essential requirements, those standards may be withdrawn *only* in accordance with the procedure set out in Article 5 of Directive 1999/5' (emphasis added).

[98] ECJ, Case C-6/05 *Medipac* [2007] ECR I-4557, paras 60–1.

[99] For an overview of different levels of harmonization in this area, see: Part I, ch 2, II, A. 'A different technical approach: substantive or procedural harmonization and mutual recognition'. See also,

According to the ECJ, mutual trust is inherent in the EU system of diploma recognition,[100] but this does not necessarily equate to an unlimited level of mutual trust. The level of trust and the corresponding duty of mutual recognition that is required in each case will depend, to a great extent, on the level of harmonization that has been obtained for the profession in question and will thus generally be higher in areas where greater harmonization has been achieved.[101] However, it would be erroneous to conclude that duties of mutual recognition are limited to situations where great harmonization—and thus great equivalence—has been achieved. Rather, it follows from the ECJ's case law that a duty of mutual recognition can also apply 'if a diploma, certificate or other evidence of formal qualification is *not necessarily substantively equivalent* in terms of the training received' (emphasis added).[102]

The regime of trust that reigns in the area of diplomas has, however, its limits. Even in the 'sectorial' directives, where a quasi-automatic mutual recognition mechanism has been established owing to extensive substantive harmonization, the trust required is not unlimited since it can be called into question whenever a Member State has, for instance, serious doubts about the authenticity of a diploma. However, a Member State may not simply refuse to recognize the diploma or document, and is instead obliged to make contact with the Member State of origin in order to request further information, such as a confirmation of authenticity. Once authenticity has been confirmed, the duty of trust will be reapplied as the Member State will be bound by such a statement unless new factors arise.[103] Just as in the goods area, a very close link therefore exists between the duty of cooperation and mutual trust.

Mutual trust also implies that Member States are not permitted to rely on prejudices. The fact that a Member State is not in favour of private teaching establishments, for example, is insufficient grounds to conclude that such institutions would be unable to provide an appropriate (equivalent) education. The directives on the mutual recognition of diplomas do indeed provide a guarantee of equivalence, and as a result, distrust arising from the mere fact that people are employed in the private sector cannot be justified.[104]

(3) *Enhancing mutual trust and mutual recognition in the area of driving licences*

In the area of mutual recognition of driving licences, an advanced level of harmonization was necessary in order to enhance mutual recognition and consequently mutual

for instance: DEFALQUE, PERTEK, STEINFELF, and VIGNERON, *Commentaire J. Mégret* (n 23) 93–145; J. PERTEK, *Diplôme et professions en Europe* (Brussels, Bruylant, 2008) 65–98.

[100] See, for instance: ECJ, Case C-110/01 *Tennah-Durez* [2003] ECR I-6239, para 69; ECJ, Case C-330/03 *Colegio de Ingenieros de Caminos, Canales y Puertos* [2006] ECR I-801, para 21.

[101] Compare for instance, in relation to DIR 2005/36/EC, Articles 13 and 14, that prescribe mutual recognition in combination with an equivalence requirement and compensatory measures, with Article 21, that imposes automatic mutual recognition.

[102] See, for instance: ECJ, Case C-421/98 *Commission v Spain* [2000] ECR I-10375, para 37; ECJ, Case C-111/12 *Ordine degli Ingegneri di Verona e Provincia and others*, nyr, para 45.

[103] ECJ, Joined Cases C-193/97 and C-194/97 *de Castro Freitas* [1998] ECR I-6747, paras 29–32; ECJ, Case C-110/01 *Tennah-Durez* [2003] ECR I-6239, paras 75–81. DIR 2005/36/EC confirms the need of a close cooperation and the need to provide each other with mutual assistance and it insists on the role of the home state to examine the veracity of the facts that are invoked (Art. 56(1) and 56(2) *in fine* DIR 2005/36/EC).

[104] ECJ, Case C-274/05 *Commission v Greece* [2008] ECR I-7969, paras 23 and 34. For a similar reasoning in the area of medical treatment and private hospitals: ECJ, Case C-444/05 *Stamatelaki* [2007] ECR I-3185, paras 36–7.

trust.[105] In this area, far-reaching harmonization has already been achieved and a clear and unconditional mutual recognition regime has been put in place that must be adhered to, in principle, without any formality. However, mutual trust can nonetheless be put on hold even in this area, and controlling activities can resume whenever a Member State becomes aware that a fundamental interest underpinning the directive is being put at risk.[106]

(4) *Enhancing mutual trust and mutual recognition in certain services sectors*

Finally, in a number of services sectors, too, the EU legislator has often emphasized the need to enhance trust through both harmonization measures and clear rules on cooperation between Member States.

For instance, the harmonization, first, of authorization procedures and prudential supervision[107] and, secondly, of cooperation measures[108] should increase trust and allow for a smoothly functioning mutual recognition mechanism in the areas covered by the relevant directives in the banking, insurance and investment sectors.

Several directives have also been issued in the areas of broadcasting and electronic commerce which prescribe clear provisions for cooperation and supervision, and which harmonize crucial elements of the relevant directive's scope.[109] Such provisions are clearly meant to enhance mutual trust among Member States. Just as in the goods area, the required level of trust is of a non-automatic nature. Indeed, the safeguard clauses contained within these directives clearly imply that—even within the harmonized field—trust (and mutual recognition) can be suspended whenever one of the explicitly mentioned public interests (justification grounds) is perceived to be in danger.[110]

(5) *Imposing mutual trust and mutual recognition in the absence of harmonization*

A number of directives (or proposals) have taken a different route, by avoiding harmonization and focusing solely on coordinating competences and enhancing cooperation

[105] § 2, 3, and 7 DIR 2006/126/EC. Prior to the coming into force of harmonization measures, the ECJ stressed in its case law the need of more harmonization in this area in order to enhance mutual recognition and mutual trust, see for instance: ECJ, Case 16/78 *Choquet* [1978] ECR 2293, para 7; ECJ, Case-193/94 *Skanavi* [1996] ECR I-929, paras 24–6.

[106] Opinion of AG Bot in Joined Cases C-329/06 and C-343/06 *Wiedemann and Funk* and C-334/06 to C-336/06 *Zerche, Schubert and Seuke* [2008] ECR I-4635, § 80–112. See also: Part I, ch 2, III. 'The Limits of the Legislative Principle of Mutual Recognition'.

[107] See, for instance, in relation to the *banking* sector: Articles 6 ff. and 56 ff. DIR 2006/48/EC. In relation to the *insurance* sector: Articles 18 and 76 ff. DIR 2009/138/EC. In relation to the *investment* sector: Articles 5 ff. and 16 ff. DIR 2004/39/EC, Article 3 ff. DIR 2006/73/EC.

[108] See, for instance, in relation to the *banking* sector: Articles 30, 31, and 42 DIR 2006/48/EC. In relation to the *insurance* sector: Article 64 ff. DIR 2009/138/EC. In relation to the *investment* sector: Articles 56–60 DIR 2004/39/EC.

[109] See, for instance, in relation to the *audiovisual media* sector: harmonization measures (Art. 5 ff. DIR 2010/13/EU) and an explicit provision for the need of close cooperation between the Member States' competent authorities (Art. 30 DIR 2010/13/EU). In relation to the *electronic commerce* sector: DIR 1999/93/EC which refers to harmonized criteria in § 20 and Annexes I and II, but which does not contain an explicit cooperation provision; or DIR 2000/31/EC, which foresees in harmonization provisions (Art. 5-14 DIR 2000/31/EC) and which has an explicit provision on cooperation (Art. 19 DIR 2000/31/EC).

[110] See, for instance, in relation to the *TV broadcasting* sector: Article 3(2) DIR 2010/13/EU. In relation to the *electronic commerce* sector: Articles 2(3)–2(5) DIR 2000/31/EC. The safeguard clauses of

between Member States' administrative and judicial authorities, while at the same time requiring a high level of mutual trust and mutual recognition.

This rare mixture, namely the imposition of a high level of trust without a guarantee of common minimum rules (which could be trust-enhancing), has faced intense opposition in relation to (the proposal of) services DIR 2006/123/EC, but can also be linked to less controversial instruments such as DIR 2001/24/CE on the reorganization and winding up of credit institutions. The preamble of this latter instrument explicitly recognizes that, owing to the difficulty of harmonizing Member States' laws and practices, it is necessary to establish Member States' mutual recognition of the measures taken by each of them to restore their authorized credit institutions.[111] In other words, rather than mutual recognition in combination with harmonization, it is mutual recognition instead of harmonization that is prevalent in this specific field.

III. The Limits of the Legislative Principle of Mutual Recognition

The preceding analysis has already revealed that it is impossible to speak of one unique principle of mutual recognition that remains constant throughout all domains and through time. Various factors, such as the sensitivity of the subject, the political atmosphere at the moment of the instrument's adoption, past experiences of a certain approach, and so on, have resulted in instruments that incorporate principles of mutual recognition of varying strengths.

The exact contours of the (legislative) principle of mutual recognition will now be determined with regard to the limits that can be deduced from the various legislative instruments and that can be categorized as follows: limits arising from the chosen harmonization approach (section III, A); limits linked to the level of control left to the host Member State (section III, B); with a special emphasis on the Member States' increased powers of control whenever mutual recognition is applied in a way that might jeopardize the free movement provisions (section III, C); and measures against fraud and/or forum shopping (section III, D).

A. Limits resulting from the chosen harmonization approach: the fine line between the Treaty's framework and the secondary legislation's framework

(1) *The starting point: the* Tedeschi *ruling*

When discussing the main limits of the judicially developed principle of mutual recognition, I began with an analysis of the Treaty-based exception grounds and the case law-based rule of reason. Following the ECJ's famous *Tedeschi* ruling, these justification grounds can no longer be invoked when EU harmonization also provides for the harmonization of the measures necessary to ensure the protection of the interest in question. The

both directives state that a Member State is obliged to contact the country of origin and the Commission *before* taking any measure, whereas in the New Approach directives (free movement of goods) such a previous step is usually not required. Other directives in the services sector do not include any safeguard clause and rely instead completely on trust and presumptions of compliance. See, for instance: Article 3 DIR 1999/93/EC.

[111] § 6 DIR 2001/24/EC.

national measure concerned must be assessed in light of the provisions of the harmonizing directive rather than those of the TFEU.[112]

However, this rule requires further clarification: only if the directive in question exhaustively and completely harmonizes the subject matter,[113] and if the directive forbids the introduction of stricter national rules, will the Member State be prevented from invoking a (Treaty-based or case law-based) justification ground. If, on the other hand, the directive in question does not harmonize a matter exhaustively or fully, or if it permits the introduction of stricter national rules, the ECJ will check the national measure against the Treaty provisions on free movement and the principle of mutual recognition incorporated therein.[114] From this perspective, the judicially developed principle of mutual recognition plays an important complementary role in the harmonized framework.

(2) *The choice between different harmonization techniques*

During the development of the internal market's legislative acquis, the European legislator switched between two principal techniques: minimum harmonization and full harmonization. Sometimes the two techniques were combined, and sometimes one was substituted for the other.[115] When the principle of mutual recognition was launched, however, it was minimum harmonization in particular that was promoted by the Commission.[116] While full harmonization measures continue to appeal in some areas,[117]

[112] See, for instance: ECJ, Case 5/77 *Tedeschi* [1977] ECR 1555, para 35; ECJ, Case C-257/06 *Roby Profumi* [2008] ECR I-189, para 14; ECJ, Case C-445/06 *Danske Slagterrier* [2009] ECR I-2119, para 25; ECJ, Case C-205/07 *Gysbrechts* [2008] ECR I-9947, para 33.

[113] On the conceptual difference between *exhaustive* harmonization (which implies a study of the objective(s) of the directive in order to check whether the directive exhaustively covers the subject matter) and *full* (or *complete*) harmonization (which refers to a harmonization technique whereby the directive leaves the Member States—safeguard clauses left aside—no margin to apply more severe norms), see: Y. HOFHUIS, *Minimumharmonisatie* (Deventer, Kluwer, 2006) 17; P.J. SLOT and G. STRAETMANS, 'Harmonisatie van wetgeving in de EG', *Tijdschrift Privaat Recht* 2003, 740–2. Both authors suggest, however, that the difference between both concepts should not be overemphasized as even in the ECJ's case law both concepts get mixed up from time to time, see for instance: ECJ, Case C-169/89 *Gourmetterie Van den Burg* [1990] ECR I-2143, para 9; ECJ, Case C-374/05 *Gintec* [2007] ECR I-9517, paras 29 and 34. See also: C. BARNARD, *The Substantive Law of the EU. The Four Freedoms* (Oxford, Oxford University Press, 2010) 626; DEFALQUE, PERTEK, STEINFELF, and VIGNERON, *Commentaire J. Mégret* (n 23) 254, who treat the concepts 'full harmonization' and 'exhaustive harmonization' as synonyms. Exhaustive harmonization is, however not exclusively linked to full harmonization, but can go hand in hand with minimum harmonization. This is clearly demonstrated in *Compassion in World Farming*: ECJ, Case C-1/96 *Compassion in World Farming* [1998] ECR I-1251, para 56, where the ECJ concluded that in adopting the directive the European legislator had laid down *exhaustively* common *minimum* standards.

[114] See, for instance: ECJ, Case C-389/96 *Aher-Wagon* [1998] ECR I-4473, para 16.

[115] For an overview of the different harmonization techniques and some examples, see, for instance: A. MATTERA, 'L'harmonisation des législations nationales: un instrument d'intégration et de reconnaissance mutuelle', *RDUE* 2010, 710; SLOT and STRAETMANS, 'Harmonisatie van wetgeving in de EG' (n 113) 720–39.

[116] Communication from the Commission to the European Parliament and the Council—Reinforcing the Effectiveness of the Internal Market (n 3) p. 4 and 21.

[117] Full harmonization can, for example, be found in DIR 2001/83/EC, interpreted by the ECJ in Case C-84/06 *Antroposana* [2007] ECR I-7609, paras 40–2. Recently, full harmonization has regained its place in the area of consumer protection. See, for instance, DIR 2008/48/EC and the analysis of the HOUSE OF LORDS, EU COMMITTEE, Consumer Credit in the EU: Harmonization and Consumer Protection (n 18) 70–100. See also: HOFHUIS, *Minimumharmonisatie* (n 113) 13–16; N. REICH, 'Wie vollständig ist die geplante Vollständige Harmonisierung im Verbrauchersrecht', *EuZW* 2008, 1; SLOT and STRAETMANS, 'Harmonisatie van wetgeving in de EG' (n 113) 723.

the majority of the internal market's legislative instruments are currently based on the minimum harmonization approach.[118]

Under the full harmonization approach, uniform rules are developed that leave Member States without any margin to act. This will, of course, be beneficial to the internal market's free movement policy, since problems of recognition are unlikely to arise if only one norm exists for the entire EU.[119]

Under a minimum harmonization approach, the common European norm represents the minimum level of protection available for the public interest, leaving the Member States free to prescribe higher norms in their national legislations. The application of stricter national norms for national products is a manifestation of the fully accepted situation of reverse discrimination within the EU.[120]

However, if a Member State decides to apply these stricter standards to goods originating from other Member States, it will become clear that there are limits to its discretionary power. This is because the national measure will be subject to the (judicially developed) principle of mutual recognition and its corresponding limits, i.e. the TFEU exceptions and the rule of reason.[121] The exact contours of a Member State's residual power in this context must be determined for each specific instrument in terms of the instrument's context, nature, content and aims.[122]

Not infrequently, explicit free movement clauses are set out in the internal market's directives in order to facilitate the internal market.[123] Such clauses limit the Member States' discretionary powers by counterbalancing their right to set higher norms in their national legislation with a duty to recognize goods or services originating from other Member States insofar as these goods or services are in line with the directive's minimum standards.[124] The national measure in question which goes beyond the minimum harmonization provision will then be examined in light of the TFEU framework and/or the rule of reason.[125]

Similarly, a Member State's margin to act can also be restricted by the presence of provisions which explicitly state that Member States are allowed to maintain or apply stricter provisions only within their own territories.[126] Conversely, in the absence of such

[118] For an evaluation of both harmonization approaches, see, for instance: W. DEVROE, 'Limits of Differentiation in European Economic Law: *ne bis in idem* and Minimum versus Maximum Harmonization', *MJ* 2009, 141–8; M. FAURE, 'Towards a Maximum Harmonisation of Consumer Contract Law?', *MJ* 2008, 433–45.

[119] See, however, SER, 'Advies 2004/06. Oneerlijke handelspraktijken op consumententerrein in de EU', 49, retrievable at: <http://www.ser.nl/nl/publicaties/adviezen/2000-2007/2004/b22670.aspx>, in which it is held that—occasionally—problems can arise, for instance, in case of non-implementation or bad implementation of the corresponding norm. See also: HOUSE OF LORDS, EU COMMITTEE, Consumer Credit in the EU (n 18) 32. In this report attention is drawn to the fact that also other elements—which are *not* related to harmonization—can hamper the mutual recognition principle, e.g. linguistic or cultural factors.

[120] ECJ, Case C-11/92 *Gallaher* [1993] ECR I-3545, para 22.

[121] ECJ, Case C-389/96 *Aher Waggon* [1998] ECR I-4473, paras 15–16; ECJ, Case C-322/01 *Deutscher Apothekerverband* [2003] ECR I-14887, paras 64–5.

[122] ECJ, Case C-324/99 *DaimlerChrysler* [2001] ECR I-9897, paras 32–42.

[123] On the link between free movement clauses and the requirement that the legislation in question must be adopted for the purpose of facilitating the internal market (Art. 114 TFEU), see, for instance: ECJ, Case C-376/98 *Germany v Parliament and Council* [2000] ECR I-2247, paras 102–5; ECJ, Case C-380/03 *Germany v Parliament and Council* [2006] ECR I-11573, paras 73–8.

[124] See, for instance: Article 5 in combination with Article 18 DIR 94/62/EC.

[125] See, for example: ECJ, Case C-309/02 *Radlberger* [2004] ECR I-11763, para 58; ECJ, Case C-322/01 *Deutscher Apothekerverband* [2003] I-14887, para 64.

[126] ECJ, Case C-1/96 *Compassion in World Farming* [1998] ECR I-1251, para 59.

clauses, Member States are allowed to apply their more stringent national standards to products or services originating from other Member States, providing such an approach is in accordance with the *ratio legis* of the instrument concerned as well as with the general rules of the TFEU framework (in particular, justification grounds, rule of reason and proportionality check).[127]

The ultimate means for a Member State to maintain stricter standards than those provided in the instrument in question and to set aside the principle of mutual recognition is described in Articles 114(4) and 114(5) TFEU. However, owing to its harshness and its demanding conditions, this procedure has rarely been applied in practice.[128]

(3) *In pursuit of the correct framework for evaluating Member States' residual power in cases of minimum harmonization*

Whenever a Member State acts upon its residual power to justify a national measure which might jeopardize the principle of mutual recognition, the question arises as to whether the invoked justification ground(s) should be analysed within the framework of the TFEU exceptions and the rule of reason (judicial justification grounds) or within the framework of the legislative instrument concerned (legislative justification grounds). Despite the clarification provided by the *Tedeschi* ruling, the line between the two frameworks is not always so clear-cut in practice. Some directives adopt a mix of the harmonization techniques; others select an exhaustive approach while leaving certain crucial elements undefined; and finally, in some cases, the national measure aims at protecting an interest which is not covered by the exhaustive harmonization. Consequently, the ECJ finds itself obliged in many judgments to evaluate a national measure in light of the Treaty framework, despite the fact that a directive is available.[129]

The crucial question of whether a matter has been harmonized enough to rule out the Treaty framework and, consequently, to accept the legislative instrument as the only relevant framework, remains difficult. It is a question that the ECJ has not always been eager to answer,[130] especially since many directives make no clear mention of the extent to which a specific interest covered by the directive's coordinated field has been harmonized.[131] Furthermore, in some (recent) legislative instruments, such as DIR 2000/31/EC and DIR 2006/123/EC, the European legislator seems to have imposed the more restrictive legislative instrument's framework of justification grounds despite the fact that the matter in question has not yet been exhaustively harmonized.[132] Such

[127] ECJ, Case C-389/96 *Aher Waggon* [1998] ECR I-4473. See, in particular, the corresponding Opinion of AG Cosmas, § 13.

[128] BARNARD, *The Substantive Law of the EU. The Four Freedoms* (n 113) 620–3.

[129] See, for instance: ECJ, Case C-51/94 *Commission v Germany* [1995] ECR I-3599, paras 33 and 41; ECJ, Case C-1/96 *Compassion in World Farming* [1998] ECR I-1251, para 65; ECJ, Case C-220/98 *Estée Lauder* [2000] ECR I-117, paras 23–32; ECJ, Case C-3/99 *Cidrerie Ruwet* [2000] ECR I-8749, para 57; ECJ, Case C-14/00 *Commission v Italy* [2003] ECR I-513, para 67 ff.; ECJ, Case C-463/01 *Commission v Germany* [2004] ECR I-11705, paras 44–5; ECJ, Case C-147/04 *De Groot* [2006] ECR I-248, para 80; ECJ, Case C-319/05 *Commission v Germany* [2007] ECR I-9811, para 97.

[130] See, for instance: ECJ, Case C-11/95 *Commission v Belgium* [1996] ECR I-4115, para 55, where the ECJ decided that it had not been demonstrated that the national system of prior authorization was necessary and proportionate, without first having checked whether either the directive or the treaty was the relevant framework (i.e. the question of whether the matter was exhaustively regulated).

[131] This leads on occasions to opposing views between the ECJ and its AG. See, for instance: ECJ, Case C-1/96 *Compassion in World Farming* [1998] ECR I-1251; ECJ, Case C-5/94 *Hedley Lomas* [1996] ECR I-2553.

[132] See, for instance: Article 3(4) DIR 2000/31/EC or Article16(1)(b) DIR 2006/123/EC. For a critique on this legislative approach, see the authors mentioned in footnotes 11, 48, and 52.

an approach, which combines the wide scope of the legislative instrument with little harmonization and only a limited number of justification grounds, seems to undermine the traditional *Tedeschi* approach and might lead to an expansive principle of mutual recognition which is not compensated for by the necessary harmonization measures. It is unclear whether the ECJ will prove entirely willing to accept this (new) legislative approach in its case law.[133]

The presence of a directive does not always lead necessarily to a more expansive principle of mutual recognition. Occasionally, the ECJ is asked to interpret the directive in light of the general principles of EU law, such as the protection of fundamental rights, international norms, or the abuse of law theory.[134] While such principles and norms are not always explicitly mentioned in the directive concerned, they clearly play a pivotal role in the directive's interpretation and might, on occasions, effect an extension of the available limits of the principle of mutual recognition.

In relation to the protection of fundamental rights, in particular, a number of distinguished authors seem convinced that an explicit reference in a directive's preamble has added value or might somehow reinforce the weight of certain justification grounds.[135] It is a fact that some directives mention the protection of fundamental rights explicitly in their preamble whereas others do not mention it at all. In my opinion, such an explicit reference is understandable in cases where a specific directive aims to concretize a specific fundamental right,[136] for example, whereas it seems less relevant to mention it in the preamble of a directive where no specific fundamental right is under discussion.[137] Such references seem completely redundant from a legal point of view, as they simply repeat the duty of primary EU law.

B. Limits linked to the level of control left to the host Member State

When interpreted absolutely, the principle of mutual trust and recognition (which requires Member States to trust in the acts or controls performed in other Member States

[133] See, for instance: ECJ, Case 304/84 *Muller* [1986] ECR 1511, para 14; ECJ, Case C-244/06 *Dynamic Medien* [2008] ECR I-505, paras 22–3 (where the ECJ ruled out the application of the directive's framework and analysed the measures in light of the Treaty provisions). See also: Opinion of AG Mengozzi in Case C-244/06 *Dynamic Medien* [2008] ECR I-505, § 23–34. AG Mengozzi seemed to go in search of the *Tedeshi* rule where he stated in § 23 that 'Whilst it is acknowledged that the sale of goods via the internet constitutes an "information society service" within the meaning of the electronic commerce directive and that a domestic rule such as the prohibition of mail order sales falls within the "coordinated field" of the directive, I have not been able to ascertain, which specific provision in the directive in question may have implemented the exhaustive harmonization of domestic legislation on the protection of young persons in connection with mail order sales of goods via the internet that would preclude verification of the compatibility of the prohibition with [old] Articles 28 EC and 30 EC'.

[134] See, for instance: ECJ, Case C-1/96 *Compassion in World Farming* [1998] ECR I-1251, paras 30–7; ECJ, Case C-245/01 *RTL Television* [2003] ECR I-12489, paras 67–73; ECJ, Case C-470/03 *AGM-COS.MET* [2007] ECR I-2749, para 72; ECJ, Case C-275/06 *Promusicae* [2008] ECR I-271, paras 62–8; ECJ, Case C-450/06 *Varec* [2008] ECR I-581, paras 44–55.

[135] Some authors seem, however, convinced that the Services Directive *should* have explicitly mentioned the protection of fundamental rights as enshrined in the Charter: DE SCHUTTER and FRANCK, 'La proposition de directive relative aux services dans le marché intérieur: reconnaissance mutuelle, harmonisation et conflits de lois dans l'Europe élargie' (n 20) 619–20.

[136] See, for instance: § 16 DIR 2010/13/EU, which refers to the freedom of expression.

[137] See, for instance: § 15 DIR 2006/123/EC which states that 'the directive respects the fundamental rights as guaranteed in the Charter of Fundamental Rights of the EU'.

and to recognize them) and the country of origin principle (which assigns responsibility for the controlling activities related to the scope of most services directives to the country of origin) would appear to suggest a lack of control on the part of the host state. I have already indicated, however, that this absolute character can be attributed neither to the principles of mutual recognition or mutual trust nor to the country of origin principle.

The country of origin principle, which is included in most directives in the services area, is manifested in a variety of forms and so are the controlling mechanisms left to the host Member State. The clear wording in some directives 'that the supervision shall be the *sole* responsibility of the home Member State' (emphasis added) is less pronounced in other directives.[138] Furthermore, the purportedly exclusive power of the country of origin should also be put into perspective by the omnipresence of duties of cooperation between Member States.[139]

With regard to the ECJ's case law on (harmonized) mutual recognition, a similar conclusion can be drawn. Even in those areas where a high degree of harmonization has been achieved, Member States are still entitled to be vigilant and to react whenever they have reasons to do so, in other words; no blind regime of mutual trust applies (section B, 1). However, they are limited in their behaviour in that they may only act in cooperation with the Member State of origin, and, if no agreement can be reached, the dispute might have to be settled by a committee set up by EU law (section B, 2). Moreover, the ECJ seems less than eager to allow a Member State any extraterritorial controlling powers (section B, 3).

(1) No automatic or blind regime: Member States can act if a risk emerges

The degree of automatism that is to be attributed to the principle of mutual recognition depends to a large extent on the level of harmonization achieved. However, the ECJ has granted some control to the host Member State, even with regard to those instruments exhibiting an advanced level of harmonization and what appears to be a quasi-automatic mutual recognition mechanism which leaves other Member States hardly any margin to act.

A clear example in this regard is DIR 2006/126/EC (and its predecessor Directive 91/439/EEC). In the early years of its case law on driving licences, the ECJ repeatedly maintained that this directive provided for a regime of mutual recognition without formality, which imposed a precise and unconditional obligation and left the host Member State with no option but to accept the driving licence issued in another Member State.[140] The ECJ also referred repeatedly, in these older judgments, to its settled case law, according to which 'the provisions of a directive which derogate from a general principle established by that directive (*in casu*, free movement) must be strictly interpreted'. Yet, in other judgments on driving licences, a somewhat different focus was noticeable as the ECJ, rather than emphasizing solely that restrictions must be

[138] Article 30 DIR 2009/138/EC is one of the few directives that stipulates this explicitly. In other directives some supervision tasks are explicitly left in hands of the host Member State, see, for instance: § 32, Article 32(7), Article 32(8), Article 61, and Article 62 DIR 2004/39/EC; or: Articles 41–3 DIR 2006/48/EC.

[139] See, for instance: Article 18 DIR 2004/22/EC; Article 10 DIR 2001/95/EC; Articles 30–3 DIR 2006/48/EC; Articles 56–60 DIR 2004/39/EC; Article 19 DIR 2000/31/EC.

[140] ECJ, Case-193/94 *Skanavi* [1996] ECR I-929, para 26; ECJ, Case C-230/97 *Awoyemi* [1998] ECR I-6781, para 41; ECJ, Case C-476/01 *Kapper* [2004] ECR I-5205, paras 45–6.

interpreted restrictively,[141] also stressed that 'Directive 91/439/EEC [was] intended to strike a *balance* between the principle of mutual recognition [...] and the directive's objective of improving road safety [...]' (emphasis added).[142] This implied that the directive had not one but two objectives, of equal importance.[143] In this alternative line of case law, the ECJ—supported by both textual[144] and teleological[145] arguments—accepted that a host Member State, when in serious doubt about the accuracy or validity of a driving licence, is entitled to verify, albeit in close cooperation with the issuing Member State, whether the driving licence in question is in full compliance with the directive's provisions and objectives and is also, under certain conditions, entitled not to recognize the foreign driving licence.[146] Admittedly, the Member State's controlling powers are limited, since it is forbidden to begin inquiries into the validity of just any driving licence on its own initiative, yet it *may*,[147] whenever objective elements are present, make contact with other Member States in order to ask for clarification of presumed irregularities. It could be argued that such an interpretation deprives the principle of mutual recognition of its usual and traditional (automatic) application in this specific context of driving licences, but then again, both the provisions included in DIR 2006/126/EC and the directive's underlying objectives provide a full assertion that a situation of (potential) fraud eliminates mutual confidence and restores the Member States' controlling powers. Furthermore, according to the logic of the principle of mutual recognition as included in this directive, it is not only the decision of a competent

[141] See, for instance: ECJ, Joined Cases C-329/06 and C-343/06 *Wiedemann and Funk* [2008] ECR I-4635, para 60; ECJ, Joined Cases, C-334/06 to C-336/06 *Zerche* [2008] ECR I-4691, para 57; ECJ, Case C-1-07 *Weber* [2008] ECR I-8571, para 29; ECJ, Case C-321/07 *Schwarz* [2009] ECR I-1113, para 84; ECJ, Case C-419/10 *Hofmann*, nyr, para 71.

[142] ECJ, Case C-321/07 *Schwarz* [2009] ECR I-1113, para 90.

[143] M. MÖSTL, 'Preconditions and Limits of Mutual Recognition', *CML Rev.* 2010, 417. Möstl's suggestion that both objectives are of equal importance is perfectly defensible, but unfortunately, difficult to reconcile with the ECJ's statement 'that any exceptions to the principle of mutual recognition which are aimed at balancing this principle with road safety objectives must be interpreted restrictively as any broad interpretation would completely undermine the principle of mutual recognition': ECJ, Case C-445/08 *Wierer* [2009] ECR I-119, para 52; ECJ, Case C-334/09 *Scheffer* [2010] ECR I-12379, para 63.

[144] See, in particular: Article 3 DIR 2006/126/EC, which imposes a duty on the Member States to take all necessary steps to avoid any risk of forgery of driving licences; Article 7(5)(c) DIR 2006/126/EC, which urges Member States to take the necessary measures and to verify with other Member States whenever there are reasonable grounds to suspect that the applicant is already the holder of another driving licence; Article 11(4) DIR 2006/126/EC, which states that a Member State shall refuse to issue a driving licence to an applicant whose driving licence is restricted, suspended, or withdrawn in another Member State (and thus implicitly requires them to be vigilant!) and Article 15 DIR 2006/126/EC, which installs a duty of mutual assistance between the Member States, i.e. a duty of exchange of information on the issuing, exchanging, replacing, renewing, and revoking of driving licences.

[145] If mutual recognition were to prevail, despite the aspect of fraud, the main objective of the directive, i.e. road security, would be seriously jeopardized. See, for instance: Opinion of AG Bott in Joined Cases C-329/06 and C-343/06 *Wiedemann and Funk* and Joined Cases C-334/06 to C-336/06 *Zerche, Schubert and Seuke* [2008] ECR I-4635, § 80–5.

[146] The ECJ accepted, for instance, that there was no duty of mutual recognition in: ECJ, Joined Cases C-329/06 and C-343/06 *Wiedemann and Funk* [2008] ECR I-4635; ECJ, Joined Cases, C-334/06 to C-336/06 *Zerche Schubert and Seuke* [2008] ECR I-4691; ECJ, Case C-1-07 *Weber* [2008] ECR I-8571; ECJ, Case C-225/07 *Möginger* [2009] ECR I-103; ECJ, Case C-321/07 *Schwarz* [2009] ECR I-1113; whereas it imposed a duty of mutual recognition in: ECJ, Case C-227/05 *Halbritter* [2006] ECR I-49; ECJ, Case C-340/05 *Kremer* [2006] ECR I-98; ECJ, Case C-445/08 *Wierer* [2009] ECR I-119; ECJ, Case C-334/09 *Scheffer*, nyr.

[147] The ECJ has firmly rejected the existence of an absolute obligation for the competent authorities to consult each other and to verify systematically whether the reasons which led to the previous withdrawal of a driving licence have disappeared: ECJ, Case C-419/10 *Hofmann*, nyr, para 82.

issuing authority that should be subject to mutual recognition: the decision of a competent Member State to revoke a driving licence may also deserve recognition from other Member States.[148] This indicates the necessity of a certain margin of control on the part of the host state.

The non-automatic nature of the principle of mutual recognition, combined with a margin of discretion for the host Member States in checking the validity of documents, can also be found in the social security area, especially in relation to the application of REG 1408/71 and what is referred to as the E-101 certificate. The ECJ's point of departure in this context is also a presumption of trust: an E-101 establishes the presumption that posted workers are properly affiliated with the social security system of the Member State in which the business is established, and that the certificate is recognized by the competent institution of the Member State in which the workers are posted.[149] A host Member State is bound by an E-101 certificate providing it is not withdrawn or declared invalid by the competent authority of the Member State of origin.[150] This recognition, however, is not based on an assumption of blind or automatic trust, since it relies on the competent institution of the Member State issuing the E-101 to reconsider the grounds for its issue and, if necessary, to withdraw the certificate if the competent institution of the Member State in which the workers are posted expresses doubts as to the correctness of the facts on which the certificate is based.[151]

Explicit safeguard measures and controlling mechanisms are built into the New Approach directives, which reveals the legislator's reluctance to grant too wide a margin of automatism to the principle of mutual recognition. Remarkably, this is the case not only in areas where the scope of harmonization is quite limited, but also in harmonized areas where equivalence has been established at least theoretically.

A certain amount of older case law that deals with the health inspections performed by the Member State of destination and their (in)compatibility with the principle of mutual recognition and mutual trust suggests that Member States are permitted to perform some marginal controls through occasional checks. The starting point that underlies this secondary legislation is a duty to take into account the checks carried out in the Member State of origin, i.e. a duty of trust. Spot check controls, however, are allowed in properly justified circumstances, i.e. whenever there are serious reasons to believe that the directive has not been complied with or when there is a reasonable presumption of irregularity.[152]

In other areas of law, too, the ECJ has demonstrated similar reasoning: host Member States are in principle bound by the declarations contained in a certificate and may not call into question the accuracy of the particulars provided therein, but when serious

[148] Opinion of AG Bott in Joined Cases C-329/06 and C-343/06 *Wiedemann and Funk* and Joined Cases C-334/06 to C-336/06 *Zerche, Schubert and Seuke* [2008] ECR I-4635, § 83; MÖSTL, 'Preconditions and Limits of Mutual Recognition' (n 143) 429.

[149] ECJ, Case C-202/97 *FTS* [2000] ECR I-883, para 53; ECJ, Case C-178/97 *Banks and Others* [2000] ECR I-2005, para 40; ECJ, Case C-2/05 *Herbosch Kiere* [2006] ECR I-1079, para 24.

[150] ECJ, Case C-202/97 *FTS* [2000] ECR I-883, paras 53–5; ECJ, Case C-178/97 *Banks and Others* [2000] ECR I-2005, paras 40–2; ECJ, Case C-2/05 *Herbosch Kiere* [2006] ECR I-1079, paras 24–6.

[151] ECJ, Case C-202/97 *FTS* [2000] ECR I-883, para 56; ECJ, Case C-178/97 *Banks and Others* [2000] ECR I-2005, para 43; ECJ, Case C-2/05 *Herbosch Kiere* [2006] ECR I-1079, para 27.

[152] ECJ, Case 35/76 *Simmenthal* [1976] ECR 1871, para 20; ECJ, Joined Cases 2/82, 3/82 and 4/82 *Delhaize* [1983] ECR 2973, paras 11–13; ECJ, Case 190/87 *Moorman* [1988] ECR 4689, paras 12–13; ECJ, Case 186/88 *Commission v Germany* [1989] ECR 3997, para 9; ECJ, Joined Cases C-277/91, C-318/91 and C-319/91 *Liguri Carni* [1993] ECR I-6621, para 25; ECJ, Case C-426/92, *Deutsches Milch-Kontor* [1994] ECR I-2757, para 23; ECJ, Case C-249/92 *Commission v Italy* [1994] ECR I-4311, paras 20–1; ECJ, Case C-105/94, *Celestini* [1997] ECR I-2971, paras 34–7.

doubts arise or when objective factors lead the host Member State to conclude that the certificate contains obvious inaccuracies, the presumption of trust can be suspended.[153] In *Tennah-Durez*, the ECJ ultimately accepted that this reasoning was not limited to the specific areas of law under consideration but that it also gave expression to a more general principle which can be applied in other areas of EU law.[154] Generally, the legislative framework grants the host Member State no discretion of its own as regards the substance of a certificate, being entitled to perform only a summary check of the certificate's formal elements.[155]

(2) *Clarifying doubts or inaccuracies through mutual cooperation and interventions by the Commission and the centralized committees set up by EU law*

The next issue that needs to be addressed is what a host Member State can do when it is confronted with (presumed) irregularities in a document issued in another Member State. In particular, I discuss whether it can decide—on its own authority—not to recognize the document or whether it is required to contact the home Member State, the Commission, or any other body or committee prior to taking a decision. The answer to this question logically depends upon the procedural framework that has been set up by the corresponding secondary legislation. Sometimes it will be the Commission's task to solve disputes via a binding dispute settlement procedure, but in the absence of such a provision it will be the Member States' responsibility either to contact each other in order to solve a dispute or to submit the dispute to the committee established by the legal instrument in question.[156]

However, a number of general guidelines can be deduced from the overall approach. Only occasionally has the ECJ accepted that a host state is not bound by a document issued by another Member State without any obligation[157] on the part of the host state to contact the home state before deciding not to recognize the document. This margin of discretion is presumably only available on very limited occasions, namely when compelling evidence erases any doubt as to the invalidity of the document in question.[158] The point of departure in most directives and in the majority of the ECJ's case law seems instead to be a duty to begin a process of cooperation that will allow the home Member

[153] ECJ, Case 130/88 *Van de Bijl* [1989] ECR 3039, paras 22–4 and the corresponding Opinion of AG Darmon at § 14–16, who is only willing to accept 'a material error or intrinsic defect in the certificate, i.e. a patent flaw in the certificate which is revealed on first examination'; ECJ, Joined Cases C-193/97 and C-194/97 *de Castro Freitas* [1998] ECR I-6747, para 30; ECJ, Case C-110/01 *Tennah-Durez* [2003] ECR I-6239, paras 75–8; Opinion of AG Geelhoed in Case C-156/04 *Commission v Hellenic Republic* [2007] ECR I-4129, § 28, who speaks in the context of taxation of 'a reasonable doubt raised by objective facts'.

[154] ECJ, Case C-110/01 *Tennah-Durez* [2003] ECR I-6239, para 80.

[155] See, for instance, the *WISAG* judgment where the ECJ held in the context of procedures for the award of public works contracts that 'it may thus check only the authenticity of the certificates, whether they were established on a sufficiently recent date and whether the authority which issued them manifestly lacked the power to do so': ECJ, Case C-74/09 *WISAG* [2010] ECR I-7271, para 64.

[156] For some examples, see, for instance: KEESSEN, *European Administrative Decisions. How the EU Regulates Products on the Internal Market* (n 57) 38–40, 53–5, 63–4, 73–4, and 77–8.

[157] ECJ, Case 130/88 *Van de Bijl* [1989] ECR 3039, para 24.

[158] For instance, in *Van de Bijl*, cited in the preceding footnote, the ECJ accepted that the host state was not bound by a certificate when it was established that a person had completed a period of insurance or employment in the host Member State during the period of professional experience which, according to the certificate, the person had completed in the home Member State (at para 25). In *Wiedemann and Funk* it accepted that a Member State was not under a duty to recognize a foreign driving licence when

State to re-examine the document and to withdraw or rectify it where necessary.[159] This cooperation mechanism must also be applied whenever new factors come to light which give rise to serious doubts as to the authenticity of a certificate. Thus, as in the judicial context but also supported by a legislative framework, the ECJ emphasizes the crucial roles of cooperation, mutual assistance, and exchange of information between Member States in order to enhance mutual trust and improve the function of the mutual recognition mechanism.[160]

The next question that arises is what a Member State can do if the mutual cooperation system does not work as it should, e.g. if a Member State fails to respond to an allegation of irregularity. Are there any alternative paths to the last resort of the Treaty infringement provisions? In the social security sector, the ECJ has made clear that even when the Member State of origin does not react to claims made by the host Member State as regards an E-101 certificate, the latter is not entitled to stop recognizing the certificate.[161] Nor is the competent authority allowed to start proceedings in the host state's national court to investigate the validity of the E-101 certificate.[162] When the competent authorities of the two Member States fail to reach an agreement, the only possible solution appears to be to refer to an administrative commission. Then, if this administrative commission does not succeed in its task, infringement proceedings may be begun under Article 259 TFEU.[163]

The setting up of specialized EU committees whose task is to deal with problems of mutual recognition and/or to ensure a central role for the Commission in circumstances where certain objectives are deemed at risk is a technique also found in several New Approach directives and in many of the other areas of law discussed in section II of this chapter. Creating specialized committees at EU level which settle disputes arising from safeguard clauses serves to rule out the risk of national authorities' producing divergent assessments. Furthermore, because of the joint approach, the establishment of a consultation and arbitration procedure at EU level is likely to be better positioned to re-establish trust among Member States when necessary.

(3) *Controlling activities in an extraterritorial context*

An interesting point for analysis is whether a Member State's controlling powers can be applied extraterritorially. I have already concluded that the ECJ and its AGs have

it was possible to determine—not in light of information supplied by the host Member State but on the basis of entries appearing in the driving licence itself or of other incontestable information supplied by the home Member State—that the condition of residence laid down by the directive had not been satisfied when that licence was issued: ECJ, Joined Cases C-329/06 and C-343/06 *Wiedemann and Funk* [2008] ECR I-4635, para 72. On the quasi-incontestable nature of the information supplied by the competent issuing authority in this context, see also: Opinion of AG Bot, Case C-184/10 *Grasser* [2011] ECR I-4057, § 39–41.

[159] See, for instance: ECJ, Case C-110/01 *Tennah-Durez* [2003] ECR I-6239, para 78; ECJ Case C-484/10 *Ascafor*, nyr, para 68, where the ECJ underlined the need for an active attitude on the part of the national authority.

[160] The ECJ referred, for instance, explicitly to the mutual assistance mechanisms laid down in secondary legislation in: ECJ, Case C-105/95 *Daut* [1997] ECR I-1877, paras 25–7. See also, on the need of exchange of information as a useful tool for enhancing mutual trust: Communication from the Commission to the Council and the European Parliament: Enhancing the Implementation of the New Approach Directives, COM (2003) 240 final, p. 6–12 and p. 14.

[161] ECJ, Case C-178/97 *Banks and Others* [2000] ECR I-2005, para 47.

[162] ECJ, Case C-2/05 *Herbosch Kiere* [2006] ECR I-1079, paras 30–2.

[163] ECJ, Case C-202/97 *FTS* [2000] ECR I-883, paras 57–8; ECJ, Case C-178/97 *Banks and Others* [2000] ECR I-2005, paras 44–5; ECJ, Case C-2/05 *Herbosch Kiere* [2006] ECR I-1079, paras 28–9. For

adopted a rather prudent approach to the extraterritorial application of Treaty-based or case law-based justification grounds in contexts that have not been harmonized completely. Now, I analyse whether this reticence is also evident in harmonized contexts. In other words, following exhaustive (minimum) harmonization, to what extent is a Member State entitled to invoke justification grounds either to protect a value which would—according to its own national legislation—come under threat in another Member State (section 3.1) or to react to another Member State's presumed misapplication of a harmonized EU standard (section 3.2)?

3.1. Protecting a public interest under threat in another Member State

As previously mentioned, many directives which provide for minimum harmonization and allow Member States to adopt stricter protective measures are accompanied by an explicit territorial restriction provision, according to which Member States may maintain or apply stricter provisions only within their territories. It is not surprising that the ECJ, when faced with such a territorial limitation clause, for instance in *Compassion in World Farming*, refuses to permit the extraterritorial application of the corresponding measure.[164] The ECJ's answer is nothing more and nothing less than a literal application of the directive's provision. However, it should not necessarily be interpreted as a general and absolute prohibition of extraterritorial applications.[165]

In cases dealing with directives in which the minimum clause does not explicitly include a territorial restriction, the ECJ's attitude towards the extraterritorial application of more severe national norms appears to be less pronounced. A number of authors seem to believe that in *Gourmetterie Van den Burg*, a case which dealt with the protection of bird species, the ECJ concluded that if a minimum clause does not explicitly include a territorial restriction, Member States may take stricter protective measures only within their own territory,[166] thus excluding extraterritorial application. I have doubts as to whether such a statement can indeed be inferred from this judgment. In my view, in *Gourmetterie Van den Burg*, the ECJ seemed to draw a crucial distinction between bird species for which the extraterritorial application of stricter protective measures was not authorized and endangered birds for which extraterritorial application was permitted.[167] It should be noted that the ECJ justified this distinction by referring to the general objectives laid out in the directive in question.[168] This suggests that in other cases, a study of the directive's objectives will also prove crucial in judging the validity of extraterritorial application.

Other judgments in which the ECJ appeared not to reject extraterritorial application out of hand include the *Werner and Leifer* cases, which dealt with the export to third countries at war of dual-use goods and products capable of being used for military purposes. The applicable regulation had laid down common rules for export

a critique on the lack of efficiency of this administrative commission, the few realistic perspectives that a Member State will start itself infringement proceedings based on Article 259 TFEU, and the alarming lack of controlling mechanisms in the host Member State, see: H. VERSCHUEREN, 'Sociale zekerheid en detachering binnen de Europese Unie. De zaak Herbosch Kiere: een gemiste kans in de strijd tegen grensoverschrijdende sociale dumping en sociale fraude', *B.T.S.Z.* 2006, 435–7 and 444.

[164] See, for instance: ECJ, Case C-1/96, *Compassion in World Farming* [1998] ECR I-1251, paras 59–60.

[165] SLOT and STRAETMANS 'Harmonisatie van wetgeving in de EG' (n 113). See, however: M. DOUGAN, 'Minimum Harmonization and the Internal Market', *CML Rev.* 2000, 878, who deduces from the ECJ's case law a general prohibition on an extraterritorial application of Article 34 TFEU.

[166] HOFHUIS, *Minimumharmonisatie* (n 113) 140.

[167] ECJ, Case C-169/89 *Gourmetterie Van den Burg* [2001] ECR I-2015, para 12.

[168] ECJ, Case C-169/89 *Gourmetterie Van den Burg* [2001] ECR I-2015, para 12

in the context of the common commercial policy, but allowed for restrictions on the freedom of exportation, inter alia, on the grounds of public policy. The crucial question was whether the public policy concept laid down in the regulation could have an extraterritorial bearing. AG Jacobs paved the way for a recognition of extraterritorial application—albeit an exceptional recognition—by stating that in certain circumstances in which human life is at stake, the extraterritorial application of the public policy concept should be justified. More specifically, where two third countries were at war, resulting in significant bloodshed, he felt it would be indefensible to block certain export restrictions that were intended to limit the loss of life.[169] Though it did not use the AG's exact wording, the ECJ implicitly accepted certain extraterritorial applications of the public policy concept when it recognized that the concept covers both a Member State's internal and external security. According to the ECJ, it was becoming less and less possible to examine a state's security in isolation, since this security is closely linked to the security of the international community at large.[170] The extraterritoriality interest was thus, once again, linked to an intraterritorial interest. The ECJ declined to comment on whether a restrictive measure could be justified independently with relation to an exclusively foreign public interest.

3.2. Reacting to a Member State's presumed misapplication of a harmonized EU standard

The *Hedley Lomas* case concerned the British Ministry of Agriculture's refusal to export live sheep to Spain for slaughter due to the British authorities' conviction that Spain did not comply with the rules contained in a directive on the stunning of animals before slaughter.[171] In refusing to issue an export licence, the United Kingdom caused a restriction on the free movement of goods and jeopardized the principles of mutual trust and mutual recognition. The United Kingdom argued that it was entitled to do so as the protection of the health and life of animals was at stake. From a mutual recognition perspective, *Hedley Lomas* raised the important question of whether a Member State can invoke a justification ground in order to protect a fundamental value in danger in another Member State when the first state believes that the second is not complying with the obligations laid down in a directive. As the ECJ concluded that the directive called for exhaustive harmonization, the only frame of reference was the directive itself, and this did not provide for justification grounds or for a monitor compliance procedure. The ECJ was clearly reluctant to grant Member States a large margin to act in cases where it was suspected that another Member State was failing in some of its European legislative duties.

The ECJ's point of departure was the presumption that national laws are consistent with EU law and that Member States should trust not only in other Member States but also in the results of any investigation performed by the Commission.[172] Such a climate of trust could be jeopardized if a Member State was entitled to question the legislation or

[169] Joined Opinion of AG Jacobs in Cases C-70/94 and C-83/94 *Werner and Leifer* [1995] ECR I-3191, § 59.

[170] ECJ, Case C-70/94 *Werner* [1995] ECR I-3189, paras 25–6 and ECJ, Case C-83/94 *Leifer* [1995] ECR I-3231, paras 27–8.

[171] ECJ, Case C-5/94 *Hedley Lomas* [1996] ECR I-2553, para 7.

[172] ECJ, Case C-5/94 *Hedley Lomas* [1996] ECR I-2553, para 19; Opinion of AG LEGER in Case C-1/96 *Compassion in World Farming* [1998] ECR I-1251, paras 83–4; D.P. FERNÁNDEZ ARROYO, 'De cómo la defensa de los animales frente al sufrimiento puede querer ocultar la falta de confianza comunitaria', *La Ley* 1996, No 6, 1676–19; S. PRECHAL, 'Annotatie *Hedley Lomas*', *SEW* 1998, 68.

behaviour of another Member State. Therefore, the ECJ insisted on several occasions that special vigilance was needed whenever questions arose that might require the national court to decide whether the legislation of another Member State was in accordance with EU law.[173]

The presumption of conformity, however, is not irrefutable, and the ECJ accepts that a Member State can act if a risk emerges.[174] Nevertheless, the way in which a Member State can react is clearly restricted, since a Member State may not unilaterally adopt corrective or protective measures on its own authority that are designed to obviate any other Member State's breach of the rules of EU law. Each Member State is also bound to act in accordance with the relevant procedures and legal remedies prescribed by the TFEU.[175] In other words, Member States have the option either to begin infringement procedures under Article 259 TFEU or to register a complaint with the Commission.[176] The ECJ thus firmly rejects the idea of a measure of reciprocity, which is proper to classical public international law[177] but irreconcilable with EU law, since Article 344 TFEU states that a Member State cannot submit a dispute concerning the interpretation or application of the Treaty to any method of settlement other than those provided for therein. A Member State's extraterritorial behaviour is thus rebutted on the grounds that a Member State may not take the law into its own hands.

However, does the ECJ's final decision in *Hedley Lomas* imply that a Member State may under no circumstances provisionally suspend an import or export measure when (more) convincing arguments arise? Not necessarily, in my opinion. It should be noted that in the *Hedley Lomas* case, the refusal to grant an export licence was based merely on the conviction that certain Spanish slaughterhouses did not comply with the directive's requirements and we should also note that the Commission had previously conducted an investigation related to this case that had resulted in the complaint's dismissal.[178] The ECJ had explicitly recognized that its answer had to be provided in this factual context.[179] Similarly, AG Léger emphasized subsequently that the outcome of the ECJ's *Hedley Lomas* judgment should be confined to cases where non-observance of a harmonizing directive's provisions was hypothetical.[180] If, however, a Member State found itself in a situation in which no investigation had yet been performed by the Commission and in which a (more) fundamental general interest such as human life or health was at stake, I believe the ECJ would be unlikely to condemn the taking of (proportionate) provisional measures, provided that two conditions were fulfilled. First, the Commission must be promptly informed of the Member State's actions and must receive a statement of reasons which demonstrate the indispensable grounds for acting promptly in order to safeguard the fundamental interest at stake. Secondly, the Member State concerned should immediately cease its actions if the Commission urges the Member State to do so. In the *Hedley Lomas* case, in my view, it was precisely the UK's continuing refusal to grant export permissions, even after the Commission's decision to dismiss the case, which

[173] ECJ, Case 244/80 *Foglia v Novello* [1981] ECR 3045, para 30; ECJ, Case C-318/00 *Bacardi-Martini* [2003] ECR I-905, para 45.

[174] ECJ, Case C-470/03 *AGM COS.MET* [2007] ECR I-2749, para 62.

[175] ECJ, Case C-5/94 *Hedley Lomas* [1996] ECR I-2553, paras 19–20; ECJ, Case C-241/01 *National Farmers' Union* [2003] ECR I-9079, paras 49–50; ECJ, Case C-111/03 *Commission v Sweden* [2005] ECR I-8789, para 66, and the case law mentioned over there.

[176] Opinion of AG Léger in Case C-5/94 *Hedley Lomas* [1996] ECR I-2553, § 30.

[177] Opinion of AG Léger in Case C-5/94 *Hedley Lomas* [1996] ECR I-2553, § 27.

[178] ECJ, Case C-5/94 *Hedley Lomas* [1996] ECR I-2553, paras 8 and 15.

[179] ECJ, Case C-5/94 *Hedley Lomas* [1996] ECR I-2553, para 16.

[180] Opinion of AG Léger in Case C-1/96 *Compassion in World Farming* [1998] ECR I-1251, § 84.

constituted the serious breach of the principle of mutual recognition (and against Art. 344 TFEU) for which the UK was correctly condemned.

C. The peculiar case of the enhanced duty of vigilance whenever the mutual recognition mechanism endangers the free movement provisions

In some rare cases, the principles of mutual recognition and mutual trust have not fulfilled their traditional roles as enhancers of the free movement provisions and have instead had some adverse effects on the internal market's objectives.

For instance, in *Commission v Spain*, Spain had refused entry to two third-country nationals who were members of the family of EU citizens for reasons of public policy on the sole ground that they had been included by Germany on the list in the Schengen Information System (SIS) of persons not to be permitted entry.[181] The Commission held that Spain had breached former Directive 64/221/EEC by failing to give adequate reasons for refusing to issue a visa and allow entry, whereas Spain contended that it had simply carried out its obligations under the Convention Implementing the Schengen Agreement (CISA). The Court started by explaining the relationship between the CISA and EU law on freedom of movement for persons and held that the provisions of the Schengen *acquis* are applicable *only if and as far as they are compatible with EU law.*[182] In view of the finding that the concept of public policy within the meaning of Article 2 Directive 64/221/EEC did not correspond to that in Article 96 CISA,[183] the ECJ held that the Spanish authorities were not justified in refusing entry to the persons concerned without having first verified whether their presence constituted a genuine, present, and sufficiently serious threat affecting one of the fundamental interests of society, as required by Directive 64/221/EEC.[184] Against this legal background, the ECJ implicitly criticized Spain's excessive trust in Germany's evaluation of the public policy exception. It concluded that 'although the principle of genuine cooperation underpinning the Schengen acquis implied that the State consulting the SIS should give due consideration to the information provided by the State which issued the alert, it also implied that the latter should make supplementary information available to the consulting State to enable it to gauge, in each case, the gravity of the threat posed by the person for whom the alert had been issued'.[185] The ECJ followed a similar approach in *Jipa*, where it was invited to interpret the public policy concept of Article 27(2) DIR 2004/38 (successor of Directive 64/221/EEC) in a case where Romania had relied exclusively on information provided by Belgium regarding the illegal residence of a Romanian citizen in order to impose on its citizen a measure prohibiting him from travelling to Belgium for a period of up to three years. The ECJ emphasized that a measure limiting the exercise of the right of free

[181] ECJ, Case C-503/03 *Commission v Spain* [2006] ECR I-1097.

[182] ECJ, Case C-503/03 *Commission v Spain* [2006] ECR I-1097, paras 32–5.

[183] ECJ, Case C-503/03 *Commission v Spain* [2006] ECR I-1097, para 48. The ECJ explained that according to Article 96 CISA, 'an alert in the SIS for the purposes of refusing entry may be based on a threat to public policy where the person concerned has been convicted of an offence carrying a penalty involving deprivation of liberty of at least one year (Article 96(2)(a)), or if he has been subject to a measure based on a failure to comply with national regulations on the entry or residence of aliens (Article 96(3)). Unlike the rules laid down by Directive 64/221/EEC, as interpreted by the Court, such circumstances justify in themselves an alert *irrespective of any specific assessment of the threat represented by the person concerned*' (emphasis added).

[184] ECJ, Case C-503/03 *Commission v Spain* [2006] ECR I-1097, para 55.

[185] ECJ, Case C-503/03 *Commission v Spain* [2006] ECR I-1097, para 56.

movement must be adopted in the light of considerations pertaining to the protection of public policy or public security in *the Member State imposing the measure*.[186] The ECJ therefore concluded that information provided by another Member State can be taken into account in the context of the assessment undertaken by the competent national authorities in order to adopt a measure restricting freedom of movement, but 'the national measure cannot be based *exclusively* on reasons advanced by another Member State [...]' (emphasis added).[187]

Both cases are a confirmation of my earlier findings that the internal market does not impose a regime of blind mutual trust. Those cases where mutual trust and mutual recognition might jeopardize the free movement provisions are likely to be exceptional areas where Member States are not only permitted but actually have a duty to be vigilant regarding decisions and information provided by other Member States and, furthermore, to take the necessary measures to verify this information.

D. Limits arising from concerns about abuse of law

As discussed above, the ECJ has allowed Member States to set the principle of mutual recognition aside whenever a striking case of abuse of law is evident, albeit within strict margins. I have also indicated that the issue of abuse of law is closely related to fears over a race to the bottom. I will now investigate how these two items are addressed by the European legislator. Concerns about abuse of law and a race to the bottom (section D, 4) have on occasions also become matters for the European legislator, though not always to the same extent. A number of secondary legislation texts contain explicit references to the abuse of law issue (section D, 1), whereas in other texts the legislator's aim of avoiding unjustified legal tourism is either only implicitly present (section D, 2) or apparently absent (section D, 3).

(1) Explicit references to abuse of law

Several directives refer explicitly in their preambles to the ECJ's case law on the circumvention of law. Whereas most preambles (e.g. in the areas of broadcasting and electronic commerce) refer, in accordance with the ECJ's case law, to a Member State's right to take measures to combat evasion of legislation,[188] others (e.g. in the areas of banking, insurance, and investment) employ far more imperative language which suggests that taking such measures is actually an obligation.[189]

[186] ECJ, Case C-33/07 *Jipa* [2008] ECR I-5157, para 25.

[187] ECJ, Case C-33/07 *Jipa* [2008] ECR I-5157.

[188] See, for instance: § 57 DIR 2000/31/EC which recalls that 'The ECJ has consistently held that a Member State retains *the right* to take measures against a service provider that is established in another Member State but directs all or most of his activity to the territory of the first Member State if the choice of establishment was made with a view to evading the legislation that would have applied to the provider had he been established on the territory of the first Member State'; or § 41 DIR 2010/13/EU, according to which 'in cases of circumvention, the codification of the case-law of the ECJ [...] would be an appropriate solution that *takes account of Member State concerns* [...]' (emphasis added).

[189] See, for instance, the similar clauses in the area of banking (§ 10 DIR 2006/48/EC) and investment (§ 22 and § 39 DIR 2004/39/EC), according to which 'the principles of mutual recognition and home Member State supervision *require* that Member States' competent authorities *should not grant or should withdraw* an authorisation where factors such as the content of the activities programmes, the geographical distribution of activities or the activities actually carried on indicate clearly that a (credit)

The relevant provisions clearly mention several objective factors which need to be taken into account. Objective elements are a crucial element of the ECJ's case law on circumvention of law and are defined more specifically in the body of legislative instruments. By requiring that a firm have both its registered office and its head office in the same Member State,[190] for example, or by establishing the criteria according to which a firm is considered to be established in a Member State,[191] the EU legislator provides precise and objective criteria which certainly assist in reducing cases of forum shopping. However, they are not necessarily all-encompassing. Therefore, it remains important that the legislative texts are interpreted in the light of the general criteria developed in the ECJ's case law on abuse of law where necessary.

(2) *Implicit references to abuse of law*

In some directives, the aim of combatting the circumvention of legislation is not explicitly mentioned in the directive's preamble but the legislator's concerns regarding circumvention of law can nevertheless be read between the lines. An example of this can be found in the *Knoors* judgment, in which the ECJ clarified that the precise conditions set out in the relevant directive for the length of periods during which the activity in question must have been pursued minimize the risk of abuse in that field.[192] No specific reference to the general abuse of law theory is required, as the question of abuse is dealt with in the legislative framework itself.

A more recent example can be found in the area of driving licences. The European legislator clearly intends to tackle cases of 'driving licence tourism', by stating that no person may hold more than one driving licence,[193] for example, or by clarifying that driving licences can only be issued to applicants who have their 'normal residence' in the territory of the Member State issuing the licence,[194] or by first allowing[195] and consequently requiring[196] a Member State to refuse to issue a driving licence to an applicant whose driving licence has been restricted, suspended, or withdrawn in another Member State. In fact, over the years, the legislator had on more than one occasion encountered situations in which citizens who had lost their driving licences in their home state following a serious offence were able to obtain new licences in another Member State, which—they argued—then had to be recognized by their home state because of the principle of mutual recognition.[197]

institution has opted for the legal system of one Member State for the purpose of evading the stricter standards in force in another Member State...' (emphasis added).

[190] See, for instance: Article 11(2)(a) DIR 2006/48EC; Article 20 DIR 2009/138/EC; Article 5(4) DIR 2004/39/EC.

[191] Article 2 DIR 2010/13/EU. Its predecessor, former Directive 97/36/EC, had introduced a precise definition of the concept 'establishment' in order to make it more difficult for broadcasters to fall within their favourite EU Member State's jurisdiction and thus to overcome cases of *forum shopping* à la *Denuit* and *VT4*: ECJ, Case C-14/96 *Denuit* [1997] ECR I-2785; ECJ, Case C-56/96 *VT4* [1997] ECR I-3143.

[192] ECJ, Case 115/78 *Knoors* [1979] ECR 399, para 26.

[193] Article 7(5) DIR 2006/126/EC.

[194] Article 7(1)(e) *juncto* Article 12 DIR 2006/126/EC.

[195] According to former Articles 8(2) and 8(4) Directive 91/439/EC 'a Member State *may* refuse to recognize the validity of any driving licence issued by another Member State to a person whose driving licence is restricted, suspended, withdrawn or cancelled in another Member State'.

[196] According to Article 11(4) DIR 2006/126/EC 'a Member State *shall* refuse to recognize the validity of any driving licence issued by another Member State to a person whose driving licence is restricted, suspended, withdrawn or cancelled in another Member State'.

[197] See, in particular, the draft text of DIR 2006/126/EC (COM (2003) 621 final, p. 5–6).

Similar problems arose in *Wiedemann and Funk, Zerche, Schubert and Seuke*,[198] and other cases.[199] *Wiedemann and Funk, Zerche, Schubert and Seuke* concerned several German citizens who had lost their German driving licences for driving under the influence of drugs and/or alcohol in Germany, where they resided. Under German law, they were only entitled to regain their licences having completed a medico-psychological test. However, because they knew that such a condition was not required in the Czech Republic, they went to the Czech Republic and were able to obtain a new driving licence without having to pass any medico-psychological tests and without having to explain why they had lost their original driving licence.

The ECJ was faced with the dilemma of whether to apply the principle of mutual recognition quasi-automatically in accordance with its previous case law in this area or to refine it in light of the principles of abuse of law and fraud. AG Bot strongly recommended that in cases of fraud and circumvention of law the principle of mutual recognition should not undergo its normal and traditional application[200] and that, in exceptional cases,[201] Member States should be entitled to set the principle of mutual recognition aside. The unequivocally fraudulent intent and behaviour of the licence holders was, in the AG's opinion, one of the crucial elements which distinguished these cases from those over which the ECJ had previously presided and which should, therefore, justify a less rigid application of the principle of mutual recognition.[202] The ECJ's reasoning initially appeared to be much less concerned with fraud or circumvention but instead with (old) Article 8(2) of former Directive 91/439/EEC,[203] which entitled Member States to restrict, suspend, withdraw, or cancel a licence held by an individual who had their normal residence in that territory under certain circumstances. The directive itself thus contained a provision sufficient to resolve the case without needing to recourse to the ECJ's abuse of law theory. However, by explicitly recognizing that the directive's residence requirement assisted in combatting 'driving licence tourism' in the absence of complete harmonization of the Member States' driving licence laws,[204] the ECJ highlighted the extent to which anti-abuse of law concerns were being addressed in this provision. Most likely because of the specific contexts of these cases (manifest non-compliance with an explicit provision in the directive and a clear threat to road safety), the ECJ concluded that the unlimited mutual recognition approach it had promoted in *Kapper* (imposing a duty of mutual recognition despite non-compliance with a residence requirement)[205] had to be refined.

[198] ECJ, Joined Cases C-329/06 and C-343/06 *Wiedemann and Funk* [2008] ECR I-4635; ECJ, Joined Cases, C-334/06 to C-336/06 *Zerche, Schubert and Seuke* [2008] ECR I-4691.

[199] See, for instance: ECJ, Case C-227/05 *Halbritter* [2006] ECR I-49; ECJ, Case C-340/05 *Kremer* [2006] ECR I-98; ECJ, Case C-1-07 *Weber* [2008] ECR I-8571; ECJ, Case C-225/07 *Möginger* [2009] ECR I-103; ECJ, Case C-321/07 *Schwarz* [2009] ECR I-1113; ECJ, Case C-445/08 *Wierer* [2009] ECR I-119; ECJ, Case C-334/09 *Scheffer* [2010] ECR I-12379; ECJ, Case C-224/10 *Apelt*, nyr.

[200] Opinion of AG Bot in Joined Cases C-329/06 and C-343/06 *Wiedemann and Funk* [2008] ECR I-4635, § 76–80.

[201] Opinion of AG Bot in Joined Cases C-329/06 and C-343/06 *Wiedemann and Funk* [2008] ECR I-4635, § 93.

[202] Opinion of AG Bot in Joined Cases C-329/06 and C-343/06 *Wiedemann and Funk* [2008] ECR I-4635, § 66–76.

[203] Currently, Article 11(4) DIR 2006/126/EC.

[204] ECJ, Joined Cases C-329/06 and C-343/06 *Wiedemann and Funk* [2008] ECR I-4635, para 69. Similarly: ECJ, Case C-184/10 *Grasser* [2011] ECR I-4057, para 27 and ECJ, Case C-419/10 *Hofmann*, nyr, para 70 ff. on the *travaux préparatoires* of DIR 2006/126/EC and the EU legislature's aim to reinforce the fight against 'driving licence tourism'.

[205] ECJ, Case C-476/01 *Kapper* [2004] ECR I-5205, para 49.

In sum, since *Wiedemann and Funk*, Member States have been entitled to set the principle of mutual recognition aside in cases when the residence condition is not fulfilled according to the information on the licence or to other incontestable information supplied by another Member State and when the purpose of the directive (road safety) would be jeopardized owing to the licence holder's probable conduct following the issue of a new licence.[206] Furthermore, in subsequent judgments it became clear that the principle of mutual recognition could also be set aside in other cases of law-evading behaviour. In *Weber*, for example, the ECJ accepted that mutual recognition was not required if a driving licence holder relied on a licence that had been obtained during a period in which a licence issued in another Member State was suspended, since the mutual recognition approach 'would have the effect of encouraging offenders likely to be subject to such withdrawal to travel without delay to another Member State in order *to evade* the administrative or criminal consequences of those offences and would ultimately destroy the confidence on which the system of mutual recognition of driving licences rests' (emphasis added).[207] In *Schwarz*, too, the ECJ did not object to the non-application of the principle of mutual recognition when the person involved was relying on an old driving licence which had been issued by another Member State before that state's accession to the EU, arguing that 'if a national withdrawal measure such as was imposed in the main proceedings could be *sidestepped* by relying on a driving licence issued earlier than the licence which was withdrawn on the ground of unfitness to drive [...] road traffic safety would be compromised' (emphasis added).[208]

The ECJ's judgments in its driving licence case law initially appear extremely concise on the fraud issue, but the similarities with the ECJ's general abuse of law theory are nevertheless striking. The irrelevance of subjective elements and the pursuit of an artificial construction, in combination with a risk that (one of) the (main) objectives of the underlying instrument (in particular, road safety) could be jeopardized, indeed confirm our previous findings on this matter. If these conditions are not fulfilled, however, the ECJ will not hesitate to impose a duty of mutual recognition.[209]

The divergence of legislative requirements related to the issuing of driving licences and the absence of any judicial data at EU level on the issuing, restriction, or withdrawal of a driving licence can certainly be considered to stimulate cases of forum shopping. It is important to emphasize that such situations of forum shopping are in themselves perfectly legitimate according to the ECJ's case law and that Member States are by default bound by the duty of mutual recognition. It is only when the forum shopping involves an artificial construction which puts the directive's objective at risk that the application of the principle of mutual recognition can be put on hold.

(3) No references to abuse of law

A final example related to the abuse of law and fraud issues can be found in the area of diplomas, where it is striking that while some Member States must have had concerns

[206] ECJ, Joined Cases C-329/06 and C-343/06 *Wiedemann and Funk* [2008] ECR I-4635, paras 58–59 and 66; ECJ, Joined Cases C-334/06 to C-336/06 *Zerche, Schubert and Seuke* [2008] ECR I-4691, paras 55–6 and 63.

[207] ECJ, Case C-1/07 *Weber* [2008] ECR I-8571, para 39.

[208] ECJ, Case C-321/07 *Schwarz* [2009] ECR I-1113, para 96.

[209] See, for instance: ECJ, Case C-445/08 *Wierer* [2009] ECR I-119; ECJ, Case C-334/09 *Scheffer* [2010] ECR I-12379.

about the potential abuse of professional titles,[210] the directives concerned did not[211]—until recently[212]—contain any specific provision aimed at addressing this problem.

Yet even under the previous directive, where no specific anti-abuse of law clauses were included, the ECJ did not hesitate to follow the path it had taken in other areas of law, namely by assessing the contested behaviour in light of the aims of the provisions in question and by verifying whether any form of artificial construction was present. In this regard, it is worth mentioning the *Consiglio Nazionale degli Ingegneri* and *Köller* judgments, where the AG and the ECJ—following precisely this reasoning—imposed the duty of mutual recognition in the latter judgment (and the application of former DIR 89/48/EC) but rejected it in the former.[213]

(4) Abuse of law and race to the bottom concerns

I now return to the issue of a race to the bottom. As discussed above, the race to the bottom argument revolves around the idea that if market participants develop a tendency to select countries with the most permissive legislation (forum shopping), Member States might be tempted to deregulate and to abolish higher standards (race to the bottom).

Logically, in a legislative framework, both the existence of harmonization measures and the translation of these essential requirements into EU standards constitute important counterweights to the process of downward harmonization[214] and guarantees of an acceptable mutual recognition mechanism.

However, as I have already pointed out, the level of harmonization actually achieved may vary substantially from one instrument to another. An explicit and far-reaching country of origin provision in combination with a low degree of harmonization could be problematic, since it might encourage forum shopping and possibly also a race to the bottom. Fortunately, in practice, this scenario seems rather unlikely, as most directives of this type exclude certain aspects from the scope of the country of origin rule (e.g. certain consumer protection laws) and/or they provide anti-evasion clauses and/or clauses which permit Member States to deviate in specific cases.[215]

[210] ECJ, Case C-19/92 *Kraus* [1993] ECR I-1663, paras 33–41, where the ECJ accepted that a Member State was—under certain circumstances—entitled to take measures to protect the public against misleading or abuse of academic titles.

[211] Unless if one assumes that the 10th recital of former Directive 89/48/EC reflected anti-abuse of law considerations where it stated that 'the general system for the recognition of higher-education diplomas is not intended to amend the rules, including those relating to professional ethics, applicable to any person pursuing a profession in the territory of a Member State'.

[212] Article 50 DIR 2005/36/EC introduced for the first time a clear anti-fraud provision, which was essentially aimed at situations of forgery in the sense of material alteration of administrative documents.

[213] ECJ, Case C-311/06 *Consiglio Nazionale degli Ingegneri* [2009] ECR 415, paras 55–7 (and the corresponding Opinion of AG Poiares Maduro, at § 44–63); ECJ, Case C-286/06 *Commission v Spain* [2008] ECR I-8025, paras 69–72; ECJ, Case C-118/09 *Köller* [2010] ECR I-13627, paras 29–36 (and the corresponding Opinion of AG Trstenjak, at § 65 ff.). Both the ECJ and its AG emphasize that the *Köller* case must be distinguished from the *Consiglio Nazionale degli Ingegneri* case as only in the former was there actually proof of possession of an additional professional qualification.

[214] F. ABRAHAM, 'Building Blocks of the Single Market', *Tijdschrift voor Economie en Management* 1991, 15; J. PELKMANS, 'Mutual Recognition in Goods. On Promises and Disillusions', *JEPP* 2007, 708, who upholds that when mutual recognition is regulatory (instead of judicial), there can be no race to the bottom via bargaining as the SHEC-type risk regulation prescribes a high level of protection; S.K. SCHMIDT, 'Mutual Recognition as a New Mode of Governance', *JEPP* 2007, 677. See also: D.C. ESTY and D. GERARDIN, *Regulatory Competition and Economic Integration* (Oxford, Oxford University Press, 2001).

[215] For the example of DIR 2000/31/EC, see, for instance: HÖRNLE, 'Country of Origin Regulation in Cross-border Media: One Step beyond the Freedom to Provide Services?' (n 56) 124. For other directives which include circumvention of law provisions, see: footnotes 188 to 191.

Furthermore, in some sectors where the mutual recognition approach goes hand in hand with *ex post* cooperation mechanisms, regulatory competition has actually led to a 'climb to the top' rather than a 'race to the bottom'. For instance, under the general system directives' regime, professionals coming from low-standards countries—who must fulfil higher compensation conditions than their counterparts from other countries—are beginning to act in order to improve the reputation of their home country's systems.[216] In doing so, conditions are created for the incremental loosening of host country compensatory requirements, and therefore for the progressive expansion of the effectiveness and automaticity of mutual recognition.[217]

[216] K. NICOLAÏDIS, 'Globalization with Human Faces: Managed Mutual Recognition and the Free Movement of Professionals', in PADO SCHIOPPA (ed.), *The Principle of Mutual Recognition in the European Integration Process* (n 68) 142. For similar arguments, in the context of plant protection products and medicines, see: KEESSEN, *European Administrative Decisions. How the EU Regulates Products on the Internal Market* (n 57) 80.

[217] NICOLAÏDIS, 'Globalization with Human Faces: Managed Mutual Recognition and the Free Movement of Professionals' (n 68) 142.

3

The Workability of the Principle of Mutual Recognition in the Internal Market

Having examined the principle of mutual recognition's main characteristics from a theoretical point of view, the question that should now be addressed is how this principle functions in a day-to-day context. In what follows, I provide an overview of the measures that have been taken (section II) in order to improve the application of the principle of mutual recognition (section I).

I. The Problematic Application of the Principle of Mutual Recognition in Daily Practice

Despite its crucial position within the internal market context, it is now beyond doubt that the principle of mutual recognition has ultimately failed to meet the high expectations set for it by the ECJ in its case law and also that it has not become the grand success predicted by the Commission in its 1985 White Paper. In many reports, some of which were exclusively dedicated to an in-depth analysis of the practical application of the principle of mutual recognition, it is consistently admitted that the principle of mutual recognition is difficult to apply in practice.[1] Weiler even concludes that while the principle of mutual recognition was perhaps an intellectual breakthrough, it has also been a colossal market failure.[2] Several reasons can be put forward in explaining the poor function of the principle of mutual recognition.

[1] See, for instance: Communication from the Commission to the European Parliament and the Council—The impact and the effectiveness of the single market, COM (1996) 520 final, p. 11–13; Report from the Commission—First biennial report on the application of the principle of mutual recognition in the market of goods and services, SEC (1999) 1106, p. 3; Communication from the Commission to the Council and the European Parliament—Mutual recognition in the context of the follow-up to the action plan for the single mark et, COM (1999) 299 final, p. 4–7; Report from the Commission—Economic Reform: Report on the functioning of Community product and capital markets, COM (2001) 736 final, p. 13; Report from the Commission to the Council, the European Parliament and the Economic and Social Committee—Second biennial report on the application of the principle of mutual recognition in the Single Market, COM (2002) 419 final, p. 2; Commission interpretative communication—Facilitating the access of products to the markets of other Member States: the practical application of mutual recognition, *O.J.* C-265, 04.11.2003, p. 2; Communication from the Commission to the Council, the European Parliament, the European Economic and Social Committee and the Committee of the Regions—Internal Market Strategy Priorities 2003–2006, COM (2003) 238 final, p. 7; and, more recently, Communication from the Commission to the Council, the European Parliament, the European Economic and Social Committee—The Internal Market for Goods: a cornerstone of Europe's competitiveness, COM (2007) 35 final, p. 7–8; Commission staff working document—Accompanying document to the Proposal for a Regulation of the European Parliament and of the Council laying down procedures relating to the application of certain national technical rules to products lawfully marketed in another Member State and repealing Decision 3052/95/EC Impact assessment, SEC (2007) 113, p. 5–6.

[2] J.H.H. WEILER, 'Mutual Recognition, Functional Equivalence and Harmonization in the Evolution of the European Common Market and the WTO', in F.K. PADOA SCHIOPPA (ed.), *The Principle of Mutual Recognition in the European Integration Process* (New York, Palgrave, 2005) 49. Likewise: K. NICOLAÏDIS, 'Trusting the Poles and Constructing Europe through Mutual

It should be stressed that the new strategy of mutual recognition necessitates a change of habits and a new way of thinking.[3] It requires that the heads of state and government ensure their administrations translate their political will into positive tangible results,[4] and, above all, that their administrations think and act 'European' rather than national.[5] Such a European attitude presupposes a good knowledge of the EU's internal market law. Its cornerstone principle of mutual recognition depends to a large extent on mutual support and cooperation between Member States and is ineffective without a degree of basic mutual trust among all Member States.

Research carried out on behalf of the Commission confirms that, nearly three decades after *Cassis de Dijon*, a number of economic operators and national administrations are (still) ignorant of the existence of the (judicial) principle of mutual recognition, while several others still fail to grasp the principle in its entirety.[6] In fact, despite the apparent simplicity which initially appears to characterize the principle of mutual recognition, an examination of the corresponding case law and legislative acts at EU level reveal that the reality is far more complex and sophisticated. Economic operators and Member State officials seem to feel a considerable degree of uncertainty about the scope and potential of the (judicial) principle of mutual recognition. The absence of specific procedural rules and the fact that there is no extra paperwork is both a strength and a weakness. The ECJ's case-by-case approach has certainly produced some useful guidelines in this respect, but the creation of a foolproof system remains far-off.[7] When problems occur there is little or no transparency, no commonly agreed approach to evaluating whether levels of protection are equivalent, and no clear procedure for a company to follow in challenging a negative decision. Even in areas where the ECJ has already delivered an unequivocal judgment condemning a specific measure or practice, national administrations often still fail to apply the principle of mutual recognition correctly owing to the weak monitoring of the ECJ's case law that is evident in several Member States.[8]

Recognition', *JEPP* 2007, 685, who compares the principle of mutual recognition with a Janus-faced norm, usually branded as the 'easy option' and yet the hardest of all.

[3] White Paper from the Commission to the European Council—Completing the Internal Market, COM (1985) 310, p. 19.

[4] Second Report from the Commission to the Council and the European Parliament—The implementation of the Commission's White Paper on completing the internal market, COM (1987) 203 final, p. 24.

[5] See, for instance: Communication from the Commission to the Council, the European Parliament, the European Economic and Social Committee and the Committee of the Regions—Internal Market Strategy Priorities 2003–2006 (n 1) p. 7. See also: J. PELKMANS, 'Mutual Recognitions in Goods: on Promises and Disillusions', *JEPP* 2007, 105, who deplores the current non-existence of a mutual recognition *culture* within the EU.

[6] The lack of knowledge and/or familiarity with the mutual recognition principle was for the first time given attention in: Communication from the Commission to the European Parliament and the Council—The impact and the effectiveness of the single market (n 1) p. 17; and was, ten years later, confirmed in: Communication from the Commission to the Council, the European Parliament, the European Economic and Social Committee—The Internal Market for Goods: a cornerstone of Europe's competitiveness (n 1) p. 2. It can also be illustrated by the fact that the number of internal market infringement procedures remains relatively high and that they take relatively long too resolve, even though in the most recent years some progress is perceptible: see the Internal Market Scoreboards, retrievable at: <http://ec.europa.eu/internal_market/score/index_en.htm>.

[7] See, for instance: A.-L. SIBONY and A. DEFOSSEZ, 'Marché intérieur (marchandises, capitaux, établissement, services et capitaux)', *RTD Eur.* 2010, 137.

[8] Report from the Commission to the Council and the European Parliament on the state of the internal market for services presented under the first stage of the Internal Market Strategy for Services, COM (2002) 441 final, p. 54–5. Fortunately, in some sectors the ECJ's progressive enforcement of the mutual recognition principle did contribute to a more generally accepted mutual recognition principle, for instance in the beers sector: Internal Market Scoreboard, May 2002, No 519, p. 23, retrievable at: <http://ec.europa.eu/internal_market/score/index_en.htm>.

It is precisely this legal uncertainty that is the greatest dilemma of the internal market. It prevents many operators from relying on the principle and frequently leads them to choose a commercial strategy of 'risk avoidance'.[9] Similarly, it may also cause national administrations to be too cautious and therefore reluctant to apply mutual recognition, except in cases where there is no doubt at all.[10] For instance, in the area of goods, national administrations have refrained from applying the principle of mutual recognition when confronted with (technically) complex products, sensitive products, or products with which they were unfamiliar, and when asked to recognize a certificate drawn up in a language not spoken in their country.[11] In the areas of services and persons, similar shortcomings were also diagnosed at one point in relation to financial services and professional qualifications.[12] Moreover, in the global area of services, surveys have indicated that certain national authorities externalize a degree of automatic suspicion towards the services of other Member States, for instance, by systematically applying the rules of the country in which the service is provided without verifying equivalence or by performing more frequent checks on providers from other Member States.[13]

All of these examples reveal a disturbing ignorance of the implications of the principle of mutual recognition as well as an alarming lack of trust in products, services, or documents originating from other Member States. This distrust may even be reinforced by dialogue between national administrations that is far from fluent, predominantly in

[9] Many economic operators expressed the view that—given a choice between adapting their products to conform to national technical specifications or arguing that mutual recognition should apply—they tend to prefer the former option. It may be costly, but it is less risky if the Member State of destination blindly sticks to its national technical rule without having regard to the level of protection offered by the product. Moreover, some economic operators consider that adapting products saves time compared to the burdensome process of convincing a reluctant national administration or, exceptionally, judicial process, saving time being a virtue when bringing a product to the market. See: Report from the Commission—Economic Reform: Report on the functioning of Community product and capital markets (n 1) p. 14. A procedure before the ECJ, which might lead to an interesting judgment from a theoretical point of view and which might even decide in their favour, is usually no option. Business people want fast and unequivocal decisions so that they can plan their commercial strategy. Even the 'expedited procedure' which was introduced following the adoption of REG 2679/98/EC, and which has speeded up the procedure before the ECJ to a considerable extent, might therefore not be appealing from a business perspective. Legal certainty is top-priority, and if an adjustment to national rules is the price to pay, business will not hesitate. See also: G. WAGNER, 'The Economics of Harmonization: the Case of Contract Law', *CML Rev.* 2002, 1004, who shows that multinational companies are not deterred from cross-border sales, even where this means that they have to adapt to local legal rules.

[10] Report from the Commission—Economic Reform: Report on the functioning of Community product and capital markets (n 1) p. 14.

[11] Communication from the Commission to the European Parliament and the Council—The impact and the effectiveness of the single market (n 1) p. 11 and 18; Communication from the Commission to the Council and the European Parliament—Mutual recognition in the context of the follow-up to the action plan for the single mark (n 1) p. 5; Report from the Commission—First biennial report on the application of the principle of mutual recognition in the market of goods and services (n 1) p. 7–8; Report from the Commission to the Council, the European Parliament and the Economic and Social Committee—Second biennial report on the application of the principle of mutual recognition in the Single Market (n 1) p. 25. *In concreto*, problems with mutual recognition have been detected for certain types of foodstuff, construction products and vehicles that were excluded from the EC type approval: Report from the Commission—Economic Reform: Report on the functioning of Community product and capital markets (n 1) p. 13.

[12] Report from the Commission of 7 December 2001: Economic Reform: Report on the functioning of Community product and capital markets (n 1) p. 13–14; and, more recently: Commission staff working document on the transposition and implementation of the Professional Qualifications Directive, SEC (2010) 1292, p. 16.

[13] Report from the Commission to the Council and the European Parliament on the state of the internal market for services presented under the first stage of the Internal Market Strategy for Services (n 8) p. 53–4.

the non-harmonized sector.[14] Rather than working closely together with other Member States' administrations within a European framework, which is after all a legal duty according to settled case law,[15] national administrations tend to fall back on a national administration's framework, which is often characterized by unpredictable decisions (due to the discretionary power of appreciation), excessive formalism, delays, procedural costs, lack of transparency, and difficulties in applying the principle of mutual recognition to technically complex products.[16]

II. Remedies for Improving How the Principles of Mutual Recognition and Mutual Trust Function

The problematic issues reviewed under the previous heading are currently being addressed. Over the years, several measures have indeed been taken in order to reduce the existing obstacles and achieve a principle of mutual recognition that functions smoothly. These measures focus on (i) a better understanding of the scope and contours of the principle of mutual recognition (section II, A); (ii) controlling (existing or imminent) impediments to the principle of mutual recognition through notification procedures (section II, B); (iii) providing a procedural framework in order to guarantee more effective and uniform application of the principle of mutual recognition (section II, C); (iv) pursuing a more European approach by stimulating administrative cooperation and dialogue among the Member States (section II, D); (v) complementing the principle of mutual recognition with harmonization measures (section II, E); and (vi) the establishment of EU committees or EU agencies for settling disputes (section II, F).

A. Striving for a better understanding of the principle of mutual recognition

A logical first step to take when aiming to improve the practical application of the principle of mutual recognition is to ensure that all parties involved in the mutual recognition system have sound knowledge of their rights and duties.

In order to address the common complaint that civil servants are unfamiliar with the principle of mutual recognition and consequently apply it incorrectly, the Commission has implemented a multitude of initiatives intended to increase the diffusion of relevant

[14] Commission staff working document—Accompanying document to the Proposal for a Regulation of the European Parliament and of the Council laying down procedures relating to the application of certain national technical rules to products lawfully marketed in another Member State and repealing Decision 3052/95/EC Impact assessment (n 1) p. 24. Administrative cooperation is, by contrast, well-organized in the harmonized area where it is put in place by secondary legislation.

[15] Commission staff working document—Accompanying document to the Proposal for a Regulation of the European Parliament and of the Council laying down procedures relating to the application of certain national technical rules to products lawfully marketed in another Member State and repealing Decision 3052/95/EC Impact assessment (n 1) p. 24–5.

[16] Report from the Commission—First biennial report on the application of the principle of mutual recognition in the market of goods and services (n 1) p. 6; Communication from the Commission to the Council and the European Parliament—Mutual recognition in the context of the follow-up to the action plan for the single market (n 1) p. 5; Report from the Commission to the Council and the European Parliament on the state of the internal market for services presented under the first stage of the Internal Market Strategy for Services (n 8) p. 45–6.

information about this principle[17] and to provide adequate training to the principal parties concerned, i.e. national administrations and businesses.[18] The interaction between these parties and the European Commission has not only raised awareness of the principle amongst the former but has also been rather beneficial to the latter, since it has contributed to a better understanding of the reasons why the principle of mutual recognition is not working as it should.[19] Recently, thanks to the institutionalization of this interaction,[20] it has been REG 764/2008 in particular which has played a major role in raising the awareness of the principle of mutual recognition among those businesses and national administrations involved in intra-EU trade and in helping the Commission to identify the problematic areas of application.[21]

Other instruments that the Commission has been keen to promote in order to raise awareness about the principle of mutual recognition among national administrations include what are called the mutual recognition clauses. These are what Member States are urged to introduce by the Commission in the framework of the notification procedure laid down in DIR 98/34/EC. Yet these clauses have given rise to some controversy, firstly over their presumed obligatory character and secondly over their actual added value. As

[17] The Commission drew up 'A practical guide to the concept and application of articles 28-30 EC' (retrievable at: <http://ec.europa.eu/enterprise/policies/single-market-goods/files/goods/docs/art34-36/new_guide_en.pdf>), delivered an interpretative communication on the practical application of the mutual recognition principle, and developed several guides to other legal instruments that are relevant for the mutual recognition principle, namely a guide on former Decision 3052/95/EC, a brochure entitled 'Maintaining the internal market. Directive 98/34/EC', and several guidance documents on the application of REG 764/2008 in particular sectors (retrievable at: <http://ec.europa.eu/enterprise/policies/single-market-goods/free-movement-non-harmonised-sectors/mutual-recognition/>). Furthermore, the Commission created several internet sites that were dedicated exclusively to these instruments. For an overview of all these initiatives, see: Report from the Commission—Economic Reform: Report on the functioning of Community product and capital markets (n 1) p. 13; Report from the Commission to the Council, the European Parliament and the Economic and Social Committee—Second biennial report on the application of the principle of mutual recognition in the Single Market (n 1) p. 7–9; Commission interpretative communication—Facilitating the access of products to the markets of other Member States: the practical application of mutual recognition (n 1); Communication from the Commission to the European Parliament and the Council— First Report on the Application of Regulation 764/2008 of the European Parliament and of the Council of 9 July 2008 laying down procedures relating to the application of certain national technical rules to products lawfully marketed in another Member State and repealing Decision 3052/95/EC, COM (2012) 292 final, p. 11–12.

[18] The Commission organized several seminars on mutual recognition in the single market and held a number of round tables to discuss the practical problems surrounding the mutual recognition principle with economic operators of a specific sector and Member State officials. See: Report from the Commission—Economic Reform: Report on the functioning of Community product and capital markets (n 1) p. 14; Report from the Commission to the Council, the European Parliament and the Economic and Social Committee of 14 December 2001—Second biennial report on the application of the principle of mutual recognition in the Single Market (n 1) p. 7–9. Moreover, the Commission underlined the importance and need for more training on European Union law and for further dissemination of information on mutual recognition, see: Communication from the Commission—A Europe of Results—Applying Community Law, COM (2007) 502 final, p. 6; Communication from the Commission to the European Parliament and the Council— First Report on the Application of Regulation 764/2008 (n 17) p. 10.

[19] Interview with H. INGELS, administrator at the European Commission, DG Enterprises, Brussels, 9 February 2007.

[20] See, in particular: Articles 6(2) and 7(2) REG 764/2008 (on notification duties for Member States), Article 12(1) (on the yearly reports from the Member States), Article 13 (on the consultative committee on mutual recognition).

[21] Communication from the Commission to the European Parliament and the Council— First Report on the Application of Regulation 764/2008 (n 17) p. 10. This report reveals that the Member States have been almost unanimously positive as regards the effectiveness of REG 764/2008 in raising the awareness of the principle of mutual recognition.

regards the first point, the ECJ has now made absolutely clear that there is no general obligation to include mutual recognition clauses in national legislation.[22] As for the second, the answer is less clear-cut. From a purely legal perspective, the introduction of such clauses is superfluous since they are simply a confirmation of the directly applicable free movement Treaty provisions.[23] From a more pragmatic point of view, however, the use of such clauses may enhance legal certainty and transparency, as they will call the attention of both traders and national authorities to the existence and application of this principle.[24] There are therefore valid arguments for both positions: mutual recognition clauses are—strictly speaking—not necessary (from a theoretical point of view), but may be useful (from a practical point of view). Nevertheless, we should be aware that legal certainty and transparency can only increase when these clauses are meticulously drafted.[25] If the mutual recognition clause makes no use of a framework with specific guidelines, the actual level of legal certainty obtained could be disappointing. Moreover, the fragmented approach intrinsic to the policy of mutual recognition clauses (drafted legislation by legislation) and their non-obligatory nature might jeopardize the coherent application of the principle of mutual recognition.

B. Gaining an overview of current or imminent hindrances to the principle of mutual recognition

It would be misguided to think that the introduction of the principle of mutual recognition in EU law alone will prevent Member States creating barriers to the free movement provisions in the future. Experience has shown that Member State governments do not

[22] In fact, it was the ECJ's *Foie gras* judgment that had cast doubts on this issue (ECJ, Case C-184/96 *Commission v France* [1998] ECR I-6197, para 28). The Commission and some authors seemed convinced that from the ECJ's wording that 'by adopting Decree No 93-999 *without including in it a mutual recognition clause* France had failed to fulfil its obligations under [former] Article 28 EC' (emphasis added), it could be deduced that Member States had a general duty to include mutual recognition clauses in their national legislation. See, for instance: L. GONZÁLEZ VAQUÉ, 'Faut-il insérer des clauses de reconnaissance mutuelle dans les législations internes', *JT Dr Eur.* 1999, 87; A. MATTERA, 'L'arrêt *Foie Gras* du 22 octobre 1998 porteur d'une nouvelle impulsion pour perfectionnement du Marché unique européen', *RMUE* 1998, 113. However, such an optimistic reading of the *Foie Gras* judgment was clearly and briefly rejected by the ECJ itself in a more recent judgment, namely: ECJ, Case C-24/00 *Commission v France* [2004] ECR I-1277, para 28. For the crucial differences between both judgments, see the corresponding Opinion of AG Mischo in Case C-24/00, at § 45–7. It seems, however, that the Commission is still figuring out what the exact nature of a mutual recognition clause ought to be: ECJ, Case C-333/08 *Commission v France* [2010] ECR I-757, paras 64, 106–9.

[23] See, for instance: M. LÓPEZ ESCUDERO, 'La aplicación del principio del reconocimiento mutuo en el derecho comunitario', *G.J.* 1993, 150–1, who argues that this 'pressing' of the Commission misses any valid legal ground. Similarly, AG Mischo concludes that the free movement Treaty provisions are sufficient as they stand: Opinion of AG Mischo in Case C-24/00 *Commission v France* [2004] ECR I-1277, §54.

[24] See, for instance: L. GONZÁLEZ VAQUÉ, 'Naturaleza y efecto de las cláusulas de reconocimiento mutuo incluidas en las normativas nacionales relativas al mercado interior', *G.J.* 1997, D-27, 140–1; M. JARVIS, 'Case Note Commission v France and Greenham and Abel', *CML Rev.* 2004, 1405; S. ROMERO MELCHOR, 'La sentencia Red Bul de 5 de febrero de 2004: un cambio de orientación jurisprudencial sobre la necesidad de incluir cláusulas de reconocimiento mutuo en las normativas de los Estados miembros', *U.E.A.* 2004, 14–16; J.S. WATSON, 'Wederzijdse erkenning binnen de interne markt: een nieuwe impuls', *NTER* 2000, 46–7.

[25] Mutual recognition clauses can indeed differ considerably. For an overview of some examples, see: GONZÁLEZ VAQUÉ, 'Naturaleza y efecto de las cláusulas de reconocimiento mutuo incluidas en las normativas nacionales relativas al mercado interior' (n 22) 141–8. Moreover, the mere presence of a mutual recognition clause is not a guarantee that a Member State complies with its obligations under the free movement provisions. See, for instance: ECJ, Case C-358/01 *Commission v Spain* [2003] ECR I-13145.

always take heed of the EU dimension in drafting their national instruments.[26] A smoothly functioning principle of mutual recognition requires that the EU be informed as early as possible by each Member State of any (potential) obstacles to the principle of mutual recognition. Indeed, it is only to the extent that the EU is aware of potential barriers that it can take specific steps to prevent any hindrance to this principle. Apart from close follow-up of the implementation of EU law in national law, both *a priori* (for instance, through regular meetings with the competent national administrators during the implementation period) and *a posteriori* [27] (for instance, through mutual evaluation),[28] a number of specific mechanisms have been developed which will enable the EU institutions to detect any shortcomings or hindrances in the mutual recognition mechanism.

(1) The notification procedures

The European legislator has developed several notification procedures: DIR 98/34/EC, which obliges Member States to inform the Commission of new draft regulations in the field of technical standards and information society services; former Decision 3052/95/EC, and its successor REG 764/2008, which obliges Member States to inform the Commission of measures taken by a Member State to prevent the free movement or placing on the market of a specific product;[29] and REG 2679/98, which obliges Member States to forward all relevant information to the Commission when obstacles to the free movement of goods (as a consequence of the actions of private individuals) look likely to arise. In establishing these instruments, the European legislator indicates its clear intention to eliminate, preferably by means of a preventive approach, unacceptable hindrances to the principle of mutual recognition. Furthermore, the constant dialogue between the Member States and the Commission that results from these procedures should also contribute to a better understanding of the principle.

In recent years, thanks to its broad scope,[30] standstill procedure,[31] and compulsory nature—which was even reinforced by the ECJ's case law[32]—DIR 98/34 has proven a

[26] Commission Communication—The non-respect of certain provisions of Council Directive 83/189/EEC of 28 March 1983 laying down a procedure for the provision of information in the field of technical standards and regulations, *O.J.* C-245, 01.10.1986, p. 4.

[27] See, for instance: Communication from the Commission—A Europe of Results—Applying Community Law (n 18) p. 5–6; A. VERHOEVEN and J.S. VAN DEN OOSTERKAMP, 'Naar een betere toepassing van het gemeenschapsrecht Nieuwe voorstellen van de Europese Commissie', *SEW* 2008, 279 ff.

[28] See, for instance: Article 39 DIR 2006/123/EC.

[29] Former Decision No 3052/95/EC of the European Parliament and of the Council of 13 December 1995 establishing a procedure for the exchange of information on national measures derogating from the principle of the free movement of goods within the Community, *O.J.* L-321, 30.12.1995, p. 1–5, repealed by REG 764/2008.

[30] The directive's scope was on repeated occasions extended. Currently it covers all industrial goods, fisheries, and agricultural goods and—since 1998—even one *services*-related sector, namely information society services (Art. 1 DIR 98/34/EC). In the near future, one might consider extending the directive's field of application to cover also the ambit of DIR 2006/123/EC, which currently provides a notification system in Article 15(7). For a plea for a convergence of both notification systems, see: F. HERLITZ, 'La politique de prévention des obstacles aux échanges de marchandises et de services de la société de l'information', *RDUE* 2008, 451. For a better understanding of the concept 'technical standard', see, for instance: ECJ, Case C-13/96 *Bic Benelux* [1997] ECR I-1753, paras 19–26; ECJ, Case C-33/97 *Colim* [1999] ECR I-3175, paras 22–30; ECJ, Case C-314/98 *Snellers Auto's* [1999] ECR I-8633, paras 35–40; ECJ Case C-37/99 *Donkersteeg* [2000] ECR I-10223, paras 21–3 and paras 30–4; ECJ, Case C-278/99 *van der Burg* [2001] ECR I-2015, paras 20–2; ECJ, Case C-390/99 *Canal Satélite Digital* [2002] ECR I-607, paras 44–50; ECJ, Case C-65/05 *Commission v Hellenic Republic* [2006] ECR I-10341, paras 60–1.

[31] Article 9 DIR 98/34/EC.

[32] The ECJ has repeatedly held that the non-notification is an infringement of EU law and that non-notified new laws can in principle not be enforced. This was decided in the landmark judgment: ECJ,

powerful and efficient instrument in facilitating the correct application of the principle of mutual recognition by blocking *ex ante* potential infringements to this principle and, as a consequence, avoiding *ex post* infringement cases.[33] This procedure enabled the Commission—with the help of the Member States—to identify a significant amount of national legislation which was potentially detrimental to the principle of mutual recognition. Following constructive dialogue between the Commission and the Member States concerned, this problematic legislation was subsequently modified and brought into line with the principle of mutual recognition. From this perspective, the procedure has been (and is) a very good promoter of the principle of mutual recognition. Furthermore, the notification procedure also helps in identifying those areas where mutual recognition cannot be implemented in the Member States and where deeply divergent national regulations seem to urge the adoption of binding EU instruments instead. In other words, the notification system confirms a number of my earlier findings, namely that the principle of mutual recognition has some limits, which must be identified and which can only be overcome by means of harmonization.

REG 2679/98 and former Decision 3052/95 have received less positive evaluations. The assessment of REG 2679/98 mainly revealed weaknesses, the principal of which was the lack of effective intervention mechanisms.[34] With regard to former Decision 3052/95, the Commission concluded that despite its pivotal role in the internal market project, this instrument had not produced the results hoped for during its first two years in effect and that it had not sufficiently enabled the Commission to become better informed of how the principle of mutual recognition should function properly.[35] The ECJ did try to enhance the strength of former Decision 3052/95, however, by clarifying which types of measure the Commission should be notified of[36] and by condemning, under the infringement procedure, a Member State for breaching the Decision.[37]

Case C-194/94 *CIA Security* [1996] ECR I-2201, para 55; and was confirmed in: ECJ, Case C-159/00 *Sapod Audic* [2002] ECR I-5031, para 50, and ECJ, Case C-20/05 *Schwibbert* [2007] ECR I-9447, para 44. However, such a drastic consequence of unenforceability only applies where the technical regulation constitutes an obstacle to trade in goods. See, in particular, on this issue: ECJ, Case C-226/97 *Lemmens* [1998] ECR I-3711, para 37.

[33] For a positive evaluation of the notification procedure under DIR 98/34/EC, see: Report from the Commission to the Council, the European Parliament and the European Economic and Social Committee—The operation of directive 98/34/EC from 1999 to 2001, COM (2003) 200 final, p. 49–51; Report from the Commission to the Council, the European Parliament and the European Economic and Social Committee—The operation of Directive 98/34/EC from 2002 to 2005, COM (2007) 125 final, p. 13–14; Report from the Commission to the Council, the European Parliament and the European Economic and Social Committee—The operation of directive 98/34/EC in 2009 and 2010, COM (2011) 853 final, p. 16. See also: J. GOOSSEN, 'Notificaties onder Richtlijn 98/34', *SEW* 2003, 98–9; HERLITZ, 'La politique de prévention des obstacles aux échanges de marchandises et de services de la société de l'information' (n 30) 403–60; R. MUÑOZ, 'The Development of the Ex ante Control Mechanism Regarding Implementation of the Internal Market', in T. TRIDIMAS and P. NEBBIA (eds.), *EU Law for the 21st Century: Rethinking the New Legal Order* (Oxford, Hart Publishing, 2004) 107–8; J. PELKMANS, E. VOS, and L. DI MAURO, 'Reforming Product Regulation in the EU: A Painstaking, Iterative, Two-Level Game', in *Regulatory Reform and Competitiveness in Europe, I. Horizontal Issues* (Cheltenham, Edward Elgar, 2003) 272–81.

[34] Report from the Commission to the Council and the European Parliament on the application of Regulation (EC) No 2679/98, COM (2001) 160 final, p. 10–13. The Commission deplores that 'the Member States have not given [this instrument] any teeth'.

[35] Report from the Commission to the Council, the European Parliament and the Economic and Social Committee—The implementation of Decision 3052/95/CE in 1997 and 1998, COM (2000) 194 final.

[36] ECJ, Joined Cases C-388/00 and C-429/00 *Radiosistemi and Prefetto di Genova* [2002] ECR I-5845, paras 67–73.

[37] ECJ, Case C-432/03 *Commission v Portugal* [2005] ECR I-9665, paras 56–62.

Ultimately, though, the negative evaluation led to the adoption of a new Regulation (REG 764/2008).[38]

Contrary to the evaluations of REG 2679/98 and former Decision 3052/95, the assessment of REG 764/2008 has been rather positive.[39] REG 764/2008's twofold approach of combining transparency—by imposing a duty to exchange information between national authorities and enterprises— and efficiency—by avoiding any duplication of checks and testing— has been successful. By monitoring regularly the application of the principle of mutual recognition on the basis of notifications, yearly reports, and meetings, the Commission is now able to identify the specific categories of goods for which mutual recognition is (still) problematic and for which further measures are needed.[40]

(2) *The institutionalization of dialogue between the Commission and the Member States on the application of a justification ground*

The ECJ's case law on the free movement provisions and the principle of mutual recognition indicates that Member States often take a protectionist stance by interpreting the concept of a 'justification ground' extremely widely. In order to discourage this trend, and to remedy the envisaged measure at an early stage wherever necessary, certain legislative instruments have called on the Commission to examine the compatibility of the measure in question with EU law within the shortest possible time frame.[41] This approach, which has previously been adopted in numerous directives relating to the application of safeguard clauses, may indeed guarantee a more impartial approach to the admissibility of the justification ground as well as a more balanced application of the principle of mutual recognition. A more universal application of the Commission's participation in this process would certainly be opportune,[42] if feasible.

C. Making the principle more effective by introducing a better-defined framework

I have already mentioned that a lack of familiarity with the principle of mutual recognition and its incorrect application are frequent causes for complaint for both businesses and individuals attempting to exercise their rights in the EU. A related cause of dissatisfaction concerns the lack of effective, equivalent, and swift mechanisms of information and enforcement in the Member States.[43] A business operator is often unaware

[38] On the content of this Regulation, see: Part I, ch 3, II, C. 'Making the principle more effective by introducing a better-defined framework'.

[39] Communication from the Commission to the European Parliament and the Council—First Report on the Application of Regulation 764/2008 (n 17) p. 1–12. This positive evaluation does not mean that there are no shortcomings at all. For instance, with regard to the notification procedure, the Commission has acknowledged that there are clear indications that the Member States do not notify all decisions.

[40] Communication from the Commission to the European Parliament and the Council—First Report on the Application of Regulation 764/2008 (n 17) p. 8–9, gives an overview of the problematic categories of goods and indicates whether—according to the Commission—further harmonization is desirable or not.

[41] See, for instance: Article 3(4) DIR 2000/31/EC; Article 35 DIR 2006/123/EC.

[42] M. TISON, 'De richtlijn Elektronische Handel en financiële diensten: een brug te ver', *in Liber amicorum Yvette Merchiers* (Bruges, Die Keure, 2001) 610.

[43] § 43 DIR 2006/123/EC; Communication from the Commission to the European Parliament and the Council—The impact and the effectiveness of the single market (n 1) p. 17–18 and p. 23.

of where the relevant information can be found in another Member State. Furthermore, long waiting periods may sometimes need to be endured before an answer is given to a request. On other occasions, quick decisions may be taken by the national administration that order the operator, by virtue of technical national rules, to withdraw a specific product—usually without offering any clear margin to appeal against such decision. The Commission has also implemented a number of initiatives designed to address some of these unsatisfactory situations.[44]

A first tool consists in a short but sound procedure that each competent authority planning to take restrictive measures in relation to goods will be obliged to follow before[45] taking such a decision.[46] What is crucial to this procedure, as set out in REG 764/2008, is the written notice that the national administration must send to the economic actor, in which it will have to explain how its intended decision can be reconciled with the principle of mutual recognition.[47] The procedure provides for a waiting period (of at least twenty working days) that enables economic operators to submit comments to the written notice if they wish. Once this term expires, the national authority is obliged to take its decision within a period of twenty working days, extendable to forty working days in exceptional cases. This decision, which the economic operator must be notified of, can be qualified as elaborate since it must be reasoned, and must include the grounds for rejecting any arguments put forward by the operator as well as the remedies available under national law and their corresponding time limits.

The question that now arises is whether such a procedural framework, which rests upon the requirement of a written notice, will indeed succeed in enhancing the practical application of the principle of mutual recognition. Purely in terms of its content, the written notice is anything but revolutionary. The burden of proof that lies with the national administration, the requirement of a public interest to set the principle of mutual recognition aside, the need for a proportionality test, and so on are all elements

Communication from the Commission to the European Parliament, the Council, the European Economic and Social Committee and the Committee of the Regions—A single market for 21st Century Europe, COM (2007) 724 final, p. 12–14. See also: § 43 DIR 2006/123/EC; HOUSE OF LORDS, EU COMMITTEE, The Single Market: Wallflower or Dancing Partner? Inquiry into the Commission's review of the Single Market, 2008, 15–16, retrievable at: <http://www.publications.parliament.uk/pa/ld200708/ldselect/ldeucom/36/36.pdf>.

[44] For a comment on these instruments, see, for instance: G. RIVEL, 'Le principe de reconnaissance mutuelle dans le marché unique du XXIème siècle', *RMCUE* 2007, 518–24.

[45] Meanwhile, temporary suspension of the marketing of a product is—in principle—*not* allowed, unless there is a serious risk to the safety and health of the users or unless the measure concerns generally prohibited products on grounds of public morality or public security. In the latter case, a suspension is allowed, but requires an immediate and well-reasoned notification to both the economic operator and the Commission (Art. 7 REG 764/2008).

[46] The procedure is included in Articles 4 to 7 REG 764/2008 and must be followed in relation to all decisions which lead to the prohibition of the placing on the market of a product, the modification or additional testing of a product before its placing on the market or the withdrawal of a product (Art. 2(1) REG 764/2008). For an evaluation of REG 764/2008, see, for instance: A. KAPPERT, 'De Verordening Wederzijdse Erkenning verbetert procedure rond handelsbelemmeringen', *Journaal Warenwet* 2010, 7–12; A. KAPOOR and T. KLINDT, 'Die Reform des Akkreditierungswesens im Europäischen Produktsicherheitsrecht', *EuZW* 2009, 134–8; R. MUÑOZ, 'Le principe de reconnaissance mutuelle et le règlement 764/2008. Chronique d'une future révolution', *RDUE* 2009, 513–607; B. RAEVENS, 'Le règlement 764/2008: vers une consolidation de la reconnaissance mutuelle des produits', *J.D.E.* 2009, 131–3.

[47] *In concreto*, the written notice must, *first*, specify the national technical rule which underpins the decision, *secondly*, set out sufficient technical or scientific evidence regarding the public interest of Article 36 TFEU or another overriding reason that the national rule aims to protect and, *thirdly*, demonstrate that the rule is appropriate and does not go beyond what is necessary (Art. 6(1) REG 764/2008).

which constitute an explicit manifestation of the principle of mutual recognition, as laid down in Article 34 TFEU and interpreted by the ECJ. From this perspective, one could argue—as I have done in the context of the mutual recognition clauses—that this procedure has little added value. Yet, from a broader perspective, I do believe that this procedural framework could be beneficial in applying the principle of mutual recognition more successfully. The European legislator has obviously understood that a successful application of the European principle of mutual recognition requires first of all that the principle of mutual recognition works well at *national* level. In explicitly including the mutual recognition mechanism in a European regulation, the invisible, intangible nature of this principle has been substituted for a concrete text, with well-defined corresponding duties.[48] Under this new instrument, both national administrations and national judges are obliged—more explicitly than ever before—first, to resolve each case using a European parameter, namely the principle of mutual recognition (which should lead to a decrease in nationally tinted decisions and judgments), secondly, to present an elaborate and reasoned written decision (which should lead to a decrease in arbitrary decisions), and thirdly, to do all of this within a short deadline (which should lead to a decrease in periods of legal uncertainty).[49]

It remains to be seen whether the explicit reference to available national judicial redress mechanisms will lead to an increase in judicial proceedings. As I have already mentioned, businesses are usually reluctant to start judicial proceedings. They, like individuals, tend to be more inclined to opt for (cheaper and faster) alternative dispute resolution mechanisms such as SOLVIT,[50] or simply adapt their commercial strategies rather than engaging in costly and potentially lengthy judicial proceedings. Moreover, the 'preventive dialogue' which is the core mechanism of REG 764/2008 is precisely aimed at preventing and amicably and effectively settling problems of free movement.[51]

In relation to the services sector, similar concerns have led to the introduction of measures aimed at simplifying administration, albeit using a different approach. DIR 2006/123/EC does not include a strictly defined procedural framework, as is the case with REG 764/2008, but instead lists what are largely the duties of EU law as drawn from the ECJ's case law from recent decades.[52] Because it states the obvious, i.e. by inserting well-known EU duties into a legislative instrument, the services directive is another illustration of how repeated breaches of law in identical cases highlighted the need for a legislative process. These so-called well-known duties were apparently less well-known than assumed.[53]

[48] However, even under REG764/2008, uncertainty about how and when to apply mutual recognition in practice still occurs: Communication from the Commission to the European Parliament and the Council— First Report on the Application of Regulation 764/2008 (n 17) p. 10.

[49] Especially the explicit stipulation of this deadline, which was not yet present in the Commission's proposal (COM (2007) 36 final), should be welcomed, as it might reduce to a considerable extent situations of legal uncertainty.

[50] SOLVIT is an on-line problem solving network in which EU Member States work together to solve without legal proceedings problems caused by the misapplication of internal market law by public authorities and has been active since July 2002. For more information on this system, which is coordinated by the European Commission, see: <http://ec.europa.eu/solvit/site/about/index_en.htm>.

[51] Communication from the Commission to the European Parliament and the Council— First Report on the Application of Regulation 764/2008 (n 17) p. 6.

[52] See, for: instead of ; § 43-52 and Articles 5 to 16 DIR 2006/123/EC.

[53] Interview with M. MIRANDA, administrator at the European Commission, DG Internal Market, Brussels, Apr. 23, 2007. On the need of a horizontal legal framework in this area, see: Report from the Commission to the Council and the European Parliament—The state of the internal market for services presented under the first stage of the Internal Market Strategy for Services (n 8) p. 10 ff. and 51 ff.

REG 764/2008 and DIR 2006/123/EC, furthermore, are intended to improve the visibility of entities in charge of providing businesses with the necessary information in the goods and services sectors. The legislator has obliged the Member States to identify what are known as the Product Contact Points (in the area of goods) and the Single Contact Points (in the area of services) and has also specified the types of information they will need to provide on request.[54] From a business perspective, it is above all crucial that these entities, once identified, provide the necessary information without delay. In this regard, it is regrettable that DIR 2006/123/EC imposes only a rather vague duty to respond 'as quickly as possible' (Art. 7(4) DIR 2006/123/EC) rather than stipulating a clear-cut time limit of, for instance, fifteen working days, by analogy with Article 10(2) REG 761/2008 in the goods area.[55]

A final element that may contribute to a better defined framework is the performance of mutual evaluation. Obliging Member States to notify the Commission of the outcomes of national legislation assessments will allow Member States to compare their regulatory approaches and to simplify, where necessary, their national legal frameworks.[56]

D. Stimulating administrative cooperation

Open dialogue, administrative cooperation, and the exchange of relevant information amongst Member States are factors that have long been recognized as crucial remedies to the impaired function of the principle of mutual recognition, since administrative cooperation that works properly represents an essential instrument for compliance control.[57]

[54] Articles 9 and 10 REG 764/2008; Articles 6 and 7 DIR 2006/123/EC; Article 57 DIR 2005/36/EC. There are also plans to create 'one stop shops' in other areas of law, e.g. tax law: Communication from the Commission to the Council, the European Parliament and the European Economic and Social Committee—Removing cross-border tax obstacles for EU citizens, COM (2010) 769, retrievable at: <http://ec.europa.eu/taxation_customs/resources/documents/taxation/gen_info/tax_policy/com(2010)769_en.pdf>.

[55] For a critique on the vagueness of the provision in DIR 2006/123/EC, see, for instance: HOUSE OF LORDS, EU COMMITTEE, The Services Directive Revisited, 2005-06, retrievable at: <http://www.publications.parliament.uk/pa/ld200506/ldselect/ldeucom/215/215.pdf>, in particular question 29 of the minutes of evidence, in which concerns are expressed with regard to the quality of the information (Will it be the same quality in every Member State?) and the uncertain time frame (How long will a business firm have to wait for an answer?).

[56] Mutual evaluation is, for instance, included in the proposal for a directive on professional qualifications. See: Proposal for a directive of the European Parliament and of the Council amending Directive 2005/36/EC on the recognition of professional qualifications and Regulation on administrative cooperation through the Internal Market Information System, COM (2011) 883 final, p. 12.

[57] Report from the Commission to the Council and the European Parliament—The implementation of the Commission's White Paper on completing the internal market, COM (1994) 55 final, p. 8–9; Communication from the Commission to the Council and the European Parliament—The development of administrative cooperation in the implementation and enforcement of community legislation in the internal market, COM (1994) 29 final, p. 1–9; Resolution of the Council—Coordination with regard to information exchange between administrations, *O.J.* C-181, 02.07.1994, p.1–2; Resolution of the Council—The development of administrative cooperation in the implementation and enforcement of Community legislation in the internal market, *O.J.* C-179, 01.07.1994, p. 1–3; Commission Recommendation of 31 March 2008 on enhanced administrative cooperation in the context of the posting of workers in the framework of the provision of services, *O.J.* C-85, 04.04.2008, p. 1–4; DIR 2011/16/EU: § 7 (on the need for clearer and more precise rules governing administrative cooperation and the exchange of information) and § 8–10 (on the need for more direct contact between the Member States' local or national offices). See also: Opinion of AG Mengozzi in Joined Cases C-316/07, C-358/07, C-359/07, C-360/07, C-409/07 and C-410/07 *Markus Stoß and others* [2010] ECR I-8069, § 103, who denounces the lack of administrative cooperation in the gambling sector which is, according

Therefore, in nearly all of the relevant secondary legislative instruments I have discussed, cooperation mechanisms have been developed between the Member States and between the Member States and the Commission.[58] Despite these instruments, certain practical barriers—such as different administrative and working cultures, language barriers, and a lack of clearly identified partners in other Member States—still hamper cooperation occasionally.[59] Deficient cooperation mechanisms have unfortunately resulted in Member States reverting to control measures which are unnecessary and/or disproportionate in light of the ECJ's interpretation of the Treaty provisions and have led to calls for them to be adapted.[60]

The Internal Market Information system (IMI) was developed precisely in order to achieve better communication between Member States' administrations. This new electronic tool provides a system for exchanging information so that Member States can engage in more effective day-to-day cooperation as they implement the internal market legislation. The system will be used first in the area of professional qualifications (DIR 2005/36/EC) and the services directive (DIR 2006/123/EC),[61] but in view of its high potential,[62] it is likely to be extended to other sectors in the near future.[63]

In the non-harmonized field, the outlook is somewhat less promising. No organized cooperation exists and cooperation between national authorities is still less than smooth, despite the ECJ's case law on the matter. If cooperation does take place, it happens on an ad hoc basis through informal contacts, for example via the standing committee set up by DIR 98/34/EC and/or through SOLVIT.[64] In the absence of informal contacts,

to him, highly detrimental for mutual trust and prevents the application of the principle of mutual recognition. Similarly, Opinion of AG Bot in Case C-347/09 *Dickinger*, nyr, § 134.

[58] See, for instance: Articles 28 to 36 DIR 2006/123/EC; Chapter IV DIR 2011/24/EU; DIR 2011/82/EU. For the legislative instruments which currently do not yet include an explicit legal basis for administrative cooperation, there have been taken initiatives, or at least expressed intentions, to implement such a legal basis. See, for instance, with regard to the New Approach directives: Communication from the Commission to the Council and the European Parliament—Enhancing the Implementation of the New Approach Directives, COM (2003) 240 final, p. 33.

[59] Report from the Commission—First biennial report on the application of the principle of mutual recognition in the market of goods and services (n 1) p. 7–8; Interview with H. INGELS, administrator at the European Commission, DG Enterprises, Brussels, 9 February 2007.

[60] See, for instance: Communication from the Commission to the Council, the European Parliament, the Economic and Social Committee and the Committee of the Regions—The implementation of Directive 96/71/EC in the Member States, COM (2003) 458 final; Communication from the Commission to the Council, the European Parliament, the European Economic and Social Committee and the Committee of the Regions—Posting of workers in the framework of the provision of services: maximising its benefits and potential while guaranteeing the protection of workers, COM (2007) 304 final, p. 9. On the need to improve the management of the goods market through strengthened market surveillance and better coordination between accreditation, certification, and surveillance bodies, see: Communication from the Commission to the European Parliament, the Council, the European Economic and Social Committee and the Committee of the Regions—A single market for 21st century Europe (n 43) p. 5.

[61] On this instrument, see: <http://ec.europa.eu/internal_market/imi-net/about_en.html>.

[62] Commission staff working document on the transposition and implementation of the Professional Qualifications Directive (n 12) p. 11–12 and 17, retrievable at: <http://ec.europa.eu/internal_market/qualifications/docs/evaluation/staff-working-doc_en.pdf>.

[63] Communication from the Commission to the European Parliament, the Council, the Economic and Social Committee and the Committee of the Regions—Towards a single market act for a highly competitive social market economy 50 proposals for improving our work, business and exchanges with one another, COM (2010) 608 final, p. 31.

[64] Commission staff working document—Accompanying document to the Proposal for a Regulation of the European Parliament and of the Council laying down procedures relating to the application of certain national technical rules to products lawfully marketed in another Member State and repealing Decision 3052/95/EC Impact assessment (n 1) p. 25.

national administrations often tend to ignore the principle of mutual recognition.[65] The active approach that the national body is supposed to take[66] is often simply absent. There is therefore an urgent need to stimulate dialogue between national administrations in the non-harmonized field. However, before any specific action is taken in this regard, it would be advisable to gain an accurate overview of the specific sectors and administrations concerned.

E. Harmonization

The principle of mutual recognition plays a pivotal role in the internal market; however, as we have seen, it is not the sole cornerstone. In its resolution on mutual recognition, the Council emphasized the need for a coherent combination of harmonization, standardization, conformity assessment instruments, and mutual recognition.[67] The ECJ's case law, the notification procedure of DIR 98/34/EC, and the round table conferences held with different sectors have all provided a multitude of examples where widely divergent national legislation has precluded the application of the principle of mutual recognition and, thus, highlighted the need for harmonization measures to enable smooth application of the principle of mutual recognition in similar cases in the future. The choice between (much or little) mutual recognition and (much or little) harmonization requires a careful assessment for each specific case of how the objectives at stake can best be achieved and will sometimes require further (harmonizing) measures following a period of enforcement.[68]

The conclusion that 'the single market for goods is today a mature construction' and that all technical barriers to goods have been lifted[69] is largely indebted to the combined approach of mutual recognition, (minimum) harmonization, and standardization, yet it would be mistaken to conclude that the job is done. Maintaining a dynamic, expanding market for goods requires that the achieved acquis is built upon and that more measures are taken, particularly with regard to market surveillance and the standardization process.[70]

As far as the services sector is concerned, DIR 2006/123/EC (especially its 'blacklisting' of certain requirements which are expressly forbidden) is a good example of an instrument that is not particularly revolutionary in itself, since it constitutes a codification of the ECJ's case law, but which nonetheless has indisputable added value from the perspective of legal certainty.[71] It is precisely this need for increased legal certainty and

[65] Interview with H. INGELS, administrator at the European Commission, DG Enterprises, Brussels, 9 February 2007.

[66] See, for instance: ECJ, Case C-432/03 *Commission v Portugal* [2005] ECR I-9665, para 47.

[67] Resolution of the Council—Mutual recognition, *O.J.* C-141, 19.05.2000, p. 5, § 6. Also the Commission—generally seen as an advocate of mutual recognition—recognized the importance of harmonization. See, for instance: Communication from the Commission to the European Parliament and the Council— First Report on the Application of Regulation 764/2008 (n 17) p. 13, where it held that 'harmonization remains one of the most effective instruments, both for economic operators and for the national administrations'.

[68] See, for instance: European Commission, *Internal Market Scoreboard*, May 2002, No 10, p. 17–24, which revealed, for instance, that in the bicycles sector persistent obstacles had led to the agreement on a European standard, whereas no such steps had been necessary in the beer sector. For another example, see: Opinion of AG Jääskinen in Case C-142/09 *Lahousse* [2010] ECR I-11685, § 123 (with regard to motor vehicles and their components).

[69] M. MONTI, *A New Strategy for the Single Market – At The Service of Europe's Economy and Society. Report to the President of the European Commission José Manuel Barroso*, 2010, 50–1, retrievable at: <http://ec.europa.eu/bepa/pdf/monti_report_final_10_05_2010_en.pdf>.

[70] MONTI, *A New Strategy for the Single Market – At The Service of Europe's Economy and Society* (n 69).

[71] H. BADINGER and N. MAYDELL, 'Legal and Economic Issues in Completing the EU Internal Market for Services: an Interdisciplinary Perspective', *JCMS* 2009, 712–13.

more automatic mutual recognition that demands additional harmonization measures in other more specific sectors, such as the health care sector and the professional qualifications sector, for example.[72] It is also worth mentioning that in this latter sector it is not only harmonization *sensu stricto* that is being pursued but also the development of 'codes of conduct' or 'common platforms'.[73] These are typically adopted by non-state, self-regulated bodies such as professional associations and aim to develop criteria for professional qualifications that can bridge the substantial differences between training conditions in different Member States.[74]

More harmonization is also foreseeable in light of the rapidly developing e-market. Mutual recognition of e-identification and e-authentication, which can be of use in widely divergent areas such as official documentation, commercial activities, and the health care sector, requires the adoption of harmonization measures that will ensure the reliability of these e-products for everyone concerned in the different Member States.[75]

It is interesting to note that harmonization measures are not limited to the characteristics of the product, service, or certificate that is the object of mutual recognition, i.e. substantive harmonization,[76] but that they also address procedural aspects[77] and tend to apply to the actors involved in the mutual recognition process. With regard

[72] MONTI, *A New Strategy for the Single Market – At The Service of Europe's Economy and Society* (n 69) 54 and 58–60. A crucial tool in reducing the complexity of mutual recognition procedures is the proposed introduction of a European Professional Card. See, on this issue: Green Paper of the Commission—Modernising the Professional Qualifications Directive, COM (2011) 367 final, p. 2–3; Proposal for a directive of the European Parliament and of the Council amending Directive 2005/36/EC on the recognition of professional qualifications and Regulation on administrative cooperation through the Internal Market Information System (n 56) p. 7–8. Communication from the Commission to the European Parliament, the Council, the Economic and Social Committee and the Committee of the Regions, 'Single Market Act. Twelve levers to boost growth and strengthen confidence. Working together to create new growth', COM (2011) 206 final, p. 7–8; Article 11 DIR 2011/24/EU; Commission Implementing Directive 2012/52/EU of 20 December 2012 laying down measures to facilitate the recognition of medical prescriptions issued in another Member State, *O.J.* L-356, 22.12.2012, p. 68–70.

[73] The concept of 'common platform' under the current directive is considered to be a failure: Green Paper of the Commission—Modernising the Professional Qualifications Directive (n 72) p. 6. Therefore, the new proposal for a directive seeks to replace it by a new concept 'common training principles', which is aimed at introducing more automaticity in the recognition of qualifications. On this new concept, see: Proposal for a directive of the European Parliament and of the Council amending Directive 2005/36/EC on the recognition of professional qualifications and Regulation on administrative cooperation through the Internal Market Information System (n 56) p. 10.

[74] Article 15 DIR 2005/36/EC. For an evaluation of these 'codes of conduct', see, for instance: P. DELIMATSIS, 'Thou Shall Not (Dis)trust: Codes of Conduct and Harmonization of Professional Standards in the EU', *CML Rev.* 2010, 1049–87.

[75] See, for instance: Communication from the Commission to the European Parliament, the Council, the Economic and Social Committee and the Committee of the Regions—Towards a Single Market Act For a highly competitive social market economy 50 proposals for improving our work, business and exchanges with one another (n 63) p. 15; Communication from the Commission to the European Parliament, the Council, the Economic and Social Committee and the Committee of the Regions—Single Market Act—Twelve levers to boost growth and strengthen confidence—Working together to create new growth (n 72) p. 12–14; Proposal for a directive of the European Parliament and of the Council amending Directive 2005/36/EC on the recognition of professional qualifications and Regulation on administrative cooperation through the Internal Market Information System (n 56) p. 11–12.

[76] See, for instance: § 20-21DIR 2009/48/EC, where it was held necessary to adopt new essential safety requirements in view of the technical progress since the adoption of the original directive; § 6 DIR 2009/40/EC, where it was held that it is necessary to adapt rapidly to technical progress the standards and methods laid down in other directives; or § 2 DIR 2009/39/EC, where it was recalled that differences between national laws relating to foodstuffs for particular nutritional uses impede their free movement.

[77] See, for instance: REG 1107/2009 which highlights, for instance, the need for strict deadlines (§ 14), good administrative cooperation (§ 28), and a system of information exchange (§ 37); DIR 2011/16/EU, which underlines the need of time limits (§ 12) and standardized forms (§ 23).

to the latter aspect, some harmonization measures aim to clarify the necessary criteria for national authorities that are in charge of allowing or controlling products on the market[78] or that are entitled to issue official documents.[79] These measures therefore reveal not only that national authorities are suspicious of goods that they are unfamiliar with but also that they seem to entertain serious doubts as to the competence of their counterparts in the other Member States.

Finally, in areas where significant differences persist and harmonization is not feasible, the EU legislator supports partial mutual recognition.[80]

F. The establishment of EU committees and EU agencies

The relatively few short references that are made to mutual trust in the majority of policy documents contrast sharply with the actual contribution of mutual trust and the principle of mutual recognition. The majority of measures that I have just discussed all aim to increase mutual trust in order to enhance how the principle of mutual recognition functions. Of all these measures, harmonization is probably the most far-reaching in its attainment of mutual trust. After all, if the same rules are applied, there seems to be no reason to suspect the other party. Distrust may arise even here, though, since an assumption that all rules are equal is still no guarantee that they will be applied equally in all Member States. This relates to the question of distrust in market surveillance, which can of course be dealt with by developing criteria that must be fulfilled by the controlling authorities of each Member State.[81] In some sectors, however, a more drastic solution has been implemented, namely the creation of central EU agencies or bodies which are authorized to take centralized decisions.[82] Their existence is an admission of the lack of trust among Member States' authorities and their subsequent unwillingness to apply the principle of mutual recognition in certain sensitive areas, even in combination

[78] In the context of market surveillance, the Commission has concluded that further harmonization leading to a more homogeneous designation system would probably be able to restore the mutual trust among the Member States in each other's conformity assessment bodies, and, consequently, enhance a smooth working of the principle of mutual recognition: Communication from the Commission to the Council and the European Parliament—Enhancing the Implementation of the New Approach Directives (n 58) p. 6–12 and p. 14.

[79] See, for instance, in the area of driving licences: § 18, Article 10 and Annex IV DIR 2006/126/EC; or in the area of mutual recognition of (medical) prescriptions in the area of cross-border health care: HOUSE OF LORDS, EU COMMITTEE, Healthcare across EU borders: a safe framework, 2008–2009, 41–2, retrievable at: <http://www.publications.parliament.uk/pa/ld200809/ldselect/ldeucom/30/9780104014356.pdf>, in which it is held that the ability of nurses to prescribe medication for patients is limited to a minority of Member States and can therefore cause problems in cross-border situations.

[80] Proposal for a directive of the European Parliament and of the Council amending Directive 2005/36/EC on the recognition of professional qualifications and Regulation on administrative cooperation through the Internal Market Information System (n 56) p. 10–11.

[81] Communication from the Commission to the Council and the European Parliament—Enhancing the Implementation of the New Approach Directives (n 58) p. 14–19 and 25; Communication from the Commission to the Council, the European Parliament, the European Economic and Social Committee—The Internal Market for Goods: a cornerstone of Europe's competitiveness (n 1) p. 8–9.

[82] See, for instance: the creation of the Food Agency (REG 178/2002), the European Medicines Agency (REG 726/2004), the European Aviation Safety Agency (REG 216/2008), or the European Chemicals Agency (REG 1907/2006). Reference can, furthermore be made to the committees created by the New Approach directives, or, for instance, the Committee for Proprietary Medicinal Products mentioned in Article 32 DIR 2001/83/EC.

with harmonization. These central authorities are often best-placed to take up a role in conflict resolution when the mutual recognition mechanism appears to work unsatisfactorily at the bilateral or multilateral level. Furthermore, their role is not necessarily restricted to that of conflict management, since they may also act as logistical hubs, relay points, catalysts, and information centres for cross-border cooperation.[83]

[83] Opinion of the European Economic and Social Committee on the Posting of workers in the framework of the provision of services—Maximising its benefits and potential while guaranteeing the protection of workers, COM (2007) 304 final, *O.J.* C-224, 30.08.2008, p. 98.

4

Conclusions on the Principle of Mutual Recognition in the Internal Market

The previous chapters have confirmed the pivotal role that the principle of mutual recognition continues to play in the internal market context despite some difficulties in daily practice. Since the ECJ's *Cassis de Dijon* ruling, the principle of mutual recognition has become the cornerstone[1] of the internal market—in both the judicial and legislative contexts—and has continued to maintain a position of interest. Recent legislative instruments which aim to enhance the workability of the principle of mutual recognition indeed confirm its value and indicate that it remains a topic of great interest for the European legislator, despite hints that the internal market is currently at a low ebb in terms of popularity.[2]

In order to draw conclusions, I will now return to the major themes developed in Part I: the legal basis (section I); the terminology (section II); the addressees of the principle of mutual recognition (section III); its object (section IV); its main characteristics (section V); and finally, its workability (section VI).

I. Legal Basis

With respect to the legal basis of the principle of mutual recognition, I started by emphasizing that the duty of mutual recognition can easily be connected to several other principles: the principles of proportionality, subsidiarity, sincere cooperation, and mutual trust, as well as the free movement provisions. Although I selected the free movement provisions as the most appropriate legal basis for the principle of mutual recognition, I also recognized the need firstly for a good cooperation mechanism (principle of sincere cooperation) and secondly for the existence of mutual trust (general principle of mutual trust) as the two main pillars upon which the principle of mutual recognition can be built, both in the legislative and judicial contexts.

II. Terminology

Regarding terminology, I examined the continual shift between various concepts: the principle of mutual recognition, the principle of equivalence, and the home country

[1] Report from the Commission—First biennial report on the application of the principle of mutual recognition in the market of goods and services, SEC (1999) 1106, p. 2; Communication from the Commission to the Council, the European Parliament, the European Economic and Social Committee and the Committee of the Regions–Internal Market Strategy Priorities 2003–2006, COM (2003) 238 final, p. 7.

[2] But also more needed than ever, see: M. MONTI, *A New Strategy for the Single Market–At The Service of Europe's Economy and Society. Report to the President of the European Commission José Manuel Barroso*, p. 20, retrievable at: <http://ec.europa.eu/bepa/pdf/monti_report_final_10_05_2010_en.pdf>.

control principle. I concluded that neither the ECJ nor the European legislator has succeeded in clarifying this matter unequivocally. Legal doctrine has a tendency to use the terms country of origin principle, principle of equivalence, and principle of mutual recognition simply as synonyms. I have tried to demonstrate that this is not necessarily wise. While these concepts are certainly related to each other, they in fact refer to different aspects of the mutual recognition mechanism.

The legislative internal market acquis is generally less about trusting or recognizing an entirely different system and more about organizing and imposing equivalence instead, thus trusting what is 'equal'. However, I have highlighted the fact that in some exceptional cases, mutual recognition has been imposed without any form of equivalence having been established. In the non-harmonized sector, I come to a similar conclusion: in some judgments, equivalence appeared to be the core of the ECJ's reasoning; in others, it initially appeared to be absent, or at most implicitly present; in yet others, equivalence was indeed entirely absent. Similarly, in some judgments 'equivalence' required truly equivalent, very similar, or quasi-identical obligations, while in others 'equivalence' referred to the protected interest in question, which often did not require equivalent protection but sufficient protection instead. I concluded that the principle of equivalence should perhaps best be seen as an application of the proportionality test. From this perspective, the equivalence test helps to determine the contours of the mutual recognition mechanism, but it cannot be put on the same footing as the principle of mutual recognition, since the equivalence requirement is omnipresent neither in the judicial context nor in the harmonized field.

Similarly, I suggested that the country of origin or home state (control) principle should not be equated with the principle of mutual recognition. In the non-harmonized context, I indicated that the ECJ has explicitly stated that no home state control principle is included in the TFEU. Furthermore, the ECJ's free movement case law clearly shows that the regulations of both the country of origin and the country of destination can be called into question while the ECJ is evaluating infringements of the free movement provisions. It would therefore be misleading to speak of a home state principle in this context. In the harmonized sector, the country of origin or home state (control) principle occupies a prominent position in certain specific sectors, e.g. the financial services sector, the audiovisual media sector, and the electronic commerce sector, whereas in other areas, such as the New Approach directives and the area of diplomas, the country of origin (or home state control) principle has a far less relevant role to play. The country of origin (or home state control) principle appears above all to be a legislative instrument which can modulate the contours of the legislative mutual recognition mechanism by attributing specific powers to the home Member State in sectors where a strong emphasis on the home state seems appropriate.

I therefore concluded that in both the judicial and legislative contexts, it is advisable to use the term 'principle of mutual recognition' whenever referring in general terms to the mechanism described in the free movement provisions. Though the ECJ seems reluctant to use this term, it is very common in the legislative context and is in my opinion the term that best reflects the mechanism that the ECJ has developed since *Cassis de Dijon*. The free movement provisions do indeed imply that Member States should, in principle, mutually recognize goods, services, persons (diplomas), and capital coming from other Member States. The other two terms ('equivalence' and 'home state'), however, are less general than the term 'mutual recognition', as they refer to two specific features of the mutual recognition mechanism, namely equivalence requirements and the mechanism for distributing powers among the home and host states.

III. Addressees

The TFEU free movement provisions and the principle of mutual recognition contained within it are primarily obligations addressed to the Member States. It is incumbent on the Member States and, in particular, on their national administrators, to put the principle of mutual recognition into practice.

The administrative and public nature of the addressees, however, is subject to two caveats. Firstly, the ECJ explicitly recognizes in its case law that not only a Member State's administrative authorities but also its judicial authorities are bound by the duty of mutual recognition. Secondly, a distinction is drawn between the TFEU provision on the free movement of goods (solely addressed to Member States) and the TFEU provision on the free movement of services (addressed to entities of a public and non-public nature). However, this distinction between 'public' and 'private' addressees must be nuanced in light of the ECJ's case law: in the area of goods, the ECJ upholds a broad interpretation of the concept 'public authority', and in the area of services, the vast majority of national regulations made subject to the mutual recognition mechanism were of a public nature or were at least derived from bodies very closely linked to a Member State's government. Therefore, the public-private divide that results from the TFEU provisions has been mitigated to some extent by the ECJ's case law.

While the principle of mutual recognition imposes potentially far-reaching duties on the Member States' authorities, it also entails significant consequences for natural and legal persons. Indeed, the direct invocability that the ECJ has attached to the TFEU free movement provisions implies that it will often be a natural or legal person who triggers the application of the mutual recognition principle in the internal market context by claiming rights related to the relevant free movement provisions.

IV. Object

The case law mentioned in Part I has revealed that the 'object' of the mutual recognition mechanism in the internal market context is extremely broad and also that it has grown significantly over the past years. The duty described in *Cassis de Dijon* to recognize alcoholic products, for example, was quickly extended to all other products produced lawfully in the country of origin. Likewise, the duty to recognize goods was quickly extended to foreign services, diplomas (persons), and capital. Furthermore, the ECJ has made it plain that not only goods, services, and persons lawfully marketed, provided, or employed in the home country must be recognized in the host country: in the same way, any document, certificate, certification, attestation, control, or any other kind of factual or legal component related to these goods, services, or persons must also be recognized insofar as these elements have been (lawfully) attested by the competent authority of a Member State.

The use of the word 'lawfully', which requires that goods, citizens, and companies meet the commercial, technical, and other requirements stipulated by the home country's regulations, hints at the fact that the mutual recognition mechanism ultimately amounts to a duty to recognize other Member States' regulations on the goods, services, or persons concerned and indicates the largely regulatory nature of the object of the mutual recognition mechanism in this context.

V. Characteristics

As regards the characteristics of the principle of mutual recognition, throughout my study in Part I, I detected four major features, which are retrievable both in the judicial context and the harmonized context, and which all help to gauge the contours of the mutual recognition mechanism: the flexible nature of the principle of mutual recognition (section V, A); the non-automatic nature of the principle of mutual recognition (section V, B); the teleological or functional nature of the principle of mutual recognition (section V, C); the versatile nature of the principle of mutual recognition (section V, D).

A. The flexible nature of the principle of mutual recognition

The principle of mutual recognition is flexible, especially because of the nature of the proportionality test that is applied to it: this test allows for the principle to be widened or narrowed depending, first of all, on the national public interest that is at stake. For instance, I have indicated that in cases where public health or human life is at risk, the ECJ tends to apply a less rigid proportionality test and consequently a weaker duty of mutual recognition than for instance in areas where consumer protection is at stake. However, stating that either a broad or narrow interpretation of the principle of mutual recognition is applied depending only on the 'sensitive' nature of the interest in question would be oversimplifying matters, since the ECJ has also accepted the application of the principle of mutual recognition in sensitive areas such as social security and health insurance. There are indeed a large variety of factors which can influence the outcome of the proportionality test and the contours of the principle of mutual recognition, and these go far beyond the nature of the interest in question. Such factors might include, for example, the inconsistent or incoherent behaviour of the Member State concerned, the European or international dimension of a national public interest, the *majoritarian* view of the Member States, particularities of a given national identity that are (or are not) deemed worthy of EU protection, and so on. In the harmonized sector, I have observed that the principle of mutual recognition tends to fluctuate according to the level of harmonization acquired, which may vary significantly from one instrument to another and even within one instrument. This can lead to different outcomes regarding the distribution of competences between the home and host states, any equivalence requirements, and the availability of grounds for non-recognition.

The principle of mutual recognition is not a static concept that will be applied identically throughout the course of time; instead, it is a dynamic concept that amounts to a process of learning by doing. Changing views in society, new scientific developments and also progress in harmonization may all influence the way in which the principle of mutual recognition is applied. This inevitably brings us to the next characteristic: the non-automatic nature of the principle of mutual recognition.

B. The non-automatic nature of the principle of mutual recognition

Perhaps the most obvious proof of the non-automatic nature of the principle of mutual recognition is the combination of traditional justification grounds (i.e. Treaty based-justification grounds and the rule of reason in the non-harmonized context; secondary legislation-based justification grounds in the harmonized context) and the more recent tendency to invoke the protection of fundamental rights in order to justify barriers to free movement.

The Treaty framework and the secondary legislation framework, as interpreted by the ECJ, both demonstrate that the internal market is clearly concerned not only with economic free movement rights (and mutual recognition) but also with the protection of non-economic interests such as safety, health, the consumer, the environment, and other relevant public interests. The fact that the latter are justification grounds, and thus exceptions to the free movement provisions, which are in principle subject to a restrictive interpretation in the ECJ's case law, does not make them any less important than the free movement provisions. This fact has become especially visible in judgments where both the free movement provisions and fundamental rights are at stake. The ECJ has emphasized that it is impossible to establish any hierarchy in these categories of fundamental rights and has repeatedly maintained that the two groups of rights should be balanced or reconciled. It has been less explicit in imposing a similar 'balancing' or 'reconciling' duty on other public interests, but it is or should be implicitly present nevertheless, particularly with regard to interests that have a European or international dimension.

The fact that the protection of fundamental rights has been recognized by the ECJ as a general principle of EU law and also that it is contained in Article 6 TEU means that it has superior status as a rule of law, and can—more than any other justification ground—be positioned on an equal footing with the fundamental free movement rights. This undoubtedly implies that even if the secondary legislation makes no explicit mention of the protection of fundamental rights as a justification ground, a compliance check may still be performed, which could in turn lead to the elimination of the principle of mutual recognition if necessary. Will the same conclusion apply to the other justification grounds, though? Can a Member State invoke 'consumer protection' as a justification ground, for example, even when the legislative instrument has not explicitly incorporated it? According to the ECJ's internal market case law, the answer to this question largely depends on the level of harmonization achieved with the legislative instrument in question. Only in cases of exhaustive harmonization will the ECJ evaluate the national measure strictly within the framework of the harmonization measure. In other cases, the Treaty framework—including the rule of reason—will be restored as the applicable framework.

It was interesting to observe that when evaluating a justification ground, the ECJ refers to a yardstick in order to assess the interest in question. In cases of both judicial and legislative mutual recognition, this yardstick is a precondition for applying the principle of mutual recognition. In a judicial context, the yardstick usually consists of an equivalence or sufficiency check (external yardstick), while in a harmonized context the yardstick is often the harmonized norm referred to in the legislative instrument (internal yardstick).

Both the equivalence test and the sufficiency test have highlighted a number of difficulties with the mutual recognition mechanism. As regards the 'equivalence' test, the ECJ's case law has revealed that while the principle of mutual recognition often concerns the mutual recognition of a national norm or a national SHEC objective, it can sometimes have a much wider scope. Indeed, in the ECJ's case law, the principle of mutual recognition has occasionally been set aside because of the incompatibility of two legislative frameworks. This case law has made clear that a national rule or an SHEC objective can therefore not be read in isolation but must be viewed within the context of a Member State's legislative system (or its underlying philosophy). As regards the 'sufficiency' test, it appears that the ECJ has sought a kind of European parameter without losing sight of certain specific national elements, however. Thus, once again, the principle of mutual recognition is not applied in an isolated way. Local food habits, linguistic issues, social or cultural singularities, and so on may all influence the application of the principle of mutual recognition.

I have observed that even in the area of fundamental rights, the ECJ still goes in search of a European concept but continues to grant the Member States some margin of discretion. It appears anxious to impose an exclusively EU standard on the Member States while remaining apprehensive about allowing one Member State to impose its own system of values on another in the name of universal standards. This latter aspect has revealed itself especially clearly in the reserved approach taken by the ECJ in judgments concerning an extraterritorial field of application. The ECJ is clearly not willing to encourage cases of regulatory or value imperialism, and is only prepared to (implicitly) accept an extraterritorial interest if an interest is simultaneously under threat in the originating Member State.

The development of the abuse of law theory is another manifestation of the non-automatic nature of the principle of mutual recognition. A direct consequence of this principle and the free movement provisions is that an individual or legal person may be drawn towards the less severe or more attractive legislation in another Member State. Such forum shopping is a direct consequence of the free movement provisions and is thus permitted, with some restrictions. Mutual recognition can be denied in cases of material fraud or in cases where artificial constructions have been set up and the parties concerned do not accept all of the legal consequences of the free movement provision in question. It is interesting to note that the European legislator has also attempted to combat this problem by providing specific provisions which restrict the application of the principle of mutual recognition in cases of fraud or abuse of law. Some of the provisions that I discussed can even be situated on the borderline between internal market legislation and criminal law. This is the case with the directive on mutual recognition of driving licences, for example, where there has been some discussion of the extent to which the confiscation of a licence following a criminal conviction can trigger the mutual recognition mechanism.

A final element that confirms the non-automatic application of the principle of mutual recognition is the margin of control that is left to a Member State upon receipt of a request for mutual recognition. The crucial point of departure here seems to be mutual trust. However, Member States are allowed to perform extra controls or to request additional information from another Member State whenever there is reasonable doubt concerning a product's compliance with the necessary requirements, or when objective factors or concrete evidence suggest that a certificate contains manifest inaccuracies. In other words, Member States are duty bound to trust and to recognize, but they may react and suspend the mutual recognition mechanism whenever substantial objective grounds are available.

C. The functional or teleological nature of the principle of mutual recognition

The ECJ's case law is not univocal, however, as some judgments exchange the duty of trust for a duty of vigilance with regard to the decisions of other Member States. This ambivalent or at least ambiguous case law brings us to another characteristic of the principle of mutual recognition: its functional, teleological nature.

In situations where the principle of mutual recognition tends to restrict the free movement provisions rather than enhancing them, especially, the ECJ no longer speaks in terms of mutual trust but seems to suggest that Member States should not take the decisions of other Member States for granted. The principle of mutual recognition was developed precisely in order to enhance (the effectiveness of) the TFEU free movement provisions, and as a result it seems odd to apply this principle to the opposite effect, namely to restrict the free movement provisions. It is therefore logical that the ECJ employ a distinctive approach to mutual trust (and mutual recognition) in both contexts: mutual trust whenever the principle of mutual recognition enhances the free movement provisions, and a more reserved, vigilant approach whenever the principle of mutual recognition jeopardizes the free movement provisions. The two approaches are perhaps not as incompatible in practice as they initially seem.

A combined reading of the two lines of case law suggests that the ECJ does not subscribe to a blind regime of trust but in fact allows (as a first hypothesis) or obliges (as a second hypothesis) Member States to be vigilant towards the decisions of other Member States. The concrete margin of action that is left to the Member States is based on cooperation and information exchange in both cases and very little or no margin for unilateral measures is granted. The principle of mutual recognition therefore requires no regime of blind trust but instead a regime of constructive trust, which is built upon mutual knowledge, mutual cooperation, and mutual monitoring. However paradoxical it sounds, it is precisely these mechanisms of cooperation and control that are the most important tools in creating a workable principle of mutual recognition.

D. The versatile nature of the principle of mutual recognition

A final characteristic of the principle of mutual recognition constitutes its versatile nature. I have observed how the principle of mutual recognition has been implemented in the four freedoms, covering a wide range of domains, in some of which the ECJ (and the EU legislator) emphasized the possibility of partial mutual recognition as opposed to full mutual recognition. Furthermore, I have observed that the principle of mutual recognition has two versions: one substantive and one procedural. Examples of both techniques can be located in the ECJ's case law as well as in the secondary legislation. I notice that there has been a change of focus from one technique to another in some harmonized domains, but in most areas the two techniques are generally used in a complementary manner. Procedural elements often fulfil an auxiliary function: they are a means of improving how the principle of mutual recognition is applied. Apparently, a (quasi-exclusive) procedural approach is a particularly attractive tool in those areas where substantive harmonization is difficult to achieve (in the pharmaceutical sector, for instance). In other areas, substantive and procedural harmonization will often be combined.

VI. Workability

Regarding the principle's workability, I concluded that while it initially appears to be a simple mechanism, the judicial principle of mutual recognition is in fact a complex instrument in daily practice. I have indicated that the problematic application of the principle of mutual recognition is attributable to a variety of factors, including insufficient knowledge and understanding of the principle, a lack of dialogue or cooperation, and a lack of trust. All of these causes can be traced back to the lack of a European attitude among the national administrations.

However, the most problematic issue is likely to be the lack of legal certainty, particularly in the non-harmonized sector. The ECJ's case law certainly provides useful guidelines but by their nature they are simply not sufficient to provide a watertight framework, which is what businesses have been calling for. Several measures have been taken in order to address the disappointing results of the principle of mutual recognition: notification procedures which provide an overview of the problematic sectors and initiate harmonization measures where necessary; measures that enhance knowledge among businesses and national administrations; and measures that improve cooperation among national administrations.

Despite all of these initiatives, which will undoubtedly have a beneficial effect on how the principle of mutual recognition is applied, we should remain realistic and be aware that an all-encompassing application of the principle of mutual recognition is perhaps beyond reach. Even if we were to succeed in achieving a quasi-perfect application of the principle to the national administrations, business people might still decide not to rely on the mutual recognition ratio for commercial reasons. After all, as far as they are concerned, the principle of mutual recognition constitutes a right they can invoke, but under no circumstances is it an obligation. This voluntary aspect of the principle of mutual recognition might restrict its penetration in the internal market context to some extent.

PART II

MUTUAL RECOGNITION IN THE EU CRIMINAL JUSTICE AREA

Upon the incorporation of 'the area of freedom, security, and justice' into the Treaty of Amsterdam (1997), a new ambitious goal was set at EU level. Since then, the competences which the ECJ has acquired under this Treaty with regard to police and judicial cooperation in criminal matters and the incorporation of the Schengen acquis into the EU[1] framework have enabled the ECJ to shed light on the basic elements upon which this new area should be constructed and developed. Under the Treaty of Lisbon, the competences of the EU institutions in this area were further increased and the area of freedom, security, and justice was confirmed as one of the main objectives of the European integration project.[2]

Part II of this book aims at tracing the essential characteristics of the principle of mutual recognition in the area of freedom, security, and justice, with particular regard to judicial cooperation in criminal matters, from both the judicial and legislative perspectives. It is divided into four chapters. First, I analyse the legal reasoning adopted by the ECJ in introducing and developing the principle of mutual recognition throughout its *ne bis in idem* case law (Chapter 1). Secondly, I investigate how this principle has been developed in the EU's secondary legislation on judicial cooperation in criminal matters (Chapter 2). Next, I evaluate the workability of the principle of mutual recognition in a day-to-day context (Chapter 3). Finally, I conclude Part II with a summary of my main findings on the fundamental characteristics of the principle of mutual recognition in the EU criminal justice area (Chapter 4).

[1] The Schengen acquis was integrated into the EU framework by a Protocol to the Amsterdam Treaty with a view to enhancing European integration and enabling the EU to develop more rapidly into an area of freedom, security, and justice. On this incorporation, see, for instance: J. DE ZWAAN, 'Schengen and its Incorporation into the New Treaty: The Negotiating Process', in M. DEN BOER (ed.), *Schengen's Final Days? The incorporation of Schengen into the new TEU, External Borders and Information Systems* (Maastricht, European Institute of Public Administration, 1998) 13–24.

[2] Article 3(2) TEU. On the crucial role of the ECJ in the area of freedom, security, and justice, see, in particular: K. LENAERS, 'The Contribution of the European Court of Justice to the Area of Freedom, Security and Justice', *ICLQ* 2010, 255–301. On the increased power of the ECJ (and the other EU institutions) in the area of criminal matters, see, for instance: B. DE WITTE, 'The European Judiciary after Lisbon', *MJ* 2008, 49 ff.; C. JANSSENS, 'Europees strafrecht en het Verdrag van Lissabon. Een verhaal van déjà vu's, dwarsliggers en compromissen', *Nullum Crimen* 2009, 19 ff.; C. LADENBURGER, 'Police and Criminal Law in the Treaty of Lisbon. A New Dimension for the Community Method', *EuConst* 2008, 30 ff.

1

The Mutual Recognition Principle as Judicial Impetus for Powerful EU-wide Application of the *Ne Bis In Idem* Principle

I. Mutual Recognition and *Ne Bis In Idem* as Two Interrelated Principles

The case law which concerns the Convention Implementing the Schengen Agreement (hereafter referred to as 'CISA')[1] constitutes an important ECJ contribution to the development of the area of freedom, security, and justice, especially with regard to the transnational *ne bis in idem* principle.

The *ne bis in idem* principle implies that a person will not be prosecuted, tried, or sentenced more than once for the same act or omission in more than one Member State. The key provision is Article 54 CISA, which states that 'a person whose trial has been finally disposed of in one Contracting Party may not be prosecuted in another Contracting Party for the same acts provided that, if a penalty has been imposed, it has been enforced, is actually in the process of being enforced or can no longer be enforced under the laws of the sentencing Contracting Party'. Moreover, in situations where Article 54 CISA is not applicable, the 'taking into consideration' or 'accounting' principle laid down in Article 56 CISA comes into play. In accordance with this provision, any imposition of a second sentence must deduct any relevant time already served in the initial sentencing state and also take account of any non-custodial sentence to the extent provided for by national law. Though the latter principle is to be distinguished from the former, they are complementary and both highly relevant in light of the mutual recognition principle.[2]

Under this heading the focus lies on the ECJ's still young but powerful *ne bis in idem* case law, in which it interprets the principle of mutual recognition as the corollary of the *ne bis in idem* principle. In what follows, I begin by referring briefly to the first judgment in which the ECJ was able to apply a broad interpretation of Article 54 CISA by understanding the latter provision as imposing the mutual recognition of final decisions in criminal matters (section I, A). Next, I proceed with an assessment of how the ECJ has interpreted the main elements of the *ne bis in idem* principle, in order to identify some of the main features of the mutual recognition mechanism in this context (section I, B). Finally, I examine the ECJ's overall approach to the *ne bis in idem* principle in order to complete the outline of the mutual recognition mechanism in this context (section I, C).

[1] The Schengen acquis—Convention implementing the Schengen Agreement of 14 June 1985 between the Governments of the States of the Benelux Economic Union, the Federal Republic of Germany and the French Republic on the gradual abolition of checks at their common borders, *O.J.* L-239, 22.09.2000, p. 19–62.

[2] On the complementary nature of both principles, see: Opinion of AG Ruiz-Jarabo Colomer in Case C-150/05 *Van Straaten* [2006] ECR I-9327, § 58. See also: W.B. VAN BOCKEL, *The ne bis in idem Principle in EU Law* (AH Alphen aan den Rijn, Kluwer Law International, 2010) 210, who considers the prohibition of double prosecution (Art. 54 CISA) the 'real' *ne bis in idem* principle; S. PEERS, *EU Justice and Home Affairs Law*, 3rd edn (Oxford, Oxford University Press, 2011) 851–2.

A. *Gözütok and Brügge*: the first manifestation of a duty of mutual recognition in criminal matters

In the *Gözütok and Brügge* cases, the ECJ was asked to rule on the scope of Article 54 CISA, and in particular on the relevance of out-of-court settlements for the application of Article 54 CISA.[3] In both cases, one of which centred on dealing in narcotics (*Gözütok*) and the other on causing grievous bodily injury to a person (*Brügge*), the suspects had agreed with the Member State's public prosecutor to a settlement of a substantial sum, upon payment of which further proceedings would be barred. Notwithstanding these settlements, however, new proceedings were begun against both individuals in another Member State.

Therefore, the ECJ was asked to decide whether an out-of-court settlement between an individual and the public prosecutor could be equated with the situation of a person 'whose trial had been finally disposed of' in the sense of Article 54 CISA. Despite the existence of certain strong arguments which weighed against this reading, such as the literal wording of Article 54 CISA, which explicitly refers to 'a trial', as well as the unequivocal intentions of the Contracting Parties, the more perilous situation of the victim, and the Council's interpretation of Article 54 CISA,[4] the ECJ ultimately returned a positive answer. Relying on the object and purpose of Article 54 CISA and the need to ensure that this provision took proper effect,[5] and without overlooking the European integration process in this area,[6] the ECJ suggested that it was somewhat inconsequential whether the principle of *ne bis in idem* enshrined in Article 54 CISA was applied to procedures whereby further prosecution was barred (regardless of whether the court was involved) or to judicial decisions. According to the ECJ, 'there is a necessary implication that each Member State [...] recognises the criminal law in force in the other Member States even when the outcome would be different if its own national law were applied'.[7]

This paragraph is fundamental to the ECJ's reasoning; in this way, the ECJ rather radically and audaciously introduced the duty of the mutual recognition of criminal law decisions in the area of freedom, security, and justice, with a strong focus on the law of the Member State in which the criminal proceedings were initiated. The ECJ's broad formulation of the duty to recognize 'the criminal law in force in the other Member State' indicates the broad scope of the object of mutual recognition in this area. Indeed, the competent authorities are not only required to recognize each other's judicial decisions,

[3] ECJ, Joined Cases C-187/01 and C-385/01 *Gözütok and Brügge* [2003] ECR I-1345.

[4] For some reflections on such a broad reading, see: A. KLIP, 'Grensoverschrijdende bescherming na voldoen transactie?', *SEW* 2004, 92; S. STEIN, 'Ein Meilenstein für das europäische *ne bis in idem*', *NjW* 2003, 1163; M.I. VELDT FOGLIA, 'Ruime uitleg van het ne bis in idem-beginsel in artikel 54 SUO', *NTER* 2003, 131. Programme of measures to implement the principle of mutual recognition of decisions in criminal matters, *O.J.* C-012, 15.01.2001, p. 12–13. The Council's suggestion to approach (also) decisions taken following penal mediation clearly indicates that—according to the Council—they were not yet covered by Article 54 CISA.

[5] ECJ, Joined Cases C-187/01 and C-385/01 *Gözütok and Brügge* [2003] ECR I-1345, para 35.

[6] ECJ, Joined Cases C-187/01 and C-385/01 *Gözütok and Brügge* [2003] ECR I-1345, para 37. The incorporation of the Schengen acquis in the EU acquis through the Amsterdam Treaty implied that Article 54 CISA had become part of a new, broader integration objective of maintaining and developing the EU as an area of freedom, security, and justice. See also: J. NARCISO DA CUNHA RODRIGUES, 'A propos du principe *ne bis in idem*. Un regard sur la jurisprudence de la Cour de Justice des Communautés européennes', in *Une communauté de droit. Festschrift für Gil Carlos Rodriguez Iglesias* (Berlin, Berliner Wissenschaftsverlag, 2003) 172–6.

[7] ECJ, Joined Cases C-187/01 and C-385/01 *Gözütok and Brügge* [2003] ECR I-1345, para 33.

but—implicitly—also each other's (substantive and procedural) criminal law provisions and prosecutorial policy.

B. The outlines of the mutual recognition mechanism in light of the core elements of the *ne bis in idem* principle enshrined in Article 54 CISA

The ECJ's choice to read a duty of mutual recognition into Article 54 CISA has had an impact on the way in which the ECJ interprets a number of the core elements of the *ne bis in idem* principle, particularly the condition that a person's trial is 'finally disposed of' ('the *finality* requirement', section B, 1), that it concerns 'the same facts' ('the *idem* requirement', section B, 2), and finally that if a penalty has been imposed, this penalty has already been enforced, is in the process of being enforced, or can no longer be enforced ('the enforcement requirement', section B, 3).

(1) The finality requirement

The ECJ has delivered several judgments in which it has clarified the types of judicial decisions that are to be considered 'finally disposing' of a trial in the sense laid down in Article 54 CISA and the types of decisions that are not. To date, the ECJ has accepted as 'final decisions' out-of-court settlements with the public prosecutor (*Gözütok and Brügge*),[8] a court acquittal based on a lack of evidence (*van Straaten*),[9] and a court acquittal arising due to the prosecution of the offence being time-barred (*Gasparini*).[10] On the other hand, it has rejected the application of Article 54 CISA in cases where a judicial authority had closed proceedings without any assessment of the unlawful conduct with which the defendant had been charged (*Miraglia*),[11] and cases where a police authority, following the expiry of the limitation period and an examination of the merits of the case, had submitted an order to suspend the criminal proceedings (*Turanský*).[12]

An interesting issue that has not yet been settled unambiguously by the ECJ is the question of the implications that the granting of amnesty has in the context of Article 54 CISA. This issue was raised in the *Bourquain* case,[13] where the AG maintained a clear stance against the application of Article 54 CISA to amnesty measures by stating that 'mutual trust (and mutual recognition) should not shelter, under the Community *ne bis in idem* principle, instances of non-enforcement of a penalty brought about by the exercise of these exorbitant national powers, since mutual recognition then ceases to operate in the sphere of the judicial application of the law and follows a different course, driven by winds with a strong sociological and political component'.[14] His unequivocal recommendation that the *ne bis in idem* principle not be applied in such circumstances, however, was not taken up by the ECJ. As the national judge had not specifically requested any explanation in this regard, and as the preliminary ruling could be settled satisfactorily without addressing this issue, the ECJ was extremely brief with regard to the amnesty issue. By cautiously noting that the granting of amnesty 'cannot be understood

[8] ECJ, Joined Cases C-187/01 and C-385/01 *Gözütok and Brügge* [2003] ECR I-1345.
[9] ECJ, Case C-150/05 *Van Straaten* [2006] ECR I-9327.
[10] ECJ, Case C-467/04 *Gasparini and others* [2006] ECR I-9199.
[11] ECJ, Case C-469/03 *Miraglia* [2005] ECR I-2009.
[12] ECJ, Case C-491/07 *Turanský* [2008] ECR I-11039.
[13] ECJ, Case C-297/07 *Bourquain* [2008] ECR I-9425.
[14] Opinion of AG Ruiz-Jarabo Colomer in Case C-297/07 *Bourquain* [2008] ECR I-9425, § 83.

as meaning that there is no first judgment for the purposes of Article 54 CISA',[15] the ECJ did not unambiguously state whether the granting of amnesty triggered the application of Article 54 CISA. In view of the ECJ's broad approach to Article 54 CISA in its *ne bis idem* case law, and of its focus on the objectives of creating legal certainty and protecting the legitimate expectations of the accused,[16] it seems in my view more than likely that the ECJ would not have shared the AG's rather narrow point of view on this matter.[17] This approach is furthermore supported by the FD EAW, which lists amnesty among the mandatory grounds for non-execution of an arrest warrant.[18]

Another relevant element of the discussion surrounding the finality requirement concerns the question of whether the application of Article 54 CISA requires a previous assessment of the merits of the case. The importance that the ECJ generally attaches to such an assessment was indicated in *Miraglia*, where the ECJ rejected the application of Article 54 CISA on the grounds that 'there had been no assessment whatsoever of the unlawful conduct',[19] and in *van Straaten*, where the ECJ imposed the application of Article 54 CISA on the grounds that a determination of the merits of the case had indeed taken place.[20] It was not until the ECJ delivered its *Gasparini* judgment, however, that the full implications of this requirement became clear. In *Gasparini*, the ECJ rejected the restrictive, substance-based approach of its AG, who had argued that a discontinuance without a substantive assessment, namely a procedural time-bar, should not be covered by the *ne bis in idem* principle.[21] The ECJ emphasized instead that Article 54 CISA made no reference to the content of the judgment[22] in order to conclude that the latter provision also applied to acquittals based on procedural arguments such as prescription. The ECJ's broad interpretation of the 'merits of the case'—which implied that Article 54 CISA is to be applied whenever a case has come to an end based either on substantive or procedural grounds—is, admittedly, controversial.[23] Yet, in light of the ECJ's point of departure in *Gözütok and Brügge*, namely that Article 54 CISA necessitates mutual recognition of the criminal laws of (other) Member States, it is likely the most

[15] ECJ, Case C-297/07 *Bourquain* [2008] ECR I-9425, para 44.

[16] See: Part II, ch 1, I, C, 4. 'A teleological and functional approach to mutual recognition in which the ECJ balances freedom, security, and justice'.

[17] In legal doctrine, opinions are divided as to the question whether amnesty should trigger the application of Article 54 CISA, or not. For an affirmative answer, see, for instance: S. BRAMMER, Case Note *Bourquain*, *CML Rev.* 2009, 1694–6; C. VAN DEN WYNGAERT and G. STESSENS, 'The International *non bis in idem* Principle: Resolving some of the Unanswered Questions', *ICLQ* 1999, 798. For a negative answer, see, for instance: VAN BOCKEL, *The ne bis in idem Principle in EU Law* (n 2) 234–5; for a similar reticent attitude, in the context of the FD EAW, see: J. PRADEL, G.J.M. CORSTENS, and G. VERMEULEN, *Droit pénal européen* (Paris, Dalloz, 2009) 619.

[18] Admittedly, two different legal instruments are at stake here (CISA and FD EAW), yet a common approach seems defensible in light of the ECJ's case law. In the context of time-barred offences, the ECJ relied in *Gasparini*, in subsidiary order, on the FD EAW in order to strengthen its argument that *ne bis in idem* was applicable in the case of a final acquittal because prosecution of the offence was time-barred (ECJ, Case C-467/04 *Gasparini and others* [2006] ECR I-9199, para 31). Furthermore, in *Mantello* the ECJ held that in view of the shared objective of Article 54 of the CISA and Article 3(2) of the FD EAW, which is to ensure that a person is not prosecuted or tried more than once in respect of the same acts, it must be accepted that an interpretation of that concept given in the context of the CISA is equally valid in the context of the FD EAW (ECJ, Case C-261/09 *Mantello* [2010] ECR I-11477, para 40).

[19] ECJ, Case C-469/03 *Miraglia* [2005] ECR I-2009, para 34.

[20] ECJ, Case C-150/05 *Van Straaten* [2006] ECR I-9327, para 60.

[21] Opinion of AG Sharpston in Case C-467/04 *Gasparini and others* [2006] ECR I-9199, § 85–120. Compare, however, with Opinion of AG Colomer in Case C-150/05 *Van Straaten* [2006] ECR I-9327, § 65, who supports the broad view that was adopted by the ECJ in *Gasparini.*

[22] ECJ, Case C-467/04 *Gasparini and others* [2006] ECR I-9199, para 24.

[23] See, for instance: A. KLIP, *European Criminal Law. An Integrative Approach,* (Antwerp, Intersentia, 2012) 255 ff.; VAN BOCKEL, *The ne bis in idem Principle in EU Law* (n 2) 42 and 159.

correct interpretation. A more limited approach based on 'the merits of the case' (i.e. an exclusively substantive approach) would obstruct this obligation of mutual recognition, as it would imply that divergent legislation could hinder to an undesirable extent the application of the principle of mutual recognition. Any concerns about the potentially pernicious consequences resulting from such a broad interpretation, such as criminal forum shopping, as hinted at by AG Sharpston in her opinion on the *Gasparini* judgment, are not necessarily ill-founded, however, and should encourage Member States to pursue more harmonizing measures.[24]

The ECJ's case law on the finality requirement calls for additional attention to be paid to the delineation of the object of the mutual recognition mechanism, namely the types of decision that are able to trigger the *ne bis in idem* principle and its underlying duty of mutual recognition. In *Gözütok and Brügge*, the ECJ embraced a wide interpretation of the object of mutual recognition, namely judicial decisions *sensu lato*, including those made by a public prosecutor in the context of out-of-court settlements. In this judgment, the ECJ made it very clear that the fact alone that the public prosecutor's decision had been taken without a court being involved did not preclude the application of Article 54 CISA. However, in a more recent judgment, *Turanský*, the ECJ dismissed the application of Article 54 CISA in a case where a police authority had decided to close criminal proceedings owing to the expiry of the limitation period. In light of this judgment, doubts have been raised as to whether the ECJ (still) prefers a wide interpretation of decisions that are the object of the mutual recognition mechanism and of the authorities that can issue such decisions, or whether it has reconsidered its position in the context of time-barred offences. A joint reading of *Turanský* and *Gasparini* initially appears to support the second hypothesis, namely that *ne bis in idem* only applies when a formal court decision has been made on the issue of prescription (*Gasparini*) and not when a police authority has decided to suspend proceedings (*Turanský*).[25] Yet, upon closer examination, the decisive element of the *Turanský* judgment was less the fact that the decision in question had been taken by a police authority and more the finding that under the national law concerned, such a decision did not definitively bring the proceedings to a close.[26] In light of this, *Gözütok and Brügge* and *Turanský* are perfectly consistent with each other. In both decisions, in fact, the crucial question was not as to which authority had taken the relevant decision, but rather whether the decision taken did indeed have the effect of withdrawing the criminal charges against the suspect. When the latter condition is met, it appears irrelevant whether a court or any other authority required to play a role in the administration of criminal justice in the legal system concerned takes the decision in question, provided that the national legislation concerned conforms to EU law.[27]

(2) *The* idem *requirement*

In a series of judgments beginning with *Van Esbroeck*, the ECJ was confronted with a number of situations in which persons who had been sentenced on the basis of a legal

[24] P. HOET, 'Ne bis in idem—nationaal en internationaal. De rechtspraak van het Hof van Justitie en van het Hof van de Rechten van de Mens getoetst aan de nationale rechtspraak', *CABG* 2008, 56. On the issue of *forum shopping*, see: Part II, ch 1, IV, D. 'Forum shopping, abuse of law, and concerns about de facto approximation around the lowest common denominator'.

[25] A. KLIP, 'Recente rechtspraak strafrecht en Europese Unie', *DD* 2006, 1064–5; A. KLIP, 'Noot onder Turanský en Bourquain', *NJ* 2009, Afl. 45, 511.

[26] ECJ, Case C-491/07 *Turanský* [2008] ECR I-11039, paras 39–40.

[27] On this latter requirement, see: Part II, ch 1, III. 'Equivalence, Country of Origin, and Mutual Recognition: which Focus?'

qualification in one Member State (for instance, export of drugs) were standing trial in another Member State on the basis of a different legal qualification (for instance, import of drugs).[28] In these judgments, the ECJ had to decide whether—notwithstanding the two different legal qualifications—the cases concerned 'the same facts' in the sense of Article 54 CISA, which would mean that the *ne bis in idem* (and mutual recognition) principle could be applied.

While ignoring the then-applicable case law of the ECtHR,[29] the ECJ concluded in *Van Esbroeck* that a factual interpretation of 'idem' (the facts are identical) was to be preferred over an interpretation based on the legal qualification (the legal provisions are identical) and over an interpretation based on the protected legal interest. The ECJ convincingly argued that within the framework of the EU, 'a criterion based on the legal qualification of the acts or on the protected legal interest might create as many barriers to freedom of movement within the Schengen territory as there are penal systems in the Contracting States'.[30] In choosing this interpretation, the ECJ clearly took the only viable option consistent with a pro-free movement and pro-mutual recognition approach, as no other interpretation would produce a result so faithfully in keeping with the nature and purpose of Article 54 CISA.[31]

In *Van Straaten*, the ECJ took its broad interpretation of Article 54 CISA even further by accepting that a person who had been convicted in one Member State for importing and possessing heroin and then subsequently convicted in a second Member State for exporting a far larger amount of heroine to the first Member State was still protected by Article 54 CISA. The ECJ held that the drug quantities quoted by the two Member States concerned did not have to be identical to allow for the application of Article 54 CISA, thus relying on the definition of 'the identity of the material facts' it had previously developed in *Van Esbroeck* as 'a set of concrete circumstances which are inextricably linked together in time, space and by their subject-matter'.[32] In *Van Straaten*, the ECJ appeared to be exploring the outer limitations of what 'idem' means and simultaneously negotiating the idea of what an area of freedom, security, and justice ought to be. Furthermore, like so many other *ne bis in idem* judgments, this case made it clear that the *ne bis in idem* principle was in urgent need of increased cooperation between the Member States (with particular regard to information exchange and evidence gathering) as well as of decisive, centralized rules on competent courts in order to avoid and/or settle positive conflicts of jurisdiction.[33]

[28] ECJ, Case C-436/04 *Van Esbroeck* [2006] ECR I-2333.

[29] In *Zolotukhin* (ECtHR, 10 February 2009, *Zolotukhin v Russia*, 14939/03), the ECtHR aligned its case law with the criteria developed by the ECJ in *Van Esbroeck*. On this development, see: W.B. VAN BOCKEL, 'Coming of age: de ontwikkeling van het ne bis in idem-beginsel in de EU-rechtsorde', *NTER* 2010, 69–71.

[30] ECJ, Case C-436/04 *Van Esbroeck* [2006] ECR I-2333, para 35; ECJ, Case C-150/05 *Van Straaten* [2006] ECR I-9327, para 47; ECJ, Case C-288/05 *Kretzinger* [2007] ECR I-6441, para 33.

[31] VAN BOCKEL, *The ne bis in idem Principle in EU law* (n 2) 46, 166 and 231. The mere finding that an interpretation based on the material facts is fully in line with the main objective of Article 54 CISA does not mean, however, that its application is exempted from problems. The application of the principle of *ne bis in idem* to offences with a particularly vague and wide scope might, according to Van Bockel, lead to problems of under-punishment.

[32] ECJ, Case C-436/04 *Van Esbroeck* [2006] ECR I-2333, para 36; ECJ, Case C-150/05 *Van Straaten* [2006] ECR I-9327, paras 48–52; ECJ, Case C-467/04 *Gasparini and others* [2006] ECR I-9199, paras 54–6; ECJ, Case C-288/05 *Kretzinger* [2007] ECR I-6441, paras 26–7.

[33] See: Part II, ch 3: 'The Workability of the Principle of Mutual Recognition in Criminal Matters'.

In her opinion on the *Kraaijenbrink* case, AG Sharpston recognized the undesirable results that could be produced by too strict a reading of the statement in *Van Straaten* that the drug quantities quoted in the two Member States concerned did not need to be identical to allow for the application of Article 54 CISA.[34] In this preliminary ruling, where the main issue was whether a common intention with regard to offences concerning the proceeds of drug trafficking operations in two Member States sufficed to justify the application of Article 54 CISA, the ECJ took up a far more reasonable and nuanced position. It continued to focus on the need for objective criteria in examining the 'identical' nature of the facts at hand, as it had done in *Van Esbroeck* and *van Straaten*, but it also rejected firmly any approach based on subjective criteria as exclusive criteria.[35]

(3) *The enforcement requirement*

The pro-mutual recognition approach can also be identified in the ECJ's interpretation of the enforcement requirement. This condition, whose rationale is to avoid impunity for absconding convicts in cases where a conviction has not been (fully) enforced,[36] has often been interpreted very generously in the ECJ's case law.

1In line with the principle of mutual recognition and with Article 54 CISA's aim of promoting free movement, the ECJ held that out-of-court settlements (*Gözütok and Brügge*) and suspended sentences (*Kretzinger*) ought to be considered penalties which are actually in the process of being enforced or which have been enforced.[37] The ECJ's broad interpretation of Article 54 CISA's enforcement condition was most striking in the *Bourquain* judgment, where the ECJ accepted it was sufficient that a penalty could no longer be enforced, regardless of whether that penalty could ever have been executed in practice.[38] Opinions diverge as to whether the ECJ took the correct approach in *Bourquain*. On one hand, the ECJ's conclusion has been criticized on the grounds that a principle such as *ne bis in idem* (and mutual recognition) should not work to render perpetrators immune from further prosecution in cases where earlier sanctions could not be enforced for specific historical reasons, such as in *Bourquain*.[39] On the other hand, it has been argued that while under the then-applicable French legislation it was indeed impossible to enforce the penalty without first holding a new trial in the defendant's presence, it is also a fact that in 1981 the limitation period for the execution of the sentence imposed on *Bourquain* had definitively expired. This meant that the

[34] Opinion of AG Sharpston in Case C-367/05 *Kraaijenbrink* [2007] ECR I-6619, § 35–7.

[35] ECJ, Case C-367/05 *Kraaijenbrink* [2007] ECR I-6619, paras 26–31.

[36] M. FLETCHER, R. LOOF, and B. GILLMORE, *EU Criminal Law and Justice* (Cheltenham, Edward Elgar, 2008) 136. On the relationship—and compatibility—between Article 54 CISA and Article 50 Charter (which does not contain an 'enforcement clause'), see, for instance: C. BURCHARD and D. BRODOWSKI, 'The Post-Lisbon Principle of Transnational *ne bis in idem*: on the Relationship between Article 50 Charter of Fundamental Rights and Article 54 Convention Implementing the Schengen Agreement. Case note on District Court Aachen, Germany, (52 Ks 9/08—"Boere"), Decision of 8 December 2010', *NJECL* 2010, 310–27. N. BURROWS, 'Harmonization of Technical Standards: Reculer pour Mieux Sauter?', *MLR* 1990, 597–603.

[37] According to the ECJ, the penalty has been enforced once the accused has complied with his obligations (ECJ, Joined Cases C-187/01 and C-385/01 *Gözütok and Brügge* [2003] ECR I-1345, para 30) or once the probation period has come to an end (ECJ, Case C-288/05 *Kretzinger* [2007] ECR I-6441, para 42).

[38] ECJ, Case C-297/07 *Bourquain* [2008] ECR I-9425, paras 45–8.

[39] VAN BOCKEL, *The ne bis in idem Principle in EU law* (n 2) 234. For a similar criticism: D. CHALMERS, G. DAVIES, and G. MONTI, *European Union Law* (Cambridge, Cambridge University Press, 2010) 611.

penalty was 'no longer enforceable' at that time and Article 54 CISA could have been applied.[40] In my view, the latter interpretation should be considered superior since it is alone in doing full justice to the objectives underpinning Article 54 CISA, namely free movement, legal certainty, and the legitimate expectations of the accused. Furthermore, such an interpretation expresses far better the idea of respect towards (and recognition of) the other Member State's legal order, which is considered one of the main features of the principle of mutual recognition[41] and of the EU legal order in general.[42]

However, the ECJ's broad interpretation of the enforcement condition is not without its limits, as the *Kretzinger* judgment demonstrates. In refusing to qualify the short length of time a suspect is in police custody and/or being held on remand pending trial as a penalty that has been enforced or is actually in the process of being enforced,[43] the ECJ wisely acknowledged that the *ne bis in idem* principle should not be taken to reckless extremes. The rejection of the application of Article 54 CISA in such cases should not necessarily be seen as a complete dismissal of the importance of the time that a suspect is held in custody.[44] As mentioned above, in the absence of Article 54 CISA, any compensation for time spent in pre-trial detention can be remedied by the national judicial authority by means of the 'lighter' version of the mutual recognition principle as enshrined in Article 56 CISA.

C. The outlines of the mutual recognition mechanism in light of the ECJ's overall approach to the *ne bis in idem* principle enshrined in Article 54 CISA

The previous section allows us to gain a better insight into the broad scope of the mutual recognition duty in the context of Article 54 CISA. In order to grasp the contours of the principle of mutual recognition fully in this context, it is advisable to pursue in greater depth a number of crucial steps inherent to the ECJ's reasoning in its *ne bis in idem* case law. First, the proper nature of the *ne bis in idem* principle, and its consequences in the procedural and substantive realms, implies a limited role for Member States' officials and has some benefit for the prosecuted person(s) involved (section C, 1). Secondly, mutual recognition goes hand in hand with mutual trust (section C, 2). Thirdly, mutual recognition is not dependent upon prior approximation (section C, 3). Finally, the ECJ embraces a teleological and functional approach to the relevant CISA and TFEU provisions (section C, 4).

(1) Mutual recognition as a (procedural) bar to fresh prosecutions and a (substantive) individual's right not to be punished twice

The *ne bis in idem* principle prevents a person from being subject to more than one penalizing procedure and from being punished repeatedly, insofar as any duplication

[40] BRAMMER, 'Case Note *Bourquain*' (n 17) 1694.

[41] See: Part II, ch 1, I, C, 3. 'Mutual recognition without the need for prior approximation: long live diversity?'

[42] According to Article 67(1) TFEU 'the Union shall constitute an area of freedom security and justice with respect for [. . .] the different legal systems and traditions of the Member States' and according to Article 4(2) TEU 'the Union shall respect the Member States' [. . .] national identities inherent in their fundamental structures, political and constitutional [. . .]'.

[43] ECJ, Case C-288/05 *Kretzinger* [2007] ECR I-6441, para 52.

[44] Precisely this preoccupation had urged the AG to suggest a less drastic solution than the ECJ finally adopted: Opinion of AG Sharpston in Case C-288/05 *Kretzinger* [2007] ECR I-6441, § 64–8.

of procedures and penalties involves the unacceptable repetition of a state's exercise of its *ius puniendi*.[45] In other words, the principal effect of a (transnational) *ne bis in idem* principle lies in not prosecuting and/or punishing those acts already judged in another Member State because of the recognition that the first judgment has finally settled the matter. Mutual recognition thus operates in the context of Article 54 CISA in an exculpatory manner vis-à-vis the defendant.[46]

The tasks entrusted to the competent authorities in relation to the mutual recognition mechanism are rather limited in this context. Here, mutual recognition implies not a duty to enforce a foreign decision[47] but something less far-reaching, namely a duty 'to take into account' a foreign judgment that has resulted either in a decision not to prosecute (Article 54 CISA) or in an alleviation of the penalties (Article 56 CISA).[48] Mutual recognition implies a proportionality test in the second supposition, whereas no such test exists in the first, since the *ne bis in idem* principle brings the enforcement powers of the (other Member) State(s) to a halt.[49] Yet, even on the basis of the first hypothesis it would be wrong to conclude that the national authorities are denied any margin of control, as they are still expected to verify whether the conditions of Article 54 CISA have been fulfilled.[50]

As for the qualification of the *ne bis in idem* principle, the question has been raised as to whether it should be considered a procedural rule or a rule of substantive criminal law.[51] Unlike its AG, the ECJ failed to qualify explicitly the *ne bis in idem* principle as an important subjective safeguard for citizens, but this should not necessarily be seen as a negation of the AG's point of view in this regard. Admittedly, by qualifying the objective of Article 54 CISA judgment upon judgment so as to ensure that no individual is prosecuted for the same facts in more than one Member States simply because he has exercised his right to freedom of movement,[52] the ECJ unquestionably

[45] Opinion of AG Ruiz-Jarabo Colomer in Joined Cases C-187/01 and C-385/01 *Gözütok and Brügge* [2003] ECR I-1345, § 48.

[46] CHALMERS, DAVIES, and MONTI, *European Union Law* (n 39) p. 607.

[47] See: Part II, ch 2: 'The Principle of Mutual Recognition as Legislative Impetus for Efficient Judicial Cooperation in Criminal Matters'.

[48] On this 'set-off' principle and AG Sharpston's suggestion to qualify it as a general principle of EU law, see: Opinion of AG Sharpston in Case C-288/05 *Kretzinger* [2007] ECR I-6441, § 65 and § 70; Opinion of AG Sharpston in Case C-367/05 *Kraaijenbrink* [2007] ECR I-6619, § 58–61. The AG's point of view on this matter was, however, not yet confirmed by the ECJ.

[49] Opinion of AG Ruiz-Jarabo Colomer in Case C-150/05 *Van Straaten* [2006] ECR I-9327, § 58. The fact that there is no proportionality 'check' as such does not impede that the proportionality principle lies at the basis of the *ne bis in idem* rule, see: Part II, ch 1, II, A. 'The principle of proportionality'.

[50] See: Part II, ch 1, IV, A. 'Limits resulting from the CISA's conditions for application of the *ne bis in idem* principle'.

[51] AG Colomer's undisputable preference for a substance-based approach is not explicitly followed by the ECJ, neither in *Gözütok and Brügge* nor in any subsequent judgment. See Opinion of AG Ruiz-Jarabo Colomer in Joined Cases C-187/01 and C-385/01 *Gözütok and Brügge* [2003] ECR I-1345, § 114; Opinion of AG Ruiz-Jarabo Colomer in Case C-436/04 *Van Esbroeck* [2006] ECR I-2333, § 33–4. See also: M. FLETCHER, 'Some Developments to the ne bis in idem Principle in the European Union: Criminal Proceedings Against Gözütok and Brügge', *MLR* 2003, 778; KLIP, *European Criminal Law* (n 23) 251.

[52] ECJ, Joined Cases C-187/01 and C-385/01 *Gözütok and Brügge* [2003] ECR I-1345, para 38; ECJ, Case C-436/04 *Van Esbroeck* [2006] ECR I-2333, para 33; ECJ, Case C-150/05 *Van Straaten* [2006] ECR I-9327, para 57; ECJ, Case C-467/04 *Gasparini and others* [2006] ECR I-9199, para 27. V. MITSILEGAS, *EU Criminal Law* (Oxford, Hart Publishing, 2009) 143; J. VERVAELE, 'The Transnational ne bis in idem Principle in the EU. Mutual Recognition and Equivalent Protection of Human Rights', *Utrecht Law Review* 2005, 100; M. WASMEIER, 'The Principle of ne bis in idem', *Revue Internationale de Droit Pénal. Le droit Pénal de l'Union Européenne* 2006, 121.

emphasizes freedom of movement as a rationale behind the *ne bis in idem* principle in the Schengen context. Notwithstanding this focus, which is in any case a perfectly legitimate statement in light of the CISA's preamble, it is difficult to see how the ECJ could not consider this 'fundamental principle of EU law'[53]—one that is explicitly laid down in Article 50 Charter—a safeguard, a form of judicial protection, and a fundamental right of citizens. Rather than qualifying the *ne bis in idem* principle as either procedural or substantive, I maintain a combined approach by suggesting that the *ne bis in idem* principle has consequences for both the procedural side (since the principle blocks a new prosecution) and for the substantive side (since the principle implies a right not to be prosecuted twice).[54]

Irrespective of any procedural or substantive qualifications of the *ne bis in idem* principle, and regardless of its limited or extensive scope for application, it is beyond any doubt that mutual recognition as embodied in the *ne bis in idem* principle works above all to the benefit of citizens facing criminal charges and to the detriment of a (second) Member State's prosecutorial interests. The ECJ's broad interpretation of Article 54 CISA leads to the prevalence of the individual's judicial protection and emphasizes the fundamental rights dimension of this provision.

(2) *Mutual recognition and mutual trust: two sides of the same coin?*

The intrinsic link between mutual trust and mutual recognition appeared for the first time in the *Gözütok and Brügge* judgment, where the ECJ stated that 'Article 54 CISA necessarily implies that the Member States have mutual trust in their criminal justice systems and that each of them recognises the criminal law in force in the other Member States'.[55] The ECJ's succinct statement on mutual trust contrasts sharply with the wide-ranging reflections and questions these statements have prompted among legal commentators, especially concerning the nature of trust, its (legal) basis, its characteristics, its limits, and the relation between mutual trust and mutual recognition.[56] Under this heading, the focus lies on the latter aspect, particularly with regard to the

[53] ECJ, Case C-436/04 *Van Esbroeck* [2006] ECR I-2333, para 40.

[54] J.-L. DE LA CUESTA, 'Concurrent National and International Criminal Jurisdiction and the Principle "ne bis in idem". General Report', *IRPL* 2002, 710.

[55] ECJ, Joined Cases C-187/01 and C-385/01 *Gözütok and Brügge* [2003] ECR I-1345, para 33. Likewise: ECJ, Case C-436/04 *Van Esbroeck* [2006] ECR I-2333, para 30; ECJ, Case C-467/04 *Gasparini and others* [2006] ECR I-9199, para 30; ECJ, Case C-150/05 *Van Straaten* [2006] ECR I-9327, para 43; ECJ, Case C-297/07 *Bourquain* [2008] ECR I-9425, para 37.

[56] G. DE KERCHOVE and A. WEYEMBERGH (eds.), *La confiance mutuelle dans l'espace pénal européen/Mutual trust in the European Criminal Area* (Brussels, Institut d'Etudes Européennes, 2005); O. DE SCHUTTER, 'The Two Europes of Human Rights: The Emerging Division of Tasks between the Council of Europe and the European Union in Promoting Human Rights in Europe', *Col. J. Eur. L.* 2008, Vol. 14:3, 542 ff.; O. DE SCHUTTER, 'L'espace de liberté, de sécurité et de justice et la responsabilité individuelle des Etats au regard de la convention européenne des droits de l'homme', in G. DE KERCHOVE and A. WEYEMBERGH (eds.), *L'espace pénal européen: enjeux et perspectives,* (Brussels, Institut d'Etudes Européennes, 2002) 227 ff.; D. FLORE, *Droit pénal européen. Les enjeux d'une justice pénale européenne* (Brussels, Larcier, 2009) 370–83; J. OUWERKERK, 'Mutual Trust in the Area of Criminal Law', in H. BATTJES, E. BROUWER, P. DE MORREE and J. OUWERKERK (eds.), *The Principle of Mutual Trust in European Asylum, Migration and Criminal Law. Reconciling Trust and Fundamental Rights* (Utrecht, Forum, 2011) 38–48; G. STESSENS, 'The Principle of Mutual Confidence between Judicial Authorities in the Area of Freedom, Justice and Security', in G. DE KERCHOVE and A. WEYEMBERGH (eds.), *L'espace pénal européen: enjeux et perspectives,* (Brussels, Institut d'Etudes Européennes, 2002) 93 ff.

question of whether trust can best be qualified as a precondition to or consequence of recognition.[57]

In the ECJ's judgments, there is a juxtaposition between the two concepts—that Member States have mutual trust in and recognize each other[58]—but the precise link between trust and recognition has not been decisively elucidated. Fortunately, some AGs' opinions go some way towards clarifying or at least addressing the issue of their meaning.

AG Sharpston stated that 'mutual trust' and 'mutual recognition' are different names for the same principle.[59] According to her, 'mutual recognition' is the term used by the European Council, the Council, and the Commission, whereas the ECJ prefers the term 'mutual trust'. In my opinion, such a conclusion suffers too much from simplification and, moreover, is simply not correct. The fact that the concept of trust is clearly comparable to the concept of mutual recognition does not necessarily imply that they are identical. The ECJ's explicit references to both recognition and trust would hardly make sense if both concepts meant the same thing. An analysis of some of the official documents issued by the European institutions in this field indicates that these institutions all refer to both concepts and also that they clearly do not treat them as identical.[60] Furthermore, a purely linguistic approach to the two concepts suggests that they are not mere synonyms but two distinct operations. 'Trust' relates in my view to the 'spirit' or 'attitude' which must govern the way in which Member States are expected to cooperate with each other within the EU,[61] whereas 'mutual recognition' refers to the legal mechanism which obliges Member State to effect the judicial decisions of other Member States.

Late AG Ruiz-Jarabo Colomer dwelled at greater length on the meaning of trust than his learned colleague and his reflections on trust (and recognition) are, in my opinion, more convincing. He stresses that mutual trust is an essential element in the development of the EU, which is a true 'common market[62] of fundamental rights' where Member States share principles and values.[63] It is precisely this common heritage that should enable Member States (and their judicial authorities) to trust each other, i.e. to have trust in the adequacy of other Member States' rules and also to trust that these rules are correctly applied. From this perspective, mutual recognition presents itself as the next logical step, or consequence. After all, if Member States are presumed to trust each other's criminal justice systems, nothing should prevent them recognizing a judicial

[57] Compare, in this regard, in particular: D. FLORE, 'La notion de confiance mutuelle: l'alpha ou l'oméga d'une justice pénale européenne?', in DE KERCHOVE and WEYEMBERGH (eds.), *La confiance mutuelle dans l'espace pénal européen/Mutual trust in the European Criminal Area* (n 56) 17 ff. with STESSENS, 'The Principle of Mutual Confidence between Judicial Authorities in the Area of Freedom, Justice and Security' (n 56) 93 ff.

[58] ECJ, Joined Cases C-187/01 and C-385/01 *Gözütok and Brügge* [2003] ECR I-1345, para 33; ECJ, Case C-436/04 *Van Esbroeck* [2006] ECR I-2333, para 30; ECJ, Case C-467/04 *Gasparini and others* [2006] ECR I-9199, para 30; ECJ, Case C-150/05 *Van Straaten* [2006] ECR I-9327, para 43; ECJ, Case C-297/07 *Bourquain* [2008] ECR I-9425, para 37.

[59] Opinion of AG Sharpston in Case C-467/04 *Gasparini and others* [2006] ECR I-9199, § 107 (in particular, fn 87 of the AG's Opinion).

[60] See: Part II, ch 2: 'The Principle of Mutual Recognition as Legislative Impetus for Efficient Judicial Cooperation in Criminal Matters'.

[61] On the close link between the principles of mutual trust, mutual recognition, and loyal cooperation, see: Part II, ch 1, II, C. 'The principle of sincere cooperation'.

[62] Mind the use of a typically economic concept ('market') in the old third-pillar context. In *Van Straaten* the Advocate General opted for a different wording, namely a common 'home' of fundamental rights: Opinion of AG Ruiz-Jarabo Colomer in Case C-150/05 *Van Straaten* [2006] ECR I-9327, § 61.

[63] Opinion of AG Ruiz-Jarabo Colomer in Joined Cases C-187/01 and C-385/01 *Gözütok and Brügge* [2003] ECR I-1345, § 124.

decision made by another Member State's legal order. In such a framework, the principle of mutual trust works at an abstract level, i.e. as a normative principle which cannot simply be set aside whenever cracks appear in the mutual trust *in concreto*.[64]

Yet, a lack of mutual trust *in concreto* is nevertheless able to jeopardize the smooth functioning of the *ne bis in idem* (and mutual recognition) principle. When reading the facts of *Gözütok and Brügge*, *Miraglia*, *Van Straaten*, *Bourquain* or any of the other *ne bis in idem* judgments, the impression cannot be avoided that the second Member State's authorities considered the 'judgment' passed by the authorities in the first Member State insufficient, or that they felt the latter's interpretation of Article 54 CISA to be incorrect, and therefore sought to impose a punishment themselves, 'properly'.[65] In other words, these judgments reveal a clear lack of trust *in concreto* which contrasts sharply with the abstract and normative nature of trust endorsed by the ECJ in its case law.[66] This case law largely prevents national judicial authorities from calling into question the duty of mutual recognition and from jeopardizing the *ne bis in idem* principle, since even in the absence of mutual trust (*in concreto*), Member States are in principle bound by a duty of mutual recognition based on the mutual trust (*in abstracto*) principle. Only when the first Member State's interpretation of the fulfilment of Article 54 CISA's conditions is not correct,[67] or when the relevant national provision is irreconcilable with the objective of Article 54 CISA,[68] is the ECJ willing to admit to a lack of trust and to set the corresponding duty of mutual recognition aside.

In sum, reading duties of mutual trust and mutual recognition into Article 54 CISA seems both logical and justifiable within the framework of the EU legal order, in which Member States share common principles and values and in which they have committed themselves to the principle of sincere cooperation (Article 4(3) TEU).[69] Member States are required to trust each other (principle of mutual trust *in abstracto*) and consequently to recognize each other's decisions (principle of mutual recognition). The existence of trust *in concreto* is thus no *conditio sine qua non* for the application of the mutual recognition principle; on the contrary, the point of departure is that the mutual recognition principle must be applied whether mutual trust *in concreto* exists or not. However, in

[64] The more abstract, theoretical nature of mutual trust as a general principle of EU law does not prevent it from being translated into a specific attitude on behalf of the actors in the criminal justice system, an attitude with, furthermore, an obligatory character, because of the normative nature of the principle. On this normative nature, see: Opinion of AG Ruiz-Jarabo Colomer in ECJ, Case C-297/07 *Bourquain* [2008] ECR I-9425, § 45.

[65] E. GUILD, 'Crime and the EU's Constitutional Future in an Area of Freedom, Security and Justice', *E.L.J.* 2004, 230–1.

[66] The finding that mutual trust *in abstracto* does not necessarily coincide with mutual trust *in concreto* and the ECJ's far-reaching reliance on 'mutual trust' which is deemed to exist between the Member States, has raised doubts as to whether, in the absence of approximation, mutual trust can and should be so easily imposed on Member States. See, in this regard, the sharp criticism of AG Sharpston on the unlimited nature of such 'a vaguely defined principle of mutual trust': Opinion of AG Sharpston in Case C-467/04 *Gasparini and others* [2006] ECR I-9199, § 108-14; H. LABAYLE, 'Architecte ou spectactrice? La Cour de Justice de l'Union dans l'espace de liberte, securite et justice', *RTD. Eur.* 2006, 26–9. Also the European institutions have become aware that a common set of values does not suffice and that mutual trust needs to be enhanced by means of confidence-building measures. See: Part II, ch 3: 'The Workability of the Principle of Mutual Recognition in Criminal Matters'. Precisely the development of trust-building measures is aimed at bridging the gap between (the general principle of) mutual trust *in abstracto* and (the required attitude of) mutual trust *in concreto*.

[67] See, for instance: ECJ, Case C-469/03, *Miraglia* [2005] ECR I-2009, para 22.

[68] See, for instance: ECJ, Case C-297/07 *Bourquain* [2008] ECR I-9425, paras 40–2.

[69] See: Part II, ch 1, II. Legal Basis, Interrelated Principles, and Consolidation of the Fundamental Role of the Principle of Mutual Recognition in the EU Criminal Justice Area.

exceptional cases, a lack of trust *in concreto* can be considered justified and may lead to the non-application of the *ne bis in idem* rule and, thus, to the lack of any duty of mutual recognition.

(3) *Mutual recognition without the need for prior approximation: long live diversity?*

In *Gözütok and Brügge* the central question was whether a settlement with the public prosecutor amounted to the final disposal of a trial in accordance with the meaning of Article 54 CISA. The ECJ itself noted that, in general, national legal systems did not consider out-of-court settlements to preclude further proceedings except in non-serious cases.[70] We might easily imagine, then, that a Member State whose criminal justice system does not consider an out-of-court settlement to amount to a bar to further proceedings would not be quick to agree to such a far-reaching interpretation of Article 54 CISA. Should we not expect that national criminal sovereignty prevails where Member States have not harmonized or approximated their national laws in this respect? The ECJ rejected such a position by pointing out that 'nowhere in Title VI of the Treaty on EU relating to police and judicial cooperation in criminal matters . . . or in the Schengen Agreement or the CISA itself, is the application of Article 54 of the CISA made conditional upon harmonisation, or at the least approximation, of the criminal laws of the Member States relating to procedures whereby further prosecution is barred'.[71] In subsequent cases, the ECJ expressed the same view: disparities between the criminal law systems of the Member States regarding definitions of drugs offences, prescription periods, or *in absentia* judgments cannot preclude the principle of mutual recognition from playing its role.[72] Furthermore, in these same judgments, the ECJ has similarly emphasized on numerous occasions that a duty to recognize the criminal law in force in the other Member States exists 'even when the outcome would be different if its own national law were applied'.[73]

The ECJ's interpretation of Article 54 CISA, which detaches mutual recognition completely from any previous approximation requirement, reflects a clear choice to give prevalence to the object and purpose of this provision and of its *effet utile*[74] and is, furthermore of great benefit to the citizen involved in this context.

Yet, questions have been raised as to how the ECJ's interpretation relates to the traditionally held view that criminal law is a delicate matter of national sovereignty. In this regard, it has been argued that the interpretation was made at the expense of great respect for the Member States' penal law systems.[75] In my view, the latter opinion slightly disregards two crucial features of the EU's integration process, namely an undeniable increase in EU competence in the area of judicial cooperation in criminal matters and a continuous and strengthened focus on respect for (criminal) diversity within the EU legal order.

[70] ECJ, Joined Cases C-187/01 and C-385/01 *Gözütok and Brügge* [2003] ECR I-1345, para 39.

[71] ECJ, Joined Cases C-187/01 and C-385/01 *Gözütok and Brügge* [2003] ECR I-1345, para 32.

[72] ECJ, Case C-436/04 *Van Esbroeck* [2006] ECR I-2333, para 29; ECJ, Case C-467/04 *Gasparini and others* [2006] ECR I-9199 para 30; ECJ, Case C-297/07 *Bourquain* [2008] ECR I-9425, para 37.

[73] ECJ, Joined Cases C-187/01 and C-385/01 *Gözütok and Brügge* [2003] ECR I-1345, para 33; ECJ, Case C-436/04 *Van Esbroeck* [2006] ECR I-2333, para 30; ECJ, Case C-467/04 *Gasparini and others* [2006] ECR I-9199, para 29; ECJ, Case C-297/07 *Bourquain* [2008] ECR I-9425, para 37.

[74] ECJ, Joined Cases C-187/01 and C-385/01 *Gözütok and Brügge* [2003] ECR I-1345, para 35.

[75] V. HATZOPOULOS, 'With or Without You . . . Judging Politically in the Field of Area of Freedom, Security and Justice', *E.L. Rev.* 2008, 60.

First, with regard to the 'sovereignty' argument,[76] it must be admitted that in light of the successive Treaty amendments, particularly those of the last two decades, which have strengthened the competences of the EU institutions in this area of law considerably, this argument has inevitably lost significance.

Secondly, with regard to the 'diversity' argument,[77] we should bear in mind that it is generally acknowledged that the principle of mutual recognition is, by its proper nature, an integrative tool aimed at respecting diversity to the fullest extent possible and, consequently, respecting the penal law systems of the Member States. In the *ne bis in idem* context, the 'second' Member State is bound to respect the national framework of the Member State in which the 'first' sentence was passed. In one area of freedom, security, and justice, a Member State's role as 'first' or 'second' state may vary from one day to another, and the principle of mutual recognition thus necessitates a clear duty of mutual respect vis-à-vis the legal frameworks of each and every Member State.

(4) A teleological and functional approach to mutual recognition in which the ECJ balances freedom, security, and justice

The *Gözütok and Brügge* judgment was the first—though certainly not unique—ruling on the former third pillar over which the ECJ has been accused, often unjustly, of having transgressed clear Treaty provisions.[78] Rather than adhering to a literal interpretation of Article 54 CISA, the ECJ decided in its *ne bis in idem* case law to defend a teleological and functional approach.[79] The ECJ did not limit itself to the object, purpose, and *effet utile* of Article 54 CISA[80] but fitted this provision into a broader framework, namely the former EU Treaty. The ECJ recalled that the EU had set itself the objective of maintaining and developing the Union as an Area of Freedom, Security, and Justice in which the free movement of persons was assured (old Art. 2 TEU).[81] This right to freedom of movement can only be guaranteed effectively if the perpetrator of an act is aware that once he or she has been found guilty and served a sentence, or, where applicable, been acquitted by a final judgment in a given Member State, he or she may travel within the Schengen territory without fear of prosecution in another Member State.[82]

The free movement of persons, which has always been one of the pillars of the internal market, is therefore also crucial to the Area of Freedom, Security, and Justice. In *Van*

[76] This aspect is developed in more detail in: Part III, ch 1, II. 'Criminal Justice and the Transfer of Sovereignty: the Paradox of National Sovereignty Claims in Light of the EU's Integration Process'.

[77] Part III, ch 1, II. 'Criminal Justice and the Transfer of Sovereignty: the Paradox of National Sovereignty Claims in Light of the EU's Integration Process'.

[78] Most language versions clearly seem to imply the necessary intervention of a judicial authority with regard to Article 54 CISA. See, for instance: the Spanish version 'quien haya sido juzgada en sentencia firme'; the Dutch version 'persoon die bij onherroepelijk vonnis is berecht'; the French version 'personne définitivement jugée' or the English version 'person who has been finally judged'.

[79] Also in other judgments related to criminal matters the ECJ took a teleological and functional approach, see for instance: ECJ, Case C-176/03 *Commission v Council* [2005] ECR I-7879; ECJ, Case C-105/03 *Pupino* [2005] ECR I-5285.

[80] ECJ, Joined Cases C-187/01 and C-385/01 *Gözütok and Brügge* [2003] ECR I-1345, para 35 and para 38; ECJ, Case C-436/04 *Van Esbroeck* [2006] ECR I-2333, para 34; ECJ, Case C-150/05 *Van Straaten* [2006] ECR I-9327, para 57; ECJ, Case C-297/07 *Bourquain* [2008] ECR I-9425, para 51 and the corresponding Opinion of AG Ruiz-Jarabo Colomer, § 67–9; ECJ, Case C-491/07 *Turanský* [2008] ECR I-11039, para 41.

[81] ECJ, Joined Cases C-187/01 and C-385/01 *Gözütok and Brügge* [2003] ECR I-1345, para 36.

[82] ECJ, Joined Cases C-187/01 and C-385/01 *Gözütok and Brügge* [2003] ECR I-1345, para 38; ECJ, Case C-436/04 *Van Esbroeck* [2006] ECR I-2333, paras 33–4; ECJ, Case C-150/05 *Van Straaten* [2006] ECR I-9327, para 46; ECJ, Case C-467/04 *Gasparini and others* [2006] ECR I-9199, para 27.

Esbroeck and subsequent judgments, the ECJ also relied on the free movement argument to maintain that a factual interpretation of 'idem' (the facts are identical) should be preferred over an interpretation based on the legal qualification (the legal provisions are identical) and over an interpretation based on the protected legal interest. In these cases, in contrast to the situation in the *Gözütok and Brügge* judgment, the language of Article 54 CISA now favoured such an interpretation. Thus, in *Van Esbroeck*, both teleological and textual arguments were combined to justify the application of the *ne bis in idem* principle. In *Van Straaten*, the ECJ was required to decide whether the *ne bis in idem* principle also applied in cases where there had been a previous acquittal. Once again, free movement arguments together with the principle of legal certainty and the protection of legitimate expectations assured the application of the *ne bis in idem* principle.[83]

However, free movement cannot always prevail and mutual recognition must be applied in a reasonable way. Therefore, the ECJ emphasized in *Miraglia* that the purpose of old Article 2 TEU, namely to maintain and develop the Union as an Area of Freedom, Security, and Justice in which the free movement of persons was assured, must be developed in conjunction with appropriate measures for preventing and combatting crime.[84] The 'security' and 'justice' aspects of this area would clearly not be served if *ne bis in idem* also applied to cases where the judicial authorities of one Member State had decided to close a case on the sole grounds that criminal proceedings had been started in another Member State against the same defendant and for the same acts, without any determination whatsoever as to the merits of the case. The same concerns about 'security' and 'justice' underpin a number of other cases: in the *Kraaijenbrink* judgment, the ECJ concluded that the same criminal intention in relation to a case of drugs trafficking and money laundering did not suffice to trigger the application of Article 54 CISA;[85] in the *Kretzinger* judgment, the ECJ stated that the purpose of Article 54 CISA is to avoid a situation in which a person whose trial has been concluded in the first state can no longer be prosecuted for the same acts and therefore ultimately remains unpunished if the state in which sentence was first passed has not actually enforced the penalty imposed;[86] and in the *Turanský* judgment, the ECJ emphasized that Article 54 CISA is not intended to protect suspects from potentially having to submit to subsequent investigations in several Contracting States.[87] In *Gasparini*, freedom, security, and justice arguments were combined. Free movement arguments clearly played a fundamental role in deciding that *ne bis in idem* applies in cases where a previous judgment was time-barred. Yet the ECJ was evidently also inspired by security and justice elements when it rightly stated in answer to the second question that the *ne bis in idem* principle cannot apply to persons other than those whose trial has been definitively concluded in a Contracting State.[88] A similar combined approach can be found in the *Kretzinger* judgment, where free movement elements prevailed with regard to suspended custodial sentences and security elements in relation to police custody and/or detention on remand pending trial.[89]

These judgments thus clearly demonstrate that mutual recognition is not an objective in itself, but rather a means to achieve another objective, namely the Area of Freedom,

[83] ECJ, Case C-150/05 *Van Straaten* [2006] ECR I-9327, para 59.

[84] ECJ, Case C-469/03 *Miraglia* [2005] ECR I-2009, para 34; ECJ, Case C-491/07 *Turanský* [2008] ECR I-11039, para 43.

[85] ECJ, Case C-367/05 *Kraaijenbrink* [2007] ECR I-6619, para 34.

[86] ECJ, Case C-288/05 *Kretzinger* [2007] ECR I-6441, para 51.

[87] ECJ, Case C-491/07 *Turanský* [2008] ECR I-11039, paras 41–4.

[88] ECJ, Case C-467/04 *Gasparini and others* [2006] ECR I-9199, para 36.

[89] ECJ, Case C-288/05 *Kretzinger* [2007] ECR I-6441, para 44 and para 52.

Security, and Justice. The ECJ was therefore right to decide not to adopt a purely formalistic view. The delicate balancing act that the ECJ has performed in its case law, by means of which the principle of mutual recognition is presented as a flexible principle that can be of interest to both the prosecution (where the focus is on security elements) and the suspected person (where the focus is on freedom elements), should be warmly welcomed.

II. Legal Basis, Interrelated Principles, and Consolidation of the Fundamental Role of the Principle of Mutual Recognition in the EU Criminal Justice Area

In the previous chapter, I analysed the principle of mutual recognition on the basis of the ECJ's general approach to the *ne bis in idem* principle of Article 54 CISA and its specific conditions. In this chapter, I continue to explore the mutual recognition principle, now in light of four fundamental principles of EU law which co-influence the meaning and scope of the principle of mutual recognition, namely the principles of proportionality (section II, A), subsidiarity (section II, B), sincere cooperation (section II, C), and mutual trust (section II, D). Finally, this chapter addresses the question of the principle of mutual recognition's legal basis in the Treaty, which since the Treaty of Lisbon came into force has highlighted the position of paramount importance occupied by this principle with regard to judicial cooperation in criminal matters (section II, E).

A. The principle of proportionality[90]

The close relationship between the principle of proportionality and the principle of mutual recognition, with particular regard to Articles 54 and 56 CISA, has been emphasized in policy documents as well as in several AGs' opinions.[91] The *ne bis in idem* principle, which imposes a duty of mutual recognition in order to avoid a duplication of sentences for one offence, and the set-off principle, which prescribes a duty when imposing a new sentence to take into account and thus recognize a previous sentence whenever the *ne bis in idem* principle does not apply, can both be considered expressions or exemplifications of the principle of proportionality in this specific area of law.[92]

The relevance of the principle of proportionality, however, is not limited to the specific *ne bis in idem* context. In relation to other instruments of EU secondary legislation that are explicitly based on the principle of mutual recognition, the principle of proportionality fulfils an equally important though slightly different function vis-à-vis the principle of mutual recognition. For instance, in relation to the surrender regime under the FD EAW, the principle of proportionality's crucial yet distinct role can be identified as in this context it operates essentially as a restriction to the principle of mutual recognition. Indeed,

[90] Article 5(4) TEU.

[91] Communication from the Commission to the Council and the European Parliament—Area of Freedom, Security and Justice: Assessment of the Tampere programme and future orientations, COM (2004) 401 final, 10. Opinion of AG Ruiz-Jarabo Colomer in Case C-436/04 *Van Esbroeck* [2006] ECR I-2333, § 20; Opinion of AG Ruiz-Jarabo Colomer in Case C-150/05 *Van Straaten* [2006] ECR I-9327, § 58 ff; Opinion of AG Sharpston in Case C-288/05 *Kretzinger* [2007] ECR I-6441, § 64 ff; Opinion of AG Sharpston in Case C-367/05 *Kraaijenbrink* [2007] ECR I-6619, § 56 ff; Opinion of AG Ruiz-Jarabo Colomer in Case C-297/07 *Bourquain* [2008] ECR I-9425, § 37 and § 49.

[92] See the cases cited in n 91.

whereas in relation to Article 54 CISA and Article 56 CISA the principle of mutual recognition is a specific manifestation of the principle of proportionality, in the context of the FD EAW the principle of proportionality is a kind of guarantee that the principle of mutual recognition will be applied moderately.[93] Indeed, by stating that a European Arrest Warrant may be issued 'for acts punishable by the law of the issuing Member State by a custodial sentence or a detention order for a maximum period of at least twelve months or, where a sentence has been passed or a detention order has been made, for sentences of at least four months',[94] a threshold is established, and mutual recognition is only deemed to apply to 'serious offences' and not to 'minor' offences, i.e. offences below this threshold. However, in view of the fact that the threshold is formulated by reference to the maximum penalty applicable to the offence in question, and not the penalty that is actually likely to be imposed, there is a risk that the threshold will fail to produce the desired effect.[95] Occasionally, despite this threshold, a number of executing judicial authorities have relied on the principle of proportionality in order to set aside the principle of mutual recognition in cases they considered minor and in which they deemed it unlikely that a (severe) sentence would follow in the issuing Member State.[96] Even though such decisions are in conflict with the distribution of powers that corresponds to the mutual recognition mechanism in the FD EAW and entail a risk of impunity, they nevertheless appear justified in some cases in light of fundamental rights considerations with regard to the person who is to be surrendered.[97] Such decisions and fundamental rights considerations also indicate the need to develop legislative measures for 'minor' cases which are less drastic than surrender proceedings but which also avoid impunity.[98]

[93] For some examples of how the principle of proportionality can play a role in relation to the EAW or other legislative instruments, see: S. ALEGRE and M. LEAF, 'Mutual Recognition in European Judicial Cooperation: A Step Too Far Too Soon? Case Study—The European Arrest Warrant', *ELJ* 2004, 210; T. LJUNGQUIST, 'Mutual Recognition of Non-custodial Pre-trial Supervision Measures in the European Union', *Le droit pénal de l'Union Européenne. Revue International de droit pénal* 2006, 175.

[94] Article 2(1) FD EAW.

[95] On this issue, see, for instance: R. DAVIDSON, 'A Sledgehammer to Crack a Nut? Should there be a Bar of Triviality in European Arrest Warrant Cases?', *C.L.R.* 2009, 31–6; J. VOGEL and J.R. SPENCER, 'Proportionality and the European Arrest Warrant', *C.L.R.* 2010, 480–1. See also: P. ASP, 'Mutual Recognition and the Development of Criminal Law Cooperation within the EU', in E.J. HUSABO and A. STRANDBAKKEN (eds.), *Harmonization of Criminal Law in Europe* (Antwerp, Intersentia, 2005) 33, who criticizes that the principle of proportionality is totally disregarded in the third pillar.

[96] Several legal practitioners insisted on the need to perform an (additional) proportionality check when confronted with EAW requests: C. JANSSENS, 'Conferentieverslag: Mutual Recognition of Judicial Decisions in Criminal Matters and the Role of the National Judge (Third Annual Forum)', *Panopticon* 2009, 73. In order to address the problematic situation whereby executing Member States refused to surrender on the basis of a proportionality test, the Council has underlined that this proportionality check needs to be performed at an earlier level, namely by the issuing Member State and prior to sending an EAW request. See: Council of the EU, *Handbook on the EAW* 2008, 14. On the risk of inserting an (additional) proportionality test and its potentially undermining effect on the objective of the EAW, see: FLETCHER, LOOF, and GILLMORE, *EU Criminal Law and Justice* (n 36) 118.

[97] For some examples, see, for instance: DAVIDSON, 'A Sledgehammer to Crack a Nut?' (n 95) 36; A. KLIP, 'Overleveringsperikelen', *DD* 2010, 552; VOGEL and SPENCER, 'Proportionality and the European Arrest Warrant' (n 95) 482. See also: ECtHR, 17 January 2012, *Vinter and others v United Kingdom*, 66069/09 and 130/10 and 3896/10, para 89, where the ECtHR accepted that a grossly disproportionate sentence could amount to ill-treatment contrary to Article 3 ECHR, but that it will only be on 'rare and unique occasions' that the test will be met.

[98] VOGEL and SPENCER, 'Proportionality and the European Arrest Warrant' (n 95) 482.

B. The principle of subsidiarity[99]

The principle of subsidiarity and the principle of mutual recognition have one crucial characteristic in common: they both attach much importance to respecting the Member State's legal and judicial traditions. From this perspective, it is logical that the two principles are often linked[100] and even that the mutual recognition approach is said to be based on the principle of subsidiarity.[101]

Respect for diversity is of the utmost importance in criminal law. It is also a subject of an extremely sensitive nature since it enshrines the values of any given society by punishing what it considers to be socially unacceptable and by leaving unpunished what it deems to be acceptable.[102] The European legislator's new legislative approach, with its strong focus on the principle of mutual recognition that has been evident since the Tampere European Council, has substantially diminished the need for approximation in the field of (substantive) criminal law.[103] Prompted by arguments that a (full) approximation approach would simply not work, this New Approach has resulted in a legislative technique that relies heavily on respect for the national legal systems of the Member States. This strong reliance on the Member States' national legislations is fully in line with the main assumption that underpins the principle of subsidiarity, namely that the EU will not intervene when an issue can be regulated effectively by the Member States themselves.

Despite these common features and a certain level of interdependence between the two principles, attention must also be given to what distinguishes them. As explained earlier,[104] the principle of subsidiarity is above all a guiding principle for dividing competences between the EU and the Member States and thus plays a pivotal role whenever approximation measures are developed. The principle of mutual recognition, on the other hand, is not dependent on approximation of the Member States' criminal laws; its raison d'être and validity is reinforced precisely because no such approximation is required. Unlike the principle of subsidiarity, which involves a vertical mechanism distributing competences between the EU and the Member States, the principle of mutual recognition largely concerns the coordination of competences among the Member States, thus a horizontal mechanism.

C. The principle of sincere cooperation[105]

The principle of sincere cooperation is not mentioned once in the case law on mutual recognition in criminal matters, neither by the ECJ nor by its AGs. In view of its general and broad scope, it has been convincingly argued that the principle itself is not adequate to serve

[99] Article 5(3) TEU.

[100] M. LÓPEZ ESCUDERO, 'El reconocimiento mutuo de sanciones pecuniarias en la Unión Europea', *Rev. Gen. Der. Eur.* 2006, 32; FLETCHER, LOOF, and GILLMORE, *EU Criminal Law and Justice* (n 36) 194 ff.

[101] Communication from the Commission to the Council and the European Parliament—Area of Freedom, Security and Justice: Assessment of the Tampere programme and future orientations (n 91) p. 10.

[102] FLETCHER, LOOF, and GILLMORE, *EU Criminal Law and Justice* (n 36) 194; M. HILDEBRANDT, 'European Criminal Law and European Identity', *Criminal law and Philosophy* 2007, 57–78; Opinion of AG Bot in Case C-348/09 *P.I.*, nyr, § 36.

[103] FLETCHER, LOOF, and GILLMORE, *EU Criminal Law and Justice* (n 36) 202.

[104] See: Part I, ch 1, II, C. 'The principle of subsidiarity'.

[105] Article 4(3) TEU.

as a legal basis for specific mutual recognition measures.[106] Yet, this conclusion does not necessarily imply that the principle of sincere cooperation, and the many aspects that it encompasses, has no influence whatsoever on the principle of mutual recognition. On the contrary, since the *Pupino* judgment,[107] in which the ECJ applied former Article 10 EC in the context of the former EU Treaty by means of a cross-pillar approach, specifically in the context of police and judicial cooperation in criminal matters,[108] legal scholars have emphasized the promising impact that this article could have on the future of the principle of mutual recognition.[109] Though Article 4(3) TEU does not sum up any specific duties on the part of the Member States, it does provide a number of clear guidelines as to the cooperative spirit and the climate of mutual respect that must govern the relationship between Member States.[110] Thus, since *Pupino*, it has been clear that all actors in the criminal justice system will be under strict obligation to guarantee the full application of the mutual recognition system. In other words, they will have an active duty to cooperate and find solutions, as well as to exchange information and provide assistance.[111]

D. The principle of mutual trust

In its *ne bis in idem* case law, beginning with *Gözütok and Brügge*, the ECJ has repeatedly maintained that the *ne bis in idem* principle necessarily implies that 'Member States *have* mutual trust in their criminal justice systems' (emphasis added).[112] However, this duty of mutual trust, which emerged during *Gözütok and Brügge* as one of the founding principles of Article 54 CISA, must be seen in a broader context. The principle of mutual trust is not only the underlying basis of the Schengen area,[113] but also of the objective to establish an area of freedom, security, and justice and of the entire EU integration project in general.[114]

[106] A. DUTTA, 'Die Pflicht der Mitgliedstaaten zur gegenseitigen Durchsetzung ihrer öffentlichrechtlichen Forderungen', *EuR* 2007, 753; A. HATJE, *Loyalität als Rechtsprinzip in der Europäischen Union* (Baden-Baden, Nomos, 2001) 40 ff.

[107] ECJ, Case C-105/03 *Pupino* [2005] ECR I-5285.

[108] The question whether the (first pillar) principle of solidarity (and trust) could also underpin cooperation in criminal matters between the EC Member States was stated in the report of MJ BIGAY, 'L'entraide judiciaire européenne: vers un espace judiciaire européen', rapport présenté au colloque du groupe national de l'AIDP, tenu à Nice, 2–4 octobre 1980, cited in: C. VAN DEN WYNGAERT, 'L'espace Judiciaire Européen: Vers une fissure au sein du Conseil de l'Europe?', *Revue de droit pénal et de criminologie* 1981, 517–18.

[109] R. BARENTS, 'De denationalisering van het strafrecht', *SEW* 2006, 373.

[110] O. DE SCHUTTER, 'La contribution du contrôle juridictionnel à la confiance mutuelle', in G. DE KERCHOVE and A. WEYEMBERGH (eds.), *La confiance mutuelle dans l'espace pénal européen* (Brussels, IEE, 2005) 103. The aspect of mutual respect was explicitly taken up by the Lisbon Treaty when reformulating former Article 10 EC into Article 4(3) TEU, which now clearly states that the Member States shall, in *full mutual respect*, assist each other in carrying out tasks which flow from the Treaties.

[111] M. FICHERA and C. JANSSENS, 'Mutual Recognition of Judicial Decisions in Criminal Matters and the Role of the National Judge', *ERA Forum* 2007, 199.

[112] ECJ, Joined Cases C-187/01 and C-385/01 *Gözütok and Brügge* [2003] ECR I-1345, para 33. Likewise: ECJ, Case C-436/04 *Van Esbroeck* [2006] ECR I-2333, para 30; ECJ, Case C-467/04 *Gasparini and others* [2006] ECR I-9199, para 30; ECJ, Case C-150/05 *Van Straaten* [2006] ECR I-9327, para 43; ECJ, Case C-297/07 *Bourquain* [2008] ECR I-9425, para 37.

[113] Opinion of AG Ruiz-Jarabo Colomer in Case C-436/04 *Van Esbroeck* [2006] ECR I-2333, § 57; Opinion of AG Sharpston in Case C-288/05 *Kretzinger* [2007] ECR I-6441, § 100; Opinion of AG Sharpston in Case C-367/05 *Kraaijenbrink* [2007] ECR I-6619, § 43.

[114] Opinion of AG Ruiz-Jarabo Colomer in Joined Cases C-187/01 and C-385/01 *Gözütok and Brügge* [2003] ECR I-1345, § 122–4; Opinion of AG Ruiz-Jarabo Colomer in Case C-150/05 *Van Straaten* [2006] ECR I-9327, § 61–2.

Trust, solidarity, and respect are the foundations upon which the ambitious EU integration project is built and these concepts are consolidated in Article 4(3) TEU.[115] Integration requires assistance and cooperation between Member States which is unlikely to occur without mutual trust and solidarity. It is precisely the ambitious nature of the EU integration project, in which Member States share common values, objectives, and principles,[116] and in which they are connected with each other by means of a refined institutional framework, that explains why there is or ought to be[117] a high degree of trust within the EU[118] which will in turn enable a high degree of cooperation between Member States through the principle of mutual recognition.

E. In search of the correct legal basis: the Treaty of Lisbon and the consolidation of the principle of mutual recognition in judicial cooperation in criminal matters

The conclusions of the Tampere European Council (1999) made clear that legal instruments for judicial cooperation in criminal matters would subsequently be based on the principle of mutual recognition. Yet, in the absence of any explicit reference to the principle of mutual recognition in the then-applicable EU Treaty, questions logically arise as to identifying an adequate legal basis (under the old and new Treaties) for this principle and must be addressed next.

Both Article 54 CISA (discussed here in Chapter 1) and the framework decision on mutual recognition in judicial cooperation in criminal matters (discussed in Chapter 2) were adopted on the legal basis of the provisions of the former EU Treaty, namely old Articles 31 (and 34)[119] TEU.[120]

In accordance with old Article 31(1)(a) TEU, the EU was entitled to take measures aimed at 'facilitating and accelerating cooperation between competent ministries and judicial or equivalent authorities of the Member States [...] in relation to proceedings and the enforcement of decisions'. From a narrow perspective, i.e. a strictly literal

[115] In several judgments the ECJ interpreted the principle of mutual recognition *in the light of* the high degree of trust and solidarity between the Member States. Not only in relation to judicial cooperation in criminal matters (for instance, ECJ, Case C-303/05 *Advocaten voor de wereld* [2007] ECR I-3633, para 57), but also in relation to other aspects of the area of freedom, security, and justice (for instance, in relation to irregular immigration: Opinion of AG Kokott in Joined Cases C-261/08 and C-348/08 *Zurita Garcia* [2009] ECR I-10143, § 60).

[116] Opinion of AG Ruiz-Jarabo Colomer in Joined Cases C-187/01 and C-385/01 *Gözütok and Brügge* [2003] ECR I-1345, § 124; Opinion of AG Ruiz-Jarabo Colomer in Case C-150/05 *Van Straaten* [2006] ECR I-9327, § 62; Opinion of AG Ruiz-Jarabo Colomer in Case C-303/05 *Advocaten voor de wereld* [2007] ECR I-3633, § 44.

[117] On the difference between trust *in abstracto* and trust *in concreto*, see: Part II, ch 1, C, 2. 'Mutual recognition and mutual trust: two sides of the same coin?'

[118] Compare, for instance, with the reference to 'a spirit of mutual confidence' in the European Convention on the transfer of proceedings in criminal matters, 15 May 1972, § 3, retrievable at: <http://conventions.coe.int/Treaty/Commun/QueVoulezVous.asp?NT=073&CM=1&CL=ENG>. The (possibly lower) degree of trust in the context of the Council of Europe should not be equated to the level of trust that is (or should be) present amongst the EU Member States.

[119] Old Article 34 TEU only referred to the *type* of measures that could be used under the old third pillar—common positions, framework decisions, decisions and conventions—and will not be discussed hereafter as it is not relevant for the question that is addressed under this heading.

[120] With regard to Article 54 CISA, the legal basis was attributed after the incorporation of the Schengen acquis into the EU legal order. See, in particular, Article 2 and Annex A of Council decision 1999/436/EC of 20 may 1999 determining, in conformity with the relevant provisions of the Treaty establishing the European Community and the Treaty on European Union, the legal basis for each of the provisions or decisions which constitute the Schengen acquis, *O.J.* L-176, 10.07.1999, p. 17–30.

interpretation of this provision, it has been argued that old Article 31 EU could cover only (traditional) mutual legal assistance instruments and that it was inappropriate for the more 'revolutionary'[121] principle of mutual recognition.[122] However, the ECJ usually favours a teleological interpretation method, particularly where a restrictive interpretation does not conform to the objective(s) of the Treaties. Thus, in light of the development of the area of freedom, security, and justice, and taking into account the principles of subsidiarity, sincere cooperation, and mutual trust, to which the principle of mutual recognition is closely related, I agree with those authors who maintain, in fact, that the principle of mutual recognition could already be identified in old Article 31 TEU.[123] In particular, three elements of old Article 31(1)(a) TEU support this view. First, the fact that the EU was entitled to take measures to facilitate and accelerate cooperation is entirely consistent with the rationale behind the principle of mutual recognition, which is itself a mechanism for facilitating and accelerating (judicial) cooperation in order to improve on the traditional forms of cooperation (MLA). Secondly, the explicit reference to a cooperation mechanism between the Member States' judicial or equivalent authorities corresponds to a crucial feature of the principle of mutual recognition in criminal matters, namely its scope *ratione personae*, which is of a pre-eminently judicial nature. Thirdly, the mention of proceedings and the enforcement of decisions reflects a broad scope *ratione materiae* which is perfectly reconcilable with the scope of the current mutual recognition instruments.

The Treaty of Lisbon removed any remaining doubts about this issue by including an explicit reference to the principle of mutual recognition and its relation to judicial cooperation in criminal matters.[124] In accordance with Article 82(1) TFEU, judicial cooperation in criminal matters in the EU shall be based on the principle of the mutual recognition of judgments and judicial decisions. Furthermore, the European Parliament and the Council shall adopt, in accordance with the ordinary legislative procedure, measures to lay down rules and procedures for ensuring recognition throughout the Union of all forms of judgment and judicial decisions (Art. 82(1)(a) TFEU). This brand new provision provides the EU legislator with an explicit legal basis for any legislative measure on mutual recognition it aims to pursue. Yet it also raises the question of whether such legislative measures are indispensable for the application of the principle of mutual recognition, or whether any duties of mutual recognition can arise directly from the Treaty provisions themselves. In this regard, it is surprising that when drafting this Treaty provision, the Member States did not choose a more rigid formulation similar to those used in other sensitive areas of law.[125] In not doing so, it is now up to the ECJ to give Article 82(1)(a) TFEU either a broad or a narrow interpretation.

[121] See, however, with regard to the purportedly 'revolutionary' character of this principle: FICHERA and JANSSENS, 'Mutual Rcognition of Judicial Decisions in Criminal Matters and the Role of the National Judge' (n 111) 179–84.

[122] P. DE HERT, 'Het einde van de Europese rechtshulp', *Justitiële verkenningen* 2004, 111.

[123] LÓPEZ ESCUDERO, 'El reconocimiento mutuo de sanciones pecuniarias en la Unión Europea' (n 100) 4–5; M. BÖSE, 'Artikel 31—Justitielle Zusammenarbeit', in J. SCHWARZE (ed), *EU Kommentar* (Baden-Baden, Nomos, 2008) 172–3.

[124] Article 67(3) TFEU and Article 82(1) TFEU.

[125] Compare, in particular, with Article 53 TFEU, which encourages the Member States to adopt measures on the mutual recognition of diplomas in order to facilitate the free movement of persons (Art. 53(1) TFEU), but which makes the application of mutual recognition only *conditional upon prior coordination* in the area of medical or pharmaceutical professions (Art. 53(3) TFEU).

III. Equivalence, Country of Origin, and Mutual Recognition: Which Focus?

In Part I, I pointed out that in the internal market context, the principles of mutual recognition, equivalence, and country of origin often become muddled. Furthermore, I emphasized that despite their undeniable interrelationship, these terms and their corresponding concepts are not interchangeable and that any requirements concerning equivalence and/or the country of origin largely determine the contours of the principle of mutual recognition.

Under this heading, I analyse the extent to which the principle of equivalence and/or the principle of country of origin have any decisive role to play in the ECJ's *ne bis in idem* case law and if so, whether the focus lies on equivalence, country of origin, or mutual recognition.

A. Equivalence

The ECJ's statements in *Gözütok and Brügge* that 'the application of Article 54 CISA is not made conditional upon approximation' and 'that each Member State must recognise the criminal law in force in another Member State even when the outcome would be different if its own law were applied', and finally 'that the application of Article 54 CISA cannot be made subject to the condition that the first State's legal system does not require such judicial involvement either'[126] are all indications of one fact, namely that a requirement of equivalence seems to be entirely absent from the ECJ's reasoning.[127] However, such a radical view must be nuanced in light of three elements, namely the wording of Article 54 CISA (section A, 1), the (divergent) opinions of certain AGs (section A, 2), and the reference to comparative law surveys (section A, 3).

(1) Identicality of the material facts

A first manifestation of an equivalence requirement can be found in the definition of *ne bis in idem* itself. *Idem* means identical which is, of course, a very advanced level of equivalence. The ECJ's decision in *Van Esbroeck* to consider the identicality of the material facts as the only relevant criterion for the application of Article 54 CISA and to reject any criterion based on the legal qualification of the acts or on the protected legal interest was clearly prompted by a wish not to hinder free movement (mutual recognition). In not requiring that the legal qualification or the protected legal interest be identical (or even equivalent), the ECJ opts for a minimalist approach to equivalence. The definition of the test as 'a set of concrete circumstances which are inextricably linked' makes it a

[126] ECJ, Joined Cases C-187/01 and C-385/01 *Gözütok and Brügge* [2003] ECR I-1345, paras 32–4. The ECJ's wording was repeated, unchanged, in more recent judgments. See, for instance: ECJ, Case C-297/07 *Bourquain* [2008] ECR I-9425, paras 36–7.

[127] For a critique on the fact that a crucial feature of the principle of mutual recognition as it has always existed in the internal market context—namely equivalence—is missing in the context of judicial cooperation in criminal matters, see, for instance: M. GUZMÁN ZAPATER, 'Un elemento federalizador para Europa: el reconicimiento mutuo en el ámbito del reconicimiento de decisions judiciales', *RDCE* 2001, 427; L. MARIN, 'The European Arrest Warrant and Domestic Legal Orders. Tensions between Mutual Recognition and Fundamental Rights: the Italian Case', *MJ* 2009, 483; S. PEERS, 'Mutual Recognition and Criminal Law in the European Union: Has the Council Got it Wrong?', *CML Rev.* 2004, 18–19.

broad and flexible criterion, which is to the benefit of the principle of mutual recognition and, in this context, to the benefit of the (natural or legal) person that is subject to (second) criminal proceedings.

(2) *The battle of the AGs: equivalence* in abstracto *versus equivalence* in concreto

In his opinions on *Gözütok and Brügge* and *Van Straaten*, late AG Ruiz-Jarabo Colomer explained that 'recognition is based on the thought that while another State may not deal with a certain matter in the same or even a similar way as one's own State, the outcome will be such that it is accepted as equivalent to a decision by one's own State because it reflects the same principles and values'.[128] It is not the equivalence of specific criminal provisions that is envisaged here by the AG, but rather the equivalence of the principles and values upon which the criminal law systems of the different Member States are founded. There is a kind of presumption of equivalence with regard to these common principles and values, which are shared by the EU Member States. By analogy with the principle of mutual trust *in abstracto*, one could speak here of a presumption of equivalence *in abstracto*.

This *in abstracto* approach, however, is not endorsed by all members of the ECJ. In particular, in her conclusion on the *Gasparini* judgment, AG Sharpston made an effort to convince the ECJ to adopt a less abstract approach. While drawing a parallel with the case law on the principle of mutual recognition in the internal market context, she insisted on the need for a kind of comparability test.[129] According to her, the concept of mutual trust should not extend so far as to provide a sensible basis for applying *ne bis in idem* to all national decisions that discontinue criminal proceedings by applying a time bar.[130] In her reasoning, the fact that no substantive assessment of the offence takes place in cases where a prosecution is terminated due to time bar was crucial in her reasoning. Therefore, she suggested that a distinction be drawn between trusting other Member States' criminal proceedings in general (including such matters as fair trial guarantees, the substantive delineation of offences, and rules on the production and admissibility of evidence) and trusting a decision that no substantive assessment of the offence can take place because the prosecution is time-barred.[131] Only with regard to the second supposition did she insist on a kind of equivalence or comparability test. Her proposal was not taken up by the ECJ, however, which imposed a duty of mutual recognition notwithstanding even great differences between Member States' legislation and, manifestly, the absence of any equivalence test.

(3) *Comparative law surveys*

A final element that hints at the relevance of equivalence is the development of and reference to comparative law surveys. Neither AG Ruiz-Jarabo Colomer nor AG Sharpston has raised objections to comparative studies of the relevant criminal law provisions in the different Member States. On the contrary, both AGs have drawn up comparative

[128] Opinion of AG Ruiz-Jarabo Colomer in Joined Cases C-187/01 and C-385/01 *Gözütok and Brügge* [2003] ECR I-1345 § 124; Opinion of AG Ruiz-Jarabo Colomer in Case C-150/05 *Van Straaten* [2006] ECR I-9327, § 61–2; P. PEITEADO MARISCAL, *El reconocimiento mutuo de resoluciones penales definitivas en la Unión Europea* (Madrid, Colex, 2006) 31.

[129] Opinion of AG Sharpston in Case C-467/04 *Gasparini and others* [2006] ECR I-9199, § 110.

[130] Opinion of AG Sharpston in Case C-467/04 *Gasparini and others* [2006] ECR I-9199, § 108.

[131] Opinion of AG Sharpston in Case C-467/04 *Gasparini and others* [2006] ECR I-9199, § 109.

surveys on crucial issues from the *ne bis in idem* judgments. In this regard, consideration was given to out-of-court settlements, prescription, the age of criminal responsibility, suspended custodial sentences, and a set-off principle in relation to detention while held on remand pending trial, from a comparative law perspective.[132] The results of these studies indicated whether significant differences existed between the Member States (i.e. no equivalence) or whether the national legal systems in fact demonstrated significant similarities (i.e. equivalence) overall.

However, the primary aim of these comparative studies is less likely to have been the pursuit of 'equivalence' between the legislation of the two Member States involved but rather the development of a tool which would allow for a better understanding of the objective of the legal criminal law concept under discussion. The rare occasions upon which the ECJ has made explicit reference to the AGs' surveys confirm this. The ECJ might rely solely upon a majority trend in Member States' legislation (i.e. where national legislation does not diverge substantially) when it serves the purpose of Article 54 CISA or when it could aid in defining the characteristics of a national legal concept in light of Article 54 CISA.[133] When the opposite is true (i.e. there is a lack of convergence between national legislation), the ECJ tends to be less willing to refer to the divergent approaches taken by the Member States.[134] This silence is significant as it confirms my previous finding that—notwithstanding AG Sharpston's powerful plea for more consideration of the 'equivalence' requirement[135]—equivalence *in concreto* is currently not a key issue for the ECJ in its *ne bis in idem* case law.

B. Country of origin

In the legal literature on judicial cooperation in criminal matters, explicit references to 'the country of origin principle' are rather infrequent.[136] It cannot be denied, though, that the application of the country of origin principle has many advantages in the area

[132] On out-of-court settlements, see the remarkably extensive survey performed in the Opinion of AG Ruiz-Jarabo Colomer in Joined Cases C-187/01 and C-385/01 *Gözütok and Brügge* [2003] ECR I-1345, § 63–77; on prescription and the age of criminal responsibility, see: Opinion of AG Sharpston in Case C-467/04 *Gasparini and others* [2006] ECR I-9199, § 66–8 and § 112; on suspended custodial sentences and mechanisms of set-off, see: Opinion of AG Sharpston in Case C-288/05 *Kretzinger* [2007] ECR I-6441, § 44–51 and § 64; on 'amnesty', see the comments of AG Ruiz-Jarabo Colomer in his Opinion in Case C-297/07 *Bourquain* [2008] ECR I-9425, § 77 ff.

[133] See, for instance: ECJ, Joined Cases C-187/01 and C-385/01 *Gözütok and Brügge* [2003] ECR I-1345, paras 39–40, where the ECJ mentions a general trend in national legal systems to develop its interpretation of Article 54 CISA; or ECJ, Case C-436/04 *Van Esbroeck* [2006] ECR I-2333, para 30; ECJ, Case C-288/05 *Kretzinger* [2007] ECR I-6441, para 40, where the ECJ points out that the suspension of a sentence is 'a feature of the criminal systems of the Contracting States'.

[134] The most striking example is undoubtedly the *Gasparini* judgment in which the ECJ does not at all address the concerns of AG Sharpston. Compare: ECJ, Case C-467/04 *Gasparini and others* [2006] ECR I-9199, paras 29–30 with the corresponding Opinion of AG Sharpston, at § 109–20. The *Bourquain* judgment is another example—this time on *in absentia* judgments—where the ECJ practically ignores the fact that diverging approaches were taken by Member States, as indicated by the AG. Compare: ECJ, Case C-297/07 *Bourquain* [2008] ECR I-9425, paras 36 ff. with the corresponding Opinion of AG Ruiz-Jarabo Colomer at § 59 ff.

[135] Opinion of AG Sharpston in Case C-467/04 *Gasparini and others* [2006] ECR I-9199, § 109–20.

[136] See, however, for some scarce examples: BARENTS, 'De denationalisering van het strafrecht' (n 109) 363; M. BÖSE, 'Das Prinzip der gegenseitigen Anerkennung in der transnationalen Strafrechtspflege in der EU', in C. MOMSEN, R. BLOY, and P. RACKOW (eds.), *Fragmentarisches Strafrecht* (Frankfurt am Main, Peter Lang, 2003) 236 ff.; D. ROHLFF, *Der Europäische Haftbefehl* (Frankfurt am Main, Peter Lang, 2003) 36; T. WEIGEND, 'Der Entwurf einer Europäischen Verfassung und das Strafrecht', *ZStW* 2004, 294.

of freedom, security, and justice, especially when compared to a principle based on the country of destination, which is far more closely linked to the traditional concept of national sovereignty.[137]

In the context of Article 54 CISA, the ECJ has clarified through its interpretation of the 'bis' and 'idem' requirements that both the country of origin (i.e. the country where the 'first' judgment was passed, hereafter 'country of origin') and the country of destination (i.e. the country dealing with the second criminal prosecution, hereafter 'country of destination') both have a crucial role to play. Admittedly, in principle, it is for the country of destination to assess the criteria enshrined in Article 54 CISA in light of the autonomous, uniform interpretation of these concepts that has been developed by the ECJ. However, with regard to some of them, I have already indicated that their exact scope is largely co-determined by the country of origin's legal framework.

As far as the concept of 'bis' is concerned, the ECJ made a strong appeal to the law of the country of origin by making it the main point of reference whenever questions arise as to the interpretation of the 'finality' and 'enforcement' requirements of Article 54 CISA. This can be deduced from the ECJ's *Gözütok and Brügge* judgment, where the ECJ stated that 'the application by one Member State of the *ne bis in idem* principle, as set out in Article 54 of the CISA, to procedures whereby further prosecution is barred, which have taken place in another Member State without a court being involved, cannot be made subject to a condition that *the first State's legal system* does not require such judicial involvement either' (emphasis added).[138] In *Turanský*, the ECJ expressed this view more explicitly and removed any remaining doubts when it stipulated that 'in order to assess whether a decision is "final" for the purposes of Article 54 of the CISA, it is necessary first of all to ascertain [...] that the decision in question is considered under the law of *the Contracting State which adopted it* to be final and binding, and to verify that it leads, in that State, to the protection granted by the *ne bis in idem* principle' (emphasis added).[139] However, the country of origin rule is not endorsed unconditionally[140] and the ECJ's *ne bis in idem* case law provides for exceptions to this rule. For instance, the fact that the decision under discussion was 'a final decision of a court' according to the national legislation of the country of origin could not convince the ECJ to apply the principle of *ne bis in idem* in *Miraglia*.[141] Similarly, in *Bourquain*, the ECJ put the importance of the country of origin's legislation into perspective when stating that 'the achievement of the objective (of Article 54 CISA) would be jeopardized if *the specific features of national proceedings* [...] did not permit an interpretation of the concept of a trial being finally disposed of within the meaning of Article 54 of the CISA which includes judgments delivered *in absentia* in accordance with national legislation' (emphasis added).[142] AG Sharpston apparently shared this point of view when she observed in her opinion on *Kretzinger* that 'the use of the word "final" in Article 54 CISA is not to be defined *solely*

[137] BARENTS, 'De denationalisering van het strafrecht' (n 109) 364.

[138] ECJ, Joined Cases C-187/01 and C-385/01 *Gözütok and Brügge* [2003] ECR I-1345, para 48.

[139] ECJ, Case C-491/07 *Turanský* [2008] ECR I-11039, paras 35 and 40. See also: Opinion of AG Sharpston in Case C-288/05 *Kretzinger* [2007] ECR I-6441, § 99. Similarly, in the context of the FD EAW: ECJ, Case C-261/09 *Mantello* [2010] ECR I-11477, para 46.

[140] The country of origin's legislation will not play a relevant role whenever one of its provisions turns out to be incompatible with the EU Treaty or the international framework on human rights. See: Part II, ch 1, IV, B. 'Mutual recognition, *ne bis in idem*, and free movement of judgments in light of fundamental rights protection'.

[141] ECJ, Case C-469/03 *Miraglia* [2005] ECR I-2009, para 22.

[142] ECJ, Case C-297/07 *Bourquain* [2008] ECR I-9425, paras 40–2.

by reference to domestic legislation' (emphasis added).[143] All of these references indicate that the country of origin decreases in importance whenever the national provision does not serve the purposes of Article 54 CISA.

With regard to the concept of 'idem', the question of whether the facts that triggered the two proceedings are identical is in essence a factual assessment to be made by the country of destination,[144] albeit in close cooperation with the country of origin.[145] For obvious reasons—namely that it concerns a factual assessment and that the ECJ has rejected a criterion based on the legal qualification—the country of origin's legal framework is far less relevant.

C. Principle of equivalence, principle of country of origin, or principle of mutual recognition?

The preceding analysis has revealed that neither 'equivalence' nor 'the country of origin' plays a dominating role in the context of the *ne bis in idem* principle enshrined in Article 54 CISA. With regard to the 'equivalence' element, the ECJ's firm statement that in the context of Article 54 CISA mutual recognition 'is not made conditional upon prior approximation' is very significant in this regard. Admittedly, on occasions, the ECJ has referred to a majority view held in the Member States, yet these references were only made where such a view supported the objectives of Article 54 CISA and it was thus far from being decisive on its own. With regard to the 'country of origin' element, I have admitted that in view of the predominantly uniform, autonomous interpretation that is given to the *ne bis in idem* concept, the relevance of the country of origin only arises with regard to the interpretation of the 'bis' requirement, and only to the extent that the country of origin's national legal framework is compatible with the objectives of Article 54 CISA.

For the aforementioned reasons, I prefer to use the term 'principle of mutual recognition', as I believe it is the crucial mechanism underpinning Article 54 CISA which leads to the application of the *ne bis in idem* principle. More generally, it is also the ideal instrument for improving integration in the area of freedom, security, and justice.

IV. Limits to the Principle of Mutual Recognition

Thus far, my analysis of the ECJ's *ne bis in idem* case law has revealed its determination to promote a very powerful principle of mutual recognition. Indeed, since previous approximation is not required and having minimized the role of equivalence, we might wonder which limits remain in force to block the *ne bis in idem* and mutual recognition principles. Under this heading, I provide an overview of the mechanisms that can produce this blocking effect. Firstly, I examine the restrictions laid down by the CISA provisions themselves (section IV, A). Next, I examine whether the protection of fundamental rights can have an impact on the mechanism of mutual recognition (section IV, B).

[143] Opinion of AG Sharpston in Case C-288/05 *Kretzinger* [2007] ECR I-6441, § 93. Also the ECJ rejected Kretzinger's argument that *by virtue of his home country's law* Article 54 CISA ought to apply: ECJ, Case C-288/05 *Kretzinger* [2007] ECR I-6441, paras 49–51.

[144] See, for instance: ECJ, Case C-367/05 *Kraaijenbrink* [2007] ECR I-6619, paras 27–9.

[145] Logically, the country of destination is dependent on information provided by the country of origin in order to perform an in-depth assessment as to whether there is indeed identity of the facts.

Subsequently, I verify whether the Member States are entitled to any margin of control (section IV, C). Finally, I investigate the role of forum shopping, if any, and the related discussions on 'abuse of law' and 'race to the bottom' (section IV, D).

A. Limits resulting from the CISA's conditions for application of the *ne bis in idem* principle

According to Article 54 CISA, 'a person whose trial has been finally disposed of in one Contracting Party may not be prosecuted in another Contracting Party for the same acts provided that, if a penalty has been imposed, it has been enforced, is actually in the process of being enforced or can no longer be enforced under the laws of the sentencing Contracting Party'. The *ne bis in idem* principle enshrined in this provision implies that four fundamental conditions need to be fulfilled: first, the trial must have been concluded in one of the Contracting States; secondly, new proceedings based on the same facts must have begun; thirdly, an enforcement requirement must be in place if a penalty has been imposed; and finally, the proceedings must have been brought against the same defendant. My previous analysis of the ECJ's *ne bis in idem* case law revealed the ECJ's tendency to adhere to a broad interpretation of these criteria which has led, so far, to intensive application of the *ne bis in idem* and mutual recognition principles. Mutual recognition has only been suspended in cases where its application was considered to be incompatible with the 'security' objective of the area of freedom, security, and justice. In the majority of cases, however, the 'freedom' aspect prevailed.

Another restriction of the *ne bis in idem* and mutual recognition principles can be found in Article 55 CISA. This article enabled each Contracting Party to declare, at the time of ratifying, accepting, or approving the CISA, that it would not recognize a foreign decision for *ne bis in idem* purposes, first on the basis of territoriality arguments (except if the offence was partially committed in that foreign state's territory), secondly because the committed offence affected national security or other equally essential interests, or thirdly in the event of offences committed by officials in violation of the duties of their office. The desirability of allowing such exceptions in the Schengen context and even in the broader EU context has been contested.[146] In view of the fact that this article's very existence conflicts with the logic of the principle of mutual recognition,[147] it is to be expected that the ECJ, when asked to interpret one of these exceptions, will interpret it very narrowly.

In any case, neither the non-fulfilment of one of Article 54 CISA's criteria—particularly the third—nor the application of Article 55 CISA entirely rules out the duty of mutual recognition. As already mentioned, Article 56 CISA stipulates that if further prosecution is brought in one Contracting State against a person whose trial for the same acts has been finally disposed of in another Contracting State, any period of deprivation of liberty served in the latter Contracting State arising from those acts shall be deducted from any penalty imposed. Furthermore, this article prescribes that penalties

[146] See, in particular: FLETCHER, LOOF, and GILLMORE, *EU Criminal Law and Justice* (n 36) 138; see, however: VAN DEN WYNGAERT and STESSENS, 'The International *non bis in idem* Principle: Resolving some of the Unanswered Questions' (n 17) 803, who argue that (most of these) exceptions seem justified as the CISA does not provide an *ordre public* clause allowing a state to refuse to recognize the *ne bis in idem* effect of foreign criminal judgments when the interests of the state concerned are at stake.

[147] FLETCHER, LOOF and GILLMORE, *EU Criminal Law and Justice* (n 36).

not involving deprivation of liberty shall also be taken into account to the extent permitted by national law. Thus, whenever Article 54 CISA cannot be applied because of the non-fulfilment of one of the conditions for application, or whenever Article 55 CISA applies, Member States still have a duty to 'take into account' the first sentence imposed by the other Contracting State.[148] This duty is still a duty of mutual recognition, albeit a more moderate form than that laid down in Article 54 CISA.

B. Mutual recognition, *ne bis in idem*, and free movement of judgments in light of fundamental rights protection

The absence of any explicit justification ground in the CISA for blocking application of the *ne bis in idem* and mutual recognition principles raises questions as to whether and to what extent Member States are entitled to set aside the *ne bis in idem* and mutual recognition principles in cases where the first sentence would be affected by a breach of fundamental rights.

Both AG Ruiz-Jarabo Colomer and AG Sharpston answered this question in the affirmative. With regard to trials *in absentia*, AG Sharpston maintained in her opinion on the *Kretzinger* case that a trial held *in absentia* which led to a final judgment must comply with the requirements laid down in Article 6 ECHR. According to her, a judgment following a trial *in absentia* which had been issued in a manner that contravened the ECHR, even when regarded as valid and final under national law, would *ipso facto* violate those general principles of EU law that encapsulate basic and fundamental rights. As a result, it could not lawfully be regarded as a judgment that 'finally disposed' of a trial for the purposes of Article 54 CISA.[149] Thus, the protection of (European) fundamental rights, in her opinion, is a limit to the *ne bis in idem* and mutual recognition principles. In the same vein, AG Ruiz-Jarabo Colomer recalled in his opinion on the *Bourquain* case that among the many facets of fundamental rights, particular relevance is attached to the limits and even exceptions which are set with regard to mutual recognition, always bearing in mind that those rights apply as common principles in the Member States.[150] Neither in *Kretzinger* nor in *Bourquain* did the facts of the cases hint at a breach of fundamental rights, and as no such arguments were put forward by the parties concerned, the ECJ was not required to take a stance on this issue.[151]

Judgments in other areas of law do indicate that the ECJ will not refrain from blocking the principle of mutual recognition (and the role of the country of origin) 'in exceptional cases where the guarantees laid down in the legislation of the State of origin [. . .] have been insufficient to protect the defendant from a manifest breach of his right to defend himself before the court of origin, as recognised by the ECHR'.[152] However, there is a crucial difference between the *Krombach* judgment, where strict

[148] On the interrelationship between Article 54 CISA, Article 55 CISA, and Article 56 CISA, see: Opinion of AG Sharpston in Case C-288/05 *Kretzinger* [2007] ECR I-6441, § 72 and Opinion of AG Sharpston in Case C-367/05 *Kraaijenbrink* [2007] ECR I-6619, § 63.

[149] Opinion of AG Sharpston in Case C-288/05 *Kretzinger* [2007] ECR I-6441, § 101.

[150] Opinion of AG Ruiz-Jarabo Colomer in Case C-297/07 *Bourquain* [2008] ECR I-9425, § 51.

[151] The ECJ's statements in *Bourquain* that Article 54 CISA applies in the case of an earlier conviction *in absentia*, should not necessarily be seen as a rejection of the AG's position, especially since in *Bourquain* the judgment *in absentia* at hand was not at all questioned on the basis of fundamental human rights grounds.

[152] ECJ, Case C-7/98 *Krombach* [2000] ECR I-1935, para 44.

application of mutual recognition would have been detrimental to the accused and his fundamental rights, and *Bourquain* or other *ne bis in idem* judgments, where giving precedence to fundamental rights protection would lead to a deterioration in the person's position as he or she would no longer be able to invoke Article 54 CISA. Advocate General Sharpston rightly pointed out in this regard that transforming this safeguard for the accused (right to a retrial) into a condition which invalidates the application of other rights (*ne bis in idem*) would lead to an absurd situation.[153] It is in the context of these considerations that the ECJ's reasoning in *Bourquain* must be read. In describing the relevant provisions of the French Code of Military Justice—somewhat disdainfully—as specific features of national proceedings, and in suggesting that they not be taken too seriously lest they endanger the application of Article 54 CISA, the ECJ minimized to a considerable extent the fundamental role that the right to a retrial generally plays in the context of *in absentia* judgments.[154] Of course, it is precisely the difference in context between Article 54 CISA (mutual recognition as a protective measure for the individual) and—for instance—the FD EAW (mutual recognition as an enforcement tool vis-à-vis the individual) which largely explains the ECJ's approach and is obviously the reason why pleas in academic writing for fundamental rights considerations in this context are extremely rare.

C. Margins of control left to the Member States when applying the *ne bis in idem* principle

In order to assure smooth application of the *ne bis in idem* and mutual recognition principles, the ECJ's logical point of departure is a strong focus on mutual trust, which results in any re-assessment of the merits of a case being prohibited (section C, 1). However, this does not mean that Member States are precluded from exercising any margin of discretion whatsoever. The verification of the conditions for application in Article 54 CISA (in light of the objectives of freedom, security, and justice) as well as the strong focus on cooperation and exchange of information in Article 57 CISA clearly indicate the need for some means of control and could be put forward as arguments for rejecting the idea of the so-called blind application of mutual recognition as enshrined in Article 54 CISA (section C, 2).

(1) No re-assessment of the merits of a case

An analysis of the ECJ's *ne bis in idem* case law has revealed that the ECJ adheres to a broad interpretation and application of the *ne bis in idem* principle. In light of this case law, Member States are required to reconcile themselves to the 'final disposal of a case' in another Member State, irrespective of whether this resulted in conviction or acquittal.

[153] Opinion of AG Ruiz-Jarabo Colomer in Case C-297/07 *Bourquain* [2008] ECR I-9425, § 64.

[154] Compare: Part II, ch 2: 'The Principle of Mutual Recognition as Legislative Impetus for Efficient Judicial Cooperation in Criminal Matters'. In particular, the question as to under which circumstances a person convicted *in absentia* is entitled to ask for a retrial— safeguard explicitly written down in the FD EAW—has caused obstacles to the principle of mutual recognition in the context of surrender and the FD EAW. In this context, which will be discussed further on in more detail, it is fully accepted that important guarantees are built in to block the principle of mutual recognition whenever a judgment *in absentia* endangers the individual's fundamental rights and when no satisfying guarantees for a retrial are available.

In *Van Straaten*, the ECJ held that Member States are also bound by Article 54 CISA when the accused is acquitted in a Member State because of a lack of evidence.[155] Thus, Member States are not entitled to re-examine or re-open the case on the basis of (new) evidence available in this Member State.

In this regard, an important qualification to the *ne bis in idem* principle is included in Article 4(2) of Protocol No 7 to the ECHR, namely that this principle 'shall not prevent the re-opening of the case in accordance with the law and penal procedure of the State concerned, if there is evidence of new or newly discovered facts, or if there has been a fundamental defect in the previous proceedings, which could affect the outcome of the case'.[156] No similar exception is included in the CISA or in the Charter,[157] though it might be argued that a very narrowly defined exception of this kind could be considered necessary for exceptional cases in a true area of freedom, security, and justice.[158] Whilst Article 4(2) of Protocol No 7 only applies to repeated prosecution in the *same* state and not in different states,[159] the EU would in my view benefit from a cross-border rule that allows 'the re-opening of the case in accordance with the law and penal procedure of the State where the person has been finally acquitted or convicted, if there is evidence of new or newly discovered facts, or if there has been a fundamental defect in the previous proceedings, which could affect the outcome of the case'. Such a rule, which would obviously require an amendment to the CISA and/or to Article 50 Charter,[160] would address the above-mentioned concerns about injustice being done without undermining the principle of mutual recognition.

Ultimately, what the CISA aims to achieve is free movement within an area of freedom, security, and justice and an integral part of that process is the identification of a *propriae naturae* definition of *ne bis in idem* that allows free movement rights within an area of freedom, security, and justice that is characterized by high levels of safety.[161] Therefore, it remains to be seen whether the ECJ will conform in each and every case to

[155] ECJ, Case C-150/05 *Van Straaten* [2006] ECR I-9327, para 61.

[156] Article 4(2) Protocol No 7 to the ECHR, E.T.S. 117, retrievable at: <http://conventions.coe.int/Treaty/EN/Treaties/Html/117.htm>.

[157] See, however, Opinion of AG Sharpston in Case C-467/04 *Gasparini and others* [2006] ECR I-9199, § 75, who states that in the EU context Article 4 of Protocol No 7 may fairly be said to embody the highest legal expression of the principle of *ne bis in idem* as a fundamental human right. Within a purely national context, several Member States foresee the legal possibility of an extraordinary re-opening of a case owing to exceptional circumstances, but often only in favour of the convicted person. See, on this issue: DE LA CUESTA, 'Concurrent National and International Criminal Jurisdiction' (n 54) 714 and the different national reports taken up in this publication.

[158] The UK's 800-year-old law on double jeopardy was changed in 2005 to include this exception following the mediatized *Dunlop* case, which dealt with a man who had been acquitted for the murder of his former girlfriend but who had shortly afterwards confessed his guilt to a prison officer and had, furthermore, showed off his horrendous deed in pubs and bars, consciously knowing that he could not be retried for the same crime. The UK's *Dunlop* case illustrates the relevance of limits to the *ne bis in idem* principle in a national context, but obviously might be of great relevance in a European context as well. Furthermore, it reveals that restrictions to *ne bis in idem* and mutual recognition are not necessarily a consequence of little approximation or lack of trust. See, on the *Dunlop* case, the press release of the UK's Crown Prosecution Service, retrievable at: <http://www.cps.gov.uk/news/latest_news/155_06/>.

[159] See, in particular: ECtHR, *Amrollahi v Denmark*, 11 July 2002, 56811/00, where the ECtHR declared inadmissible a case where an individual alleged that prosecution for the crime for which he had already been punished would await him if expelled.

[160] In *Gözütok and Brügge* the ECJ clearly stated that Article 55 CISA constitutes an exhaustive list of exceptions to the *ne bis in idem* principle included in Article 54 CISA: ECJ, Joined Cases C-187/01 and C-385/01 *Gözütok and Brügge* [2003] ECR I-1345, para 44.

[161] Opinion of AG Sharpston in Case C-467/04 *Gasparini and others* [2006] ECR I-9199, § 84.

the *Van Straaten* ruling in its future case law or whether it may adjust its view in light of international (and national) legislation that provides for exceptions to this rule by giving the principle appropriate but not unlimited scope.[162]

One of the crucial elements that convinced the ECJ to apply Article 54 CISA in *Van Straaten* was the fact that a determination as to the merits of the case had taken place.[163] When *Van Straaten* is read in combination with the previous *Miraglia* judgment, where the ECJ rejected the application of Article 54 CISA on the basis that no assessment of the unlawful conduct with which the defendant was charged had taken place,[164] the impression is formed that Member States regain the power and authority to prosecute when no assessment of the merits of the case has taken place. In *Gasparini*, however, as mentioned above, the ECJ did not follow this line of reasoning. Instead, it imposed the application of Article 54 CISA in a case where the accused was acquitted because of a procedural time-bar. Such an application does not necessitate any examination of the merits of the case in principle. In sum, a Member State's freedom to prosecute can be halted by a final disposal based on either substantive or procedural grounds. In adhering to such a broad interpretation of Article 54 CISA, the ECJ reduces the controlling powers of the Member States rather considerably.

(2) No blind application of Article 54 CISA

The previous findings do not imply, however, that a Member State has no margin at all to act or examine the facts of the case whenever it is aware of a (possible) application of Article 54 CISA. On the contrary, Article 54 CISA provides for several conditions whose fulfilment should be verified prior to the application of Article 54 CISA. Moreover, a joint reading of Article 57 CISA and the ECJ's *ne bis in idem* case law indicates that a Member State that is aware of a (possible) application of Article 54 CISA (the country of destination) plays a key role with regard to the verification of those conditions, albeit in close cooperation with the Member State in whose territory a judgment has already been passed (the country of origin). Article 57 CISA imposes on the country of destination a duty to request relevant information from the country of origin and to take this information into consideration, but the actual responsibility to decide whether the conditions of Article 54 CISA have indeed been fulfilled lies with the country of destination. The latter's margin of appreciation is largely inviolable, except via the ECJ's final control.

The true margin of control that the country of destination is entitled to will logically depend upon the kind of question it is dealing with. If a Member State has doubts as to the scope or interpretation of the country of origin's criminal law, the margin of discretion will be rather limited, in my view: the country of destination's criminal

[162] Opinion of AG Sharpston in Case C-467/04 *Gasparini and others* [2006] ECR I-9199. See also: ECJ, Case C-617/10 *Fransson*, nyr, with regard to the *ne bis in idem* principle included in Article 50 Charter and, in particular, the question whether the *bis in idem* principle also applies if a Member States imposes a combination of an administrative and a criminal penalty. In its search for an adequate scope of the *ne bis in idem* principle, the ECJ was clearly willing to grant the Member States a margin of discretion on this sensible issue as it concluded that Article 50 Charter 'does not preclude a Member State from imposing successively, for the same acts [...] a tax penalty and a criminal penalty in so far as the first penalty is not criminal in nature' (at para 37). AG Cruz Villalón had taken a similar view in his opinion under this case, paying due regard to the constitutional traditions of the Member States on this point of law (at § 82 and 86), rather than adhering strictly to the ECtHR's case law (at § 81–5).

[163] ECJ, Case C-150/05 *Van Straaten* [2006] ECR I-9327, para 60.

[164] ECJ, Case C-469/03 *Miraglia* [2005] ECR I-2009, para 35.

court will be required to ask the country of origin's national court to clarify this point of law and, in principle, to accept the latter court's answer. If a Member State has doubts as to whether a decision is to be considered 'final' under the country of origin's legal system, a similar line of reasoning is imposed. In both cases, it is more than likely that the country of destination would only be able to set aside the country of origin's point of view if it contradicted the objectives of the area of freedom, security, and justice. Whether a Member State is entitled to decide this issue for itself, however, is highly questionable.[165] It is likely that a preliminary question will be required in order to set aside the country of origin's conclusion.

In some circumstances, a Member State's margin of control is somewhat greater, for instance when a Member State needs to decide whether the (second) proceedings refer to the 'same acts'. AG Sharpston's opinion on the *Kraaijenbrink* case is very instructive in this regard. She clearly suggests that the guidelines developed by the ECJ in its *ne bis in idem* case law should not be considered strict rules but rather as statements that afford the national court discretion in assessing what constitutes the 'same acts' in the circumstances of the case in question. In particular, with regard to drugs offences, the AG rightly observed that a literal application of the ECJ's statements that 'the quantities of the drugs are not required to be identical' to all drug trafficking offences might produce undesirable results.[166]

In sum, despite a uniform and autonomous interpretation of the *ne bis in idem* concept, the country of destination still has some margin of discretion at its disposal when interpreting this concept and is certainly not bound by a blind application of Article 54 CISA.

D. Forum shopping, abuse of law, and concerns about de facto approximation around the lowest common denominator

The ECJ's statement that Article 54 CISA is not conditional upon harmonization or approximation of the Member States' criminal laws, which assumes respect for the co-existence of different national criminal laws, has given rise to abundant legal discussion of issues of forum shopping, 'abuse' of the *ne bis in idem* principle and a possible race to the bottom. These three elements are closely connected and are all related to one major theme, namely the question of whether and under which circumstances individuals and/or public prosecutors (are entitled to) benefit from the diversity of national criminal justice systems (forum shopping; abuse of ne bis in idem provisions) and whether this entails any practical consequences (in the field of de facto approximation).

Firstly, from a purely theoretic point of view,[167] 'forum shopping' or 'criminal jurisdiction shopping' can be carried out by both offenders and the public

[165] See the reserved attitude of the ECJ in: ECJ, Case C-38/98 *Renault* [2000] I-2973, para 33, where the ECJ stated in the context of REG 44/2001 that 'the court of the State in which enforcement is sought cannot, without undermining the aim of Regulation No 44/2001, refuse recognition of a judgment emanating from another Member State solely on the ground that it considers that national or Community law was misapplied in that judgment'. On the contrary, the ECJ argues that in such cases, the system of legal remedies in each Member State, together with the preliminary ruling procedure provided for in Article 267 TFEU, affords a sufficient guarantee to individuals. Similarly: ECJ, Case C-420/07 *Apostolides* [2009] ECR, I-3571, para 60.

[166] Opinion of AG Sharpston in Case C-367/05 *Kraaijenbrink* [2007] ECR I-6619, § 36.

[167] From a more practical view, it is highly questionable whether criminal activities are indeed likely to be so strategically planned and to follow such clear cost/profit calculations. In fact, there is very little criminological evidence that supports the view that offenders indeed exploit the differences between various legal orders: K. NUOTIO, 'Harmonization of Criminal Sanctions in the European Union.

prosecution.[168] From the (shrewd) offender's perspective, it might be of interest to move to a state in which the conduct concerned does not constitute an offence or is not prosecuted in practice, where the chances of arrest are small, or where the penalties imposed for that offence are mild.[169] In light of the *ne bis in idem* principle, individuals might be tempted to deliberately court prosecution in a Member State where proceedings are known to result necessarily in an acquittal, and then rely on *ne bis in idem* to move freely within the EU.[170] From the public prosecutor's point of view, forum shopping might be used intentionally in a way that would significantly affect the punishment of the accused and complicate his defence considerably.[171] It is difficult to see how either of these options—insofar as they actually occur in practice—might be blocked under the current legal regime. The only effective means of putting a halt to such practices are the highly recommended and oft-repeated demands in legal literature, first for the development of (binding) criteria which will guide the choice of the forum and secondly for some form of judicial control over this choice.[172]

The next question that needs to be addressed is the extent to which offenders are entitled to benefit from the *ne bis in idem* principle and whether this principle can be set aside whenever it is abused or applied inappropriately. In my view, both Article 54 CISA and the ECJ's case law exhibit anti-abuse of law elements, though the word 'abuse' itself is not mentioned. The ECJ's refusal to apply Article 54 CISA in *Miraglia* and their statement that the application of the *ne bis in idem* principle in that case 'would run counter to the very purpose of the provisions of Title VI of the Treaty on EU as it was the very bringing of proceedings in the second Member State that justified the discontinuance of the

Criminal Law Science Fiction', in HUSABO and STRANDBAKKEN (eds.), *Harmonization of Criminal Law in Europe* (n 95) 92. This does not exclude, however, that on some occasions, and with regard to some criminal activities it actually does occur. See, for instance: Opinion of AG Sharpston in Case C-467/04 *Gasparini and others* [2006] ECR I-9199, fn 86, who sustains that it is far from a theoretical issue and refers, by way of illustration, to Belgium and the Netherlands which have long been the preferred location for dealers who trade in stolen works of art because of their lenient treatment of these offences.

168 DE LA CUESTA, 'Concurrent National and International Criminal Jurisdiction' (n 54) 727.

169 A. BERNARDI, 'Europe sans frontières et droit pénal', *Rev. Sc. Crim.* 1994, 5; P. BERNASCONI, 'Les infractions transfrontalières: terrorisme, trafic de stupéfiants, délits financiers', in M. DELMAS-MARTY (ed.), *Quelle politique pénale pour l'Europe* (Paris, Economia, 1993) 81–91; H. FUCHS, 'Bemerkungen zum gegenseitigen Anerkennung justizieller Entscheidungen', *ZStW* 2004, 369; W. PERRON, 'Perspectives of the Harmonization of Criminal Law and Criminal Procedure in the European Union', in HUSABO and STRANDBAKKEN (eds.), *Harmonization of Criminal Law in Europe* (n 95) 17; H. VAN DER WILT, 'Harmonisatie van strafrecht in Europa: gewogen en te licht bevonden', *NJb.* 2002, 747–52. On the possible risks of miscarriages of justice which might occur following an expansive application of the *ne bis in idem* principle and a comparison to the US system, see: M. RICHARD, 'The US Approach to Mutual Confidence,' in DE KERCHOVE and WEYEMBERGH (eds.), *La confiance mutuelle dans l'espace pénal européen/Mutual trust in the European Criminal Area* (n 56) 273–5.

170 Opinion of AG Sharpston in Case C-467/04 *Gasparini and others* [2006] ECR I-9199, § 104. See also: DE LA CUESTA, 'Concurrent National and International Criminal Jurisdiction' (n 54) 724–5, who links the risk of fraud and the possibility of sham trials to the fact that national courts are not allowed to examine the foreign decision and who denounces the absence of mechanisms to prevent abuses.

171 FUCHS, 'Bemerkungen zum gegenseitigen Anerkennung justizieller Entscheidungen' (n 169) 369; C. NESTLER, 'Europäisches Strafprocessrecht', *ZStW* 2004, 341; WEIGEND, 'Der Entwurf einer Europäischen Verfassung und das Strafrecht' (n 136) 293.

172 S. GLESZ, 'Zum Prinzip der gegenseitigen Anerkennung', *ZStW* 2004, 361–2; T. VANDER BEKEN, *Forumkeuze in het internationaal strafrecht. Verdeling van misdrijven met aanknopingspunten in meerdere staten* (Ghent, RUG, 1998–99) 459; A. WEYEMBERGH, 'Le principe ne bis in idem: pierre d'achoppement de l'espace pénal européen?', *C.D.E.* 2004, 364–69. And, in relation to the *Corpus Iuris* project: C. VAN DEN WYNGAERT, 'Eurojust and the European Public Prosecutor in the Corpus Iuris Model: Water and Fire?', in N. WALKER (ed.), *Europe's Area of Freedom, Security and Justice* (Oxford, Oxford University Press, 2004) 237. See also: Part II, ch 3: 'The Workability of the Principle of Mutual Recognition in Criminal Matters'.

prosecution by the public prosecutor in the first Member State'[173] ultimately amounted to a clear statement that the *ne bis in idem* principle cannot be invoked in an abusive way, i.e. in a way that runs counter to one of the main objectives of the TFEU, namely the prevention and combatting of crime. A close link therefore exists between compliance with EU objectives and prohibition of any abusive invocation of Article 54 CISA. Similar lines of reasoning can be found in the *Gasparini* judgment, where the ECJ declined to apply the *ne bis in idem* principle to persons other than those whose trial had been officially concluded in a Contracting State,[174] and in the opinion of AG Sharpston on the *Kraaijenbrink* case, where it was emphasized that the ECJ's statement that 'the quantities of the drug that are at issue are not required to be identical' should not be interpreted literally as such a reading might produce undesirable results.[175] Furthermore, the criteria of Article 54 CISA (final judgment, new proceedings, same offender, and enforcement requirements) should also be interpreted in this light and considered conditions that must be fulfilled in order to prevent the abusive application of the mutual recognition principle. They are aimed at constructing a workable and reasonable *ne bis in idem* principle and in my view are therefore perfectly compatible with the logic of mutual recognition.

Thirdly, the extensive interpretation of the principle of mutual recognition in criminal matters may raise concerns about de facto approximation around the lowest common denominator. So far, 'race to the bottom' preoccupations in legal literature have mainly been voiced in the context of framework decisions where mutual recognition is applied in order to enforce or enhance prosecutions or convictions. In this context, it is often said that the application of the principle of mutual recognition entails the dominance of the most punitive criminal legislation and the lowest level of procedural guarantees.[176] However, in the *ne bis in idem* context, where extensive interpretation of the principle of mutual recognition actually works in favour of the offender, this issue has often been neglected. Yet it has also been argued that in the latter context, a quasi-unlimited approach to the principle of mutual recognition may also lead to de facto approximation around 'the lowest common denominator', but here with entirely different results. In this context, the 'lowest common denominator' refers not to the most punitive criminal legislative provision but to the most lenient. This was illustrated by AG Sharpston in her opinion on the *Gasparini* case, where she took the age of criminal responsibility as an example: it is a deliberate societal choice that varies significantly from one Member State to another.[177] In accordance with the ECJ's extensive interpretation of the principle of mutual recognition—to which the AG made some clear objections—the discontinuance of criminal proceedings in a first Member State caused by the defendant's being under the age of criminal responsibility (most lenient legislation) will trigger the application of *ne bis in idem* in any other Member State where the age of criminal responsibility is lower (more punitive legislation). However, in my view, this does not mean that the most lenient provision will always prevail; it only means that if the Member State with the most lenient legislation deals with the case first, other Member States will also be bound by this decision. Once again, the question of jurisdictional competence and the need for criteria in determining the most appropriate forum arise.[178]

173 ECJ, Case C-469/03 *Miraglia* [2005] ECR I-2009, para 34.

174 ECJ, Case C-467/04 *Gasparini and others* [2006] ECR I-9199, paras 36–7.

175 Opinion of AG Sharpston in Case C-367/05 *Kraaijenbrink* [2006] ECR I-9199, § 36.

176 See: Part II, ch 2, III, D. 'Forum shopping, abuse of law, and concerns about de facto approximation around the lowest common denominator'.

177 Opinion of AG Sharpston in Case C-467/04 *Gasparini and others* [2006] ECR I-9199, § 112.

178 See: Part II, ch 3: 'The Workability of the Principle of Mutual Recognition in Criminal Matters'.

2

The Principle of Mutual Recognition as Legislative Impetus for Efficient Judicial Cooperation in Criminal Matters

In the late 1990s, judicial cooperation in criminal matters between the Member States of the EU was hampered for a variety of reasons. Deeply embedded differences in Member States' criminal law traditions clashed with a level of approximation that had not yet made much progress owing to institutional constraints and the highly sensitive nature of the subject matter. Furthermore, serious shortcomings of efficiency were revealed in the 'traditional' international instruments adopted within the Council of Europe for cooperation in criminal matters. Not only were these instruments overwhelmingly characterized by what could be termed a non-committal 'request principle',[1] they were also rather seldom enforced in all Member States owing to a lack of ratification by national parliaments.[2] The Treaty of Amsterdam had reinforced the powers of the EU in criminal matters to a considerable extent,[3] but the European Council was aware that more initiatives were needed to make the new Treaty provisions useful tools for truly effective judicial cooperation in criminal matters within the EU. Borrowing from concepts that had worked well in the creation of the single market[4] and combining them with elements from some Council of Europe conventions, a 'new'[5] strategy was developed: the principle of mutual recognition for judicial cooperation in criminal matters.[6] The European Council's statement that 'the principle of mutual recognition should become

[1] Communication from the Commission to the Council and the European Parliament—Mutual recognition of final decisions in criminal matters, COM (2000) 495 final, p. 2.

[2] Green Paper of the Commission—The approximation, mutual recognition and enforcement of criminal sanctions in the European Union, COM (2004) 334 final, p. 35–46.

[3] See, for instance: P. ALBRECHT and S. BRAUN, 'Deficiencies in the Development of European Criminal Law', *E.L.J.* 1999, 298; G. DE KERCHOVE, 'L'Europe pénale: bilan et perspectives', in M. CHIAVARO and A. MOORE (eds.), *Police and Judicial Co-operation in the EU. FIDE 2004 National Reports* (Cambridge, Cambridge University Press, 2004) 338; D. FLORE, 'Une justice pénale après Amsterdam', *J T Dr Eur.* 1999, 121–9; A. KLIP, 'Amsterdams Uniestrafrecht. Beschouwingen over de internationaal strafrechtelijke samenwerking na het Verdrag van Amsterdam', *NJb* 1998, 811–16; A. KLIP, 'Uniestrafrecht is op hol geslagen', *NJb* 1997, 663–70; H. NILSSON, 'From Classical Judicial Cooperation to Mutual Recognition', *Revue Internationale de Droit Pénal. Le droit Pénal de l'Union Européenne* 2006, 56; D. ORDOÑEZ SOLIS, 'El espacio judicial de libertad, seguridad y justicia en la Unión Europea', *R.E.P.* 2003, 456–8; J. VERVAELE, 'The Europeanization of Criminal Law and the Criminal Law Dimension of European Integration', 2005, <http://www.coleurop.be/content/studyprogrammes/law/studyprog/pdf/ResearchPaper_3_2005_Vervaele.pdf>.

[4] According to Jack Straw, then UK Home Secretary, 'one could be inspired from the way in which the internal market was unblocked in the 1980s and, instead of opting for total approximation, conceive a situation where each Member State recognises the validity of decisions of courts from other Member States in criminal matters with a minimum of procedure and formality': V. MITSILEGAS, *EU Criminal Law* (Oxford, Hart Publishing, 2009) 116; Ministère de la Justice, *L'espace judiciaire européen. Actes du Colloque d'Avignon* (Paris, La documentation française, 1999) 89.

[5] Precisely because of these two factors the truly 'new' or 'revolutionary' nature of this principle should be put into perspective: M. FICHERA and C. JANSSENS, 'Mutual Recognition of Judicial Decisions in Criminal Matters and the Role of the National Judge', *ERA Forum* 2007, 179–84.

[6] Tampere European Council—Presidency Conclusions, 15 and 16 October 1999, <http://ue.eu.int/ueDocs/cms_Data/docs/pressData/en/ec/00200-r1.en9.htm>, § 33; and, more cautiously: Cardiff

the cornerstone of judicial cooperation in (both civil and) criminal matters within the EU'[7] has undoubtedly become one of the most popular quotations in legal literature on European criminal law. What may be of equal importance, though, is the European Council's less-cited preceding statement that 'enhanced mutual recognition of judicial decisions and judgments *and the necessary approximation* of legislation would facilitate co-operation between authorities and the judicial protection of individual rights' (emphasis added).[8] At least two crucial features of the European Council's view on mutual recognition can be perceived in this sentence. First, mutual recognition should not operate in a legal vacuum but should be supplemented—where necessary—by approximation measures; in this way, the complementary nature of mutual recognition and approximation can be identified. Secondly, mutual recognition serves a dual purpose: it not only aims to enhance judicial cooperation, but also pursues the judicial protection of fundamental rights. Both of these aspects will be treated in greater detail later in this chapter. The European Council's new strategy was immediately taken up and developed by the Commission and the Council.[9] According to the Commission, the mutual recognition of court judgments, i.e. free movement of legal acts, was a practical solution to the deeply embedded differences in Member States' judicial traditions and structures.[10] It is founded on the idea that while one Member State may not deal with a certain matter identically or even similarly to another state, the results will be such that they can be accepted as equivalent.[11] What is crucial in the Commission's reasoning here is that Member States share a solid set of common legal principles.[12] Therefore, a decision taken by an authority in one Member State can in principle be accepted in another Member State, though a comparable authority may not even exist in that state, or may exist but would not be authorized to take such a decision, or would have taken an entirely different decision in a comparable case.[13] Equivalence is taken to its extreme here. Another crucial aspect of the mutual recognition mechanism in the Commission's point of view is mutual trust, not only in the adequacy of one's partner's rules, but also in these rules being applied correctly.[14] I will return to these elements of equivalence and trust later.

European Council—Presidency Conclusions, 15 and 16 June 1998, <http://ue.eu.int/ueDocs/cms_Data/docs/pressData/en/ec/00200-r1.en9.htm>, § 39.

[7] Tampere European Council—Presidency Conclusions, 15 and 16 October 1999 (n 6) § 33.

[8] Tampere European Council—Presidency Conclusions, 15 and 16 October 1999 (n 6).

[9] Action Plan of the Council and the Commission—How best to implement the provisions of the Treaty of Amsterdam on an area of freedom, security, and justice. Text adopted by the Justice and Home Affairs Council of 3 December 1998, *O.J.* C-019, 23.01.1999, p. 13; Programme of measures to implement the principle of mutual recognition of decisions in criminal matters, *O.J.* C-012, 15.01.2001, p. 10–22.

[10] Communication from the Commission to the Council and the European Parliament—Biannual update of the scoreboard to review progress on the creation of an area of 'freedom, security and justice' in the European Union (Second half of 2001), COM (2001) 628 final, p. 5; Communication from the Commission to the Council and the European Parliament—Biannual update of the scoreboard to review progress on the creation of an area of 'freedom, security and justice' in the European Union (First half of 2002), COM (2002) 261 final, p. 7.

[11] Communication from the Commission to the Council and the European Parliament—Mutual recognition of final decisions in criminal matters (n 1) p. 4.

[12] Green Paper of the Commission—Criminal law protection of the financial interests of the Community and the establishment of a European Prosecutor, COM (2001) 715 final, p. 56 and 62.

[13] Communication from the Commission to the Council and the European Parliament—Mutual recognition of final decisions in criminal matters (n 1) p. 4.

[14] Communication from the Commission to the Council and the European Parliament—Mutual recognition of final decisions in criminal matters (n 1).

This chapter aims at tracing the contours of the legislative principle of mutual recognition through an analysis of the relevant framework decisions and directives on mutual recognition in judicial cooperation in criminal matters. First, I focus on the different terminology that can be used to describe the characteristics of the mutual recognition mechanism (section I). Subsequently, I examine the fluctuating nature of the relationship between approximation and mutual recognition in various instruments, whilst paying specific attention to the techniques of mutual recognition (procedural versus substantive mutual recognition) that have been put in place (section II). Finally, I turn to the legislative mechanisms not discussed previously that have a tendency to limit the application of the principle of mutual recognition in order to better define the scope of the legislative mutual recognition principle in this context (section III).

I. A Conceptual Appraisal: Mutual Recognition, Equivalence, or Country of origin?

In Chapter 1 of Part II, I explained why I prefer the term 'principle of mutual recognition' over the terms 'principle of country of origin' or 'principle of equivalence' as the most appropriate description of the judicially developed principle of mutual recognition.

In what follows, I analyse whether and to what extent the principles of equivalence and country of origin have any significant role to play in the legislative context of judicial cooperation in criminal matters, particularly in the relevant framework decisions on mutual recognition. My analysis begins with the legislator's unmistakable selection of the principle of mutual recognition (section I, A). I then proceed with an attempt to identify any features typical of a country of origin principle (section I, B) and/or an equivalence principle (section I, C) in this area, before reaching a conclusion on the meaning of these principles in the legislative context of judicial cooperation in criminal matters (section I, D).

A. The legislator's preference of 'recognition and execution' clauses

The legislator's decision to include an explicit reference to the principle of mutual recognition was evident even prior to the adoption of any specific mutual recognition instrument, with the launching of the 'Programme of measures to implement the principle of mutual recognition of decisions in criminal matters', which referred to the principle of mutual recognition both in its title and in its content.[15]

Subsequently, almost all instruments that were adopted following this Programme referred in their preambles to the Programme and/or to the principle of mutual recognition enshrined in it.[16] Furthermore, some framework decisions' titles refer explicitly to the principle of mutual recognition,[17] while others stipulate explicitly in their main text that the order is to be executed on the basis of the principle of mutual recognition.[18] The

[15] Programme of measures to implement the principle of mutual recognition of decisions in criminal matters (n 9) p. 10–22.

[16] § 2 and 6 FD EAW; § 1–4 EOFPE; § 1–3 FD MRFP; § 1–4 and § 8–9 FD MRCO; § 1–3 FD MRCS; § 2–4 FD ESO (post-trial); § 1–3, § 6, and § 8 FD EEW; § 2 FD ESO (pre-trial); § 2–5 DIR EPO.

[17] See, for instance: FD MRFP; FD MRCO; FD MRCS; FD ESO (post-trial); FD ESO (pre-trial).

[18] See, for instance: Article 1(2) FD EAW; Article 1(2) FD EEW; Article 1(2) PROP DIR EIO.

majority contain a standard clause entitled 'obligation to execute',[19] or a 'recognition and enforcement' clause,[20] according to which the competent judicial authorities of the executing Member State are to recognize an order transmitted in accordance with the framework decision's provisions, without any further formality being required, and to take the necessary measures for its immediate execution. Only in a minority of instruments is the relevant clause entitled 'decision of the executing state', and despite the misleading title, which wrongfully suggests that the executing Member State has a choice in its decision, the obligation to recognize and execute is usually just as obligatory as in the other clauses.[21]

Finally, a number of instruments also exist that barely mention the principle of mutual recognition. For instance, in the FD TIA, the duty imposed on competent authorities to take convictions into account is remarkably less stringent than in the more explicit mutual recognition instruments. This instrument clearly imposes a minimum obligation, namely a duty just to take into account a foreign judgment by attaching to it effects that are equivalent to those attached by a decision handed down by the first Member State's own courts.[22] The combined approach of 'recognition and execution' so typical of the other instruments is absent in this instrument, since Member States are under no obligation whatsoever to execute foreign decisions.

B. Country of origin

For the sake of clarity, I begin this section by emphasizing that by 'country of origin', in the context of the framework decisions on judicial cooperation in criminal matters, I understand the Member State in which the relevant orders for arrest, evidence, supervision, protection, investigation, or otherwise originates, irrespective of the nationality of the person to whom such orders apply (hereafter country of origin or issuing Member State). Similarly, by 'country of destination', I understand the Member State that is asked to execute the corresponding orders for arrest, evidence, supervision, protection, investigation, or otherwise (hereafter country of destination or executing Member State).[23] In the context of the FD TIA, by 'country of origin' I understand the Member State in which a previous conviction was handed down, and by 'country of destination' I understand the Member State that is required to take the previous conviction into account.

Whenever the country of origin issues an order, and no grounds for non-recognition or non-execution are applicable, the country of destination is in principle obliged to recognize and execute the corresponding order without any significant margin of control. With regard to the issue of an order, the partial abolition of the dual criminality requirement and the proportionality check left to the issuing Member State are two clear examples of the country of origin's paramount position in the mutual recognition instruments (section B, 1). With regard to the execution of an order, the crucial questions

[19] See, for instance: Article 1 FD EAW; Article 1 FD EEW; Article 1 PROP DIR EIO.

[20] See, for instance: Article 5 FD EOFPE; Article 6 FD MRFP; Article 7 FD MRCO; Article 8 FD MRCS; Article 11 FD EEW; Article 8 PROP DIR EIO.

[21] Article 8 FD ESO (post-trial), Article 12 FD ESO (pre-trial), and Article 9 DIR EPO clearly indicate that the competent authority of the executing state *shall* recognize the judgment and *shall*, without delay, take all necessary measures.

[22] Article 3 FD TIA.

[23] This new terminology 'issuing Member State' (instead of requesting Member State) and 'executing Member State' (instead of requested Member State) clearly reflects the decreased level of discretion in hands of the executing Member State under the new mutual recognition regime, compared to the traditional international cooperation in criminal matters.

pertain to the law that will govern the execution and to whether the country of origin has any significant role to play in this regard (section B, 2). As I will explain in what follows, many mutual recognition instruments indicate that the execution is in principle to be governed by the executing Member State's law (section B, 2.1), but do quite often leave some important residual power of competence to the country of origin nevertheless (section B, 2.2).

(1) *Some crucial checks to be made by the country of origin when issuing a warrant or an order*

One of the central and most controversial elements of the application of the principle of mutual recognition has undoubtedly been the partial abolition of one of the cornerstones of traditional international cooperation in criminal matters, rooted in state sovereignty and the principle of reciprocity, namely the requirement of dual criminality.[24] With the partial abolition of the dual criminality check in the FD EAW and in many subsequent mutual recognition instruments,[25] the country of origin gained a much stronger role than it had played in traditional international cooperation in criminal matters. Indeed, in requiring the mutual recognition of a list of 'offences' as defined by the issuing Member State, without any possibility for the executing Member State to check whether the conduct in question constitutes an offence under its own national criminal legislation, this latter Member State's margin of control becomes severely limited.

Another element which emphasizes the enhanced position of the country of origin concerns the issue of proportionality checks. In this regard, the executing Member State's margin of discretion has been the subject of much debate in relation to the application of the FD EAW. Apparently, national judges are occasionally issued with EAWs concerning facts that are considered trivial from their (national) perspective, and thus unworthy of a EAW.[26] It may only be a matter of time until similar concerns arise in relation to the other mutual recognition instruments. The FD EAW does not explicitly mention such a proportionality check, but it is obvious that—when applied—the responsibility for this should lie with the issuing Member State.[27] In another mutual recognition instrument, the FD EEW, and also its successor the PROP DIR EIO, a more explicit approach was

[24] E. VAN SLIEDREGT, 'The Dual Criminality Requirement', in N. KEIJZER and E. VAN SLIEDREGT (eds.), *The European Arrest Warrant in Practice* (The Hague, TMC Asser press, 2009) 51–2.

[25] See, for example: Article 2(2) FD EAW; Article 3(2) FD EOFPE; Article 5 FD MRFP; Article 6(1) FD MRCO; Article 14 FD EEW; Article 10 PROP DIR EIO. See, however, the more prudent approach in Article 7(4) FD MRCS; Article 14(4) FD ESO (pre-trial); Article 10(1)(c) DIR EPO.

[26] R. DAVIDSON, 'A Sledgehammer to Crack a Nut? Should there be a Bar of Triviality in European Arrest Warrant Cases?', *C.L.R.* 2009, 31–6; J. VOGEL and J.R. SPENCER, 'Proportionality and the European Arrest Warrant', *C.L.R.* 2010, 474–82; C. JANSSENS, 'Conferentieverslag: Mutual Recognition of Judicial Decisions in Criminal Matters and the Role of the National Judge (Third Annual Forum)', *Panopticon* 2009, 72–4. At ERA's Third Annual Forum conference, a German judge gave the example of a Lithuanian who had been prosecuted in Lithuania for not having repaid a 130 Euro loan. The man in question had no criminal record, had made considerable efforts to reimburse the money, and had been living for many years in Germany where he had built up a family life. At the same conference, a British judge mentioned the case of a EAW that was based on the theft of a pig.

[27] The FD EAW explicitly refers back to the issuing Member State's legislation with regard to the minimum threshold that needs to be fulfilled (Art. 2(1) FD EAW). Furthermore, the Council confirmed the crucial role of the issuing Member State in this regard in its *Handbook on the European Arrest Warrant*, document number 8216/1/08, p. 14, retrievable at: <http://www.consilium.europa.eu/documents/access-to-council-documents-public-register?lang=en>.

taken in literally requiring that necessity and proportionality checks be performed by the issuing Member State as a condition for the issue of a warrant.[28] By not allowing the executing Member State any margin to question the proportionality or necessity of the measure at stake, these issues confirm the country of origin's crucial position. Thus, once an order has been issued, in principle the executing Member State will not be entitled to perform a proportionality check. Despite this fact, the country of destination is by no means prevented from performing a proportionality check in relation to any mutual recognition instrument. For instance, the FD TIA grants the country of destination permission to perform a proportionality check in stipulating that 'if the national court in the new criminal proceedings, when taking into account a previously imposed sentence handed down in another Member State, is of the opinion that imposing a certain level of sentence within the limits of national law would be *disproportionately* harsh on the offender, considering his circumstances, and if the purpose of the punishment can be achieved by a lower sentence, it may reduce the level of sentence accordingly if doing so would have been possible in purely domestic cases' (emphasis added).[29] Similar examples can be found in framework decisions that entitle the executing Member States to adapt the original order, as such an adaptation is usually the consequence of a previous proportionality check, especially with regard to the sentence imposed or the measure required by the issuing Member State.[30]

(2) The interaction of competence between the issuing Member State and the executing Member State with regard to the law governing execution

2.1 The basic principle: the executing Member State's law governs execution

In light of the concepts of state sovereignty and territoriality,[31] and taking into account the simple fact that execution takes place on the executing Member State's territory, entrusting the execution of the order to the executing Member State's legislation seems to be a logical choice.

In some framework decisions, referral to the executing Member State's law is pointedly made, especially regarding specific decisions related to execution.[32] Other framework decisions include a more general clause on the law governing execution which states that the execution of the respective order shall be governed by the law of the executing state and that its authorities alone have the authority to decide on the procedures for execution and to determine all of the measures relating to it.[33] Some of these instruments specify moreover that once the competent authority of the executing state

[28] Article 7(a) FD EEW; Article 5a(1)(a) PROP DIR EIO.

[29] § 9 TIA.

[30] See: Part II, ch 2, III, A. 'Limits resulting from the *de minimis* rule'.

[31] On the meaning and evolution of these concepts in the EU legal order and its 'new' mutual recognition regime in this area, see: Part III. 'Mutual Recognition from a Cross-Policy Perspective: Investigating the Viability of the Internal Market Analogy'.

[32] See, for instance, in relation to the FD EAW: Article 11 (on the rights of a requested person), Article 12 (on keeping the person in detention), Article 13 (on consent to surrender), Article 14 (on the hearing of the requested person), Article 20 (on privileges and immunities), and Article 29 (on the handing over of property); in relation to the FD EEW: Article 11(2) (on choosing the (coercive) measures that are made necessary by the EEW request); in relation to the FD EOFPE on the execution of orders freezing property or evidence: Articles 5(1) and 5(2) (on the necessary (coercive) measures to be taken); in relation to the PROP DIR EIO: Articles 8(3a), 9(1)(a), 9(3) and 12(1).

[33] See, in this regard, the very similar provisions in: Article 12(1) FD MRCO; Article 9(1) FD MRFP; Article 17 FD MRCS; Articles 13 and 14 FD ESO (post-trial); Article 10 FD TIA; Article 11 DIR EPO.

has recognized the judgment and has informed the issuing state's competent authority of this recognition, the issuing state no longer has any authority in relation to the execution of the decision and will also not be entitled to take any subsequent measures.[34] A similar approach can be found in the FD TIA, where the dominant role of the legal framework belonging to the Member State in which new criminal proceedings are taking place—thus not the country of origin—is equally clear.[35]

2.2. Some necessary modifications to the basic principle

The significant power that the executing Member State seems to have at its disposal whenever it is in charge of executing an order must be put into perspective. The issuing Member State's power to act during execution has not been entirely abolished in the mutual recognition instruments under discussion, as most of them require the issuing Member State to give its opinion and/or consent regarding important execution issues. The issuing Member State's crucial role is especially evident in relation to the following elements: the executing state's adaptation of an order (section 2.2.1); the application of the country of origin's formalities and procedures (section 2.2.2); legal remedies to an order made on substantive grounds and requests for review (section 2.2.3); follow-up in cases of an order being breached (section 2.2.4); and the termination of an order (section 2.2.5).

2.2.1. The adaptation of an order

In principle, an executing Member State is required to recognize and execute an order in strict compliance with the order's form and content as issued by the country of origin. However, circumstances may arise in which this rule could be difficult to apply. The sentence imposed by the issuing Member State may be difficult to reconcile with the legal framework of the executing Member State or it might transpire that a decision is impossible to enforce. Thus, the question of imposing alternative sanctions arises. In order to address these situations, several instruments provide the executing Member State with the power to make certain modifications to the original order, albeit in exceptional cases and subject to strict conditions.[36] It is precisely because such adjustments are only permitted in exceptional cases that they are frequently made conditional upon receiving the consent of the issuing Member State,[37] and also that some framework decisions entitle the issuing Member State to withdraw an order following an executing Member State's proposal to implement a modification.[38] These elements also indicate the country of origin's non-negligible role in this regard.

[34] See, for instance: Article 15 FD MRFP; Article 22 FD MRCS; Article 7 FD ESO (post-trial). See, however, Article 14 FD MRCO, which stipulates that the transmission of a confiscation order to one (or more) executing states does not restrict the right of the issuing state to execute the confiscation order itself.

[35] Article 3(1) FD TIA.

[36] See, for instance: Article 8 FD MRFP (where it is established that the executing Member State may decide to reduce the amount of the penalty enforced to the maximum amount provided for acts of the same kind under the national law of the executing state, provided that, first, the decision is related to acts which were not carried out within the territory of the issuing state and that, second, the acts fall within the jurisdiction of the executing state); Article 13 FD ESO pre-trial (where it is explicitly mentioned that the adapted supervision measure shall correspond *as far as possible* to that imposed in the issuing state and that it shall not be more severe than the supervision measure which was originally imposed); Articles 8(2), 8(3), and 8(4) FD MRCS; Article 9(2) DIR EPO (where it is held that the measure shall *to the highest degree possible* correspond to the protection measure adopted in the issuing state); Article 9 PROP DIR EIO.

[37] See, for instance: Article 10 FD MRFP; Articles 7(2) and Article 12(4) FD MRCO.

[38] See, for instance: Articles 8(2) and 8(3) FD MRCS in combination with Article 13 FD MRCS (on modifications as to the nature or duration of custodial sentences) and Article 17(3) FD MRCS (on the

2.2.2. *The taking into account and application of (aspects of) the country of origin's legal framework*

Despite the fundamental principle according to which the executing Member State's rules govern the execution, several framework decisions stipulate that, on occasions, the rules of the issuing Member State may penetrate the executing Member State's legal order.

In certain framework decisions, this 'influence' is limited to specific aspects of the criminal justice system. For instance, both the FD MRFP and the FD MRCO impose a duty to execute orders issued against legal persons even when the executing state does not recognize the principle of legal persons' criminal liability.[39] The latter framework decision also imposes a duty to take into account the issuing Member State's rules on early or conditional release.[40]

In other instruments, the influence of the issuing Member State's legal framework is of a more general nature. In this regard, reference can be made to the area of gathering and freezing evidence, where the relevant instruments put into perspective the axiom that the executing Member State governs the execution of an order. In accordance with the FD EOFPE, 'the judicial authority of the executing Member State shall also observe the formalities and procedures expressly indicated by the competent judicial authority of the issuing state in the execution of the freezing order whenever it is necessary to ensure that the evidence taken is valid and provided that such formalities and procedures are not contrary to the fundamental principles of law in the executing State'.[41] The FD EEW and the PROP DIR EIO go one step further by abandoning the first condition and stating that 'the executing authority shall comply with the formalities and procedures expressly indicated by the issuing authority [. . .] provided that such formalities and procedures are not contrary to the fundamental principles of law of the executing State'.[42] Thus, under the latter instrument, the issuing Member State's legal framework clearly prevails as its formalities and procedures can only be set aside when they conflict with the *fundamental*[43] principles of the executing state's law. The basic concept that the executing Member State's law governs the execution can no longer be upheld in this context: in relation to the area of evidence gathering, the *forum regit actum* principle (country of origin) reigns.[44]

2.2.3. *The handling of requests for review and other legal remedies*

The execution of an order may provide cause for displeased individuals to contest its validity or to request, after some time, a review of the measure in question. As the execution will be performed in the executing Member State, it would be tempting for the

application of provisions on early or conditional release); Articles 9(2) and 9(4) FD ESO post-trial (on adaptations of the nature or duration of probation measures or alternative sanctions); Article 13(3) FD ESO (pre-trial); Article 9(2) PROP DIR EIO.

[39] See, for instance: Article 9(3) FD MRFP; Article 12(3) FD MRCO.

[40] Article 17(4) FD MRCS.

[41] Article 5 FD EOFPE.

[42] Article 12 FD EEW; Article 8(2) PROP DIR EIO.

[43] For a critique on the fact that it only concerns *fundamental* principles of the executing law and no other rules of the executing Member State's procedural system, see: C. HEARD and D. MANSELL, 'The European Investigation Order: Changing the face of Evidence-gathering in EU Cross-border Cases', p. 7, retrievable at: <http://www.fairtrials.net/publications/lectures-and-articles/njecl-article-on-european-investigation-order/>.

[44] S. GLESZ, 'Mutual Recognition, Judicial Inquiries, Due Process and Fundamental Rights', in J. VERVAELE (ed.), *European Evidence Warrant. Transnational Judicial Inquiries in the EU* (Antwerp,

individual involved to assume that all of the judicial proceedings related to the order's execution will be controlled by the executing Member State.

Yet the principle of mutual recognition appears to demand another approach with a stronger emphasis on the country of origin and it therefore tends to distinguish between matters related to procedural claims[45] (executing or issuing Member State's competence) and matters related to substantive claims[46] and requests for review[47] (both issuing Member State's competence). This legislative policy indicates the legislator's strong belief in a powerful issuing Member State that should at all times remain the 'owner' of the order whenever substantial issues are at stake.[48]

2.2.4. *Follow-up in cases where one of the obligations included in the (supervision) order is breached*

In a limited number of instruments, a relatively high burden rests on the executing Member State whenever it is put in charge of an (intensive) duty of supervision, either in the pre-trial or post-trial phase of criminal proceedings. When performing this duty of supervision, the executing state may find that at a certain moment (one of) the obligation(s) imposed on the person subject to the supervision measure is breached. This raises the question of whether the executing Member State can take any measures in such an event or whether it is once again the issuing Member State that has the final word.

As far as the post-trial phase is concerned, the legal situation is in line with the basic principle: the executing Member State has jurisdiction over all subsequent decisions related to the execution, particularly in cases of non-compliance with a probation measure or alternative sanction, yet the executing Member State can declare that it will refuse to take responsibility for certain decisions on the revocation of a suspended sentence or the imposition of a custodial sentence, in which case jurisdiction is to be transferred back to the issuing Member State for these specific decisions.[49]

With regard to the pre-trial phase, the point of departure is entirely different: it is not the executing Member State but the issuing Member State that is required to take a decision in accordance with its law as soon as the executing Member State passes on information about a breach.[50] Here, again, the country of origin's substantial role is confirmed.

Intersentia, 2005) 126–7; C. WILLIAMS, 'The European Evidence Warrant', *Revue Internationale de Droit Pénal. Le droit Pénal de l'Union Européenne* 2006, 158.

45 Compare, for instance, Article 11(1) FD EOFPE, which states that actions shall be brought before a court in the issuing state *or* in the executing state (in accordance with the national law of each) with Article 18(1) FD EEW which states that actions shall be brought before a court in the executing state in accordance with the law of that state and, in similar wording: Article 9(1) FD MRCO.

46 See, for instance: Article 11(2) FD EOFPE; Article 18(2) FD EEW; Article 9(2) FD MRCO; Article 13(3) PROP DIR EIO.

47 See, for instance: Article 11(2) FD MRFP; Article 13(2) FD MRCO; Article 19(2) FD MRCS; Article 19(2) FD ESO (post-trial); Article 18(1)(a) and 18(1)(b) FD ESO (pre-trial); Article 13(1)(a) DIR EPO.

48 For instance, the ECJ confirmed the issuing state's crucial role in the context of the FD EAW in: ECJ, Case C-168/13 PPU *Jeremy F.*, nyr, para 50.

49 Article 14(1) FD ESO (post-trial). A similar approach was taken in the DIR EPO, an instrument which can apply both before and after the trial. Whilst it is in the DIR EPO in principle up to the executing state to impose a specific (criminal or other) measure in case of a breach (Articles 11(1) and 11 (2) DIR EPO), the competent issuing authority regains its power when there is no measure available in the executing state (Art. 11(3) DIR EPO *juncto* Art. 13 DIR EPO).

50 Articles 18 and 19(3) FD ESO (pre-trial).

2.2.5. The termination of an order

A final element that highlights the crucial role of the country of origin during the entire recognition and execution process is its power to decide upon the termination of an order.

An order can come to an end for a variety of reasons and on the initiative either of the executing Member State or the issuing Member State, yet their respective margins of discretion vary to a considerable extent. An executing Member State that has decided not to invoke any ground for non-recognition or non-execution is bound to proceed with the execution until it is complete, except for in certain well-described circumstances.[51] By contrast, it appears from many framework decisions that an issuing Member State may withdraw an order or decide that it has ceased to be enforceable at any moment and for any reason.[52] The position of the issuing Member State as 'owner' of the order thus remains undisputed.

In the FD TIA there is no 'order' and no 'execution', yet similar concerns also arise here whenever the country of origin decides to remove an EU offender's conviction from its criminal records database. Under such circumstances, is a Member State to which this conviction has previously been communicated under a similar duty to remove the offence from its criminal records database? Or is this Member State entitled to apply its own national criminal law provisions on this matter? Of course, this is a very sensitive issue in relation to Member States' national sovereignty, as it raises questions about the extent to which it is legitimate to apply foreign criminal (procedural) law in another Member State's territory. In accordance with the rationale behind the principle of mutual recognition, it is clear that it is the country of origin that should govern such a decision, but the framework decision does not take a clear stance and Member States whose criminal justice systems do not enable deletion of offences following a certain period of time do not seem eager to share such a point of view.[53]

C. Equivalence

With regard to judicial cooperation in criminal matters, the point of departure is that mutual recognition should be based on the idea that while another Member State may not deal with a certain criminal matter identically or even similarly to one's own state, and while a comparable authority may not even exist in that state, or would not be authorized to take such a decision, or would have taken an entirely different decision in a comparable case, the results will be such that decisions in criminal matters can be accepted as equivalent to decisions taken in one's own State.[54] In other words, there is a

[51] Jurisdiction can be transferred back to the competent authority of the issuing state if, for instance, the sentenced person absconds or no longer has a lawful and ordinary residence in the executing state: Article 20(1) FD ESO (post-trial).

[52] See, for instance, the non-committal wording of Articles 12(1) FD MRFP, 15 FD MRCO, and 13 (1) (a) DIR EPO. Many other framework decisions do not specify this issue and only two of the 'mutual recognition' instruments that are currently in force explicitly restrict the issuing Member State's power to withdraw an order, namely Article 13 FD MRCS, which states that an issuing state may withdraw the certificate as long as the enforcement of the sentence in the executing state has not begun and by giving reasons for doing so, and Article 20(2) FD ESO (post-trial), which suggests that jurisdiction can only be transferred back to the issuing state when new criminal proceedings are taking place in this state.

[53] In particular, the United Kingdom and Ireland made objections against such point of view. See, the opinions expressed by British and Irish judges at the ERA Conference on 'Exchanging Criminal Records in the EU' held at Trier on 13 and 14 September 2007.

[54] Communication from the Commission to the Council and the European Parliament—Mutual recognition of final decisions in criminal matters (n 1) p. 4.

presumption of equivalence *in abstracto* ('the decisions are accepted as equivalent'), even in the absence of equivalence *in concreto* ('a Member State may not deal with a matter in the same way or in a similar way' or 'a comparable authority may not exist').

The equivalence requirement's reach is not limited to judicial decisions themselves but also extends implicitly to the underlying (substantive and procedural) criminal law provisions of the different Member States. However, in view of the occasionally stark differences between Member States' criminal legislation, a gap is emerging between equivalence *in abstracto* and equivalence *in concreto*. The European legislator has addressed this issue in the various mutual recognition instruments either by allowing for a kind of equivalence check (section C, 1) or, in exceptional cases, by imposing mutual recognition in the absence of equivalence (section C, 2). Moreover, in some legal instruments the ECJ has established equivalence through approximation.[55] It is also noteworthy that in the context of judicial cooperation in criminal matters, the equivalence requirement does not necessarily play its role exclusively on the executing Member State's own initiative (section C, 3), and more generally that equivalence concerns not only the similarity of legislation but also the compatibility of systems (section C, 4).

(1) Mutual recognition with an equivalence check

1.1. Equivalence and the partial abolition of the dual criminality check

The relevance of the partial abolition of the dual criminality requirement was mentioned above in order to emphasize the issuing Member State's crucial position in the mutual recognition mechanism. The traditional dual criminality requirement is also closely related to the issue of equivalence since dual criminality requires that an act amounts to a criminal offence under the laws of both the requesting (issuing) state and the addressed (executing) state. In other words, it requires equivalence concerning the criminal nature of the act in two states. This being the case, it is tempting to conclude that with the (partial) abolition of the dual criminality check in many mutual recognition instruments, beginning with the FD EAW, the equivalence requirement is no longer an issue for the application of the principle of mutual recognition. Yet an analysis of the rationale behind the partial abolition of the dual criminality check and the legislative history of Article 2(2) FD EAW reveals a more complex picture and illustrates, in my view, that the European legislator does not consider equivalence to be entirely insignificant.

In fact, both the Commission's original proposal and the framework decision's final text hint at the relevance of equivalence. The former suggested abolishing the dual criminality check,[56] but allowed each Member State to establish, individually, an exhaustive list of acts which might be considered offences in some Member States but in respect of which its judicial authorities were entitled to refuse to execute a EAW on the grounds that it would contravene the fundamental principles of the legal system in that state (sometimes called the 'negative' list).[57] While the idea of a negative list was eventually abandoned, its significance remains. It demonstrates the Commission's recognition that not all legal systems are built on the same values and that mutual recognition should not be taken to extremes,[58] i.e. by ignoring the relevance of equivalence altogether. The

[55] On the impact of approximation and equivalence on the principle of mutual recognition, see: Part II, ch 2, II, B. 'Approximation measures and cooperation duties for enhancing trust and mutual recognition'.

[56] Article 2 COM (2001) 522 final.

[57] Article 27 COM (2001) 522 final.

[58] VAN SLIEDREGT, 'The Dual Criminality Requirement' (n 24) 54.

final text abolished the dual criminality check for a list of thirty-two offences unanimously agreed upon by the Council and explicitly included in the framework decision itself (sometimes called the 'positive list').[59] It is noteworthy that with regard to these offences it was not the dual criminality requirement that was abolished, but rather the dual criminality check. An irrefutable assumption is evident here, namely that each act on this list is punishable in every Member State—thus, presumption of equivalence—and that dual criminality is fulfilled whenever a competent authority lists one of these acts as an offence in a specific arrest warrant.

Admittedly, in both situations the assumption of equivalence is to some extent theoretical. With regard to the (rejected) negative list, it is difficult to see how much equivalence could be guaranteed, as a Member State could obviously not be aware of the criminal law provisions of all twenty-seven Member States. Mutual recognition would nevertheless have to be applied to every offence not on the list, even if this contradicted the fundamental principles of the legal system in that state, i.e. where equivalence was lacking. Under the regime of the (current) positive list, however, problems of equivalence may also still arise. Owing to the vague and generic description of the offences, it has repeatedly been argued that it is relatively straightforward to identify examples in which double criminality would not be fulfilled and in which equivalence therefore fails in practice.[60] Concerns have been expressed particularly with regard to non-harmonized offences (in relation to which the Council attempted to develop a number of 'common' definitions in the draft minutes of a meeting),[61] but problems related to equivalence and harmonized offences have not been ruled out in practice.[62]

The crucial question is whether such a lack of equivalence *in concreto* can suffice to suspend the principle of mutual recognition. Let us take the example of abortion which in some Member States is categorized as murder. Should the literal meaning of the framework decision be stuck to rigidly (i.e. should the issuing Member State's legislation be considered the only relevant framework?) or should a more teleological approach be adopted (i.e. by looking at the intentions and objectives discussed in the Council when the list of thirty-two offences was being drawn up?). In selecting those thirty-two offences 'which are punishable in all Member States', it could be argued that the Council intended only to target offences which threatened the public order of all Member States or of the EU as a whole, i.e. a European public order concept. This perspective would require the national judge, perhaps supported by a preliminary ruling procedure, to investigate the common traditions of the Member States in order to decide whether abortion could be considered as conduct that posed a threat to the Union legal order and whether it therefore required protection and cooperation under the EAW's regime. For instance, if it was found that abortion was not a criminal offence in the majority of

[59] Article 2(2) FD EAW.

[60] R. BLEXTOON, 'Comment on an Article by Article Basis', in R. BLEXTOON and W. VAN BALLEGOOIJ (eds.), *Handbook on the European Arrest Warrant* (The Hague, TMC Asser Press, 2005) 229–32; N. KEIJZER, 'The Double Criminality Requirement', in BLEXTOON and VAN BALLEGOOIJ, *Handbook on the European Arrest Warrant* (n 60) 152–60.

[61] VAN SLIEDREGT, 'The Dual Criminality Requirement' (n 24) 58.

[62] See, for instance: C. JANSSENS, 'De burger, de Unie en het Europees aanhoudingsbevel: op zoek naar het juiste evenwicht tussen vrijheid, veiligheid en rechtvaardigheid', in J. MEEUSEN and G. STRAETMANS (eds.), *Politiële en justitiële strafrechtelijke samenwerking in de Europese Unie. Welk evenwicht tussen vrijheid, veiligheid en rechtvaardigheid?* (Antwerp, Intersentia, 2007) 41; M. PLACHTA, 'European Arrest Warrant: Revolution in Extradition?', *Eur. Journ. Crime Cr.L. Cr.J.* 2003, 190, who believes that 'terrorism' would create considerable difficulties in the practical application of this instrument.

Member States, and that it was rarely prosecuted even in those states where it was still punishable,[63] it would be doubtful whether abortion could be thought to pose a threat to the European public order and therefore constitute a 'list offence'. However, it is highly unlikely that the ECJ would adopt such a progressive view of the European public order concept, since it has thus far maintained a prudent hands-off approach in cases which touch upon moral or criminal policy questions.[64] This case law indicates that the ECJ is reluctant to interfere in the criminal law policy of a Member State or to impose specific moral values upon a Member State. Instead, it permits a considerable margin of discretion in these sensitive areas. Furthermore, a well-founded answer to the question of whether the facts in question amount to the offence 'murder' would require an in-depth analysis and evaluation of the factual elements of the case and an understanding of the different legal elements that constitute the offence. This seems to lie beyond the scope of the executing judicial authority's responsibilities, and is certainly no task for the ECJ.

In this light, it is not surprising that in *Advocaten voor de wereld* the ECJ applied a literal, rather than a teleological, approach to the interpretation of the list offences. In this judgment, the ECJ did not examine the rationale behind the double criminality requirement or its link to equivalence and neither did it attempt to formulate a 'common' definition of the listed offences, as the Council had done in the draft minutes mentioned above. Instead, it focused on the actual wording of the framework decision and emphasized that according to this instrument, the issuing Member State's legal framework is the only relevant (and sufficient) criterion for satisfying the legality principle.[65] In doing so, the ECJ took a different approach to that of the Council, specifically an approach based not upon (presumed) equivalence but upon a non-uniform interpretation of offences, as required by the framework decision.

Does this mean, though, that an executing judicial authority which has serious doubts about the legal qualification of the acts which form the basis of a warrant and about whether they are covered by any of the listed offences (and thus whether they comply with the equivalence rationale) is prevented from taking any action and then obliged to execute the warrant? Not necessarily, in my view. It should not be overlooked that in *Advocaten voor de wereld*, the validity of a legal instrument whose final text had been the result of a difficult compromise was questioned in light of its compatibility with two fundamental rights (the principle of legality and the principle of legal certainty). It was clear both to the ECJ and to its AG that neither of these principles had been violated by the FD EAW, and so the FD EAW's validity was upheld. However, this finding does not exclude the possibility that in future, less highly charged cases where it is not the validity of the instrument itself that is at stake but its application in day-to-day practice, the ECJ will expand on the subtle distinction made by its AG in the very last paragraph

[63] At the ERA Conference held in Trier on 23-25 October 2006, an Irish judge commented that in Ireland, traditionally known as one of the big opponents to abortion practices, abortion cases are, in recent years, dismissed on a regular basis by the public prosecutors.

[64] See, for instance: ECJ, Case C-159/90 *Grogan* [1991] ECR I-4685; ECJ, Case C-243/01 *Gambelli* [2003] ECR I-13031; ECJ, Case C-36/02 *Omega* [2004] ECR I-9609; ECJ, Joined Cases C-483/09 and C-1/10 *Valentín Salmerón Sánchez*, nyr.

[65] ECJ, Case C-303/05 *Advocaten voor de wereld* [2007] ECR I-3633, para 53. See, in this regard: D. FLORE, *Droit pénal européen. Les enjeux d'une justice pénale européenne* (Brussels, Larcier, 2009) 416; G. STESSENS, 'Het Europees aanhoudingsbevel en het wederzijds vertrouwen', in F. DERUYCK, M. DE SWAEF, J. ROZIE, M. ROZIE, P. TRAEST, and R. VERSTRAETEN (eds.), *De wet voorbij. Liber amicorum Luc Huybrechts* (Antwerp, Intersentia, 2010) 387, who qualifies the 'dual criminality' requirement as a form of legal chauvinism rather than as a requirement that follows from the principle of legality.

of the opinion on *Advocaten voor de wereld*.[66] In this paragraph, the AG emphasized that besides discussion of the principle of legality, nothing prevented an executing court from clarifying its remaining doubts as to the interpretation of a specific listed offence by applying for a preliminary ruling. Furthermore, if the national court remained uncertain whether the acts in question were indeed covered by the list, nothing prevented it from relying on Articles 2(1) and (4) FD EAW (a ground for non-recognition based on a lack of dual criminality/equivalence for non-list offences). If the ECJ did indeed follow the AG on this point, it would mean a revival of the equivalence element in this context.

1.2. Equivalence and the taking into account of previous convictions for different facts

The duty to take into account any previous convictions against the same person for different facts in other Member States, as stipulated in the FD TIA, is a clear example of how this instrument is based on equivalence, as this duty is only obligatory to the extent that previous national convictions are taken into account, and as it requires only that legal effects are attached to them equivalent to previous national convictions in accordance with national law.[67] In other words, the receiving Member State is obliged to treat these foreign convictions as equivalent to similar national convictions. Yet in order to afford this duty appropriate effect, it is necessary to perform a comparability analysis, i.e. to determine what the foreign conviction would correspond to under national law. If a comparable offence exists in national law, the duty applies; if no comparable offence exists, there is no such duty. It is clear that in practice this comparability test will sometimes prove complex.[68]

1.3. Equivalence concerning the types of measure that can be imposed and/or the formalities that must be followed in the context of recognition and execution

Equivalence elements are sometimes evident in the types of measure that can be imposed and/or the formalities that must be followed.

What is perfectly in line with the equivalence idea from the executing Member State's perspective is the requirement that any measures which would be available under national law in a similar domestic case in the executing state must also be available for the purposes of executing a European Evidence Warrant,[69] or a European Protection Order,[70] and *a contrario* the possibility that the executing authority might have recourse to an investigative measure other than that provided for in a European Investigation Order when that measure does not exist under the law of the executing state.[71] However, another requirement in the instruments on evidence gathering is less convincing in terms of equivalence, namely that measures—including search or seizure—must be available for the purposes of executing the order where it is related to any of the listed offences.[72] Due to the vague and generic description of the listed offences, it is perfectly conceivable that by analogy with the FD EAW a European Evidence Warrant or—more likely—a

[66] Opinion of AG Ruiz Jarabo Colomer in Case C-303/05 *Advocaten voor de wereld* [2007] ECR I-3633, § 106.

[67] Article 3(1) FD TIA.

[68] J.B. JACOBS and D. BLITSA, 'Sharing Criminal Records: The United States, the European Union and Interpol Compared', *Loy. L.A. Int'l and Comp. L. Rev.* 2008, 166, who warn that the complexity of the comparability analysis that has been developed in the United States should raise a serious caution for the EU Member States' courts.

[69] Article 11(3)(i) FD EEW.

[70] Article 9(1) DIR EPO.

[71] Article 9(1)(a) PROP DIR EIO.

[72] Article 11(3)(ii) FD EEW; Article 10(1a)f PROP DIR EIO.

European Investigation Order could in fact be issued in relation to facts that are not punishable in the executing Member State. In such a case, mutual recognition would be imposed in the absence of equivalence.

Furthermore, equivalence can also play a role in the context of the MRCO in circumstances where confiscation of property is ordered under the 'extended' powers of confiscation. Under such a far-reaching and sensitive measure, which is regulated in a different framework decision,[73] 'the executing Member State shall execute the confiscation order *at least* to the extent provided for in similar domestic cases under national law' (emphasis added).[74] It may thus be possible—though theoretically not obligatory—to apply the equivalence test, as the executing Member State seems to be entitled to go further than what is permitted for similar domestic cases under its national law when applying the mutual recognition mechanism.

A final example of equivalence can be found in the FD EEW and PROP DIR EIO provisions, according to which an executing Member State is entitled not to comply with formalities and procedures of the issuing Member State that are contrary to the fundamental principles of its own law.[75] Here, we are confronted with a rather demanding test, as it is insufficient to demonstrate that the formalities in the Member States are divergent (and thus not-equivalent) in order to suspend mutual recognition. Instead, the executing Member State will have to demonstrate that applying the issuing Member State's formalities and procedures contradicts the *fundamental* principles of its own law.

1.4. Equivalence and the substitution of sanctions

Equivalence is also relevant in the FD MRFP in relation to the imposition of imprisonment or other sanctions as compensation for the non-recovery of a financial penalty. Here, this imposition appears rather imperative, as it indicates that such substituting sanctions may only be applied by the executing state in such cases *if its laws allow*.[76] Imposing custodial sentences on its territory in cases where the national law is not in accordance would likely be incompatible with the fundamental aspects of its criminal justice system, yet it is significant that the framework decision itself makes mutual recognition in this context subject to equivalence in an imperative way and that the executing Member State itself has no choice in the matter.

Another binding mechanism can be identified in the FD MRCO, where the executing Member State is obliged to verify equivalence whenever it proposes to substitute the confiscation order with a requirement to pay a sum of money corresponding to the value of the property. The framework decision only allows for such a conversion if this is permitted by the law of that state.[77]

1.5. Modifications and validations as a contribution to equivalence concerns

Specific mechanisms have been integrated in a small number of instruments to address equivalence concerns without jeopardizing the mutual recognition principle.

Under the FD MRFP, the degree of the penalty to be enforced can be made more 'equivalent' to the executing Member State's criminal framework by reducing it to the maximum amount specified for acts of the same kind under the national law of the

[73] Council Framework Decision 2005/212/JHA of 24 February 2005 on Confiscation of Crime-Related Proceeds, Instrumentalities and Property, *OJ.* L-68, 15.03.2005, p. 49–51.

[74] Article 8(3) FD MRCO.

[75] Article 12 FD EEW; Article 8(2) PROP DIR EIO.

[76] Article 10 FD MRFP.

[77] Article 7(2) FD MRCO.

executing state. However, carrying out such an alignment by modifying the original order is only permitted if it has been established that the decision is related to acts not carried out on the territory of the issuing state and when those acts fall within the jurisdiction of the executing state.[78] Thus, as far as this provision is concerned, equivalence is limited to those situations in which the issuing Member State is not deemed—at least from an EU perspective—to be the most suitable party for dealing with the case in the first place; similarly, equivalence is intended to be of benefit to the person subject to the measure, since the executing state is able only to reduce the amount. Similar provisions are also present in the FD MRCS, the FD ESO (post-trial), and the FD ESO (pre-trial), which all enable the executing Member State to adapt the sentence, probation measure, alternative sanction, supervision measure, or protection order if it is incompatible with the law of the executing state in terms of its nature or duration.[79] In principle, as in the previous instrument, equivalence can only be applied where an adaptation favours the person involved, as the majority of these instruments explicitly stipulate that the adaptation should not aggravate the sentence, probation measure, or alternative sanction passed in the issuing Member State.[80]

Another mechanism that may help to remedy a lack of equivalence is the validation procedure. In cases where an EEW has been issued by an issuing authority other than a court, investigating magistrate, or public prosecutor, and where the measures necessary for executing the EEW would be ordered or supervised by a judge, court, investigating magistrate, or public prosecutor under the law of the executing state in a similar domestic case, the FD EEW entitles Member States to make a general declaration to the Council requesting validation by the corresponding authority in the issuing state before the warrant is executed.[81] In enabling Member States to make such a declaration, the legislator implicitly recognizes how equivalence between the capacities of Member States' authorities can be decisive for the application of the principle of mutual recognition and it was precisely this concern that the validation procedure was brought in to address. Under PROP DIR EIO it has even been proposed that this validation become mandatory.[82]

(2) *Mutual recognition without an equivalence requirement*

Occasionally, framework decisions impose mutual recognition in the absence of equivalence. For instance, the FD MRFP and the FD MRCO oblige the executing Member State to enforce, respectively, a financial penalty or a confiscation order that has been imposed on a legal person, even if the executing Member State's law does not recognize the principle of legal persons' criminal liability.[83]

Another example where mutual recognition is imposed without equivalence can be found in the FD ESO (post-trial) and the FD ESO (pre-trial), which both accept that Member States may designate non-judicial bodies as competent authorities for taking decisions under these instruments.[84] The issuing Member State will therefore be

[78] Article 8(1) FD MRFP.

[79] Articles 8(2) and 8 (3) FD MRCS; Articles 9(1) and 9(2) FD ESO (post-trial); Article 13(1) FD ESO (pre-trial); Article 9 DIR EPO.

[80] Article 8(4) FD MRCS; Article 9(3) FD ESO (post-trial) and Article 13(2) FD ESO (pre-trial). On the contrary, DIR EPO does not foresee any provision in this regard.

[81] Article 11(5) FD EEW.

[82] Article 5a(3) PROP DIR EIO states that 'the EIO *shall* be validated' (emphasis added).

[83] Article 9(3) FD MRFP, Article 12(3) FD MRCO.

[84] Article 3(2) FD FD ESO (post-trial), Article 6(2) FD ESO (pre-trial).

required to recognize the competence of non-judicial bodies that take relevant decisions over the order, even though a similar (equivalent) power may not be conferred to the competent authorities in the issuing Member State.

The preceding examples illustrate that the European legislator has neither imposed a general and absolute equivalence requirement nor excluded the possibility of equivalence playing a relevant role where it might be considered appropriate. In fact, it has chosen to impose equivalence requirements only in relation to those elements that are extremely sensitive for the Member States, while insisting on imposing mutual recognition without equivalence checks in relation to elements that are less sensitive for the Member States.

(3) The particular case of equivalence checks performed by the issuing Member State

Under the previous headings, we have just seen how those instruments that provide for an equivalence test usually enable the executing Member State to perform it. This is logical, as it is the executing Member State that will have to 'execute' the foreign order on its own territory and it is also this state that could be confronted with incompatibilities between the foreign order and its own legal system, possibly leading to an adaptation of the original order.

However, on occasions, equivalence may also play a role in the issuing Member State. In accordance with a number of framework decisions, issuing Member States are entitled to withdraw certificates if rules are too divergent or if an executing Member State's proposed adaptation to the original order is not considered acceptable by the issuing Member State.[85] In the FD EEW and the PROP DIR EIO, this entitlement even begins to resemble an obligation.[86] Thus under the latter instruments, the issuing Member State is obliged to perform an equivalence test prior to issuing the warrant.

(4) Equivalence in a broader context: from the compatibility of rules to the compatibility of systems

So far, I have mainly focused on the equivalence or compatibility of rules. However, in judicial cooperation in criminal matters, it might be just as important to examine the compatibility of entire legal systems in the context of certain instruments.

For instance, with regard to evidence, it could be argued that relatively 'easy' rules on evidence gathering (which contain few procedural guarantees) might be compensated for in Member State A by 'tougher' rules on the admissibility of evidence (which would contain a range of procedural guarantees for the defendant). Meanwhile, the reverse situation could be in effect in Member State B. Provided the evidence circulates within one Member State alone, there are, in principle, certain checks and balances which guarantee a fair trial. However, in a transnational context, the situation might become more complex and fair trial rights could be jeopardized, for example if evidence from one

[85] See, for instance: Article 17(3) FD MRCS, Article 9(4) FD ESO (post-trial), Article 13(3) FD ESO (pre-trial).

[86] Article 7(b) FD EEW stipulates that 'the issuing Member State *shall ensure* that the objects, documents or data can be obtained under the law of the issuing state in a comparable case if they were available on the territory of the issuing state, even though different procedural measures might be used' and Article 5a (1) (b) PROP DIR EIO states that 'an EIO may be issued only when the issuing authority *is satisfied that* the following conditions have been met: [. . .] the investigative measure(s) mentioned in EIO could have been ordered under the same conditions in a similar national case' (emphasis added).

Member State were to be admitted in another Member State without specific guarantees being taken into account at any stage. It is therefore crucial that the executing Member State does not look at isolated rules, but also keeps a sharp eye on the broader context, i.e. the legal systems of both Member States. In addition, the combination of two systems might also be to the advantage of the accused, namely in those circumstances where he or she benefits from the greatest degree of protection in each Member State.

Similarly, in the context of sentencing, a harsh sentencing system in Member State A might be compensated for by softer rules on early or conditional release, with the reverse situation again in effect in Member State B. In a transnational context, the combination of two different systems might, once again, be either of benefit or of detriment to the individual concerned. Here, too, different rules on a specific aspect of the criminal process—in this case rules on early or conditional release—should not be considered in isolation but in a broader context.

D. The equivalence requirement and the distribution of competences as flexible tools for enhancing balanced application of the principle of mutual recognition

This section began by focusing on the legislator's explicit decision to apply a principle of mutual recognition. An analysis of the relevant framework decisions has indicated that both the country of origin and the equivalence requirement play significant roles in the application of mutual recognition in this context.

First, with regard to the country of origin, it has been emphasized that in both the issuing and executing phases of the warrant, the role of the country of origin's legal framework cannot be ignored. This general tendency to assign a significant role to the country of origin, which continues even after the order is issued, constitutes a major step beyond traditional international cooperation in criminal matters in the context of the Council of Europe. Yet, reading this strong position simply as a consolidation of the 'country of origin' principle would be failing to acknowledge the considerable power that remains in the hands of the executing Member State. In the instruments under discussion, the principle of mutual recognition relies on a sophisticated mechanism for distributing competences between the issuing and executing Member States, whereby the power of control may vary from one instrument to another depending on the instrument in question and on the specific consequences entailed by that instrument for the executing Member State's legal order. In this regard, in my view, it is entirely legitimate to assign the executing authorities more powers of control in the context of, for instance, the FD ESO (post-trial) than in the context of the FD EAW, as the consequences that the order's execution entails on the executing Member State's territory in the former example are far more significant than in the latter. It is precisely in light of these differences that a sophisticated mechanism for distributing competences between the two Member States is to be preferred above the more simple country of origin principle.

Secondly, with regard to the relevance of equivalence in this context, and despite general statements that equivalence has been neglected in judicial cooperation in criminal matters, I have argued that equivalence does matter in many instruments and that the European legislator is fully aware that a certain level of equivalence is required in order to achieve mutual trust among legal practitioners and thus enhance the principle of mutual recognition. Admittedly, in some instruments, mutual recognition is imposed without equivalence requirements, yet I have demonstrated that the majority of framework decisions include mechanisms designed to address problems of non-equivalence in this context. A relevant question for distinguishing between areas of law where equivalence should play a decisive role and where it should not, in my view, is whether the element in question touches upon a fundamental issue of the executing Member State's national legal framework. Equivalence checks should not be performed for every small difference in legislation, but reserved for those issues which involve key aspects of one of the national legal orders concerned. Only in this way can the principle of equivalence contribute constructively to an efficient and workable but not unlimited principle of mutual recognition.

In sum, in the framework decisions under discussion, no 'full' equivalence principle or 'full' country of origin principle exists, as for each instrument the legislator was forced to strike a balance between various factors and to strive for mutual recognition instruments that both respected and reconciled the legal frameworks of the Member States involved. The European legislator has thus applied the mechanism for distributing competences and the equivalence requirement as facilitators of a smoothly working mutual recognition principle, without granting an absolute status to either.

II. Examination of the Approximation and Mutual Recognition Tandem

In the above sections, I have emphasized the crucial role of a well-developed mechanism for distributing competences between the issuing and executing Member States as well as a number of basic equivalence requirements for improving how the principle of mutual recognition functions and for enhancing mutual trust. In what follows, I examine two additional elements that also play crucial roles in the mutual recognition mechanism: the approximation and cooperation mechanisms. Before giving an overview of how these elements are incorporated in the relevant framework decisions (section II, B), I provide a brief outline of the difference between substantive and procedural mutual recognition (section II, A).

A. A different technical approach: substantive versus procedural approximation and mutual recognition

When the principle of mutual recognition was launched at the meeting of the European Council in Tampere, the Council and the Commission were asked to investigate which aspects of procedural law would require common minimum standards in order to facilitate the application of the principle of mutual recognition.[87] The European Council was of the opinion that establishing minimum rules for aspects of procedural rule was permitted by the Treaties in order to facilitate the mutual recognition of judgments and judicial decisions as well as police and judicial cooperation in criminal matters with a cross-border dimension.[88]

The European Council's rather one-sided focus on procedural approximation was counterbalanced by the Hague Programme, where it was stated that the approximation

[87] Tampere European Council—Presidency Conclusions, 15 and 16 October 1999 (n 6).

[88] The Hague Programme—Strengthening freedom, security and justice in the European Union, *O.J.* C-53, 03.03.2005, p. 12.

of substantive criminal law ultimately served the same purpose.[89] The Commission confirmed this view on repeated occasions by arguing that mutual trust and mutual recognition could be reinforced by legislative measures, i.e. the approximation of criminal procedures and (also) the approximation of substantive criminal law.[90]

Despite the significant importance it attaches to both aspects of approximation, the Commission has also stressed from the outset that approximation is no *conditio sine qua non* for mutual recognition.[91] Mutual recognition and approximation are seen as two distinct but complementary mechanisms for realizing the European area of justice: on some occasions they will both be indispensable in ensuring that the mutual recognition principle functions smoothly; on other occasions, one or both of them may be less useful.

(1) Substantive mutual recognition

By substantive mutual recognition in the context of judicial cooperation in criminal matters, I understand the mechanism for recognizing a Member State's substantive rules on criminal law. The duty to recognize arrest warrants, supervision orders, freezing orders, confiscation orders, and (financial and custodial) penalties, as enshrined in the mutual recognition instruments that I have examined, inevitably implies a duty to recognize, at least to some extent, the underlying relevant national or approximated criminal law provisions on e.g. incrimination, sentencing, mitigating, and aggravating circumstances, incitement, aiding and abetting and attempt, justification grounds, criminal liability, and the enforcement of sanctions.

In the following sections, I demonstrate that despite the explicit legal basis,[92] common rules largely remain absent and mutual recognition is imposed in the absence of any (substantive) approximation at EU level. Several instruments on judicial cooperation in criminal matters explicitly emphasize that 'the instrument at stake is not aimed at approximation', 'there is no need for Member States to adapt their internal systems', 'the instrument is not designed to set up legal equivalences', and 'the instrument respects the variety of domestic solutions'.[93] In this way, the impression is created that approximation is being resisted in a certain specific field or that approximation is simply considered unnecessary. Another element supporting this view is the fact that

[89] The Hague Programme—Strengthening freedom, security and justice in the European Union (n 88).

[90] Green Paper of the Commission—The approximation, mutual recognition and enforcement of criminal sanctions in the European Union (n 2) p. 10; Communication from the Commission to the Council and the European Parliament—The mutual recognition of judicial decisions in criminal matters and the strengthening of mutual trust between Member States, COM (2005) 195 final, p. 6.

[91] Green Paper of the Commission—The approximation, mutual recognition and enforcement of criminal sanctions in the European Union (n 2) p. 10. This position was furthermore confirmed in: G. VERNIMMEN-VAN TIGGELEN, L. SURANO, and A. WEYEMBERGH (eds.), *The Future of Mutual Recognition in Criminal Matters in the European Union—L'avenir de la reconnaissance mutuelle en matière pénale dans l'Union européenne* (Brussels, IEE, 2009) 557; but had previously been subject to much criticism. See, for instance: A. WEYEMBERGH, *L'approximation des législations: condition de l'espace pénal européen et révélateur de ses tensions* (Brussels, IEE, 2004).

[92] Article 83(1) TFEU and former Article 31(1)(e) TEU.

[93] See, for instance: § 5 and § 13 FD TIA; § 16 Council Framework Decision 2009/315/JHA on the organisation and content of the exchange of information extracted from criminal records between Member States, *O.J.* L-93, 07.04.2009, p. 23–32; § 10 and § 14 Council Decision 2009/316/JHA on the establishment of the European Criminal Records Information System (ECRIS) in application of Framework Decision 2009/315/JHA, *O.J.* L-93, 07.04.2009, p. 33–48.

the legislator refers only very rarely to related instruments on approximation in the framework decisions on mutual recognition.[94]

Very occasionally, the duty of substantive mutual recognition does relate to approximated EU norms. For instance, as regards the list of thirty-two offences mentioned in the FD EAW and in many subsequent framework decisions, the mutual recognition mechanism refers to both harmonized and non-harmonized norms.

It could be argued that substantive mutual recognition is easier to achieve where substantive approximation is available, yet such a statement only paints half of the picture. The approximation technique used in relation to judicial cooperation in criminal matters is generally one of minimum approximation,[95] and leaves Member States a considerable margin of discretion.[96] Furthermore, legal norms always require a certain amount of interpretation, which may vary from one judge to another within a single Member State let alone from judge to judge in two different Member States.

(2) *Procedural mutual recognition*

Under procedural mutual recognition in the context of judicial cooperation in criminal matters, I would classify the recognition of national or approximated criminal procedural law-related standards, which contain both procedural rules *sensu stricto* (rules related to the national criminal procedure) and procedural rules *sensu lato* (rules on conditions and procedures for regulating the function of the mutual recognition principle).

To date, little procedural approximation *sensu stricto* has taken place, in view of the EU's contested competence in criminal procedural law prior to the coming into force of the Treaty of Lisbon.[97] Furthermore, as in the area of substantive approximation, the legislator has sometimes emphasized that the instrument at stake 'is not designed to harmonise national legislation'.[98] Such statements are not always convincing, however. It is difficult to see, for instance, how in the FD IAJ, where the criteria precluding the executing authority's refusal to execute an arrest warrant are harmonized,[99] it could be convincingly argued that the framework decision does not pursue approximation. The fact that the framework decision refers to further procedural requirements as outlined in the national law of the issuing Member State while defining these criteria does not necessarily mean that no approximation has taken place. In my view, it only influences the level of

[94] See, for instance: § 8 FD MRCO which underlines that this framework decision is linked to Council Framework Decision 2005/212/JHA of 24 February 2005 on Confiscation of Crime-Related Proceeds, Instrumentalities and Property (n 73) p.49–51.

[95] Both Article 83(1) TFEU (substantive approximation) and Article 82(2) TFEU (procedural approximation) speak in terms of common 'minimum' norms.

[96] Green Paper of the Commission—The approximation, mutual recognition and enforcement of criminal sanctions in the European Union (n 2) p. 14–22.

[97] There were different views and, consequently, uncertainty as to whether old Article 31(1)(c) TEU provided a sufficient legal basis for instruments on criminal procedural law: M. BOSE, 'Artikel 31. Justizielle Zusammenarbeit', in J. SCHWARZE (ed.), *EU-Kommentar* (Baden-Baden, Nomos, 2008) 1757; HOUSE OF LORDS, EU COMMITTEE, Procedural Rights in Criminal Proceedings. Report with Evidence, 2004–05, 60, retrievable at: <http://www.parliament.the-stationery-office.co.uk/pa/ld/ldeucom.htm>. This unsatisfactory situation was remedied by the introduction of an explicit legal basis in the Treaty of Lisbon, namely Article 82(2) TFEU.

[98] § 14 FD IAJ.

[99] See also: ECJ Case C-399/11 *Melloni*, nyr, para 62, where the ECJ unambiguously stated that FD IAJ '*effects a harmonisation* of the conditions of execution of a European arrest warrant in the event of a conviction rendered in absentia' (emphasis added).

approximation that has taken place, and in doing so leaves the Member States a considerable margin of discretion.

Conversely, almost all mutual recognition instruments contain a strict legal framework of procedural rules *sensu lato*.[100] Steps such as introducing a standard form and content, imposing common time limits, and developing both common criteria for forwarding judgments and common justification grounds for non-recognition and non-execution, which are present in nearly all mutual recognition instruments, appear to be much easier to achieve and are at the same time crucial to a feasible principle of mutual recognition.

B. Approximation measures and cooperation duties for enhancing trust and mutual recognition

The intrinsic link between mutual trust and mutual recognition has already been discussed above, in my comments on the ECJ's case law on the *ne bis in idem* principle.[101]

The Commission also confirmed at an early stage the crucial role that mutual trust plays in an effective principle of mutual recognition.[102] In some policy documents, the Commission has referred rhetorically to the assumed level of trust that should exist among the Member States,[103] while in other documents the Commission and the European legislator have displayed a more realistic approach by stressing the need to develop confidence-building measures that will stimulate the principle of mutual recognition.[104]

In this section, I examine the elements of substantive and procedural approximation that have been developed (or neglected) as well as the mechanisms of cooperation that have been put in place in order to foster trust and enhance the way in which the principle of mutual recognition functions. In order to do this, I refer to measures relating to various aspects of judicial cooperation in criminal matters, particularly the new surrendering mechanism introduced under the FD EAW (section B, 1); the duty to take into account foreign criminal records (section B, 2); the regime of European protection measures (section B, 3); and other measures covering both the pre-trial phase (section B, 4) and the post-trial phase (section B, 5).

[100] The restrictive old Article 31(1)(c) TEU did not serve as a legal basis, but rather the more broadly defined former Article 31(1)(a) TEU.

[101] See: Part II, ch 1, I, C, 2. 'Mutual recognition and mutual trust: two sides of the same coin?'

[102] Communication from the Commission to the Council and the European Parliament—Mutual recognition of final decisions in criminal matters (n 1) p. 4.

[103] Communication from the Commission to the Council and the European Parliament—Mutual recognition of final decisions in criminal matters (n 1); Green Paper of the Commission—Criminal law protection of the financial interests of the Community and the establishment of a European Prosecutor (n 12) p. 56; § 10 and Article 2(2) FD EAW; § 4 FD EOFPE; § 9 FD MRCO; § 5 FD MRCS.

[104] See, for instance: Communication from the Commission to the Council and the European Parliament—Towards enhancing access to information by law enforcement agencies, COM (2004) 429 final, p. 12; Communication from the Commission to the Council and the European Parliament—Area of Freedom, Security and Justice: Assessment of the Tampere Programme and future orientations, COM (2004) 401 final, p. 12; Recommendation of the European Parliament to the Council and to the European Council on the future of the area of freedom, security, and justice as well as on the measures required to enhance the legitimacy and effectiveness thereof (2004/2175 (INI)), *O.J.* 166 E, 07.07.2005, p. 5; § 5 Council Framework Decision 2008/977/JHA of 27 November 2008 on the protection of personal data processed in the framework of police and judicial cooperation in criminal matters, *O.J.* L-350, 30.12.2008, p. 60–71; § 8 FD EEW.

(1) Mutual recognition and the surrender of persons

With regard to the mutual recognition of EAWs, which can be issued in both the pre- and post-trial phases, the European legislator established a standard that has been followed in the majority of subsequent instruments, namely procedural approximation *sensu lato*, specifically: the approximation of rules relating to the conditions, procedures, and effects of surrender between national authorities,[105] in combination with a cooperation mechanism based on direct contact[106] and a duty to exchange information.[107] Moreover, reference should be made to the FD IAJ which has introduced—with the aim of improving mutual recognition of judicial decisions between Member States—clear and common grounds for non-recognition of decisions rendered following a trial at which the person concerned did not appear in person.[108] By harmonizing exhaustively the circumstances in which the execution of a European Arrest Warrant must be regarded as not infringing the rights of the defence—and thus by creating equivalence amongst Member States in this regard—the EU legislator has reinforced to a considerable effect the principle of mutual recognition. This reinforcing effect can be illustrated by the *Melloni* case where one of the central questions was whether—despite approximation—an executing judicial authority is still entitled to place limits to the principle of mutual recognition.[109] In the case at hand, the Spanish Constitutional Court wondered whether the surrender of Mr Melloni could be made conditional on the right to have his conviction *in absentia* reviewed. The ECJ answered this question in the negative. According to the ECJ, the exhaustive list created by the EU legislator was incompatible with any retention of the possibility for the executing judicial authority to make the execution conditional on the conviction being open to review.[110] In other words, the existence of a definition at EU level of the degree of protection which had to be afforded to the fundamental right at stake, was in this case a crucial element in denying any moderation to the principle of mutual recognition.[111]

Some very basic procedural rights—approximation *sensu stricto*—are also available in the framework decision,[112] but these deal only with the phase prior to surrender. Because of this, these provisions are generally considered to be insufficient and measures have therefore been taken in an attempt to work out more specific legal instruments that will address this issue better.[113] Procedural approximation *sensu stricto* can also be

[105] The FD EAW approximated the rules related to: the categories of listed offences in respect of which there is no verification of double criminality (Art. 2 (2) FD EAW), the grounds for mandatory or optional non-execution of the European Arrest Warrant (Art. 3 and Art. 4 FD EAW), the content and form of that warrant (Art. 8 FD EAW), the transmission of such a warrant and the detailed procedures governing such transmission (Art. 9 and Art. 10 FD EAW), the time limits and procedures for the decision to execute that warrant (Art. 17 FD EAW), and the time limits for surrender of the person sought (Art. 23 FD EAW).

[106] See: Articles 9(1) and 10(5) FD EAW.

[107] See: Articles 10(5), 15(2), 15(3), 17(4), 23(4), 25, 26(2), 27(4), and 28(3)(a) FD EAW.

[108] Article 1 FD IAJ.

[109] ECJ, Case C-399/11 *Melloni*, nyr. Another crucial question in the *Melloni* judgment related to the relationship between fundamental rights and mutual recognition. See: Part II, ch 2, III, B. 'Limits resulting from mechanisms aimed at eliminating or restricting the principle of mutual recognition'.

[110] ECJ, Case C-399/11 *Melloni*, nyr, para 44.

[111] See also: Opinion of AG Bot in Case C-399/11 *Melloni*, nyr, § 70, 86, and 124–7.

[112] See: Articles 11 to 14 FD EAW (on the minimum guarantees which must be granted to a requested or arrested person).

[113] See, in particular: Resolution of the Council—A Roadmap for strengthening procedural rights of suspected or accused persons in criminal proceedings, *O.J.* C-295/1, 04.12.2009, p. 1–3. The first instruments that have been adopted following this Roadmap, are: Directive 2010/64/EU of the

located in the ECHR and the ECtHR's case law, yet here too the framework is not felt to offer sufficient protection. Furthermore, it has been stressed that even this minimum approach is all too often not respected in practice.[114] From this perspective, it has been argued that owing to the lack of sufficient procedural rights protection, both in theory and in practice, the idea of mutual trust is at risk of collapse. Thus arises the issue of more approximation and/or limits to the principle of mutual recognition.[115]

Minimum substantive approximation is available with regard to some of the listed offences for which the dual criminality check has been abolished. These approximation measures can be identified in certain older framework decisions and in other former third-pillar instruments,[116] but are not mentioned in the FD EAW itself—an indication of the fact that no tight bonds exist between substantive approximation and mutual recognition in this context. The lack of well-defined criteria for all thirty-two listed offences in the framework decision has been criticized extensively,[117] and a case has been lodged before the ECJ. The fact that the offences set out in the list are not accompanied by their legal definitions, in addition to the fact that some of them—it was argued—indeed constitute very vaguely defined categories of undesirable conduct, was said to be in breach of the principle of legality. This argument was correctly rejected by the ECJ in *Advocaten voor de wereld* on the basis of the clear provisions included in the FD EAW, which unequivocally state that the definition of offences and of the penalties applicable is a matter to be determined by the law of the issuing Member State.[118] One of the core elements of the ECJ's reasoning, by analogy with its *ne bis in idem* case law, was 'that it is not the objective of the Framework Decision to harmonise the substantive criminal law of the Member States and that nothing in Title VI of the EU Treaty [. . .] makes the application of the European Arrest Warrant conditional on approximation of the criminal laws of the Member States within the area of the offences in question'.[119] In this way, the ECJ

European Parliament and of the Council of 20 October 2010 on the right to interpretation and translation in criminal proceedings, *O.J.* L-280, 26.10.2010, p. 1–7; Directive 2012/13/EU of the European Parliament and of the Council of 22 May 2012 on the right to information in criminal proceedings, *O.J.* L-142, 01.06.2012, p. 1–10. Another instrument is currently still in progress, namely: Proposal for a directive of the European Parliament and of the Council on the right of access to a lawyer in criminal proceedings and on the right to communicate upon arrest, COM (2011) 326 final.

[114] S. ALEGRE, 'Human Rights and the Future of Extradition in the European Union: Implications of Recent Case Law in the United Kingdom, France and Spain', *ERA Forum* 2003–04, 63–9; R. LAWSON, 'Collection of Evidence and Fair Trials. A Human Rights Perspective', lecture held at the ECLAN conference on 'Evidence in Criminal Matters in the EU: Admissibility and Acquisition', 22 October 2009, Brussels; A. SMEULERS and J. DE VRIES, 'Het Europees aanhoudingsbevel: gerechtvaardigd vertrouwen?', *N.J.C.M. Bull.* 2003, 428–60.

[115] See: Part II, ch 2, III, B. 'Limits Resulting from Mechanisms Aimed at Eliminating or Restricting the Principle of Mutual Recognition'.

[116] See, for instance: BOSE, 'Artikel 31. Justizielle Zusammenarbeit' (n 97) 175; L. MOREILLON and A. WILLI-JAYET, *Coopération judiciaire pénale dans l'Union européenne* (Brussels, Bruylant, 2005) 341 ff.

[117] See, for instance: S. ALEGRE and M. LEAF, 'Mutual Recognition in European Judicial Cooperation: A Step Too Far Too Soon? Case Study—the European Arrest Warrant', *E.L.J.* 2004, 208–9; J. APAP and S. CARRERA, 'Judicial Cooperation in Criminal Matters. European Arrest Warrant. A Good Testing Case for Mutual Recognition in the Enlarged EU?', CEPS Policy Brief No 46, 2004, retrievable at: <http://www.ceps.be>, 8–9; D.-J. DIEBEN, 'The Academic Assessment of the European Arrest Warrant. A Review of the Literature', in E. GUILD (ed.), *Constitutional Challenges to the European Arrest Warrant* (Nijmegen, Wolf Legal Publishers, 2006) 233–41; S. DOUGLAS-SCOTT, 'The Rule of Law in the European Union—Putting the Security into the Area of Freedom, Security, and Justice', *E.L.R.* 2004, 225–6; B. SCHÜNEMANN, 'Europäischer Haftbefehl und EU-Verfassungsentwurf auf schieber Ebene', *ZRP* 2003, 187–8.

[118] ECJ, Case C-303/05 *Advocaten voor de wereld* [2007] ECR I-3633, para 52.

[119] ECJ, Case C-303/05 *Advocaten voor de wereld* [2007] ECR I-3633, para 59.

confirms the legislator's view that mutual recognition cannot be made conditional upon prior substantive approximation. In accordance with the TFEU, the European legislator is thus at liberty to select the approximation approach deemed most appropriate and to apply it where it is deemed necessary.

However, this approach does not mean that no flaws in the mutual recognition mechanism will arise in practice, especially when we consider the divergent national legislation. Legal research shows, though, that despite heavy debate among academics, problems resulting from the partial abolition of the dual criminality requirement are exceptional rather than commonplace.[120] There are also indications that obstacles are more likely to occur in relation to other elements of substantive criminal law, such as the age of criminal responsibility, the limitation period, the liability of legal persons, and judgments *in absentia*.[121] In providing explicit grounds for non-recognition and non-execution,[122] the European legislator has recognized that in cases where legislation is too divergent on certain aspects of the criminal justice system, and in the absence of further approximation, the principle of mutual recognition may be suspended.

(2) Mutual recognition and taking (foreign) criminal records into account

The FD TIA, which applies at every stage of criminal proceedings, takes a slightly different route to approximation.

The only approximation measures that have been taken in this context relate to purely cooperation-based elements, such as procedural approximation *sensu lato*, namely an obligation to store convictions, register them, update them, and transmit this information to other Member States.[123] Two elements are crucial to this approach. First, there is a duty to transmit information since awareness of existing convictions is a prerequisite for according them any effect. Secondly, there is a need to establish a standardized European format since improving the free movement of information on convictions is of little use if this information cannot be understood. However, neither this instrument nor any related instrument addresses the lack of approximation with regard to the consequences attached to a previous conviction in another Member State by the different national legislations. It is the fact that Member States' legislations contain very divergent legislative solutions that is likely to have prevented the implementation of a far-reaching

[120] JANSSENS, 'De burger, de Unie en het Europees aanhoudingsbevel: op zoek naar het juiste evenwicht tussen vrijheid, veiligheid en rechtvaardigheid' (n 62) 39–42; A. VAN DORST, 'Het Europees aanhoudingsbevel', in G.J.M. CORSTENS (ed.), *Europeanisering van het Nederlands recht* (Deventer, Kluwer, 2004) 423; N. VENNEMANN, 'The European Arrest Warrant and its Human Rights Implications', *ZaöRV* 2003, 111. See also: Part II, ch 3. 'The Workability of the Principle of Mutual Recognition in the Area of Freedom, Security, and Justice'.

[121] See, for instance: JANSSENS, 'De burger, de Unie en het Europees aanhoudingsbevel: op zoek naar het juiste evenwicht tussen vrijheid, veiligheid en rechtvaardigheid' (n 62) 60 (on judgments *in absentia*); G. VERNIMMEN-VAN TIGGELEN and L. SURANO (eds.), *Study. Analysis of the Future of Mutual Recognition in Criminal Matters in the European Union. Final Report,* 2008, 9, retrievable at <http://ec.europa.eu/justice_home/doc_centre/criminal/recognition/docs/mutual_recognition_en.pdf>. See also: Part II, ch 3: 'The Workability of the Principle of Mutual Recognition in the Area of Freedom, Security, and Justice'.

[122] See: Part II, ch 2, III. 'Limits to the Principle of Mutual Recognition'.

[123] The FD TIA must be read together with Council Framework Decision 2009/315/JHA on the organization and content of the exchange of information extracted from criminal records between Member States (n 93) p. 23–32 and Council Decision 2009/316/JHA on the establishment of the European Criminal Records Information System (ECRIS) in application of Framework Decision 2009/315/JHA, *O.J.* L-93, 07.04.2009, p. 33–48.

mutual recognition mechanism.[124] As a departure from the approach taken by the FD EAW, this framework decision does not impose mutual recognition in combination with grounds for non-recognition or non-execution,[125] but sets up a mutual recognition mechanism that is somewhat weaker with regard to the effects that it produces in the other Member States. Indeed, rather than establishing an obligation to execute judicial decisions taken in other Member States, the framework decision aims instead to enforce the consequences attached to a previous conviction in one Member State in the course of new criminal proceedings in another Member State by applying a duty to take them into account on the basis of the assimilation principle. Member States are required to act on prior convictions in other Member States as if they were equivalent to prior domestic convictions. The fact that the main focus lies on the legislative framework of the Member State where new proceedings are being conducted is the unavoidable result of overly divergent national approaches to this issue and of the current unwillingness to adopt far-reaching approximation in this matter.

(3) Mutual recognition and European protection orders

The assimilation principle mentioned under the previous heading is also present in the DIR EPO. As compensation for the lack of detailed substantive approximation with regard to the types of protection measure that can be imposed,[126] the assimilation principle weakens an otherwise far-reaching duty of mutual recognition. In explicitly stating that an executing authority is required to take measures that would be available under its national law in a similar case,[127] the mutual recognition mechanism ultimately implies in this context that a national authority must do no more and no less in a cross-border situation than what would be required in an internal situation. The mutual recognition mechanism included in this instrument is thus presented as one that fully recognizes and respects national diversity in the criminal law systems of the Member States, in accordance with Article 4(2) TEU.[128]

The only 'new' elements that national authorities must take into account upon receiving or issuing a European protection order are the duties on cooperation and information exchange,[129] as well as the procedural approximation measures *sensu stricto* (e.g. the right of the person causing danger to be heard and to challenge the protection measure)[130] and the approximation measures *sensu lato* (with particular regard to the content and form of the European protection order),[131] as laid down in the DIR EPO.

[124] A. LIPSKA, Lecture held at the ERA Conference on 'Exchanging Criminal Records in the EU', Trier, 13 September 2007, who deplores the limited result of the finally adopted instrument.

[125] The original proposal contained mandatory and optional grounds for not taking into account a conviction handed down in another Member State (Art. 4 and Art. 5 COM (2005) 91 final), yet these were not maintained in the finally adopted instrument.

[126] See, in this regard, the very broad wording of Article 5 DIR EPO.

[127] Article 9(1) DIR EPO.

[128] Prior to the coming into force of this instrument, the ECJ had already shown respect vis-à-vis the national criminal justice system in a very closely related area of law: ECJ, Joined Cases C-483/09 and C-1/10 *Valentín Salmerón Sánchez*, nyr; C. JANSSENS, 'Annotatie *Magatte Gueye* and *Valentín Salmerón Sánchez*', *SEW* 2012, 159–63.

[129] See, in particular: Articles 9(4), 11(3), 13(5), 14(3), and 16 DIR EPO.

[130] Article 6(4) DIR EPO.

[131] Article 7 DIR EPO.

(4) Mutual recognition in the pre-trial phase

The FD EAW, the FD TIA, and the DIR EPO all play a role at different stages during the criminal proceedings. Under this heading, however, the focus lies on mutual recognition instruments that play a role exclusively in the pre-trial phase, namely the FD EOFPE, the FD EEW, the PROP DIR EIO, and the FD ESO (pre-trial).

The approximation approach chosen in all of these instruments is very similar to that adopted in relation to the above-mentioned instruments: cooperation duties that imply a mechanism of direct contact, dialogue, and information exchange[132] in combination with procedural approximation *sensu lato*, including, in the majority of instruments, a standard form and content;[133] a standard procedure;[134] common grounds for non-recognition, non-execution and postponement,[135] and tight deadlines, while incorporating a high degree of flexibility where necessary.[136]

It remains to be seen whether flaws in mutual trust and thus in mutual recognition will arise with regard to these pre-trial instruments due to the lack of both substantive and procedural approximation *sensu stricto* (i.e. the lack of approximation on procedural safeguards).

4.1. The European freezing order

The FD EOFPE is a clear example of an instrument founded on cooperation-based approximation in the absence of common substantive rules and accompanied by a very limited range of procedural rules.

Both the executing and issuing Member States are required to put in place the necessary arrangements to ensure that any interested parties, including bona fide third parties, have access to legal remedies with no suspensive effect for freezing orders executed in order to preserve their legitimate interests.[137] In explicitly stating that adequate information must be provided to interested parties in order to facilitate the exercise of their rights, and in stipulating that any time limits must be applied in such a way that an effective legal remedy is guaranteed, the framework decision takes a first—albeit tentative—step towards a basic level of procedural approximation *sensu stricto*.[138]

The lack of common norms in this area, especially with regard to the freezing of evidence, not only raises general concerns over trust but might also jeopardize the validity of evidence that is gathered in the executing Member State but subsequently used in the issuing Member State. In order to address this problem, the framework decision has developed a flexible principle of mutual recognition based on a combined approach, by applying both the executing and issuing Member States' legal frameworks.[139]

[132] Articles 4, 6(2), 6(3), 7, and 11(3) FD EOFPE; Articles 8 and 17 FD EEW; Articles 19, 20, and 22 FD ESO (pre-trial); Articles 8 (4), 9(2), 10(2), 13(5), 14(2), 15, 27(d), and Y PROP DIR EIO.

[133] Article 4(1) FD EOFPE (a *national* order, but accompanied by a uniform certificate); Article 6(1) FD EEW (uniform warrant); Article 10(1) FD ESO (pre-trial); Article 5(1) PROP DIR EIO.

[134] Articles 4 ff. FD EOFPE; Articles 7 ff. EEW; Article 10 ff. FD ESO (pre-trial); Article 5a ff. PROP DIR EIO.

[135] Articles 7 and 8 FD EOFPE; Articles 13 and 16 FD EEW; Article 15 FD ESO (pre-trial); Articles 10, 14, 19(2), 21(1)(a), 27(1), 27a(3), 27b(4) PROP DIR EIO.

[136] Article 5(3) FD EOFPE; Articles 12(1), 13(1), 15, and 20(1) FD EEW; Article 12 FD ESO (pre-trial); Article 11 PROP DIR EIO.

[137] Article 11 FD EOFPE.

[138] Article 11 FD EOFPE.

[139] Article 5 FD EOFPE.

4.2. The European evidence warrant

An instrument that is clearly inspired by the FD EOFPE, and which contains a very similar basic procedural rights provision, is the FD EEW and its future successor, the PROP DIR EIO.

Under these instruments, too, Member States have a duty to provide any interested parties, including *bona fide* third parties, with legal remedies to the recognition or execution of an evidence warrant in order to preserve their legitimate interests.[140] As in the FD EOFPE, the FD EEW requires that adequate information is provided and that the applicable (national) time limits are able to guarantee an effective legal remedy.[141]

With regard to the area of evidence gathering, it could be argued that the ECHR and the corresponding ECtHR's case law serve as a further (procedural law) yardstick, though upon closer examination this solution appears to have certain limitations. The key vehicle in the development of evidentiary human rights standards has been Article 6 ECHR's right to a fair trial, but throughout its case law the ECtHR has maintained that it is for the competent national authorities to determine the relevance of proposed evidence and that rules on the admissibility of evidence are primarily a matter for regulation under national law.[142]

In view of the dominant position of the gathering and use of evidence in the domestic criminal justice systems and of the apparently powerful mutual recognition mechanism which has been put in place, according to which 'the executing authority shall recognise a European Evidence Warrant *without any further formality* being required and shall *forthwith* take the necessary measures for its execution' (emphasis added),[143] it might be tempting to conclude that the FD EEW is in fact the most far-reaching mutual recognition instrument available. Such a view is erroneous, however, in view of the framework decision's limited scope,[144] and the potentially difficult 'joint' application of rules on evidence that originate from both the issuing and executing Member States.[145]

[140] Article 18 FD EEW; Article 13 PROP DIR EIO.

[141] Article 18 FD EEW. This specification has not yet been withheld in the PROP DIR EIO. For a critique on the vagueness of current Article 13 PROP DIR EIO, see: J. BLACKSTOCK, 'Briefing on the European Investigation Order for Council and Parliament. Partial General Approach', July 2011, p. 5–6, retrievable at: <http://www.statewatch.org/news/2010/aug/eu-justice-briefing-eio.pdf>.

[142] J.D. JACKSON, 'The Effect of Human Rights on Criminal Evidentiary Process: Towards Convergence, Divergence or Realignment?', *MLR* 2005, 748–50; C. NESTLER, 'Europäisches Strafprozessrecht', *ZStW* 2004, 347 and the references made therein.

[143] Article 11(1) FD EEW.

[144] The instrument does not address questions of admissibility and an evidence warrant can only be used to obtain evidence that *already exists* and that is *directly available*, thus excluding the interception of telephone calls, the monitoring of bank accounts, the taking of fingerprints or DNA samples, etc. (Art. 4 FD EEW). This instrument was part of a step-by-step approach whose final aim was to cover all types of evidence gathering that are currently excluded from the framework's decision and are dealt with by the mutual legal assistance procedures (§ 25 FD EEW). This step-by-step approach, which would unavoidably lead to a fragmentation of the system for obtaining evidence in the transitional period, has been criticized by legal commentators from the very beginning. See, for instance: C. WILLIAMS, 'The European Evidence Warrant: the Proposal of the European Commission', *ERA Forum: Special Issue on European Evidence* 2005, 17–18; J. SPENCER, 'An Academic Critique of the EU Acquis in Relation to Trans-Border Evidence Gathering', *ERA Forum: Special Issue on European Evidence* 2005, 29; S. GLESZ, 'Eine akademische Kritik des "EU-Acquis" zur grenzüberschreitende Beweissammlung', *ERA Forum: Special Issue on European Evidence* 2005, 52. Moreover, it has led to the launching of a new proposal with a far broader scope, namely the PROP DIR EIO, with is meant to replace the FD EEW.

[145] Article 12 FD EEW.

Only time and practical experience will tell whether and how much more approximation will be necessary in order to pursue better compatibility between the criminal law systems of the Member States and thus better mutual recognition. The explicit legal basis for the adoption of minimum rules on the mutual admissibility of evidence, as laid down in the Treaty of Lisbon and in the Stockholm Programme's provisions, are in any case a clear indication that the Member States have considered the option of further approximation in this area with some seriousness.[146]

4.3. The European supervision order

An explicit provision on legal remedies, discussed in relation to the FD EOFPE and the FD EEW, is not actually included in the FD ESO (pre-trial); similarly, an extensive provision on requests for review, which contained some basic procedural safeguards for the individual and which was present in the original proposal,[147] was not retained in the final version of the framework decision but replaced by a simple reference to the issuing Member State's legal framework.

The close relationship between common norms and (an advanced degree of) mutual recognition is especially evident in Article 8 FD ESO (pre-trial), which deals with the types of supervision measure that can be imposed. This article distinguishes a closed list of 'common' measures, for which the Member States have agreed to apply the framework decision and its principle of mutual recognition,[148] from other additional measures, which are not necessarily available in all Member States and for which each Member State must notify the Council as to whether it is prepared to monitor them.[149] The Member States' manifest concern over imposing measures which are unacceptable or unknown in the executing Member State's legal order is also addressed by a provision that enables an executing authority to adapt a supervision measure whenever it is incompatible with the law of the executing state.[150]

Distrust that might arise from a lack of approximated supervision measures for this instrument can best be explained in light of the highly responsible role that it ascribes to the competent national authorities. Under the FD ESO (pre-trial), the executing state's duty is not limited to a mere 'recognition' of the supervision order but also extends to its day-to-day execution and enforcement, which assigns a greater role to the authorities than in many other mutual recognition instruments.[151] A Member State that does not trust the efficiency of another Member State's legal system will not be tempted to issue a

[146] Article 82(2)(a) TFEU. European Council, The Stockholm Programme—An open and secure Europe serving and protecting citizens', *O.J.* C-115, 04.05.2010, 12; Communication from the Commission to the Council, the European Parliament, the European Economic and Social Committee and the Committee of the Regions—Delivering an area of freedom, security, and justice for Europe's citizens. Action Plan implementing the Stockholm Programme, COM (2010) 171 final, p. 18. See also: I. GONZÁLEZ CANO in V. MORENO CATENA and L. ARROYO ZAPATERO (eds.), *La prueba en el Espacio Europeo de Libertad, Seguridad y Justicia Penal* (Navarre, Aranzada, 2006) 116.

[147] The original proposal, which is retrievable via: <http://www.europarl.europa.eu/oeil/search.jsp>, included in old Article 13 (on requests for review)—amongst other things—a personal right for the subject to request the issuing authority to review the ESO within 15 days of receipt of the request, a right to be heard by the issuing authority prior to the final decision on the request, and a right to interpretation and legal advice.

[148] Article 8(1) FD ESO (pre-trial).

[149] Article 8(2) FD ESO (pre-trial).

[150] Article 13 FD ESO (pre-trial).

[151] HOUSE OF LORDS, EU COMMITTEE, European Supervision Order. Report with evidence, 2007, 18, retrievable at: <http://www.publications.parliament.uk/pa/ld200607/ldselect/ ldeucom/145/145.pdf>.

supervision order as there is a risk that the individual subject to criminal proceedings will not return. With regard to the FD ESO, as the House of Lords has rightly pointed out, the required level of trust is therefore likely to be higher than that required for the operation of the FD EAW: the latter requires the executing Member State to trust the issuing Member State's warrant, whereas the former requires the issuing Member State to trust the executing Member State's judicial authority to carry out functions in relation to the issuing Member State's investigations and prosecutions as well as to return the suspect for trial in the issuing Member State if necessary.[152]

(5) Mutual recognition in the post-trial phase

The mutual recognition instruments applied in the post-trial phase, namely the FD MRFP, the FD MRCO, the FD MRCS, and the FD ESO (post-trial), display a pattern that is similar to the instruments discussed earlier: a cooperation mechanism based on direct contact, dialogue and information exchange,[153] complemented with procedural approximation *sensu lato*, largely including a standard form and content,[154] a standard procedure,[155] common criteria to be applied for forwarding an order,[156] common grounds for non-recognition and non-execution,[157] and tight deadlines.[158]

In these post-trial instruments, too, both substantive and procedural approximation *sensu stricto* are usually very limited if not entirely absent, as I will illustrate in the next section.

5.1. Financial penalties

The FD MRFP takes an approach to mutual recognition that neglects to account for (substantive) approximation. It has been argued that this approach was chosen either because its drafters believed that approximation had in fact been achieved or because the lack of approximation with regard to some offences would not create any problems in the particular circumstances of this framework decision.[159]

Examples of European approximation measures that include financial sanctions are very rare, though this should be seen in the context of the European legislator's marked preference for custodial sentences.[160] As regards the approximation of penalties, the

[152] HOUSE OF LORDS, EU COMMITTEE, European Supervision Order. Report with evidence (n 151).

[153] Articles 4, 7(3), 12, and 14 FD MRFP; Articles 4, 8(4), 8(5), 15, and 17 FD MRCO; Articles 5, 20, and 21 FD MRCS; § 20 and Articles 6, 11(3), 15, 16, 17, and 18 FD ESO (post-trial).

[154] In contrast to the FD EAW and the FD EEW (both mutual recognition of a single *European* warrant), all these instruments concern the recognition of a *national* decision that is accompanied by a uniform certificate: Article 4 FD MRFP; Article 4 FD MRCO; Article 4 FD MRCS; Article 6 FD ESO (post-trial).

[155] Article 4 FD MRFP; Article 4 FD MRCO; Articles 4 to 6 FD MRCS; Article 6 FD ESO (post-trial).

[156] Article 4 FD MRCS; Article 5 FD ESO (post-trial).

[157] Article 7 FD MRFP; Article 8 FD MRCO; Article 9 FD MRCS; Article 11 FD ESO (post-trial).

[158] Articles 12 and 23 *in fine* FD MRCS; Article 12 FD ESO (post-trial). See, however, '*without delay*' (Art. 4 FD MRFP) and a duty to take '*forthwith*' all necessary measures for its execution (Art. 7 FD MRCO).

[159] I. BANTEKAS, 'The Principle of Mutual Recognition in EU Criminal Law', *E.L. Rev.* 2007, 371.

[160] Green Paper of the Commission—The approximation, mutual recognition and enforcement of criminal sanctions in the European Union (n 2) p. 18. For some examples, see: M. LOPEZ ESCUDERO, 'El reconocimiento mutuo de sanctiones pecuniarias en la Unión Europea', *Rev. Gen. Der. Eur.* 2006, 18; MOREILLON, and WILLI-JAYET, *Coopération judiciaire pénale dans l'Union européenne* (n 116) 341 ff.

exercise has thus far been confined to defining the applicable penalties either as effective, proportionate, and dissuasive, or in terms of the minimum level of the maximum penalty. Besides imprisonment, a wide range of penalties are available in the Member States' criminal systems.

In order to ascertain the situation in the Member States, it is necessary to compile an inventory and perform a comparative analysis of their legislation on financial penalties. The Commission's Green Paper on the approximation, mutual recognition, and enforcement of criminal sanctions in the EU shows that the differences between the Member States' legislations are considerable.[161]

The current lack of approximation at EU level, in combination with heterogeneous national legislations on financial penalties, has led to the inclusion of a moderated mutual recognition mechanism in the corresponding framework decision. Indeed, it is from this angle that we must consider both the executing state's power to reduce the penalty under certain conditions and the fact that imposing imprisonment or alternative sanctions by way of substitution for non-recovery of the financial penalty is made subject to two conditions: first, that the executing state's laws provide for such a substitution and secondly, that the issuing state has also allowed for it.

5.2. Confiscation orders

The FD MRCO is a rare example of an instrument which is accompanied by another framework decision establishing common rules on the confiscation of proceeds from crime,[162] and which has thus introduced some fundamental substantive approximation in this matter.

The approximation approach is minimal, however, as the framework decision provides for the use of a variety of confiscation means, some of which are not binding.[163] This is rather striking in an instrument which attempts to approximate criminal law, but can be explained as a necessary step in achieving a compromise—and the unanimous agreement of the Council—in light of the different national legal approaches to confiscation.[164] This limited approximation approach, in an instrument whose primary aim is to suppress Member States' conversion of the confiscation order into a national form, results once again in a limited mutual recognition mechanism. This is especially the case with regard to extended confiscation powers, as the executing Member State is entitled in specific circumstances to execute the confiscation order to the extent provided for in similar domestic cases under national law.

Procedural approximation *sensu stricto* is limited in the mutual recognition framework decision to a standard clause on legal remedies in the executing state[165] but this should be read together with the approximation framework decision, which requires interested parties to have access to effective legal remedies in order to preserve their rights following the issue of confiscation orders.[166] Given the very general description of both

[161] Green Paper of the Commission—The approximation, mutual recognition and enforcement of criminal sanctions in the European Union (n 2) p. 30.

[162] Council Framework Decision 2005/212/JHA of 24 February 2005 on Confiscation of Crime-Related Proceeds, Instrumentalities and Property (n 73) p. 49–51.

[163] Compare Articles 3(1) and 3(2) FD MRCO (each Member State *shall*...) with Article 3(3) FD MRCO (each Member State *may*...).

[164] For a similar conclusion regarding the approximation at EU level of 'organized crime', see: V. HATZOPOULOS, 'The Third Wave of Third Pillar Law', *E.L. Rev.* 2009, 528.

[165] Article 9 FD MRCO. [166] Article 4 FD MRCO.

provisions, it is obvious that the protection of procedural rights in this context remains to a large extent a Member State's own affair.

5.3. Transfer of sentenced persons

At EU level, the formula used to approximate custodial sentences consists in setting minimum levels for maximum penalties; however, neither common minimum penalties nor common maximum penalties currently exist.[167]

On the basis of the Commission's inventory and of a comparative analysis of the Member States' criminal law systems, major differences can be discerned among Member States regarding the maximum penalty. It is also clear that Member States have a relatively large variety of means to enforce custodial sentences.[168] Furthermore, the huge differences in day-to-day prison situations have also been denounced and this has led to calls for a set of binding minimum prison rules.[169]

In order to address potential conflicts arising from the diversity of criminal justice systems, several mechanisms were introduced in the FD MRCS that led to a watered down version of the principle of mutual recognition. Apart from the 'traditional' grounds for non-recognition or non-execution,[170] an executing state is—though only under certain conditions—entitled to adapt the sentence if it is incompatible with its own law in terms of duration or nature.[171] Another option is that the two Member States reach an agreement on partial recognition and enforcement.[172] Furthermore, the transfer may be cancelled when the issuing Member State does not agree with the executing Member State's applicable provisions on possible early or conditional release.[173] Finally, this framework decision was the first instrument on mutual recognition in effect in criminal matters in which Member States were given the option of whether to abolish dual criminality or not.[174]

The lack of substantive approximation is barely compensated for by procedural approximation *sensu stricto* in the FD MRCS. With the abolition of the sentenced individual's consent, his procedural rights are ultimately limited to a right to be heard and a right to be notified.[175]

5.4. Supervision of probation measures and alternative sanctions

On the basis of the inventory and of the comparative analysis of Member States' legislation on alternative sanctions performed by the Commission, it is clear that as of

[167] For some examples, see, for instance: Green Paper of the Commission—The approximation, mutual recognition and enforcement of criminal sanctions in the European Union (n 2) p. 15–16 and p. 51; MOREILLON and WILLI-JAYET, *Coopération judiciaire pénale dans l'Union européenne* (n 116) 341 ff.

[168] Green Paper of the Commission—The approximation, mutual recognition and enforcement of criminal sanctions in the European Union (n 2) p. 29–30 and Annex 1.

[169] S. SNACKEN and D. VAN ZYL SMIT, *Principles of European Prison Law and Policy* (Oxford, Oxford University Press, 2009). See also: the speeches of A. VAN KALMTHOUT and C. MORGENSTERN, at the ERA Conference 'Pre-trial Detention, Enforcement and Supervision of Sentences', Trier, 15 and 16 May 2008.

[170] See: Part II, ch 2, III, B. 'Limits resulting from mechanisms aimed at eliminating or restricting the principle of mutual recognition'.

[171] Article 8 FD MRCS.

[172] Article 10 FD MRCS.

[173] Article 17(3) FD MRCS.

[174] Article 7(4) FD MRCS.

[175] Article 6 FD MRCS. For criticism on the sentenced person's reduced involvement in the FD MRCS, see, for instance: V. MITSILEGAS, 'The Limits of Mutual Trust in Europe's Area of Freedom,

2004 most Member States had recently introduced alternative sanctions or were in the process of doing so.[176] The study has shown that significant differences exist between the Member States' criminal law: not only are there considerable differences regarding the function and legal nature of alternative sanctions, but there are also a large range of alternative sanctions themselves. Some of these alternative sanctions, such as social supervision and the related supervisory bodies, do not exist in all Member States. In sum, the term 'alternative sanction or penalty' is not being interpreted consistently in all Member States'.[177] Furthermore, references to alternative penalties are scarce in EU instruments.[178] Generally speaking, no EU legislation on the approximation of alternative sanctions is currently in evidence.

In light of these two findings, it is not surprising that the mutual recognition of alternative sanctions can cause conflicts, all the more since the authorities of the executing Member State are required to assume an active role in the supervision of the probation arrangements and since trust in this context is not limited to judicial authorities but also extends to probation officers and their reports.[179]

Both substantive and procedural approximation *sensu stricto* are almost entirely absent from the FD ESO (post-trial).[180] This instrument addresses the potential difficulties in a number of ways which all result in a fairly moderate application of the principle of mutual recognition. In imitation of the FD MRCS, which was adopted on

Security and Justice: From Automatic Inter-State Cooperation to the Slow Emergence of the Individual', *Y.E.L.* 2012, 328–80, who argues that this framework decision 'has introduced a system of maximum automaticity with little consideration for the position of the affected individual'.

[176] Green Paper of the Commission—The approximation, mutual recognition and enforcement of criminal sanctions in the European Union (n 2) p. 32 and Annex 2.

[177] Green Paper of the Commission—The approximation, mutual recognition and enforcement of criminal sanctions in the European Union (n 2) p. 20–1 and p. 42–3. A judicial system which foresees in alternative sanctions, is an element subject to evaluation in the negotiations in the framework of the enlargement strategy, and is clearly not self-evident for some candidate-Member States. See, for instance: Commission staff working document Turkey 2009 progress report accompanying the communication from the Commission to the European Parliament and the Council enlargement strategy and main challenges 2009–2010, SEC (2009) 1334, p. 26 and 83; Commission staff working document Croatia 2009 progress report accompanying the communication from the Commission to the European Parliament and the Council enlargement strategy and main challenges 2009–2010, SEC (2009) 1334, p. 13, 46–7, 54, and 64.

[178] For a scarce reference to alternative sanction, see, for instance: Article 10 former Council Framework Decision 2001/220/JHA of 15 March 2001 on the standing of victims in criminal proceedings, *O.J.* L-82, 22.03.2001, p. 1–4 (replaced by Directive 2012/29/EU of the European Parliament and of the Council of 25 October 2012 establishing minimum standards on the rights, support and protection of victims of crime, and replacing Council Framework Decision 2001/220/JHA, *O.J.* L-315, 14.11.2012, p. 57–73), leaving the Member States, however, a great margin of discretion by stipulating that each Member State shall seek to promote mediation in criminal *cases for offences which it considers appropriate for this sort of measure* (emphasis added). Compare also Article 6(4) Proposal for a Council Framework Decision on combatting racism and xenophobia, COM (2001) 664 final, which requires Member States to ensure that ancillary or alternative sanctions such as community service or participation in training courses, deprivation of certain civil or political rights, or publication of all or part of a sentence may be imposed or foreseen for some of the offences referred to in the framework decision, with the finally adopted Council Framework Decision 2008/913/JHA of 28 November 2008 on combatting certain forms and expressions of racism and xenophobia by means of criminal law, *O.J.* L-328, 06.12.2008, p. 55–8, which no longer makes any reference to alternative sanctions.

[179] Article 3(2) FD ESO (post-trial) foresees that Member States may designate *non-judicial* authorities as the competent authorities for taking decisions under this framework decision.

[180] The traditional 'legal remedies' clause according to which Member States are required to ensure that the sentenced persons are subject to a set of legal rights and remedies in accordance with their national law, is, in this instrument, only mentioned in the preamble § 21 FD ESO (post-trial).

the same day, the FD ESO (post-trial) permits executing Member States to adapt the original measure,[181] reject some of its responsibilities,[182] and retain the dual criminality verification.[183]

III. Limits to the Principle of Mutual Recognition

In the previous chapter, I touched upon various elements that influence the strength of the principle of mutual recognition, such as the scope of the framework decision, the requirement of equivalence, and the distribution of power between the issuing Member State and the executing Member State.

In order to ensure the effectiveness of judicial cooperation in criminal matters, especially the principle of mutual recognition, grounds for non-recognition and non-execution, as well as grounds for postponing its execution are restricted. Yet, a demanding unanimity requirement in the Council, in combination with limited approximation in a very sensitive area, has led to the creation of a considerable number of mechanisms that limit the principle of mutual recognition in the relevant framework decisions. In the next section, I discuss these mechanisms under the following headings: limits resulting from the *de minimis* rule (section III, A); limits resulting from mechanisms aimed at eliminating or restricting the principle of mutual recognition (section III, B); limits linked to the level of control left to the executing Member State (section III, C); and limits arising from concerns about abuse of law (section III, D).

A. Limits resulting from the *de minimis* rule

Given the far-reaching consequences that some of the mutual recognition instruments have for the individual and the sometimes demanding role to be played by the competent judicial authority in the executing Member State, it is not surprising that questions have been raised (and heavily debated) as to whether the application of the principle of mutual recognition should be made subject to a proportionality test.[184]

The FD EAW introduced a *de minimis* rule, in which it stipulates that an arrest warrant may be issued for acts punishable under the law of the issuing Member State by a custodial sentence or a detention order for a maximum period of at least twelve months or, where a sentence has already been passed or a detention order issued, for sentences of at least four months.[185] In introducing this threshold, the legislator clearly aimed at avoiding situations where arrest warrants could be issued for minor offences. However,

[181] Article 9 FD ESO (post-trial).

[182] Articles 11(4) and 14(3) FD ESO (post-trial).

[183] Article 10(4) FD ESO (post-trial).

[184] Conference on Mutual Recognition of Judicial Decisions in Criminal Matters: The Role of the National Judge (fourth annual forum), ERA, Trier, 28–30 October 2009; Conference on Mutual Recognition of Judicial Decisions in Criminal Matters: The Role of the National Judge (third annual forum), ERA, Trier, 22–24 October 2008; Conference on Mutual Recognition of Judicial Decisions in Criminal Matters: The Role of the National Judge (second annual forum), ERA, Trier, 21–23 November 2007.

[185] Article 2(1) FD EAW. If the arrest warrant relates to an offence for which the dual criminality verification has been abolished, the required threshold is higher: the offence must be punishable in the issuing Member State by a custodial sentence or a detention order for a *maximum period of at least three years* (Art. 2(2) FD EAW). Similarly, in all the framework decisions the partial abolition of the dual criminality check is compensated by the requirement that under the issuing Member State's legal

with twenty-seven legislators and widely divergent rules on custodial sentences, it is doubtful whether a (national) proportionality test which would have to be performed on the basis of the issuing Member State's legal framework could achieve this aim.

At a forum where national legal practitioners discussed the pros and cons of this new instrument, several participants insisted on the need to perform an (additional) proportionality check at the moment when an executing Member State receives an EAW order.[186] Yet such a practice, whereby executing authorities could refuse to surrender on the basis of a so-called proportionality test, has been widely condemned. In particular, the Council has emphasized that the proportionality check should be performed at an earlier stage, namely prior to the sending of an order, and only by the issuing Member State.[187] It is clear that introducing an (additional) proportionality test to be carried out by the executing Member State could undermine the objectives of the FD EAW and its underlying principle of mutual recognition.[188]

In the FD EEW and the PROP DIR EIO, the legislator took a different route by introducing an explicit 'necessity and proportionality' clause. Here, it is the *issuing* Member State which must be satisfied that providing the objects, documents, or data requested is both necessary and proportionate for the purposes of the proceedings covered by the legal instrument.[189] Once again, we might wonder whether such clause could be successful in light of the range of possible ways to interpret what is 'proportionate' and 'necessary', and taking into account the fact that it is the issuing Member State's sole responsibility to verify this against its own legal framework.[190] In the area of evidence gathering, however, the executing authority is not deprived of any margin of discretion. Under the FD EEW, the executing authority is at liberty to select the measures that it deems necessary for obtaining the objects, data, or documents required and to decide whether or not coercive measures will be necessary.[191] The PROP DIR EIO seems to go a step further than the FD EEW by allowing the executing authority to make use of an investigative measure which will produce the same results as the measure provided for in the EIO, but which is less intrusive.[192] This does indeed come rather close to a proportionality test carried out by the executing authority.

A slightly different approach is adopted in the FD MRCS and the FD ESO (post-trial), where no necessity or proportionality checks are imposed on the issuing authorities. Yet two mechanisms have been put in place in these instruments which allow the executing Member State to verify two aspects of proportionality. First, under these instruments an executing authority is entitled not to recognize an order on the basis of the limited duration of the (probation or alternative) measure (less than six

framework 'the offence must be punishable by a custodial sentence of a measure involving deprivation of liberty for a maximum period of at least three years'. Such clause is clearly prompted by *de minimis* considerations as it only allows an abandonment of the dual criminality check for offences that are—in view of the issuing Member State—serious enough. See, for instance: Article 3(2) FD EOFPE; Article 14(1) FD ESO (pre-trial); Article 7(1) FD MRCS.

186 JANSSENS, 'Conferentieverslag: Mutual Recognition of Judicial Decisions in Criminal Matters and the Role of the National Judge (Third Annual Forum)' (n 26) 73.

187 Council of the EU, *Handbook on the EAW* (n 27) p. 14.

188 M. FLETCHER, R. LOOF, and B. GILLMORE, *EU Criminal Law and Justice* (Cheltenham, Edward Elgar, 2008) 118.

189 Article 7 FD EEW. Similarly: Article 5a(1)(a) PROP DIR EIO.

190 Article 7 FD EEW: '... these conditions shall be assessed *only* in the *issuing* State in each case' (emphasis added).

191 Article 11(2) FD EEW.

192 Article 9 (1bis) PROP DIR EIO.

months' duration),[193] or where the major part of the sentence has already been executed in the issuing Member State (less than six months of the sentence remains to be served).[194] In view of the limited (remaining) duration of the sentence, execution may be considered disproportionate, hence the ground for non-recognition or non-execution. Secondly, questions can arise in the executing Member State as to whether the sanction imposed in the issuing Member State is proportionate to the executing Member State's own standards. Under both framework decisions, the executing authority is entitled to adapt the sentence whenever it is incompatible with its own state law in terms of duration or nature.[195] However, in my view, the qualification 'incompatible' indicates that the proportionality test it involves will not necessarily be 'light'. Only further case law, guided by the ECJ, will tell to what extent 'disproportionate' sentences can be considered 'incompatible' with the executing Member State's framework and subsequently adapted.

Another, less controversial example can be found in the FD MRFP. In this instrument, the legislator stipulates that the competent authority in the executing state may refuse to recognize or execute a decision when the financial penalty is below 70 Euro or equivalent to that amount,[196] and thus established a proportionality test that is not open to further discussion.

Leaving aside the finding that *de minimis* considerations are relevant in all framework decisions with regard to the partial abolition of the dual criminality check, the preceding analysis reveals two major trends in the framework decisions. In the first category, the proportionality test is of an obligatory nature and must be performed by the issuing Member State (for example: FD EAW; FD EEW; PROP DIR EIO), whereas in a second category it is optional and the responsibility of the executing Member State (for example: FD MRCS and the FD ESO post-trial). In my view, this difference in approach is perfectly justified in light of the different roles fulfilled by the principle of mutual recognition in each category. Next, in the first category, the criminal investigation centres around the issuing Member State, as individuals will need to be surrendered (FD EAW) and evidence must be transferred (FD EEW) in order to enable the issuing Member State to finalize or execute the criminal proceedings. It is therefore perfectly logical that in these contexts, it is essentially the issuing authority that has to handle the proportionality issue. However, in the second category, the responsibilities related to the execution of sentences are mostly transferred to the executing authorities in the state where the (remaining) sanction will be carried out. In the latter context, it is therefore more than justifiable that the executing authority has a larger say in the proportionality issue.

B. Limits resulting from mechanisms aimed at eliminating or restricting the principle of mutual recognition

The framework decisions include a variety of mechanisms that limit the scope of the principle of mutual recognition, including (mandatory or optional)[197] justification grounds for

[193] Article 11(1)(j) FD ESO (post-trial). [194] Article 9(1)(h) FD MRCS.

[195] Article 8 FD MRCS; Article 9 FD ESO (post-trial). [196] Article 7(2)(h) FD MRFP.

[197] The technique of *mandatory* grounds was adopted only once, namely in the first mutual recognition instrument (Art. 3 FD EAW, in relation to *ne bis in idem*; underage; and amnesty). It was abandoned and substituted for a mere 'optional' approach in the subsequent framework decisions.

non-recognition or non-execution;[198] grounds for postponement of execution;[199] guarantees;[200] provisions on partial recognition and enforcement;[201] temporary derogations;[202] and grounds for the discontinuation of measures taken on the basis of the principle of mutual recognition.[203]

In my view, taking into account these different mechanisms, a *summa divisio* can be made between two main categories, namely limits linked to the need to safeguard domestic criminal justice interests (section B, 1) and limits linked to the need to safeguard international interests (section B, 2).

(1) Limits linked to the need to safeguard domestic criminal justice concerns

As mentioned above, the framework decisions on mutual recognition include several mechanisms that are able to block the principle of mutual recognition on either a temporary or peremptory basis.[204]

Characteristics that are inherent to organizational, institutional, or constitutional aspects of a Member State's criminal justice system have been decisive in allowing for a temporary (e.g. Austria and Poland) or more permanent derogation (e.g. Germany) of certain specific provisions of the FD EAW,[205] FD MRCS,[206] and FD EEW.[207] Besides these country-based derogations, the principle of mutual recognition can also be suspended provisionally when such a suspension is in the interests of an ongoing criminal

[198] All instruments that are currently in force include grounds for non-recognition or non-execution. See, for instance: Articles 3 and 4 FD EAW; Article 7 FD EOFPE; Article 7 FD MRFP; Article 8 FD MRCO, Article 9 FD MRCS; Article 11 FD ESO (post-trial) and Article 13 FD EEW; Article 15 FD ESO (pre-trial); Article 10 DIR EPO. It is, however, strange to see that several grounds for non-recognition—in particular, amnesty and pardon, immunities and privileges—are in some of these instruments not enshrined in the specific provision on grounds for non-recognition and non-execution, but in a separate provision. See, for instance: Article 20 FD EAW (specific provision on immunity); or Article 11 FD MRFP and Article 13 FD MRCO (both specific provisions on amnesty and pardon).

[199] All instruments that are currently in force, with the exception of the FD MRFP, foresee situations in which the decision to recognize and execute can be postponed. See, for instance: Article 23(4) FD EAW, Article 8 FD EOFPE; Article 10 FD MRCO; Article 11 FD MRCS; Article 8(2) FD ESO (post-trial); Article 16 FD EEW; Article 12(4) FD ESO (pre-trial).

[200] 'Guarantees' are only explicitly written down in Article 5 FD EAW, namely guarantees in relation to (1) judgments *in absentia*, (2) custodial life sentences, and (3) the return of nationals and residents to the executing state. However, in several other instruments, safeguards regarding these same topics are taken up through other mechanisms, see, for instance: grounds for non-recognition or non-execution in case of judgments *in absentia* (Art. 9(i) FD MRCS; Art. 11(h) FD ESO post-trial) or a right for the executing Member State to adapt the duration of the sentence, for instance, in case of a custodial life sentence (Art. 8 FD MRCS; Art. 9 FD ESO post-trial).

[201] Provisions on partial recognition and enforcement are not present in the first mutual recognition instruments. Probably, the ambitious point of departure (strong belief in the full application of mutual recognition) has gradually decreased and has been transformed into a more realistic approach according to which it is better to recognize *something* instead of *nothing*. For examples of provisions on partial recognition, see, for instance: Article 8(3) FD MRCO; Article 10 FD MRCS; Articles 11(4) and 13(4) FD ESO (post-trial); Article 13(5) FD EEW; Article 13 FD ESO (pre-trial).

[202] In order to enable (some) Member States to make the necessary constitutional, legal, institutional, or practical arrangements to comply with the obligations following from the framework decisions, some instruments included temporary derogations in relation to some provisions: Article 33 FD EAW; Articles 20(2)–20(4) FD MRFP; Article 6(5) FD MRCS.

[203] See, for instance: Article 14 DIR EPO.

[204] For a detailed overview of the mechanisms that can put limitations to the principle of mutual recognition in accordance with the framework decisions on mutual recognition in this area, see, for instance: FLORE, *Droit pénal européen. Les enjeux d'une justice pénale européenne* (n 65) 430–62.

[205] Article 33 FD EAW. [206] Article 6(5) FD MRCS. [207] Article 23(4) FD EEW.

investigation in the executing Member State[208] or when certain legal or factual formalities must be arranged beforehand.[209]

However, in many cases, limitations will arise from the invocation of a permanent ground for non-recognition or non-execution (or of another mechanism for restricting the principle of mutual recognition) in order to compensate for divergent provisions in national legislations on certain delicate aspects of the national criminal justice system, such as: amnesty and immunity,[210] prescription,[211] the age of criminal responsibility,[212] judgments *in absentia*,[213] custodial life sentences,[214] measure of psychiatric or health care involving deprivation of liberty,[215] and extended confiscation measures.[216] These derogation grounds are an illustration of the European legislator's pursuit of an acceptable balance between enhancing cooperation through mutual recognition and maintaining respect for a number of basic elements of the Member States' criminal law systems, as required by Article 67 TFEU.

In legal literature, the debate appears to have centred less on the mechanisms that have actually been set in place and more on the grounds for non-recognition that are felt to be missing in the new instruments on mutual recognition. In particular, when the first mutual recognition instrument—the FD EAW—was adopted, concerns were voiced about the partial abolition of the verification of dual criminality as well as the absence of yet another traditional ground for refusal, namely the 'public policy' exception.[217]

Leaving aside the dual criminality requirement, which was discussed in paras 29–34, the question that we now need to address is the extent to which the public policy exception may have been neglected in the various mutual recognition instruments. Indeed, it cannot be denied that none of these instruments include an explicit public policy ground, which is clearly a different approach from that adopted in a number of instruments on mutual recognition in the field of judicial cooperation in civil matters.[218] Yet this different approach does not necessarily and automatically imply that concerns of 'public policy',

[208] See, for instance: Article 8(1) FD EOFPE; Article 10(1)(c) FD MRCO; Article 10(1)(d) and (e) DIR EPO.

[209] See, for instance: Article 11 FD MRCS; Article 8(2) FD ESO (post-trial); Articles 11(4) and 16 FD EEW; Article 10(1)(f) DIR EPO.

[210] See, for instance: Articles 3(1) and 20 FD EAW; Article 7(1)(b) FD EOFPE; Article 7(2)(e) FD MRFP; Article 8(2)(c) FD MRCO; Articles 9(1)(f) and 19 FD MRCS; Articles 11(1)(f) and 19 FD ESO (post-trial); Article 13 FD EEW; Article 15(1)(f) FD ESO (pre-trial); Article 10(1)(h) DIR EPO; Article 10(1)(a) PROP DIR EIO.

[211] See, for instance: Article 4(4) FD EAW; Article 7(2)(c) FD MRFP; Article 8(2)(h) FD MRCO; Article 9(1)(e) FD MRCS; Article 11(1)(e) FD ESO (post-trial); Article 15(1)(e) FD ESO (pre-trial).

[212] See, for instance: Article 3(3) FD EAW; Article 7(2)(f) FD MRFP; Article 9(1)(g) FD MRCS; Article 11(1)(g) FD ESO (post-trial); Article 15(1)(g) FD ESO (pre-trial).

[213] See, for instance: Article 5(1) FD EAW; Article 7(2)(g) FD MRFP; Article 8(2)(e) FD MRCO; Article 9(1)(i) FD MRCS; Article 11(1)(h) FD ESO (post-trial). See also: FD IAJ.

[214] See, for instance: Article 5(2) FD EAW.

[215] See, for instance: Article 9(1)(k) FD MRCS.

[216] See, for instance: Article 8(3) FD MRCO.

[217] On the lack of a public policy exception, see, for instance: G.L. TOSATO, 'Some Remarks on the Limits to Mutual Recognition of Judicial Decisions in Civil and Criminal Matters within the European Union', *Rivista di diritto internazionale privato e prozessale* 2003, 869–78; W. VAN BALLEGOOIJ and G. GONZALES, 'Mutual Recognition and Judicial Decisions in Criminal Matters. A "Rule of Reason" for Surrender Procedures?', in A. SCHRAUWEN (ed.), *Rule of Reason. Rethinking another Classic of European Legal Doctrine* (Groningen, Europa Law Publishing, 2005) 176; J. VERVAELE, 'European Criminal Law and General Principles of Union Law', 2005, retrievable at: <http://www.coleurop.be/content/studyprogrammes/law/studyprog/pdf/ResearchPaper_5_2005_Vervaele.pdf>, 7.

[218] See, for instance: Article 34(1) REG 44/2001; Article 26 Regulation 1346/2000 of 29 May 2000 on insolvency proceedings, *O.J.* 2000 L-160, 30.06.2000, p. 1–18.

meaning measures that protect a rule of law or a right regarded as essential or fundamental in the legal order of the state in which enforcement is sought,[219] plays no role at all in the criminal law sphere. On the contrary, in my view there are several mechanisms that address this concern.

First, it is striking to note how all of the relevant framework decisions explicitly state in their preambles that they 'do not prevent a Member State from applying its constitutional rules relating to due process [...]'.[220] Admittedly, a preamble's provision is not binding in itself if its content is not also repeated in the main text, yet it cannot be denied that it is a first indication of certain 'public policy' considerations. A Member State's margin of discretion in applying its national constitutional rules is not unlimited however. Not only will it depend on the question whether there is a definition at EU level of the degree of protection of the fundamental right in question,[221] but it will also be influenced by the objectives of the legislative instrument at stake.[222]

Secondly, a more general reference to the Member States' constitutions can be found in Article 53 Charter, which states that 'nothing in the Charter shall be interpreted as restricting or adversely affecting human rights and fundamental freedoms as recognised in their respective fields of application, by [...] and by the Member States' constitutions'. In *Melloni* the ECJ has clarified that this provision does *not* give general authorization to a Member State to apply the standard of protection of fundamental rights guaranteed by its constitution when that standard is higher than that deriving from the Charter nor to give it priority over the application of provisions of EU law.[223] Whilst Member States have some freedom in fixing the level of protection for the fundamental rights which they wish to guarantee in the implementation of EU law, this room for manoeuvre is limited by fundamental principles of the EU legal order, in particular primacy, unity, and effectiveness of EU law.[224] Consequently, in areas where the EU legislator has established definitions at EU level—such as Article 4a(1) a FD EAW as interpreted in the *Melloni* case—the Member States' margin of action under Article 53 Charter will be smaller than in cases where no common definitions exist.[225] This confirms my previous finding that the principle of mutual recognition will be more powerful—and thus that exceptions to this principle will be more limited—where approximation is available.[226]

Thirdly, some obvious examples of mechanisms that take public policy concerns seriously can also be identified in the main text of the relevant legal instruments on mutual recognition in criminal matters. One can think of the grounds for non-recognition or non-execution that were introduced in order to overcome conflicts arising from divergent

[219] Admittedly, the exact definition of 'public order' can vary depending upon the context of EU law in which it is used. Our definition is inspired by the ECJ's interpretation of 'public policy' exceptions that are used in the context of mutual recognition in civil matters: ECJ, Case C-341/04 *Eurofood* [2006] ECR I-4137, para 63. For an in-depth analysis of the 'public policy' concept in EU law, see: T. CORTHAUT, *EU ordre public* (The Hague, Kluwer Law International, 2012).

[220] See, for instance: § 12 FD EAW; § 6 FD EOFPE; § 6 FD MRFP; § 14 FD MRCO; § 14 FD MRCS; § 6 FD ESO (post-trial); § 28 FD EEW; § 17 FD ESO (pre-trial). FLORE, *Droit pénal européen* (n 65) 440–1, who rightly questions the national—and not international—nature of the constitutional rules that are mentioned in the preambles.

[221] See, for instance: Opinion of AG Bot in Case C-399/11 *Melloni*, nyr, § 123–4 *juncto* § 91.

[222] See, for instance: ECJ, Case C-168/13 PPU *Jeremy F.*, nyr, para 53.

[223] ECJ, Case C-399/11 *Melloni*, nyr, paras 55–63.

[224] ECJ, Case C-399/11 *Melloni*, nyr, para 60.

[225] Opinion of AG Bot in Case C-399/11 *Melloni*, nyr, § 124–7.

[226] See: Part II, ch 2, II, B. 'Approximation measures and cooperation duties for enhancing trust and mutual recognition'.

legislation on delicate aspects of the criminal justice system[227] or the mechanisms for adapting sentences when they are considered incompatible with the executing Member State's legal system.[228] However, the FD EEW and the PROP DIR EIO do come closest to an authentic public policy concept in their stipulation that the 'formalities and procedures of the issuing Member State must be applied, but only in so far as they are not contrary to the fundamental principles of law of the executing State',[229] and in their introduction of a ground for the non-recognition and non-execution of an order 'where in a specific case, its execution would harm essential national security interests'.[230] In referring to 'fundamental principles of law' and 'essential national security interests', the legislator highlights characteristics that are very often attributed to a (national) public policy concept by the ECJ in other areas of EU law.

(2) Limits linked to the need to safeguard EU or international interests

Some grounds for non-execution and non-recognition, together with a number of other mechanisms that limit the principle of mutual recognition, were introduced in order to protect rights or principles developed at European or international level. In the same way that Member States share common values which justify the application of the principle of mutual recognition, they also share common grounds upon which the principle of mutual recognition must be blocked.

A first example is the *ne bis in idem* principle, which is included as a ground for non-recognition and non-execution in all relevant framework decisions.[231] Next are the humanitarian grounds for postponement[232] and the return guarantee,[233] based on internationally recognized standards on a convicted person's reintegration in society, both of which are included in the FD EAW.

A last example, and one that has given rise to much debate, is the provision included in all framework decisions on mutual recognition and according to which 'the framework decision at stake shall not have the effect of amending the obligation to respect the fundamental rights and fundamental legal principles as enshrined in Article 6 TEU'.[234] A public outcry was provoked by the fact that this provision has not been retained as a

[227] E.g. grounds related to amnesty and immunity, prescription, the age of criminal responsibility, judgments *in absentia*, custodial life sentences, measure of psychiatric or health care involving deprivation of liberty, and extended confiscation measures.

[228] See: Part II, ch 2, I, C, 1.5. 'Modifications and validations as a contribution to equivalence concerns'.

[229] Article 12 FD EEW; Article 8(2) PROP DIR EIO.

[230] Article 13(1)(g) FD EEW; Article 10(1)(a) PROP DIR EIO.

[231] See, for instance: Article 3(2) FD EAW; Article 7(1)(c) FD EOFPE; Article 7(2)(a) FD MRFP; Article 8(2)(a) FD MRCO; Article 9(1)(c) FD MRCS; Article 11(1)(c) FD ESO (post-trial); Article 13(1)(a) FD EEW; Article 15(1)(c) FD ESO (pre-trial); Article 10(1)(g) DIR EPO; Article 10(1)(e) PROP DIR EIO.

[232] Article 23(4) FD EAW.

[233] Article 5(3) FD EAW.

[234] See, for instance: § 10 and § 12 and Article 1(3) FD EAW; § 6 and Article 1 FD EOFPE; § 13 and Article 1(2) FD MRFP; § 13 and Article 3(4) FD MRCS; § 5 and Article 1(4) FD ESO (post-trial); § 27 and Article 1(3) FD EEW; § 16 and Article 5 FD ESO (pre-trial); § 16 DIR EPO; § 17 and Article 1(3) PROP DIR EIO. For a critique on this approach and the controversial nature of this issue, see, for instance: ALEGRE and LEAF, 'Mutual Recognition in European Judicial Cooperation: A Step Too Far Too Soon?' (n 117) 202; APAP and CARRERA, 'Judicial Cooperation in Criminal Matters. European Arrest Warrant (n 117) 13–14; M.-H. DESCAMPS, 'La reconnaissance mutuelle des décisions judiciaires pénales', *Actualités de droit pénal européen* 2003, 104; HEARD and MANSELL, 'The European Investigation Order: Changing the face of Evidence-gathering in EU Cross-border Cases' (n 43) 10–11;

legitimate 'ground for non-recognition or non-execution'—with one exception[235]—and is only mentioned in the preamble and provisions on the scope of the relevant framework decisions. Authors who have pleaded for the insertion of a (national) public policy exception, mentioned earlier, have often also campaigned for the adoption of a proper 'fundamental rights exception' clause or a 'European public order' clause.[236]

In what follows, I will argue that an explicit ground for non-recognition and non-execution is not indispensable for setting aside the principle of mutual recognition. In my view, an opposing reasoning sells short the true scope of fundamental rights in the framework of the EU. The protection of fundamental rights is considered to be one of the general principles on which the EU is founded[237] and the ECJ had explicitly recognized the protection of fundamental rights in its case law long before Articles 6 and 7 were introduced in the TEU.[238] In other words, fundamental rights penetrate to the very heart of EU law and their enforcement should under no circumstances be made conditional upon inclusion in an instrument of secondary legislation. Framework decisions (secondary EU law) must be applied in such a way that is consistent with the protection of fundamental rights (the core of primary EU law), even if they are 'only' mentioned in a framework decision's preamble or in the provisions on the framework decision's scope. In the context of the implementation or application of a framework decision or another instrument of secondary legislation, Member States simply may not infringe upon EU law. National legislative and judicial authorities have a duty to take into account and respect the broader framework (TEU; TFEU; general principles of EU law; Charter) when implementing and applying an instrument of secondary legislation.[239] This reasoning finds support in the ECJ's case law. For instance, in *Advocaten voor de wereld*, the first judgment on the FD EAW, the ECJ's point of departure when answering the second question was that 'by virtue of Article 6 EU, the Union is founded on the principle of the rule of law and that it respects fundamental rights, as guaranteed by the ECHR, and as they result from the constitutional provisions common to the Member States, as general principles of Community law', and that 'it follows that the institutions are subject to review of the conformity of their acts with the Treaties and the general principles of law, *just like the Member States when they implement the law of the Union*' (emphasis added).[240]

E. SANFRUTOS CANO, 'Coopération policière et judiciaire en matière pénale. Advocaten voor de wereld', *RDUE* 2007, 2, 480.

[235] Article 20(3) FD MRFP includes an explicit human rights exception where it states that 'Each Member State may, where the certificate gives rise to an issue that fundamental rights or fundamental legal principles as enshrined in Article 6 of the Treaty may have been infringed, oppose the recognition and the execution of decisions'. For a critique on the formulation of this provision, see: S. PEERS, *EU Justice and Home Affairs Law*, 3rd edn (Oxford, Oxford University Press, 2011) 725, who argues that the provision, when read literally, will be impossible to apply in practice as there appears to be no way that the *certificate* could *as such* give rise to concerns that human rights have been infringed.

[236] See, for instance: TOSATO, 'Some Remarks on the Limits to Mutual Recognition of Judicial Decisions in Civil and Criminal Matters within the European Union' (n 217) 869–78; VAN BALLEGOOIJ and GONZALES, 'Mutual Recognition and Judicial Decisions in Criminal Matters. A "Rule of Reason" for Surrender Procedures?' (n 217) 176; VERVAELE, 'European Criminal Law and General Principles of Union Law' (n 217) 7.

[237] See, for instance: ECJ, Joined Cases C-402/05 P and C-415/05 P *Kadi and Al Barakaat International Foundation* [2008] ECR I-6351, para 303.

[238] See, for instance: ECJ, Case 11/70 *Internationale Handelsgesellshaft* [1970] ECR 1125.

[239] In *Fransson* the ECJ's grand chamber made it very clear that—despite the opposing views of the AG, the Commission, and five Member States—it was not willing to accept a restrictive interpretation of the scope of the Charter and, in particular, of the 'implementation' requirement written down in Article 51 Charter, see: ECJ, Case C-617/10 *Fransson*, nyr, paras 17–31.

[240] ECJ, Case C-303/05 *Advocaten voor de wereld* [2007] ECR I-3633, para 45. On the bearing of this judgment, see, for instance: A. HINAREJOS, 'The Lisbon Treaty Versus Standing Still: A View from

A less abstract formulation of this duty in the context of FD EAW can be found in the *Wolzenburg*, *Lopes Da Silva Jorge*, *Radu*, *Melloni*, and *Jeremy F.* judgments. In *Wolzenburg* the ECJ held that Member States' legislative authorities were obliged to comply with provisions of the former *first* pillar—in particular former Article 18 EC—when implementing former *third*-pillar (secondary law) instruments—in particular FD EAW—into their national legislation.[241] A few years later, after the coming into force of the Lisbon Treaty—which abolished the former pillar structure and introduced one legal order—the ECJ confirmed in *Lopes Da Silva Jorge* the Member States' duty to implement FD EAW in compliance with current Article 18 TFEU.[242] Following these judgments an important question arose: if the application of the FD EAW was governed by a rule of primary law from a legal order that was different—albeit linked—at that time, would a more fundamental rule of primary law—the Charter—from the now unified legal order not then govern the application of the FD EAW *a fortiori*, even in the absence of a specific ground for non-recognition?

Before addressing the *Radu* and *Melloni* judgments, it is highly recommendable to have first a look at the *N.S. and M.E.* judgment.[243] Even though the *N.S. and M.E.* cases do not concern EU *criminal* law, but EU *asylum* law, a short reference to the ECJ's legal reasoning in *N.S. and M.E.* is—in my view—highly relevant. There are indeed very close analogies with the issues that I am discussing under this heading, in particular the question whether a Member State can set aside its duties under EU secondary law and its obligations under the principle of mutual trust when fundamental rights are at stake. In *N.S. and M.E* the ECJ had to decide whether a Member State was entitled to set aside the duty of transferring an asylum seeker to another Member State (in accordance with REG 343/2003), when such a transfer could jeopardize the fundamental rights (in particular Article 4 Charter). The ECJ recalled first of all the Member States' duty to interpret secondary legislation in a manner consistent with fundamental rights.[244] Subsequently, it examined REG 343/2003 and its underlying principle of mutual trust in light of Article 4 Charter. Finally, it concluded that a Member State, may *not*—pursuant to Article 4 Charter—transfer an asylum seeker to another Member State if there are substantial grounds for believing that there are systemic flaws in the asylum procedure in that Member State.[245] The *N.S. and M.E.* judgment was—paradoxically—at the same time predictable and refreshing. It was predictable, as it was difficult to imagine another outcome in view of the groundbreaking ECtHR's *M.S.S. v Belgium and Greece* judgment.[246] But, it was also refreshing, as it was the first time that the ECJ acknowledged in the area of freedom, security, and justice explicitly the need of limits to mutual trust on fundamental rights grounds.

In the aftermath of the *N.S. and M.E.* judgment the question was raised whether the ECJ's reasoning in asylum matters could be applied *mutatis mutandis* to criminal

the Third Pillar', *EuConst* 2009, 107; C. JANSSENS, 'Case Note under ECJ, 3 May 2007, *Advocaten voor de wereld*, Case C-303/05', *Col. J. Eur. L.* 2007/2008, 169–87. More sceptical: V. FRANSSEN, 'Het Europees aanhoudingsbevel gered, hoera?', *R.W.* 2008, 1138–44; F. GEYER, 'European Arrest Warrant. Court of Justice, Judgment of 3 May 2007, *Advocaten voor de wereld*', *EuConst*, 2008, 149, 161; R. MICHALKE, 'EU-Vertragskonformität des Rahmenbeschlusses über Europäischen Haftbefehl', *EuZW* 2007, 373–8; D. SARMIENTO, 'European Union: The European Arrest Warrant and the Quest for Constitutional Coherence', *IJCL* 2008, 171–83.

[241] ECJ, Case C-123/08 *Wolzenburg* [2009] ECR I-9621, para 45.

[242] ECJ, Case C-42/11 *Lopes Da Silva Jorge*, nyr, para 39.

[243] ECJ, Joined Cases C-411/10 and C-493/10 *N.S. and M.E.*, nyr.

[244] ECJ, Joined Cases C-411/10 and C-493/10 *N.S. and M.E.*, nyr, paras 77 and 99.

[245] ECJ, Joined Cases C-411/10 and C-493/10 *N.S. and M.E.*, nyr, paras 86–106.

[246] ECtHR, 21 January 2011, *M.S.S. v Belgium and Greece*, 30696/09.

matters and thus whether in the latter context fundamental rights could set a limit to the principles of mutual trust and mutual recognition.[247] Expectations ran high when the ECJ was about to deliver its *Radu* and *Melloni* judgments, in particular in light of the AG's promising opinions.

In *Radu* the ECJ was asked to decide whether a national court is entitled not to execute a European Arrest Warrant if there is a breach with fundamental rights, even if that ground for non-execution is not provided in the FD EAW.[248] Contrary to its AG—who built up a general theory as to whether and under which circumstances Member States should be entitled to refuse arrest warrants on the basis of breaches of fundamental right—[249] the ECJ focused on the compliance of the right to be heard as included in FD EAW with the Charter. The ECJ first had a look at the specific issues of the case at hand: Mr Radu had been subject to several arrest warrants issued for the purpose of conducting criminal investigations related to the offence of robbery, he had not consented to his surrender to Germany and he had argued before the Romanian (referring) judge that the fact that he had not been heard by the issuing judge before the arrest warrants were issued, constituted a breach of Articles 47 and 48 Charter and Article 6 ECHR. The ECJ then started by recalling the purpose of FD EAW, its obligatory nature and the exhaustive[250] nature of the list of the non-execution grounds, before observing that the right to be heard *before* an arrest warrant is issued is *not* included in that list. If the exhaustive nature of the list of grounds of non-recognition had been vital, the ECJ could have concluded its judgment here. Yet, instead, the ECJ continued its reasoning—in order to examine the relevance of Articles 47 and 48 Charter for the present case. It stated that 'the observance of *Articles 47 and 48 of the Charter* of Fundamental Rights of the European Union *does not require* that a judicial authority of a Member State should be able to refuse to execute a European Arrest Warrant issued for the purposes of conducting a criminal prosecution on the ground that the requested person was not heard by the issuing judicial authorities before that arrest warrant was issued' (emphasis added)[251] and it gave some convincing arguments to support this finding.[252] This paragraph is a crucial point in the judgment for at least two reasons. First, it refers to the above-mentioned duty to interpret and to apply secondary legislation in conformity with fundamental rights. Secondly, it explains—in my view—the different outcome in *Radu* when compared to the *N.S. and M.E.* judgment. Indeed, whilst in *N.S. and M.E.* a moderation of the principle of mutual trust was necessary in order to avoid a breach of Article 4 Charter, in *Radu* there was simply no breach of the Charter and therefore no need to moderate the principles of mutual recognition and trust.

[247] See, for instance: G. DE BAERE, 'N.S. v. Secretary of State for the Home Department', *American Journal of International Law* 2012, 622; M. DEN HEIJER, 'Case Note N.S. and M.E.', *CML Rev.* 2012, 1745; S. PEERS, 'Analysis Court of Justice: The NS and ME Opinions—The Death of "Mutual Trust"?', 1, retrievable at: <http://www.statewatch.org/analyses/no-148-dublin-mutual-trust.pdf>.

[248] ECJ, Case C-396/11 *Radu*, nyr. Prior to the *Radu* judgment, this question had also been raised—but left unanswered—in *I.B.*: ECJ, Case C-306/09 *I.B.* [2010] ECR I-10341, para 63.

[249] Opinion of AG Sharpston in Case C-396/11 *Radu*, nyr, § 68–72. With regard to the important role that fundamental rights ought to play in this context, see also: Opinion of AG Cruz Villalón in Case C-306/09 *I.B.* [2010] ECR I-10341, § 43; Opinion of AG Mengozzi in Case C-42/11 *Lopes Da Silva Jorge*, nyr, § 27–9.

[250] ECJ, Case C-396/11 *Radu*, nyr, para 36. The ECJ stated—with reference to previous case law on the FD EAW—that 'the Member State may refuse to execute such a warrant *only* in the cases of [...] Article 3 and [...] Articles 4 and 4a' (emphasis added).

[251] ECJ, Case C-396/11 *Radu*, nyr, para 39.

[252] ECJ, Case C-396/11 *Radu*, nyr, paras 40–3.

In *Melloni*, the ECJ is not only asked to decide whether a Member State is entitled to rely on national constitutional law pursuant to Article 53 Charter,[253] but it is also confronted with the national court's argument that 'the obligation to respect fundamental rights as enshrined in Article 6 TEU allows the executing judicial authorities to refuse to execute the European Arrest Warrant including in the situation of Article 4(a) FD EAW'.[254] The ECJ neither rejects not confirms such a general margin of discretion to the executing authority; it chooses to reformulate this argument into a question of the compatibility of Article 4(a) FD EAW with Articles 47 and 48 Charter.[255] After scrutinizing Article 4(a) FD EAW in light of the ECtHR's case law, it concludes—like in *Radu*—that FD EAW is compatible with Articles 47 and 48 Charter.[256]

Unlike the two preceding judgments, *Jeremy F.* does not concern the issue whether an executing judicial authority is entitled not to recognize a European Arrest Warrant on the basis of fundamental rights grounds, but concerns the question whether Articles 27 and 28 FD EAW prevent a Member State from providing for an appeal suspending the execution of a decision extending the effects of a European Arrest Warrant.[257] The ECJ observes, first of all, that such an appeal is not explicitly foreseen in the FD EAW. It is noteworthy that the ECJ—prior to analysing whether the inclusion of such an appeal in a national implementation legislation falls within a Member State's margin of discretion in the context of the FD EAW—[258] starts by examining whether the absence of such an appeal in the FD EAW is reconcilable with the Charter (Art. 47 Charter).[259] By taking this approach the ECJ confirms—by analogy with *Radu* and *Melloni*—the strict obligation to interpret and apply the FD EAW in harmony with the Charter.

Admittedly, a more explicit position of the ECJ in *Radu* and *Melloni* vis-à-vis an executing judicial authority's power not to recognize a European Arrest Warrant in exceptional circumstances where fundamental rights are under threat, in line with the *N.S. and M.E.* judgment, would have been enlightening and most welcome in view of the current debate. However, *Radu* and *Melloni* should not overly disappoint us either for not having given a clear answer yet.[260] They were simply—in my view—not the right cases in which to introduce this line of reasoning. If fundamental rights had truly been in danger, the outcome and the legal reasoning would doubtless have been different. Thus, if we are to learn anything at all from the *N.S. and M.E.*, *Radu*, and *Melloni* judgments it is that the FD EAW must be interpreted and applied in light of the Charter and that one of the most difficult tasks of constructing an area of freedom, security, and justice—which rests on both the ECJ and the national judicial authorities—consists of distinguishing between cases where fundamental rights are truly under threat (e.g. *N.S. and M.E.*) and

[253] See: Part II, ch 2, III, B, 1. 'Limits linked to the need to safeguard domestic criminal justice concerns'.

[254] ECJ, Case C-399/11 *Melloni*, nyr, para 45.

[255] ECJ, Case C-399/11 *Melloni*, nyr.

[256] ECJ, Case C-399/11 *Melloni*, nyr, paras 48–54.

[257] ECJ, Case C-168/13 PPU *Jeremy F.*, nyr, para 27.

[258] ECJ, Case C-168/13 PPU *Jeremy F.*, nyr, paras 54–74, where the ECJ accepts that Member States are entitled—but not obliged—to foresee an appeal in the context of Articles 27 and 28 FD EAW, but only to the extent that they respect the time limits foreseen in Article 17 FD EAW.

[259] ECJ, Case C-168/13 PPU *Jeremy F.*, nyr, paras 42–7, where the ECJ concludes that the FD EAW is in perfect agreement with Article 47 Charter.

[260] For some disappointment, see: L. DELGADO, 'Droits fondamentaux et reconnaissance mutuelle: une jurisprudence troublante ou simplement prudente?', February 2013, retrievable at: <http://www.gdr-elsj.eu/>; H. LABAYLE, 'Mandat d'arrêt européen et degré de protection des droits fondamentaux, quand la confiance se fait aveugle', March 2013, retrievable at: <http://www.gdr-elsj.eu/>.

cases where a suspected person is trying to place himself outside the reach of the law (e.g. *Radu* and *Melloni*).[261]

To conclude, I come back to the question that I posed at the beginning of this heading: is an explicit fundamental rights exception ground needed? I agree with the Commission that it would be superfluous to introduce an explicit fundamental rights exception in an EU instrument established between Member States which are all members of the ECHR, which have all adopted the EU Treaty (including its explicit reference to the protection of fundamental rights in Articles 6 and 7 TEU), and which have all subscribed to the Charter.[262] In such a system, breaches of fundamental rights should remain exceptional. Yet, exceptionally, they do occur,[263] and when they occur, such breaches can and should constitute a bar to the application of the principle of mutual recognition. As I see it, the thorny question is not whether the European *ordre public* can constitute a limit to the principle of mutual recognition. In view of the reasons I exposed above, I believe it can. Questions relate more to the extent to which an executing Member State is entitled to control 'fundamental rights'-based arguments, and also to which elements are considered sufficient for setting aside the principle of mutual recognition. In this regard, it has been argued that a slight difference in the degree of protection afforded by two Member States would not have to amount to a ground for non-recognition, whereas a 'sufficient' breach of a fundamental right would.[264] This latter issue will be discussed in more detail under the next heading.[265]

C. Limits linked to the level of control left to the executing Member State

The introduction of the principle of mutual recognition in the FD EAW has on some occasions created the false impression that this new system is based on blind surrender.[266] Under this heading, I first demonstrate that despite the limited powers of control granted to the executing Member States, it would be incorrect to state that the principle of mutual recognition that is included in the framework decisions is based on a blind or fully automatic regime of recognition and execution (section C, 1). Secondly, I assess the extent to which an executing Member State can carry out certain controlling

[261] On the need of reconciling the different objectives underlying the creation of an area of freedom, security and justice, see: Opinion of AG Bot, in Case C-399/11 *Melloni*, nyr, § 107–19.

[262] Report from the Commission based on Article 34 of the Council Framework Decision of 13 June 2002—The European arrest warrant and the surrender procedures between Member States, COM (2005) 63 final, p. 6. Slightly surprising was the Commission's more recent position with regard to the PROP DIR EIO in which it suggested to introduce one more ground for refusal namely 'when there are substantial grounds that indicate that the person to be transferred would face the real risk of being subjected to inhuman or degrading treatment or punishment': <http://ec.europa.eu/justice/news/intro/doc/comment_2010_08_24_en.pdf>, p. 25.

[263] The ECJ has acknowledged this explicitly in the area of asylum law in: ECJ, Joined Cases C-411/10 and C-493/10 *N.S. and M.E.*, nyr, paras 80–1 and paras 100–4. See also: Opinion of AG Sharpston in Case C-396/11 *Radu*, nyr, § 41, who stated that 'while the record of the Member States in complying with their human rights obligations may be commendable, it is also not pristine'.

[264] G. CORSTENS, 'Europeanisering van het strafrecht en de steun van de bevolking', in DERUYCK, DE SWAEF, ROZIE, ROZIE, TRAEST, and VERSTRAETEN (eds.), *De wet voorbij. Liber amicorum Luc Huybrechts* (n 65) 29.

[265] See: Part II, ch 2, III, C. 'Limits linked to the level of control left to the executing Member State'.

[266] G.VERMEULEN 'U vraagt, wij draaien ... Europees aanhoudingsbevel leidt tot blinde overlevering verdachten en veroordeelden', *De Juristenkrant* 2003, No. 57, 3–4; SCHÜNEMANN, 'Europäischer Haftbefehl und EU-Verfassungsentwurf auf schieber Ebene' (n 117) 185–9.

activities in the extraterritorial context that the mutual recognition instruments imply (section C, 2).

(1) Margin of control left to the executing Member State

As I have already indicated, most framework decisions contain a standard clause according to which the competent authorities in the executing state are to recognize a decision transmitted in accordance with the relevant provisions of the framework decision without any further formality being required and take all the necessary measures for its execution, unless the competent authority decides to invoke one of the grounds for non-recognition or non-execution.

This type of clause, especially the wording 'without any further formality' and 'forthwith', gives a first indication of the limited power of control that is left to the executing Member State. The executing court is not entitled to examine the substance of the case and must, for instance when surrendering proceedings, refrain from assessing the evidence and from delivering a judgment as to guilt. The partial abolition of the verification of the dual criminality requirement runs along these lines: whenever an order or warrant concerns a 'list offence', the executing Member State is not entitled to verify whether this offence is also forbidden under its own law.

However, the standard clause on recognition and execution that I mentioned at the beginning of this section also contains two elements that hint at some degree of controlling power for the executing Member State, namely (i) a chance to check whether the warrant or order is complete and satisfying (section 1.1) and (ii) a chance to invoke grounds for non-recognition and non-execution (section 1.2). The FD EAW also contains a number of other elements which influence the margin of control left to the executing Member State (section 1.3).

1.1. Presumed inaccuracy or incompleteness of a European warrant or order

Unlike all subsequent framework decisions on mutual recognitions in criminal matters, the FD EAW does not explicitly include within the list of grounds for non-recognition a specific ground for refusing to recognize and execute a decision if the warrant is incomplete or evidently fails to correspond to the decision. This has raised questions about the extent to which an executing judicial authority is entitled to verify and/or react to presumed inaccuracies in an EAW.

The FD EAW contains several provisions which suggest that the executing authority retains a certain margin of control with regard to the completeness and accuracy of the EAW file. This is evidenced by Article 1(2) FD EAW (which requires Member States to execute an EAW in accordance with the relevant provision of the FD) when read together with Article 8 FD EAW (which gives a detailed overview of the information that a EAW must contain) and Article 15(1) FD EAW (which stipulates that if the executing judicial authority considers the information communicated by the issuing Member State insufficient to allow it to decide on surrender, it shall request that the necessary supplementary information is supplied).

Before examining the relevant ECJ case law, which is still being developed in this area, it may be interesting to observe how national judicial authorities have dealt with this issue in their day-to-day application of the FD EAW. An analysis of this national case law does indeed reveal that the inaccuracy (e.g. wrong date of birth, a careless translation, an extremely vague description of the offence) or incompleteness (e.g. a missing fax number or e-mail address for the issuing authority) of an EAW file has frequently been invoked by defendants in an attempt to prevent their surrender.[267] The way in which the various executing authorities have reacted to these arguments show signs of both convergence and divergence,[268] yet some general conclusions can nevertheless be drawn from this case law. First, national judicial authorities generally appear to be unconcerned about minor shortcomings in the system, especially where the EAW applies to serious offences. Secondly, they tend to make a distinction between major and minor shortcomings depending on the objective that is being pursued with the required information and whether this objective can be achieved with alternative information. Thirdly, most national judicial authorities perform their controlling activities in a spirit of cooperation by contacting the issuing authority in order to enable it to rectify any erroneous information and/or supply additional information. Next, leaving aside a small number of dubious judgments, national judicial authorities appear fully aware that they may only ask for the information that is required by the FD EAW itself and that under no circumstances may they proceed to reassess the facts underpinning the case or to interpret the foreign legislation in light of their own national legislation. This summary[269] demonstrates, in my view, that national judicial authorities have generally been performing their controlling activities in accordance with both the spirit and the provisions of the FD EAW and the EU acquis.

Furthermore, the guidelines provided are not only relevant for the FD EAW but—*mutatis mutandis*—may also apply in relation to the other framework decisions. In sum, an executing Member State is entitled to verify, prior to recognizing and executing an EU order, that the conditions for recognition and execution as described in the relevant framework decision have been met and, especially, that the file is complete. An executing court which receives an incomplete or obviously incorrect file is entitled to refuse to recognize the order or warrant, though not—in principle[270]—after having consulted the competent authority in the issuing Member State and having requested that any necessary information be supplied where appropriate. A preceding duty of cooperation and direct contact therefore exists between the two Member States. If the executing authority remains convinced that the order is incomplete or incorrect following consultation, however, it is again entitled to refuse to recognize and execute the order. In view of the fact that, according to settled national case law, restrictions to the principle of mutual recognition are to be interpreted restrictively, it should be assumed that only serious shortcomings or manifest inaccuracies will suffice to suspend the principle of mutual recognition. Furthermore, there are also reasons to argue that in cases of minor

[267] JANSSENS, 'De burger, de Unie en het Europees aanhoudingsbevel: op zoek naar het juiste evenwicht tussen vrijheid, veiligheid en rechtvaardigheid' (n 62) 32–9.

[268] JANSSENS, 'De burger, de Unie en het Europees aanhoudingsbevel: op zoek naar het juiste evenwicht tussen vrijheid, veiligheid en rechtvaardigheid' (n 62).

[269] JANSSENS, 'De burger, de Unie en het Europees aanhoudingsbevel: op zoek naar het juiste evenwicht tussen vrijheid, veiligheid en rechtvaardigheid' (n 62), for an in-depth analysis and reference to the relevant national case law.

[270] In the FD EOFPE and the DIR EPO a prior consultation of the issuing Member State's competent authority does not seem to be mandatory as the relevant provisions respectively state that 'the competent judicial authority *may* specify a deadline for its presentation, completion or correction' (Art. 7 (2) (a) FD EOFPE), and that an authority may refuse to recognize a EPO if it 'is not complete *or* has not been completed within the time limit set by the competent authority of the executing State'. By contrast, in all other instruments there is clear duty to do so. See, for instance: '… the executing Member State *shall* consult the issuing authority and ask it to supply any necessary information' (Art. 7(3) FD MRFP).

shortcomings or irregularities, national authorities should be entitled to perform an *a posteriori* correction.[271]

In sum, the executing judicial authority does have some powers of control with regard to warrants or orders issued by another Member State's competent judicial authority, though these powers are not unlimited.

1.2. The application of grounds for non-recognition and non-execution

The duty of mutual recognition also applies unless the competent authority decides to invoke one of the grounds for non-recognition or non-execution. This description of the process reveals, once again, that the executing Member State does have some discretionary power to examine the order or warrant, particularly in order to verify whether one of the grounds for non-recognition and non-execution can be applied.

Questions arise in this regard, first as to the margin of discretion that is left to the executing Member State in implementing the grounds for non-recognition in its national legislation (section 1.2.1) and secondly as to the executing judicial authority's discretionary powers in applying these grounds to a specific case (section 1.2.2). Both aspects have come under discussion in the ECJ's case law on the FD EAW.

1.2.1. Margin of discretion in implementing the grounds for non-recognition and non-execution in national law

The way in which the national legislators have implemented the framework decisions' grounds for non-recognition and non-execution may be very decisive for the competent courts' discretionary powers of control and must therefore be discussed first.[272] In this regard, it is, first of all, necessary to highlight the difference between situations in which there is a definition at EU level and those in which there is no common definition. If a ground for non-recognition and non-execution has been the subject of a common definition within the EU, Member States will have little room for manoeuvre in applying national standards, whereas their margin of action will be considerably greater in the absence of approximation.[273]

The FD EAW provides for a system of *mandatory* grounds for non-recognition and non-execution ('the executing judicial authority *shall* refuse to execute')[274] and *optional* grounds ('the executing judicial authority *may* refuse')[275] which initially appears to grant the executing judicial authority a significant margin of discretion. However, many Member States have interpreted the article on 'optional' grounds to mean that they can decide in their national implementation legislation whether or not a judicial authority is required to refuse surrender whenever one of these grounds is applicable.[276] Following

[271] See, for instance, by analogy with the area of judicial cooperation in civil matters: ECJ, Case C-92/12PPU *Health Service Executive*, nyr, para 95.

[272] In fact, some of the Member States' legislation on the EAW's grounds for non-recognition and non-execution are a gold mine for potential infringement procedures by the Commission once the Treaty of Lisbon's temporary derogation with regard to the competences of the Commission and the ECJ will have expired (Art. 10 Protocol No 36 on transitional provisions). For some examples of bad implementation in this regard, see: Report from the Commission based on Article 34 of the Council Framework Decision of 13 June 2002—The European arrest warrant and the surrender procedures between Member States (revised version), COM (2006) 8 final.

[273] See, for instance: Opinion of AG Bot, in Case C-399/11 *Melloni*, nyr, § 124–7. See also: Part II, ch 2, II, B. 'Approximation measures and cooperation duties for enhancing trust and mutual recognition'.

[274] Article 3 FD EAW. [275] Article 4 FD EAW.

[276] Commission staff working document—Annex to the Report from the Commission based on Article 34 of the Council Framework Decision of 13 June 2002 on the European arrest warrant and the surrender procedures between Member States (revised version), SEC (2006) 79, p. 10.

this interpretation, many Member States have converted the system of optional grounds into a system of mandatory grounds, thus restricting the executing judicial authority's margin of discretion.

In the *Wolzenburg* case,[277] the ECJ was forced to take a position on this issue in relation to one of the FD EAW's optional grounds, namely that which stipulates that 'the executing judicial authority may refuse to surrender if the European Arrest Warrant has been issued for the purpose of the execution of a custodial sentence [. . .] where the requested person is *staying in* or *is a national* or *a resident* of the executing Member State and that State undertakes to execute the sentence [. . .]' (emphasis added).[278]

Dutch implementation legislation had converted this optional ground into a mandatory one. Dutch law essentially stipulated that surrender of a Dutch national for the purposes of executing a custodial sentence would not be permitted (i.e. an unconditional mandatory ground), whereas the surrender of a resident would only be blocked provided that certain conditions were fulfilled, among which being the resident's possession of a permanent residence permit of indefinite duration and having been lawfully resident for a continuous period of five years (i.e. a conditional mandatory ground). It was precisely this different approach to nationals (automatic application of the ground for non-recognition) and residents (conditional application of the ground for non-recognition) and the subsequent question of whether such differentiation amounted to a form of discrimination prohibited by Article 18 TFEU, that formed the crucial elements of the ECJ's judgment.

The ECJ could not avoid addressing the issue of a Member State's discretionary power when implementing optional grounds for non-recognition into national legislation, and it explicitly recognized that 'the Member States have, of necessity, a certain margin of discretion'.[279] Starting from this premise, the ECJ examined the national provisions in light of the framework decision's purpose and of the EU acquis (in particular, Art. 18 TFEU) and finally decided to uphold—to a large extent—the Dutch provision at stake. The ECJ was indeed of the opinion that (only) the Dutch supplementary administrative requirements, especially the possession of a residence permit of indefinite duration, were incompatible with Article 4(6) FD EAW. Its conclusion, as in the preceding *Kozlowski* judgment,[280] appeared to be supported and balanced by two main elements: the principle of mutual recognition and the objective of enhancing a person's chances of (re) integrating into society. On the one hand, the ECJ appears to be in favour of a system that applies grounds for non-recognition conditionally (in the present case, a five-year residence requirement), based on the argument that such a system limits situations in which the executing judicial authority may refuse to surrender a requested person and thus reinforces[281] the system of surrender to the advantage of an area of freedom,

[277] ECJ, Case C-123/08 *Wolzenburg* [2009] ECR I-9621.

[278] Article 4(6) FD EAW.

[279] ECJ, Case C-123/08 *Wolzenburg* [2009] ECR I-9621, para 61.

[280] ECJ, Case C-66/08 *Kozlowski* [2008] ECR I-6041, paras 43 and 45. On the need of reconciling both objectives, see: Opinion of AG Mengozzi in Case C-42/11 *Lopes Da Silva Jorge*, nyr, § 36.

[281] Whether such a 'conditional' (but rigid) system indeed reinforces the principle of mutual recognition is not so convincing in my view. Admittedly, in the *Wolzenburg* case the application of the five-year residence requirement enhances the principle of mutual recognition. This is, however, not necessarily true in all cases. There might be other situations where the requested person complies with a five-year residence requirement, but does not speak the language of the Member State concerned, has no family ties over there, and has no job prospects. In such a context both the principle of mutual recognition and the reintegration objective would militate against the application of Article 4(6) FD EAW. However, since the national judge has been deprived of any margin of discretion, he simply cannot

security, and justice (i.e. a focus on the principle of mutual recognition).[282] On the other hand, however, the ECJ does not seem to resist a system which applies grounds for non-recognition to nationals automatically, as according to the ECJ nationals have a connection with their Member State of origin which is such that their social reintegration following enforcement of a sentence ought to be ensured (i.e. focus on reintegration in society).[283]

The ECJ's *Wolzenburg* decision is remarkable for two reasons. First, the ECJ's decision to accept the automatic application of a ground of non-recognition in the case of a national is a rare example of a non-restrictive attitude on the part of the ECJ towards limits to the principle of mutual recognition. It is striking, especially in light of the 'mutual recognition' approach and the new surrender regime within the EU, one of the most significant achievements of which is the generalization of the surrender of nationals.[284] It is hard to see how the ECJ will be able to maintain this rigid view[285] when confronted with future judgments on citizens with dual nationality or 'nationals' who have lived abroad for their entire lives. These cases are anything but straightforward in an EU which promotes the free movement of persons so intensively, as illustrated by the *Rottman* case.[286] Second, the ECJ's decision to allow Member States a considerable margin of discretion when converting optional grounds for non-recognition into conditional grounds for non-recognition in the case of non-nationals raises questions as to the outer limits of this margin of discretion.

Since the ECJ's more recent *Lopes Da Silva Jorge* judgment, it has become clear that the margin of discretion granted in *Wolzenburg* must be interpreted in light of the particular national context at issue in that case.[287] Unlike the *Wolzenburg* case, where the national legislation at stake actually implemented Article 4(6) FD EAW in relation to nationals of other EU Member States (by providing a conditional ground for non-recognition for non-national EU citizens), the French provisions under discussion in *Lopes Da Silva Jorge* automatically excluded all EU citizens who did not have the French nationality from the ground for non-recognition contained in Article 4(6) FD EAW. The ECJ, following its AG, examined the national provision in light of the FD EAW (taking into account the objectives of both mutual recognition and social reintegration) and the EU acquis (in particular Art. 18 TFEU) and ultimately condemned the French provision.

surrender and will be forced to apply Article 4(6) FD EAW: C. JANSSENS, 'Case Note *Wolzenburg*', *CML Rev.* 2010, 842. For a similar critique, see: S. DE BIOLLEY and A. WEYEMBERGH, 'Chronique de jurisprudence consacrée à l'espace de liberté, de sécurité et de justice. Jurisprudence de la Cour de justice relative au 3ème pilier du Traité sur l'Union européenne (2006–2009)', *C.D.E.* 2010, 204.

282 ECJ, Case C-123/08 *Wolzenburg* [2009] ECR I-9621, paras 56–9. For a previous mentioning of this main objective of the FD EAW, see for instance: ECJ, Case C-303/05 *Advocaten voor de wereld* [2007] ECR I-3633, para 31; ECJ, Case C-296/08 PPU *Goicoechea* [2008] ECR I-6307, paras 51, 55, and 76; ECJ, Case C-66/08 *Kozlowski* [2008] ECR I-6041, para 31.

283 ECJ, Case C-123/08 *Wolzenburg* [2009] ECR I-9621, para 70.

284 Council of the EU, *Handbook on the EAW* (n 27) p. 12. See also: Opinion of AG Bot in Case C-123/08 *Wolzenburg* [2009] ECR I-9621, § 126.

285 This formalistic view vis-à-vis dual nationality cases is also present in other areas of law (see, for instance: ECJ, Case C-168/08 *Hadadi* [2009] ECR, I-6871, para 55). However, the ECJ's (and AG's) reasoning in the more recent *McCarthy* judgment seems to hint at a more teleological approach and is to be welcomed: ECJ, Case C-434/09 *McCarthy*, [2011] ECR I-3375, paras 54–6 and the corresponding Opinion of AG Kokott at § 32–45.

286 ECJ, Case C-135/08 *Rottman* [2010] ECR I-1449.

287 Opinion of AG Mengozzi in Case C-42/11 *Lopes Da Silva Jorge*, nyr, § 38 and 43, who warns that care must be exercised when relying upon the *Wolzenburg* judgment.

In sum, by condemning both the requirement of a residence permit of indefinite duration (*Wolzenburg*) and a national legislation that prevented all nationals of other Member States from reaping the benefits provided by Article 4(6) FD EAW (*Lopes Da Silva Jorge*), the ECJ limited to a reasonable extent the margin of discretion that Member States could make use of in implementing framework decisions into their national legislation.

1.2.2. Margin of discretion in applying the grounds for non-recognition and non-execution

An executing authority's margin of control when deciding upon EAW requests is to a large extent determined by the national provisions implemented by the national legislator. Indeed, a national provision that includes detailed conditions for the application of a ground for non-recognition (such as a five-year residence requirement for non-nationals or an unconditional application of the ground for non-recognition for nationals, both in the *Wolzenburg* case) will leave a smaller margin of discretion to the national competent authority than a national provision that does not include such requirements (such as in the *Kozlowski* case).

Prior to *Wolzenburg*, the ECJ had already been asked to clarify the meaning of the terms 'resident' and 'staying' included in Article 4(6) FD EAW. In *Kozlowski*, the ECJ began by stating unequivocally that it followed from the need for uniform application of EU law and from the principle of equality that the terms of an EU provision which made no express reference to Member States' laws in order to determine its meaning and scope must normally be given autonomous and uniform interpretation throughout the Union with regard to the context of the provision and the objective pursued by the legislation in question.[288] Consequently, since the terms 'resident' and 'staying' constitute autonomous concepts of EU law, Member States are not entitled to give those terms a broader meaning in their national law than that which derives from such a uniform interpretation.[289] Thus, in underlining in this judgment that Member States are not entitled to give those terms a *broader*[290] meaning, the ECJ seems to confirm its traditional view that restrictions to the principle of mutual recognition must be interpreted restrictively.

Subsequently, the ECJ goes on to explain the contours of the executing authority's margin of discretion. The *Kozlowski* case is indeed a neat illustration of how the ECJ understands the executing authority's tasks when deciding upon the application of a ground for non-recognition. The executing authority is not entitled to apply 'blindly' a ground for non-recognition to a person who is 'staying' in that Member State; it may only refuse to execute an EAW when it has been ascertained whether the requested person is indeed 'staying' in that Member State in accordance with the guidelines developed by the ECJ. This implies that it is necessary for the competent authority of the executing Member State to make an overall assessment of various objective factors characterizing the situation of that person, which include, especially, the length, nature, and conditions of his or her stay and any family or economic connections held within the executing Member State.[291] Furthermore, once the executing authority has come to the conclusion that the requested person is indeed 'staying' in that Member State, it

[288] ECJ, Case C-66/08 *Kozlowski* [2008] ECR I-6041, para 42.

[289] ECJ, Case C-66/08 *Kozlowski* [2008] ECR I-6041, para 43.

[290] However, the ECJ did not yet address in this judgment the question whether Member States are entitled to give a more *restrictive* meaning to a uniform concept, which might, in the case of 'a resident', enhance the principle of mutual recognition. In the light of the subsequent *Wolzenburg* case, it has become clear that more restrictive conditions will only be accepted as far as these provisions are held compatible with the FD EAW's objectives and with the EU acquis.

[291] ECJ, Case C-66/08 *Kozlowski* [2008] ECR I-6041, para 48.

will still not be entitled to apply the ground for non-recognition automatically, as it will first need to be decided whether a legitimate interest exists which would justify the sentence imposed in the issuing Member State being executed on the territory of the executing Member State.[292] In sum, the *Kozlowski* judgment demonstrates that the executing Member State's task in deciding upon a ground for non-recognition is anything but passive or automatic.

When examining the application of a ground for non-recognition, the executing judicial authority will sometimes require information to be provided by the issuing judicial authority in order to make an adequate decision. For instance, in *Mantello*,[293] where the executing judicial authority had doubts as to whether it could refuse to surrender a person based on the *ne bis in idem* ground, it became clear just how influential the issuing authority's information could be.

The *Mantello* case raised interesting questions about the extent to which executing judicial authorities faced with incoming European Arrest Warrants are entitled to verify compliance with the principle of *ne bis in idem* (margin of control), especially in cases where the acts described—in this case, offences related to participation in a criminal organization—have already been judged in the *issuing* Member State. Most intervening Member States claimed 'that the judicial authorities which issue a European Arrest Warrant are required to ensure observance of it' and argued in light of the principles of mutual recognition and trust and of the prohibition of dual burdens that these principles also necessitate that 'those authorities are best placed to verify that the person against whom a European Arrest Warrant is issued has not already been sentenced in their State for the same acts'.[294] AG Bot opposed the Member States' point of view, arguing that it went against the system of the European Arrest Warrant as defined by the Framework Decision and that Article 3(2) FD EAW is the expression of a fundamental right.[295] AG Bot deduced from Article 3(2) FD EAW that it is not incumbent on the executing judicial authorities to ascertain of their own accord whether or not the acts referred to in the European Arrest Warrant have already been judged in the issuing Member State or elsewhere (no verification duty *ex ante*).[296] However, an executing judicial authority is obliged to begin an examination in order to assess whether or not Article 3(2) FD EAW is applicable upon being informed that the requested person has already been conclusively judged for the same acts (verification duty *ex post*).[297] This assessment, which implies verifying compliance with the EU *ne bis in idem* principle as defined by the ECJ,[298] will lead to the non-recognition of the EAW if the executing judicial authority concludes that the acts referred to in the European Arrest Warrant have already been the subject of a final judgment in the issuing Member State, or if, having received information to that effect and having questioned the issuing judicial authority in order to ascertain the accuracy of that information, the executing judicial authority receives no satisfactory response from the issuing judicial authority.[299]

[292] ECJ, Case C-66/08 *Kozlowski* [2008] ECR I-6041, para 44.
[293] ECJ, Case C-261/09 *Mantello* [2010] ECR I-11477.
[294] Opinion of AG Bot in Case C-261/09 *Mantello* [2010] ECR I-11477, § 72–4.
[295] Opinion of AG Bot in Case C-261/09 *Mantello* [2010] ECR I-11477, § 76.
[296] Opinion of AG Bot in Case C-261/09 *Mantello* [2010] ECR I-11477, § 82.
[297] Opinion of AG Bot in Case C-261/09 *Mantello* [2010] ECR I-11477, § 82.
[298] Opinion of AG Bot in Case C-261/09 *Mantello* [2010] ECR I-11477, § 93.
[299] Opinion of AG Bot in Case C-261/09 *Mantello* [2010] ECR I-11477, § 95.

In view of the fact that the exact contours of an executing authority's controlling powers are among the most delicate issues related to the principle of mutual recognition,[300] it is unsurprising that AG Bot's interesting and extensive elaborations on the controlling powers of the executing authority were not expanded on in the ECJ's *Mantello* judgment.[301] There is, furthermore, a legal argument which explains why the ECJ appeared far less concerned in *Mantello* with the controlling powers of the executing judicial authority and why it focused instead on the issuing authority's competence. In contrast to the AG, who examined the case in light of both the *idem* ('does it concern the same facts?') and *bis* ('does it concern a final judgment?') requirements, the ECJ analysed the case only from the latter perspective. This difference in approach had important consequences, not necessarily for the final outcome of the case (both the AG and the ECJ concluded that the *ne bis in idem* ground could not be applied here), but certainly for the delineation of the issuing and executing authorities' competences. In confirmation of the ECJ's traditional *ne bis in idem* case law,[302] the ECJ stated in *Mantello* that the executing authority's competence is considerably broader in the context of an *idem* approach (which requires autonomous EU interpretation rather than a focus on the legislation of one Member State) than in that of a *bis* approach (which is exclusively governed by the law of the Member State where the first judgment was passed). In line with this distinction, both the AG[303] and the ECJ[304] conclude that the issuing authority is responsible for replying to the question of whether a final judgment has taken place or not (*bis* requirement) and that the issuing authority's decision is in principle binding for the executing authority.[305]

It is certainly regrettable that *Mantello* did not shed more light on the contours of the executing authority's competence with regard to the interpretation of the *idem* requirement in the context of the FD EAW,[306] and more importantly on the relevant role and influence of fundamental rights in the application of grounds for non-recognition. This question—which was also passed by in other judgments,[307] despite strong insistence

[300] A. WEYEMBERGH, 'Arrêts *IB* et *Mantello*: le mandat d'arrêt européen', *J.D.E.* 2011, 73.

[301] For a critique on the limited attention paid to this issue in the ECJ's judgment, see: J. OUWERKERK, 'Case note *Mantello*', *CML Rev.* 2011, 1695; WEYEMBERGH, 'Arrêts *IB* et *Mantello*: le mandat d'arrêt européen' (n 300) 73.

[302] See: Part II, ch 1, IV, C. 'Margins of control left to the Member States when applying the *ne bis in idem* principle'.

[303] Opinion of AG Bot in Case C-261/09 *Mantello* [2010] ECR I-11477, § 131.

[304] ECJ, Case C-261/09 *Mantello* [2010] ECR I-11477, para 50.

[305] In *Mantello* the ECJ first recalled that Article 15(2) FD EAW, just like Article 57 CISA, allows the executing judicial authority to request from the judicial authority in whose territory a judgment has been delivered legal information on the precise nature of the judgment. Subsequently, it found that it was clear from the reply given by the issuing judicial authority that the first judgment could not be regarded as having definitively barred further prosecution at national level. Finally, it concluded that the executing judicial authority was obliged to draw all the appropriate conclusions from the assessments made by the issuing judicial authority in its response: ECJ, Case C-261/09 *Mantello* [2010] ECR I-11477, paras 48–50. The fact that in *Mantello* the concept of 'same facts' did not relate to a cross-border situation might have influenced the outcome of this specific case, yet at the same time it cannot be denied that the ECJ's focus on the prior consultation mechanism, which is installed in nearly all framework decisions (see, for instance: Art. 8(4) FD MRCO; Art. 9(3) FD MRCS; Art. 11(3) FD ESO (post-trial); Art. 13 (5) FD EEW), is a clear indication that decisions on non-recognition cannot just take place at random or automatically, but that they must be well-founded and are subject to cooperation duties.

[306] It is questionable whether the ECJ's traditional *ne bis in idem* case law (ECJ, Case C-367/05 *Kraaijenbrink* [2008] ECR I-6619, para 28) which confers a considerable power to the executing authority, is transposable to the specific context of the *Mantello* case where the relevant facts had all taken place in the issuing Member State.

[307] With regard to *Radu* and *Melloni*, see: Part II, ch 2, III, B, 2. 'Limits linked to the need to safeguard EU or international interests'.

by a number of AGs[308]—will inevitably return and will need to be addressed in future case law.

Finally, the executing judicial authority's decision regarding the application of a ground for non-recognition is not (only) dependent on prior feedback from the issuing Member State's judicial authority (*Mantello*), but is on some occasions also made subject to a prior consultation of Eurojust.[309] The mandatory nature of the consultation of a specialized, centralized EU body will prompt the executing authorities to examine the facts behind the ground for non-recognition carefully before referring it to Eurojust, and is thus a better guarantee of a well-founded decision on non-recognition.

1.3. The speciality rule, the guarantees and the executing authority's consent in cases of onward surrender as elements that influence the executing Member State's margin of control

In addition to the application of grounds for non-recognition, the executing authority's margin of discretion can also be deduced from other mechanisms that are contained in the FD EAW, particularly the speciality rule (Art. 27 FD EAW), the guarantees to be given by the issuing authority (Art. 5 FD EAW), and the consent needed in cases of onward surrender (Art. 28 FD EAW). The importance of the executing authority's controlling power results from these provisions in that they enable the executing authority to protect the rights and interests of the person surrendered, either by requesting application of the speciality rule, or by asking for guarantees, or by consenting (or refusing to consent) to onward surrender.

In *Leymann and Pustovarov*[310] and *Jeremy F.* (both on the speciality rule), *I.B.*[311] (on the guarantee for *in absentia* judgments), and *Melvin West*[312] (on consent in cases of onward surrender), the ECJ confirmed—by analogy with its case law on the grounds for non-recognition—that in the context of the FD EAW, the principle of mutual recognition does not imply an absolute obligation to recognize and execute a warrant.[313] By means of a contextual and teleological interpretation, the ECJ urges the executing authorities to pursue the objectives aimed at by the FD EAW.[314] While recognizing that efficient and expeditious surrender is the FD EAW's essential objective,[315] the ECJ does not at any point consider the other objectives to be of lesser importance or that exceptions to the main objective should be interpreted strictly.[316] Only by reconciling the

[308] See, for instance: View of AG Bot in Case C-66/08 *Kozlowski* [2008] ECR I-6041, § 106–7; Opinion of AG Cruz Villalón in Case C-306/09 *I.B.* [2010] ECR I-10341, § 43–5; Opinion of AG Bot in Case C-261/09 *Mantello* [2010] ECR I-11477, § 76; Opinion of AG Mengozzi in Case C-42/11 *Lopes Da Silva Jorge*, nyr, § 28; Opinion of AG Sharpston in Case C-396/11 *Radu*, nyr, § 63–97.

[309] Article 13(4) FD EEW.

[310] ECJ, Case C-388/08 PPU *Leymann and Pustovarov* [2008] ECR I-8993.

[311] ECJ, Case C-306/09 *I.B.* [2010] ECR I-10341.

[312] ECJ, Case C-192/12 PPU *Melvin West*, nyr.

[313] See, for instance: ECJ, Case C-306/09 *I.B.* [2010] ECR I-10341, para 50; ECJ, Case C-192/12 PPU *Melvin West*, nyr, para 64; ECJ, Case C-168/13 PPU *Jeremy F.*, para 36 and para 45, where the ECJ even underlines the need for sufficient judicial controls in EAW proceedings, as indicated in the FD EAW's Preamble.

[314] See, for instance: ECJ, Case C-388/08 PPU *Leymann and Pustovarov* [2008] ECR I-8993, paras 46–51; ECJ, Case C-306/09 *I.B.* [2010] ECR I-10341, paras 52 and 58; ECJ, Case C-192/12 PPU *Melvin West*, nyr, paras 53 and 70; ECJ, Case C-168/13 PPU *Jeremy F.*, paras 56–74.

[315] See, for instance: ECJ, Case C-388/08 PPU *Leymann and Pustovarov* [2008] ECR I-8993, para 42; ECJ, Case C-192/12 PPU *Melvin West*, nyr, para 53; ECJ, Case C-168/13 PPU *Jeremy F.*, para 58.

[316] Instead of focusing on either a restrictive or a non-restrictive interpretation, the ECJ has emphasized in its case law that it goes in search of an interpretation 'that does not prejudice the FD EAW's

different objectives involved will the executing authority be able to discharge its relevant duty, namely to protect the rights and interests of the person surrendered.[317]

(2) Controlling activities in an extraterritorial context

The application of the FD EAW has fostered debate on the relationship between mutual recognition and extraterritoriality in the context of judicial cooperation in criminal matters. In particular, two questions should be addressed here, namely the extent to which an executing authority is entitled to invoke a ground for non-recognition (i) in order to protect a value which—according to its national legislation—would come under threat in another Member State (section 2.1) and (ii) in order to react to another Member State's presumed misapplication of fundamental rights included in European or international instruments (section 2.2).

2.1. Protecting a (national) public interest under threat in another Member State

Of all of the relevant instruments on mutual recognition, the FD EAW is perhaps the most useful in demonstrating how an executing authority's decision not to recognize a European Arrest Warrant or to subject it to certain conditions entails extraterritorial consequences which may lead to the 'export' of national values related to either substantive or procedural national criminal law.

As far as *substantive* criminal law is concerned, we can take the example of a fictitious surrender case in which an issuing judicial authority from Member State B has issued a European Arrest Warrant to an executing judicial authority of Member State A concerning a performed abortion in Member State B which the latter Member State categorized under the FD EAW as 'murder'. If we assume that performing an abortion is perfectly legal in Member State A but prohibited by criminal law in Member State B, these different views as regards the reprehensibility of the behaviour at hand reveal a conflict of values and beg the question as to which criminal law system of values should prevail. Should a judge from Member State A be entitled to refrain from surrendering the defendant to Member State B (export and extraterritorial impact of the criminal law system of values of Member State A on the criminal proceedings in Member State B)? Or should a judge from Member State A be obliged to surrender (priority to the criminal law system of values of Member State B)? As discussed above,[318] the FD EAW's relevant provisions do not allow much room for discussion: it is the issuing Member State's legislation which will be the relevant framework for deciding whether the conduct in question is a list offence.[319] Consequently, if in our example the issuing authority of Member State B decides that it is a list offence, then mutual recognition must—in principle[320]—be applied and the

objectives': ECJ, Case C-388/08 PPU *Leymann and Pustovarov* [2008] ECR I-8993, para 56; ECJ, Case C-306/09 *I.B.*[2010] ECR I-10341, para 58; ECJ, Case C-192/12 PPU *Melvin West*, nyr, paras 56 and 77. Moreover, some AGs have made an explicit plea for a non-restrictive interpretation. See, for instance: Opinion of AG Cruz Villalón in Case C-306/09 *I.B.*[2010] ECR I-10341, § 43–5; Opinion of AG Sharpston in Case C-396/11 *Radu*, nyr, § 69.

[317] On this role of the executing authority, see: View of AG Cruz Villalón in Case C-192/12 PPU *Melvin West*, nyr, § 73 and § 80.

[318] See: Part II, ch 2, I, C, 1.1 'Equivalence and the partial abolition of the dual criminality check'.

[319] Article 2(1) FD EAW.

[320] See, in more detail: Part II, ch 2, I, C, 1.1 'Equivalence and the partial abolition of the dual criminality check'.

person must be surrendered. In other words, Member State A's legal framework will have no extraterritorial impact on the criminal investigations in Member State B.[321]

As far as *procedural* criminal law is concerned, we can refer to the *Melloni* judgment. In this case, a Spanish judge wondered whether it could make the surrender of Mr Melloni to Italy conditional on the right to have his conviction *in absentia* reviewed as required by the Spanish Constitution. This question—which, in case of an affirmative answer, would have amounted in my view to an extraterritorial application of the Spanish constitutional rule on judgments *in absentia*—was rejected by the ECJ. The ECJ's reason for refusing the prevalence of the Spanish constitutional provision was that the European legislator had exhaustively harmonized the circumstances in which the execution of a European Arrest Warrant issued for decisions rendered *in absentia* must be regarded as not infringing the rights of the defence. In this regard, the *Melloni* case distinguishes itself from the previous, fictitious example, where the conflict between the two national criminal justice systems concerned an issue which had not been harmonized by the EU legislator.

The existence of grounds for non-recognition linked to essential aspects of the national criminal justice system implies thus that national criminal justice systems can have extraterritorial consequences when these grounds are applied or invoked in the context of surrender. In view of the examples discussed above and taking into account that the ECJ has a tendency to interpret restrictions restrictively, it is to be expected that the ECJ will seek to limit the extraterritorial workings of national public policy exceptions as far as possible. Moreover, in cases where the national public interest has been harmonized at EU level, the extraterritorial dimension of the national public interest will be in principle non-existing.

2.2. Reacting to another Member State's presumed misapplication of fundamental rights

According to a literal reading of the framework decisions, no explicit grounds for non-recognition based on fundamental rights breaches exist besides the FD MRFP. I have already explained why I do not believe this necessarily implies that an executing authority would be prevented, in any event, from refusing to apply the principle of mutual recognition when faced with a serious breach of a fundamental right.[322] As the ECJ has not yet taken a clear stance on this issue,[323] it seems useful to refer to some of the ECtHR's relevant cases (section 2.2.1) as well as to some of the ECJ's judgments on two other fields of the area of freedom, security and justice—namely mutual recognition of judicial cooperation in civil matters (section 2.2.2) and asylum (section 2.2.3)—in order to sustain an argument in favour of the extraterritorial though well-defined application of an EU-wide fundamental rights protection ground.

[321] However, if the abortion had been performed (in whole or in part) on the territory of Member State A, the outcome would be different as Member State A would be entitled to refuse to surrender on the basis of the territoriality exception (Article 4(7)(a) FD EAW). In the latter hypothesis the conduct would have taken place in Member State A, therefore *this* Member State's public order would be affected or not affected and not Member State B's public order as in the first hypothesis.

[322] See: Part II, ch 2, III, B, 2. 'Limits linked to the need to safeguard EU or international interests'.

[323] See, however, the opinions of some AGs who have touched upon this issue: View of AG Bot in Case C-66/08 *Kozlowski* [2008] ECR I-6041, § 106–7; Opinion of AG Cruz Villalón in Case C-306/09 *I.B.* [2010] ECR I-10341, § 43–5; Opinion of AG Bot in Case C-261/09 *Mantello* [2010] ECR I-11477, §76; Opinion of AG Sharpston in Case C-396/11 *Radu*, nyr, § 63–97. See also: Part II, ch 2, III, B, 2. 'Limits linked to the need to safeguard EU or international interests'.

2.2.1. Guidelines provided by the ECtHR's case law

An analysis of national case law on the FD EAW reveals that in many surrender proceedings, defendants invoke a (potential) breach of one of their fundamental rights, especially Article 3 ECHR, Article 6 ECHR, and/or Article 8 ECHR, in order to preclude their surrender.[324] Likewise, in relation to the other framework decisions, possible interferences with these fundamental rights are more than likely to occur in the near future. It is therefore relevant to examine the extent to which a national judicial authority is entitled to refuse to execute a warrant whenever a breach of one of these rights appears imminent. In view of the frequent contact between the ECJ and the ECtHR and the mutual influence each has on the other's case law,[325] it may be interesting to assess which guidelines the ECtHR has developed in its case law, first with regard to a Contracting State's international obligations (under extradition and surrender regimes), and secondly with regard to a Contracting Party's duty to afford due significance to individuals' protection of their fundamental rights.

Answering questions about the extent to which a Contracting State can be obliged to set aside its international obligations of cooperation in order to prevent the potential violation of a fundamental right is no simple matter, as became clear in the ECtHR's reasoning in the *Soering* case, in which both Articles 3 and 6 ECHR came under discussion.[326] Before reaching its conclusion, the ECtHR made three crucial statements. First, the ECtHR recognized that as movement around the world becomes easier and crime takes on a larger, more international dimension, it is increasingly in the interests of all nations that suspected offenders who flee abroad should be brought to justice (hence the need for a powerful extradition mechanism which will curb the use of safe havens).[327] Secondly, it is not normally for the Convention institutions to make statements about the occurrence or otherwise of potential violations of the Convention.[328] Thirdly, the establishment of such a responsibility inevitably involves a comparison of the requesting country's conditions with the standards of Article 3 of the Convention (thus the extraterritorial application of 'European' standards).[329] In light of these findings, the ECtHR proposed a rather severe test: a Contracting State's decision to extradite a fugitive will only give rise to an issue under Article 3 where there are substantial grounds to believe that the person concerned is at genuine risk of being subjected to torture or to inhuman or degrading treatment or punishment in the receiving country,[330] or where

[324] JANSSENS, 'De burger, de Unie en het Europees aanhoudingsbevel: op zoek naar het juiste evenwicht tussen vrijheid, veiligheid en rechtvaardigheid' (n 62) 50–8. For an overview of these (and other) ECHR's rights that have been discussed in the ECtHR's case law in the context of extradition, see: ECtHR Press Unit, 'Expulsions and extraditions', October 2012, retrievable at:<http://www.echr.coe.int/Documents/FS_Expulsions_Extraditions_ENG.pdf>.

[325] Declaration on Article 6(2) of the Treaty on European Union (attached to the Treaty of Lisbon); SIR NICOLAS BRATZA, 'Interface between the EU and the ECHR', speech given at the Conference 'Mutual trust—A Mutual Challenge', London, Aire Centre, 12 February 2010; K. LENAERTS, 'European Justice as a Control of Mutual Cooperation of EU Member States: the Principle of *ne bis in idem* and Conflicts of Competences as Challenges', speech given at the Conference 'Criminal Justice in Europe: Challenges, Principles and Perspectives', Luxembourg, University of Luxembourg, 22–23 October 2010.

[326] On the relevance—still today—of the *Soering* judgment as the first judgment in which the ECtHR authoritatively stated that extradition may raise issues under Article 3 and engage the responsibility of the extradition state, see, for instance: C. NICHOLLS, C. MONTGOMERY, and J. KNOWLES, *The Law of Extradition and Mutual Assistance* (Oxford, Oxford University Press, 2007) 121 ff.

[327] ECtHR, 7 July 1989, *Soering v United Kingdom*, 14038/88, para 89.

[328] ECtHR, 7 July 1989, *Soering v United Kingdom*, 14038/88, para 90.

[329] ECtHR, 7 July 1989, *Soering v United Kingdom*, 14038/88, para 91.

[330] ECtHR, 7 July 1989, *Soering v United Kingdom*, 14038/88, para 91.

the facts of the case comprise substantial grounds for believing that the applicant could genuinely be exposed to a flagrant denial of Article 6 rights in the receiving country.[331]

In relation to Article 3 ECHR, the use of the terms 'substantial grounds' and 'genuine risk' is a clear indication that a Contracting State is not required to set aside its duties of international cooperation for just any suspicion of a potential breach; this should be done only in cases where the risk can be identified precisely and where the evidence is serious and confirmed.[332] The ECtHR made it clear that this test not only applies in cases where third countries are involved, but also in cases between two Contracting States, or two EU Member States.[333] The assumption that Contracting States ought to apply the Convention correctly is not irrefutable,[334] and Contracting States are required to set this assumption aside and abstain from extraditing a person to another Contracting State whenever it has been established beyond reasonable doubt that at the time of the decision to extradite there were serious and well-founded reasons to believe that extradition would expose the person(s) involved to real, personal risk of inhuman or degrading treatment.[335] In determining whether there are substantial grounds to believe that a real risk of treatment that contravenes Article 3 exists, the ECtHR examines the facts as a whole through a detailed and in-depth examination which renders the decision a serious task for the requested state, since it will be obliged to take all precautions necessary throughout its consideration of whether to extradite.[336] Whilst in *Soering* the ECtHR held that the risk of ill-treatment should be balanced against the danger the person involved posed,[337] the ECtHR rejected such a balancing test explicitly in

[331] ECtHR, 7 July 1989, *Soering v United Kingdom*, 14038/88, para 113.

[332] ECtHR, 12 April 2005, *Chamaïev v Georgia and Russia*, 3678/02, paras 352, 366–7 and 372; ECtHR, 21 January 2011, *M.S.S. v Belgium and Greece*, 30696/09, para 353; ECtHR, 10 February 2011, *Dzhaksybergenov v Ukraine*, 12343/10, para 37. This case law clearly indicates that denouncing a general situation in a state will not easily be accepted as 'serious' evidence, whereas the availability of several international reports will be far more convincing evidence for a breach of Article 3 ECHR. See also: ECtHR, 7 June 2007, *Garabayev v Russia*, 38411/02, para 76, where the ECtHR 'adopts the standard of proof "beyond reasonable doubt" but adds that such proof may follow from the coexistence of sufficiently strong, clear and concordant inferences or of similar unrebutted presumptions of fact'.

[333] See, for instance, albeit not within the context of extradition, but with regard to the application of the Dublin II Convention: ECtHR, 21 January 2011, *M.S.S. v Belgium and Greece*, 30696/09 (which should be read together with ECtHR, 2 December 2008, *K.R.S. v UK*, 32733/08).

[334] ECtHR, 21 January 2011, *M.S.S. v Belgium and Greece*, 30696/09, paras 354 and 359, where—in the presence of a large amount of reliable sources which had reported practices which were manifestly contrary to the ECHR—the ECtHR held that Belgium 'could not merely assume that the applicant would be treated in conformity with the Convention standards but, on the contrary, that first it had to verify how the Greek authorities applied their legislation on asylum in practice'. With regard to the implications of this judgment for the EU legal order, see: Part II, ch 2, III, C, 2.2.3. 'Guidelines provided by the ECJ's case law in the area of asylum'. More generally, on the 'assumption' of trust amongst Contracting States, which is highly relevant in the context of the EU, see, for instance: J. CALLEWAERT, 'Het EVRM en de Europese Unie: van Bosphorus naar Lissabon', *NTER* 2010, 105–6; O. DE SCHUTTER, 'The Two Europes of Human Rights: The Emerging Division of Tasks between the Council of Europe and the European Union in Promoting Human Rights in Europe', *Col. J. Eur. L.* 2008, 543.

[335] In view of the relatively high burden of proof, the ECHR has concluded, on several occasions, that the potential breach was not sufficiently demonstrated. See for instance ECtHR, *Chamaïev v Georgia and Russia*, 12 April 2005, 3678/02; ECtHR, *Mamatkulov and Askarov v Turkey*, 4 February 2005, 46827/99 and 46951/99.

[336] D. AZARIA, 'Part II. Minimum Standards—Protecting Individuals Involved in Transnational Criminal Proceedings', in Extradition. European Standards. Explanatory notes on the Council of Europe convention and protocols and minimum standards protecting persons subject to transnational criminal proceedings, Strasbourg, Council of Europe, 2006, retrievable at: <http://www.coe.int/t/dghl/standardsetting/pc-oc/978-92-8716076-8.pdf>, 126.

[337] ECtHR, 7 July 1989, *Soering v United Kingdom*, 14038/88, paras 89 and 110.

more recent case law where it underlined that 'the assessment of whether the minimum level of severity has been met for the purposes of Article 3 ECHR, can only be assessed independently of the reasons for removal or extradition'.[338] Despite the relatively high threshold,[339] Contracting States (including EU Member States) have occasionally been condemned by the ECtHR on the basis of Article 3 ECHR for extraditing or expelling persons to other Contracting Parties. Structural problems in certain EU Member States, such as overcrowding and inadequate living conditions in detention facilities[340] and the excessive length of pre-trial detention,[341] can raise issues under Article 3 ECHR. Similarly, in the EU context, executing judicial authorities will be required to keep the ECtHR's case law in mind when deciding upon European arrest or other warrants that originate from Member States where structural problems have been assessed on the basis of ECtHR judgments and/or other reliable sources. Moreover, it remains to be seen whether the ECJ will adopt rigorously the test laid down by the ECtHR or whether it will take another approach.

In relation to Article 6 ECHR, the burden of proof for a 'flagrant' denial is even more difficult to demonstrate. Not only has the ECtHR given a very narrow interpretation to both the concept of a 'flagrant' denial[342] and Article 6's application to extradition proceedings,[343] but it has also closely linked the requirement of a 'flagrant' denial to the question of whether an effective judicial remedy is available in the requesting (issuing) state.[344] Taking into account the fact that the ECtHR starts in its case law from the premise that a Contracting State is presumed[345] to comply with the requirement of having an effective judicial remedy,[346] and also that the ECtHR is of the opinion that it is

[338] ECtHR, 17 January 2012, *Harkins and Edwards v United Kingdom*, 9146/07 and 32650/07, paras 124–5, where the ECtHR held that it 'must be taken to have departed from the approach contemplated by paragraphs 90 and 110 of the *Soering* judgment'.

[339] For some examples of cases falling foul of Article 3, see, for instance: AZARIA, 'Part II. Minimum Standards' (n 336) 127; NICHOLLS, MONTGOMERY, and KNOWLES, *The Law of Extradition and Mutual Assistance* (n 326) 125. On the ECtHR's cautious attitude in finding that removal from the territory of a Contracting State would be contrary to Article 3, see: ECtHR, 17 January 2012, *Harkins and Edwards v United Kingdom*, 9146/07 and 32650/07, paras 129–31.

[340] See, for instance: ECtHR, 19 April 2001, *Peers v Greece*, 28524/95; ECtHR, 20 January 2009, *Slawomir Musical v Poland*, 28300/06; ECtHR, 16 July 2009, *Sudlejmanovic v Italy*, 22635/03; ECtHR, 22 January 2010, *Orchowski v Poland*, 17885/04. For an overview of some specific areas of concern, see: G. VERMEULEN, A. VAN KALMTHOUT, N. PATERSON, M. KNAPEN, P. VERBEKE, and W. DE BONDT, *Cross-border Execution of Judgements Involving Deprivation of Liberty in the EU: Overcoming Legal and Practical Problems through Flanking Measures* (Antwerp, Maklu, 2011) 70.

[341] See, for instance: ECtHR, 3 February 2009, *Kauczor v Poland*, 45219/06.

[342] See, for instance: ECtHR, 16 October 2001, *Einhorn v France*, 71555/01; ECtHR, 4 February 2005, *Mamatkulov & Askarov v Turkey*, 46827/99 and 46951/99; ECtHR, 9 May 2006, *Salem v Portugal*, 26844/04. See also: AZARIA, 'Part II. Minimum Standards' (n 336) 129; M.K.M. BOSCH, 'De flagrante schending van Artikel 6 EVRM anno 2010', *DD* 2010, 717.

[343] AZARIA, 'Part II. Minimum Standards' (n 336) 128; C. VAN DEN WYNGAERT, 'Applying the European Convention on Human Rights to Extradition: Opening Pandora's Box?', *ICLQ* 1990, 775.

[344] This will, in case of an affirmative answer, often lead to the verdict that there has been no violation of Article 6 ECHR. See, for instance: ECtHR, 16 October 2001, *Einhorn v France*, 71555/01. For a critical assessment of this *procedural* approach towards the interpretation of a 'flagrant' denial instead of a more substantive-based approach, see: BOSCH, 'De flagrante schending van Artikel 6 EVRM anno 2010' (n 342) 724–6.

[345] A presumption which the ECtHR seems to apply in this context more rigidly than in the context of absolute rights (Article 3 ECHR), where the ECtHR is not willing to tolerate any risks: A. KLIP, 'Noot bij HR 25 mei 2004', *N.J.* 2005, 243.

[346] See, for instance: ECtHR, 4 October 2007, *Cenaj v Greece and Albania*, 12049/06, and the comments on this judgment by V. GLERUM and N. ROZEMOND, in E. VAN SLIEDREGT, J.M. SJÖCRONA, and A.M.M. ORIE (eds.), *Handboek internationaal strafrecht* (Deventer, Kluwer, 2008) 225.

more appropriate for the issuing court to hear and determine the applicant's complaints in relation to the alleged unfairness caused by a breach of Article 6 ECHR than to leave this to be decided by the executing state,[347] it appears very difficult—yet not impossible[348]—to condemn a Contracting State on the basis of Article 6 ECHR.[349] Here too, it remains to be seen whether the ECJ will adopt rigorously the test laid down by the ECtHR or whether it will apply a less stringent test.[350]

A similar conclusion can be drawn with regard to the application of another non-absolute right in the context of extradition and/or surrender, namely Article 8 ECHR. In light of the ECtHR's case law in this specific area and of its Article 8 compliance test,[351] it is clear that the ECtHR is reluctant to identify breaches of Article 8 in cases where prisoners are kept at a great distance from their families for extended periods.[352] It is also clear that only extreme personal circumstances,[353] or cases where the procedure is manifestly disproportionate to the seriousness of the offence and the penalty that is

[347] ECtHR, 4 May 2010, *Stapleton v Ireland*, 56588/07, paras 29–30.

[348] See, for instance: ECtHR, 17 January 2012, *Othman v United Kingdom*, 8139/09.

[349] The ECtHR has confirmed this view recently in its *Stapleton v Ireland* decision with regard to a surrender case based on a FD EAW procedure between two EU Member States, Ireland and the UK. In this case the applicant had argued that a delay in prosecuting a crime in the UK had amounted to a breach of Article 6 ECHR and that, therefore, Ireland's decision to surrender him to the UK would be unlawful. The ECtHR disagreed considering that 'the facts of the present case did not disclose substantial grounds for believing that there would be a real risk that the applicant would be exposed to a flagrant denial of his Article 6 rights in the UK' and underlining that it would be more appropriate for the courts within the UK to hear and determine the applicant's complaints in relation to the alleged unfairness caused by delay as 'these issues are factually and legally more pertinent to the issuing state (the UK)'. ECtHR, 4 May 2010, *Stapleton v Ireland*, 56588/07, para 26 and paras 29–30. For a similar reticent attitude with regard to the application of Article 6 ECHR in the context of the FD EAW, see: ECtHR, 7 October 2008, *Monedero Angora v Spain*, 41138/05, where the ECtHR dismissed the case, holding that since the surrender procedure does not involve the assessment of criminal charges against the accused, Article 6 ECHR could not be held applicable.

[350] See, in this regard: Opinion of AG Sharpston in Case C- 396/11 *Radu*, nyr, § 79–97, who agrees that the test for refusal must be a rigorous one, but who is nevertheless of the opinion that the current ECtHR's test is unduly stringent. AG Sharpston therefore suggests a new test. Her point of departure is that 'the competent judicial authority of the State executing a European arrest warrant can refuse the request for surrender without being in breach of the obligations authorised by the founding Treaties and the other provisions of Community law, where it is shown that the human rights of the person whose surrender is requested have been infringed, or will be infringed, as part of or following the surrender process'. AG Sharpston makes, however, some refinements to this rule. First, such a refusal will be competent only in exceptional circumstances. Secondly, in cases involving Articles 5 and 6 of the Convention and/or Articles 6, 47, and 48 of the Charter, the infringement in question must be such as fundamentally to destroy the fairness of the process. Thirdly, the person alleging infringement must persuade the decision-maker that his objections are substantially well-founded. Finally, past infringements that are capable of remedy will not found such an objection.

[351] The ECtHR has established four criteria in order to verify the compatibility of the State's action with Article 8: (i) the existence of a family life; (ii) an interference with the right to private life; (iii) an interference which is in accordance with the law; (iv) a proportionality test (measure is founded on a legitimate aim and necessary in a democratic society). On these criteria and the elements that the ECtHR takes into account when applying the proportionality test, see: AZARIA, 'Part II. Minimum Standards' (n 336) 129–30.

[352] So far, the ECtHR has usually accepted that the proportionality test was met. See, for instance: ECtHR, 4 September 1995, *Raidl v Austria*, 25342/94; ECtHR, 8 December 1997, *Launder v UK*, 27279/95; ECtHR, 26 January 2010, *King v UK*, 9742/07. In *Boultif v Switzerland* the ECtHR accepted a breach of Article 8, but the latter case is less relevant as it concerned deportation (instead of extradition) and the prison sentence to which the person had been sentenced was served satisfactorily (ECtHR, 2 August 2001, *Boultif v Switzerland*, 54273/00, para 51).

[353] See, for instance: S. ALEGRE, Lecture in the International Seminar for Experts 'Justice and Home Affairs—Toward the Full Implementation of the Amsterdam Treaty', organized by the Cicero Foundation in Paris in the series *Great Debates* on 14–15 February 2002; NICHOLLS, MONTGOMERY

likely to be passed,[354] will lead to a violation of Article 8 ECHR in this context. The latter aspect, in particular, is highly relevant in the context of the FD EAW, where EAWs are sometimes issued for minor offences, with the result that offenders are released in the issuing Member State just a few days later. Such practices could possibly fall foul of Article 8 ECHR.

To date, the ECJ has not yet explicitly adopted the ECtHR's standpoint in any of its judgments on judicial cooperation in criminal matters. However, in two other policy fields of the area of freedom, security and justice, namely judicial cooperation in civil matters (in particular, the Brussels I Regulation and its predecessor, the Brussels Convention, section 2.2.2) and asylum (in particular, the Dublin Regulation, section 2.2.3), the ECJ's case law provides some interesting insights into how the ECJ's position in this area might develop in the future.

2.2.2. *Guidelines provided by the ECJ's case law in the area of mutual recognition in civil matters*

In *Krombach*, one of the crucial questions that the ECJ had to address was whether the court of a Member State in which enforcement of a civil claim was being sought in criminal proceedings was entitled to refuse this execution on the basis of a public policy ground, especially since the defendant had been denied access to legal representation.[355] The ECJ began by emphasizing that recourse to the public policy clause in former Article 27(1) of the Brussels Convention can be permitted only 'where recognition or enforcement of the judgment delivered in another Contracting State would be at variance to an unacceptable degree with the legal order of the State in which enforcement is sought inasmuch as it infringes a fundamental principle' and it continued by explaining that 'the infringement would have to constitute a manifest breach of a rule of law regarded as essential in the legal order of the State in which enforcement is sought or of a right recognised as being fundamental within that legal order'.[356] The ECJ's clear focus on a national public policy clause ('within *that* legal order') is converted into a European public policy concept towards the end of the judgment as the ECJ concludes that 'recourse to the public policy clause must be regarded as being possible in exceptional cases where the guarantees laid down in the legislation of the State of origin and in the Convention itself have been insufficient to protect the defendant from a manifest breach of his right to defend himself before the court of origin, *as recognised by the ECHR*' (emphasis added).[357] In establishing this close link between the fundamental

and KNOWLES, *The Law of Extradition and Mutual Assistance* (n 326) 134; M. SUMMERS, 'Interface between the EU and the ECHR', speech given at the Conference 'Mutual trust—A Mutual Challenge', London, Aire Centre, 12 February 2010.

[354] AZARIA, 'Part II. Minimum Standards' (n 336) 130, who refers to a recommendation issued by the Committee of Ministers to the States Parties to the ECHR, in which the states are required to bear in mind in extradition cases the hardship that might be caused by the extradition procedure to the person concerned and his or her family in cases where the procedure is manifestly disproportionate to the seriousness of the offence and when the penalty likely to be passed will not significantly exceed the minimum period of one-year detention or will not involve deprivation of liberty.

[355] ECJ, Case C-7/98 *Krombach* [2000] ECR I-1935.

[356] ECJ, Case C-7/98 *Krombach* [2000] ECR I-1935, para 37.

[357] ECJ, Case C-7/98 *Krombach* [2000] ECR I-1935, para 44. On the great relevance of the 'European' nature of the public policy concept in this judgment, see, for instance: S. ÁLVAREZ GONZÁLEZ, 'Orden público y reconocimiento de resoluciones extranjeras: límites a la valoración del juez nacional y orden público comunitario', *La Ley* 2000, No 5, 2005–09; R. GONZÁLEZ GONZÁLEZ, 'Límites a la construcción de un "orden público europeo" en materia de derechos fundamentales', *RDCE* 2000, 593–617.

rights protected by the ECHR at international level and national public policy, it has been argued that *Krombach* saw the ECJ translate a factor of resistance to integration (the public policy concept) into a factor of European integration.[358] The public policy clause should not, then, be seen as an expression of distrust, but rather as an element which might increase trust, as it is a useful instrument for remedying situations where unacceptable legislative divergences exist.[359] From this perspective, true integration among EU Member States not only implies common understanding of certain values and rights, in order to apply the principle of mutual recognition, but also common understanding of grounds that may constitute a bar to mutual recognition.

Before proceeding with an analysis of certain subsequent judgments in this area, we should first address the question of whether the *Krombach* ruling can be transposed to the area of judicial cooperation in criminal matters. Admittedly, none of the discussed framework decisions contains an explicit public policy clause like that of former Article 27(1) Brussels Convention or its successor Article 34(1) REG 44/2001.[360] However, this does not necessarily imply that *Krombach* as a whole would not be relevant for these framework decisions. In my view, it should be relevant at least as far as the European public policy concept is concerned. I have already highlighted the crucial role of fundamental rights within the EU legal order, and with the Treaty of Lisbon now in force, the major role that the ECJ is expected to play in the area of freedom, security, and justice can only increase, especially in relation to the approximation of fundamental (procedural) guarantees. Given the fact that the *Krombach* case exhibits so many (procedural) criminal law elements, it is hard to see how it could not have influence on the ECJ's future case law on the mutual recognition of criminal law judgments.[361] Furthermore, a number of the guarantees in Article 6 ECHR apply to both civil and criminal proceedings, which explains why the ECJ has occasionally referred to an ECtHR judgment on criminal matters when dealing with a civil procedure based on the former Brussels Convention or its successor REG 44/2001.[362]

Notwithstanding the ECJ's major contribution to the establishment of a European public policy concept in *Krombach*, several questions remained open, such as the extent to which an executing judicial authority is entitled to assess foreign proceedings in order to decide whether or not to apply the public policy argument. In *Krombach*, the situation was clear and unambiguous in fact and in law: the defendant was not heard at any time, had no opportunity to defend himself and had no means of appeal. Therefore, an in-depth assessment of the proceedings in the country of origin was redundant. In contrast, the proceedings of more recent cases held before state of origin courts have been more complex and the ECJ has been asked to provide some guidelines on how an executing judicial authority is to verify any alleged infringements. In *Eurofood*, the

[358] M. DELMAS-MARTY, 'Conclusions de l'ouvrage «Variations autour d'un droit commun. Premières rencontres de l'UMR de droit comparé de Paris »', in E. ALEJANDRO ALVAREZ et al (eds.), *Mireille Delmas-Marty et les années UMR* (Paris, Société de Législation Comparée, 2005) 232.

[359] L. CARBALLO PIÑEIRO, 'Orden jurídico comunitario, derechos fundamentales e interpretación del artículo 27.1 del Convenio de Bruselas', *La Ley* 2000, No 3, 1748–53.

[360] From 10 January 2015, the public policy (*ordre public*) clause included in Article 45(1)(a) REG 1215/2012 shall apply (Art. 81 REG 1215/2012).

[361] K. LENAERTS, 'Préface', in G. DE KERCHOVE and A. WEYEMBERGH (eds.), *La reconnaissance mutuelle des décisions judiciaires pénales dans l'Union européenne* (Brussels, Institut d'Etudes Européennes, 2001) 15–16, who also points at the *Krombach* judgment when evaluating the ECJ's role in the area of mutual recognition of criminal matters.

[362] ECJ, Case C-283/05 *ASML* [2006] ECR I-12041, para 28 and Opinion of AG Léger in Case C-283/05 *ASML* [2006] ECR I-12041, § 105–6. See also: ECJ, Case C-168/13 PPU *Jeremy F.*, nyr, para 50, where the ECJ refers to a judgment on civil matters when dealing with a case on the FD EAW.

ECJ explained that the question of the foreign measure's compatibility with the public policy concept had to be assessed 'having regard to the proceedings *as a whole* in the light of *all* the circumstances' (emphasis added).[363] Subsequently, in *Gambazzi*, the ECJ clarified this by stating that 'the assessment's sole purpose is to identify any *manifest and disproportionate* infringement of the right to be heard' (emphasis added).[364] For this purpose, 'the court must confine itself to identifying the legal remedies which were available and verifying that they offered the person involved the possibility of being heard, in compliance with the adversarial principle and the full exercise of the rights of defence'.[365] Needless to say, the ECtHR's case law may, in this regard, serve as an important yardstick.[366]

The ECJ has stated since *Krombach* that any review of the court's assessment of the merits of the case is not permitted as it would constitute a review of the judgment's substance, which is expressly prohibited in the applicable European legislation.[367] Moreover, in *Renault*, the ECJ explained that the principle of mutual recognition cannot be set aside solely on the ground that the executing court believes national or EU law to have been misapplied in the decision in question, unless such an error of law constitutes a manifest breach of a particular rule of law that is regarded as essential in the state's legal order.[368] The ECJ thus aims at striking a proper balance between guaranteeing that the principle of mutual recognition can be blocked whenever a fundamental breach of an essential rule of law occurs and avoiding an executing judicial authority's being able to claim the role of 'final arbiter' of how judges in other Member States apply European or national law.[369] With regard to the latter issue, namely where a foreign judicial authority has serious concerns about the application of a national or European provision by a judge in another Member State, the system of legal remedies in each Member State and the preliminary proceeding should afford sufficient guarantee to individuals.[370]

In sum, the ECJ's case law that was analysed here indicates that the objectives of the Brussels I Regulation—namely, mutual trust, mutual recognition, efficient and rapid procedures—cannot be attained by undermining in any way the right to a fair hearing. Moreover, a fair balance is required between, on the one hand, mutual trust in the administration of justice in the EU, and, on the other, respect for the rights of the defence.[371] This legal reasoning—which imposes with regard to the Brussels I Regulation a duty to interpret and apply the provisions in conformity with fundamental rights—can *mutatis*

[363] ECJ, Case C-341/04 *Eurofood* [2006] ECR I-3813, para 40.

[364] ECJ, Case C-394/07 *Gambazzi* [2009] ECR I-2563, para 46.

[365] ECJ, Case C-394/07 *Gambazzi* [2009] ECR I-2563.

[366] See, for instance: ECJ, Case C-283/05 *ASML* [2006] ECR I-12041, para 28.

[367] ECJ, Case C-7/98 *Krombach* [2000] ECR I-1935, para 36; ECJ, Case C-394/07 *Gambazzi* [2009] ECR I-2563, para 46

[368] ECJ, Case C-38/98 *Renault* [2000] ECR I-2973, paras 33–4; ECJ, Case C-420/07 *Apostolides* [2009] ECR, I-3571, para 60.

[369] This argument also played a role in another judgment on mutual recognition and REG 44/2001: ECJ, Case C-185/07 *Allianz* [2009] I-663, paras 29–30.

[370] ECJ, Case C-38/98 *Renault* [2000] ECR I-2973, paras 33–4; ECJ, Case C-420/07 *Apostolides* [2009] ECR, I-3571, para 60.

[371] See, for instance: ECJ, Case C-619/10 *Trade Agency*, nyr, paras 42–3 and 55, where the ECJ also held, with reference to previous case law, that fundamental rights do not constitute unfettered prerogatives and may be subject to restrictions, which must correspond to the objectives of public interest pursued by the measure in question and must not constitute, with regard to the aim pursued, a disproportionate interference with the rights thus guaranteed.

mutandis be applied to other mutual recognition based instruments on judicial cooperation in civil matters, and to other fundamental rights.[372]

2.2.3. *Guidelines provided by the ECJ's case law in the area of asylum*

The Common European Asylum System—and in particular REG 343/2003—is the area of freedom, security and justice's field of law in which the ECJ has set—so far—the clearest limits to mutual trust and mutual recognition on the basis of fundamental rights considerations. In the *N.S. and M.E.* judgment, which was discussed earlier,[373] the ECJ held for the first time that the presumption that 'asylum seekers will be treated in a way which complies with fundamental rights' must be rebuttable.[374] Moreover, the ECJ—inspired by the ECtHR's approach in *M.S.S. v Belgium and Greece*—found that if there is 'substantial ground' for believing that due to systemic flaws in the asylum procedure the asylum seeker would face 'a real risk' of being subjected to inhuman or degrading treatment within the meaning of Article 4 Charter, Member States have a duty ***not*** to transfer the asylum seeker to the Member State responsible under REG 343/2003.[375] In order to demonstrate that the risks to which the applicant was exposed were proved, the ECJ referred to elements that the ECtHR had taken into account in its *M.S.S. v Belgium and Greece* judgment, e.g. regular and unanimous reports of international non-governmental organizations, correspondence sent by the United Nations High Commissioner for Refugees to the national minster responsible, and Commission reports on the evaluation of the Dublin system.[376]

Both the ECJ's point of departure ('fundamental rights can constitute a limit to mutual recognition and mutual trust') in *N.S. and M.E.* and the criteria that must be taken into account in order to conclude that there is a breach of the Charter, are—in my view—relevant for the criminal law context too.[377] The question whether there is a real risk of ill treatment contrary to Article 4 Charter should indeed not depend on the legal basis for removal to another Member State.[378] Neither the Charter nor the secondary legislation, nor the ECJ's case law provide any convincing argument for an opposing view on this issue. In fact, both the Dublin Convention and the FD EAW start from the same premise, namely that 'fundamental rights will be observed in the Member States'. The ECJ's refinement of this statement in *N.S. and M.E.* that 'the mere ratification of conventions by a Member State cannot result in the application of a conclusive presumption that that State observes those conventions'[379] should therefore be transposable to the context of the FD EAW and should open the door for possible limits to mutual recognition in the

[372] See, for instance, with regard to the Brussels II bis Regulation on matrimonial matters and parental responsibility, the obligation to interpret Article 42 REG 2201/2003 (namely, the child's right to be heard) in light of Article 24 Charter: ECJ, Case C-403/09 PPU *Detiček* [2009] ECR I-12193, paras 53–5; ECJ, Case C-400/10 PPU *MCB* [2010] ECR I-8965, para 60; ECJ, Case C-491/10 PPU *Zarraga* [2010] ECR I-14247, paras 59–60. See also, with regard to Regulation No 1393/2007 (on the service of documents): ECJ, Case C-325/11 *Alder*, nyr, para 35.

[373] See: Part II, ch 2, III, B, 2. 'Limits linked to the need to safeguard EU or international interests'.

[374] ECJ, Joined Cases C-411/10 and C-493/10 *N.S. and M.E.*, nyr, paras 103–4.

[375] ECJ, Joined Cases C-411/10 and C-493/10 *N.S. and M.E.*, nyr, paras 86 and 94.

[376] ECJ, Joined Cases C-411/10 and C-493/10 *N.S. and M.E.*, nyr, para 90.

[377] See also: MITSILEGAS, 'The Limits of Mutual Trust in Europe's Area of Freedom, Security and Justice: From Automatic Inter-State Cooperation to the Slow Emergence of the Individual' (n 175) 359, who states that 'the ruling in *N.S.* has thus introduced a *fundamental rights mandatory ground for refusal* in criminal and civil matters [...]'.

[378] Similarly, with regard to the ECHR: ECtHR, *Harkins and Edwards v United Kingdom*, 17 January 2012, 9146/07 and 32650/07, para 120.

[379] ECJ, Joined Cases C-411/10 and C-493/10 *N.S. and M.E.*, nyr, para 103.

latter context. Therefore, I would argue that if there are regular and unanimous reports of international non-governmental organizations and, possibly, (repeated) convictions by the ECtHR which confirm systemic flaws in a Member State's detention system which amount to substantial grounds for believing that the person would face a real risk of being subjected to inhuman or degrading treatment, the executing judicial authority should refrain from surrendering the person.[380] It is important to underline—once more—that such a scenario must be distinguished from cases like *Radu* and *Melloni*.[381] In these cases the suspected persons basically argued that provisions of the FD EAW were in breach with the Charter/ECHR (*Radu*) and that a more protective national constitutional standard should prevail over a harmonized EU standard (*Melloni*). However, once it was established that the EU standard was in line with the Charter and the ECHR (and with the ECtHR's case law), the issue of limits to mutual recognition became irrelevant in these cases. Therefore, it was understandable and correct for the ECJ not draw any parallels with *N.S. and M.E.* in *Radu* and *Melloni*. It will become more interesting if the ECJ has to deal with surrender cases related to issuing Member States that are experiencing major operational or structural problems regarding detention conditions. At that time, the question of the analogy with the *N.S. and M.E.* line of reasoning will rise again and become unavoidable.

D. Forum shopping, abuse of law, and concerns about approximation around the lowest common denominator

The current legislative mutual recognition acquis is characterized, first, by a considerable lack of substantive approximation, and can therefore be qualified as a promoter of the co-existence of different national criminal laws, which could encourage forum shopping. Individuals, criminal organizations, prosecutors, and other judicial authorities might be tempted to take advantage of (or abuse) such a situation. The first instrument in which the principle of mutual recognition was introduced, the FD EAW, was aimed at developing a system of swift judicial cooperation and surrender in respect of persons fleeing justice (abuse of the free movement provisions). According to some legal commentators, the focus on prosecution found in this instrument and in many more subsequent instruments necessarily leads to instances of race to the bottom. In my view, however, the framework decisions have introduced several mechanisms which address these concerns.

As far as forum shopping is concerned, I would like to start by repeating the arguments I introduced when discussing this element in the context of the ECJ's *ne bis in idem* case law.[382] In principle, individuals and criminal organizations are entitled to settle in Member States where a specific type of behaviour has not been criminalized (free movement of persons). Needless to say, this is not a case of abuse of law, but the logical consequence of co-existing divergent legislation (individuals' and criminal organizations' use of forum shopping). However, individuals and criminal organizations are not immune to criminal prosecution in this situation, since in the absence of binding criteria for determining the choice of the forum, judicial authorities largely remain free to begin

[380] Similarly: Report from the Commission to the European Parliament and the Council on the implementation since 2007 of the Council Framework Decision of 13 June 2002—The European arrest warrant and the surrender procedures between Member States, COM (2011) 175 final, 7.

[381] See: Part II, ch 2, III, B, 2. 'Limits linked to the need to safeguard EU or international interests'.

[382] See: Part II, ch 1, IV, D. 'Forum shopping, abuse of law, and concerns about de facto approximation around the lowest common denominator'.

proceedings on the basis of a variety of connecting factors (judicial authorities' use of forum shopping).[383] In order to address the latter phenomenon, the European legislator introduced in one of the more recent instruments on mutual recognition, namely the FD EEW and its successor the PROP DIR EIO, a provision which aims to prevent situations whereby judicial authorities seek out the Member State which has the most interesting or flexible rules on gathering evidence. Indeed, the requirement that the issuing authority must be satisfied that 'the objects, documents or data can be obtained under the law of the issuing State in a comparable case if they were available on the territory of the issuing State'[384] and that 'the investigating measure could have been ordered under the same conditions in a similar national case'[385] have clearly been introduced to address this concern about evidence-related forum shopping.

As far as abuse of law is concerned, there are, in my view, at least two crucial mechanisms in the instruments on mutual recognition that address this issue, namely the partial abolition of the dual criminality verification and the principle of speciality.[386] The rationale behind the partial abolition of the dual criminality verification was clearly to prevent individuals who have committed a crime within one Member State being able to find refuge in another Member State where such acts are not punishable, or not punishable to the same extent. Intentionally going to a Member State where a certain behaviour is tolerated is one thing (acceptable use of the free movement provisions); fleeing to a Member State where a crime is not punishable, having committed this offence in another Member State where it is, is clearly another (abuse of the free movement provisions). These latter instances of abuse are something that cannot be tolerated in a single area of freedom, security, and justice.

Under the traditional extradition system, the motivation behind the speciality rule was a fear that the requesting state would limit its requests to acts for which extradition would most likely be granted and conceal its intent to try the requested person for other acts.[387] The speciality rule may thus be considered as a tool for preventing certain forms of judicial authorities' abuse of law.

Abuse of law can also occur via the public prosecution, for instance when an EAW is issued not with the aim of prosecuting or executing a sentence upon the person involved, but only for interrogation purposes or for other reasons not covered by the FD EAW,[388] or where a temporary transfer is requested by an issuing authority under the PROP DIR

[383] On the negative consequences of such *forum shopping*, see, for instance: NESTLER, 'Europäisches Strafprocessrecht' (n 142) 341; H. FUCHS, 'Bemerkungen zum gegenseitigen Anerkennung justizieller Entscheidungen', *ZStW* 2004, 369.

[384] Article 7(b) FD EEW. WILLIAMS, 'The European Evidence Warrant: the Proposal of the European Commission' (n 144) 24.

[385] Article 5a(1)(b) PROP DIR EIO.

[386] Article 27 FD EAW; Article 18 FD MRCS.

[387] O. LAGODNY and C. ROSBAUD, 'Speciality Rule', in KEIJZER and VAN SLIEDREGT (eds.), *The European Arrest Warrant in Practice* (n 24) 265. The rule itself was, traditionally, clearly based on a kind of mistrust between states and one might wonder to what extent such rule is compatible with the basic idea of mutual trust that underpins the new area of freedom, security, and justice. The Commission's initial proposal (COM (2001) 522 final) to abolish the speciality rule (COM (2001) 522 final), is more convincing in the light of the mutual recognition's rationale.

[388] See, for instance: A. KLIP, 'Noot onder Leymann and Pustovarov', *NJ* 2009, 3922; E. KURTOVIC and P. LANGBROEK, 'Uitgeleverd aan overlevering? De Nederlandse overleveringspraktijk beschreven, gevolgd door een discussie over de effectuering van fundamentele rechten van verdachten en veroordeelden', *DD* 2010, 836; J. PRADEL, G. CORSTENS, and G. VERMEULEN, *Droit pénal européen* (Paris, Dalloz, 2009) 614; G. SULLIVAN, 'The European Arrest Warrant: Abuse of Process as a Bar to Extradition', *NJECL* 2009, 37–53.

EIO and the person is subsequently prosecuted and/or tried in the issuing Member State.[389] In my view, there is little doubt that if objective elements demonstrated the improper use of the FD EAW, the PROP DIR EIO, or any other mutual recognition instrument, the ECJ would qualify such practices as incompatible with both the aim and the wording of the legal instrument in question.

A final element for discussion in relation to situations of abuse of law is the criticism that has been aimed at 'abusive' application of EAWs for minor offences, such as the theft of 20 cauliflowers.[390] In my view, however, it is erroneous to qualify these situations as 'abuse' of law. The FD EAW explicitly refers to the law of the issuing Member State as an adequate legal framework. Therefore, if certain conduct meets the framework decision's threshold in the issuing Member State's legislation, the issue of a European Arrest Warrant represents the correct application of the framework decision. Concerns might be expressed in relation to proportionality, but this concept also varies from one Member State to another and is certainly not a case of abuse of law.

As regards race to the bottom arguments and concerns about approximation around the lowest common denominator, it is striking to observe how a lack of approximation in combination with a swift mechanism for judicial cooperation has stimulated the belief among legal commentators that the new legal mechanism of mutual recognition will unavoidably lead to a race to the bottom, i.e. higher punishment and lower procedural standards.[391] In my opinion, however, such a view must be nuanced in light of three elements. First, cases in which Member States refuse to apply the principle of mutual recognition based on a ground for non-recognition might actually have the opposite effect, namely a levelling up rather than a race to the bottom.[392] Secondly, the mutual recognition acquis also contains instruments which are of benefit to the individual.[393] In the same way, a number of instruments which initially appear to be predominantly of benefit to the judicial authorities might also have positive consequences for the individual.[394] Thirdly, many framework decisions contain explicit

[389] On these unacceptable methods of circumventing extradition mechanisms, see: HEARD and MANSELL, 'The European Investigation Order: Changing the face of Evidence-gathering in EU Cross-border Cases' (n 43) 9.

[390] Ignacio Gonzalez, judge at the Spanish Audiencia Nacional, complained about 'many abusive European Arrest Warrants' stemming from East European countries, in particular Romania, at the ERA Conference, 28–30 October 2009, Trier. For other examples of 'abuse' of the European Arrest Warrant System, see: K. SUGMAN and P. GORKIC, 'Abuse of the European Arrest Warrant System', in KEIJZER and VAN SLIEDREGT (eds.), *The European Arrest Warrant in Practice* (n 24) 245–63.

[391] S. GLESZ, 'Zum Prinzip der gegenseitigen Anerkennung', *ZStW* 2004, 359; M. KAIAFA-GBANDI, 'The Treaty Establishing a Constitution for Europe and Challenges for Criminal Law at the Commencement of 21st Century', *Eur. Journ. Crime Cr.L.Cr.J.* 2005, 496; A. NIETO MARTIN, 'Modelos de organización del sistema europeo de derecho penal', in L. ARROYO ZAPATERO and A. NIETO MARTIN (eds.), *El derecho penal de la Unión Europea. Situación actual y perspectivas de futuro* (Cuenca, Ediciones de la Universidad de Castilla-La Mancha, 2007) 170; G. ORMAZABAL, *Espacio penal europeo y mutuo reconocimiento* (Madrid, Marcial Pons, 2006) 72; A.J. SANZ MORAN, 'La orden europea de detención y entrega: algunas consideraciones de carácter jurídico-material', in C. ARANGUENA FANEGO (ed.), *Cooperación judicial penal en la UE: La orden europea de detención y entrega* (Valladolid, Editorial Lex Nova, 2005) 88; SCHÜNEMANN, 'Europäischer Haftbefehl und EU-Verfassungsentwurf auf schieber Ebene' (n 117) 187; VERVAELE, 'The Europeanisation of Criminal Law and the Criminal Law Dimension of European Integration' (n 3) 7.

[392] J.R. SPENCER, 'The European Arrest Warrant', *CYELS* 2003–04, 216; Y BURUMA, 'Radikale Toleranz', *ZStW* 2004, 428.

[393] See, for instance: FD MRCS; FD ESO (post-trial); FD ESO (pre-trial).

[394] For instance, a swift surrender regime in accordance with the FD EAW, can be to the benefit of the individual: I. JEGOUZO, 'Le mandat d'arrêt européen: premiers pas d'un espace judiciaire européen en matière pénale', *R.A.E.* 2003–04, 358. Another example is the FD EEW: several authors indicate that it could also be used on the initiative (and thus to the benefit of) the individual concerned,

provisions which state that the executing authority is not entitled to aggravate the sentence imposed.[395] It is difficult to see how these provisions could lead to a race to the bottom; they are in fact guarantees that the accused or prosecuted person will be punished in accordance with the most lenient system.

see, for instance: SPENCER, 'An Academic Critique of the EU Acquis in Relation to Trans-Border Evidence Gathering' (n 144) 34.

[395] See, for instance: Article 8 FD MRFP (the executing authority may decide *to reduce* the amount); § 9 and Article 3(5) FD TIA (on *reducing* the level of the sentence); Article 8 FD MRCS (the adapted sentence shall not aggravate the sentence passed in the issuing state); Article 9 FD MRCS (the adapted probation measure shall not be more severe or longer than the one that was originally imposed).

3

The Workability of the Principle of Mutual Recognition in Criminal Matters

Both the ECJ's *ne bis in idem* case law and the legislator's mutual recognition strategy are still being developed. At the time of writing, many mutual recognition instruments are still undergoing implementation in some Member States, one instrument is still in the negotiation phase, and only a small number of instruments have actually been implemented in *every* Member State and applied in practice. Yet, despite the instruments' newness, a number of both small- and large-scale evaluation and research projects have already been set up in order to measure the workability of the (legislative) principle of mutual recognition in criminal matters. In what follows, I assess the extent to which the (legislative) principle of mutual recognition can be considered a success story, the advantages and drawbacks that can be attributed to this principle in day-to-day practice (section I), and the remedies needed to further improve any inefficacies related to its operation (section II).

I. The Workability of the Principle of Mutual Recognition: an Ambivalent Success Story?

In a legislative context, the workability of a mutual recognition instrument essentially depends on two conditions, namely (i) accurate implementation of the legislative EU instruments into national legislation and (ii) the competent national authorities' proper application of this legislation in a day-to-day context. In light of these two conditions, there is currently a remarkable discrepancy between the workability of the FD EAW (section I, A) and of the other mutual recognition instruments (section I, B).

A. The European Arrest Warrant: a promising and leading example of mutual recognition in the EU's criminal justice approach

Despite the delayed and inaccurate implementation of the FD EAW in some Member States,[1] and the constitutional difficulties to be overcome in certain Member States with regard to the surrender of nationals,[2] it is reasonable to state that the FD EAW is generally considered to be a success story, both in quantitative[3] and qualitative[4] terms.

[1] Report from the Commission based on Article 34 of the Council Framework Decision of 13 June 2002—The European arrest warrant and the surrender procedures between Member States, COM (2005) 63 final, p. 2–3.

[2] Report from the Commission on the implementation since 2005 of the Council Framework Decision of 13 June 2002—The European arrest warrant and the surrender procedures between Member States, COM (2007) 407 final, p. 5–6.

[3] With a *quantitative* success, I refer, in essence, to the increasing volume of requests and the percentage of them that has resulted in effective surrender. See, for instance, the annual publications of the replies to the questionnaire on quantitative information on the practical operation of the European arrest warrant, retrievable at: <http://www.consilium.europa.eu/showPage.aspx?id=549andlang=EN>.

[4] With a *qualitative* success, I refer, in essence, to a correct implementation of the FD EAW and an application in compliance with the FD EAW in light of the core values of 'freedom', 'security', and

Day-to-day practice of the FD EAW's new system of surrender has eradicated many of the criticisms that had been voiced in legal doctrine prior to its enforcement.[5] For instance, some predicted a complete lack of mutual trust among legal practitioners but this has failed to emerge in practice; similarly, the partial abolition of the dual criminality check has not proved too problematic in reality; and the issue of protecting fundamental rights has not become a major impediment to a smooth procedure of surrender. In fact, most practitioners have welcomed the new system as it has replaced a procedure that was overly cumbersome and often hindered by too wide a margin of discretion and sovereignty. It has also introduced a far more efficient system of surrender, which is based on direct contact between judicial authorities and built upon a clear legal framework (with limited grounds for refusal, considerable limitations to double criminality checks, tight deadlines, and standard forms) which enhances legal certainty without jeopardizing individual rights.

Besides the obvious need for a more efficient procedure,[6] and the factual circumstances which favoured the rapid enforcement of this instrument,[7] several other factors have also contributed to the FD EAW success story. For example, the implementation of the FD EAW was monitored intensively both during and after the implementation period.[8] Large-scale evaluations of the FD EAW's implementation and its practical application took place in each Member State and highlighted the benefits and pitfalls

'justice'. See, for instance: Report from the Commission on the implementation since 2005 of the Council Framework Decision of 13 June 2002—The European arrest warrant and the surrender procedures between Member States (n 2) p. 2 ff.; Council of the European Union—Final report on the fourth round of mutual evaluations. The practical application of the European Arrest Warrant and corres ponding surrender procedures between Member States', document number 8302/1/09, p. 5, retrievable at: <http://www.consilium.europa.eu/documents/access-to-council-documents-public-register?lang=en>; Council of the European Union, Follow-up of the Mutual Recognition instruments, document number 13405/1/10, p. 4 (with reference to the fourth round of mutual evaluations), retrievable at: <http://www.consilium.europa.eu/documents/access-to-council-documents-public-register?lang= en>; Report from the Commission to the European Parliament and the Council on the implementation since 2007 of the Council Framework Decision of 13 June 2002—The European arrest warrant and the surrender procedures between Member States, COM (2011) 175 final.

[5] See, for instance: S. ALEGRE and M. LEAF, 'Mutual Recognition in European Judicial Cooperation: A Step Too Far Too Soon? Case Study—The European Arrest Warrant', *E.L.J.* 2004, 200–17; M. ANDERSON and J. APAP, *Striking a Balance between Freedom, Security and Justice in an Enlarged European Union* (Brussels, CEPS, 2002); J. APAP and S. CARRERA, 'Progress and Obstacles in the Area of Justice and Home Affairs in an Enlarged European Union', CEPS Working paper 2004, No 194, retrievable at: <http://www.ceps.be>; P. BEKAERT, 'Europees aanhoudingsbevel is knoeiwerk op alle niveau's', *De Juristenkrant* 2005, No. 117, 3; R. BLEXTOON, 'Haastige spoed is zelden goed (of het Europees aanhoudingsbevel)', *NTER* 2004, 23–9; S. DOUGLAS SCOTT, 'The Rule of Law in the European Union—Putting the Security into the Area of Freedom, Security, and Justice', *E.L. Rev.* 2004, 219–42; P. MONVILLE, 'Le mandat d'arrêt européen: remise en cause du mécanisme de la simple remise', *JT Dr Eur.* 2003, 168–72; B. SCHÜNEMANN, 'Europäischer Haftbefehl und EU-Verfassungsentwurf auf schieber Ebene', *ZRP* 2003, 185–9; A. SMEULERS and J. DE VRIES, 'Het Europees aanhoudingsbevel: gerechtvaardigd vertrouwen?', *N.J.C.M. Bull.* 2003, 445–62; R. SMITH, 'Old Wine in New Bottles: Human Rights, Legal Aid and the New Europe', *Justice Journal* 2005, <http://www.eurowarrant.net/documents/cms_eaw_id821_1_04%20Smith%20Old%20Wine%20in%20New%20Bottles.doc>; G.VERMEULEN 'U vraagt, wij draaien… Europees aanhoudingsbevel leidt tot blinde overlevering verdachten en veroordeelden', *De Juristenkrant* 2003, No. 57, 3–4.

[6] The FD EAW was already mentioned in the 1999 Tampere European Council Conclusions.

[7] The adoption of the FD EAW was given a top priority on the EU agenda in the aftermath of the 9/11 terrorist attacks. On this influence, see, for instance: B. GILMORE, 'The Twin Towers and the Third Pillar: Some Security Agenda Developments', European University Institute Working Papers, 2003, 1–14, retrievable at: <http://cadmus.eui.eu/bitstream/handle/1814/202/law03-7.pdf>.

[8] Council of the European Union, Follow-up of the Mutual Recognition instruments (n 4) p. 6.

of the new system.[9] Furthermore, various fora were set up for discussion and useful exchange of information, such as regular meetings of the FD EAW's dedicated working group on cooperation in criminal matters, regional seminars, and expert meetings, all of which complemented continued dialogue between national administrations and institutions with input from external experts.[10] Moreover, training sessions on the FD EAW and on EU law in general were organized within most Member States.[11] Finally, the workability of the FD EAW was also enhanced by the development of certain practical tools, such as national factsheets on how cooperation must apply in practice for both the issuing and executing states (called the *fiches françaises*), an instrument for identifying which authority was locally responsible for receiving the executed decision (called the 'atlas'), and a guide for assisting practitioners in issuing arrest warrants (the handbook on the EAW).[12] All of these instruments were considered extremely useful by practitioners dealing with the FD EAW either on a day-to-day basis or more sporadically.[13]

The switch from an extradition system between sovereign states to an EU cooperation-based surrender system between Member States has necessitated a change in habits and a new mentality, particularly for the national judicial authorities, who have become the main actors in the new system. In this regard, it is encouraging to note that the majority of judicial authorities have made themselves familiar with this new form of EU cooperation-based thinking in a relatively short period of time, following the example of their respective superior courts, which have mostly done extremely well in reading the FD EAW (and its national implementation legislation) in light of the EU acquis.[14]

The largely positive assessment of the workability of the FD EAW in day-to-day practice does not necessarily mean, however, that problems with its day-to-day application

[9] See, in particular the evaluation reports on the fourth round of mutual evaluations 'The practical application of the European Arrest Warrant and corresponding surrender procedures between Member States' for each Member State and the corresponding final report, retrievable at: <http://www.consilium.europa.eu/documents/access-to-council-documents-public-register?lang=en>.

[10] See 'The practical application of the European Arrest Warrant and corresponding surrender procedures between Member States' for each Member State and the corresponding final report (n 9).

[11] See, the studies on the different Member States in: G. VERNIMMEN-VAN TIGGELEN, L. SURANO, and A. WEYEMBERGH (eds.), *The Future of Mutual Recognition in Criminal Matters in the European Union* (Brussels, IEE, 2009).

[12] Council of the European Union, Follow-up of the Mutual Recognition instruments (n 4) p. 10–11.

[13] This was indeed underlined by the majority of legal practitioners participating in the ERA Annual forum on the application of the EAW, held in Trier in 2007, 2008, 2009, and 2010.

[14] On the predominantly pro-EU approach of some Member States' (Supreme) courts, see, for instance: E. FAHEY, 'How to be a Third Pillar Guardian of Fundamental Rights? The Irish Supreme Court and the European Arrest Warrant', *E.L. Rev.* 2008, 563–76 (on the Irish Supreme Court); C. JANSSENS, 'De burger, de Unie en het Europees aanhoudingsbevel: op zoek naar het juiste evenwicht tussen vrijheid, veiligheid en rechtvaardigheid', in J. MEEUSEN and G. STRAETMANS (eds.), *Politiële en justitiële strafrechtelijke samenwerking in de Europese Unie: welk evenwicht tussen vrijheid, veiligheid en rechtvaardigheid?* (Antwerp, Intersentia, 2007) 31–64 (with regard to the Belgian *Cour de Cassation,* the French *Cour de Cassation*, the Dutch *Rechtbank van Amsterdam* and *Hoge Raad*, and the British *High Court* and *House of Lords*); E. KURTOVIC and P. LANGBROEK, 'Uitgeleverd aan overlevering? De Nederlandse overleveringspraktijk beschreven, gevolgd door een discussie over de effectuering van fundamentele rechten van verdachten en veroordeelden', *DD* 2010, 473–92; V. MITSILEGAS, 'The Reception of the Principle of Mutual Recognition in the Criminal Justice Systems of EU Member States. The Case of Greece', in VERNIMMEN-VAN TIGGELEN, SURANO, and WEYEMBERGH, *The Future of Mutual Recognition in Criminal Matters in the European Union* (n 11) 184–5; J. SPENCER, 'Implementing the European Arrest Warrant: A Tale of How Not to Do it', *SLR* 2009, 184–202 (with regard to the House of Lords). See also the national case law discussed in: N. KEIJZER and E. VAN SLIEDREGT (eds.), *The European Arrest Warrant in Practice* (The Hague, TMC Asser Press, 2009) 8, 34, 63, 153–4, and 205.

do not exist.[15] A number of recurring problems have indeed been highlighted by the large-scale evaluation projects, the many conferences held on this topic, and the annual reports published by various entities and organizations.

First, we can identify problems of a substantive nature. These problems may result from different national views on how to interpret and implement certain aspects of the FD EAW,[16] from (in)surmountable[17] differences between the Member States' legal systems (such as problems of 'disproportionate' EAWs or EAWs based on judgments *in absentia*),[18] or from discrepancies between the ways in which Member States adhere to the rights set out in the ECHR or the Charter.[19] Secondly, we can identify issues of a more practical nature. For instance, in some Member States, the principle of direct contact and information exchange still needs further development,[20] whereas in other Member States more training is required on certain practical, technical, or administrative aspects related to the FD EAW[21] or on (practical) elements of the other Member States' legal systems.[22] However, perhaps one of the most problematic practical elements, recurring

[15] See, in particular: Report from the Commission to the European Parliament and the Council on the implementation since 2007 of the Council Framework Decision of 13 June 2002—The European arrest warrant and the surrender procedures between Member States (n 4) p. 7–10, in which the Commission acknowledges that 'despite its operational success, the EAW system is far from perfect'.

[16] E.g. discussions regarding the mandatory versus the optional nature of the grounds for non-recognition or discussions regarding different national practices vis-à-vis own nationals and EU-residents. See, for instance: Council of the European Union, Final report on the fourth round of mutual evaluations (n 4) p. 12–13; Eurojust, Annual Report 2009, retrievable at: <http://www.eurojust.europa.eu/doclibrary/corporate/Pages/annual-reports.aspx>, p. 32–3. At the annual forum on the FD EAW, organized in Trier by ERA, some judicial authorities complained about rigid national implementation legislations which prevented a smooth application of the mutual recognition principle. Other issues regarding national implementation legislations that were criticized—such as the territoriality exception or the exception based on a breach of fundamental rights—did not really lead to a problematic application in practice. It can of course also be argued that leaving the application of an optional ground for non-recognition on a case-by-case basis to the national judicial authorities entails risks of legal uncertainty, see, for instance: G. STESSENS, 'Het Europees aanhoudingsbevel en het wederzijds vertrouwen', in F. DERUYCK, M. DE SWAEF, J. ROZIE, M. ROZIE, P. TRAEST, and R. VERSTRAETEN (eds.), *De wet voorbij. Liber amicorum Luc Huybrechts* (Antwerp, Intersentia, 2010) 387.

[17] Only insurmountable differences will lead to the intervention of the European legislator. Other differences will be accepted as being part of the mutual recognition operation, either directly by the judicial authorities involved or after mediation by Eurojust, see: Eurojust, Annual Report 2009 (n 16) p. 33. These annual reports underline the crucial role of Eurojust in overcoming differences in legal systems.

[18] The problem of 'disproportionate' EAWs is often linked to a Member State's choice to adhere either to the legality principle or to the discretionary principle. See, for instance: Council of the European Union, Final report on the fourth round of mutual evaluations, (n 4) p. 13–14; Eurojust, Annual Report 2009 (n 16) p. 32. For possible solutions to this problematic issue, see, for instance: R. DAVIDSON, 'A Sledgehammer to Crack a Nut? Should there be a Bar of Triviality in European Arrest Warrant Cases?', *C.L.R.* 2009, 31–6; M. SOTTO MAIOR, 'The Principle of Proportionality: Alternative Measures to the EAW', in KEIJZER and VAN SLIEDREGT (eds.), *The European Arrest Warrant in Practice* (n 14) 213–28; J. VOGEL and J.R. SPENCER, 'Proportionality and the European Arrest Warrant', *C.L.R.* 2010, 480–1. The problem surrounding insurmountable differences between the national legislations on *in absentia* judgments led to the adoption of FD IAJ.

[19] For some regrettable examples, see, for instance, the examples given by Fair Trials International at their website: <http://www.fairtrials.net/campaigns/justice_in_europe>. This overview also indicates that in a transnational context—like in a national context—errors of justice are likely to occur. See also: Part II, ch 2, III, C, 2.2.1 'Guidelines provided by the ECtHR's case law'.

[20] See, for instance: Council of the European Union, Final report on the fourth round of mutual evaluations (n 4) p. 7–8 and p. 18; Eurojust, Annual Report 2009 (n 16) p. 33.

[21] See, for instance: Council of the European Union, Final report on the fourth round of mutual evaluations (n 4) p. 9–11 and p. 19–20.

[22] See, for instance: Council of the European Union, Final report on the fourth round of mutual evaluations (n 4) p. 8–9 and p. 11–12.

again and again, is the issue of language.[23] It seems that both short-term and long-term measures are urgently required to tackle the problem of delayed, inaccurate, incomplete, or incorrect translations as well as other linguistic problems such as difficulties in communication between judicial authorities of different Member States and the lack of (adequate) interpretation facilities during the course of legal proceedings. The need to take both categories of problems seriously is highlighted by the fact that issues of a practical nature frequently have a major influence on issues of a more substantive nature.[24]

B. The other mutual recognition instruments: a long road ahead?

As the implementation deadlines for the other mutual recognition instruments passed, it became apparent that the state of play in this area was very far from satisfactory in all Member States.[25] The workability of these instruments was not only being hindered by delays and deficiencies in the implementation process, but also by the practical and legal difficulties being encountered in their day-to-day application. Furthermore, with regard to mutual recognition instruments whose prescribed implementation periods have not yet expired or have recently expired, the Council's forecasts for timely implementation can be viewed with some scepticism.[26] Finally,

[23] See, for instance: Council of the European Union, Final report on the fourth round of mutual evaluations (n 4) p. 10; Eurojust, Annual Report 2009 (n 16) p. 33; J. GINTER, 'The content of a European Arrest Warrant', in KEIJZER and VAN SLIEDREGT (eds.), *The European Arrest Warrant in Practice* (n 14) 15–16; G. VERNIMMEN-VAN TIGGELEN and L. SURANO, 'Quel futur pour la reconnaissance mutuelle en matière pénale? Analyse transversale', in G. VERNIMMEN, L. SURANO, and A. WEYEMBERGH (eds.), *The Future of Mutual Recognition in Criminal Matters in the European Union* (Brussels, IEE, 2009) 567–8. The language issue was also mentioned by the majority of legal practitioners participating in the ERA Annual forum on the application of the EAW, held in Trier in 2007, 2008, 2009, and 2010.

[24] For instance, deficiencies in the regular flow of information and the absence of appropriate coordination between the competent authorities (issues of a practical nature), have led to a number of problems with the operation of the speciality rule (issue of a substantive nature).

[25] Report from the Commission based on Article 14 of the Council Framework Decision 2003/577/JHA of 22 July 2003—The execution in the European Union of orders freezing property or evidence, COM (2008) 885 final, p. 7; Report from the Commission based on Article 20 of the Council Framework Decision 2005/214/JHA of 24 February 2005—The application of the principle of mutual recognition to financial penalties, COM (2008) 888 final, p. 9; Report from the Commission to the European Parliament and the Council based on article 22 of the Council Framework Decision 2006/783/JHA of 6 October 2006—The application of the principle of mutual recognition to confiscation orders, COM (2010) 428, p. 13; Council of the European Union—Follow-up of the Mutual Recognition instruments (n 4) p. 18–19.

[26] Council of the European Union—Follow-up of the Mutual Recognition instruments (n 4) p. 5; Council of the European Union—Implementation of the Framework Decision of the Council of the European Union of 6 October 2006 (2006/783/JHA) on the application of the principle of mutual recognition to confiscation orders—Information provided to the General Secretariat, document number 9006/12, retrievable at: <http://www.consilium.europa.eu/documents/access-to-council-documents-public-register?lang=en>; Council of the European Union—Implementation of the Council Framework Decision 2008/675/JHA of 24 July 2008 on taking account of convictions in the Member States of the European Union in the course of new criminal proceedings, document number 14292/1/12, retrievable at: <http://www.consilium.europa.eu/documents/access-to-council-documents-public-registe r?lang=en>; Council of the European Union—Implementation of the Framework Decision of the Council of the European Union of 24 February 2005 (2005/214/JHA) on the application of the principle of mutual recognition to financial penalties—Information provided to the General Secretariat, document number 9015/2/12, retrievable at: <http://www.consilium.europa.eu/documents/access-to-council-documents-public-register?lang=en>; Council of the European Union—Implementation of the Council Framework Decision 2008/909/JHA on the application of the principle of mutual recognition to judgments in criminal matters imposing custodial sentences

the difficult negotiations[27] surrounding one of the prominent mutual recognition instruments currently still under discussion, the PROP DIR EIO, indicate that the driving force and enthusiasm that accompanied the adoption of the FD EAW have been lost somewhat.

Yet it would be erroneous to conclude from this that a general lack of belief in the principle of mutual recognition persists or that legal practitioners are still unwilling to co-operate with one other. On the contrary, research has demonstrated that Member States' judicial authorities await the coming into force of mutual recognition instruments—especially those that have added value[28]—with some enthusiasm, and also that a great willingness to trust counterparts in other Member States is evident.[29]

Any pessimism or reticence towards the implementation or application of any of the more recent mutual recognition instruments can be ascribed to a variety of factors. First, judicial authorities are often unaware whether a specific mutual recognition instrument has been implemented in another Member State and, if it has, how this affects the other Member State and the judicial authority to be addressed.[30] Secondly, many judicial authorities have criticized the step-by-step approach of the European institutions, which can lead to complex situations during a transitional period as judicial authorities are required to combine different procedures. This has become especially clear with regard to the FD EOFPE[31] and

or measures involving deprivation of liberty for the purpose of their enforcement in the European Union—Information provided to the General Secretariat, document number 6345/3/12, retrievable at: <http://www.consilium.europa.eu/documents/access-to-council-documents-public-register?lang=en>; Council of the European Union—Implementation of Framework Decision of the Council of the European Union of 27 November 2008 on the application of the principle of mutual recognition to judgments and probation decisions with a view to the supervision measures and alternative sanctions—Information provided to the General Secretariat, document number 7334/1/12, retrievable at: <http://www.consilium.europa.eu/documents/access-to-council-documents-public-register?lang=en>.

27 The Council only reached a partial general approach (17 June 2011) following difficult, lengthy negotiations (the original initiative dates from 29 April 2010) and negotiations with the European Parliament under the co-decision procedure present a real challenge due to the proposal's high level of human rights implications.

28 See, for instance, for positive expectations vis-à-vis the application of the FD MRFP and/or the FD MRCO: R. KERT, 'The Implementation and Application of Mutual Recognition Instruments in Austria', in VERNIMMEN, SURANO, and WEYEMBERGH (eds.), *The Future of Mutual Recognition in Criminal Matters in the European Union* (n 23) 40; J.R. SPENCER, 'Mutual Recognition of Decisions in Criminal Justice and the United Kingdom', in *The Future of Mutual Recognition in Criminal Matters in the European Union* (n 23) 538–9; A. WEYEMBERGH and V. SANTAMARIA, 'La reconnaissance mutuelle en matière pénale en Belgique', in *The Future of Mutual Recognition in Criminal Matters in the European Union* (n 23) 76–7.

29 See, in particular, the very positive outcome of the study on EU cross-border gathering and use of evidence in criminal matters: G. VERMEULEN, W. DE BONDT, and Y. VAN DAMME, *EU Cross-border Gathering and Use of Evidence in Criminal Matters* (Antwerp, Maklu, 2010).

30 Council of the European Union—Follow-up of the Mutual Recognition instruments (n 4) p. 8–11; A. SUOMINEN, 'The Finnish Approach to Mutual Recognition in Criminal Matters and its Implementation', in VERNIMMEN, SURANO, and WEYEMBERGH (eds.), *The Future of Mutual Recognition in Criminal Matters in the European Union* (n 23) 236. On the lack of information and the lack of knowledge with regard to the cross-border execution of judgments involving deprivation of liberty, see: G. VERMEULEN, A. VAN KALMTHOUT, N. PATERSON, M. KNAPEN, P. VERBEKE, and W. DE BONDT, *Cross-border Execution of Judgments Involving Deprivation of Liberty in the EU* (Antwerp, Maklu, 2011) 56–7.

31 The scarce application of the FD EOFPE was highlighted by R. MORAN MARTÍNEZ, 'The Freezing of Property and Evidence in Criminal Proceedings', in M. DE HOYOS SANCHO (ed.), *Criminal Proceedings in the European Union: Essential Safeguards* (Valladolid, Lex Nova, 2008) 407, as well as by a German judicial authority at the annual ERA Conference in Trier (2009) who confirmed that he was only aware of *one* freezing order under his jurisdiction. The order had been successfully

the FD EEW.[32] In the presence of a rather well-functioning system of mutual legal assistance (MLA), judicial authorities are often inclined to fall back on traditional instruments with which they are familiar (MLA) rather than combining the MLA and MR procedures. The FD EEW was also criticized in view of what was seen as the legislator's significant reliance on the FD EAW in drafting the FD EEW. The copy-and-paste approach has resulted in an FD EEW which constitutes a step backwards in several regards in comparison with the MLA regime. Thirdly, judicial authorities have expressed concerns about some of the (upcoming) mutual recognition instruments, which require significant efforts on the part of the executing Member State: it is felt that their implementation and day-to-day application might be seriously hindered in some Member States owing to the (current) lack of operational capacities and/or human resources.[33] Finally, it can clearly be argued that many—if not all—of the practical and legal problems described when discussing the practical application of the FD EAW are also likely to occur here in the absence of effective remedies.

II. Remedies for Improving the Efficacy of the Principle of Mutual Recognition and for Enhancing Mutual Trust

The majority of policy documents issued after the principle of mutual recognition was launched in relation to criminal matters not only refer to the objective of promoting mutual recognition (of judicial decisions and judgments), but have also stressed from the outset the need to take legislative measures and other measures which support and enhance the workability of the principle of mutual recognition.[34] These 'enhancing'

recognized and executed, yet the judicial authority complained about the procedure that had to be followed and, more precisely, the fact an additional MLA request had been necessary to transfer the frozen evidence. See also: M. CHINOVA and M. ASSENOVA, 'L'application du principe de la reconnaissance mutuelle en matière pénale en Bulgarie', in VERNIMMEN, SURANO, and WEYEMBERGH, *The Future of Mutual Recognition in Criminal Matters in the European Union*, (n 23) 96; M. POELEMANS, 'Bilan et perspectives du principe de reconnaissance mutuelle en matière pénale en France', in *The Future of Mutual Recognition in Criminal Matters in the European Union* (n 23) 253.

[32] In view of the EEW's limited scope, the need to combine the EEW with other MLA instruments has become crystal-clear and there is a difficulty in convincing legal practitioners of the added value of this new instrument. See, for instance: D. FLORE, *Droit pénal européen. Les enjeux d'une justice pénale européenne* (Brussels, Larcier, 2009) 395–6 and 478; M. POELEMANS, 'Bilan et perspectives du principe de reconnaissance mutuelle en matière pénale en France' (n 31) 253–4; J.R. SPENCER, 'Mutual Recognition of Decisions in Criminal Justice and the United Kingdom' (n 28) 546; T. WAHL, 'The Perception of the Principle of Mutual Recognition of Judicial Decisions in Criminal Matters in Germany', in *The Future of Mutual Recognition in Criminal Matters in the European Union* (n 23) 137; A. WEYEMBERGH and V. SANTAMARIA, 'La reconnaissance mutuelle en matière pénale en Belgique', in *The Future of Mutual Recognition in Criminal Matters in the European Union* (n 23) 62. In view of the huge amount of resistance amongst legal practitioners, a new instrument, with a broader scope has been developed with the aim of substituting the FD EEW, namely the PROP DIR EIO.

[33] K. LIGETI, 'The Principle of Mutual Recognition in Criminal Matters in Hungary', in VERNIMMEN, SURANO, and WEYEMBERGH, *The Future of Mutual Recognition in Criminal Matters in the European Union* (n 23) 266; T. WAHL, 'The Perception of the Principle of Mutual Recognition of Judicial Decisions in Criminal Matters in Germany' (n 32) 136.

[34] See, for instance: Communication from the Commission to the Council and the European Parliament—Towards enhancing access to information by law enforcement agencies, COM (2004) 429 final; Communication from the Commission to the Council and the European Parliament—Area of Freedom, Security and Justice: Assessment of the Tampere Programme and future orientations, COM (2004) 401 final; Recommendation of the European Parliament to the Council and to the European

measures, which have been codified to a large extent by the Treaty of Lisbon,[35] can be classified in six main categories, as follows: measures that pursue a better understanding of the principle of mutual recognition (section II, A); measures that aim to gain an overview of any current hindrances (section II, B); measures that strive for an adequate procedural framework (section II, C); measures that stimulate cooperation, communication and coordination among the competent authorities (section II, D); approximation measures (section II, E); and finally, measures that address the issue of costs (section II, F).

A. Striving for good knowledge and understanding of the principle of mutual recognition and of any related issues

A principle of mutual recognition that works smoothly is chiefly dependent upon a thorough knowledge of how this principle should work in practice. The existence of a specific legal framework, namely the framework decision combined with the corresponding national implementation legislation, undoubtedly provides the competent judicial authorities with a sound footing, but it has become clear that the mere existence of these legal texts is inadequate for ensuring successful application of the principle.

As mentioned above, the development of the Handbook on the EAW and the creation of what are called the *fiches françaises,* which contain practical and relevant information on the national systems and the EAW, have proved very useful in familiarizing the national practitioners with this new instrument and are certainly worth following in relation to the other instruments.[36] Compared to the FD EAW, where regular meetings were held with national experts both during and after the implementation of the framework decisions in order to provide a forum for discussion and information exchange, contact has been less frequent with the other instruments, which may explain practitioners' lack of knowledge about the existence and potential of these other instruments.[37]

It has been rightly argued that the principle of mutual recognition makes every national judge or prosecutor a European actor, a status which requires greater familiarly with the reality of European integration in addition to the sharing of a common

Council on the future of the area of freedom, security, and justice as well as on the measures required to enhance the legitimacy and effectiveness thereof (2004/2175(INI)), *O.J.* 166 E, 07.07.2005, p. 58–63; Communication from the Commission to the Council and the European Parliament—The mutual recognition of judicial decisions in criminal matters and the strengthening of mutual trust between Member States, COM (2005) 195 final.

[35] Article 70 TFEU (on mutual evaluations); Article 82 TFEU (in particular the provisions on training, cooperation, and approximation of criminal procedural law); and Article 83(1) TFEU (on approximation of substantive criminal law).

[36] Council of the European Union—Follow-up of the Mutual Recognition instruments (n 4) p. 10–12.

[37] Council of the European Union—Follow-up of the Mutual Recognition instruments (n 4) p. 3; Council of the European Union, Follow-up of the Mutual Recognition instruments. Outcome of the discussions based on the results of the questionnaire on implementation, document number 17998/10, p. 5, retrievable at: <http://www.consilium.europa.eu/documents/access-to-council-documents-public-register?lang=en>. On the need to create a handbook and to provide more information, see, for instance, in the area of prisoner transfer: VERMEULEN, VAN KALMTHOUT, PATERSON, KNAPEN, VERBEKE, and DE BONDT, *Cross-border Execution of Judgments Involving Deprivation of Liberty in the EU* (n 30) 85; and in the area of probation measures and alternative sanctions: D. FLORE, S. BOSLY, A. HONHON, and J. MAGGIO (eds.), *Probation measures and alternative sanctions in the European Union* (Antwerp, Intersentia, 2012) 552.

European culture.[38] Therefore, a thorough knowledge of the principle of mutual recognition itself does not suffice: the competent authorities must also gain a clear insight into the EU legal order as a whole[39] and must familiarize themselves with the legal and judicial systems of the other Member States.[40] In order to attain these objectives, adequate training should be provided at both national and EU level.[41] Such training initiatives could take the form of traditional conferences, seminars, or workshops, but could also consist of Erasmus-style exchange programmes or participation in networks of judicial organizations and institutions.[42]

Finally, the principle of mutual recognition and the free movement of judicial decisions, which entail a duty to take foreign criminal convictions into account, especially through the FD TIA, can only be successful if judicial authorities in the different Member States are aware of such decisions and of the different types of offence and penalty recognized in other Member States. In order to address these issues, the EU institutions have been working on the development of an EU criminal records database.[43]

B. Gaining an overview of any current or imminent obstacles to the principle of mutual recognition

Smooth application of the principle of mutual recognition can be hindered by obstacles in the national implementation process or by problems in applying the national legislation in practice. In order to overcome such difficulties, the EU institutions have

[38] See, for instance: G. VERNIMMEN-VAN TIGGELEN and L. SURANO, 'Analysis of the future of mutual recognition in criminal matters in the European Union. Final Report', 59, retrievable at: <http://ec.europa.eu/justice/doc_centre/criminal/recognition/docs/mutual_recognition_en.pdf>; Communication from the Commission to the Council, the European Parliament, the European Economic and Social Committee and the Committee of the Regions—Delivering an area of freedom, security, and justice for Europe's citizens. Action Plan implementing the Stockholm Programme, COM (2010) 171 final, p. 8.

[39] See, for instance: Resolution of the Council and of the Representatives of the Governments of the Member States meeting within the Council—The training of judges, prosecutors and judicial staff in the European Union, *O.J.* C-299, 22.11.2008, p. 3, which emphasizes the need to improve the knowledge of the EU's primary and secondary law among judges, prosecutors, and judicial staff.

[40] See, for instance: Communication from the Commission to the European Parliament and the Council—Judicial training in the European Union, COM (2006) 356 final, p. 7; Resolution of the Council and of the Representatives of the Governments of the Member States meeting within the Council—The training of judges, prosecutors and judicial staff in the European Union (n 39) p. 3.

[41] Article 82(1)(c) TFEU. For some examples of European support for judicial training, see, for instance: Communication from the Commission to the European Parliament and the Council—Judicial training in the European Union (n 40) p. 4–6. On the need for more workshops and seminars in order to raise awareness of the FD 2005/214/JHA, see, for instance: Council of the European Union, Follow-up of the Mutual Recognition instruments—outcome of the discussions based on the results of the questionnaire on implementation (n 37) p. 5.

[42] The Hague Programme—Strengthening freedom, security and justice in the European Union *O.J.* C-53, 03.03.2005, p. 11–12; Communication from the Commission to the Council, the European Parliament, the European Economic and Social Committee and the Committee of the Regions—Delivering an area of freedom, security, and justice for Europe's citizens. Action Plan implementing the Stockholm Programme' (n 38) p. 8; FLORE, BOSLY, HONHON, and MAGGIO (eds.), *Probation measures and alternative sanctions in the European Union* (n 37) 552–3; VERMEULEN, VAN KALMTHOUT, PATERSON, KNAPEN, VERBEKE, and DE BONDT, *Cross-border Execution of Judgments Involving Deprivation of Liberty in the EU* (n 30) 88.

[43] See, in particular: Council Framework Decision 2009/315/JHA on the organisation and content of the exchange of information extracted from criminal records between Member States, *O.J.* L-93, 07.04.2009, 23–32; Council Decision 2009/316/JHA on the establishment of the European Criminal Records Information System (ECRIS) in application of Framework Decision 2009/315/JHA, *O.J.* L-93, 07.04.2009, 33–48.

reiterated that evaluating both the implementation and effects of all measures is essential to the effectiveness of Union action.[44] Evaluating or monitoring both elements thoroughly therefore constitutes a key tool in a successful principle of mutual recognition.

As for monitoring correct and timely transposition into national legislation, the mutual recognition instruments usually include an explicit provision according to which Member States are obliged to transmit to both the Council and the Commission the text of their national implementation laws, so that the Commission can draw up an implementation report on the basis of this information when the implementation period comes to an end.[45] These reports highlight any shortcomings in a Member State's implementation legislation and assess the need for amendments or new initiatives. Using this 'name and shame' approach, the Commission's clearly intends to urge the Member States addressed in the report to take the necessary steps to bring their national legislation into line with the report's recommendations. However, in the current situation, where infringement procedures are still missing,[46] this form of pressure might be insufficient and may also arrive too late.[47]

In order to address implementation problems in a timely manner, the Commission has decided to intervene at an earlier stage by giving Member States assistance before they are monitored.[48] The reason behind this New Approach is that incorrect national implementation legislation is not necessarily the consequence of bad faith and may be due to a lack of expertise. Therefore, the Commission decided to organize workshops with Member States in order to exchange best practices and to issue guidance papers for legislators that would enable them to be better prepared for the actual implementation. This new strategy, with its strong emphasis on prevention together with the Commission's forthcoming enforcement powers,[49] is likely to be more beneficial to the immediate effectiveness of mutual recognition instruments than *ex post* implementation reports.

As for the evaluation of the law in practice, the need for an objective and impartial evaluation of the implementation of policies in the area of freedom, security, and justice, especially to promote the full application of the principle of mutual recognition, has been emphasized on repeated occasions. The consolidation of this tool in the Treaty of Lisbon[50] highlights its importance, but it is not innovative, let alone revolutionary, in itself. In fact, over the years, the EU has gained considerable experience of performing

[44] See, for instance: The Hague Programme: strengthening freedom, security and justice in the European Union (n 42) p. 11; Council and Commission Action Plan implementing the Hague Programme on strengthening freedom, security and justice in the European Union, *O.J.* C-198, 12.08.2005, p. 17; Communication from the Commission to the Council and the European Parliament—The mutual recognition of judicial decisions in criminal matters and the strengthening of mutual trust between Member States (n 34) p. 8; European Council—The Stockholm Programme—an open and secure Europe serving and protecting citizens, *O.J.* C-115/01, 04.05.2010, p. 1–38. Communication from the Commission to the Council, the European Parliament, the European Economic and Social Committee and the Committee of the Regions—Delivering an area of freedom, security, and justice for Europe's citizens. Action Plan implementing the Stockholm Programme (n 38) p. 8.

[45] See, for instance: Article 34 FD EAW, Article 20 FD FD MRFP, Article 22 FD MRCO.

[46] Article 10 Protocol No 36 on transitional provisions, Treaty of Lisbon.

[47] M. MIRANDA, 'Implementation of EU Criminal Justice Instruments', Lecture held at the Annual Forum on Mutual Recognition of Judicial Decisions in Criminal Matters, ERA, Trier, 28 October 2008.

[48] See, in particular: Communication from the Commission—A Europe of Results—Applying Community Law, COM (2007) 502 final.

[49] Article 10 Protocol No 36 on transitional provisions, Treaty of Lisbon.

[50] Article 70 TFEU.

evaluation projects, both in the area of criminal law itself[51] and in other policy areas.[52] This experience may be of use during the development of an efficient evaluation mechanism for the future area of freedom, security, and justice.

One of the main objectives of evaluation projects—which are based on the well-established system of peer-evaluation—is to facilitate a better understanding of national systems in order to identify best practices and obstacles to cooperation.[53] The final reports of the evaluations, as well as the handbooks that have been and will be issued as a result of such evaluations, should therefore be compulsory reading for any competent practitioner in the corresponding area of law.

With regard to monitoring the correct transposition of a directive or the evaluation of the national law in practice, it is important that these are not one-off events but are carried out periodically with an efficient follow-up system. In view of the time-consuming and expensive nature of many evaluation projects, however, it is worth mentioning that the information gathered using these methods can also be supplemented by information obtained using less intensive instruments, such as the Council's annual (quantitative) questionnaires on the EAW[54] or Eurojust's annual reports.[55]

C. A workable and well-defined legal framework that permits swift and fair procedures

One of the strengths of the FD EAW regime is that it contains a workable and well-defined legal framework with specific rules on the instrument's scope, criteria for application, and governing law, and also that it stipulates an easily manageable standard form, strict deadlines, restricted number of grounds for refusal, and thus a limited margin of discretion for the competent judicial authorities. These characteristics, which are also evident in the other mutual recognition instruments, are prerequisites for a workable principle of mutual recognition.

A workable principle of mutual recognition also requires that the decisions taken are fair, with due regard to fundamental rights considerations.[56] Therefore, the (limited)

[51] See, for instance: S. DE BIOLLEY and A. WEYEMBERGH, 'L'évaluation dans le cadre du troisième pilier du traité sur l'Union européenne', in S. DE BIOLLEY and A. WEYEMBERGH (eds.), *Comment évaluer le droit pénal européen?* (Brussels, Editions de l'Université de Bruxelles, 2006) 75–98; H. NILSSON, 'Eight Years of Experience of Mutual Evaluation within the EU', in DE BIOLLEY and WEYEMBERGH (eds.), *Comment évaluer le droit pénal européen?*, 115–24; A. ZARZA, 'Evaluations of Member States in the Third Pillar of the European Union. The Specific Case of the European Arrest Warrant', in *Comment évaluer le droit pénal européen?* (n 51) 99–113.

[52] See, for instance: A. KLIP and M. DANE, 'Improving Mutual Trust amongst European Union Member States in the Areas of Police and Judicial Cooperation in Criminal Matters Lessons from the Operation of Monitoring, Evaluation and Inventory Mechanisms in the First and Third Pillars of the European Union' (Maastricht, WODC, 2009).

[53] Communication from the Commission to the Council and the European Parliament—The mutual recognition of judicial decisions in criminal matters and the strengthening of mutual trust between Member States (n 34) p. 8; Communication from the Commission to the Council and the European Parliament—Evaluation of EU Policies on freedom, security and justice, COM (2006) 332 final, p. 2. On the need of identifying best practices, see: FLORE, BOSLY, HONHON, and MAGGIO (eds.), *Probation measures and alternative sanctions in the European Union* (n 37) 552–3; VERMEULEN, VAN KALMTHOUT, PATERSON, KNAPEN, VERBEKE, and DE BONDT, *Cross-border Execution of Judgments Involving Deprivation of Liberty in the EU* (n 30) 87–8.

[54] The replies to the Council's questionnaires are retrievable at: <http://www.consilium.europa.eu/documents/access-to-council-documents-public-register?lang=en>.

[55] These reports are retrievable at: <http://www.eurojust.europa.eu/press_annual.htm>.

[56] See, for instance: Green Paper of the Commission—Strengthening mutual trust in the European judicial area. A Green Paper on the application of EU criminal justice legislation in the field of detention,

margin of discretion that is left to the executing judicial authority must be exploited with care, to facilitate the taking of swift (but not too swift) and fair decisions which reflect sound reasoning in which all relevant elements and objectives are balanced.[57] A mutual recognition model that is too rigid or automated presents a threat to individual rights. As a result, instruments that pay due regard to the necessary safeguards of individual rights are required.

Another related feature of the FD EAW is that it provides the practitioner with a single, well-organized regime for the surrender of persons within the EU, which contrasts sharply with the patchwork of rules on evidence gathering. In view of the FD EEW's limited scope, national practitioners are required to send requests on the basis of both the MLA instruments and the FD EEW, which makes the cooperation mechanism in this area rather cumbersome instead of efficient. It is perfectly understandable that this system came in for severe criticism among practitioners, academics, and administrators, with the result that the FD EEW and the related instruments on MLA will be replaced with a single comprehensible instrument (PROP DIR EIO).

D. Stimulating cooperation, communication, and coordination among the competent authorities

The principle of mutual recognition is the driving force behind judicial cooperation in criminal matters and its successful application is therefore largely dependent on effective and smooth cooperation between the competent authorities. In this regard, it is not surprising that the TFEU explicitly allows for the taking of measures that will facilitate cooperation between Member States' judicial or equivalent authorities in relation to proceedings in criminal matters and enforcement of decisions.[58]

The duty of cooperation applies in both the harmonized and non-harmonized contexts, as the duty to cooperate applies even in the absence of any explicit legal provision on cooperation, pursuant to Article 4(3) TEU (principle of sincere cooperation). Yet the majority of legislative measures on mutual recognition do include specific provisions in which different components of the duty of cooperation are clarified, specifically: a duty to communicate with colleagues in the other Member States (principle of direct contact between judicial authorities), a duty to request any (additional) information that might be required, and a duty on the part of the other Member State to supply the required information (principle of information exchange or free movement of information).[59]

COM (2011) 327 final, which gives some clear examples as to how the application of mutual recognition instruments can pose a threat to human rights protection. See also: Resolution of the Council—A Roadmap for strengthening the rights and protection of victims, in particular in criminal proceedings, *O.J.* 28.06.2011, C-187, p. 1–5.

[57] In this regard, the PROP DIR EIO's regime of grounds for non-recognition can be considered as a good example of a balanced compromise. See: Articles 10, 19(2), 21(1a), 27(b), 27a(3), 27b(4) PROP DIR EIO.

[58] Article 82(1)(d) TFEU. It follows, furthermore, from Article 74 TFEU that not only cooperation amongst *judicial* authorities is envisaged, but that also measures to ensure (better) *administrative* cooperation can be adopted.

[59] See, for instance: Articles 11(3), 15, 17, and 18 FD ESO (post-trial); Articles 8(4), 8(5), 15, and 17 FD MRCO. On the need of information exchange, see, for instance: Communication from the Commission to the Council and the European Parliament—Towards enhancing access to information by law enforcement agencies (n 34).

Smooth cooperation and direct contact between the competent authorities requires, first of all, that the issuing authority is able to identify the authority locally competent to receive the decision to be executed and is also able to contact this authority to discuss any practical issues regarding the execution of the order.[60] In this regard, authorities can make the necessary inquiries via the contact points of the European Judicial Network. Furthermore, a number of specific databases have been developed by the European Judicial Network on the basis of data provided by the Member States, such as 'atlas', which relates to the FD EAW. A similar instrument is currently under construction for the FD EOFPE and it is predicted that in the future each instrument will have a corresponding atlas containing relevant data on the competent authorities per Member State.[61]

Good cooperation also requires smooth communication between the competent authorities, but these may be severely affected by linguistic barriers. As mentioned in the previous chapter, recurring problems include the paucity of some Member States' translation capacities, the associated costs, difficulties of translating into less common languages in short periods of time, and translations of poor quality, mainly because only a small number of Member States accept a certificate written in a language other than their own official language(s).[62] For this reason, the proposal to allow only a limited number of vehicular languages for issuing EAWs (and other warrants or orders)[63] and to supply supplementary corresponding information[64] should be given serious thought, in my view, in combination with language training for all competent authorities involved in EU judicial cooperation in criminal matters.

Good cooperation also benefits from the various networks[65] that have been set up in order to enable permanent dialogue between the Member States' (highest) courts[66] and between law enforcement authorities.[67] For this kind of 'permanent dialogue'[68] it

[60] Council of the European Union, Follow-up of the Mutual Recognition instruments (n 4) p. 11.

[61] In this regard, a good example of a balanced compromise is the regime on grounds for non-recognition in the PROP DIR EIO that foresees in different grounds for non-recognition depending on the sensitive nature of the measure at stake.

[62] See, for instance, with regard to the FD EAW: Council of the European Union, Final report on the fourth round of mutual evaluations (n 4) p. 10.

[63] See, for instance: § 14a and Article 5(2) PROP DIR EIO which encourages Member States to accept at least one language which is commonly used in the European Union other than their official language(s).

[64] The calls that have been made for a more practical and flexible approach to language requirements through the acceptance of languages other than the Member State's own official language for (arrest) warrants and any additional information was expressed by a great number of authorities during the fourth round of mutual evaluations on the EAW and taken over by the Council in its recommendations in the final report on this evaluation: Council of the European Union, Final report on the fourth round of mutual evaluations (n 4) p. 10.

[65] On the need of promoting networking, see for instance: Communication from the Commission to the Council and the European Parliament—The mutual recognition of judicial decisions in criminal matters and the strengthening of mutual trust between Member States (n 34) p. 9; Communication from the Commission—The creation of a Forum for discussing EU justice policies and practice, COM (2008) 38 final, p. 3.

[66] See, for instance: the network that was created and that consists of the presidents of the supreme judicial courts of the European Union, retrievable at: <http://www.network-presidents.eu>.

[67] See, for instance: the yearly conferences on the practical application of mutual recognition instruments organized by ERA, which offer a forum where law enforcement authorities and judicial authorities can discuss controversial issues and where they can exchange best practices.

[68] Recommendation of the European Parliament to the Council and to the European Council on the future of the area of freedom, security, and justice as well as on the measures required to enhance the legitimacy and effectiveness thereof (n 34) p. 61.

is not sufficient that competent authorities simply know of each other: they should also communicate with each other, read each other's judicial decisions, and learn from each other's experience.[69] Provided that such a threefold approach is maintained, judicial authorities will become more familiar with other Member States' judicial systems as well as with the EU legal order, which will be of benefit to their general understanding and knowledge of the principle of mutual recognition.

A final, major element which should not be overlooked when discussing the issue of good cooperation, and which came to the fore when discussing both the judicial principle of mutual recognition developed in the ECJ's *ne bis in idem* case law and the legislative principle of mutual recognition, is the need for an effective coordination tool with clear rules on the allocation of jurisdiction.[70] Judicial authorities will only be inclined to step into a far-reaching cooperation mechanism when they can accept that the issuing authority is indeed competent in dealing with the matter in question. A legislative measure has been taken to address this issue,[71] and Eurojust has thus far done everything in its power to solve any conflicts that have arisen in this context.[72] However, we might still wonder whether the current instrument, with its non-committal wording and Eurojust's non-binding competences, suffice to eradicate scepticism and the corresponding hindrances to a smooth cooperation mechanism. The question of whether more stringent rules are indeed necessary, however, will largely depend upon further evaluation of the mutual recognition instruments (and of judicial cooperation in criminal matters in general), and more importantly upon the willingness of the Member States and the EU legislator to adopt rules of a more obligatory nature, something that has already been carried out in other areas of law in order to facilitate mutual recognition.[73]

[69] See, for instance: Communication from the Commission to the Council, the European Parliament, the European Economic and Social Committee and the Committee of the Regions—Freedom, security and justice in Europe since 2005: an evaluation of the Hague Programme and Action Plan, COM (2009) 263 final, p. 11; and in the context of detention: Green Paper of the Commission—Strengthening mutual trust in the European judicial area. A Green Paper on the application of EU criminal justice legislation in the field of detention (n 56) p. 2 ff.

[70] Article 82(1)(b) TFEU and see, for instance: Communication from the Commission to the Council and the European Parliament—Mutual recognition of final decisions in criminal matters, COM (2000) 495 final, p. 9–10; Communication from the Commission to the Council and the European Parliament—Area of Freedom, Security and Justice: Assessment of the Tampere Programme and future orientations (n 34) p. 12; S. CLAVEL, 'L'approximation des règles de competence et des procedures de règlement des conflits (exception de litispendance)', in F. JAULT-SESEKE, J. LELEUR, and C. PIGACHE (eds.), *L'espace judiciaire européen civil et penal. Regards croisés* (Paris, Dalloz, 2009) 45–61; M. DEITERS, 'Gegenseitige Anerkennung von Strafgesetzen in Europa', *ZRP* 2003, 361; R. KERT, 'The Implementation and Application of Mutual Recognition Instruments in Austria' (n 28) 26; M. LUCHTMAN, 'Choice of Forum in an Area of Freedom, Security, and Justice', *Utrecht Law Review* 2011, 101; L. SURANO, 'The approach of Swedish practitioners to the principle of mutual recognition in criminal matters', in VERNIMMEN, SURANO, and WEYEMBERGH, *The Future of Mutual Recognition in Criminal Matters in the European Union* (n 23) 496–7; G. SVEDAS and D. MICKEVICIUS, 'Future of Mutual Recognition in Criminal Matters in the European Union: Lithuania', in *The Future of Mutual Recognition in Criminal Matters in the European Union* (n 23) 347–8.

[71] Framework Decision 2009/948/JHA on the prevention and settlement of conflicts of jurisdiction in criminal proceedings, *O.J.* L-328, 15.12.2009, p. 42–7.

[72] On the crucial role of Eurojust with regard to judicial cooperation in criminal matters, see: Article 85 TFEU; E. BARBE, 'Comment pallier l'absence de règles harmonisées de conflit de compétence en matière pénale?', in JAULT-SESEKE, LELEUR, and PIGACHE (eds.), *L'espace judiciaire européen civil et pénal. Regards croisés* (n 70) 88–92. For an overview of some of its interventions, see the annual reports from Eurojust, retrievable at:<http://www.eurojust.europa.eu/doclibrary/corporate/Pages/annual-reports.aspx>.

[73] See, for instance, with regard to judicial cooperation in civil matters: S. CLAVEL, 'L'harmonisation des règles de competence et des procedures de règlement des conflits (exception de litispendance)', in

E. Approximating substantive and procedural criminal law where necessary

As discussed above, much has been said and written about the relationship between mutual recognition and approximation.[74] However, in light of the Treaty provisions and the many policy documents that have addressed this issue, it seems clear that since the Tampere summit (1999) the EU has opted for a complementary approach which combines the two integration mechanisms.[75] While the focus has always been on the approximation of procedural criminal law,[76] with the aim of facilitating mutual recognition, there can be little doubt that the approximation of substantive criminal law may also serve the same purpose.[77]

The relationship between mutual recognition and approximation is not only characterized by complementarity: it also has a subsidiary or reactive nature. By this I mean that, in principle, approximation only comes into play when specific problems with the application of the principle of mutual recognition, or with judicial cooperation in criminal matters in general, have been identified in advance.[78] This can be evidenced by the 'list offences' mentioned in the FD EAW where, despite severe criticism in legal literature over the lack of approximation, the Commission seems determined not to

JAULT-SESEKE, LELEUR, and PIGACHE (eds.), *L'espace judiciaire européen civil et pénal. Regards croisés* (n 70) 45–61; and BARBE, 'Comment pallier l'absence de règles harmonisées de conflit de compétence en matière pénale?' (n 72) 79–92, who underlines that the different nature between private law and public law explains to a large extent the limited progress on this point of law in criminal matters.

[74] See: Part II, ch 2, II. 'Examination of the Approximation and Mutual Recognition Tandem'.

[75] See: Part II, ch 2, II. 'Examination of the Approximation and Mutual Recognition Tandem'.

[76] Tampere European Council—Presidency Conclusions, 15 and 16 October 1999, retrievable at: <http://www.consilium.europa.eu/uedocs/cms_data/docs/pressdata/en/ec/00200-r1.en9.htm>. See also: Article 82(2) TFEU which foresees the adoption of measures on approximation of criminal *procedural* law *to the extent necessary to facilitate mutual recognition* in three well-defined areas (mutual admissibility of evidence; rights of individuals in criminal procedure; rights of victims of crime). See also: Resolution of the Council—A roadmap for strengthening procedural rights of suspected or accused persons in criminal proceedings, *O.J.* C-295/1, 04.12.2009, and the instruments that are adopted or in the process of being adopted on the basis of this Resolution. In respect of the development of minimum standards with regard to victims of crime as an instrument to enhance mutual trust and mutual recognition, see: Communication from the Commission to the European Parliament, the Council, the Economic and Social Committee and the Committee of the Regions—Strengthening victims' rights in the EU, COM (2011) 274 final; Resolution of the Council—A Roadmap for strengthening the rights and protection of victims, in particular in criminal proceedings (n 56) p. 2; Directive 2012/29/EU of the European Parliament and of the Council of 25 October 2012 establishing minimum standards on the rights, support and protection of victims of crime, and replacing Council Framework Decision 2001/220/JHA, *O.J.* L-315, p. 57–73.

[77] The fact that Article 83(1) TFEU, which foresees the adoption of measures on approximation of criminal *substantive* law, does not explicitly mention that these measures must be adopted *to the extent necessary to facilitate mutual recognition*, does not exclude that such measures can be adopted with this aim. In several policy documents, the link between mutual recognition and the approximation of substantive criminal law has been underlined. See, for instance: Recommendation of the European Parliament to the Council and to the European Council on the future of the area of freedom, security, and justice as well as on the measures required to enhance the legitimacy and effectiveness thereof (n 34) p. 63; Communication from the Commission to the Council and the European Parliament—Communication on the mutual recognition of judicial decisions in criminal matters and the strengthening of mutual trust between Member States (n 34) p. 8.

[78] The latter can be deduced from the specification that (procedural) approximation will only be deployed 'to the extent necessary to facilitate mutual recognition' (Art. 82(2) TFEU), and that (substantive) approximation will only apply to 'the definition of criminal offences and sanctions in the areas of particularly serious crime with a cross-border dimension resulting from the nature of impact of such offences or from the need to combat them on a common basis' (Art. 83(1) TFEU). See, for instance: Communication from the Commission to the European Parliament and the Council—Coordination on drugs in the European Union, COM (2003) 681 final, p. 5–6.

take any legislative initiatives unless genuine difficulties[79] are identified.[80] With regard to another more delicate area of law,[81] namely evidence gathering, and in particular the admissibility of evidence, there seems to be more of a need and more willingness to take approximating measures in the near future.[82] These examples again demonstrate the crucial role of evaluation and research projects, as it is on the basis of such projects and also the ECJ's case law, of course, that the need for approximation measures can be highlighted.

Finally, it should not be overlooked that wherever approximation is found to be desirable and necessary in order to facilitate mutual recognition, it must still pass the legal basis test, which means that approximation will only be possible if a particular Treaty provision grants the EU power to take legislative measures in the area of law in question.[83]

F. Addressing the issue of costs

A final element for discussion is the issue of costs. In the majority of cases, problematic application of the mutual recognition instruments is not caused by bad faith or a lack of trust, but rather by a lack of financial means or human resources.[84] Problematic

[79] It is important to underline that the mere existence of any differences between Member States' legislations does not suffice to put the approximation mechanism into action, but that it is required that the established differences lead to specific difficulties in practice. See, for instance, in relation to FD 2005/214 JHA: Council of the European Union, Framework decision 2005/214/JHA on the application of the principle of mutual recognition to financial penalties—Follow up of the mutual recognition instruments, document number 17205/1/10, p. 3–4, retrievable at: <http://www.consilium.europa.eu/documents/access-to-council-documents-public-register/search-in-the-register?lang=en>. Here it was stated that differences exist amongst Member States regarding alternative sanctions to financial penalties on the one hand and with regard to compensation to victims on the other. However, whereas with regard to the first category, no particular difficulties were reported (and thus no specific measures are deemed necessary), it was considered that with regard to the second category, problems might arise and that a common approach would thus be desirable.

[80] Communication from the Commission to the Council and the European Parliament—The mutual recognition of judicial decisions in criminal matters and the strengthening of mutual trust between Member States (n 34) p. 8–9. On the basis of the study of Vernimmen, Surano, and Weyembergh, it seems that the existence of differences in substantive criminal law does not seem to be very problematic for the application of the principle of mutual recognition: VERNIMMEN, SURANO, and WEYEMBERGH, *The Future of Mutual Recognition in Criminal Matters in the European Union* (n 23); J. PRADEL, G. CORSTENS and G. VERMEULEN, *Droit pénal européen* (Paris, Dalloz, 2009) 465.

[81] O.L. KNÖFEL, 'Judizielle Loyalität in der Europäischen Union—Zur Rechts- und Beweishilfe im Verhältnis der Unionsgerichtbarkeit zu den Gerichten der Mitgliedstaaten', *EuR* 2010, 620, who qualifies the law on evidence in cross-border cooperation as 'das heiszeste Eisen'.

[82] Article 82(2)(a) TFEU; European Council, The Stockholm programme—An open and secure Europe serving and protecting citizens (n 44) 12; Communication from the Commission to the Council, the European Parliament, the European Economic and Social Committee and the Committee of the Regions—Delivering an area of freedom, security, and justice for Europe's citizens. Action Plan implementing the Stockholm Programme (n 38) p. 18.

[83] See, for instance, the plea for more approximation in the area of detention and prisoners' rights, as suggested by VERMEULEN, VAN KALMTHOUT, PATERSON, KNAPEN, VERBEKE, and DE BONDT, *Cross-border Execution of Judgments Involving Deprivation of Liberty in the EU* (n 30) 96–105. As EU law currently stands doubts have raised as to the existence of a valid legal basis in view of the fact that Article 82(2) TFEU limits procedural harmonization in criminal matters to aspects related to (i) mutual admissibility of evidence, (ii) rights of individuals in criminal procedure, and (iii) rights of victims of crime. Approximation on any other element of procedural criminal law would require a previous unanimous decision of the Council, after obtaining the consent of the European Parliament (Art. 82(2)(c) TFEU).

[84] See, for instance, with regard to the FD EAW and the use of this instrument for minor offences which puts a serious strain on limited resources: DAVIDSON, 'A Sledgehammer to Crack a Nut?' (n 18) 35.

application of the principle of mutual recognition is therefore less a problem of trust and more a question of costs.

The point of departure in most legislative instruments is that, in principle, costs resulting from the application of the corresponding instrument are to be borne by the executing state, except for those arising exclusively within the territory of the issuing state.[85] This in itself is perfectly defensible in a single area of freedom, security, and justice, where it seems logical to take the approach that what is in the interests of the issuing judicial authority is necessarily also in the interests of the executing judicial authority, and vice versa.[86] Every Member State may fulfil the role of either issuing or executing Member State at any one time, with the result that the costs incurred ultimately balance out. However, they do not usually balance out exactly and when there is a considerable and sustained discrepancy of work related to the execution of mutual recognition instruments between Member State A and Member State B, it is understandable that frictions might arise, especially in cases where Member States are already faced with tight internal deadlines and the need to prioritize incoming cases due to a short age of staff or limited resources. In such cases, problems of a practical nature (such as limited resources) risk becoming issues of a more substantive nature (for instance, foreign requests do not seem 'proportionate' in light of the national agenda).

In this respect, it is necessary that future legislative work at EU level duly takes into account the capacities available at national level to implement the instruments concerned, especially the effort required to prepare practitioners for the application of new instruments, including possible organizational changes.[87] In this context, Member States are encouraged to make use of the funding opportunities available through financial programmes, particularly within the Commission's dedicated programmes on 'criminal justice' and 'the prevention and fight against crime'.[88] Moreover, if the issue of costs leads to an unacceptable discrepancy in practice, it seems unavoidable that the EU legislator will need to reconsider, for each instrument separately, the point of departure that costs are to be borne by the executing Member State. It may have to develop a slightly more detailed mechanism which enables the reimbursement of (certain) costs, as in other areas of law.[89]

[85] See, for instance: Article 30 FD EAW, Article 22 FD ESO (post-trial), Article 25 FD ESO (pre-trial), Article Y PROP DIR EIO. See also: Opinion of AG Sharpston in Case C-179/11 *Cimade*, nyr, § 84 (on the area of visa, asylum, and immigration).

[86] E. BARBE, at the Conference on 'The European Investigation Order: Towards the Next Level of Obtaining Evidence Across the EU', 14 and 15 December 2010, Brussels, organized by ERA in cooperation with the then Belgian Presidency of the Council of the EU.

[87] Council of the European Union, Follow-up of the Mutual Recognition instruments (n 4) p. 4.

[88] Council of the European Union, Follow-up of the Mutual Recognition instruments (n 4) p. 4.

[89] See, for instance: Article 18 REG 1206/2001, as discussed in ECJ, Case C-283/09 *Weryński* [2011] ECR I-601; Article 54 REG 4/2009.

4

Conclusions on the Principle of Mutual Recognition in the EU Criminal Justice Area

The preceding chapters have illustrated the position of paramount importance that the principle of mutual recognition has occupied in the EU criminal justice area since the Tampere conclusions, both in the ECJ's case law and in the legislative instruments that have been adopted in the intervening time. Despite the finding that the principle's application in daily practice has not proven to be an unqualified success story, certain policy documents, legislative instruments currently in development, and the Treaty of Lisbon all indicate that there is a strong belief among Member States and in EU institutions that the future of EU criminal justice lies in the generalized application of the principle of mutual recognition.

In conclusion, I will now return to the major themes developed in Part II with regard to the principle of mutual recognition: its legal basis (section I); the terminology (section II); its addressees (section III); its object (section IV); its main characteristics (section V); and finally, its workability (section VI).

I. Legal Basis

Since the coming into force of the Treaty of Lisbon, the principle of mutual recognition has gained an explicit legal basis, namely Article 82(1) TFEU. Notwithstanding this clarification, it is helpful to keep in mind the other general principles to which the principle of mutual recognition is closely related and which may help clarify its scope and meaning, namely the principles of proportionality, subsidiarity, sincere cooperation and mutual trust.

II. Terminology

In the EU criminal justice context, there is a strong trend in legislation, case law, and academic writing to refer to '(the principle of) mutual recognition', seemingly avoiding any reference to a 'principle of equivalence' or a 'country of origin' principle. Yet, my analysis of the ECJ's *ne bis in idem* case law and of the relevant framework decisions has revealed that a study of the relevance of both concepts in the EU criminal justice area does yield interesting results.

It has been argued on many occasions that (the principle) of equivalence (unfortunately) has no relevant role to play in this context. I have attempted to illustrate that the truth is somewhat more complex, both in the ECJ's *ne bis in idem* case law and in the relevant legislative instruments. With regard to the former, I recognized that in its *ne bis in idem* case law, the ECJ generally focuses on a presumption of equivalence *in abstracto*, firmly rejecting any suggestions that it might be better to adopt a more concrete test; however, it must be noted that equivalence is not entirely absent from this case law, as the *ne bis in idem* concept itself refers to a kind of equivalence requirement, admittedly watered down by an approach based on the material facts (rather than the legal qualifications). With regard to the latter, I have illustrated that in the majority of legislative instruments, several mechanisms have been developed that address any problematic issues related to lack of equivalence in this context. In this regard, it should be kept in mind that equivalence checks are not intended to be performed for every minor legislative difference, but only where fundamental aspects of one Member State's legal order are at stake, especially where that Member State is required to execute the order on its own territory.

In academic writing, little attention has been paid to the role that the 'country of origin' (the issuing Member State) could potentially play in this context. Yet one of the major achievements of the principle of mutual recognition's introduction in the framework decisions is precisely that it has attributed such a significant role to the issuing Member State while also leaving considerable powers to the executing Member State. This has resulted in a sophisticated mechanism for distributing competences between the two Member States. Similarly, in the ECJ's *ne bis in idem* case law, the assessment of the *ne bis in idem* criteria relies on close cooperation and the well-balanced distribution of competences between the two Member States involved.

In sum, while I have no intention of calling the adequacy of the term 'principle of mutual recognition' into question, I do believe that (more) attention should be paid to the relevant roles of both the 'equivalence' aspect and the system of 'distribution of competences' in the ECJ's *ne bis in idem* case law and in the framework decisions on mutual recognition, as they provide useful information on how the principle of mutual recognition works and also help to clarify its scope and meaning.

III. Addressees

Article 82(1) TFEU imposes a duty of mutual recognition on Member States in the context of judicial cooperation in criminal matters. Since the introduction of the FD EAW (and certain preceding policy documents), it has become clear that, in essence, it is the judicial authorities that will play a pivotal role in applying the mutual recognition instruments. It would, however, be inaccurate to conclude on this basis that the duties related to the mutual recognition mechanism are exclusively directed at public judicial authorities. In fact, it seems far more correct to assume that all actors involved in criminal proceedings which are subject to a mutual recognition mechanism are bound by the duties arising from the principle of mutual recognition. In other words—and this is implicitly confirmed in a number of framework decisions—private and semi-private entities attributed a relevant role under one of the framework decisions on mutual recognition can also be bound by mutual recognition duties.

The principle of mutual recognition not only imposes duties on (judicial) authorities, but also has a significant effect on the natural (or legal) person who is subject to the mutual recognition mechanism. Contrary to what is often assumed, these individuals are not necessarily mere passive subjects who 'undergo' the mutual recognition process: in relation to certain instruments, they may actually be the ones who trigger the mutual recognition mechanism in the first place.

IV. Object

Both Article 54 CISA and Article 82 TFEU impose a duty to recognize judgments and judicial decisions, which illustrates the predominantly judicial nature of the principle of mutual recognition's object in the EU criminal justice context.

Yet there are a number of clear signs in the ECJ's case law, EU policy documents, and EU legislation that the concept of 'judicial authority' must be interpreted broadly and that decisions made by non-judicial authorities can also be made subject to the duty of mutual recognition on certain occasions. For instance, in the context of alternative sanctions, which is characterized in several Member States by a combined public-private cooperation approach, I have drawn attention to the fact that the corresponding framework decision explicitly recognizes that Member States may designate non-judicial authorities as the competent authorities for taking decisions. In light of growing privatization trends in other key areas of the Member States' criminal justice systems, we cannot rule out the possibility that yet more non-judicial decisions will be subject to the mutual recognition mechanism in the future.

V. Characteristics

The scope and meaning of the principle of mutual recognition can best be explained by examining its main characteristics, particularly the fact that it is flexible (section V, A), non-automatic (section V, B), teleological (section V, C), and versatile (section V, D).

A. The flexible nature of the principle of mutual recognition

The principle of mutual recognition is an instrument for constructing an area of freedom, security, and justice, which necessitates the performance of a careful balancing act involving each of these three valuable elements (freedom, security, and justice). This requirement therefore results in a flexible principle.

The ECJ's *ne bis in idem* case law is a first illustration of how the ECJ performs this balancing act. While free movement—and thus mutual recognition—can be seen as the CISA's primary aim, the ECJ has also given significant thought to the 'security' and 'justice' pillars in order to counterbalance the 'freedom' element and thus preclude too rigid an application of the principle of mutual recognition.

With regard to the framework decisions on mutual recognition, the number of judgments in which the ECJ has performed such a balancing act is still rather limited. However, in the small number of judgments that are available, a clear trend of counterbalancing the principle of mutual recognition with other valuable interests can be identified. Thus far, the proportionality test applied by the ECJ has granted a relatively wide margin of discretion to the Member States, yet it remains to be seen whether the ECJ will apply the same soft test in each and every case. It seems far more likely that the proportionality test (and thus the principle of mutual recognition) will be applied with some flexibility depending on the interest at stake and the specific circumstances of the case in question.

Another element which indicates the flexible nature of the principle of mutual recognition relates to my previous finding that many framework decisions allow for adaptations of an original order whenever recognition and/or execution of this order is considered incompatible with fundamental aspects of the Member State's criminal justice system. Such clauses introduce the possibility of partial mutual recognition (rather than full mutual recognition) and highlight the fact that the application of the principle of mutual recognition is not a case of all or nothing, but rather a gradual, flexible system which—in cases where full recognition is not feasible—a little recognition is preferable to none at all. Furthermore, the provisions of other framework decisions discussed in Part II also reflect the flexible nature of the principle of mutual recognition. Examples of these include the optional nature of the majority of grounds for non-recognition and non-execution (optional (non) recognition), the possibility of postponing recognition (postponed recognition), and the possibility of making recognition subject to the fulfillment of certain guarantees (conditional recognition).

B. The non-automatic nature of the principle of mutual recognition

The flexible nature of the principle of mutual recognition is closely related to its non-automatic nature, as it is precisely the existence of a range of interests (the grounds for non-recognition and non-execution that are included in the framework decisions)—which must be counterbalanced with the principle of mutual recognition—that illustrates how the principle of mutual recognition does not operate automatically. In view of the fact that case law in this area of law remains rather scarce, a number of questions are still open for discussion and will need to be clarified in the ECJ's future case law. A first question relates to the general rule that exceptions must be interpreted narrowly. To date, the ECJ has not yet explicitly imposed this rule in the context of the FD EAW, though a number of implicit indications hint that things may be moving in that direction. A second question is whether two different approaches are needed for grounds that address a purely national interest and grounds that address an EU or international interest. A particularly interesting example concerns the protection of fundamental rights. I have argued above that in very exceptional circumstances, fundamental rights obligations—which constitute one of the foundations of the EU legal order—must take priority over the principle of mutual recognition and that in this regard the case law of both the ECJ and the ECtHR may prove relevant.

The non-automatic nature of the principle of mutual recognition can also be recognized in cases where abuse of law is under discussion. While the ECJ has not yet referred explicitly to the term 'abuse of law' in either its *ne bis in idem* case law or its case law on the FD EAW, there have been judgments in both contexts in which the principle of mutual recognition has been set aside by the ECJ precisely because its application would run counter to one of the main objectives of the TFEU (or the legislative framework). In cases where a natural (or legal) person or a Member State's representative relies on the principle of mutual recognition (or on its non-application), while manifestly disregarding one the fundamental objectives underlying the legal framework at stake, this amounts to abusive application of the provision at stake, which cannot be accepted.

A final illustration of the non-automatic application of the principle of mutual recognition can be found in the ECJ's approach to a Member State's margin of discretion when faced with a mutual recognition issue. In the ECJ's *ne bis in idem* case law, the point of departure is mutual trust and the unequivocal prohibition of reassessing the merits of a case. However, duties of cooperation and information exchange were explicitly included in order to enable the (second) Member State to properly assess whether the *ne bis in idem* criteria have been fulfilled in each specific case. 'Blind' or automatic application of the principle of mutual recognition is also rejected in the legislative instruments discussed in Part II of this book. Here, too, the essential point of departure is mutual trust, but the legislative instruments leave the executing Member States some margin for suspending the principle of mutual recognition and for questioning the accuracy, completeness, or authenticity of the mutual recognition file or any other related document, provided, first, that there are objective and substantive reasons to do so and, secondly, that this margin of control remains subject to cooperation and information exchange duties between the Member States involved.

C. The functional or teleological nature of the principle of mutual recognition

In the EU criminal justice context, the principle of mutual recognition can be seen as the ideal tool for establishing the area of freedom, security, and justice. Mutual recognition pursues the free movement of (judicial) decisions, though not at the expense of other valuable interests underpinning this area. My analysis of the ECJ's *ne bis in idem* case law and the adopted framework decisions on mutual recognition in criminal matters has illustrated that the principle of mutual recognition can work in two diametrically opposed ways, namely either as an instrument that aims to facilitate the enforcement of penalties (mutual recognition which benefits the Member State's public prosecution services) or as an instrument that aims to make an individual exempt from further prosecution by applying the *ne bis in idem* principle (mutual recognition which benefits a natural or legal person involved in criminal proceedings). Either way, correct application of the principle of mutual recognition requires that the main objective(s) of the legal instrument behind the principle is (are) duly taken into account and counterbalanced with other crucial objectives underpinning the area of freedom, security, and justice.

D. The versatile nature of the principle of mutual recognition

The previous finding that the principle of mutual recognition can interact with occasionally opposing objectives brings me to another feature of this principle, namely its versatility. The principle of mutual recognition described in the TFEU and the many available policy documents has an ambitious scope and is intended to be applied to all of the phases of a criminal law proceeding, even having an impact beyond the criminal law sphere *sensu stricto*.

The principle of mutual recognition's versatile nature is also reflected firstly in its inclusion in Article 54 CISA and the *ne bis in idem* grounds for refusal in the framework decisions and secondly in its position as the actual point of departure for these framework decisions. While both versions of the principle of mutual recognition are essential in creating the area of freedom, security, and justice and while the point of departure is identical in both scenarios (namely that the decisions of other Member States must be recognized), their primary focus and outcomes are different. Whereas the first version of the principle entails an obligation on the part of a Member State's competent authority not to do something and is mainly of benefit to a convicted or acquitted person (freedom and justice considerations as main focus), the second version imposes an obligation on a Member State's competent authority to actively do something and is, in the majority of legislative instruments, principally in the interests of the issuing Member State (security and efficient cooperation as central focus).

The versatile nature of the principle of mutual recognition also results from the fact that it can be realized to different degrees (full recognition, partial recognition, no recognition) and in different forms (substantive mutual recognition and procedural mutual recognition).

VI. Workability

In view of the relative newness of many mutual recognition instruments, it may be unwise to draw far-reaching conclusions about the workability of (all of) these instruments in general, yet certain points that have emerged from my analysis on the workability of the principle of mutual recognition are worth mentioning.

Thus far, at least one instrument based on the principle of mutual recognition has proven extremely useful in practice, namely the FD EAW. The success of this instrument can be explained by a variety of factors: it provides a single, well-defined legal framework with clear duties and tight deadlines (legal certainty) which has replaced (all) previously applicable legal instrument in this field of law; its implementation was followed-up very closely by the competent EU institutions, both during its implementation period and afterwards by means of a thorough evaluation procedure (in order to identify any existing obstacles); numerous forums for discussion, training, and exchange of information were set with regard to the practical application of this instrument (in order to assure good knowledge and understanding of the FD EAW); and practical tools were also developed (in order to enhance cooperation among judicial authorities). All of these elements contributed to the principle of mutual recognition's functioning well through the FD EAW and should also be taken into account as useful guidelines for the other framework decisions. Of course, the FD EAW system is not without its flaws and some of the problematic elements that were highlighted during the follow-up—such as linguistic problems, insurmountable differences in legal systems, and cost-related issues—will need to be addressed not only with regard to the FD EAW but also with regard to the other framework decisions.

PART III

MUTUAL RECOGNITION FROM A CROSS-POLICY PERSPECTIVE

Investigating the Viability of the Internal Market Analogy

In the preceding two parts of this book I analysed the principle of mutual recognition in two different EU policy domains: the internal market (Part I) and criminal justice in the area of freedom, security, and justice (Part II). In this third and final part, I rely largely on the results obtained from these analyses in order to identify the peculiarities, parallels, and (in)compatibilities that arise from a cross-policy application of the principle of mutual recognition. The main research question underpinning this book, which I discuss in more detail in Part III, is whether the internal market analogy is viable (and if so, to what extent) and whether any potential benefits and/or pitfalls are related to a cross-policy analysis. I examine this question with reference to three key issues: the introduction of the principle of mutual recognition in two distinct but intertwined policy areas (Chapter 1); the mutual recognition mechanism and whether its main characteristics can be attributed to the principle of mutual recognition (Chapter 2); and the extent to which the principle of mutual recognition succeeds in each area and which elements are crucial to its success (Chapter 3). Finally, I summarize the main findings of Part III and of the book as a whole by drawing a number of general conclusions (Chapter 4).

1

The Introduction of the Principle of Mutual Recognition in Two Distinct but Intertwined Policy Areas

In an area without internal borders, whether economic (the internal market) or judicial (the area of freedom, security, and justice), divergent national legislation can constitute a serious barrier to the free movement of economic or non-economic factors, especially when each Member State attempts to uphold its own standards based on arguments of host state control or sovereignty.

In the initial phase of the internal market strategy, as in the early years of EU judicial cooperation in criminal matters, the European legislator decided upon an exclusively harmonizing approach in order to tackle this problem of disparity between Member States' laws. Yet in both areas, such an approach led to disappointing results. It was precisely in order to overcome the difficulties arising from a straightforward harmonization approach, and with the aim of stimulating the integration process, that the ECJ underlined in *Cassis de Dijon*[1] the Member States' duty to recognize goods that are lawfully produced and marketed in another Member State. Similarly, in *Gözütok and Brügge*,[2] it was reiterated that each Member State should recognize the criminal law in force in another Member State. These judgments saw the introduction of the principle of mutual recognition, first in the internal market context and two decades later in the area of freedom, security, and justice. In addition to this judicial impetus, the principle of mutual recognition was also taken up by the Commission,[3] the Council,[4] and the European Council,[5] who had all become aware of the fact that in view of the impossibility of agreeing on detailed harmonization, the only[6] viable alternative for more integration was an approach based on the coordination of national legal systems through mutual recognition. In both contexts, these EU institutions therefore made a strong case for the introduction of the principle of mutual recognition in combination with minimum harmonization.[7]

However, the fact that similar motives lay behind the principle of mutual recognition's adoption in each area does not necessarily demonstrate that the principle is equally suitable for each context. In view of the significant differences in the objectives pursued in each area, and of the peculiar nature of criminal justice, it has been repeatedly argued that transferring a key concept from an economic integration project to the area of criminal justice was a regrettable mistake. In what follows, I verify whether this critique is indeed justified and whether arguments based on the objectives pursued in each area

[1] ECJ, Case 120/78 *Rewe-Zentral AG (Cassis de Dijon)* [1979] ECR 649, para 14.

[2] ECJ, Joined Cases C-187/01 and C-185/01 *Gözütok and Brügge* [2003] ECR I-1345, para 33.

[3] Communication from the Commission concerning the consequences of the judgment given by the ECJ on 20 February 1979 in Case 120/78 ('Cassis de Dijon'), *O.J.* C-256, 03.10.1980, p. 2–3; White Paper from the Commission to the European Council—Completing the Internal Market , COM (1985) 310 final.

[4] Resolution of the Council—A new approach to technical harmonisation and standards, *O.J.* C-136, 04.06.1985, p.1–9.

[5] Tampere European Council—Presidency Conclusions, 15 and 16 October 1999, retrievable at: <http://ue.eu.int/ueDocs/cms_Data/docs/pressData/en/ec/00200-r1.en9.htm>.

[6] See, in this regard, Nicolaïdis who rightly points out that 'recognition was not one of several options available but the only game in town for effective free movement short of harmonization'. K. NICOLAIDIS, 'Kir Forever? The Journey of a Political Scientist in the Landscape of Mutual Recognition', in M. POIARES MADURO and L. AZOULAI (eds.), *The Past and Future of EU Law. The Classics of EU Law Revisited on the 50th Anniversary of the Rome Treaty* (Oxford, Hart Publishing, 2010) 449. See also the triple classification of Poiares Maduro, the decentralized model of host state control, the centralized model of harmonization, and the competitive model of mutual recognition, in: M. POIARES MADURO, *We The Court—The European Court of Justice and the European Economic Constitution* (Oxford, Hart Publishing, 1998) 103–49 and J. PELKMANS, 'Mutual Recognition: Economic and Regulatory Logic in Goods and Services. Bruges European Economic Research Papers 24/2012', 2012, retrievable at: < http://www.coleurope.eu/sites/default/files/research-paper/beer24.pdf>, 5–7, who speaks in terms of 'the EEC's free-movement-of-goods trilemma'.

[7] In the internal market context the terms 'harmonization' and 'approximation' are used as synonyms (see, in particular Art. 114 TFEU) whereas in the Treaty provisions on judicial cooperation in criminal matters only the term 'approximation' is used (Articles 82 and 83 TFEU). Hereinafter I will, however

(section I), and on their intrinsically different natures (section II), do indeed have any weight as regards the application of the principle of mutual recognition in the context of judicial cooperation in criminal matters.

I. Policy Aims Underpinning the Internal Market and the Area of Freedom, Security, and Justice: Towards a Citizens' Europe?

Some authors have highlighted the fact that the purpose of the criminal justice system is entirely different—and arguably more important—than the purpose of the internal market: the former seeks to ensure public safety, whereas the latter aims at regulating economic development. Thus, in the internal market, mutual recognition serves to facilitate the exercise of the fundamental freedoms in favour of the individual, thus supporting freedom (the individual as the subject of rights in a mutual recognition procedure which serves private interests). In the area of freedom, security, and justice, however, it is not the free movement of (goods, services, or capital of) individuals that is at stake, but the free movement of judicial (enforcement) decisions against individuals, thus mutual recognition is said to threaten freedom (the individual as the object in a mutual recognition procedure which serves public interests).[8] Needless to say, the aims pursued by the area of freedom, security, and justice, especially the criminal justice area, are indeed different from the aims pursued by the internal market area. Yet in view of the TFEU provisions and the ECJ's case law, it seems mistaken to reduce the internal market to a simple economic matter without highlighting the relevance of non-economic interests in this context. In the same way, it would be equally incorrect to uphold the view that mutual recognition in criminal justice is exclusively based on security grounds, threatening the citizen's freedom. The need to take into account and balance different objectives in each context requires an urgent reconsideration of the dichotomy 'public versus private interests' (section I, A). Furthermore, it would be oversimplifying matters in light of the EU acquis to state that 'the application of mutual recognition is treating individuals as subjects in the internal market context and as objects in the area of freedom, security, and justice' (section I, B).

A. Mutual recognition and the need to balance different objectives

(1) Balancing different objectives in the internal market

The free movement provisions on goods, persons, services, and capital are undoubtedly the driving force behind the internal market project, but the TFEU, the ECJ's case law and the EU legislation clearly illustrate that the free movement provisions, and the underlying principle of mutual recognition, only apply to their full extent insofar as safety, health, consumer, environmental, and fundamental rights as well as other non-economic interests—many of which have now been explicitly included in the Charter—are sufficiently

use the term 'harmonization' to refer to both concepts (approximation and harmonization) in both areas of law (internal market and judicial cooperation in criminal matters). I feel supported by the ECJ, who also uses the term 'harmonization' in a criminal justice context. See, for instance: ECJ, Case C-399/11 *Melloni*, nyr, para 43 ('armonización' in the language of the case).

[8] See, for instance: V. MITSILEGAS, *EU Criminal Law* (Oxford, Hart Publishing, 2009) 117–18; M. MÖSTL, 'Preconditions and Limits of Mutual Recognition', *CML Rev.* 2010, 409; S. PEERS, 'Mutual Recognition and Criminal Law in the European Union: Has the Council got it wrong?', *CML Rev.* 2004, 24.

protected at national (or European) level. Indeed, the Treaty exceptions, the rule of reason and the provisions on the protection of fundamental rights have implicitly created a balancing test[9] whereby 'the fundamental freedoms' are balanced against other fundamental, non-economic values. The EU could have promoted integration at the expense of (one of) these non-economic interests, or maintained (one of) these non-economic interests at the expense of integration, yet for the most part,[10] it has managed to avoid either extreme.[11]

The key to the EU's ability to balance economic integration and non-economic interests lies largely in its decision to combine free movement (mutual recognition) with regulation (harmonization). Undoubtedly, it is the continual expansion of the EU's role and competence in regulatory policy fields through successive Treaty amendments and new legislation that has played a crucial role in preventing the completion of the internal market from undermining national non-economic interests or from privileging economic interests over non-economic interests.[12]

The ECJ, too, has contributed significantly to establishing an EU that aims to improve free movement, without putting principal interests at risk. For instance, the ECJ's willingness to consider consumer and environmental issues as worthy of protection at a time when neither had any basis in the Treaty[13] is significant in this regard. It illustrates the ECJ's determination not to pursue the notions of free movement, mutual recognition, and economic integration to a reckless extreme, but to strike a balance with any non-economic interest that is deemed worthy of protection from the EU perspective.[14]

The ECJ's decision to consider the free movement provisions directly applicable was another important step in the case law that is worth mentioning here. It gave the integration process an important boost, and in this way, to some extent, the ECJ individualized provisions which were essentially directed towards the Member States and thus public in nature.[15] Owing to the direct effect of the free movement provisions, the ECJ has dealt with a huge number of preliminary proceedings in which it was required to balance a private economic interest (a natural or legal person's claim based on one of the free

[9] In fact, the ECJ only explicitly used the term 'balancing' in judgments where free movement and fundamental rights were at stake. See, for instance: ECJ, Case C-112/00 *Schmidberger* [2003] ECR I-5659, para 81, where the ECJ stated that 'the interests involved must be *weighed* having regard to all the circumstances of the case in order to determine whether a fair *balance* was struck between those interests' (emphasis added); ECJ, Case C-391/09 *Vardyn-Wardyn* [2011] ECR I-3787, paras 87 and 91. However, the ECJ's analysis of the Treaty-based justification grounds and the *rule of reason* in combination with a proportionality test also comes down to a similar balancing test, namely between the free movement provision on the one hand and the non-economic interest on the other.

[10] With regard to some judgments, however, the ECJ's unilateral concern with free movement (at the expense of safety) has been rightly criticized. See, for instance: N. REICH, 'AGM-COS.MET or: Who is Protected by EC Safety Regulation?', *E.L. Rev.* 2008, 85 ff.

[11] D. VOGEL, *Trading Up. Consumer and Environmental Regulation in a Global Economy* (Cambridge, Massachussetts, Harvard University Press, 1995) 53 and 95.

[12] VOGEL, *Trading Up* (n 11) 53–5. For a strong plea on the harmonization of non-economic aims in the internal market legislation, see: B. DE WITTE, 'A Competence to Protect: The Pursuit of Non-Market Aims through Internal Market Legislation', in P. SYRPIS (ed.), *The Judiciary, the Legislature and the EU Internal Market* (Cambridge, Cambridge University Press, 2012) 25–46.

[13] Currently: Article 168 TFEU and Article 169 TFEU. The importance of both interests and policy domains is also underlined by Article 37 Charter and Article 38 Charter.

[14] S. WEATHERILL, 'Recent Case Law Concerning the Free Movement of Goods: Mapping the Frontiers of Market Deregulation', *CML Rev.* 1999, 59.

[15] Moreover, Article 15 Charter has taken this individualization process even further by upgrading the *fundamental freedoms*—in particular the free movement of establishment and the free movement of services—to *fundamental rights* in hands of the EU citizen.

movement provisions) with a non-economic public interest (a Member State invoking a Treaty exception or a rule of reason). Yet it would be erroneous to conclude that the mutual recognition principle always necessitates a private interest's being taken into consideration in the internal market context. The free movement provisions are essentially duties imposed on the Member States, and thus represent a public interest, namely the economic integration process. Therefore, in all infringement proceedings initiated by the Commission, the ECJ will be asked to rule on a conflict between two public interests, namely the free movement provision *in abstracto* (this time independent of any specific private or subjective right) and a non-economic interest (Treaty exception or rule of reason). Besides these two scenarios, it is also conceivable that the ECJ will be asked to rule in cases where two private interests are at stake, as illustrated by the *Schmidberger* case.[16] In sum, it is not the private or public nature of the interest(s) at stake that should be considered the main feature of the mutual recognition principle in the internal market context, but rather the balancing mechanism itself.

(2) *Balancing different objectives in the criminal justice area*

Since the European Council meeting in Tampere, the principle of mutual recognition or the free movement of judgments in criminal matters has become the guiding principle in the criminal justice area. In this domain, mutual recognition aims first and foremost to promote smooth cooperation at the levels of criminal investigation, prosecution, and sentencing in order to ensure a high level of security in the EU, as required by Article 67 TFEU.[17] In line with this objective, the European legislator has adopted much security-driven legislation in past years, including a great number of mutual recognition instruments.[18]

Yet it would be erroneous to conclude that the EU's criminal justice area, and especially the mutual recognition mechanism embedded within it, is solely concerned with enhancing the free movement of enforcement decisions and facilitating cooperation between authorities. As far back as the European Council's conclusions from Tampere it has been stressed that the protection of individual rights is essential to the principle of mutual recognition, as these conclusions clearly state that 'enhanced mutual recognition [...] would facilitate cooperation between authorities and the judicial protection of individual rights'.[19]

[16] ECJ, Case C-112/00 *Schmidberger* [2003] ECR I-5659.

[17] Article 67 TFEU states that 'the Union shall endeavour to ensure a high level of security [...]'.

[18] For a critique and analysis of such a security-based approach, see, for instance: M. ANDERSON and J. APAP, *Striking a Balance between Freedom, Security and Justice in an Enlarged European Union* (Brussels, CEPS, 2002) 7 ff.; S. DOUGLAS SCOTT, 'The Rule of Law in the European Union—Putting the Security into the Area of Freedom, Security, and Justice', *E.L. Rev.* 2004, 219–42; B. GILMORE, 'The Twin Towers and the Third Pillar: Some Security Agenda Developments', EUI Working Paper Law 2003, retrievable at: <http://cadmus.iue.it/dspace/bitstream/1814/202/1/law03-7.pdf>; MITSILEGAS, *EU Criminal Law* (n 8) 323; C. SAFFERLING, 'Europe as Transnational Law—A Criminal Law for Europe: Between National Heritage and Transnational Necessities', *German Law Journal* 2009, 1393.

[19] Tampere European Council—Presidency Conclusions, 15 and 16 October 1999 (n 5) § 33. See also: Communication from the Commission—Towards an area of freedom, security, and justice, COM (1998) 459. More recently, under the Stockholm Programme, striking the right balance between law enforcement measures and measures to safeguard individual rights has become a political priority: European Council—The Stockholm Programme—An open and secure Europe serving and protecting citizens, *O.J.* C-115, 04.05.2010, p. 4.

The importance of fundamental rights is not limited to declarations in non-binding policy documents, though. Article 67 TFEU states—unlike its predecessor, former Article 29 TEU—that 'the Union shall constitute an area of freedom, security and justice *with respect for fundamental rights* [...]' (emphasis added). Furthermore, the Member States—when implementing or applying framework decisions and other instruments related to judicial cooperation in criminal matters—are bound by the Charter.[20]

EU secondary legislation, on the other hand, displayed in the early 'mutual recognition' years remarkably less focus on fundamental rights.[21] Whilst most mutual recognition instruments were adopted swiftly, procedural rights initiatives were usually—partly owing to the lack of an unambiguous legal basis in the old Treaties—[22] turned down. Yet the coming into force of the Treaty of Lisbon has given an important boost to the legislative process by the introduction of a clear legal basis for the adoption of EU legislation in the area of procedural criminal law in a cross-border context (Art. 82(2) TFEU). Following the adoption of a roadmap for strengthening procedural rights of suspected or accused persons, a number of instruments have been adopted and others are still in progress.[23] However, it must be clear that the harmonization work will not stop here. The mutual recognition and harmonization tandem is—like in the internal market context—in constant progress and the more mutual recognition will be applied, the more obstacles to mutual recognition will become visible and the more harmonization will be required.

The ECJ's case law—in particular on the *ne bis in idem* principle and on the FD EAW—is a final example of how 'freedom', 'security', and 'justice' objectives cannot be read in isolation, but must be seen in conjunction with each other.[24] Admittedly, free movement and mutual recognition are the point of departure,[25] yet they are constantly balanced against other interests, e.g. reintegration objectives[26] or fundamental rights.[27]

[20] Article 51(1) Charter. On the growing importance of this Charter, in particular after the coming into force of the Treaty of Lisbon, see: D. LECZYKIEWICZ, 'Effective Judicial Protection of Human Rights after Lisbon: Should National Courts be Empowered to Review EU Secondary Law?', *E.L. Rev.* 2010, 328–32. See also: Opinion of AG Cruz Villalón in Case C-306/09 *IB* [2010] ECR I-10341, § 44; Opinion of AG Sharpston in Case C-396/11 *Radu*, nyr, § 51, who does not believe that the Treaty of Lisbon altered EU law to a material degree in the area of fundamental rights.

[21] For a criticism on this delay, see, for instance: S. PEERS, *EU Justice and Home Affairs*, 3rd edn (Oxford, Oxford University Press, 2011) 753.

[22] On the issue of the legal basis, see for instance: V. MITSILEGAS, 'The Constitutional Implications of Mutual Recognition in Criminal Matters in the EU', *CML Rev.* 2006, 1305–6.

[23] Resolution of the Council—A Roadmap for strengthening procedural rights of suspected or accused persons in criminal proceedings, *O.J.* C-295, 04.12.2009, 1–3; Directive 2010/64/EU of the European Parliament and of the Council of 20 October 2010 on the right to interpretation and translation in criminal proceedings, *O.J.* L-280, 26.10.2010, p. 1–7; Directive 2012/13/EU of the European Parliament and of the Council of 22 May 2012 on the right to information in criminal proceedings, *O.J.* L-142, 1.6.2012, p. 1–10; Proposal for a directive of the European Parliament and of the Council on the right of access to a lawyer in criminal proceedings and on the right to communicate upon arrest, COM (2011) 326 final.

[24] See: Part II, ch 1, I, C, 4. 'A teleological and functional approach to mutual recognition in which the ECJ balances freedom, security, and justice'; Part II, ch 2, III, B. 'Limits resulting from mechanisms aimed at eliminating or restricting the principle of mutual recognition'.

[25] See, for instance: ECJ, Case C-66/08 *Kozlowski* [2008] ECR I-6041, para 32; ECJ, Case C-123/08 *Wolzenburg* [2009] ECR I-9621, para 57; ECJ, Case C-396/11 *Radu*, nyr, para 35; ECJ, Case C-399/11 *Melloni*, nyr, para 38; ECJ, Case C-168/13 PPU *Jeremy F.*, paras 34–6.

[26] See, for instance: ECJ, Case C-66/08 *Kozlowski* [2008] ECR I-6041, para 45; ECJ, Case C-123/08 *Wolzenburg* [2009] ECR I-9621, paras 62 and 67; ECJ, Case C-306/09 *I.B.* [2010] ECR I-10341, para 52.

[27] The fact that the ECJ has not yet explicitly confirmed that there are human rights exceptions to the principle of mutual recognition in the criminal justice context, does not mean that fundamental rights

Due to its direct impact on civil liberties and human rights, it is likely that much of the balancing act will need to be performed between private interests (individual fundamental rights) and public interests (enforcement decisions). However, under the Treaty of Lisbon, the Commission is entitled—or will be entitled[28]—to set up infringement proceedings against Member States in this area of law. Therefore, it is only a matter of time before the ECJ will need to strike a balance between two public interests (EU free movement and law enforcement objectives versus a national public interest). A conflict between two 'public' interests may even take place at an earlier stage, namely within the European Council in the framework of alarm bell proceedings.[29]

Consequently, both public and private interests can also be at stake here in different combinations and it would therefore be misleading and futile to focus on the public or private nature of the interest(s) in question with the aim of characterizing the principle of mutual recognition. Instead, it also seems useful in this context to focus on the balancing mechanism, which implies a duty to take fundamental rights considerations into account when pursuing security objectives.

(3) *Balancing different interests as an intrinsic feature of the principle of mutual recognition in both contexts*

In the preceding paragraphs I have concluded that one of the major characteristics of the principle of mutual recognition is its non-automatic nature, which results from a mandatory balancing act between the free movement provisions (and the principle of mutual recognition) and an interest of paramount importance.

In view of the fact that mutual recognition in the criminal justice area touches upon citizens' fundamental rights, thus raising issues of constitutional importance,[30] it has been argued that the application of the principle of mutual recognition is more problematic in the criminal justice context and that the internal market analogy is therefore difficult to draw.[31] In my view, however, such assertions are inaccurate for two main reasons: first, they wrongly suggest that the interests that are at stake in the internal market context are of a lesser value than those at stake in the criminal justice context (section 3.1) and secondly, they lead to the mistaken view either that protecting fundamental rights is incompatible with the principle of mutual recognition or that mutual recognition is being applied with no regard for fundamental rights issues (section 3.2).

are not considered important in this context, see, for instance: ECJ, Case C-303/05 *Advocaten voor de wereld* [2007] ECR I-3633, para 45; ECJ, Case C-396/11 *Radu*, nyr, paras 39–42; ECJ, Case C-399/11 *Melloni*, nyr, paras 48–52; ECJ, Case C-168/13 PPU *Jeremy F.*, paras 40–9. See also: Opinion of AG Cruz Villalón in Case C-306/09 *I.B.* [2010] ECR I-10341, § 43, who underlines that when interpreting the FD EAW, one must take into consideration *all* of the objectives sought by the text; Opinion of AG Sharpston in Case C-396/11 *Radu*, nyr, § 71.

[28] Article 258 TFEU and Article 10 Protocol (No 36) on transitional provisions.

[29] Articles 82(3) and 83(3) TFEU.

[30] H. HIJMANS, 'De derde pijler in de praktijk: leven met gebreken. Over de uitwisseling van informatie tussen de lidstaten', *SEW* 2006, 377–8.

[31] See, for instance: M. LÓPEZ ESCUDERO, 'El reconocimiento mutuo de sanciones pecuniarias en la Unión Europea', *Rev. Gen. Der. Eur.* 2006, No 10, 6; MITSILEGAS, *EU Criminal Law* (n 8) 117–18; MÖSTL, 'Preconditions and Limits of Mutual Recognition', (n 8) 409; PEERS, 'Mutual Recognition and Criminal law in the European Union' (n 8) 24; J. SIEVERS, 'Too Different to Trust? First Experiences with the Application of the European Arrest Warrant', in E. GUILD and F. GEYER (eds.), *Security versus Justice? Police and Judicial Cooperation in the European Union* (Hampshire, Ashgate, 2008) 113.

3.1. The role of fundamental non-economic interests in the internal market context

Part I of this book described the relevance of issues of a fundamental rights nature in the internal market context. On the basis of the case law that I discussed there, three conclusions can be drawn.[32] First, it cannot be denied that certain major internal market cases—such as *Schmidberger, Omega, Viking Line,* and *Laval un Partneri*—were decided with due regard to fundamental rights arguments. Second, fundamental rights fulfil a dual role in the internal market context: they are able to set aside the free movement provisions (fundamental rights as restriction to mutual recognition) but in other cases they can also reinforce these provisions (fundamental rights as facilitator of mutual recognition). Third, fundamental rights issues may refer to national constitutional provisions,[33] national interpretations of EU fundamental rights,[34] or EU fundamental rights grounds.[35] In all three cases, the ECJ appears willing to accept that fundamental rights may constitute a bar to mutual recognition provided that—in the first and second cases—the (national) fundamental rights provisions are reconcilable with the EU acquis.

Apart from fundamental rights issues—which obviously come up less frequently in the internal market context than in the criminal justice context—there are important other fundamental interests of a non-economic nature that can trigger the balancing test of the principle of mutual recognition.[36] For example, consumer protection and environmental protection which are written down in the TFEU and the EU's secondary legislation have now also been included explicitly in the Charter.[37] Even though they have not acquired a status that is equal to that of human rights,[38] they constitute an important counterweight for the principle of mutual recognition. Another example of a fundamental interest that is playing a significant role in the internal market context, concerns public health. Not only does it rank foremost among the assets and interests protected by the Treaty according to the ECJ[39] and is it closely related to the EU's main objective, namely to promote the well-being of its peoples,[40] but it must also be safeguarded in order to guarantee the fundamental rights, human dignity, the right to life, and the right to physical and mental integrity, referred to in Articles 1 to 3 of the Charter.[41]

All of these elements clearly demonstrate that non-market values do play a profound role in the internal market and that it is therefore inappropriate to consider the purpose of the criminal justice system *ipso facto* 'more important' than the purpose of the internal market.

[32] See: Part I, ch 1, IV, A, 3. 'Balancing conflicting interests: free movement versus fundamental rights. In search of a European public order concept?'

[33] See, for instance: ECJ, Case C-274/05 *Commission v Greece* [2008] ECR I-7969; ECJ, Case C-147/08 *Römer* [2011] ECR I-3591.

[34] See, for instance: ECJ, Case C-36/02 *Omega* [2004] ECR I-9609.

[35] See, for instance: ECJ, Case C-112/00 *Schmidberger* [2003] ECR I-5659; ECJ, Case C-341/05 *Laval un Partneri* [2007] ECR I-11767.

[36] See: Part I, ch 1, IV, A. 'The ECJ's evaluation of justification grounds'.

[37] Articles 37 and 38 Charter.

[38] On the difference between 'rights' and 'principles', see: 'Explanations relating to the Charter of Fundamental Rights', *O.J.* C-303,14.12.2007, 35. This difference should, however, not be overestimated. See, for instance: A.W. HERINGA and L. VERHEY, 'The EU Charter: Text and Structure', *MJ* 2001, 14; C. HILSON, 'Rights and Principles in EU Law: A Distinction without foundation?', *MJ* 2008, 193–215.

[39] ECJ, Joined Cases C-570/07 and C-571/07 *Blanco Pérez* [2010] ECR I-4629, para 44.

[40] Article 3(1) TEU.

[41] On the first-class position of 'the right to life' in the system of protection of fundamental rights, see: Opinion of AG Jääskinen in Case C-249/09 *Novo Nordisk* [2011] ECR I-3155, § 45–50; AG Mengozzi in Case C-42/11 *Lopes Da Silva Jorge*, nyr, § 28; R. ALEXY, 'On Balancing and Subsumption. A Structural Comparison', *Ratio Juris* 2003, No 4, 440.

3.2. The role of fundamental rights in the criminal justice context

It goes without saying that fundamental rights occupy a position of paramount importance in the EU legal order in general,[42] in the area of freedom, security, and justice, and, especially, in relation to judicial cooperation in criminal matters. This latter aspect was discussed at length in Part II.[43] By analogy with the internal market context, I concluded that fundamental rights have a dual role in this context, namely either as a stimulus[44] or a limit[45] to mutual recognition.

Yet there initially appears to be a striking difference between the two contexts, with regard to the protection of fundamental rights. In the internal market context, both the TFEU and a number of legislative instruments provide an explicit public order exception which enables the setting aside of the free movement provisions and its underlying duty of mutual recognition on human rights grounds. With regard to the area of judicial cooperation in criminal matters, however, no similar 'public order' or 'fundamental rights' exception exists—strictly speaking—either in the TFEU provisions on criminal matters[46] or in the (majority of the) corresponding secondary EU legislation.

Following closer investigation, I concluded in Part II, however, that both the legislator and the ECJ have given due regard to concerns of (national) public policy and (EU or internationally protected) human rights. First, with regard to the absence of a national public policy clause, it should be recalled that certain legal instruments include provisions which come very close to a public order clause.[47] Moreover, nearly all instruments include mechanisms which enable a Member State to take specific, delicate aspects of the executing Member States' national (constitutional) legislation into account, either through justification grounds (for instance on amnesty, immunity, and criminal age), equivalence checks, or mechanisms for adapting the initial sentence.[48] Additionally, Article 53 Charter, which includes an important reference to the Member States' constitutions, can play an important role, even though its scope will be rather limited in areas that have been exhaustively harmonized at EU level.[49] Secondly, with regard to the absence of a fundamental rights exception, I concluded in Part II—after paying due regard to the *Radu* and *Melloni* judgments and some of the ECJ's case law in civil matters and asylum—that there is no reason to believe that the ECJ will not accept in the

[42] In its *Kadi* judgment the ECJ classified 'the respect for human rights and fundamental freedoms enshrined in Article 6(1) TEU as *a foundation* of the Union' (emphasis added): ECJ, Joined Cases C-402/05 P and C-415/05 P *Kadi and Al Barakaat International Foundation* [2008] ECR I-6351, para 303.

[43] See: Part II, ch 2, III, B. 'Limits resulting from mechanisms aimed at eliminating or restricting the principle of mutual recognition'.

[44] See, in particular: the case law on Article 54 CISA, as discussed in Part II, ch 1, I, C, 1. 'Mutual recognition as a (procedural) bar to fresh prosecutions and a (substantive) individual's right not to be punished twice'.

[45] See, in particular: the role to be fulfilled by Article 6 TEU and the Charter, as discussed in Part II, ch 2, III, B, 2. 'Limits linked to the need to safeguard EU or international interests'.

[46] Admittedly, there is Article 72 TFEU, which states that the Treaty provisions on the area of freedom, security, and justice 'shall not affect the exercise of the responsibilities incumbent upon Member States with regard to the maintenance of law and order and the safeguarding of internal security', yet it is difficult to see how this general provision could serve as a sufficient legal ground to set aside the principle of mutual recognition.

[47] See, in particular: Article 13(1)(g) FD EEW and Article 10(1)(a) PROP DIR EIO, as discussed in Part II, ch 2, III, B, 1. 'Limits linked to the need to safeguard domestic criminal justice concerns'.

[48] See: Part II, ch 2, III, B, 1. 'Limits linked to the need to safeguard domestic criminal justice concerns'.

[49] ECJ, Case C-399/11 *Melloni*, nyr, paras 55–63.

criminal justice context a human rights exception to the principle of mutual recognition by analogy with its *N.S. and M.E.* judgment.[50]

3.3. The protection of fundamental interests as a link between the two contexts

Arguments based on catchy statements or scornful slogans, such as *Bier ist Bier und Schnapps ist Schnapps* and *Courts are not supermarkets*, underestimate the importance of non-economic interests in the internal market context and also seem to minimize the need for preconditions and limits to mutual recognition in this area. Rather than focusing on the difficult balancing act that is required in both contexts, these slogans suggest that the principle of mutual recognition is an 'easy and logical choice' in the internal market context, but a 'difficult and unacceptable solution' as regards criminal justice. With the aid of a specific example, I hope to demonstrate that such a perspective is ultimately not convincing. Indeed, why should there be less scrutiny of a decision about the recognition of a product which potentially affects the life and health of millions of people (scenario 1) than of a decision about the recognition of a European Arrest Warrant which potentially jeopardizes an offender's right to trial within a reasonable period (scenario 2)? It is difficult to see why the application of the principle of mutual recognition should be 'obvious' in the first scenario, but 'problematic' in the second. Is the right to a high level of human health and consumer protection (for millions of people) really of lesser value than the right to a fair trial (for one person)? Here, it is by no means my intention to undermine the crucial role played by the protection of fundamental rights in the criminal justice context; fundamental rights fulfil an important role in both contexts, arguably more frequently in the criminal justice area. Yet I do believe that the existence and relevance of crucial non-economic values in the internal market context have been erroneously confined to a second-class position by some authors.

It is all too often forgotten that both the internal market and criminal justice areas are essentially concerned with one fundamental objective, namely the well-being of EU citizens in an open yet secure area where fundamental rights are protected and where the cornerstone principles of free movement and mutual recognition are balanced with other essential interests.[51]

The internal market and the area of freedom, security, and justice should therefore not be seen as two entirely distinct areas, but rather as two complementary and converging areas for which the free movement of persons constitutes a binding link.[52] In the past, the latter instrument was employed to achieve the completion of the internal market and can now serve to promote the relatively new objective of the area of freedom, security, and justice.[53]

In view of the foregoing considerations, I am not convinced that the principle of mutual recognition would be acceptable in the internal market context but not in the criminal

[50] See: Part II, ch 2, III, B, 2. 'Limits linked to the need to safeguard EU or international interests'; Part II, ch 2, III, C, 2. 'Controlling activities in an extraterritorial context'.

[51] On the crucial position of the EU citizen in the EU legal order, see, for instance: Article 3(1) which states that 'The Union's aim is to promote [...] the well-being of its peoples'; Article 3(2) TEU which states that 'the Union shall offer *its citizens* an area of freedom security and justice' (emphasis added) or Article 13(1) TEU which states that 'The Union shall have an institutional framework which shall aim to [...] *serve* its *interests*, those *of its citizens* and those of the Member States [...]' (emphasis added).

[52] R. BARENTS, 'De denationalisering van het strafrecht', *SEW* 2006, 360; S. PRECHAL, *Juridisch cement voor de Europese Unie* (Groningen, Europa Law Publishing, 2006) 19–29.

[53] On the close link between both areas, see: Opinion of AG Bot in Case C-137/09, *Josemans* [2010] ECR I-13019, § 92.

justice context on the sole ground that the two areas pursue different objectives. The very fact that paramount interests exist in both areas which must be balanced against the principle of mutual recognition is—in my view—an argument that favours a cross-policy application of the principle of mutual recognition. Therefore, rather than being seen as a disruptive factor for the application of the principle of mutual recognition in the criminal justice context, the protection of fundamental rights and other fundamental interests should be seen as a factor that unifies the two contexts.[54] Furthermore, and precisely because of the cross-policy relevance of non-economic values, it must be accepted that the principle of mutual recognition is less an economic principle and more of a modus operandi for the EU in both economic (e.g. the internal market) and non-economic areas (e.g. judicial cooperation in criminal matters). In fact, it is an implicit principle useful for improving the function of any integrated economic or political order.[55]

B. Citizens at the heart of the mutual recognition mechanism

Another argument that is often invoked in order to undermine a cross-policy application of the principle of mutual recognition is the allegedly different position occupied by the individual in each context. Natural or legal persons are usually seen as subjects of individual rights, namely free movement claims, in the internal market context, and as mere objects of the free movement arrangements between Member States in the transnational criminal justice context.[56] According to some, this is problematic because criminal law—unlike the regulation of trade—not only serves state interests but is also—or should be—concerned with individual rights and freedoms.[57]

(1) The individual: subject or object in the internal market context?

As mentioned above, the Treaty provisions on free movement are primarily directed at the Member States as these are required to ensure the free movement of legal objects (goods, services, capital, and labour) and legal subjects (natural persons and legal persons) between Member States. From this perspective, the free movement provisions primarily serve state interests.

Yet at the same time, the Treaty provisions on free movement constitute fundamental (individual) rights of citizens owing to the fact that they can be directly invoked by citizens. From this perspective, natural persons and legal persons can be considered the true 'subjects' of rights.

However, being a subject of rights in the EU context does not necessarily mean that an individual is genuinely treated as such in the national context. My analysis of the workability of the principle of mutual recognition in the internal market context was

[54] K. LENAERTS, 'The Contribution of the European Court of Justice to the Area of Freedom, Security and Justice', *ICLQ* 2010, 301; PRECHAL, *Juridisch cement voor de Europese Unie* (n 52) 24–8.

[55] K. NICOLAIDIS and G. SHAFFER, 'Transnational Mutual Recognition Regimes: Governance without Global Government', *Law and Contemporary Problems* 2005, 288 and 317; P. PEITEADO MARISCAL, *El reconocimiento mutuo de resoluciones penales definitivas en la Unión Europea* (Madrid, Colex, 2006) 31–2.

[56] See, for instance: PEERS, 'Mutual Recognition and Criminal law in the European Union' (n 8) 24; A.H.J. SWART, 'Politie en justitie in de Europese Unie', *AA* 2001, 18; on the question of the norm addressees in the mutual recognition mechanism, see: Part III, ch 2: 'The Mutual Recognition Mechanism: Object, Actors, Mechanism, and Characteristics'.

[57] MITSILEGAS, 'The Constitutional Implications of Mutual Recognition in Criminal Matters in the EU' (n 22) 1280.

rather illuminating in this regard, as it showed how citizens and companies have often been deprived of an effective right to free movement in the past.[58] Indeed, if we consider that in day-to-day practice, free movement requests have been denied on a large scale without motivation after a considerable amount of time has already passed and often without any possibility of national judicial redress, we might wonder how far individuals can really be considered true 'subjects' of free movement rights in this context.

(2) The individual: subject or object in the criminal justice context?

As regards the criminal justice area, concerns about and criticisms of the individual's position were voiced long before the introduction of the principle of mutual recognition in the criminal justice area.[59] In the European or international context of cooperation in criminal matters, criticisms were largely directed at the fact that suspects and convicted persons were treated as mere objects of cooperation and that their corresponding individual rights were not protected at European or international level.[60]

It remains to be seen whether such a criticism is still valid today in a Union which is founded on the rule of law and on the protection of fundamental rights,[61] and which aims 'to offer its citizens an area of freedom, security, and justice'.[62] Both the Treaty of Lisbon[63] and the Stockholm Programme[64] have put the citizen, more than ever, at the centre of the EU's integration process.

Even prior to the coming into force of the Treaty of Lisbon, however, there were elements of the ECJ's case law that were inconsistent with the view that the principle of mutual recognition treats individuals as mere objects in the criminal justice context. For example, it cannot be denied that the ECJ's case law on Article 54 CISA represents at least one aspect of criminal justice where the application of mutual recognition has led to the development of a subjective right for citizens.[65] A pro-citizen approach can also be

[58] See: Part I, ch 3: 'The Workability of the Principle of Mutual Recognition in the Internal Market'.

[59] The problematic nature of an individual's position as 'object' is thus neither a direct consequence nor a specific feature of the principle of mutual recognition itself, but rather follows from the nature of the underlying policy domain (criminal justice) to which the principle applies.

[60] See, for instance: C. HARDING and B. SWART, 'Intergovernmental Cooperation in the Field of Criminal Law', in P. FENNELL, C. HARDING, N. JORG, and B. SWART (eds.), *Criminal Justice in Europe. A Comparative Study* (Oxford, Clarendon Press, 1995) 103 ff.; and, more recently: V. MITSILEGAS, 'The Limits of Mutual Trust in Europe's Area of Freedom, Security and Justice: From Automatic Inter-State Cooperation to the Slow Emergence of the Individual', *Y.E.L.* 2012, 319–72.

[61] See, in particular: Article 6 TEU and the Charter, as mentioned in: ECJ, Case C-303/05 *Advocaten voor de wereld* [2007] ECR I-3633, para 45.

[62] Article 3(2) TEU. Furthermore, Article 3(2) TEU *juncto* Article 67(3) TFEU indicate that the 'security' objective is precisely pursued for the benefit of the EU citizens: T. MARGUERY, 'La citoyenneté européenne joue -t- elle un rôle dans l'espace de liberté, de sécurité et de justice?', *C.D.E.* 2010, 404.

[63] MARGUERY, 'La citoyenneté européenne' (n 62). See also: J.-C. PIRIS, *The Lisbon Treaty. A Legal and Political Analysis* (Cambridge, Cambridge University Press, 2010) 189, who focuses on the full judicial control of the ECJ which will ensure a better protection of citizens' rights in matters related to the area of freedom, security, and justice.

[64] The full title of the Stockholm Programme is significant in this regard 'An open and secure Europe *serving and protecting its citizens*' and one of its political priorities is precisely the protection of its citizens' rights. See, in more detail: European Council, The Stockholm Programme—An open and secure Europe serving and protecting citizens', *O.J.* C-115, 04.05.2010, p. 1–38. See also: Communication from the Commission to the Council and the European parliament—An area of freedom, security, and justice serving the citizens, COM (2009) 262 final. See, on the change in focus from 'security' objectives to 'justice' objectives: C. RIJKEN, 'Rebalancing security and justice: protection of fundamental rights in police and judicial cooperation in criminal matters', *CML Rev.* 2010, 1455–92.

[65] See: Part II, ch 1, I, C, 1. 'Mutual recognition as a (procedural) bar to fresh prosecutions and a (substantive) individual's right not to be punished twice'.

found in a number of the ECJ's judgments on the FD EAW, in which significant consideration is given to the right to reintegration,[66] the principle of non-discrimination,[67] and—despite the negative outcome in some of the cases at hand—the right to be heard,[68] the rights surrounding a judgment *in absentia*,[69] and the right to an effective remedy.[70] Furthermore, in recent years both the ECJ and the EU legislator have taken decisive steps towards developing instruments that duly take the citizen's position and his or her subjective rights into account, such as the FD ESO (pre-trial) and the DIR EPO, but also the more controversial PROP DIR EIO.[71]

Two conclusions can be drawn from the above arguments. Firstly, it should now be clear that it is not the principle of mutual recognition itself that is either beneficial or detrimental to the protection of fundamental rights. Both in the internal market context and in the area of criminal justice there are examples where, depending on the object being recognized, the application of the principle of mutual recognition leads either to a restriction or to an enhancement of an individual's position against the state. Secondly, in order to verify whether a person is indeed being recognized and treated as a full subject of rights and not merely as an object in a mutual recognition mechanism, a crucial question, in my view, is whether the person involved can enjoy—in practice—the rights and freedoms that he or she is entitled to.[72] In this regard, one of the innovations introduced by the principle of mutual recognition in criminal matters is highly relevant, namely the transfer of the competent authority which means that it is no longer political or administrative bodies that take decisions on mutual recognition, but judicial authorities.[73] In the Western legal tradition, courts are seen as the ultimate guarantors of individual rights and freedoms, whereas national executives are deemed

[66] ECJ, Case C-66/08 *Kozlowski* [2008] ECR I-6041, para 45; ECJ, Case C-123/08 *Wolzenburg* [2009] ECR I-9621, paras 62 and 67; ECJ, Case C-306/09 *I.B.* [2010] ECR I-10341, para 52; ECJ, Case C-192/12PPU *Melvin West*, nyr, para 70.

[67] ECJ, Case C-123/08 *Wolzenburg* [2009] ECR I-9621, para 46; ECJ, Case C-42/11 *Lopes Da Silva Jorge*, nyr, para 39.

[68] ECJ, Case C-396/11 *Radu*, nyr, paras 39–42.

[69] ECJ, Case C-399/11 *Melloni*, nyr, paras 47–52.

[70] ECJ, Case C-168/13 PPU *Jeremy F.*, paras 42–7.

[71] § 4 FD ESO (pre-trial) where it is stated that cooperation between Member States is not the main objective of this instrument, but rather the right to liberty and the presumption of innocence; § 6 DIR EPO, where it is underlined that in a common area of justice without internal borders, it is necessary to ensure that the protection provided to a person in one Member State is maintained and continued in any other Member State to which the person moves or has moved. With regard to the PROP DIR EIO the Council has explicitly held that this instrument cannot be seen as an instrument directed against the accused person, but that it is an instrument that can result in two directions, demonstrating the innocence or the guilt of the accused person. See: Council of the EU, 'Initiative of the Kingdom of Belgium, the Republic of Bulgaria, the Republic of Estonia, the Kingdom of Spain, the Republic of Austria, the Republic of Slovenia and the Kingdom of Sweden for a Directive of the European Parliament and of the Council regarding the European Investigation Order in criminal matters—Frequently Asked Questions', document number 8182/12, 4 April 2012, p. 5, retrievable at: <http://register.consilium.europa.eu/servlet/driver?typ=&page=Simple&lang=EN&cmsid=638>.

[72] Far less relevant—in my view—should be the question whether the suspected, accused, or convicted person does or does not have a final say on specific aspects related to the criminal justice process. In a criminal law setting it seems quite evident that the person is deprived of some of his or her rights, also in a transnational context. See, for instance—in this regard—the discussions surrounding the abolition of the convicted person's consent in the FD MRCS. It should not be forgotten that this instrument too is aimed at safeguarding a person's reintegration (Art. 3(1) FD MRCS), which restricts to a considerable extent the Member State's freedom to act. See, however: MITSILEGAS, 'The Limits of Mutual Trust' (n 60) 328–30, for a more sceptical view.

[73] On the crucial role of the national judge in this context, see, for instance: H. LABAYLE, 'Le juge de l'espace de liberté, sécurité et justice de l'Union européenne', in *Le dialogue des juges. Mélanges en l'honneur du président Bruno Genevois* (Paris, Dalloz, 2009) 591–615.

to be the ultimate guarantors of national interests.[74] For this reason, this transfer of competence might be beneficial to the individual and his or her position as the subject of rights in the criminal justice area.

In light of the above, I believe it is difficult to maintain the sharp dichotomy between 'individual as object' (in the criminal justice context) and 'individual as subject' (in the internal market context), as it no longer corresponds fully to the instruments, case law and practical experience now available and recognized in each area. Therefore, in my view, this argument is not sufficient to refute a cross-policy application of the principle of mutual recognition.

II. Criminal Justice and the Transfer of Sovereignty: the Paradox of National Sovereignty Claims in Light of the EU's Integration Process

Obstacles to the full acceptance of the principle of mutual recognition in the area of freedom, security, and justice are sometimes fostered by the argument that criminal law is essentially a matter of national sovereignty.[75] Without calling into question the widely held view that criminal law is traditionally seen as a delicate area of national sovereignty insofar as it codifies the moral and social values of national societies[76] and in that it grants a national state the monopoly of force within its territory,[77] in what follows I argue that the concepts of 'sovereignty' and 'territoriality' should be reconsidered in light of the European integration process (section II, A), without underestimating the importance of protecting diversity and national identity within the EU legal order (section II, B).

A. Rethinking 'sovereignty' and 'territoriality' in light of the EU's integration process

(1) From national sovereignty towards the EU and Member States' joint exercise of sovereignty

First, it should be noted that the traditional meaning of 'national sovereignty'—namely 'being in the possession of the entire range of public powers in a specific territory'—is no longer sustainable.[78] Since the development of an international and a European legal

[74] M. FLETCHER, R. LOOF, and B. GILMORE, *EU Criminal Law and Justice* (Cheltenham, Edward Elgar, 2008) 14.

[75] Opinion of AG Sharpston in Case C-467/04 *Gasparini and others* [2006] ECR I-9199, § 111; J. APAP and S. CARRERA, 'Progress and Obstacles in the Area of Justice and Home Affairs in an Enlarging Europe: An Overview', in A. APAP (ed.), *Justice and Home Affairs in the EU* (Cheltenham, Edward Elgar, 2004) 12; BARENTS, 'De denationalisering van het strafrecht' (n 52) 358–9; M. DEL POZO PÉREZ, 'La órden europea de detención y entrega: un avance en el principio de reconocimiento mutuo de resoluciones judiciales entre los Estados de la Unión Europea', *La Ley* 2005 No 1, 1551–68; E. SANFRUTOS CANO, 'The Third Pillar and the European Court of Justice: A Praetorian Communitarization of Police and Judicial Cooperation in Criminal Matters', in E. GUILD and F. GEYER (eds.), *Security versus Justice?* (n 31) 53.

[76] On the 'different' nature of criminal law when compared to other areas of law, see, for instance: Opinion of AG Mazák in Case C-440/05 *Commission v Council* (ship source pollution case) [2007] ECR I-9097, § 67–9. M. HILDEBRANDT, 'European Criminal Law: United in Diversity? (Art. I-6a draft Constitution EU)', paper presented at the IVR World Congress, Granada, 2005.

[77] M. DELMAS-MARTY, 'The European Union and Penal Law', *E.L.J.* 1998, 87; K. NUOTIO, 'Criminal Law of a Transnational Polity' in *Festschrift für Heike Jung zum 65. Geburtstag* (Baden-Baden, Nomos, 2007) 688.

[78] D. GRIMM, 'Comments on the German Constitutional Court's Decision on the Lisbon Treaty. Defending Sovereign Statehood against Transforming the European Union into a State', *EuConst*

order, the term 'state sovereignty' inevitably includes compatibility with supranational public powers. Consequently, in the current situation, sovereignty is no longer a question of 'all or nothing' but of 'more or less'.

Since *Van Gend and Loos*, there has been no doubt that the EU—at that time, the European Community—constitutes a new legal order for whose benefit the Member States have agreed to limit their powers.[79] This transfer of powers to the EU has led to a case law which favours both positive and negative influences of EU law on national (criminal) law and which makes clear that criminal law was by no means seen by the ECJ as a *domaine réservé* for the Member States.[80]

The 'sovereignty' argument has not only lost weight in light of the ECJ's classical (former first pillar) case law,[81] but also following successive Treaty amendments. The scope of 'national sovereignty' has, in fact, changed significantly over the last two decades in the area of freedom, security, and justice on the Member States' own initiative.[82] Whereas before—and even, to a large extent, after—the coming into force of the Treaty of Maastricht (1992), national sovereignty over criminal matters was very closely safeguarded by the Member States, things changed rather drastically with the Treaty of Amsterdam (1997). The Treaty of Amsterdam represented a normative shift away from the full preservation of national sovereignty towards the partial pooling of the EU's and the Member States' sovereignty.[83] However, at that time, many of the intergovernmental features which characterized the pre-Amsterdam era remained completely intact, which created the impression that Member States were in some way reluctant to enter into an increasingly supranational framework. Yet barely a decade later, with the Treaty of Lisbon (2009), the Member States took another decisive step towards relinquishing sovereignty in criminal matters to the EU.[84] The Treaty of Lisbon did away with many, if not all, of the remaining intergovernmental characteristics of the Amsterdam era,[85] transferred more competences to EU level, and confirmed explicitly that the area of freedom, security, and justice—like the internal market—was an area

2009, 365–7. For a more detailed analysis of the concept 'sovereignty', see: D. GRIMM, *Souveränität. Herkunft und Zukunft eines Schlüsselbegriffs* (Berlin, Berlin University Press, 2009) and the different contributions in: N. WALKER (ed.), *Sovereignty in Transition* (Oxford, Hart Publishing, 2003). Also other areas of law that have traditionally been related to 'sovereignty', such as fiscal law, or rules on the monetary system, have not been immune to the Europeanization process, see: E. BARBE, *Justice et affaires intérieures dans l'Union Européenne* (Paris, La documentation française, 2002) 23.

[79] ECJ, Case 26/62 *Van Gend and Loos* [1963] ECR 1.

[80] See, for instance: ECJ, Case 203/80 *Casati* [1981] ECR 2595, para 27; ECJ, Case 186/87 *Cowan* [1989] ECR 195, para 19; and, more recently: ECJ, Case C-61/11 PPU *Hassen El Dridi alias Soufi Karim* [2011] ECR I-3015, para 53.

[81] DELMAS-MARTY, 'The European Union and Penal Law' (n 77) 87–115.

[82] C. KAUNERT, 'The Area of Freedom, Security and Justice: the Construction of a European Public Order', *European Security* 2005, 477.

[83] C. KAUNERT, 'The Area of Freedom, Security and Justice: the Construction of a European Public Order' (n 82) 469. See also: L. GRÖNING, 'A Criminal Justice System or a System Deficit? Notes on the System Structure of the EU Criminal Law', *Eur. Journ. Crime Cr.L.Cr.J.* 2010, 116 ff.; U. SIEBER, 'Die Zukunft des Europäischen Strafrechts', *ZStW* 2009, 65.

[84] The same transfer of sovereignty was envisaged by the Constitutional Treaty, see, for instance: F. HOPFEL, 'The main features of the Constitutional Treaty for a European Criminal Justice System', in J.A.E. VERVAELE (ed.), *European Evidence Warrant. Transnational Judicial Inquiries in the EU* (Antwerp, Intersentia, 2005) 164.

[85] For an overview of the major changes brought about by the Lisbon Treaty, see, for instance: T. CORTHAUT, 'Plus ça change, plus ç'est la même chose? A Comparison with the Constitutional Treaty', *MJ* 2009, 21–34; C. JANSSENS, 'Europees strafrecht en het Verdrag van Lissabon. Een verhaal van déjà vu's, dwarsliggers en compromissen', *Nullum Crimen* 2009, 14–27; PIRIS, *The Lisbon Treaty* (n 63) 180 ff.; SAFFERLING, 'Europe as Transnational Law, (n 18) 1383–97; A.-L. SIBONY, 'Les

of shared competences.[86] In light of these developments, national sovereignty claims appear less and less convincing.

The Treaty of Lisbon is not only noteworthy for its progress in the vertical transfer of sovereignty (from the Member States to the EU), but also—and perhaps even more so—for its firm consolidation of the horizontal transfer of sovereignty by giving the principle of mutual recognition an explicit legal basis. Indeed, under mutual recognition, the situation is not one in which sovereign states cooperate in an intergovernmental framework or in which a Member State is required to apply a supranational, harmonized norm without taking another Member State's legislation into consideration; instead, it is one in which an EU Member State is required to recognize, apply, and enforce the rules of another Member State within its own jurisdiction. Thus, one Member State can be said to transfer, in part, some of the exercise of its sovereign powers to another Member State (horizontal transfer of sovereignty).[87] This transfer of sovereignty in fact assumes an agreement between Member States to compromise local regulatory autonomy (national sovereignty) by accepting that the exporting state's regulations are sufficient.[88]

The arguments above illustrate that a predominantly national view on criminal law based on arguments of national sovereignty fails to take due heed of the EU's integration process and is therefore no longer sustainable in the modern EU. It is now beyond any doubt that (judicial cooperation in) criminal matters constitutes an area of shared competence between the Member States and the EU, which means that once the EU has legislated in a specific area, Member States can no longer exercise sovereignty in it.[89] Furthermore, the principle of primacy of EU law prevents them from applying any national (constitutional) law which conflicts with the newly adopted EU measure.[90] The fact that several national (constitutional) courts still struggle with this transfer of sovereignty became evident shortly after the coming into force of the FD EAW and its national implementation legislations. The abolition of the principle of non-surrender of own nationals, one of the remnants of national sovereignty, was clearly difficult to accept for some national (constitutional) courts.[91] Even the ECJ appeared to recognize the sensitivity of the matter. In its *Wolzenburg* judgment, for example, it displayed a remarkably mild attitude towards the Member States' margin of discretion when it maintained that

avancées du traité de Lisbonne en matière de coopération judiciaire', *Revue de la Faculté de droit de l'Université de Liège* 2008, 249–63.

[86] Article 2(2) TFEU in combination with Article 4 TFEU.

[87] K. NICOLAIDIS, 'Trusting the Poles? Constructing Europe through Mutual Recognition', *JEPP* 2007, 685; M. POIARES MADURO, 'So Close and Yet So Far: the Paradoxes of Mutual Recognition', *JEPP* 2007, 819.

[88] J.P. TRACHTMAN, 'Embedding Mutual Recognition at the WTO', *JEPP* 2007, 783.

[89] Article 2(2) TFEU and Article 4 TFEU.

[90] For an example of a recent case where primacy and national constitutional provisions are discussed in the context of European criminal law context, see: ECJ, Case C-399/11 *Stefano Melloni*, nyr. Even prior to the coming into force of the Lisbon Treaty, it was argued that the principle of primacy also applied to the (old) third pillar. See, in particular: R. BARENTS, 'Annotatie *Pupino*', *SEW* 2006, 78; K. LENAERTS and T. CORTHAUT, 'Of Birds and Hedges: the Role of Primacy in Invoking Norms of EU Law', *E.L. Rev.* 2006, 287–315. *Contra*: A. HINAREJOS, 'The Lisbon Treaty versus Standing Still: A view from the Third Pillar', *EuConst* 2009, 101–2.

[91] See, for instance: M. FICHERA, 'The European Arrest Warrant and the Sovereign State: a Marriage of Convenience?', *E.L.J.* 2009, 70–97; C. JANSSENS, 'Het Europees aanhoudingsbevel onder vuur: hebben de nationale grondwettelijke hoven het laatste woord?', *RW* 2006–07, 415–18; J. KOMAREK, 'European Constitutional Pluralism and the European Arrest Warrant: Contrapunctual Principles in Disharmony', Jean Monnet Working Paper 2006/10, retrievable at: <http://papers.ssrn.com/sol3/papers.cfm?abstract_id=934067>; K. KOWALIK-BANOZIK, 'Should we Polish it Up? The Polish Constitutional Tribunal and the Idea of Supremacy of EU Law', retrievable at: <http://www.GermanLawJournal.com>.

'the [national] rule that a European Arrest Warrant may not be executed against nationals of the Member State of execution does not seem to be excessive'.[92]

In sum, the transfer of sovereignty, which characterizes the EU legal order as a whole, has resulted in a network of local, national, and supranational normative systems with a plurality of sovereign powers that co-exist and interact in a variety of ways.[93] This form of joint or shared sovereignty means that certain characteristics of national sovereignty will sometimes be upheld and sometimes dismissed in the legislative process or in the ECJ's case law.[94] While the authors of the Treaties may have deliberately avoided the term 'national sovereignty' throughout the Treaties, they did emphasize the respect retained for the Member States' national identities and also introduced in the Treaty of Lisbon a specific procedure which enables each Member State to interrupt the legislative procedures whenever a draft directive would affect a fundamental aspect of its criminal justice system.[95] Finally, the ECJ's case law in other areas of law also illustrates that it does not refrain from referring to the 'sovereign powers of Member States' where necessary.[96]

(2) We are many but not one: on the relevance of territorial limits in a borderless area

2.1. Extraterritoriality as an intrinsic feature of the principle of mutual recognition

With the introduction of the principle of mutual recognition, the traditional territorial application of national law—based on the age-old notion of 'When in Rome, do as the Romans do'—has reached a conclusion.[97] Mutual recognition creates extraterritoriality, in the sense that national standards, not EU standards, must in principle[98] be recognized

[92] ECJ, Case C-123/08 *Wolzenburg* [2009] ECR I-9621, para 70. Compare with the more audacious, but well-founded approach of AG Bot in his opinion in this case, § 121 ff.

[93] S. BERTEA, 'Looking for Coherence within the European Community', *E.L.J.* 2005, 155. See also: T. KOOPMANS, 'The Birth of European Law at the Crossroads of Legal Traditions', *Am. Journal of Comp. Law* 1991, 505–6, who speaks of a 'two-way influence' and 'one many-sided legal edifice'.

[94] The European Arrest Warrant is a good example of an instrument in which national sovereignty clearly lost strength, among other things due to the introduction of the principle of mutual recognition, but where typically sovereign characteristics remained in force either in the instrument itself (for instance, the territoriality exception or the principle of speciality) or through national case law (for instance, the principle of reciprocity). For examples of national case law, see: C. JANSSENS, 'De burger, de Unie en het Europees aanhoudingsbevel: op zoek naar het juiste evenwicht tussen vrijheid, veiligheid en rechtvaardigheid', in J. MEEUSEN and G. STRAETMANS (eds.), *Politiële en justitiële strafrechtelijke samenwerking in de Europese Unie. Welk evenwicht tussen vrijheid, veiligheid en rechtvaardigheid?* (Antwerp, Intersentia, 2007) 58; K. LENAERTS, 'De Rome à Lisbonne: la constitution européenne en marche?', *C.D.E.* 2009, 237.

[95] Article 4(2) TEU. R. BIEBER, 'An Association of Sovereign States', *EuConst* 2009, 399. See also: Part III, ch 1, II, B. '(Criminal) diversity and respect for national identity as integral features of the EU's legal order'.

[96] See, for instance: ECJ, C-135/08 *Rottmann* [2010] ECR I-1449, para 32, on nationality law, where the ECJ refrains from 'striking at the heart of the sovereign powers of the Member States'; ECJ, Case C-385/99 *Müller-Fauré and van Riet* [2003] ECR I-4509, para 102, on social security law, where the ECJ searches for a solution that does not 'undermine the Member States' sovereign power in this field'; ECJ, Case C-16/05 *Tum and Dari* [2007] ECR I-7415, para 58, on national immigration policy, where the ECJ reassures the Member State by stating that the standstill clause 'does not mean that the very substance of their sovereign competence in respect of aliens should be regarded as being undermined'; ECJ, Case C-336/96, *Gilly/Directeur des services fiscaux du Bas-Rhin* [1998] ECR 1998, I-2793, para 48, on direct taxation, where the ECJ rejects a view which 'would encroach on the Member States' sovereignty'.

[97] H. LABAYLE, 'Le bilan du mandat de Tampere et l'espace de liberté, sécurité et justice de l'Union européenne, *C.D.E.* 2004, 641; PEITEADO MARISCAL, *El reconocimiento mutuo de resoluciones penales definitivas en la Unión Europea* (n 55) 30; A. WEYEMBERGH, 'Droit pénal et reconnaissance mutuelle', *JT Dr Eur.* 2001, 193.

[98] See, however: Part III, ch 1, II, A, 2.2. 'Territoriality-based exception grounds: an acceptable compromise between the principle of mutual recognition and the remnants of national sovereignty?'.

and applied extraterritorially.[99] Mutual recognition implies a horizontal re-allocation of authority in order to prescribe and enforce laws,[100] which results in the Member State of destination losing on its own territory some of its sovereign powers over the full control of foreign persons, goods, services, and capital (in the internal market context) or in the executing state losing on its territory some of its sovereign powers over foreign criminal justice decisions (in the area of freedom, security, and justice). Following the ECJ's acceptance of situations of reverse discrimination, Member States remain free to maintain and enforce their own regulations for products produced within their jurisdiction and to apply their national criminal codes to criminal investigations that fall within their exclusive jurisdiction. However, they cannot prevent their citizens from consuming on their territory foreign products that meet the legal standards of another Member State (extraterritorial effect of goods) in the same way that they may be obliged to take into account or to bear the consequences on their territory—to a certain extent—of foreign criminal law (extraterritorial effect of criminal law).

2.2. Territoriality-based exception grounds: an acceptable compromise between the principle of mutual recognition and the remnants of national sovereignty?

Both the internal market and the area of freedom, security, and justice represent European 'areas' without borders, but still consist of Member States with their own cultural, moral, religious, or other differences.[101] In view of these differences, it has been considered necessary to allow the Member States some margin to act whenever a clash emerges between the fundamental values underpinning a Member State's legal order and the extraterritorial effects of a foreign law having direct implications on that Member State's territory.

In the internal market context, the Treaty exceptions, rule of reason, and protection of fundamental rights can play mitigating roles vis-à-vis the potentially harsh effects of an extraterritorial application of foreign legislation. In the absence of harmonization, Member States are in principle entitled to choose the level of protection they deem to be most appropriate for their territory, albeit within the limits described by the Treaties and checked by the ECJ by means of the proportionality test. The ECJ has always refused to qualify such powers as a *réserve de souveraineté,* but it is difficult not to interpret these justification grounds, and especially the ECJ's acceptance of unwritten justification reasons beyond what is explicitly laid down in the Treaties, as an expression of deep respect for exactly that original responsibility or sovereign power of the Member States.[102]

In the area of criminal justice, grounds for non-recognition and non-execution are included in all legislative instruments on mutual recognition. As in the internal market context, they allow a Member State to limit the extraterritorial effect of foreign legislation on their territory. Among these grounds for non-recognition is the 'territoriality

[99] BARBE, *Justice et affaires intérieures dans l'Union européenne* (n 78) 136; MITSILEGAS, 'The Constitutional Implications of Mutual Recognition in Criminal Matters in the EU' (n 22) 1281.

[100] NICOLAIDES, 'Trusting the Poles?' (n 87) 685.

[101] On the co-existence and thus compatibility of the concept '(national) territory' and '(European) area', see: G. DE KERCHOVE, 'L'espace pénal européen après Amsterdam et le sommet de Tampere', in G. DE KERCHOVE and A. WEYEMBERGH (eds.), *Vers un espace judiciaire penal européen. Towards a European Judicial Criminal Area* (Brussels, Institut d'Etudes Européennes, 2000) 4–6. See, however: BARENTS, 'De denationalisering van het strafrecht' (n 52) 366 ff.; D. FLORE, 'Reconnaissance mutuelle, double incrimination et territorialité', in G. DE KERCHOVE and A. WEYEMBERGH (eds.), *La reconnaissance mutuelle des décisions judiciaires pénales dans l'Union européenne* (Brussels, Institut d'Etudes Européennes, 2001) 74, who both argue that the notion of 'territoriality' is in fact incompatible with the notion of 'area'.

[102] MÖSTL, 'Preconditions and Limits of Mutual Recognition' (n 8) 411.

exception', which essentially aims to safeguard the right of a Member whose social order has been disrupted to intervene by re-establishing social order within its territory through the application of its criminal law. Bearing in mind that the principle of territoriality is recognized in all Member States as the preferred basis for judicial competence and thus represents a common principle shared by all Member States,[103] it could serve as an acceptable solution in cases where criminal conduct has mainly taken place within one Member State.[104] By upholding the territoriality exception, the principle of mutual recognition is, in this context, a mark of respect for each Member State's criminal law. The territoriality exception thus allows for a revival of the old dictum 'When in Rome, do as the Romans do' and yields to some extent to the argument that citizens should be required to accept external standards. It is also a manifestation of the non-importation principle, which holds that a state should not be required to import the criminal policies or procedures of another jurisdiction if it is substantially different from its own,[105] at least when criminal proceedings or investigations are taking place within its territory.

It has been argued correctly that the territoriality exception, along with any other ground for non-recognition, reclaims some of the sovereignty that the mutual recognition system intends to restrict.[106] Two contrasting concepts are at stake here: the territoriality exception, like any other ground for non-recognition, is protective of sovereignty and the host (or executing) Member State's regulations, whereas the principle of mutual recognition erodes sovereignty and obliges the host state to accept the home (or issuing) Member State's standards. In fact, the introduction of grounds for non-recognition and the combination of home and host state country control are consistently the result of an unavoidable compromise, a delicate balancing act between the principle of mutual recognition (free movement) and national interests that are deemed worthy of protection (national sovereignty). It is the very existence of these national interests, as codified in the TFEU and in the ECJ's case law, which indicates that the 'territoriality' exception and the concept of 'national territory' are not in themselves irreconcilable with the idea of one internal market or one area of freedom, security, and justice. Instead, they are indispensable elements that bound the limits of the principle of mutual recognition in both areas.

[103] A. KLIP, *European Criminal Law An Integrative Approach* (Antwerp, Intersentia, 2012) 423–4; S. PEERS, *EU Justice and Home Affairs* (n 21) 455; T. VANDER BEKEN, *Forumkeuze in het internationaal strafrecht. Verdeling van misdrijven met aanknopingspunten in meerdere staten* (Ghent, RUG, 1998–99) 458.

[104] There is, however, discussion on the question whether the principle of territoriality should also apply in cases of controversial (criminal) conduct such as abortion or euthanasia. Compare in this regard: Y. BURUMA, 'Radikale Toleranz. Auf dem Weg zu einem zweidimensionalen Raum der Freiheit, der Sicherheit und des Rechts', *ZStW* 2004, 429–30 and FLORE, 'Reconnaissance mutuelle, double incrimination et territorialité' (n 101) 74.

[105] On the meaning of this principle in the context of the European Arrest Warrant, see: P. ASP and A. VON HIRSCH, 'Double Criminality and Transnational Investigative Measures in EU Criminal Proceedings: Some Issues of Principle', *Zeitschrift für Internationale Strafrechtsdogmatik* 2006, 518.

[106] M. DE HOYOS SANCHO, 'Euro-orden y causas de denegación de la entrega', in C. ARANGUENA FANEGO (ed.), *Cooperación judicial penal en la Unión Europea* (Valladolid, Lex Nova, 2005) 293–5.

2.3. Extraterritoriality-based exception grounds: an unjustified means of extrapolating a Member State's system of values?

Member States are not only tempted to set aside the principle of mutual recognition by claiming that fundamental interests would be under threat within *their territory* (territoriality-based argument), but also that fundamental interests would be under threat in *another Member State's territory* (extraterritoriality-based argument).[107]

In the EU criminal justice context, it is interesting to examine the example of a surrender order issued for a person who performed an abortion in a Member State where abortion was considered a criminal offence and was thus categorized under the list offence 'murder' (Art. 2(2) FD EAW).[108] A Member State that does not criminalize abortion might be tempted to refuse to surrender the individual in question, arguing that the criminal proceedings underlying the surrender order ran counter to its system of values and/or that it is required by national and/or public international law to protect its citizens.[109] By refusing to surrender a person to the Member State where the facts occurred and where the criminal proceedings are taking place, the Member State is in fact judging the surrender request in light of its own system of values and thus seeking to export its own scale of values to another Member State's territory. This is not permitted under the FD EAW regime at least as far as the conduct constitutes one of the list offences according to the issuing judge. If we support the view that criminal law is essentially concerned with safeguarding the right of a Member State whose social order has been disrupted to intervene by re-establishing social order within its territory through applying its criminal law, non-recognition of the surrender order seems inappropriate in the example provided. It would not only be disrespectful of the national values of the Member State upon whose territory the criminal conduct occurred,[110] but would also frustrate smooth cooperation between Member States. In accordance with the principle of sincere cooperation, Member States are required to assist each other in full mutual respect in the tasks distributed by the Treaties (Art. 4(3) TEU)[111] and any attempt to impose values on another Member State would clearly constitute a breach of this founding principle of the EU legal order. It is therefore essential that Member States reflect on the protection of national values within their own jurisdictions, but also that they desist from applying such choices extraterritorially.[112] Moreover, the argument that

[107] De Hoyos Sancho speaks in this regard of '*Verfassungsexport*' whereas Asp and Von Hirsch use the term 'the non-importation principle': DE HOYOS SANCHO 'Euro-orden y causas de denegación de la entrega' (n 106) 244; P. ASP and A. VON HIRSCH (n 105) 518.

[108] This example was also discussed above with regard to the equivalence requirement, see: Part II, ch 2, I, C, 1.1 'Equivalence and the partial abolition of the dual criminality check'.

[109] PEERS, 'Mutual Recognition and Criminal law in the European Union' (n 8) 25, who seems to suggest that in view of (i) the different nature of both fields of law; (ii) the involvement of human rights elements; and (iii) the Member States different roles in both contexts, an executing Member State should be entitled to refuse to surrender in the above-mentioned case.

[110] See, for instance: E. BARBE, 'El principio de doble incriminación', in L. ARROYO ZAPATERO and A. NIETO MARTIN (eds.), *La orden de detención y entrega europea* (Cuenca, Ediciones de la Universidad de Castilla-La Mancha, 2006) 204–5, who states that the respect for another Member State's criminal law system is the greatest paradox of the EAW; G. DE KERCHOVE, 'La reconnaissance mutuelle des décisions pré-sentencielles en général', in G. DE KERCHOVE and A. WEYEMBERGH (eds.), *La reconnaissance mutuelle des décisions judiciaires pénales dans l'Union européenne* (n 101) 119.

[111] On the important role of the principle of sincere cooperation for both areas of law, see for instance: BARENTS, 'De denationalisering van het strafrecht' (n 52) 373–4; A. DUTTA, 'Die Pflicht der Mitgliedstaaten zur gegenseitigen Durchsetzung ihrer öffentlichrechtlichen Forderungen', *EuR* 2007, 744–67.

[112] N.N. SHUIBHNE, 'Margins of Appreciation: National Values, Fundamental Rights and EC Free Movement Law', *E.L. Rev.* 2009, 231. See, however: FLORE, 'Reconnaissance mutuelle, double incrimination et territorialité' (n 101) 74.

national or public international law generally requires Member States to protect 'their' citizens, must be revisited in the EU context. By creating the list of thirty-two offences and by including a rule that refers to the issuing Member State's legal framework, the FD EAW clearly imposes a duty on the executing Member States' authorities to trust the issuing Member State's criminal law framework, in particular its definition of offences. Ultimately, if free movement, mutual recognition, and sincere cooperation work as they should in the EU, then making sacrifices in the reach of national sovereignty and perhaps in national constructions of morality may seem justified.[113] In my fictitious example about abortion, this would mean that the executing Member State would not be entitled not to recognize the EAW order.

The preceding arguments apply all the more in the case of exhaustive harmonization, as illustrated by the *Melloni* judgment. Contrary to my example on abortion which was related to an issue that had not been harmonized by the FD EAW (namely, the constituent elements of a criminal offence and its penalties),[114] the *Melloni* case concerned an issue that had been harmonized exhaustively at EU level (namely, the circumstances in which the execution of a European Arrest Warrant issued for judgments *in absentia* must be considered as not infringing the rights of the defence).[115] Precisely because of the fact that there was exhaustive harmonization—which reflected the consensus reached by all the Member States on the issue of *in absentia* judgments[116]—the ECJ refused an extraterritorial application of the Spanish constitutional provision.

The *Melloni* judgment shows strong similarities with a very famous internal market judgment, the *Hedley Lomas* case, regarding the United Kingdom's refusal to export calves to Spain on the grounds of dissatisfaction with Spain's animal welfare standards.[117] In *Hedley Lomas*, the ECJ was very reluctant to agree to such an extraterritorial claim as it would not only allow a Member State to impose its system of universal values on another Member State, but may well have amounted to a Member State taking unilateral measures vis-à-vis another Member State, which is firmly prohibited under the Treaties.[118] The ECJ's first and most authoritative argument was, however, that since the directive provided for exhaustive harmonization of the issue at stake, recourse to the justification grounds included in former Article 36 EC was simply no longer possible.[119] A joint reading of *Hedley Lomas* (internal market context) and *Melloni* (criminal justice context) thus suggests that—if there is exhaustive harmonization—it will be extremely difficult for a Member State to impose limits to mutual recognition.

However, the examples above do not necessarily preclude the possibility of obtaining a different outcome in cases where there are substantive grounds for believing that a fundamental right is under serious threat in another Member State. In accordance with Article 6 TEU, the EU is bound by the rights, freedoms, and principles set out in the Charter and by fundamental rights as guaranteed by the ECHR and resulting from the constitutional traditions common to the Member States. In light of Article 6 TEU,

[113] N.N. SHUIBHNE, 'Margins of Appreciation' (n 112) 256.
[114] ECJ, Case C-303/05 *Advocaten voor de wereld* [2007] ECR I-3633, para 52.
[115] ECJ, Case C-399/11 *Melloni*, nyr, paras 61–3.
[116] ECJ, Case C-399/11 *Melloni*, nyr, para 62.
[117] ECJ, Case C-5/94 *Hedley Lomas* [1996] ECR I-2553. For an analysis of this judgment and other relevant case law, see: Part I, ch 1, IV, B, 2. 'The ECJ's hesitant attitude towards accepting Member States' arguments for protecting extraterritorial interests'; and Part I, Chapter 2, III, B, 3. 'Controlling activities in an extraterritorial context'.
[118] ECJ, Case C-5/94 *Hedley Lomas* [1996] ECR I-2553, para 20.
[119] ECJ, Case C-5/94 *Hedley Lomas* [1996] ECR I-2553, para18.

which is one of the foundations upon which the EU is built, and which implies a duty for Member States to comply with, it is difficult to see how a Member State could under no circumstances be entitled to set aside the principle of mutual recognition when objective factors reveal that a fundamental right is under serious threat in another Member State. The *Krombach* and *N.S. and M.E.* judgments are very instructive in this regard.[120] Yet it should not be overlooked that patent breaches like that under discussion in *Krombach* and *N.S. and M.E.* are rare and that the burden of proof is very high. In moments of doubt it is highly unlikely that the ECJ would favour Member States' passing judgments on the (criminal) justice systems of other Member States. Given the ECtHR's case law,[121] the ECJ's internal market case law,[122] and the ECJ's case law on judicial cooperation in civil matters and asylum,[123] it is clear that besides patent breaches, both courts prefer to leave it up to the issuing Member State to pass judgment on a violation of fundamental rights. In sum, a Member State that has doubts about the correctness of another Member State's behaviour has, in principle, only one legitimate way to react, namely by bringing proceedings against the Member State that is thought to have failed in its duties according to the Treaty framework.[124]

B. (Criminal) diversity and respect for national identity as integral features of the EU's legal order

European criminal law has been criticized not only on the ground that criminal justice is part of (national) sovereignty, but also on the ground that it is constitutive of the identity of a people and their values.[125] On these grounds, it has been argued that criminal law is—and should be—an aspect of the national legal tradition.

An assessment of national legislations reveals both convergent and divergent approaches to various aspects of substantive[126] and procedural criminal law,[127]

[120] ECJ, Case C-7/98 *Krombach* [2000] ECR I-1935; ECJ, Joined Cases C-411/10 and ECJ, Case C-493/10 *N.S. and M.E.*, nyr. See: Part II, ch 2, III, C, 2.2.2. 'Guidelines provided by the ECJ's case law in the area of mutual recognition in civil matters'; and Part II, ch 2, III, C, 2.2.3. 'Guidelines provided by the ECJ's case law in the area of asylum'.

[121] See: Part II, ch 2, III, C, 2.2.1. 'Guidelines provided by the ECtHR's case law'.

[122] See: Part I, ch 1, IV, B, 2. 'The ECJ's hesitant attitude towards accepting Member States' arguments for protecting extraterritorial interests'; and Part I, ch 2, III, B, 3. 'Controlling activities in an extraterritorial context'.

[123] See: Part II, ch 2, III, C, 2.2.2. 'Guidelines provided by the ECJ's case law in the area of mutual recognition in civil matters'; and Part II, ch 2, III, C, 2.2.3. 'Guidelines provided by the ECJ's case law in the area of asylum'.

[124] Article 258 and Article 259 TFEU. However, as regards criminal matters, infringement proceedings under Article 258 TFEU, are subject to a five-year transitional period (Art. 10 Protocol No 36 to the Treaty of Lisbon).

[125] FLORE, 'Reconnaissance mutuelle, double incrimination et territorialité' (n 101) 68.

[126] For instance: What is being criminalized? Preparation of a crime or only the crime itself? Criminal intention or only accomplished crime or only the attempt or only serious attempt? Rape outside or also inside a marriage? Selling and/or use of which drugs? Which varieties of fraud? Euthanasia? Abortion? Can the penal law be applied to acts committed abroad (principle of territoriality versus principle of extraterritoriality)? Is there a regime of mandatory prosecution or discretionary prosecution? See: HILDEBRANDT, 'European Criminal Law: United in Diversity?' (n 76) 23; P. HOBBING, 'Uniforms without Uniformity: A Critical Look at European Standards in Policing', in E. GUILD and F. GEYER (eds.), *Security versus Justice? Police and Judicial Cooperation in the European Union* (Hampshire, Ashgate, 2008) 255.

[127] For instance: What positions do prosecutors, judges and defendants have in the trial? Who is being heard at what point? What counts as evidence? How is the burden of proof distributed? Is a defendant protected against self-incrimination? Is the trial public? Does the defendant have access to

characteristics which are also in constant evolution.[128] Thus, despite sharing a core of common values, and perhaps even some common penal culture,[129] the EU's (criminal justice) identity is inherently pluralist and European criminal law should therefore be constructed in a pluralistic way, with respect for national diversity.[130] In this regard, it is noteworthy that the Treaty of Lisbon stresses that the EU is to constitute an area of freedom security and justice 'with respect for [...] the different legal systems and traditions of the Member States' (Art. 67(1) TFEU), a description that is also repeated in a paragraph on procedural harmonization of criminal law (Art. 82(2) TFEU). Respect for criminal diversity follows, furthermore, from the alarm bell procedure introduced by the Treaty of Lisbon as compensation for the abolition of the unanimity requirement. According to this new procedure, a Member State is in a position to suspend the ordinary legislative procedures by requiring that a draft directive be referred to the European Council whenever it is thought that this draft would affect fundamental aspects of its criminal justice system (Art. 82(3) TFEU and Art. 83(3) TFEU). Member States are therefore required to be vigilant during legislative proceedings and to compare any future European directives with their national criminal law frameworks. As in the pre-Lisbon era, it will be crucial that Member States are fully aware of which aspects of their criminal justice system they deem to be fundamental as early as during the legislative negotiations. Otherwise, there is a risk that an instrument could be adopted which will eventually rekindle feelings of sovereignty in a constitutional context and create unnecessary tensions between the national constitutional court and the ECJ.

The EU's integration process has shown that both criminal law and many other branches of law are interwoven with certain society-related values which characterize a Member State's identity at any given time.[131] In the internal market context, intense debate has surrounded a variety of subjects, ranging from national culinary traditions[132] to issues of a more substantive nature, such as health care services, and other more controversial themes such as gambling, prostitution, abortion, and drugs.[133] In its internal market case law, the ECJ has often seen non-harmonized areas in which significant moral, religious, and cultural differences existed and it has consistently maintained that it is for each Member State to determine in those areas, in accordance with its own scale of values, what is required to protect the interest in question. The only margin

relevant information in time? Which checks and balances have been incorporated to supply the defendant with equality of arms? Is the trial contradictory or adversarial? How are judges recruited? Which safeguards have been installed to guarantee the impartiality of the judge? Is the prosecutor a crime fighter or is he required to defend the possible innocence of the defendant? See: HILDEBRANDT, 'European Criminal Law: United in Diversity?' (n 76) 24; HOBBING, 'Uniforms without Uniformity' (n 126) 255.

[128] P. HOBBING, 'Uniforms without Uniformity' (n 126) 258–9, who points to the fact that with regard to criminal law 'these eternal national traditions are not that old and deeply rooted after all'.

[129] E. BACIGALUPO, 'Bemerkungen zu strafrechtlichen Fragen des Verfassungsentwurfs', *ZStW* 2004, 330.

[130] M. DELMAS MARTY, 'Les défis d'un droit pénal européen', in E. ALEJANDRO ALVAREZ et al (eds.), *Mireille Delmas-Marty et les années UMR* (Paris, Société de Législation Comparée, 2005) 425; G. GRASSO, 'Derechos fundamentales y derecho penal en el nuevo tratado por el que se establece una Constitución para Europa', in M. BAJO FERNÁNDEZ (ed.), *Constitución Europea y Derecho Penal Económico. Mesas redondas derecho y economía* (Madrid, Centro de estudios Ramón Areces, 2006) 247.

[131] For some specific examples, see: BARENTS, 'De denationalisering van het strafrecht' (n 52) 362; H. HIJMANS, 'De Europese Unie, verdwijnende grenzen en elektronische diensten', *SEW* 2004, 352; HOBBING, 'Uniforms without Uniformity' (n 126) 258–9.

[132] On the 'heated' nature of these discussions, see: VOGEL, *Trading Up* (n 11) 41 ff.

[133] See: Part I, ch 1, IV, A. 'The ECJ's evaluation of justification grounds'.

of control retained by the ECJ in these sensitive areas is a considerably watered down proportionality test.[134]

The EU's general duty to respect Member States' national identities not only results from the EU's motto '*United in Diversity*',[135] but also from Article 4(2) TEU, according to which 'the Union shall respect the Member States' [...] national identities inherent in their fundamental structures, political and constitutional [...]'.[136] Furthermore, in the context of the internal market, respect for national identities can also be read in Articles 114(4) and 114(5) TFEU, which enable a Member State to maintain existing national provisions or to introduce new national provisions that contravene a harmonization measure adopted under Article 114 TFEU. Like the above-mentioned alarm bell proceedings, these provisions were the price paid for the switch to qualified majority voting.[137] Despite some obvious differences in the nature of the two procedures (*ex ante* versus *ex post*) and between the institutions involved (European Council versus Commission) the rationale behind each provision's introduction was identical, namely to guarantee respect for national diversity. In sum, the fact that the TFEU does not only include in both contexts free movement and mutual recognition obligations, but also provisions that reflect respect for the distinctiveness of the national legal systems, is yet another element that favours a cross-policy application of the principle of mutual recognition.

Both in the internal market context and in the criminal justice area, the principle of mutual recognition has been criticized for threatening national identity and culture, or national sovereignty.[138] However, the principle of mutual recognition has neither the object nor the effect of challenging the legal and judicial traditions of the Member States.[139] In fact, it pursues precisely the opposite aim, namely respect in a non-harmonized world for the quality and validity of other sovereign states' laws.[140] From this

[134] See: Part I, ch 1, IV, A. 'The ECJ's evaluation of justification grounds'.

[135] This motto was explicitly recognized by a majority of Member States in an additional declaration to the Treaty of Lisbon: Declaration 52 by the Kingdom of Belgium, the Republic of Bulgaria, the Federal Republic of Germany, the Hellenic Republic, the Kingdom of Spain, the Italian Republic, the Republic of Cyprus, the Republic of Lithuania, the Grand-Duchy of Luxembourg, the Republic of Hungary, the Republic of Malta, the Republic of Austria, the Portuguese Republic, Romania, the Republic of Slovenia and the Slovak Republic on the symbols of the EU.

[136] The ECJ attaches great importance to this provision without, however, granting it absolute protection. See, for instance: ECJ, Case C-208/09 *Sayn-Wittgenstein* [2010] ECR I-13693, paras 92–4; ECJ, Case C-391/09 *Vardyn-Wardyn* [2011] ECR I-3787, para 86; Opinion of AG Bot in Case C-399/11 *Stefano Melloni*, nyr, § 138–42. See also: L. BESSELINK, Case Note Sayn-Wittgenstein, *CML Rev.* 2012, 688–9, who qualifies *Sayn-Wittgenstein* as part of a development in constitutional relations in which the ECJ respects the national constitutional orders as interpreted by national constitutional courts and in which it no longer thinks in terms of strict hierarchy.

[137] C. BARNARD, *The Substantive Law of the EU: the Four Freedoms* (Oxford, Oxford University Press, 2010) 585–6.

[138] See, for instance: V. HATZOPOULOS, 'With or Without You ... Judging Politically in the Field of Area of Freedom, Security and Justice', *E.L. Rev.* 2008, 60; VOGEL, *Trading Up* (n 11) 41 ff. The latter gives examples of how mutual recognition was threatening, according to some, national *cuisine*: See also the abundant critiques on the abolition of the dual criminality requirement as discussed in: Part II, ch 2, I, B. 'Country of origin'.

[139] Opinion of AG Sharpston in Case C-467/04 *Gasparini and others* [2006] ECR I-9199, § 109. See also: G. CORSTENS, 'Europeanisering van het strafrecht en de steun van de bevolking', in F. DERUYCK, M. DE SWAEF, J. ROZIE, M. ROZIE, P. TRAEST, and R. VERSTRAETEN (eds.), *De wet voorbij. Liber amicorum Luc Huybrechts* (Antwerp, Intersentia, 2010) 27, who underlines that European criminal law does not encroach on national criminal law as it merely coordinates and facilitates.

[140] Opinion of AG Sharpston in Case C-467/04 *Gasparini and others* [2006] ECR I-9199, § 109; Communication from the Commission to the Council and the European Parliament—Area of

perspective, preference for mutual recognition is often expressed in terms of its being an instrument of political and economic integration which is more respectful of diversity and a Member State's autonomy.[141] In view of the extraterritorial effects of the principle of mutual recognition, which lead to increasing 'denationalization'[142] of a Member State's law, the link between mutual recognition and the preservation of diversity should perhaps not be exaggerated.[143] Yet limits incorporated in the Treaty and in the legislative instruments on mutual recognition as well as in the ECJ's case law do guarantee, to a considerable extent, that national identity claims can be sufficiently taken into consideration.

Freedom, Security and Justice: Assessment of the Tampere programme and future orientations, COM (2004) 401 final, 10.

[141] See, in particular: A. MATTERA, 'L'article 30 du traité CEE, la jurisprudence Cassis de Dijon et le principe de la reconnaissance mutuelle. Instruments au service d'une Communauté plus respectueuse des diversités nationales', *RMUE* 1992, 13 ff.; and, more recently: A. MATTERA, 'La reconnaissance mutuelle: une valeur historique ancienne, un principe juridique intégrationniste, l'asile politique d'un modèle de société humaniste', *RDUE* 2009, 414–15; NICOLAIDIS and SHAFFER, 'Transnational Mutual Recognition Regimes' (n 55) 316.

[142] R. BARENTS, 'The Precedence of EU Law from the Perspective of Constitutional Pluralism', *EU Const* 2009, 446.

[143] POIARES MADURO, 'So Close and Yet So Far' (n 87) 818–19.

2

The Mutual Recognition Mechanism: Object, Actors, Mechanism, and Characteristics

In the previous chapter, I concluded that an examination of the different natures of each area of law and their corresponding objectives does not result in convincing arguments against the viability of the internal market analogy. Therefore, I now turn again to the operation of the principle of mutual recognition in a cross-policy approach, in an analysis comprising four key questions: What is recognized under the principle of mutual recognition (object of the mutual recognition mechanism, section I)? Who is involved in the mutual recognition process (relevant actors, section II)? Which duties does the mutual recognition principle impose on the actors involved (section III)? Which characteristics can be attributed to the principle of mutual recognition (section IV)?

In essence, all of these questions were addressed in Parts I and II of this book, either briefly or in more detail. The main results of these previous analyses will be taken up again in this chapter, and examined again using a comparative, functional approach. Similarities and differences found between the elements that characterize the mutual recognition mechanism in each context will be discussed in this chapter with the aim of clarifying whether the internal market analogy is viable or not in light of arguments that relate to the mutual recognition mechanism.

I. The Object of the Mutual Recognition Mechanism

It has been argued, on repeated occasions, that a world of difference exists between the object of the mutual recognition mechanism in the internal market context and in the area of judicial cooperation in criminal matters. Admittedly, if we take a prototype from each context—a bottle of beer (internal market) and an arrest warrant (judicial cooperation in criminal matters)—few will disagree that a bottle of beer initially appears not to have a lot of common ground with an arrest warrant. Yet on closer examination, it must be acknowledged that mutual recognition is not limited to the recognition of these explicit objects, but also concerns the recognition of the national regulations and legislation upon whose basis the beer is produced and the arrest warrant issued. This more implicit object of the mutual recognition mechanism (the underlying legislation and regulations) reveals an important common feature of the object of the mutual recognition mechanism in both contexts, namely its predominantly public nature (section I, B). The alleged difference in nature between regulatory public acts (internal market) and judicial public acts (judicial cooperation in criminal matters) (section I, A) does not undermine the finding that mutual recognition is essentially concerned with the mutual recognition of states' acts.

A. Regulatory and judicial acts

Both the ECJ and the EU legislator have contributed to a clarification of what is to be considered the object of the mutual recognition mechanism.[1]

In the internal market context, the ECJ has made it plain that not only must goods, services, and persons lawfully marketed, provided, or employed in their home country be recognized in the host country, but equally any document, certificate, certification, attestation, control or, ultimately, any other factual or legal element regarding these goods, services, or persons insofar as these elements have been (lawfully) attested by a Member State's competent authority.[2] It is precisely the requirement of 'lawfulness',[3] which demands that goods, citizens, or companies meet the commercial, technical, or other requirements stipulated by the home country's regulatory framework, that implies that the mutual recognition mechanism amounts to a duty to recognize the other Member State's regulations on the goods, services, or persons concerned. It also explains the mainly[4] regulatory nature of the object of the mutual recognition mechanism in this context.[5]

In relation to criminal matters, both the *ne bis in idem* provisions (Art. 54 CISA) and the provisions on judicial cooperation in criminal matters (Art. 82 TFEU) unequivocally impose a duty to recognize judgments and judicial decisions, which highlights the judicial nature of the object of mutual recognition in this area of law. Yet despite the strong focus on 'judicial decisions' in both provisions, it cannot be denied

[1] As discussed in Part I (in the internal market context), it has been—first and foremost—the ECJ's case law with its broad interpretation of the free movement Treaty provisions that has helped clarifying what is to be considered as 'object' of the mutual recognition mechanism. In addition to the ECJ's case law, the European legislator too has contributed to the delineation of the object of the mutual recognition mechanism in this context. Yet, even though some instruments can be mentioned in which relatively new 'objects' were added to the mutual recognition list, in many more instruments the legislator simply consolidated judicial developments, often in combination with a more refined mutual recognition mechanism. By contrast, in relation to criminal matters, I pointed out in Part II that, so far, leaving aside the ECJ's *ne bis in idem* case law, it has been mainly the European legislator that has explained the scope of the mutual recognition mechanism through the gradual realization of an ambitious legislative programme.

[2] Report from the Commission—First biennial report on the application of the principle of mutual recognition in the market of goods and services, SEC (1999) 1106, p. 3 and 12; V. GOTZ, 'Der Grundsatz der gegenseitigen Anerkennung im europäischen Binnenmarkt,' in *Liber amicorum Günther Jaenicke—Zum 85. Beburtstag* (Berlin, Springer, 1998) 779; V. HATZOPOULOS, 'Le principe de reconnaissance mutuelle dans la libre prestation de services', 2009, 24–30, retrievable at: <www.coleurope.eu>.

[3] On this requirement, see: White Paper from the Commission to the European Council—Completing the Internal Market, COM (1985) 310, p. 19; N. STOFFEL VALLOTTON, *La prohibición de restricciones a la libre circulación de mercancías en la Comunidad Europea* (Madrid, Dykinson, 2000) 423–4 and the authors cited therein.

[4] It is not excluded, however, that—in this context too—*judicial* acts related to goods, services, or persons, stemming for the country of origin, can be put on the table during administrative or judicial proceedings in the host state and, consequently, made subject to a duty of mutual recognition.

[5] However, on some occasions the mutual recognition mechanism can also apply in the absence of a specific piece of national legislation. For instance, in the area of free movement of goods, some goods can be put on the market—in some Member States—without any specific legislation or authorization requirements. H. Ingels gave the example of children's beds. Apparently, at a given time, the United Kingdom was one of the only EU Member States that had developed specific regulations regarding children's beds, in particular regarding its inflammability, in view of the fact that in the past some children had passed away owing to the highly inflammable nature of some children's beds (Interview with H. INGELS, administrator at the European Commission, DG Internal Market, 9 February 2007). In those cases it is a Member State's policy *not* to regulate that must be recognized provided, of course, that there are no justification grounds available.

that the ECJ's case law,[6] EU policy documents,[7] and EU legislation[8] all contain some indications of the fact that the wording 'judgments and judicial decisions' must, in principle, be interpreted broadly and that the mutual recognition mechanism should not always be restricted to decisions made solely by judicial authorities *sensu stricto*. Thus, despite the predominantly judicial nature of the object of the mutual recognition mechanism, a duty of mutual recognition may also apply on occasions to decisions made by administrative or non-judicial authorities, i.e. decisions of a non-judicial nature.

Some authors have argued that what is crucial is the difference in nature of the origins of the mutual recognition mechanism's object, namely regulatory acts (internal market) and judicial acts (criminal matters). According to these authors, Member State laws that enshrine regulatory standards are clearly discernible legal texts, whereas the object of mutual recognition in criminal matters has a much greater reach since it applies to acts of the judiciary in their interpretation and application of an entire set of materials and procedural laws.[9] I do not completely agree that so much weight should be given to this distinction, for two reasons. First, as mentioned above, the distinction itself is not actually as sharp as is often assumed, since judicial decisions can be the object of mutual recognition in the internal market context and non-judicial decisions can be the object of mutual recognition in the context of judicial cooperation in criminal matters. Secondly, my analysis of the principle's workability in Parts I and II raised doubts as to the sustainability of the argument about the apparent opposition between so-called clearly discernible texts (internal market) and the so-called difficult task of interpreting and applying an entire set of norms (criminal matters). In fact, my analysis of the principle's workability in the internal market context reveals that instead of 'clearly discernible texts', national administrators are often faced with goods that have been allowed onto the market without any specific requirements or that are subject to obscure national provisions developed in a very specific national context.[10] Furthermore, my analysis of

[6] See, in particular: ECJ, Joined Cases C-187/01 and C-385/01 *Gözütok and Brügge* [2003] ECR I-1345.

[7] Policy documents have stated from the very beginning that the (legislative) principle of mutual recognition is intended to cover not only decisions by courts but also other decisions like, for instance, decisions resulting from victim-offender mediation or agreements between a suspect and prosecution services. Communication from the Commission to the Council and the European Parliament—Mutual recognition of final decisions in criminal matters, COM (2000) 495 final, p. 5.

[8] In some of the legislative instruments that have been adopted so far there is a clear and deliberate choice to restrain the scope of the mutual recognition mechanism to judicial decisions issued by *criminal courts* such, as for instance, the FD TIA. However, many of the other legislative instruments put into perspective the requirement of 'judicial authority (in criminal matters)'. First of all, most instruments refer back to the issuing Member State's law for the definition of 'judicial authority' which implies that on occasions orders must be recognized when they are stemming from authorities which are not necessarily considered to be 'judicial' authorities in some of the other Member States. Furthermore, some instruments emphasize the broad meaning of 'judicial authority'. For instance, § 2 and Article 1(a) FD MRFP state that the principle of mutual recognition should apply to financial penalties imposed by judicial *or administrative authorities*. Article 3(1) DIR EPO states 'judicial *or* equivalent authorities' and Article 3 FD ESO (post-trial) goes a step further by stating that Member States may designate *non-judicial authorities* as the competent authorities for taking decisions under these framework decisions. However, Article 2 PROP DIR EIO foresees that only judicial authorities—a judge, a court, an investigating magistrate, or a public prosecutor—are allowed to act as *issuing* authority. A European investigation order issued by another type of authority needs validation by a judicial authority (Art. 5a (3) PROP DIR EIO).

[9] S. LAVENEX, 'Mutual recognition and the monopoly of force: limits of the single market analogy', *JEPP* 2007, 765; P. PEITEADO MARISCAL *El reconocimiento mutuo de resoluciones penales definitivas en la Unión Europea* (Madrid, Colex, 2006) 30.

[10] See: Part I, ch 3: 'The Workability of the Principle of Mutual Recognition in the Internal Market'.

its workability in criminal matters, especially in relation to the application of the FD EAW, has revealed that problems with interpreting legal texts are almost non-existent, owing to the limited role granted to the executing judge.[11] In sum, the probability of attaining a smoothly working mutual recognition principle has likely been overestimated in the internal market context and underestimated in the context of criminal matters, especially with regard to the FD EAW.

Given this conclusion, it does not seem appropriate to focus on the difference in object (judicial acts versus regulatory acts) or to consider this a relevant feature for distinguishing the mutual recognition mechanism in each area. It seems far more suitable to emphasize the common thread that unites the object of the principle of mutual recognition in the two areas, namely the (predominantly) public nature of the regulations which impose a duty of mutual recognition.

B. The object of the mutual recognition mechanism: always acts of states?

Under the previous heading, I discussed the regulatory nature (internal market) and judicial nature (judicial cooperation in criminal matters) of the object of the mutual recognition principle. In both contexts, the object of the principle of mutual recognition therefore relates to acts of states and is, in principle, public in nature. However, this predominantly public nature is not always so easily discernible, either in the internal market context or in the area of judicial cooperation in criminal matters.

In the internal market context, legal scholars have drawn attention to the fact that a crucial difference exists here between the mutual recognition of provisions related to the free movement of goods (which always concerns acts of states, thus acts of a public nature) and the mutual recognition of provisions related to the free movement of services (which can also include acts of a non-public—i.e. private—nature).[12] Yet the difference between the public nature of rules related to goods and the (sometimes) private nature of rules related to services should be put into perspective. First, in the area of goods, the ECJ has maintained in its case law a broad interpretation of the concept '(acts stemming from a) public authority'[13] and the European legislator's New Approach to goods has revealed a degree of openness towards the involvement of the private sector in developing norms that can be made subject to the internal market provisions and the

[11] See: Part II, ch 3: 'The Workability of the Principle of Mutual Recognition in Criminal Matters'.

[12] HATZOPOULOS, 'Le principe de reconnaissance mutuelle dans la libre prestation de services' (n 2) 4–5. Such an argument is of course perfectly in line with the general view that the ECJ has accepted that the provisions on free movement of persons have horizontal (as well as vertical) direct effect, whereas it is generally assumed that the provisions on free movement of goods only have vertical direct effect. See, however, the nuances made by: P.J.G. KAPTEYN, A.M. McDONNELL, K.J.M. MORTELMANS, and C.W.A. TIMMERMANS, *The Law of the European Union and the European Communities with Reference to Changes Made by the Lisbon Treaty* (Alphen aan den Rijn, Wolters-Kluwer, 2008) 636; C. KRENN, 'A Missing Piece in the Horizontal Effect "Jigsaw": Horizontal Direct Effect and the Free Movement of Goods', *CML Rev*. 2012, 177–215; S. VAN DEN BOGAERT, 'Horizontality: The ECJ Attacks?', in C. BARNARD and J. SCOTT (eds.), *The Law of the Single European Market. Unpacking the Premises* (Oregon, Hart Publishing, 2002) 129. It remains, however, unclear whether the Treaty provisions on establishment and services are *fully* horizontally applicable in the sense of imposing legal obligations on all individuals and not only on powerful, self-regulating collective actors such as sporting organizations which possess power akin to public law: P. CRAIG and G. DE BURCA, *EU Law. Text, Cases and Materials* (Oxford, Oxford University Press, 2011) 767–8.

[13] U. BECKER, 'Artikel 28', in J. SCHWARZE (ed.), *EU-Kommentar* (Baden Baden, Nomos, 2009) 462.

application of the principle of mutual recognition.[14] Secondly, in the area of services, the vast majority of national regulations that are subject to the mutual recognition mechanism have a public nature, or at least derive from bodies closely linked to a Member State's government.[15] In sum, while rules stemming from 'private' organizations, such as sporting organizations[16] and trade unions,[17] have occasionally come under examination in the ECJ's case law, it cannot be denied that the majority of regulations made subject to the mutual recognition mechanism to date were issued by public bodies, bodies with a delegated public authority, or powerful, self-regulating collective actors.

Similarly, in the area of judicial cooperation in criminal matters, a cautious but undeniable trend of privatization is taking place in some Member States, which must be understood as part of a much wider ideological shift that has occurred over the last two decades. This shift has seen the rolling back of the state in many spheres of public life and the re-designation of its responsibilities to regulation rather than provision of certain services.[18] The area of alternative sanctions, with its strong focus on public-private cooperation, may be one of the areas where decisions made by non-public entities will first come to the fore, yet in view of the growing number of private prisons in the United Kingdom and of the coming into force of semi-private models in several other Member States,[19] it is clear that—even in the sacrosanct field of custodial sentences—potential seems to exist for private or semi-private decisions to become objects of the mutual recognition mechanism. While this might be controversial for some Member States, whose constitutional arguments will no doubt include the view that enforcing state punishment is a state responsibility and should not be delegated to private organizations, it is unclear whether such objections will be upheld in light of certain aspects of internal market case law.[20]

II. Actors Involved in the Mutual Recognition Mechanism

A. Actors in charge in the mutual recognition mechanism

The difference between regulatory (acts) and judicial (acts) described above again arises in relation to the actors responsible for correct application of the principle of mutual recognition, namely national administrative authorities (in the context of the internal market) and national judicial authorities (in the context of criminal matters). The dichotomy between 'regulatory' and 'judicial' should once again be put into perspective here.

In the internal market context, the ECJ has explicitly recognized that both a Member State's administrative and judicial authorities are bound by the duty of mutual

[14] See, for instance: ECJ, Case C-171/11 *Fra.bo SpA*, nyr, paras 24–31. See also, on the horizontal effect of the free movement of goods: Opinion of AG Trstenjak in Case C-171/11 *Fra.bo SpA*, nyr, § 29–35.

[15] CRAIG and DE BURCA, (n 12) 768.

[16] See, for instance: ECJ, Case C-415/93 *Bosman* [1995] ECR I-4921.

[17] See, for instance: ECJ, Case C-341/05 *Laval un Partneri* [2007] ECR I-11767.

[18] E. GENDERS, 'Legitimacy, Accountability and Private Prisons', *Punishment and Society* 2002, 286.

[19] EUROFEDOP, 'Private Prisons in Europe. UK leads the way', retrievable at: <http://www.infedop-eurofedop.com/IMG/pdf/Privegevangenissen_in_Europa_-_Het_VK_is_de_koploper_en_fr_nl.pdf>.

[20] See, in particular: ECJ, Case C-274/05 *Commission v Greece* [2008] ECR I-7969 para 23 (in relation to private teaching establishments); ECJ, Case C-444/05 *Stamatelaki* [2007] ECR I-3185, paras 36–7 (in relation to private hospitals).

recognition.[21] Vice versa, in the area of criminal matters, it can be assumed—irrespective of the key role that is to be fulfilled by the judicial authorities under the new regime—that the duties related to the mutual recognition mechanism are not limited to judicial authorities but incumbent, in principle, on all actors involved in criminal proceedings subject to a mutual recognition mechanism.[22] It is indeed difficult to see how the free movement provisions or the provisions on judicial cooperation in criminal matters, when read in light of the principle of sincere cooperation, can be carried out efficiently if certain entities are exempt from the mutual recognition duty. It should therefore be concluded that in both contexts, all actors involved in the mutual recognition mechanism, irrespective of their specific backgrounds, are bound by the duties arising from this principle, unless a legislative instrument explicitly states otherwise.

Finally, and as mentioned above, in view of the privatization trend that is taking place in some Member States in very divergent sectors, and which touches on aspects of the internal market (for instance: private health insurance funds and private schools/universities) as well as on criminal law policy (for instance: alternative sanctions which necessitate public-private cooperation and privatized prisons), it should not be overlooked that (semi-)private parties may also come to play a decisive role in the mutual recognition mechanism in both contexts.

B. Actors that 'undergo' or trigger the mutual recognition mechanism

The principle of mutual recognition not only imposes potentially far-reaching duties on the Member States' authorities, but also entails significant consequences for natural and legal persons who can either trigger the mutual recognition mechanism or simply 'undergo' it.

I described above how in the internal market context, in addition to the Commission, it is often a natural or legal person who triggers the application of the mutual recognition principle by claiming rights related to the relevant free movement provisions. This active position of a natural or legal person initially appears less evident in relation to the legal instruments on judicial cooperation in criminal matters, where the initiative is generally taken by a judicial authority and where a natural or legal person will simply undergo, rather passively, the mutual recognition mechanism. However, under some of these instruments, there is nothing to prevent a national or legal person adopting a more active approach by making suggestions to the competent judicial authority which may influence the mutual recognition mechanism. For instance, a natural or legal person may suggest that a foreign legal document be taken into account on the basis of the FD TIA or insist on the availability of relevant foreign evidence, which might trigger the application of the FD EEW. Similarly, in relation to the PROP DIR EIO, an investigation order may be used by competent authorities to collect evidence in another Member State when requested by defence lawyers.[23] Moreover, in Article 6(2) DIR EPO, it is even stated

[21] See, for instance: ECJ, Case C-336/94 *Dafeki* [1997] ECR I-6761, para 19.

[22] See, for instance: FD ESO (post-trial) and FD ESO (pre-trial), which both accept that Member States may designate non-judicial authorities as the competent authorities for taking decisions under these instruments (Art. 3(2) FD ESO (post-trial), Art. 6(2) FD ESO (pre-trial)). In some framework decisions the role for non-judicial authorities is, however, limited to *executing* orders, but not allowed for *issuing* authorities, see, for instance: Article 2 FD EEW, Article 2 PROP DIR EIO.

[23] Initiative of the Kingdom of Belgium, the Republic of Bulgaria, the Republic of Estonia, the Kingdom of Spain, the Republic of Austria, the Republic of Slovenia and the Kingdom of Sweden for a

that the competent authority of the issuing Member State 'shall *only at the request of the protected person* issue a European protection order' (emphasis added). Finally, in relation to Article 54 CISA, it will generally be a natural or legal person who informs the judicial authority of any previous judgments. Here, again, the mutual recognition is triggered by a natural or legal person, though of course it will be the judicial authority that ultimately decides on the fulfilment of the *ne bis in idem* criteria.

In view of the fact that in both areas of law, the principle of mutual recognition operates in a conditional and non-automatic way by means of a balancing mechanism, a natural or legal person involved in the mutual recognition mechanism will therefore be largely dependent in both contexts on the margin of appreciation left to the host country (executing Member State).

In this regard, we might wonder whether the fact that a natural or a legal person is involved in the mutual recognition mechanism makes any difference to the outcome of the case. In relation to the internal market, I concluded in Part I that in view of the ECJ's case law, it does not appear highly significant whether the case concerns a natural or legal person.[24] Admittedly, there have been cases in which the ECJ was seen to be very generous in its protection of natural persons,[25] but it is likely that an equal number of cases exist in which the outcome of the mutual recognition mechanism was more beneficial to legal persons.[26] Therefore, it appears to be less the natural or legal status of the person concerned that is decisive for the outcome of the mutual recognition mechanism[27] and more other factors such as (the sensitive nature of the) subject matter at stake, harmonization measures, justification grounds, or any other relevant factors of the specific case in question.

In relation to criminal matters, differing views within the Member States on legal persons' criminal liability would initially appear to suggest that the ECJ might take a more cautious approach to imposing duties of mutual recognition on legal persons. Yet most relevant instruments on mutual recognition explicitly state that orders must be recognized and executed even if the executing state does not recognize the principle of legal persons' criminal liability,[28] and this reveals the EU legislator's unequivocal decision to support mutual recognition, a position the ECJ is also keen to adopt. This duty of mutual recognition without equivalence, however, is markedly less far-reaching in relation to natural persons in most legal instruments,[29] which is understandable in light

Directive of the European Parliament and of the Council regarding the European Investigation Order in criminal matters—Frequently Asked Questions, document number 8182/12, 4 April 2012, p. 5, retrievable at: <http://www.consilium.europa.eu/documents/access-to-council-documents-public-register?lang=en>.

[24] See: Part I, ch 1, I, C. 'Mutual recognition and the free movement of persons'.

[25] See, for instance: ECJ, Case C-148/02 *Garcia Avello* [2003] ECR I-11613; ECJ, Case C-200/02 *Zhu and Chen* [2004] ECR I-9925.

[26] See, for instance: ECJ, Case C-212/97 *Centros* [1999] ECR I-1459; ECJ, C-208/00 *Uberseering* [2002] ECR I-9919; ECJ, Case C-167/01 *Inspire Art* [2003] ECR I-10155.

[27] In some judgments the ECJ even draws parallels between natural persons and legal persons, see, for instance: ECJ, Case C-210/06 *Cartesio* [2008] ECR I-9641, para 109.

[28] Article 9(3) FD MRFP; Article 12(3) FD MRCO. Furthermore, even in relation to framework decisions on mutual recognition that do not explicitly specify whether the mutual recognition duty also applies in case of legal persons, there are generally other provisions in the framework decision that clearly hint at such an interpretation. For instance, Article 19(2) FD EEW and Article 12(2) FD EOFPE both foresee in the possibility of claims by natural *or* legal persons for compensation of damage. See also: Article 4(d) PROP DIR EIO.

[29] See, for instance: Article 10 FD MRFP which allows imprisonment (as alternative to a financial penalty) only when it is permitted by the legislation of *both* the issuing *and* the executing Member State.

of the significant impact custodial sentences (compared to financial penalties) can have on a natural person's life.[30]

III. The Mutual Recognition Mechanism under Scrutiny

Regardless of whether mutual recognition is defined in terms of internal market law or in terms of judicial cooperation in criminal matters, and whether it is described in light of the judicially developed mutual recognition or in light of the legislatively developed mutual recognition, the mechanism behind it in all of these contexts always centres around the effective transfer of regulatory authority or jurisdiction between the home state (or issuing Member State) and the host state (or executing Member State) (section III, A). The mutual recognition mechanism requires of the host state, in principle, that it grants a product or judgment issued by the home state the same or at least similar effects to those granted in the home state. In what follows, I deal with the question of what this effect granting actually entails in practice (section III, B).

A. The transfer of regulatory and jurisdictional authority: mutual recognition as a form of joint governance between the host state (executing Member State) and home state (issuing Member State)

Earlier in this book, I discussed how mutual recognition creates extraterritoriality and how it requires Member States to be 'other Member State regarding'. Mutual recognition constitutes some form of joint governance, since Member States agree to recognize, subject to certain limits, their respective norms, rules, documents, and judgments as valid in each others' territories.

In the internal market context, the mutual recognition mechanism—in its original and most basic form—requires that, subject to certain conditions, the competent authority of the host state accepts a product, person, firm, service, or document originating from another Member State provided that it has been lawfully produced or marketed (goods), regulated (professional qualifications), set up (firms), performed (services), or issued (documents) in the home Member State. Given this definition's strong focus on regulation in the country from which a product, person, firm, service, or document originates (home state or country of origin), it is hardly surprising that in legal literature 'the principle of mutual recognition' has often been identified with 'the principle of country of origin'. In Part I, I outlined my arguments against treating 'the principle of mutual recognition' as synonymous to 'the principle of country of origin'. First, the ECJ has stated that the former is a principle laid down in the free movement Treaty provisions,[31] whereas the latter is not.[32] Second, within the large amount of EU legislation on mutual recognition, we find abundant examples in which the European legislator

[30] See, for instance: ECJ, Case C-467/05 *Dell'Orto* [2007] ECR I-5557, paras 51–60; ECJ, Case C-205/09 *Eredics* [2010] ECR I-10231, para 29, in relation to former FD 2001/220/JHA on the standing of victims in criminal proceedings, where the ECJ discarded the argument of discrimination and held that 'the EU legislator could legitimately establish a body of rules designed to protect only natural persons, since such persons are objectively in a situation which differs from that of legal persons because of their greater vulnerability and because of the nature of the interests which can be harmed by offences which can be committed only against natural persons, such as the victim's life and physical well-being'.

[31] ECJ, Case C-110/05 *Commission v Italy* [2009] ECR I-519, para 34.

[32] ECJ, Case C-233/94 *Commission v Germany* [1997] ECR I-2405, para 64.

has refrained from adopting an 'exclusive' country of origin approach, which entails full transfer of competence to the country of origin. Rather than imposing a one-sided country of origin approach, the European legislator's preferred solution is instead a division of competences between the home state and the host state. In fact, using a variety of mechanisms—such as the possibility of invoking justification grounds, the distribution of supervisory competences between the home State and the host state, and the duty to exchange information and cooperation—the European legislator (and the ECJ) have assured in divergent areas that Member States have a joint task in ensuring the smooth and responsible application of the principle of mutual recognition.

In relation to criminal matters, the ECJ's view of mutual recognition in *Gözütok and Brügge*[33] and the Commission's interpretation in one of its major communications on mutual recognition[34] both highlight, once again, the paramount position of the Member State from which the judgment originates (issuing Member State). Yet here, too, a note of caution is in order as an overt focus on the country of origin's role indicates a failure to comprehend the true content of the mutual recognition mechanism. On several occasions, both the ECJ[35] and the European legislator[36] have eased the omnipotence of the issuing Member State's legal framework to a certain extent. My analysis of the legislative instruments adopted in this area has also revealed that with regard to the execution of foreign orders, most instruments depart from an understanding that the executing Member State's framework governs the execution, albeit with the issuing Member State and its legal framework fulfilling either a minor or major complementary role depending on the instrument at stake.

In sum, a comparative analysis of the two contexts produces several interesting results. First, neither the ECJ nor the European legislator has embraced the country of origin's playing an omnipotent role. In fact, the ECJ's main concern is less about allowing the country of origin or issuing Member State's legal framework to prevail automatically over the other Member States' legal frameworks, and more about ensuring that all national legal frameworks comply with the Treaty provisions, even if this entails setting aside certain provisions of the country of origin (issuing Member State). Secondly, mutual recognition is a mechanism in which the legal framework of both Member States can be relevant, and in which the authorities of both Member States have a relevant role to play. Mutual recognition instruments pursue an optimal, well-balanced combination of home (issuing Member State) and host (executing Member State) country control rather than an exclusive focus on the country of origin. Thirdly, in order to describe the exact contours of the powers of the home state (issuing Member State) vis-à-vis the host state (executing Member State), a thorough scrutiny of each individual directive or framework decision (legislative context) and the ECJ's case law (judicial context) is required, since the exact distribution of competences varies from one instrument to another and may also evolve with time and across domains.

[33] '... that there is a necessary implication that the Member States [...] recognize the criminal law in force in the other Member States ...'.

[34] '... that a decision taken by a judge [...] in one Member State [...] would have to be accepted in all other Member States'. Communication from the European Commission to the Council and the European Parliament—Mutual Recognition of final decisions in criminal matters (n 7) p. 2.

[35] See: Part II, ch 1, IV, C. 'Margins of control left to the Member States when applying the *ne bis in idem* principle'.

[36] See: Part II, ch 2, I, B. 'Country of origin'.

B. Giving effect to foreign decisions: the various facets of mutual recognition

In light of the flexible nature of the principle of mutual recognition, it is a challenge to provide a faithful overview of the different phases that a national authority belonging to the host state (executing Member State) might expect to undergo in each individual mutual recognition process. In this section, I discuss what can be seen as the four major phases of a mutual recognition process: the duty to take into account (section B, 2); the examination procedure (section B, 3); the recognition (section B, 4); and the execution (section B, 5). However, there is one important caveat, namely that these phases may not necessarily take place in relation to each mutual recognition operation. Furthermore, in some areas of law, free movement can take place without any prior assessment being performed by a national competent authority, owing to the distinction between mutual recognition *ex ante* and mutual recognition *ex post* (section B, 1).

(1) Mutual recognition ex ante *and mutual recognition* ex post

It should be recalled that the principle of mutual recognition consists of a rule (free movement, mutual recognition) and an exception (Treaty-based, case law-based or legislatively developed justification grounds) and that a national authority in charge of taking a decision on mutual recognition will thus be entitled or even required to set aside the rule (mutual recognition) if it concludes following its assessment that the exception should be upheld. An important question in this regard, however, is when the competent authority's assessment should take place. In fact, an interesting difference exists between certain sectors in the internal market context and in the area of judicial cooperation in criminal matters. In relation to the latter sector, the assessment will always be carried out before any effect is given to the foreign judgment, as it is precisely the executing judge's decision on recognition and execution that will give effect to the foreign decision (mutual recognition *ex ante*). By contrast, in relation to certain internal market sectors, foreign goods or services may have an effect in another Member State's territory prior to any assessment by the host Member State's competent authorities.[37] In the latter case, any issues related to the control of the mutual recognition requirements will arise in a later stage, namely during market surveillance (mutual recognition *ex post*).

Mutual recognition *ex post* is undoubtedly of great benefit to the free movement rationale behind the corresponding Treaty provisions as it allows for the immediate and smooth application of the mutual recognition principle. It also has its risks, however, as the absence of any prior controlling mechanism might produce harmful consequences for the host state which would not necessarily have occurred under an *a priori* system. Therefore, it seems advisable to implement an *a priori* system in those internal market areas where risk-bearing goods or services are involved.[38]

[37] In relation to the free movement of goods, see, for instance: Commission staff working document—Accompanying document to the Proposal for a Regulation of the European Parliament and of the Council laying down procedures relating to the application of certain national technical rules to products lawfully marketed in another Member State and repealing Decision 3052/95/EC Impact assessment, SEC (2007) 112, p. 8–9. In relation to the free movement of services, see, for instance: Article 7 DIR 2005/36/EC on the recognition of professional qualifications, according to which a mere declaration to the host state's authorities is sufficient to start executing services in the host country (mutual recognition *ex post*).

[38] In this regard, it is noteworthy that according to Article 7(4) DIR 2005/36/EC a mere declaration by the service provider might be considered not to be sufficient in the case of regulated professions *having public health or safety implications* which do not benefit from automatic recognition. In the latter hypothesis,

(2) *The duty to take into account*

In the majority of legal literature that deals with the principle of mutual recognition, a link is only seldom made to the duty to take into account. Yet in my view, the duty to take into account is an important aspect of the mutual recognition mechanism, in both of the contexts now under discussion. The duty to take into account is best seen as a continuation of the duty 'to be other Member State regarding', as it implies an openness towards the decisions and regulations of other Member States and a willingness to act upon these foreign elements when taking a decision on mutual recognition. 'Taking into account' thus goes further than simply acknowledging the existence of the foreign regulation or judicial decision, since it requires an acceptance that the foreign element may influence or determine the outcome of the local decision. In the internal market context, the entire case law on the prohibition of dual burdens is based on the duty to take the foreign element into account. Furthermore, in the ECJ's case law on the mutual recognition of diplomas, the first obligation that rests on a Member State in the context of a mutual recognition procedure is that 'the Member State must take into consideration the diplomas, certificates and other evidence of qualification'.[39] Examples of a duty to take into account can also be found in the area of criminal matters, however, for instance in the *ne bis in idem* provisions, where the mutual recognition of a decision means that other Member States must take that decision into account by ensuring that a person will not be prosecuted again for the same acts and that a final court decision will not be challenged.[40] Similarly, mutual recognition can require that a national judge take foreign criminal judgments into account in order to assess a person's criminal record and their status as a persistent offender.[41]

The question of whether the duty to take into account constitutes a far-reaching duty of mutual recognition for the host state (executing Member State) does not have a straightforward answer, since it depends upon various factors such as—most importantly—the underlying objectives,[42] the existence (or non-existence) of justification grounds for setting aside the duty to take into account,[43] any possible equivalence requirements,[44] and the rules that determine which Member State's legal framework will govern the duty to take into account.[45]

the host Member State's competent authority can decide to perform some checks which are aimed at avoiding serious damage to the health or safety of the service recipient owing to a lack of professional qualification of the service provider.

[39] See, for instance: ECJ, Case C-340/89 *Vlassopoulou* [1991] ECR I-2357, para 16.

[40] Programme of measures to implement the principle of mutual recognition of decisions in criminal matters, *O.J.* C-12/10, 15.01.2001, p. 11.

[41] Programme of measures to implement the principle of mutual recognition of decisions in criminal matters (n 40).

[42] See, for instance: ECJ, Case C-33/07 *Jipa* [2008] ECR I-5157, para 25, where there is no duty but a mere *possibility* to take the foreign assessment into account. The ECJ's mild attitude can be explained by the fact that a too strong reliance on the foreign assessment in the case at hand would potentially threaten the free movement objective.

[43] Compare in this regard the grounds for non-recognition written down in Articles 3 and 4 PROP FD TIA with the finally adopted FD TIA in which no grounds for non-recognition are withheld.

[44] For instance, in relation to the mutual recognition of diplomas, the duty to take into account will, in principle, only lead to a far-reaching mutual recognition requirement to the extent that the knowledge and qualifications certified by the foreign diploma correspond to those required by the national provisions. In other words, equivalence requirements determine—to a large extent—the scope of the duty to take something into account. See, however: ECJ, Case C-421/98 *Commission v Spain* [2000] ECR I-10375; ECJ, Case C-111/12 *Ordine degli Ingegneri di Verona e Provincia and others*, nyr, both mentioned: Part I, ch 2, II, B, 2. 'Enhancing mutual trust and mutual recognition in the area of diplomas'.

[45] For instance, in relation to the FD TIA, it is first and foremost the legal framework of the Member State where new criminal proceedings are taking place that is decisive as the duty to take into account

(3) The examination procedure

In a subsequent phase, the competent national authority involved in a mutual recognition process goes through a number of checks, which I will refer to as the 'examination procedure'. The mutual recognition mechanism enables, and sometimes obliges, a national administrator or a national judicial authority to examine different aspects relating to the mutual recognition proceedings in question, especially: questions related to presumed inaccuracies or shortcomings (section 3.1), equivalence checks (section 3.2), examination of justification grounds including the corresponding proportionality checks (section 3.3), and other issues related to the broader Treaty framework (section 3.4). It is plain that this phase of investigation puts the supposed automatic nature of the mutual recognition principle into perspective, as it often allows the host (executing) state a considerable margin of discretion and confirms my previous statement that it would be misleading in most cases to reduce the principle of mutual recognition to a country of origin principle.

3.1. How to reconcile a presumption of trust with suspected inaccuracies or shortcomings?

In the internal market context, it might happen that a national authority asked to recognize a foreign certificate, inspection document, driving licence, or social security document has doubts about the accuracy of the document. Similarly, in relation to criminal matters, a national judicial authority asked to recognize an arrest warrant, evidence warrant, or supervision order might question the correctness or adequacy of the information contained within it. In both contexts, then, national authorities may have doubts about the accuracy or reliability of the document they are required to recognize. But what can they do next? Are they entitled to reject it? Or obliged to accept it blindly? Is there an alternative solution? In what follows I argue that, with certain refinements, the approach taken by the ECJ in the internal market context may be a useful reference for the path that is currently being explored in criminal matters.

The ECJ has stressed from the outset that the relationship between Member States' authorities should be based on a general principle of mutual trust.[46] In a Union where Member States share common values and principles, and are bound by the principle of sincere cooperation, it is perfectly reasonable that mutual trust of the decisions and documents issued in other Member States should be the starting point. It can be deduced from the ECJ's case law that the principle of sincere cooperation works both ways in this context: it requires the competent authority in the home country to carry out a proper assessment of the facts relevant for the application of the legislation in question and to guarantee the correctness of the information contained in the certificate it issues, but it also requires the competent authority in the host country to rely on (the presumption of) the certificate's correctness.[47] Yet there is always a risk, in every Member State, since no system is flawless. An unlimited principle of trust might therefore be inadequate. As a result, and rather wisely, the ECJ has never applied the principle of mutual trust excessively. Rather than imposing a blind regime of mutual trust on the Member States, the ECJ's case law

only applies to the extent previous national convictions are taken into account, and equivalent legal effects are attached to the foreign convictions as to previous national convictions, in accordance with national law (Art. 3(1) FD TIA).

[46] See, for instance: ECJ, Case 46/76 *Bauhuis* [1977] ECR 5, para 22; ECJ, Case 25/88 *Bouchara* [1989] ECR 1105, para 18.

[47] See, for instance: ECJ, Case C-202/97 *FTS* [2000] ECR I-883, paras 51–3; Opinion of AG Bot in Case C-184/10 *Grasser* [2011] ECR I-4057, § 39–41, who underlines that simple drafting errors cannot be presumed.

has left Member States some scope for control, even in harmonized areas of law which include a far-reaching duty of mutual recognition. Trust is the point of departure, yet for well-founded reasons, a national authority is entitled, and sometimes obliged, to set aside the presumption of trust, albeit in accordance with the standards set out by the ECJ in its case law.[48]

3.1.1. *The point of departure: alert, but not suspicious*

The presumption of trust requires that a Member State's competent authorities are in principle bound by documents and decisions originating from other Member States and that they do not systematically call into question the accuracy of particulars provided by the competent authorities in the home state on their own initiative and motivated by general suspicion.[49] However, the fact that there is no all-round *a priori* right, let alone duty, to scrutinize each and every foreign element thoroughly does not imply that competent authorities should behave passively. On the contrary, in light of the far-reaching consequences that the mutual recognition mechanism entails, it seems appropriate, in my view, that an administrative or judicial authority should adopt an alert attitude and that whenever it identifies obvious errors, inconsistencies, or shortcomings that could jeopardize one of the main objectives underlying the instrument or the Treaty provision in question,[50] it should have not only a *right*[51] but also a *duty* to react[52]

[48] See: Part I, ch 1, IV, B. 'Margins of control left to the Member States when applying the principle of mutual recognition'; Part I, ch 2, III, B. 'Limits linked to the level of control left to the host Member State'; Part II, ch 1, IV, C. 'Margins of control left to the Member State when applying the *ne bis in idem* principle'; Part II, ch 2, III, C. 'Limits linked to the level of control left to the executing Member State'.

[49] In the *internal market* context, see for instance: ECJ, Case 130/88 *Van de Bijl* [1989] ECR 3039, paras 22–3 (and the corresponding Opinion of AG Darmon at § 16); Opinion of AG La Pergola in Case C-336/94 *Dafeki* [1997] ECR I-6761 § 9. In the area of *judicial cooperation in criminal matters*, see for instance: Opinion of AG Bot in Case C-261/09 *Mantello* [2010] ECR I-11477, § 10.

[50] See, in this regard, for instance in the *internal market* context: ECJ, Case C-105/94 *Celestini* [1997] ECR I-2971, para 34, where the ECJ underlines that the measures of verification carried out must be necessary for the objectives pursued. Furthermore, in relation to *criminal matters*, the ECJ's *ne bis in idem* case law has revealed that a too strong reliance on the assessments made by the first Member State can jeopardize one of the objectives underlying the *ne bis in idem* provisions, or, more broadly, one of the objectives of the area of freedom, security, and justice. See, for instance: *Miraglia*, where the ECJ agreed that the Public Prosecutor's Office of the Rechtbank Amsterdam's view on 'final judgment' for the application of the *ne bis in idem* provisions jeopardized the security objective of the area of freedom, security, and justice: ECJ, Case C-469/03 *Miraglia* [2005] ECR I-2009, paras 22 and 35.

[51] See, for instance, in relation to the *internal market*: ECJ, Case 130/88 *Van de Bijl* [1989] ECR 3039, paras 22 and 26; ECJ, C-194/97 *de Castro Freitas* [1998] ECR I-6747, para 29. The ECJ's statements that 'in case of manifest inaccuracies, the national authority *may, if it so wishes*, approach the other Member State for additional information' (emphasis added) hint in my view at a too wide margin of discretion, which was perhaps justified in the cases at hand, but should certainly not be taken as the standard. In the area of *criminal matters*, I discussed a number of framework decisions that include provisions which enable the executing authority not to recognize and/or execute a certificate which is incomplete or manifestly does not correspond to the judgment and has not been completed or corrected within a reasonable deadline (see: Part II, ch 2, III, C, 1.1. 'Presumed inaccuracies or incompleteness of a European warrant or order'). Furthermore, I indicated that in accordance with the ECJ's *ne bis in idem* case law, the second Member State is not expected to blindly follow the assessments made by the first Member State and that it is entitled to raise questions as to the correct application of *ne bis in idem* which is after all an autonomous EU concept whose interpretation cannot be left in the sole hands of the first Member State (Part II, ch 1, IV, C, 2. 'No blind application of Article 54 CISA').

[52] The obligatory nature comes in particular to the fore in the ECJ's case law which refers to legislation in which such *duty* is explicitly written down. See, for instance: ECJ, Case C-470/03 *AGM-COS MET* [2007] ECR I-2749, para 62, where the ECJ states that 'that presumption of conformity does not mean that the Member States cannot act if risks appear. On the contrary, under the first subparagraph of

a fortiori where these shortcomings potentially violate the fundamental values of the EU legal order.[53]

Thus far, the ECJ has only occasionally imposed a mandatory duty on the host state's national authorities to reassess, on its own terms, the findings made by the country of origin. In particular, in *Commission v Spain* and *Jipa*,[54] the ECJ emphasized the national authority's duty to verify *in concreto* the circumstances that had led to the application of the public order exception by the country of origin, rather than allowing it to rely exclusively on the assessment made by the country of origin. As I argued earlier, the reason for the difference of approach between the non-committal wording of the earlier cited case law and *Commission v Spain* and *Jipa* may lie in the fact that in the latter judgments, the measures of verification were beneficial to the principle of mutual recognition and to the free movement of the persons involved (free movement objective), whereas in the earlier judgments the measures of control had been seen as detrimental to the free movement provisions and the mutual recognition principle. Hence, the objectives that are pursued by the measures of verification seem to determine to some extent the national authority's margin of discretion and are thus an important element for the competent authorities to bear in mind.

3.1.2. *Formal and substantive checks*

Measures of control may refer either to a summary check of formal elements, such as the authenticity of the certificate, its date of issue, and the authority of the issuing body (formal check),[55] or to more in-depth verification as regards (one of) the substantive requirement(s) underlying the certificate (substantive check).[56]

In relation to criminal matters, and under the new legislative regime with its standardized forms and short deadlines, a national judicial authority will mostly perform formal checks, namely verifications of whether (all of) the information required in the framework decision's annex is provided. However, it is not only strictly formal checks that are likely to occur. Admittedly, foreign judgments may not be reviewed as to their substance,[57] but it would be erroneous to conclude that substantive checks will never take place. Taking into account the range of grounds available for non-recognition of the FD EAW and other instruments, we cannot but conclude that a judicial authority of the executing Member State will still be entitled to perform certain substantive checks. For instance, the refusal ground based on the lack of dual criminality (for non-list offences)

Article 7(1) of the Directive, a Member State *is required* to take all appropriate measures to withdraw machinery from the market if it ascertains that the machinery, used in accordance with its intended purpose, is liable to endanger the safety of persons or property' (emphasis added).

[53] For an in-depth analysis of the related question whether fundamental rights can constitute an exception to the principle of mutual recognition, see: Part I, ch 1, IV, A, 3. 'Balancing conflicting interests: free movement versus fundamental rights. In search of a European public order concept?'; Part II, ch 2, III, B. 'Limits resulting from mechanism aimed at eliminating or restricting the principle of mutual recognition'; and Part III, ch 2, III, B, 3.3. 'A Member State's margin of discretion when applying justification grounds'.

[54] ECJ, Case C-503/03 *Commission v Spain* [2006] ECR I-1097, para 56; ECJ, Case C-33/07 *Jipa* [2008] ECR I-5157, para 25. Both discussed in: Part I, ch 2, III, C. 'The peculiar case of the enhanced duty of vigilance whenever the mutual recognition mechanism endangers the free movement provisions'.

[55] See, for instance: ECJ, Case C-74/09 *WISAG* [2010] I-7271, para 64.

[56] See, for instance, in the area of social security law where the Member State to which workers are posted can express doubts as to the correctness of the facts on which the certificate is based and on the information contained therein: ECJ, Case C-202/97 *FTS* [2000] ECR I-883, para 56.

[57] See: Part II, ch 2, I, B, 2.2.3. 'The handling of requests for review and other legal remedies'; and Part II, ch 2, III, C. 'Limits linked to the level of control left to the executing Member State'.

and the refusal ground that is based on territoriality considerations (Art. 4(1) and Art. 4(7) FD EAW) both require some form of substantive check. In the first case, the executing judicial authority is permitted to verify whether the facts included in the order constitute an offence in its own legal order; in the second case, the executing judicial authority is permitted to verify whether the facts actually occurred (in their entirety or in part) on its own territory.[58] Similarly, in the ECJ's *ne bis in idem* case law, a review of the substance of the judgment is prohibited, but the judicial authority of the second Member State is still required to verify—in close cooperation with the first Member State—whether the conditions for application ('idem' and 'bis') have been fulfilled. This implies an investigation which evidently goes further than a simple formal check and which might also expose differing points of view in the two Member States involved.[59]

If we take into account that formal checks are often limited to factual errors or substantial defects which are immediately obvious, without the need for any additional proof or investigation on the competent authority's part, whereas substantive checks often do require additional proof or further investigation, it should come as no surprise that the ECJ (and the European legislator) have generally been more open to formal (superficial) checks than to substantive (in-depth) checks. The latter are seen to put the relationship of trust at greater risk, especially if the host Member State pursues the investigative measures independently.[60] In order to prevent this situation occurring, the ECJ has emphasized on numerous occasions the need to cooperate and exchange information with the country of origin before any decision is made.[61]

3.1.3. Obvious inaccuracies

The ECJ's internal market case law has revealed that, in principle, a national authority may only take action when it is aware of objective factors or concrete evidence which reveal obvious inaccuracies.[62] This implies, first, that national authorities cannot act upon general suspicions, and secondly, that national authorities should not concern themselves with minor shortcomings. Both of these elements may also be relevant in the context of criminal matters.

[58] Article 4(1) FD EAW and Article 4(7) FD EAW.

[59] In *Mantello* this verification was taken to its extreme as the executing judicial authority wondered to what extent it was entitled to verify—in the framework of a European Arrest Warrant—whether the *ne bis in idem* criteria were fulfilled in a case where the underlying facts had *all* occurred in the *issuing* Member State: ECJ, Case C-261/09 *Mantello* [2010] ECR I-11477, discussed: Part II, ch 2, III, C, 1.2.2. 'Margin of discretion in applying the grounds for non-recognition and non-execution'.

[60] Inaccuracies can be detected by a variety of channels: on the basis of the document itself, on the basis of information available in the host state, or on the basis of information provided by the home State. In some areas of law, the ECJ seems reluctant to allow information that is supplied by the host state itself. For instance, in the area of driving licences, it has stipulated that '***not** in the light of information supplied by the **host** Member State* but on the basis of entries appearing in the driving licence itself or of other incontestable information supplied by the Member State of issue [...]' (emphasis added) the host Member State is entitled not to recognize the driving licence (ECJ, Joined Cases C-329/06 and C-343/06 *Wiedemann and Funk* [2008] ECR I-4635, para 72, discussed: Part I, ch 2, III. 'The Limits of the Legislative Principle of Mutual Recognition'). This restriction, which is not imposed in all other areas of law, can be explained by the far-reaching mutual recognition duty that is imposed in that directive, but should also be seen in the light of a more general trend that requires Member States to cooperate and to exchange information when doubts arise as to the accuracy of some documents.

[61] See: Part III, ch 2, III, B, 3.1.4. 'Duties of cooperation and information exchange'.

[62] See, for instance: ECJ, Case 130/88 *Van de Bijl* [1989] ECR 3039, para 24; ECJ, Case C-336/94 *Dafeki* [1997] ECR I-6761, para 21; ECJ, Case C-105/94 *Celestini* [1997] ECR I-2971, para 35; ECJ, Case C-110/01 *Tennah Durez* [2003] ECR I-6239, para 80, discussed: Part I, ch 1, IV, B, 1. 'Presumed inaccuracies in controls, certificates, or documents subject to mutual recognition'; and Part I, ch 2, III, B, 1. 'No automatic or blind regime: Member States can act if a risk emerges'.

To date, the ECJ has not yet had the opportunity to examine which types of inaccuracy or shortcoming justify the suspension of mutual recognition in criminal matters. An analysis of national case law from the early years of the FD EAW's application exposes a wide variety of attitudes, with a combination of national judicial authorities that refused to recognize warrants when elements were missing (even when those elements were not required in accordance with a strict reading of the framework decision) and national judges who simply passed over any inconsistencies or shortcomings that arose.[63] Whereas the latter group evidently believed that the high level of trust sustaining the principle of mutual recognition prevented any in-depth examination of the warrant, the former group's stance stressed how the simplification of the new system could not be detrimental to the protection of rights and emphasized that this protection could only be earned by careful observance of the procedures laid down. It remains to be seen which approach the ECJ will favour in the coming years, but in light of the ECJ's internal market case law, the guidelines provided above certainly appear to be of use.[64] First, there must be concrete evidence or objective factors that reveal the shortcoming and national judicial authorities should not rely on general suspicions. Secondly, if the shortcoming refers to information that is missing on the warrant or that is inconsistent, the judicial authority should look into the objective of the information required and only take action where 'manifest' shortcomings or inaccuracies jeopardize this objective.[65] Thirdly, the fact that a legal instrument, such as the FD EAW, does not explicitly include a ground for non-recognition in the case of an incomplete warrant[66] should not prevent a judicial authority from taking action.[67] Finally, in any case, promptly deciding not to recognize seems disproportionate in light of the fact that authorities have both an opportunity and responsibility to contact the judicial authority in the other Member State prior to taking a decision.[68]

3.1.4. Duties of cooperation and information exchange

General duties of cooperation and information exchange are included in many—if not all—legal instruments on the internal market and judicial cooperation in criminal matters, and have been explicitly mentioned in the ECJ's case law in both contexts, e.g.

[63] C. JANSSENS, 'De burger, de Unie en het Europees aanhoudingsbevel: op zoek naar het juiste evenwicht tussen vrijheid, veiligheid en rechtvaardigheid', in J. MEEUSEN and G. STRAETMANS (eds.), *Politiële en justitiële strafrechtelijke samenwerking in de Europese Unie. Welk evenwicht tussen vrijheid, veiligheid en rechtvaardigheid?* (Antwerp, Intersentia, 2007) 32–9, discussed: Part II, ch 2, III, C, 1. 'Margin of control left to the executing Member State'.

[64] See: Part I, ch 1, IV, B, 1. 'Presumed inaccuracies in controls, certificates, or documents subject to mutual recognition'; and Part I, ch 2, III, B, 1. 'No automatic or blind regime: Member States can act if a risk emerges'.

[65] For instance, information on an issuing authority's telephone number or its e-mail address pursues another objective (it is mainly in the interest of a smooth cooperation between the authorities) than identification requirements concerning the suspected or accused person (identification requirements can help to avoid miscarriages of justice). In my view, if one of the former elements is missing but the smooth cooperation was not hampered, the sanction should not necessarily be the same as when one of the latter elements is missing and there are doubts as to the correct identification of the person involved.

[66] Compare in this regard the FD EAW with, for instance, Article 7 FD EOFPE, Article 7 FD MRFP, and Article 7 FD MRCO. These articles explicitly accept the non-recognition of an order in case the certificate provided for in Article 4 is not produced, is incomplete, or manifestly does not correspond to the decision.

[67] In particular, in light of the *Tennah Durez* judgment, see: Part I, ch 2, III, B. 'Limits linked to the level of control left to the host Member State'; and Part III, ch 2, III, B, 3.1.4. 'Duties of cooperation and information exchange'.

[68] See: Part III, ch 2, III, B, 3.1.4. 'Duties of cooperation and information exchange'.

Wiedemann and Funk (internal market) and *Mantello* (criminal justice).[69] Besides the general provisions on duties of cooperation and information exchange, certain instruments also contain more specific provisions according to which 'in the event of justified doubts, the host state (executing Member State) *may*[70] require of the competent authorities of another Member State confirmation of the authenticity or accuracy of a document' (emphasis added). In *Tennah Durez*, the ECJ recognized that 'this mechanism gives expression to a more general principle which can also be applied in other areas of [EU] law' and that it implies that 'the issuing authority *must*, on the application of the first authority, re-examine the basis of the document concerned and, where appropriate, withdraw it' (emphasis added).[71] The host (executing) Member State's right ('may') vis-à-vis the home (issuing) Member State's duty ('must'), as described in the above-mentioned cooperation mechanism, should be put into perspective. In light of the principle of sincere cooperation, a restrictive interpretation of the host state's (executing Member State's) 'right' or margin of discretion seems logical. In my view, the host state (executing Member State) should only be entitled not to contact its counterpart in two circumstances. The first of these involves the host state's being convinced that the shortcoming is not obvious and that proceeding with mutual recognition, despite the shortcoming, will not jeopardize (one of) the fundamental objectives underlying the relevant provisions, for instance if an issuing judicial authority's telephone number is missing on the European Arrest Warrant form but other relevant contact information is available. The second involves the document itself revealing an unmistakable error or shortcoming which cannot be rectified by the home state (issuing Member State) and which jeopardizes one of the main objectives of the provisions at stake to the extent that non-recognition seems the only acceptable solution.[72] In all other circumstances, it seems preferable that the host state (executing Member State) contact the home state (issuing Member State) prior to taking any decision. It should not be forgotten that many inaccuracies are due to typing errors, which can (and should) be rectified easily through simple contact between the authorities of the Member States involved. In such a case, deciding not to recognize without having attempted to contact the home state's (issuing Member State's) competent authority in order to verify this matter would be highly disproportionate in my view and potentially amount to a breach of the principle of sincere cooperation. Similarly, a decision to recognize without having attempted to verify the matter by contacting the home state may also jeopardize one of the (non-economic) objectives underlying the internal market, or one of the objectives underlying the area of freedom, security, and justice.

Cooperation and information exchange usually lead to satisfying outcomes, yet it has been and likely will be the case again that the cooperation mechanism is hampered either because the home state (issuing Member State) fails in its duties to react or because the competent authorities of the two Member States fail to reach an agreement. Centralized entities, such as EU institutions (e.g. the Commission), specific commissions (in the internal market context), or other EU bodies (such as Eurojust for criminal matters), may then intervene with a view to solving the bilateral impasse.

[69] ECJ, Joined Cases C-329/06 and C-343/06 *Wiedemann and Funk* [2008] ECR I-4635, para 57; ECJ, Case C-261/09 *Mantello* [2010] ECR I-11477, paras 48–9.

[70] This facultative nature also appeared in the *Van de Bijl* judgment where the ECJ had stated that 'a state may, *if it so wishes*, approach the other Member State [. . .] with a view to requesting additional information' (emphasis added): ECJ, Case 130/88 *Van de Bijl* [1989] ECR 3039, para 24.

[71] ECJ, Case C-110/01 *Tennah Durez* [2003] ECR I-6239, para 80, and the case law cited therein.

[72] See, for instance: ECJ, Joined Cases C-329/06 and C-343/06 *Wiedemann and Funk* [2008] ECR I-4635.

3.2. The comparative examination procedure and the fluctuating relevance of equivalence checks

At times, in the internal market context, the examination procedure amounts to a comparative examination procedure which gives the host Member State the opportunity to verify the equivalence of the level of protection provided by the home Member State with that provided by its own national rules.

One of the criticisms of the principle of mutual recognition's transfer from the internal market context to the area of criminal matters has been that in the latter context, the Council made the error of assuming that the underlying law need not be equivalent or even comparable.[73] Thus it was argued that the application of the principle as developed in criminal matters should be reconsidered in order to align it with its application in the internal market, which usually requires some level of compatibility in the underlying national laws or even the adoption of EU legislation which will ensure that those laws are sufficiently comparable.[74]

Following my analysis in Parts I and II,[75] it has become clear that this criticism must be seen in the context of three findings. First, we should distinguish in both contexts between equivalence *in abstracto* and equivalence *in concreto*, keeping in mind that only the former is always present in both contexts (section 3.2.1). Secondly, contrary to what is often assumed, equivalence (*in concreto*) and its comparative examination procedure are not mandatory *a priori* tests for correct application of the principle of mutual recognition in the internal market context (section 3.2.2). Thirdly, contrary to what has been argued, equivalence *in concreto* and its comparative examination procedure are far from being entirely absent in relation to criminal matters (section 3.2.3). In sum, equivalence is an important parameter, but it does not play a ubiquitous role in either context, except in its abstract form (section 3.2.4).

3.2.1. Equivalence in abstracto *versus equivalence* in concreto

In both contexts, the principle of mutual recognition essentially relies on the idea that while another Member State may not deal with a certain matter in the same way or even similarly, the outcome will be accepted as equivalent because the same principles and values underpin the process.[76] It is not the equivalence of specific legislative or regulatory provisions that is envisaged here, but equivalence of the principles and values upon which the legal systems of the different Member States are founded. Both the ECJ and the legislator maintain an assumption of equivalence with regard to these common principles and values, which seems to rule out any comparative examination procedure. In this regard, I therefore prefer to speak in terms of 'equivalence *in abstracto*'.

However, the fact that Member States share common values, such as safety, health, and environmental protection, consumer protection, and protection of fundamental rights, does not necessarily imply that the specific ways in which a Member State develops its national legislation in order to safeguard these values is equivalent or even compatible with the legislation issued in another Member State. In what follows, I explain

[73] S. PEERS, 'Mutual Recognition and Criminal law in the European Union: Has the Council got it wrong?', *CML Rev.* 2004, 5.

[74] PEERS, 'Mutual Recognition and Criminal law in the European Union' (n 73).

[75] See: Part I, ch 1, III, A. 'Equivalence'; Part II, ch 1, III, A. 'Equivalence'; and Part II, ch 2, I, C. 'Equivalence'.

[76] See: Part I, ch 1, III, A. 'Equivalence'; and Part II, ch 1, III, A. 'Equivalence'.

how the point of departure in both areas, namely equivalence *in abstracto* (presumption of equivalence), can sometimes be replaced with an equivalence check *in concreto*.

3.2.2. Comparative examination procedures and the role of equivalence in the internal market context

In relation to the mutual recognition of diplomas, the ECJ has consistently and vigorously prescribed a comparative examination procedure which requires national authorities to verify whether the knowledge and qualifications certified by a foreign diploma correspond to those required by the national rules.[77] Similarly, in the ECJ's case law on the inspection of goods[78] and the protection of social rights,[79] the comparative examination check occupies a pivotal role. However, this is not the case in many other internal market areas. I demonstrated in Part I that besides obvious cases in which the existence of dual burdens was beyond doubt, judgments in which the ECJ has actually performed an (extensive) comparative test are extremely rare.[80] In some judgments, the ECJ opted to delegate the task of comparing the two legal frameworks to the national judge,[81] yet in many of the other judgments I have discussed the ECJ resolved the mutual recognition issue without making any reference to equivalence requirements. The ECJ's ambivalent and dubious relationship with the 'equivalence' requirement can also be illustrated by judgments where mutual recognition was imposed in the absence of equivalence[82] or where mutual recognition was set aside in spite of the fact that equivalence may have been present.[83] I therefore concluded in Part I that—except in certain well-defined areas—the mutual recognition mechanism is in the non-harmonized sector less concerned with verifying equivalent levels of protection in the home and host states, and instead requires an analysis performed by the competent authority of the host Member State on the necessity and proportionality of its own rules in light of the underlying objectives. The parameter for assessing necessity and proportionality will only be the equivalence test in a limited number of cases and the ECJ will more likely use European or international standards to verify whether the national measure is acceptable.[84]

Harmonization has often lead to the creation of common, substantive norms and thus 'equivalence'.[85] The ECJ has repeatedly held that in case of exhaustive harmonization, Member States are no longer entitled to invoke the justification grounds

[77] See, for instance: ECJ, Case C-340/89 *Vlassopoulou* [1991] ECR I-2357, discussed: Part I, ch 1, I, C, 1. 'Mutual recognition of diplomas'.

[78] See, for instance: ECJ, Case 132/80 *United Food* [1981] ECR 995; ECJ, Case 272/80 *Biologische Producten* [1981] ECR 3277, discussed: Part I, ch 1, III, A. 'Equivalence'.

[79] See, for instance: ECJ, Joined Cases C-369/96 and C-376/96 *Arblade* [1999] ECR I-8453; ECJ, Case C-113/89 *Rush Portuguesa* [1990] ECR I-01417; ECJ, Joined Cases C-94/98, C-50/98, C-52/98, C-54/98 and C-68/98 to C-71/98 *Finalarte* [2001] ECR I-7831, discussed: Part I, ch 1, IV, A, 2. 'Verifying equivalent and/or sufficient levels of protection'.

[80] See, for instance: ECJ, Case 124/81 *Commission v U.K.* [1983] ECR 203; ECJ, Case 188/84 *Type approval for woodworking machines* [1986] ECR 419, discussed: Part I, ch 1, IV, A, 2. 'Verifying equivalent and/or sufficient levels of protection'.

[81] See, for instance: ECJ, Case 27/80 *Fietje* [1980] ECR 3839; ECJ, Case 272/80 *Biologische Producten* [1981] ECR 3277; ECJ, Case C-340/89 *Vlassopoulou* [1991] ECR I-2357; ECJ, Case C-165/98 *Mazzoleni* [2001] ECR I-2189.

[82] See, for instance: ECJ, Case C-76/90 *Säger* [1991] ECR I-4221; ECJ, Case C-288/89 *Gouda* [1991] ECR I-4007.

[83] See, for instance: ECJ, Case C-124/97 *Läärä* [1999] ECR I-6067; ECJ, Case C-67/98 *Zenatti* [1999] ECR I-7289.

[84] See: Part III, ch 2, III, B, 3.3.3. 'The national measure must be examined against a comparative parameter, a European parameter, or an international parameter'.

[85] See: Part I, ch 2, II. 'The Harmonization and Mutual Recognition Tandem under Scrutiny'.

included in the legal instruments at stake.[86] In other words, equivalence—through harmonization—has had an important (reinforcing) impact on mutual recognition. Yet in some legal instruments, the legislator has imposed a duty of mutual recognition in the absence of equivalence. Mutual recognition will then prevail, not because of equivalent rules (as they do not exist), but simply because the European legislator imposed it.[87] Moreover, in some legal instruments harmonization is not concerned with creating substantive norms, but solely with elaborating a procedural framework to make mutual recognition work.[88] With regard to the latter instruments, mutual recognition will again often prevail, despite the lack of (substantive) equivalence.

3.2.3. *Comparative examination procedures and the role of equivalence in the context of criminal matters*

In the context of criminal matters, the ECJ's point of departure is identical to that in the context of the internal market, namely that in case of exhaustive harmonization, Member States must refrain from imposing limits on mutual recognition.[89] In other words, if there are common (minimum) rules, and thus equivalence—like the rules on *in absentia* judgments in the *Melloni* judgment—mutual recognition must prevail. Yet mutual recognition is not limited to situations where equivalence reigns. Despite the absence, to date, of extensive harmonization of substantive and procedural criminal law within the EU—and thus a lack of equivalence—Member States have agreed in primary *and* secondary EU legislation that mutual recognition must play a significant role in the EU legal order.

The ambiguous position that the equivalence requirement occupies in the internal market context is similar to that which it occupies in relation to criminal matters. Whilst in some mutual recognition instruments equivalence requirements are implicitly or explicitly included, in others mutual recognition is imposed by the European legislator in the absence of equivalence. For instance, in the ECJ's *ne bis in idem* case law, the 'idem' requirement obviously refers to a kind of equivalence check, albeit a limited one, as the ECJ only requires similarity of the material facts.[90] A similar approach can be expected with regard to the dual criminality check enshrined in Article 2(4) FD EAW.[91] The FD EAW has often been depicted as the prototype of the instrument that largely abolished dual criminality (along with the equivalence test) owing to its introduction of the 'list offences'. Yet it is equivalence considerations that lie at the basis of this list, as it concerns offences that are punishable in all Member States, as implicitly confirmed by the ECJ in *Advocaten voor de wereld* where it was stated that these offences are contrary to the EU *ordre public*.[92] Furthermore, it was even suggested by one of the ECJ's AGs that an executing judge who harbours suspicions

[86] See, for instance: ECJ, Case 5/77 *Tedeschi* [1977] ECR 1555, para 35, as discussed: Part I, ch 2, III, A, 1. 'The starting point: the *Tedeschi* ruling'.

[87] See, for instance, in the area of diplomas (in particular, former DIR 85/384): ECJ, Case C-421/98 *Commission v Spain* [2000] ECR I-10375, para 37; ECJ, Case C-111/12 *Ordine degli Ingegneri di Verona e Provincia and others*, nyr, para 45, where the ECJ held that 'a migrant architect holding a diploma, certificate or other evidence of formal qualifications coming within the scope of the directive must also be able to pursue such an activity, *even if his diploma*, certificate or other evidence of formal qualifications *is not necessarily substantively equivalent* in terms of the training received' (emphasis added).

[88] See: Part I, ch 2, II, A. 'A different technical approach: substantive or procedural harmonization and mutual recognition'.

[89] See, in particular: ECJ, Case C-399/11 *Melloni*, nyr, para 44. See also: Part II, ch 2, II, B. 'Approximation measures and cooperation duties for enhancing trust and mutual recognition'.

[90] See: Part II, ch 1, III, A. 'Equivalence'.

[91] See: Part II, ch 2, I, C. 'Equivalence'.

[92] ECJ, Case C-303/05 *Advocaten voor de wereld* [2007] ECR I-3633, para 57, discussed: Part II, ch 2, I, C, 1.1. 'Equivalence and the partial abolition of the dual criminality check'.

about the (issuing judge's) legal classification of certain acts may rely on Article 2(4) FD EAW in order to set aside the duty of mutual recognition.[93] It is this article that constitutes an equivalence check for offences that are not common to all Member States. Other instruments prescribe a more straightforward equivalence check which allows—and sometimes obliges—the executing judge to compare the two legal frameworks with regard to the specific issues at stake and which, in cases of non-equivalence, may result either in the adaptation of the original order in order to bring it into line with the executing Member State's legal framework or in a decision not to recognize the order.[94] Yet in these same instruments it has also become clear that not all aspects of the order can be made subject to an equivalence check, since some provisions explicitly impose mutual recognition in the absence of equivalence, apparently for those aspects which, in the European legislator's view, are not important enough to justify setting the mutual recognition mechanism aside.[95]

3.2.4. Comparative examination procedures and the role of equivalence for the mutual recognition mechanism

The preceding paragraphs have revealed that both the ECJ and the European legislator have held back from imposing a generalized comparative examination procedure. Consequently, no convincing arguments exist to support the view that equivalence is a *conditio sine qua non* for the examination procedure, either in the internal market context or in relation to criminal matters. Yet the finding that equivalence does not constitute an *a priori* condition needing to be fulfilled and checked every time mutual recognition issues arise, does not prevent equivalence playing a significant role on many occasions—indeed, it can and it should. Yet the exact contours of this role are far from clear, especially in the judicially developed mutual recognition context.

In relation to the legislatively developed mutual recognition mechanism, the European legislator does at least indicate in the legislative instruments which aspects are (or are not) subject to an equivalence check by providing a national administrator or a national judge with sufficient guidance as to what exactly should be examined before a decision is taken on mutual recognition. Where common rules have been developed through harmonization, the *Tedeschi* and *Melloni* rulings imply that the common (minimum) rules will prevail, together with the principle of mutual recognition, and that comparative examination procedures are excluded.

The situation is far less straightforward in relation to the judicially developed mutual recognition mechanism in the internal market. Not only is the national authority obliged to operate with no clear legislative guidelines, but it is also confronted with a huge amount of case law which unfortunately lacks clear judicial guidelines on how and when the 'equivalence' requirement should best be approached. One of the judgments in which the ECJ has performed its most detailed equivalence check should not be without mention here. In the *Type approval for woodworking machines* judgment,[96] the ECJ shattered the illusion of equivalence *in abstracto* (similar standards of safety) by

[93] Opinion of AG Ruiz-Jarabo Colomer in Case C-303/05 *Advocaten voor de wereld* [2007] ECR I-3633, § 106.

[94] See, for instance: Articles 8(2) and 8(3) FD MRCS; Articles 9(1) and 9(2) FD ESO (post-trial) and Article 13(1) FD ESO (pre-trial). See: Part II, ch 2, I, C. 'Equivalence'.

[95] E.g. the application of the mutual recognition principle to legal persons despite huge differences between the Member States' legislations regarding this issue (see, for instance: Art. 9(3) FD MRFP; Art. 12(3) FD MRCO).

[96] ECJ, Case 188/84 *Type approval for woodworking machines* [1986] ECR 419, discussed: Part I, ch 1, IV, A, 2.1. 'Lack of equivalent protection in the country of origin'.

analysing the rules in a broader context (lack of compatibility between two different systems of protection). Such a perspective might prove helpful, and possibly indispensable, when a national judicial authority is asked to judge a mutual recognition issue which involves a comparison of different systems of procedural criminal law which—though both are protective of the essential safeguards (equivalence *in abstracto*)—are ultimately incompatible because the safeguards are in place at different levels of the respective systems (incompatibility between systems).

3.3. A Member State's margin of discretion when applying justification grounds

In both contexts, the justification grounds of the Treaty framework, the ECJ's case law, and the legislative instruments all enable a national authority to set aside the principle of mutual recognition. This ability is maintained within certain limits, however, since national authorities will be required to submit well-founded arguments that justify the application of the ground for non-recognition in each particular case.

In Part I, I proposed that the application of a justification ground in the internal market context is subject to an assessment of the national measure, which hinders the principle of mutual recognition in its enforcement of suitability, necessity, and proportionality requirements. In practice, this is rarely a straightforward exercise, since it involves complex assessment on a case-by-case basis. It can also lead to very different conclusions in very similar cases (for instance, owing to the inconsistency test) and may vary with time (for instance, owing to the fact that scientific knowledge and technical development evolve at high speeds), across domains (for instance, in areas in which significant moral, religious, and cultural differences exist between the Member States and national authorities enjoy a broader margin of appreciation), and from place to place (for instance, because of the fact that national consumption habits or climatic conditions influence the outcome of the mutual recognition decision).[97] In sum, if one thing is certain about this assessment test in the internal market context, it is the fact that its outcome is highly unpredictable.

To date, only a small number of judgments have dealt in detail with a Member State's margin of discretion in criminal matters and it would therefore be incautious to draw any far-reaching conclusions at present. Nevertheless, in what follows, I demonstrate that the basic criteria applied by the ECJ in verifying the validity of a derogation that sets aside the principle of mutual recognition in each context are rather similar.

3.3.1. The point of departure: derogations from the principle of mutual recognition must be interpreted restrictively

In the internal market context, the majority of justification grounds—such as public health, public policy, and consumer protection—constitute potentially wide categories of national[98] interests which might seriously endanger the application of the principle of mutual recognition if interpreted broadly. It is therefore not surprising that the ECJ has consistently maintained that these exceptions, like all derogations from a fundamental Treaty principle, must be interpreted restrictively.[99] This does not necessarily mean, however, that the principle of mutual recognition will always prevail in the internal

[97] See: Part I, ch 1, IV, A. 'The ECJ's evaluation of justification grounds'.

[98] Admittedly, most of these grounds, if not all, are also relevant from an EU perspective, but a Member State is, in principle, entitled to give this ground for non-recognition a national interpretation, which is subject to scrutiny by the ECJ.

[99] See, for instance: ECJ, Case C-355/98 *Commission v Belgium* [2000] ECR I-1221, para 28; ECJ, Case C-348/96 *Calfa* [1999] ECR I-11, para 23.

market context. It is telling, in this regard, that the ECJ refrains from explicitly describing this point of departure in its internal market judgments. On many occasions, this rather severe point of departure almost seems to have been forgotten, especially in areas where significant moral, religious, and cultural differences exist,[100] where public health is at risk,[101] or in cases that concern vulnerable citizens.[102] Rather than emphasizing in these judgments that the justification grounds must be interpreted restrictively, the ECJ drastically reduced the weight of this condition by granting the Member States a considerable margin of discretion by means of a very mild proportionality test. Furthermore, in judgments where fundamental rights were invoked to set aside the free movement provisions, the ECJ's point of departure that 'exceptions to the fundamental freedoms must be interpreted restrictively' seems to have been substituted for a duty to reconcile the free movement provisions (mutual recognition) with the fundamental right at stake.[103]

In criminal matters, it is important to emphasize that the ECJ's case law has not yet provided a clear statement that the grounds for non-recognition must be strictly interpreted.[104] In this regard, the ECJ seems to have drawn on its experience in the internal market context, where too strict an adherence to this point of departure occasionally proved untenable. Furthermore, in view of the range of grounds for non-recognition available in this context, it seems far more appropriate to differentiate according to the specific ground for non-recognition that is at stake. In my view, it would be appropriate to distinguish between five general categories of grounds for non-recognition.

A *first category* of grounds consists of rather specific grounds for non-recognition, which refer to the executing Member State's legislation for their definition and which therefore leave only a limited margin of control to the ECJ. Examples of such grounds might include, for example, amnesty,[105] age,[106] and statutory limits.[107] It is plain that in view of the well-defined criteria linked to the executing Member State's legislation, the question of broad or restrictive interpretation will not cause significant problems with regard to these grounds.

This first group contrasts sharply with a *second category* of exceptions which do not refer to the executing Member State's legislation and which are clearly susceptible to either broad or restrictive interpretation, such as grounds based on dual criminality[108] or territoriality arguments.[109] In view of the fact that these exceptions essentially serve national interests, rather than EU interests, a broad interpretation of these grounds

100 See, for instance: ECJ, Case C-275/92 *Schindler* [1994] ECR I-1039 and the subsequent judgments in the area of gambling, discussed: Part I, ch 1, IV, A. 'The ECJ's evaluation of justification grounds'.

101 See, for instance: ECJ, Case 304/84 *Muller* [1986] ECR 1511; ECJ, Case 42/90 *Bellon* [1990] ECR I-4863, discussed: Part I, ch 1, IV, A. 'The ECJ's evaluation of justification grounds'.

102 See, for instance: ECJ, Case 286/81 *Oosthoek* [1982] ECR 4575, para 18; or ECJ Case C-382/87 *Buet* [1989] ECR 1235, para 13; ECJ, Case C-244/06 *Dynamic Medien* [2008] ECR I-505, discussed: Part I, ch 1, IV, A. 'The ECJ's evaluation of justification grounds'.

103 See, for instance: ECJ, Case C-112/00 *Schmidberger* [2003] ECR I-5659, para 81; ECJ, Case C-438/05 *Viking Line* [2007] ECR I-10779, para 79, discussed: Part I, ch 1, IV, A, 3. 'Balancing conflicting interests: free movement versus fundamental rights. In search of a European public order concept?'.

104 Compare in this regard: View of AG Bot in Case C-66/08 *Kozlowski* [2008] ECR I-6041, § 139 (who argues that Article 4(6) FD EAW must be interpreted restrictively) with Opinion of AG Cruz Villalón in Case C-306/09 *I.B.* [2010] ECR I-10341, § 42–44 and Opinion of AG Sharpston in Case C-396/11 *Radu*, nyr, paras 69–73 (who both reject a narrow approach). See also: Part II, ch 2, III, C, 1. 'Margin of control left to the executing Member State'.

105 See, for instance: Article 3(1) FD EAW.

106 See, for instance: Article 3(3) FD EAW.

107 See, for instance: Article 4(4) FD EAW.

108 See, for instance: Article 4(2) FD EAW.

109 See, for instance: Article 4(7) FD EAW.

might seriously jeopardize the principle of mutual recognition. In accordance with the ECJ's internal market case law, and the preambles of certain framework decisions,[110] it therefore seems advisable to impose for this category of exceptions the basic assumption that they be interpreted restrictively.[111] The ECJ has not yet been required to take a stance on any of these grounds, but in *Leymann and Pustovarov* (concerning the speciality principle) and in *Melvin West* (on consent in cases of onward surrender)—two concepts closely linked to states' interests and the sovereignty idea[112]—the ECJ's emphasis on the principle of mutual recognition as the main objective of the FD EAW[113] is indicative in this regard and seems to suggest that a restrictive interpretation is already in place, though the ECJ did not confirm this explicitly.[114]

A *third category* constitutes limitations to the principle of mutual recognition that relate to the reintegration objective,[115] which bears comparison with the previous category in that it does not refer to the executing Member State's legislation and that it is a concept which can be interpreted either broadly or narrowly. However, it can also be differentiated from the previous category in two respects. First, the underlying interest serves the citizen's interests rather than the state's interests, namely a convicted individual's reintegration, which has been recognized as worthy of protection at European and international level.[116] Secondly, the application of this ground for non-surrender does not suspend the principle of mutual recognition entirely, as the executing judicial authority is still required to execute the decision itself. For these two reasons, I would be tempted to argue that a mandatory restrictive interpretation may be less useful as a point of departure for this third category. Instead, it could be employed more effectively as a kind of balancing test, like the one described above in the internal market context. Some support for this argument can be identified in the ECJ's recent case law, where the ECJ and its AGs stress the importance of the reintegration objective.[117] Admittedly, in *Wolzenburg*—a case in which a Member State had given the reintegration concept an

[110] See, for instance: § 17 FD FD ESO (post-trial) and § 21 FD MRCS, which both state that 'the ground for refusal relating to territoriality should be applied *only in exceptional cases* [. . .]' (emphasis added).

[111] See, for instance: Article 4(7)(a) FD EAW which foresees that the execution of the EAW can be refused where the offences have been committed in whole or in part in the territory of the executing Member State. For a pro-European approach, and thus a restrictive interpretation of the terms 'committed in whole or in part in the territory of the executing Member State', as interpreted and applied by some national judicial authorities, see, for instance: JANSSENS, 'De burger, de Unie en het Europees aanhoudingsbevel: op zoek naar het juiste evenwicht tussen vrijheid, veiligheid en rechtvaardigheid' (n 63) 44–7. With regard to the dual criminality assessment, a restrictive interpretation could be inspired by the test that the ECJ applies in its *ne bis in idem* case law.

[112] View of AG Cruz Villalón in Case C-192/12PPU *Melvin West*, nyr, § 65.

[113] ECJ, Case C-388/08 PPU *Leymann and Pustovarov* [2008] ECR I-8993, paras 46–51; ECJ, Case C-192/12PPU *Melvin West*, nyr, paras 53–6, where the ECJ underlines that Member States are in principle obliged to act upon a European Arrest Warrant.

[114] Instead of using its traditional formula that 'restrictions must be interpreted narrowly' the ECJ states that the FD EAW should not be interpreted in a way that would jeopardize the objective pursued by this instrument, namely a smooth and fast surrender mechanism: ECJ, Case C-192/12PPU *Melvin West*, nyr, para 77.

[115] See, in particular: Articles 4(6) and 5(3) FD EAW.

[116] Opinion of AG Bot in Case C-306/09 *I.B.* [2010] ECR I-10341, § 43–4. See also: Joint partly dissenting opinion of judges Tulkens, Cabral Barreto, Fura-Sandström, Spielmann, and Jebens, ECtHR, 12 February 2008, *Kafkaris v Cyprus*, 21906/04.

[117] See, for instance: ECJ, Case C-66/08 *Kozlowski* [2008] ECR I-6041, para 45 and corresponding Opinion of AG Bot, § 68–76; ECJ, Case C-123/08 *Wolzenburg* [2009] ECR I-9621, paras 62 and 67 and corresponding Opinion of AG Bot, § 63–68; ECJ, Case C-306/09 *I.B.* [2010] ECR I-10341, para 52, and corresponding Opinion of AG Cruz Villalón, § 43.

interpretation in its own national legislation that was narrower than the more generous EU version—the reintegration objective seems to have been reduced somewhat to an exception subordinate to the general rule of mutual recognition.[118] However, in my view, the fact that Member States are indeed entitled but not obliged to interpret this concept restrictively highlights above all the importance that the ECJ attaches both to the reintegration objective and to the principle of mutual recognition. It also indicates that the ECJ is willing to grant the Member States a considerable margin of discretion in striking a sensible balance between the two principles.[119]

The non-restrictive interpretation, possibly in combination with a balancing test—as discussed with regard to the third category—should also apply to a *fourth category*, namely where fundamental rights are involved.[120] The analysis of the ECJ's internal market case law has revealed that fundamental rights can play an important role in limiting the principle of mutual recognition.[121] Similarly, in the area of judicial cooperation in civil matters and asylum, the ECJ has accepted that in case of a serious breach fundamental rights can set aside duties of mutual recognition.[122] Following this line of case law, I have argued above that there is no reason to believe that the ECJ will not accept in the criminal justice context a human rights exception to the principle of mutual recognition if manifest, serious breaches occur.[123] Moreover, in light of the prominent role that fundamental rights occupy in the EU legal order,[124] I am of the opinion that fundamental rights—that are protected by the EU legal order, in particular by the Charter—should be able to set aside the principle of mutual recognition without being reduced to a mere 'exception' to the principle of mutual recognition. In this context, instead of emphasizing that 'restrictions [to mutual recognition] must be interpreted restrictively', the point of departure should be that 'the principle of mutual recognition must be interpreted in the light of fundamental rights'.[125] This is, in fact, precisely what the ECJ has been doing in *Radu* and *Melloni*, where it has examined the right to be heard (*Radu*) and the guarantees surrounding a conviction rendered *in absentia* (*Melloni*)—as written down in the FD EAW and FD 2009/299—in light of the Charter.[126] As in both *Radu* and *Melloni* the ECJ found that there was no breach of a fundamental right, the ECJ's legal

[118] See, in this regard the ECJ's statements in *Wolzenburg* that 'by limiting the situations in which the executing judicial authority may refuse to execute a European Arrest Warrant, such legislation only facilitates the surrender of requested persons, in accordance with the principle of mutual recognition [...] which constitutes *the essential rule* introduced by that decision' (emphasis added): ECJ, Case C-123/08 *Wolzenburg* [2009] ECR I-9621, para 59. See also: M. BORGERS, 'Mutual Recognition and the European Court of Justice: The Meaning of Consistent Interpretation and Autonomous and Uniform Interpretation of Union Law for the Development of the Principle of Mutual Recognition in Criminal Matters', *Eur. Journ. Crime Cr.L.Cr.J.* 2010, 110.

[119] See: Part II, ch 2, III, C, 1.2.2. 'Margin of discretion in applying the grounds for non-recognition and non-execution'.

[120] See, for instance: Opinion of AG Cruz Villalón in Case C-306/09 *I.B.* [2010] ECR I-10341, § 43–5; Opinion of AG Sharpston in Case C-396/11 *Radu*, nyr, § 69.

[121] See: Part I, ch 1, IV, A, 3. 'Balancing conflicting interests: free movement versus fundamental rights. In search of a European public order concept?'

[122] See: Part II, ch 2, III, C, 2. 'Controlling activities in an extraterritorial context'.

[123] See: Part II, ch 2, III, B, 2. 'Limits linked to the need to safeguard EU or international interests'; Part II, ch 2, III, C, 2. 'Controlling activities in an extraterritorial context'.

[124] Respect for human rights is enshrined in Article 6(2) TEU as a foundation of the EU legal order: ECJ, Joined Cases C-402/05 P and C-415/05 P *Kadi and Al Barakaat International Foundation* [2008] ECR I-6351, para 303.

[125] See, for instance: Opinion of AG Mengozzi in Case C-42/11 *Lopes Da Silva Jorge*, nyr, § 29; Opinion of AG Cruz Villalón in Case C-306/09, *IB* [2010] ECR I-10341, § 44; Opinion of AG Sharpston in Case C-396/11 *Radu*, nyr, § 69–73.

[126] ECJ, Case C-396/11 *Radu*, nyr, paras 38–42; ECJ, Case C-399/11 *Melloni*, nyr, paras 48–53. See also, with regard to the right to an effective remedy: ECJ, Case C-168/13 PPU *Jeremy F.*, paras 42–7.

reasoning could stop here and the ECJ was not required to expand on the executing judicial authorities' duties in case of a serious breach. This will certainly be different if in future case law the ECJ is confronted with actual conflicts between mutual recognition and fundamental rights. Then it would be desirable that the ECJ would either opt for a balancing test or—with regard to some specific fundamental rights[127]—give precedence to the fundamental right at hand, if certain conditions are fulfilled.[128]

A *fifth* and final *category* of grounds for non-recognition encompasses a specific fundamental right, namely the mandatory *ne bis in idem* ground,[129] in relation to which neither a restrictive point of departure nor a balancing act seem appropriate. Provided that the preconditions for *ne bis in idem* are fulfilled, the *ne bis in idem* exception (and thus mutual recognition) should always prevail, irrespective of any balancing test.[130] Here, the principle of mutual recognition is not ruled out since two mutual recognition duties are at stake, namely the FD EAW and the *ne bis in idem*. Logically, only one can ultimately prevail.

3.3.2. The national measure must be adequate and proportionate for achieving the objective(s) that motivate the justification ground

The true scope of the principle of mutual recognition only becomes clear following an assessment of the adequacy and proportionality of a national measure in light of the justification ground at stake. In the ECJ's internal market case law, it has been the proportionality test, in particular, which has played a crucial role in demarcating the principle of mutual recognition.

This two-step reasoning—adequacy and proportionality—seems less suitable for cases of judicial cooperation in criminal matters where well-defined justification grounds with a small margin for interpretation are at stake (see para 59, category one), but on the other hand, it does seem fairly transposable to cases involving justification grounds which do imply a certain margin of appreciation. If this margin of discretion has been taken up by the national legislator, rather than being left open to the national judicial authority, we see that the ECJ attempts to pursue the underlying objective of the relevant justification ground. We also see that it does not refrain from subjecting the national measure to the two-step adequacy and proportionality test in light of the underlying objective.[131] Logically, in cases where the breach of the principle of proportionality is more visible, the ECJ's analysis will be more limited.[132]

[127] In this regard, inspiration can be drawn from the ECtHR's case law on Articles 3, 6, and 8 ECHR. See: Part II, ch 2, III, C, 2.2.1. 'Guidelines provided by the ECtHR's case law'.

[128] See: Part II, ch 2, III, C, 2.2. 'Reacting to another Member State's presumed misapplication of fundamental rights'.

[129] Article 3(2) FD EAW.

[130] See, in this regard the far-reaching powers that AG Bot was ready to concede to an executing judicial authority with regard to *ne bis in idem* as ground for non-recognition (Opinion of AG Bot in Case C-261/09 *Mantello* [2010] ECR I-11477, § 95), but in which he was not followed by the ECJ, that focused far more on the issuing Member State's role: ECJ, Case C-261/09 *Mantello* [2010] ECR I-11477, paras 48–50, discussed: Part II, ch 2, III, C, 1.2.2. 'Margin of discretion in applying the grounds for non-recognition and non-execution'.

[131] See, for instance: ECJ, Case C-123/08 *Wolzenburg* [2009] ECR I-9621, para 68 (on adequacy) and paras 69–73 (on proportionality). It is noteworthy in this regard that the proportionality test applied by the ECJ in *Wolzenburg* was not the traditionally severe test generally applied in internal market cases but—unsurprisingly—the more lenient version reserved by the ECJ in its internal market case law for sensitive areas of law.

[132] Particularly where the ECJ is confronted—in the internal market context—with a national legislation that *absolutely and automatically* prohibits the marketing of products lawfully marketed in another

Besides being a useful shield against excessive use of national grounds for non-recognition, the proportionality test may also be necessary for avoiding excessive use of the mutual recognition instruments themselves in relation to criminal matters. Unlike in the internal market context, the EU legislator clearly prefers a *de minimis* approach for most of its instruments in the area of judicial cooperation in criminal matters. As regards this kind of proportionality test, it is not the executing state but the issuing state which should preferably be in charge, since there may otherwise be a risk that value judgments are performed on other Member States' legal systems. This could jeopardize the '*united in diversity*' philosophy that underpins the principle of mutual recognition and the EU legal order in general.

3.3.3. *The national measure must be examined against a comparative parameter, a European parameter, or an international parameter*

The ECJ employs various parameters in its internal market case law in order to verify whether a national measure is indeed adequate and proportionate in terms of its underlying objective. In some areas of law, the ECJ has used a comparative parameter to assess the national measure, yet in many more judgments a European or international parameter was employed, though also taking specific national characteristics into account where relevant.[133] The ECJ has thus made it very clear that in the internal market context, the existence of national justification grounds will not be assessed exclusively in light of the national context (though specific national features can be taken into account) and will instead be judged in a broader EU/international context, thereby considerably limiting the Member States' margin of discretion.

In judicial cooperation in criminal matters, the identification of the most adequate parameter will largely depend on the type of justification ground that is at stake. Some grounds are so specific and well-defined that there seems hardly any need for interpretation or assessment, whereas other grounds do require some further interpretation. Therefore, the ECJ applied in some of its judgments—by analogy with its internal market case law[134]—a European parameter, namely EU legislation, in order to decide whether the criteria included in the national legislation fulfilled the requirements of the proportionality test.[135]

3.3.4. *The margin of control in a broader EU context*

Ultimately, a national authority's margin of control is not limited to a check of the grounds for non-recognition but also entails an assessment of the mutual recognition file in a broader context. In other words, the file should be assessed not only in light of the legislative instrument involved, if applicable, but also in light of the EU Treaty framework and the entire EU acquis. Indeed, the national authority will need to bear all of the objectives(s) behind the relevant legislation or Treaty provisions in mind as well as respect for the values constituting the foundations of the EU legal order. This latter point

Member State (e.g. ECJ, Case C-385/10 *Elenca*, nyr, para 28) or—in the criminal justice context—a national legislation that *automatically and absolutely* excludes the nationals of other Member States who are staying or resident in its territory (e.g. ECJ, Case C-42/11 *Lopes Da Silva Jorge*, nyr, para 52).

[133] See, for instance: ECJ, Case 42/90 *Bellon* [1990] ECR I-4863, para 14; ECJ, Case 94/83 *Heijn* [1984] ECR 3263, para 13; ECJ, Case 304/84 *Muller* [1986] ECR 1511, para 24; ECJ, Case 247/84 *Motte* [1985] ECR 3887, para 20; ECJ, Case C-473/98 *Toolex* [2001] ECR I-5681, paras 42–4.

[134] See: Part I, ch 1, IV, A, 2. 'Verifying equivalent and/or sufficient levels of protection'.

[135] See, for instance: ECJ, Case C-123/08 *Wolzenburg* [2009] ECR I-9621, paras 71–2.

implies that—even in relation to legislation that takes no stance on issues of fraud, abuse of law, non-discrimination, or the protection of fundamental rights—non-compliance with one of these objectives or values may seriously influence the outcome of the mutual recognition decision.

(4) Recognition, non-recognition, and the golden mean of partial recognition

It would be erroneous to state that the principle of mutual recognition is an all or nothing issue of either 'full recognition' or 'complete non-recognition'. In this regard, I emphasized in relation to the internal market context the crucial role played by the proportionality principle, which has often led to a duty of partial mutual recognition. Compensatory measures in the area of diplomas, for example, and labelling requirements in the area of free movement of goods, have allowed national authorities to avoid the stark choice between unconditional full recognition and complete exclusion.[136]

In the area of criminal matters, similar mechanisms—such as the conversion of foreign sentences[137]—included in several framework decisions, as well as the 'taking into account' mechanism enshrined in Article 56 CISA, clearly respond to similar concerns, namely that an executing judicial authority should be permitted to realize the partial recognition of a foreign decision rather than rejecting the order's recognition completely. Such conversion mechanisms, often depicted as 'regrettable remnants of the Council of Europe instruments which are not really compatible with the mutual recognition spirit',[138] are not contrary to the mutual recognition philosophy per se, in my view, as they constitute effective tools in making the mutual recognition mechanism viable to a certain extent, despite the lack of equivalence and in the absence of further harmonization.

(5) Execution

In the area of criminal matters, a crucial stage in the mutual recognition mechanism of most[139] framework decisions constitutes the 'execution' of foreign judgments.

Most framework decisions in criminal matters include very close ties between the 'recognition' and 'execution' phases, which sometimes makes it difficult to distinguish between the two. This is particularly true of the FD EAW, where 'a duty to recognize' is not even mentioned explicitly. Here, the legislator imposes a duty (only) to execute a European Arrest Warrant and provides grounds (only) for non-execution (not grounds for non-recognition), so the phases of recognition and execution seem to coincide somewhat. In subsequent instruments, the sequential nature of the two phases becomes more evident when it is stipulated that 'the competent authorities in the executing State shall recognise a decision [...] and shall forthwith take all the necessary measures for its execution'. Furthermore, the grounds for refusal in these instruments refer not only to grounds for non-execution (as in the FD EAW) but also to grounds for non-recognition. Yet the fact that these grounds are included under a single heading reinforces their connection and suggests that, on many occasions, a decision (not) to execute will be the

[136] Opinion of AG Bot in Case C-200/08 *Commission v France*, § 29 (case removed from the register). See also: Part I, ch 1, I, C, 1. 'Mutual recognition of diplomas'.

[137] See, for instance: Article 10 FD MRCS, Article 11(4) FD FD ESO (post-trial).

[138] Green paper from the Commission—The approximation, mutual recognition and enforcement of criminal sanctions in the European Union, COM (2004) 334 final.

[139] See, however: FD TIA which only imposes *a duty to take into account* instead of a duty *to execute*.

logical and immediate consequence of a decision (not) to recognize, rather than these decisions taking place in distinct stages, as is the case in other areas of law.[140]

However, investigating the internal market analogy also raises the more fundamental question of whether the execution phase of the mutual recognition mechanism (in criminal matters) is a feature that distinguishes it from the mutual recognition mechanism in the internal market area, where no 'execution phase' generally takes place.[141] 'Execution' initially appears to go a step further than 'recognition', as execution implies in this context the actual involvement of the public forces in enforcing or applying the foreign decision on the executing state's territory, rather than just taking the foreign decision into account. Yet if we examine more closely the actual consequences of a duty to take into account and a duty to execute, we find that the crucial characteristic of the mutual recognition mechanism in both contexts is the ways in which elements of a foreign legal order can have an effect in another Member State. It is also difficult to discern whether a crucial difference exists between taking a foreign element into account and actually applying it. Consequently, the role of mutual recognition—i.e. far-reaching or limited—depends less on the distinction between a duty to take into account and a duty to enforce and more on the specifications of each duty in the particular case, especially the available justification grounds, any equivalence requirements, and the distribution of competences between the two Member States. For instance, a national authority's (hypothetical) duty to take into account a foreign decision by granting it effects identical to those granted by the country of origin, without an equivalence check or the possibility of invoking justification grounds, seems far more drastic than a duty to execute a foreign decision according to local law, though subject to severe equivalence requirements.

IV. The Main Features of the Mutual Recognition Mechanism

The previous analysis of the mutual recognition mechanism's operation permits the identification of four major characteristics that can be attributed to this mechanism: it is versatile (section IV, A), functional or teleological (section IV, B), flexible (section IV, C), and non-automatic (section IV, D).

A. The versatile nature of the mutual recognition mechanism

When the principle of mutual recognition was transferred from the (old) first pillar to the (old) third pillar, many concerns were raised about the transposal of an 'economic' concept to the area of criminal matters. In my view, the focus lay too much on the apparently economic nature of this principle, since the fact that it was originally introduced in the context of the internal market project does not imply that the concept itself may only serve economic interests or that it is a liberal principle in itself. My analysis of the operation of the principle of mutual recognition in criminal matters reinforced this point of view and led me to conclude that the principle of mutual recognition should not be seen as a

[140] The distinction between recognition and execution does not have in criminal matters the importance that it has gained in other areas of law, in particular in judicial cooperation in civil matters. On this distinction, see, for instance: F. JAULT-SESEKE, J. LELEUR and C. PIGACHE (eds.), 'Les différences d'approche de l'espace judiciaire européen sur les plans civil et pénal', in *L'espace judiciaire européen civil et pénal. Regards croisés* (Paris, Dalloz, 2009) 9–10.

[141] In view of the distinction between mutual recognition *ex ante* and mutual recognition *ex post* mutual recognition can, in this context even take place tacitly, without any formal decision of the host state's competent authority.

concept of an intrinsically economic nature, but rather as a modus operandi for the EU in both economic and non-economic areas. It is in fact the diversity of areas of law which can be made subject to the principle of mutual recognition that largely demonstrates the 'versatile' nature of the mutual recognition mechanism.

Versatility follows, furthermore, from the fact that the principle of mutual recognition is not limited to a case law-based principle, but has also been developed as a legislative tool. In addition, in the latter context, the European legislator has used two different techniques: one which focuses on substantive mutual recognition (in combination with substantive harmonization) and another which focuses on procedural mutual recognition (in combination with procedural harmonization). While examples of both techniques are present in both contexts, it cannot be denied that the procedural mutual recognition technique has gained more ground, especially in recent years.

B. The functional or teleological nature of the mutual recognition mechanism

A good understanding of the principle of mutual recognition requires a thorough knowledge of the objective(s) that the principle pursues and with which it interacts. The principle of mutual recognition is not an objective in itself but a means of reaching an ultimate objective, namely the internal market and the area of freedom, security, and justice, both of which are themselves composed of several sub-objectives. Free movement is a crucial objective in both areas of law, but it is not permitted to dominate ubiquitously in either the internal market context or in the area of criminal matters. In every piece of legislation, and in each judgment, a balancing mechanism is introduced and applied in order to guarantee that free movement is achieved neither at the expense of consumer, safety, health, or environmental concerns (internal market) nor at the expense of security or justice-related objectives (area of freedom, security, and justice).

C. The flexible nature of the mutual recognition mechanism

The outcome of the balancing mechanism is never guaranteed. Not only does it work on the basis of a flexible proportionality test, which allows the principle of mutual recognition to be widened or narrowed depending on the objectives at stake, but its outcomes are also largely dependent on evolutions within the Member States and at EU level.

In the legislative context, the flexible nature of the principle of mutual recognition is further strengthened by the fact that rules on (substantive or procedural) harmonization, equivalence, distribution of competence, and grounds for non-recognition do not constitute rigid or invariable prerequisites to the application of the principle of mutual recognition. Instead, they are seen simply as elements which may enhance or restrict the smooth operation of the mutual recognition mechanism. The fluctuating nature of each of these elements, in varying combinations, grants the European legislator a considerable margin of flexibility in developing a mutual recognition duty that is either limited, moderate, or far-reaching.

D. The non-automatic nature of the mutual recognition mechanism

The preceding analysis of the mutual recognition mechanism, and especially its examination procedure, has emphasized the non-automatic nature of the mutual recognition principle in various ways, namely the available grounds for non-recognition (Treaty-based, rule of reason, legislation-based), the host state's (executing Member State's) margin of control, and the more global requirement that the application of the mutual recognition principle comply with the objectives underpinning the instrument and the EU acquis, in particular the protection of fundamental rights. This wide range of elements to be taken into account implies that even systems with an extremely far-reaching mutual recognition duty[142] may in exceptional cases lead to the non-application—and thus non-automaticity—of the principle of mutual recognition.[143] Non-automaticity applies *a fortiori* in areas where directives or framework decisions include a considerable number of justification grounds, as is currently the case with the framework decisions on judicial cooperation in criminal matters.[144] Indeed, while automaticity initially appears to be implied by a competent executing state authority's duty to recognize 'without further formality' an order or warrant and 'to take forthwith all the necessary measures for its execution', this is in fact attenuated by the authority's being permitted first to verify whether the order or warrant has been transmitted in accordance with the provisions of the framework decision and whether any grounds for non-recognition or non-execution can be invoked.

[142] In relation to the driving licence sector, the corresponding directive has been described by the ECJ as a regime without any formality, which imposes a precise and unconditional obligation and which leaves the host Member State with no discretion but to accept the document issuing in another Member State. See, in particular: ECJ, Case-193/94 *Skanavi* [1996] ECR I-929, para 26; ECJ, Case C-230/97 *Awoyemi* [1998] ECR I-6781, para 41; ECJ, Case C-476/01 *Kapper* [2004] ECR I-5205, paras 45–6.

[143] ECJ, Joined Cases C-329/06 and C-343/06 *Wiedemann and Funk* [2008] ECR I-4635.

[144] The ECJ has therefore rightly underlined that 'while the system established by FD EAW is based on the principle of mutual recognition, *that recognition does **not***, as is clear from Articles 3 to 5 FD EAW, *mean that there is an absolute obligation to execute* the arrest warrant that has been issued' (emphasis added): ECJ, Case C-306/09 *I.B.* [2010] ECR I-10341, para 50.

3

The Workability of the Principle of Mutual Recognition

The viability of a cross-policy approach to the principle of mutual recognition can also be assessed from a third and final angle, namely in light of the principle's workability, specifically the types of problem encountered in its day-to-day application as well as the solutions that have been developed in order to remedy any deficiencies. A joint reading of the corresponding chapters in Parts I and II permits the identification of six elements that ultimately appear crucial for the successful application of the principle of mutual recognition in both of the contexts now under discussion.

A first requirement that is essential to a 'workable' principle of mutual recognition is that any imminent or existing hindrances to the principle are rapidly assessed and addressed. Imminent difficulties can be addressed by means of pro-active measures, such as thorough follow-up and monitoring during the implementation of directives and framework decisions and the notification procedures used in what are referred to as the New Approach sector. Any existent and persistent problems can be assessed and addressed by means of re-active measures, such as peer-review evaluation mechanisms and infringement proceedings.

A second element that is crucial to the successful application of the principle of mutual recognition is good knowledge and understanding not only of the principle of mutual recognition itself but also of the broader EU legal context within which it operates. For both areas, I have illustrated how thorough knowledge and understanding enhances the principle of mutual recognition's function (e.g. FD EAW) whereas a lack of knowledge and understanding hampers its application (e.g. the judicially developed principle of mutual recognition in the internal market context). In both contexts, national administrative and judicial authorities are now European actors, and ought to be aware of the consequences that such a metamorphosis entails. In this regard, the adequate legal training of all competent authorities is a first measure of vital importance that should be taken when addressing flaws in the mutual recognition mechanism. However, legal training alone is insufficient and should go hand in hand with the development of more practical measures, such as tools or instruments which provide useful information on how to apply the instrument(s) in question.

A third element that is highly relevant in assessing the workability of the principle of mutual recognition concerns the issue of legal certainty. In the internal market context, the principle of mutual recognition has long operated mainly on the basis of general, open-ended Treaty provisions that may remain difficult to grasp even today, despite their having been clarified and refined throughout the years in the ECJ's case law. This lack of legal certainty has all too often led to a strategy of risk avoidance (and thus a decision not to rely on the principle of mutual recognition) on the part of the natural or legal persons precisely because they may trigger the principle of mutual recognition (if they wish) but they are certainly under no obligation to do so (voluntary nature of the principle in this context). In order to overcome problems of legal certainty, several legislative measures have been taken recently which set out the duties and rights related to the principle of mutual recognition in a tangible legislative text. While these instruments are far from revolutionary in terms of content, their very existence is a major step forward in terms of legal certainty. The situation is slightly different in criminal matters, as here the principle of mutual recognition operates largely on the basis of instruments with a clear and detailed legal framework, including well-defined duties and tight deadlines. As a result, the problematic issue of legal certainty is far less relevant in the criminal context. Furthermore, the success of the FD EAW can be explained in part by the fact that the principle of mutual recognition is triggered in the criminal context by judicial authorities that are required to apply the mutual recognition mechanism in order to realize the (national) criminal proceedings they are in charge of satisfactorily (mandatory nature of the principle).

A fourth element that has a major impact on the workability of the principle of mutual recognition in both contexts is the existence of a well-developed cooperation mechanism which essentially relies on direct contact between the authorities involved and of a fluent mechanism for exchanging information. Such cooperation first requires that the competent authorities know who they are required to contact in the other Member States (hence the need to develop tools for identifying the competent authorities in other Member States). It also requires that authorities are able to communicate with each other despite differences in national languages (hence the need for language training and, preferably, the selection of vehicular languages). A successful cooperation mechanism will also require the involvement of centralized organs which can and will intervene, in both contexts, where problems between two national authorities cannot be resolved independently (combination of horizontal and vertical cooperation mechanisms). Certain problems, especially in the area of judicial cooperation in criminal matters, will be related to conflicts of competence, hence the necessity of developing a system for the criminal justice area that draws up clear and binding rules on the allocation of jurisdiction.

A fifth element that needs serious consideration is the issue of costs. Though the issue of costs was mainly discussed in the criminal justice context, where its relevance may vary substantially from one instrument to another, it is possible to identify areas in the internal market context where one-sided application of the principle of mutual recognition (and the related burden of costs) may have a negative effect on an authority's willingness to execute mutual recognition orders (e.g. cross-border providence of medical health services and social security related issues). A clear mechanism for distributing costs therefore seems both desirable and inevitable, especially in areas where the execution of mutual recognition instruments is cost-intensive.

A sixth and final element that may influence the workability of the principle of mutual recognition relates to the level of harmonization accompanying the principle of mutual recognition in question. Harmonization is no *conditio sine qua non* for the application of the principle of mutual recognition in either the internal market context or the criminal justice context, yet in both contexts this technique may—in all its different forms—greatly facilitate the principle of mutual recognition. Harmonization is to be pursued neither systematically nor at random, but only after it has been acknowledged that insurmountable differences between the Member States' legal systems are hampering the application of the principle of mutual recognition in a considerable and unacceptable manner.

4

General Conclusions

In this study I have discussed the principle of mutual recognition's function in two key areas of the EU legal order, namely the internal market (Part I) and EU judicial cooperation in criminal matters as an aspect of the area of freedom, security, and justice (Part II). In Parts I and II I explained how the principle functions in each area on the basis of a number of parameters. Taking examples from the ECJ's case law and legal instruments from the EU legislator, I outlined the mechanism of the principle, its characteristics, its interaction with other principles, its limits, and its workability. Subsequently, in Part III, I relied on the results drawn from the two preceding parts in order to address this study's central question.

It is my opinion that the principle of mutual recognition, an instrument traditionally seen as a tool for economic cooperation and initially used to handle problems such as product requirements or service authorization, can also serve a useful purpose in the area of freedom, security, and justice, especially with regard to judicial cooperation in criminal matters, for a variety of reasons. I stressed in Part III that the principle of mutual recognition should be seen as a cross-policy integrative tool for the EU legal order (section I), and I also demonstrated through an assessment of various parameters that the mechanism behind this principle is indeed able to stand the test of the internal market analogy (section II). I have shown that the problems and difficulties faced in the principle's day-to-day application, together with the solutions considered suitable for remedying these shortcomings, in fact prove remarkably similar in the two contexts (section III).

I. Mutual Recognition as a Cross-policy Integrative Tool for the EU Legal Order

First, I pointed out that—in both areas—the principle of mutual recognition was brought in to handle the inevitable disparities between Member States' laws that arise as a result of the plurality of legal orders characterizing the EU. In a Union where the introduction of a decentralized system based on exclusive host or executing state control would seriously hamper the smooth application of the relevant Treaty provisions, and where a centralized system based on harmonization had already proven unattainable, the principle of mutual recognition and its relatively strong focus on control by the home (or issuing) Member State came to be seen as the only viable alternative for pursuing free movement and smooth cooperation as well as more respectful of national diversity than a system based on harmonization.

I went on to argue that the internal market and the area of freedom, security, and justice should not be seen as two isolated, widely divergent projects, but rather as two consecutive and complementing projects that are both crucial to the EU's integration process. Notwithstanding the different goals pursued by the internal market project and the area of freedom, security, and justice, I have demonstrated that in view of the fact that one of the EU's aims is to promote the well-being of its peoples (Art. 3(1) TEU), the EU citizen occupies a central position in both areas. This position is promoted through a range of diverse objectives, including some of a non-economic nature, as listed in Article 3 TEU. Admittedly, the 'four freedoms' primarily serve the internal market objective, i.e. one of the EU's economic goals, while judicial cooperation in criminal matters endeavours first and foremost to ensure a high level of security. However, these are not the only guidelines that the EU must take into account when pursuing the Treaty objectives. In accordance with the Treaties and with the Charter, the EU is required to protect fundamental rights (such as the right to an effective remedy, the right to a fair trial, and other justice-related fundamental rights) and to pursue a high level of safety, health, environmental, social, and consumer protection. Thus, in both contexts, the EU legislator, the ECJ, and the national (judicial and administrative) authorities are essentially required to strike delicate balances. No absolute priority must be given either to the principle of mutual recognition or to any of the other fundamental values; instead, the fundamental value at stake must be balanced against the principle of mutual recognition in each case. This conclusion indicates an important unifying factor between the two areas and demonstrates that free movement (or mutual recognition) is not taken to an extreme in either context.

Another element that argues in favour of a cross-policy application of the principle of mutual recognition is the gradual process of transferring sovereignty in criminal matters that has taken place in the EU over the last two decades. Criminal law is no longer the sole privilege of the sovereign state; judicial cooperation in criminal matters has become an area of shared competences, which means that Member States—no longer sovereign states—are required to assist each other in fulfilling the tasks and objectives proceeding from the Treaties. The application of mutual recognition must be seen in the light of important principles of EU law, such as primacy, sincere cooperation, non-discrimination, effectiveness, subsidiarity, and proportionality, and this represents another unifying factor in the contours of the principle of mutual recognition in both areas of law.

In light of all these findings, I conclude that the principle of mutual recognition should not be seen as an intrinsically economic concept but rather as an appropriate modus operandi for the EU in both economic and non-economic areas of law; it is a principle suitable for application in an integrated economic or political order which strives for further integration without unduly jeopardizing the national identities or specific features of the different Member States. Rather than asking whether mutual recognition is the most appropriate path to take in judicial cooperation in criminal matters, then, we should ask which circumstances, preconditions and characteristics justify a Member State's acceptance of the mechanism in this context, and how the approach taken in the internal market context can be instructive.

II. A Cross-policy Mechanism that Stands the Test of the Internal Market Analogy

In Part III, I examined the mutual recognition mechanism's operation with reference to four key aspects: its object, the actors involved, the constituents of the mutual recognition mechanism, and its major characteristics (the four parameters). This exercise revealed some differences but—more importantly—many similarities which may prove useful in the transferral of ideas between the two areas of law. Indeed, it is not only the judicial or legislative developments of the internal market context that may offer guidance to the area of criminal matters: *vice versa*, certain developments in the latter context may also be sources of inspiration for the former.

A first major finding in this chapter was that mutual recognition is, in essence, a mechanism that operates between the Member States' competent authorities and that applies to acts of states. Admittedly, certain distinctions were drawn in order to clarify how the apparently public nature of this mechanism has been altered somewhat by privatization trends taking place in some Member States and at EU level. Yet it cannot be denied that in both areas of law, this evolution remains an exception. The overall conclusion is that the final responsibility for a well-functioning mutual recognition mechanism remains with the Member States and their (regulatory and judicial) authorities.

Given the flexible, versatile nature of the principle of mutual recognition, it is difficult to summarize its core elements in just a few lines. Traditionally, the mutual recognition mechanism has been depicted both as a mechanism that prioritizes the country of origin's legal framework and as a mechanism that ultimately amounts to an equivalence test. Yet the results of my research demonstrate that neither of these views is entirely satisfactory. First, in both contexts, the mechanism is driven not by a choice between the home state (issuing Member State) and the host state (executing Member State), instead, it is concerned with a combination of the two, as they are required to act in a kind of partnership in order to guarantee the effective application of the principle of mutual recognition. Furthermore, the equivalence test is ubiquitous in neither of these contexts and instead fulfils a fluctuating role which ranges from strict equivalence scrutiny via presumptions of equivalence to complete indifference to equivalence arguments. Mutual recognition is therefore concerned neither with granting unconditional prevalence to the home country's legislation nor with exclusively checking equivalent levels of protection in the home and host states.

The central point of the mutual recognition mechanism is that, in both contexts, it consists of a rule (free movement, mutual recognition) and an exception (Treaty-based justification grounds, rule of reason, or legislation-based justification grounds). One of the key questions, then, will always be how the rule and the exception(s) are to relate to each other in each individual case. In this regard, the internal market's point of departure that 'exceptions must be interpreted restrictedly' has not yet been taken up explicitly by the ECJ in the context of judicial cooperation in criminal matters. In view of the different categories of justification ground available in this latter context, however, the implicit preference of a non-restrictive approach deserves approval, in my opinion. The point of departure is then no longer that 'exceptions must always be interpreted restrictively', but rather that the objectives underpinning the rule and exception(s) in question must first be investigated and then reconciled and brought into balance. Such an approach may also be of interest to the internal market context, where some recent case law developments have already seemed to be moving in this direction.

The main conclusion to be drawn from Part III is that both the preconditions and major implications of the mutual recognition mechanism are, for the most part, very similar in the two areas of law. The ECJ applies similar criteria when examining whether national measures are sufficient to set aside the principle of mutual recognition (a suitability, necessity, and proportionality test in light of a comparative, European or international parameter) and the different phases of the mutual recognition mechanism (duties to take into account and duties to recognize and execute) also have a major connection, namely the acceptance that foreign rules may have a decisive influence on decisions to be taken on the national territory, which confirms the suitability of the suggested working definition set out in the Introduction to this study.

Several aspects of the mutual recognition mechanism still require further development in the ECJ's case law on judicial cooperation in criminal matters, yet it is more than likely that the ECJ will draw on its internal market case law in order to do this. For instance, with regard to the question of how large a margin of control an executing judicial authority has access to, the ECJ's challenging pursuit of a fair balance between mutual trust (as a point of departure) and an acceptable margin of control (in cases of obvious breaches or shortcomings) in the internal market context could provide an instructive point of reference. Similarly, with regard to the question of how intensely a national measure must be assessed in light of the broader EU framework, for instance with regard to issues of abuse of law or non-discrimination, the ECJ's well-established internal market case law may prove invaluable.

III. Recurring Difficulties and Cross-policy Solutions for Enhancing the Workability of the Principle of Mutual Recognition

The viability of a cross-policy approach to the principle of mutual recognition was also assessed in Part III in light of the principle's workability. It was striking to observe how in both contexts, successful application of the principle of mutual recognition depends on six major elements. First, a workable principle of mutual recognition requires that any imminent or existing hindrances to the principle are assessed in time. Therefore, in both contexts, *ex ante* and *ex post* mechanisms have been developed to detect, as early as possible, any shortcomings in the practical application of the principle of mutual recognition. Secondly, a crucial prerequisite for a principle of mutual recognition that functions effectively is a thorough knowledge and understanding of the principle itself as well as of the general EU legal order in which this principle takes effect. This requires both adequate legal training and the development of practical tools which assist national (administrative and judicial) authorities in carrying out tasks as European actors. Thirdly, the success of the principle of mutual recognition is largely determined by elements that either support or undermine legal certainty. In particular, those legislative mutual recognition instruments which set out clear and well-defined duties and rights have proven most beneficial to the principle of mutual recognition. The fourth element constitutes a well-developed cooperation mechanism based on direct contact between the competent authorities, an efficient system of information exchange, and a back-up position for centralized EU institutions and EU bodies. This will require the arrangement of a number of practical issues, such as the development of tools that provide information about who to contact as well as the selection of a common language to prevent cooperation being hindered by purely linguistic misunderstandings. The fifth element concerns the fact that implementing the principle of mutual recognition is rather cost-intensive in some contexts. Both the EU and the Member States should take this issue seriously, for instance, by developing a mechanism for distributing costs. Finally, the sixth major element which has a major effect on the success of the principle of mutual recognition's application is the development of common rules (harmonization). The relationship between the two integration tools is in constant evolution in both contexts but it is already clear that harmonization measures will be imposed only where major differences between Member States' legal systems threaten to result in considerable hindrances to the application of the principle of mutual recognition.

IV. Final Conclusion

In the Introduction to this study I expounded on my central research question, specifically whether a cross-policy approach to the principle of mutual recognition is either feasible or desirable. In Parts I and II, I investigated the function, characteristics, and workability of the principle of mutual recognition, first, in the internal market context (Part I) and, secondly, in the context of judicial cooperation in criminal matters (Part II). These investigations subsequently enabled me to perform an analysis of a cross-policy approach to the function, characteristics, and workability of the principle of mutual recognition (Part III). On the basis of my results, I conclude that a cross-policy approach to the principle of mutual recognition is indeed both feasible and desirable.

Selected Bibliography

LITERATURE RELATED TO THE INTERNAL MARKET (AND EU LAW IN GENERAL)

ABRAHAM, F., 'Building Blocks of the Single Market', *Tijdschrift voor Economie en Management* 1991, retrievable at: <http://www.econ.kuleuven.be/tem/jaargangen/1991-2000/1991/TEM1991-4/TEM1991-4_395-415p.pdf>.

ACKERMANN, T., 'Case Note *Omega*', *CML Rev.* 2005, 1107–20.

ALBATH, L. and GIESLER, M., 'Das Herkunftslandprinzip in der Dienstleistungsrichtlinie—eine Kodifizierung der Rechtsprechung?' *EuZW* 2006, 38–42.

ALBIN, W. and VALENTIN, F., '*Dassonville* oder doch *Keck*—Zwei anstehende Urteile des EuGH zur Anwendung des Art. 28 EG auf Verwendungsbeschränkungen', *EWS* 2007, 533–40.

ALEMANNO, A., 'Libre circulation des personnes', *RDUE* 2003, 521–7.

____, 'A la recherché d'un juste équilibre entre libertés fondamentales et droits fondamentaux dans le cadre du marché intérieur', *RDUE* 2004, 709–51.

____, 'Le principe de la reconnaissance mutuelle au-delà du marché intérieur: phénomène d'exportation normative ou stratégie de 'colonialisme' réglementaire?', *RDUE* 2006, 273–311.

ALLEN, B., 'Ladies and Gentlemen, No More Bets Please', *LIEI* 2000, 201–06.

ALTER, K. and MEUNIER-AITSAHALIA, S., 'Judicial Politics in the European Community. European Integration and the Pathbreaking *Cassis de Dijon* Decision', *Comparative Political Studies* 1994, 535–61.

ANDENAS, M. and ROTH, W.-H. (eds.), *Services and Free Movement in EU Law*, Oxford: Oxford University Press, 2002.

ARNULL, A., 'Anyone for Tripe?', *E.L. Rev.* 1993, 314–23.

____, *The European Union and its Court of Justice*, Oxford: Oxford University Press, 2006.

AUDIT, M., 'Régulation du marché intérieur et libre circulation des lois', *J.D.I.* 2006, 2–33.

AVBELJ, M., 'European Court of Justice and the Question of Value Choices. Fundamental Human Rights as an Exception to the Freedom of Goods', Jean Monnet Working Paper 2004, retrievable at: <http://centers.law.nyu.edu/jeanmonnet/archive/papers/04/040601.pdf>.

BADINGER, H. and MAYDELL, N., 'Legal and Economic Issues in Completing the EU Internal Market for Services: An Interdisciplinary Perspective', *JCMS* 2009, 693–717.

BALLON, E., 'Case Note *Gebhard*', *Col. J. Eur. L.* 1997, 145–51.

BARAV, A., 'Omnipotent Courts', in *Institutional Dynamics of European Integration. Essays in Honour of Henry G. Schermers. II*, CURTIN, D. and HEUKELS, T. (eds.), Dordrecht: Martinus Nijhoff Publishers, 1994, 265–302.

BARENTS, R., 'The Precedence of EU law from the Perspective of Constitutional Pluralism', *EUConst* 2009, 421–446.

BARNARD, C., 'An Irish Solution', *New Law Journal* 1992, 526–33.

____, 'Sunday Trading: A Drama in Five Acts', *MLR* 1994, 449–60.

____, 'Unravelling the Services Directive', *CML Rev.* 2008, 323–94.

____, *The Substantive Law of the EU: the Four Freedoms*, Oxford: Oxford University Press, 2010.

____ and ODUDU, O. (eds.), *The Outer Limits of European Union Law*, Oxford: Hart Publishing, 2009.

____ and SCOTT, J. (eds.), *The Law of the Single European Market. Unpacking the Premises*, Oxford: Hart Publishing, 2002.

BASEDOWN, J., 'Dienstleistungsrichtlinie, Herkunftslandprinzip und Internationales Privatrecht', *EuZW* 2004, 423–5.

BATES, St. J., FINNIE, W., USHER, J.A., and WILDBERG, H. (eds.), *European Governmental Studies. In Memoriam J.D.B. Mitchell*, London: Sweet and Maxwell, 1983.

BEHRENS, P., 'Die Konvergenz der wirtschaftlichen Freiheiten im europäischen Gemeinschaftsrecht', *EuR* 1992, 145–62.

____, 'The Economic Order in the Treaty Establishing a Constitution for Europe. A Critical Assessment', in *30 Years of European Legal Studies at the College of Europe*, DEMARET, P., GOVAERE, I., and HANF, D. (eds.), Brussels: Peter Lang, 2005, 173–83.

BELHADJ, E., EVANS, S.J.H., and VAN DE GRONDEN, J.W., 'De Dienstenrichtlijn: de gebreken van de deugden? Een eerste verkenning van de Dienstenrichtlijn', *SEW* 2007, 141–53.

BERCUSSON, B., 'The Trade Union Movement and the European Union: Judgment Day', *E.L.J.* 2007, 296–305.

BERENDS, G. and CARREÑO, I., 'Safeguards in Food Law–Ensuring Food Scares are Scarce', *E.L. Rev.* 2005, 386–405.

BERNARD, N., 'Discrimination and Free Movement in EC Law', *ICLQ* 1996, 82–108.

____, *Multilevel Governance in the European Union*, The Hague: Kluwer, 2002.

BERNEL, A., *Le principe d'équivalence ou de reconnaissance mutuelle en droit communautaire*, Zurich: Schulthess polygraphischer Verlag, 1995.

BERTEA, S., 'Looking for Coherence within the European Community', *E.L.J.* 2005, 154–72.

BESSELINK, L., 'Case Note *Sayn-Wittgenstein*', *CML Rev.* 2012, 678–93.

BIEBER, R., 'An Association of Sovereign States', *EU Const* 2009, 391–406.

____, DEHOUSSE, R., PINDER, J., and WEILER, J.H.H., *1992: One European Market?*, Baden-Baden: Nomos, 1988.

BIONDI, A., 'In and Out of the Internal Market: Recent Developments on the Principle of Free Movement', *Y.E.L.* 1999–2000, 469–91.

____, 'Free Trade, a Mountain Road and the Right to Protest: European Economic Freedoms and Fundamental Individual Rights', *EHRLR* 2004, 51–61.

BLANPAIN, R. (ed.), *Freedom of Services in the European Union. Labour and Social Security Law: The Bolkestein Initiative*, The Hague: Kluwer, 2006.

BLANQUET, M., *L'article 5 du Traité CEE. Recherché sur les obligations de fidélité des états membres de la communauté*, Paris: Librairie Générale de Droit et de Jurisprudence, 1994.

BLOBEL, F. and SPATH, P., 'The Tale of Multilateral Trust and the European Law of Civil Procedure', *E.L. Rev.* 2005, 528–47.

BROHMER, J., 'Zulässige Untersagung eines Tötungsspiels (Rs C-36/02 Omega Spielhallen-GmbH)', *EuZW* 2004, 755–7.

BROUWER, O., 'Free Movement of Foodstuff and Quality Requirements: Has the Commission got it Wrong?', *CML Rev.* 1988, 237–262.

BULTERMAN, M.K. and KRANENBORG, H.R., 'What if Rules on Free Movement and Human Rights Collide? About Laser Games and Human Dignity: the Omega Case', *E.L. Rev.* 2006, 93–101.

BURCHARD, C. and BRODOWSKI, D., 'The Post-Lisbon Principle of Transnational *ne bis in idem*: on the Relationship between Article 50 Charter of Fundamental Rights and Article 54 Convention Implementing the Schengen Agreement. Case Note on District Court Aachen, Germany, (52 Ks 9/08—"Boere"), Decision of 8 December 2010', *NJECL* 2010, 310–27.

BURROWS, N., 'Harmonization of Technical Standards: Reculer pour Mieux Sauter?', *MLR* 1990, 597–603.

CABRAL, P. and CUNHA, P., 'Presumed Innocent: Companies and the Exercise of the Right of Establishment under Community Law', *E.L. Rev.* 2000, 157–66.

CACHARD, O., 'The Field Coordinated by the Directive on e-Commerce and Private International Law', *IBLJ* 2004, 161–79.

CANDELA SORIANO, M., 'Les exigences linguistiques: une entrave légitime à la libre circulation?', *C.D.E.* 2002, 9–44.

CAPELLI, F., 'Les malentendus provoqués par l'arrêt sur le Cassis de Dijon', *RMC* 1981, 421–35.

____, 'La libre circulation des produits alimentaires à l'intérieur du marché unique européen', *RMCUE* 1993, 790–811.

CHALMERS, D., 'Free Movement of Goods within the European Community: an Unhealthy Addiction to Scotch Whisky?', *ICLQ* 1993, 269–94.

____, 'Repackaging the Internal Market: the Ramifications of the Keck Judgment', *E.L. Rev.* 1994, 385–403.

____, 'Food for Thought: Reconciling European Risks and Traditional Ways of Life', *MLR* 2003, 532–62.

____, DAVIES, G., and MONTI, G., *European Union Law*, Cambridge: Cambridge University Press, 2010.

CHITI, E., 'An Important Part of the EU's Institutional Machinery: Features, Problems and Perspectives of European agencies', *CML Rev.* 2009, 1395–442.

CHU, G., 'Playing at Killing Freedom of Movement', *LIEI* 2006, 85–94.

COLVIN, C., 'Irish Abortion Law and the Free Movement of Services in the European Community', *Fordh. Int. L. J.* 1991–92, 476–526.

CONNOR, T., 'Accentuating the Positive: the "Selling Arrangement", the First Decade, and Beyond', *ICLQ* 2005, 127–60.

CONSTANTINESCO, V., 'L'article 5 CEE, de la bonne foi à la loyauté communautaire', in *Du droit international au droit de l'intégration. Liber amicorum Pierre Pescatore*, Baden-Baden: Nomos, 1987, 97–114.

CORTHAUT, T., *EU Ordre Public*, The Hague: Kluwer Law International, 2012.

CRAIG, P., *The Lisbon Treaty. Law, Politics and Treaty Reform*, Oxford: Oxford University Press, 2010.

____ and DE BURCA, G., *The Evolution of EU Law*, Oxford: Oxford University Press, 1999.

____ and ____, *The evolution of EU Law*, 2nd edn, Oxford: Oxford University Press, 2011.

____ and ____, *EU Law. Text, Cases and Materials*, Oxford: Oxford University Press, 2011.

CRISCUOLO, A., 'The TV without Frontiers Directive and the Legal Regulation of Publicity in the European Community', *E.L. Rev.* 1998, 357–63.

CRISHAM, C.A., 'Case Note *Thieffry* and *Patrick*', *CML Rev.* 1978, 359–70.

D'ACUNTO, S., 'La proposition de directive sur les services dans le marché intérieur', *RDUE* 2004, 201–48.

____, 'Directive Services (2006/123/EC): radiographie juridique en dix points', *RDUE* 2007, 261–328.

DASHWOOD, A., '*Cassis de Dijon*. A Major Step in the Liberalisation of Trade', *E.I.P.R.* 1981, 268–70.

____, 'The Cassis de Dijon Line of Authority', in *European Governmental Studies. In Memoriam J.D.B. Mitchell*, BATES, St. J., FINNIE, W., USHER, J.A,. and WILDBERG, H. (eds.), London: Sweet and Maxwell, 1983, 145–61.

____, 'The Limits of European Community Powers', *E.L. Rev.* 1996, 113–28.

____, 'The Relationship between the Member States and the European Union/European Community', *CML Rev.* 2004, 355–81.

DAVIES, G., *EU Internal Market Law*, London: Cavendish Publishing Limited, 2003.

____, 'Can Selling Arrangements be Harmonised?', *E.L. Rev.* 2005, 370–85.

____, 'Subsidiarity: the Wrong Idea, in the Wrong Place, at the Wrong Time', *CML Rev.* 2006, 63–84.

____, 'The Services Directive: Extending the Country of Origin Principle and Reforming Public Administration', *E.L. Rev.* 2007, 232–45.

____, 'Process and Production Method'-based Trade Restrictions in the EU', *CYELS* 2007–08, 70–97.

DAWES, A. and STRUCKMANN, K., 'Rien ne va plus? Mutual Recognition and the Free Movement of Services in the Gambling Sector after the *Santa Casa* Judgment', *E.L. Rev.* 2010, 246–51.

DEAKIN, S., 'Two Types of Regulatory Competition: Competitive Federalism versus Reflexive Harmonisation. A Law and Economics Perspective on Centros', *CYELS* 1999, 231–60.

____, 'Regulatory Competition after *Laval*', *CYELS* 2007–08, 581–609.

DE BAERE, G., 'Is this a Conflict Rule which I see Before Me? Looking for a Hidden Conflict Rule in the Principle of Origin as Implemented in Primary Community Law and in the Directive on Electronic Commerce', *MJ* 2004, 287–319.

DE BURCA, G. and WEILER, J.H.H., *The European Court of Justice*, Oxford: Oxford University Press, 2001.

DE CECCO, F., 'Room to Move? Minimum Harmonisation and Fundamental Rights', *CML Rev.* 2006, 9–30.

DEFALQUE, L., PERTEK, J., STEINFELD, Ph., and VIGNERON, Ph., *Commentaire J. Mégret. Marché intérieur. Libre circulation des personnes et des capitaux. Rapprochement des législations*, Brussels: IEE, 2006.

DE LA FERIA, R., 'Prohibition of Abuse of (Community) Law: the Creation of a New General Principle of EC Law through Tax', *CML Rev.* 2008, 398–441.

____ and VOGENAUER, S., *Prohibition of Abuse of Law: A New General Principle of EU Law*, Oxford: Hart Publishing, 2011.

DE LA ROSA, S., 'The Directive on Cross-border Healthcare or the Art of Codifying Complex Case Law', *CML Rev.* 2012, 15–46.

DELIMATSIS, P., 'Thou Shall Not (Dis)trust: Codes of Conduct and Harmonization of Professional Standards in the EU', *CML Rev.* 2010, 1049–87.

DERLEN, M. and LINDHOLM, J., 'Article 28 EC and Rules on Use: a Step towards a Workable Doctrine on Measures Having Equivalent Effect to Quantitative Restrictions', *Col. J. Eur. L.* 2010, 191–231.

DE RUYT, J., *L'Acte Unique européen. Commentaire*, Brussels: Editions de l'Université de Bruxelles, 1989.

DE SADELEER, N., 'Procedures for Derogations from the Principle of Approximation of Laws under Article 95 EC', *CML Rev.* 2003, 889–915.

____, 'L'examen, au regard de l'article 28 CE, des règles nationales régissant les modalités d'utilisation de certains produits', *J.D.E.* 2009, 247–250.

DE SCHRYVER, V., 'Enige vragen bij de Richtlijn Elektronische handel', *Financieel forum. Bank en financieel recht*, 2002, 63–79.

DE SCHUTTER, O. and FRANCQ, S., 'La proposition de directive relative aux services dans le marché intérieur: reconnaissance mutuelle, harmonisation et conflits de lois dans l'Europe élargie', *C.D.E.* 2006, 603–60.

DEVROE, W., 'Limits of Differentiation in European Economic Law: *ne bis in idem* and Minimum versus Maximum Harmonisation', *MJ* 2009, 141–8.

DE WITTE, B., 'Setting the Scene: How did Services get to Bolkestein and Why?', EUI Working Papers Law 2007, retrievable at: <http://cadmus.iue.it/dspace/bitstream/1814/6929/1/LAW_2007_20.pdf>.

DONNER, J.P.H., 'Articles 30-36 EEC in General', *SEW* 1982, 362–73.

DOUGAN, M., 'Minimum Harmonization and the Internal Market', *CML Rev.* 2000, 853–85.

DRIJBER, B.J., 'De bezems van Bolkestein', *NTER* 2004, 112–20.

____, 'The Country of Origin Principle in the proposed Directive on Services in the Internal Market', *European Consumer Law Review* 2005, 14–22.

DUBOUIS, L., 'L'interruption volontaire de grossesse au regard du droit communautaire', *Rev. dr. san. soc.* 1992, 52–7.

EDWARDS, V. and FARMER, P., 'The Concept of Abuse in the Freedom of Establishment of Companies: a Case of Double Standards?', in *Continuity and Change in EU Law. Essays in Honour of Sir Francis Jacobs*, ARNULL, A., EECKHOUT, P., and TRIDIMAS, T. (eds.), Oxford: Oxford University Press, 2008, 206–27.

EGAN, M., *Constructing a European Market. Standards, Regulation and Governance*, Oxford: Oxford University Press, 2001.

____, 'Mutual Recognition and Standard Setting: Public and Private Strategies for Governing Markets', in *Transatlantic Governance in the Global Economy*, POLLACK, M. and SHAFFER, G. (eds.), Oxford: Rowman and Littlefield Publishers, 2002, 179–209.

EIJSBOUTS, W.T., JANS, J.H., SENDEN, L.A.J., and PRECHAL, A., *Europees Recht. Algemeen deel. Sinds het Verdrag van Lissabon*, Groningen: Europa Law Publishing, 2010.

EMILIOU, N., *The Principle of Proportionality in European Law. A Comparative Study*, The Hague: Kluwer, 1996.

ENCHELMAIER, S., 'The Awkward Selling of a Good Idea, or a Traditionalist Interpretation of Keck', *Y.E.L.* 2003, 249–321.

____, 'Four Freedoms, How Many Principles?', *OJLS* 2004, 155–72.

____, 'Consumer Interests and Contract Law in the Draft Directive on Services in the Internal Market', *ERA Forum* 2005, 232–45.

____, 'The ECJ's Recent Case Law on the Free Movement of Goods: Movement in All Sorts of Directions', *Y.E.L.* 2007, 133–56.

ENGSIG SORENSEN, K., 'Abuse of Rights in Community Law: a Principle of Substance or Mere Rhetoric?', *CML Rev.* 2006, 423–59.

ENRIQUES, L., 'EC Company Law and the Fear of a European Delaware', *E.B.L.R.* 2004, 1259–74.

ESTY, D. and GERARDIN, D. (eds.), *Regulatory Competition and Economic Integration*, Oxford: Oxford University Press, 2001.

EVERLING, U., *Die Cassis de Dijon Rechtsprechung und ihre Auswirkungen auf die Ernährungswirtschaft*, Bonn: BLL, 1987.

FABRA VALLS, M., 'Régimen fiscal aplicable a los dividendos entrantes percibidos por personas físicas y relaciones entre el Derecho Comunitario y los Convenios de Doble Imposición', *Noticias de la UE* 2009, 73–80.

FACENNA, G., '*Schmidberger*: Freedom of Expression and Assembly vs. Free Movement of Goods', *EHRLR* 2004, 79.

FALLON, M., 'Variations sur le principe d'origine, entre droit communautaire et droit international privé', in *Nouveaux itinéraires en droit. Hommage à François Rigaux*, Brussels: Bruylant, 1993, 187–221.

____, *Droit matériel général de l'Union Européenne*, Louvain-la-Neuve: Bruylant, 2002.

____ and MANIET, F. (eds.), *Sécurité des produits et mécanismes du contrôle dans la communauté européenne*, Ghent: Story-Scientia, 1990.

____ and MEEUSEN, J., 'Private International Law in the European Union and the Exception of Mutual Recognition', in *Yearbook of Private International Law. Volume IV*, SARCEVIC, P. and VOLKEN, P. (eds.), The Hague: Kluwer Law International, 2002, 37–66.

____ and MEEUSEN, J., 'Le commerce électronique, la directive 2000/31/CE et le droit international privé', *Revue critique de droit international privé* 2002, 435–90.

____ and SIMON, A.-C., 'La directive "services": quelle contribution au marché intérieur', *JT Dr Eur.* 2007, 33–42.

FARRAR, C., 'EC Broadcasting Law Clarified: The *Paul Denuit* and *VT4* Cases and the Television Without Frontiers Directive', *Entertainment Law Review* 1998, 16–20.

FAURE, M., 'Towards a Maximum Harmonisation of Consumer Contract Law?', *MJ* 2008, 433–45.

FAVRET, J.-M., 'Le système général de reconnaissance des diplômes et des formations professionnelles en droit communautaire: l'esprit et la méthode', *RTD. Eur.* 1996, 259–80.

FEIDEN, S., *Die Bedeutung der 'Keck'-Rechtsprechung im System der Grundfreiheiten*, Berlin: Duncker & Humblot, 2003.

FENGER, N., 'Article 28 EC and Restrictions on Use of a Legally Marketed Product', *E.L.R.* 2009, 326–37.

FERNÁNDEZ ARROYO, D.P., 'De cómo la defensa de los animales frente al sufrimiento puede querer ocultar la falta de confianza comunitaria', *La Ley* 1996, No 6, 1676–9.

FISHER, E., 'Precaution, Precaution Everywhere: Developing a Common Understanding of the Precautionary Principle in the European Community', *MJ* 2002, 7–28.

FLYNN, L., 'Coming of Age: the Free Movement of Capital Case Law 1993–2002', *CML Rev.* 2002, 773–805.

FOUASSIER, C., 'Le système général de reconnaissance des diplômes: la confiance mutuelle et ses limites', *RAE* 2005, 3151.

FRANCQ, S., 'Chronique de jurisprudence du Tribunal de la Cour de Justice des CE. Circulation de personnes et des services', *J.D.I.* 2007, 657–8.

FUKUYAMA, F., *Trust. The Social Virtues and the Creation of Prosperity*, London: Penguin, 1995.

GALLI, G. and PELKMANS, J. (eds.), *Regulatory Reform and Competitiveness in Europe, I*, Cheltenham: Edward Elgar, 2000.

GAMBETTA, D., 'Can We Trust Trust?', in *Trust Making and Breaking Cooperative Relations*, GAMBETTA, D. (ed.), Oxford: Basil Blackwell, 1988, 213–37.

GARABIOL-FURET, M.-D., 'La directive Bolkestein, bouc émissaire d'une Europe incertaine', *RMCUE* 2005, 295–302.

____, 'Plaidoyer pour le principe du pays d'origine', *RMCUE* 2006, 82–7.

____, 'Vrais et faux semblants de la directive services', *RMCUE* 2006, 219–20.

GARDEÑEZ SANTIAGO, M., *La aplicación de la regla del reconocimiento mutuo y su incidencia en el comercio de mercancías y servicios en el ámbito comunitario e internacional*, Madrid: Eurolex, 1999.

GEKIERE, W., 'Towards a European Directive on Services in the Internal Market: Analysing the legal repercussions on the Draft Services Directive and its Impact on National Services Regulations. Research report commissioned by Anne Van Lancker. 24 September 2004', retrievable at: <http://openbarediensten.acv-online.be/Images/2004-10%20EU%20 Diensten%20-%20Impact%20Draft%20final1_tcm86-67173.pdf>.

GENSCHEL, P., 'Why No Mutual Recognition of VAT? Regulation, Taxation and the Integration of the EU's Internal Market for Goods', *JEPP* 2007, 743–61.

GIESEN, R., 'Posting: Social Protection vs. Fundamental Freedoms?', *CML Rev.* 2003, 143–58.

GONZÁLEZ VAQUÉ, L., 'Naturaleza y efectos de las cláusulas de reconocimiento mutuo incluidas en las normativas nacionales relativas al mercado interior', *G. J.* 1997, 117–51.

____, 'Marché intérieur: renforcer l'efficacité de la reconnaissance mutuelle', *JT Dr Eur.* 1999, 230–2.

____, 'Faut-il insérer des clauses de reconnaissance mutuelle dans les législations internes? A propos de l'arrêt *Foie Gras* rendu par la Cour de justice des Communautés européennes', *JT Dr Eur.* 1999, 87–8.

____, 'La jurisprudence relative à l'article 28 CE (ex article 30) après l'arrêt *Keck et Mithouard*', *RDUE* 2000, 395–415.

____, 'La sentencia *Mickelsson y Roos* del TJCE: Good Bye, *Keck y Mithouard!*', *Rev. Esp. Der. Eur.* 2009, 389–406.

GOOSSEN, J., 'Notificaties onder Richtlijn 98/34. Preventieve controle op het vrije verkeer van goederen: stand van zaken 2003', *SEW* 2003, 94–9.

GORMLEY, L., '*Cassis de Dijon* and the Communication from the Commission', *E.L. Rev.* 1981, 454–9.

____, *Prohibiting Restrictions on Trade within the EEC*, Amsterdam: Elsevier, 1985.

____, 'Recent Case Law on the Free Movement of Goods: Some Hot Potatoes', *CML Rev.* 1990, 825–57.

____, 'Reasoning Renounced? The Remarkable Judgment in *Keck and Mithouard*', *E.B.L.R.* 1994, 63–7.

____, 'Pay your Money and Take your Chance?', *E.L. Rev.* 1994, 644–53.

____, 'The Definition of Measures Having Equivalent Effect', in *Continuity and Change in EU Law. Essays in Honour of Sir Francis Jacobs*, ARNULL, A., EECKHOUT, P., and TRIDIMAS, T. (eds.), Oxford: Oxford University Press, 2008, 189–204.

____, 'Silver Threads among the Gold... 50 Years of the Free Movement of Goods', *Fordh. Int L. J.* 2008, 1637–91.
____, *EU Law of Free Movement of Goods and Customs Union*, Oxford: Oxford University Press, 2009.
GOTZ, V., 'Der Grundsatz der gegenseitigen Anerkennung um europäischen Binnenmarkt', in *Liber amicorum Günther Jaenicke—Zum 85. Geburtstag*, Berlin: Springer, 1998, 763–91.
GOVAERE, I., 'The Future Direction of the EU Internal Market: on Vested Values and Fashionable Modernism', *Col. J. Eur. L.* 2009, 67–80.
GRAHAM, R., 'Mutual Recognition and Country of Origin in the Case Law of the European Court of Justice', in *Freedom of Services in the European Union. Labour and Social Security Law: The Bolkestein Directive*, The Hague: Kluwer, 2006.
GRANDPIERRE, A., *Herkunftsprinzip kontra Marktortanknüpfung. Auswirkung des Gemeinschaftsrecht auf die Kollisionregeln im Wettbewerbsrecht*, Frankfurt am Main: Peter Lang, 1999.
GREAVES, R., 'Advertising Restrictions and the Free Movement of Goods and Services', *E.L. Rev.* 1998, 305–19.
GREGOR, S., 'Why Market Freedoms are no Fundamental Rights: a Competence Approach', *CYELP* 2010, 1–21.
GUZMÁN ZAPATER, M., 'El principio de reconocimiento mutuo: un nuevo modelo para el derecho internacional privado comunitario?', *Rev. Der. Com. Eur.* 1998, 137–70.
HAIBACH, G., 'The Mutual Recognition of Decisions in Civil and Commercial Matters in the Light of the Full Faith and Credit Clause of the US Constitution', *MJ* 2003, 291–300.
HAMMER, C., *Handbuch zum freien Wahrenverkehr*, Vienna: Manzsche Verlags- und Universitätsbuchandlung, 1998.
HATJE, A., *Loyalität als Rechtsprinzip in der Europäischen Union*, Baden-Baden: Nomos, 2001.
HATZOPOULOS, V., 'Case Note *Alpine Investments*', *CML Rev.* 1995, 1433–45.
____, 'Exigences essentielles, impératives ou impérieuses: une théorie, des théories ou pas de théorie du tout?', *RTD. Eur.* 1998, 191–236.
____, *Le principe communautaire d'équivalence et de reconnaissance mutuelle dans la libre prestation de services*, Brussels: Bruylant, 1999.
____, 'The Case Law of the ECJ in the Field of Services', *CML Rev.* 2000, 43–82.
____, 'Trente ans après les arrêts fondamentaux de 1974, les quatre libertés: quatre?', in DEMARET, P., GOVAERE, I., and HANF, D. (eds.), *30 Years of European Legal Studies at the College of Europe*, Brussels: Peter Lang, 2005, 187–201.
____, 'The Case Law of the ECJ Concerning the Free Movement Provision of Services: 2000–2005', 2006, retrievable at: <http://www.coleurope.eu/template.asp? page name = lawpapers>.
____, 'Que reste -t- il de la directive sur les services', *C.D.E.* 2007, 200–355.
____, 'Assessing the Services Directive', *CYELS* 2007–08, 215–61.
____, 'Le principe de reconnaissance mutuelle dans la libre prestation des services', 2009, retrievable at: <http://www.coleurope.eu/template.asp?pagename=lawpapers>.
HERINGA, A.W. and VERHEY, L., 'The EU Charter: Text and Structure', *MJ* 2001, 11–32.
HERITIER, A., 'Mutual Recognition: Comparing Policy Areas', *JEPP* 2007, 800–13.
HERLITZ, F., 'La politique de prévention des obstacles aux échanges de marchandises et de services de la société de l'information. Les vingt-cinq ans d'un instrument révolutionnaire: la directive 98/34/CE', *RDUE* 2008, 403–60.
HIGGINS, I., 'The Free and Not so Free Movement of Goods since *Keck*', *I.J.E.L.* 1997, 166–80.
HIJMANS, H., 'De Europese Unie, verdwijnende grenzen en elektronische diensten', *SEW* 2004, 350–62.
HILSON, C., 'Discrimination in Community Free Movement Law', *E.L. Rev.* 1999, 445–62.
____, 'Rights and Principles in EU Law: A Distinction without Foundation?', *MJ* 2008, 193–215.
HOFHUIS, Y., *Minimumharmonisatie*, Deventer: Kluwer, 2006.

HORNG, D.-C., 'The Principle of Mutual Recognition. The European Union's Practice and Development', *World Competition* 1999, 135–55.

HÖRNLE, J., 'Country of Origin Regulation in Cross-border Media: One Step beyond the Freedom to Provide Services?', *ICLQ* 2005, 89–126.

HOUSE OF LORDS, EU COMMITTEE, 'Procedural Rights in Criminal Proceedings. Report with Evidence', 2004–05, retrievable at: <http://www.parliament.the-stationery-office.co.uk/pa/ld/ldeucom.htm>.

____, 'Completing the Internal Market in Services', 2005–06, retrievable at: <http://www.publications.parliament.uk/pa/ld200506/ldselect/ldeucom/ldeucom.htm>.

____, 'The Services Directive Revisited', 2005–06, retrievable at: <http://www.publications.parliament.uk/pa/ld200506/ldselect/ldeucom/ldeucom.htm>.

____, 'Consumer Credit in the EU: Harmonization and Consumer Protection', 2005–06, retrievable at: < http://www.publications.parliament.uk/pa/ld200506/ldselect/ldeucom/210/210i.pdf>.

____, 'European Supervision Order. Report with Evidence', 2007, retrievable at: <http://www.publications.parliament.uk/pa/ld200607/ldselect/ldeucom/145/145.pdf>.

____, 'Television without Frontiers? Report with Evidence', 2007, retrievable at: <http://www.publications.parliament.uk/pa/ld200607/ldselect/ldeucom/27/27.pdf>.

____, 'The Treaty of Lisbon. An Impact Assessment', 2007–08, retrievable at: <http://www.parliament.the-stationery-office.co.uk/pa/ld200708/ldselect/ldeucom/62/62.pdf>.

____, 'The Single Market: Wallflower or Dancing Partner? Inquiry into the Commission's Review of the Single Market', 2008–09, retrievable at: <http://www.publications.parliament.uk/pa/ld200708/ldselect/ldeucom/36/36.pdf>.

____, 'EU Consumer Rights Directive: Getting it Right', 2008–09, retrievable at: <http://www.publications.parliament.uk/pa/ld200809/ldselect/ldeucom/126/12602.htm>.

____, 'Health care across EU borders: a Safe Framework', 2008–09, retrievable at: <http://www.publications.parliament.uk/pa/ld200809/ldselect/ldeucom/30/9780104014356.pdf>.

HUELIN MARTINEZ DE VELASCO, J. (ed.), *Libre circulación de personas en el ámbito comunitario*, Madrid: Consejo General del Poder Judicial, 2007.

JACOBS, F.G., 'Human Rights in the European Union: the Role of the Court of Justice', *E.L. Rev.* 2001, 331–41.

JANS, J., 'Annotatie *Omega*', *SEW* 2005, 185–6.

JANSSENS, C., 'Annotatie *P.I.*', *SEW* 2012, 479–82.

____ and HOORNAERT, L., 'Annotatie *Liga Portuguesa*', *SEW* 2010, 372–9.

JARVIS, M., 'Case Note *Commission v France* and *Greenham and Abel*', *CML Rev.* 2004, 1395–408.

JENNAR, R.M., 'La proposition de directive Bolkestein', *Courrier Hebdomadaire* 2005, 5–68.

JOLIET, R., 'La libre circulation des marchandises: L'arrêt *Keck et Mithouard* et les nouvelles orientations de la jurisprudence', *JT Dr Eur.* 1994, 145–51.

JONSSON, C.-M., 'Comparing the Mutual Recognition Principle and the Country of Origin Principle', 2005, retrievable at: <http://www.epsu.org/IMG/pdf/Mutual_recognition_prin EN.pdf>.

KAPOOR, A. and KLINDT, T., 'Die Reform des Akkreditierungswesens im Europäischen Produktsicherheitsrecht', *EuZW* 2009, 134–8.

KAPPERT, A., 'De verordening Wederzijdse Erkenning verbetert procedure rond handelsbelemmeringen', *Journaal Warenwet* 2010, 7–12.

KAPTEYN, P.J.G., McDONNELL, A.M., MORTELMANS, K.J.M., TIMMERMANS, C.W.A, and GEELHOED, L.A. (eds.), *The Law of the European Union and the European Communities with Reference to Changes Made by the Lisbon Treaty*, Alphen aan den Rijn: Wolters-Kluwer, 2008.

KEESSEN, A.M., *European Administrative Decisions. How the EU Regulates Products on the Internal Market*, Groningen: Europa Law Publishing, 2009.

KERBER, W. and VAN DEN BERGH, R., 'Mutual Recognition: Misunderstandings, Inconsistencies and a Suggested Reinterpretation', *Kyklos* 2008, 447–65.

KHAN, A. and SAP, J.W., 'Sociale zekerheid en gezondheidszorg: zijn de verwachtingen van EU-migranten financieel haalbaar?', *SEW* 2011, 18–28.

KOOPMANS, T., 'The Birth of European Legal Law At the Crossroads of Legal Traditions', *Am. Journal Comp. L.* 1991, 493–507.

____, 'Concurrentie tussen rechtstelsels', *SEW* 1992, 446–50.

KOUTRAKOS, P., 'On Groceries, Alcohol and Olive Oil: more on Free Movement of Goods after *Keck*', *E.L. Rev.* 2001, 391–407.

KOVAR, R., '*Dassonville, Keck* et les autres: de la mesure avant toute chose', *RTD Eur.* 2006, 213–47.

KRAMER, L., MICKLITZ, H.-W., and TONNER, H. (eds.), *Law and Diffuse Interests in the European Legal Order. Liber amicorum Norbert Reich*, Baden-Baden: Nomos, 1997.

KRENN, C., 'A Missing Piece in the Horizontal Effect "Jigsaw": Horizontal Direct Effect and the Free Movement of Goods', *CML Rev.* 2012, 177–215.

KUGELMANN, D., 'Die Dienstleistungs-Richtlinie der EG zwischen der Liberalisierung von Wachstumsmärkten und europäischen Sozialmodell', *EuZW* 2005, 327–31.

KUIPERS, J.J., 'The Right to a Fair Trial and the Free Movement of Civil Judgments', *CYELP* 2010, 23–51.

____, 'Case Note *e-date Advertising GmbH*', *CML Rev.* 2012, 1220–31.

LANGENFELD, C. and ZIMMERMANN, A., 'Interdependenzen zwischen nationalem Verfassungsrecht,EuropäischerMenschenrechtskonventionundEuropäischemGemeinschafts recht', *ZaöRV* 1992, 259–317.

LASOK, D., *The Professions and Services in the European Economic Community*, Deventer: Kluwer, 1986.

LAVENEX, S., 'Mutual Recognition and the Monopoly of Force: Limits of the Single Market Analogy', *JEPP* 2007, 762–79.

LAWSON, R., 'Miscarriage of Justice?', *NTM* 1992, 47–55.

LEGER, P., *Commentaire article par article des traités UE et CE*, Brussels: Bruylant, 2000.

LENAERTS, K., 'Le devoir de loyauté communautaire', in *La Loyauté. Mélanges offerts à Etienne Cerexhe*, VERHOEVEN, J. (ed.), Brussels: Larcier, 1997, 229–47.

____, 'De Europese Unie: doel of middel?', *R.W.* 1998–99, 689–710.

____, 'The Rule of Law and the Coherence of the Judicial System of the European Union', *CML Rev.* 2007, 1625–59.

____, 'Du Rome à Lisbonne, la constitution européenne en marche?', *C.D.E.* 2009, 229–53.

____ and BERNARDEAU, L., 'L'encadrement communautaire de la fiscalité directe', *C.D.E.* 2007, 19–109.

____ and VAN NUFFEL, P., *Europees recht*, Antwerp: Intersentia, 2011.

____ and ____, *European Union Law*, London: Sweet and Maxwell, 2011.

LITTLER, A., 'Regulatory Perspectives on the Future of Interactive Gambling in the Internal Market', *E.L. Rev.* 2008, 211–30.

LOMNICKA, L., 'The Financial Services Single Market and the Interface between Community Law and Domestic Law', in *Continuity and Change in EU Law. Essays in Honour of Sir Francis Jacobs*, ARNULL, A.(ed.), Oxford: Oxford University Press, 2008, 260–83.

LONBAY, J., 'Case Note *Gebhard*', *CML Rev.* 1996, 1073–87.

LÓPEZ ESCUDERO, M., *Los obstáculos técnicos al comercio en la Comunidad Europea*, Granada: Servicio de Publicaciones de la Universidad de Granada, 1991.

____, 'La aplicación del principio del reconocimiento mutuo en el derecho comunitario', *G. J.* 1993, 119–65.

LUCHTMAN, M., *European Cooperation between Financial Supervisory Authorities, Tax Authorities and Judicial Authorities*, Antwerp: Intersentia, 2008.

LUHMANN, N., *Vertrauen. Ein Mechanismus der Reduktion sozialer Komplexität*, Stuttgart: UTB—Lucius and Lucius, 2000.

MAJONE, G., 'Mutual Recognition in Federal Type Systems', EUI Working Papers 1993, 1–22.

____, 'Mutual Trust, Credible Commitments and the Evolution of Rules for a Single European Market', EUI Working Papers 1995, 1–33.

____, *Regulating Europe*, London: Routledge, 1996.

MANKOWSKI, P., 'Wider ein Herkunftslandprinzip für Dienstleistungen im Binnenmarkt', *IPRax* 2004, 385–95.

MARTIN, D., 'Case Note *Arblade*', *Eur. J. Migration and L.* 2000, 104–7.

MASCLET, J.-C., 'Les articles 30, 36 et 100 du traité CEE à la lumière de l'arrêt *Cassis de Dijon*', *RTD. Eur.* 1980, 611–34.

MATHISEN, G., 'Consistency and Coherence as Conditions for Justification of Member State Measures restricting Free Movement', *CML Rev.* 2010, 1021–48.

MATTERA, A., 'L'arrêt *Cassis de Dijon*: une nouvelle approche pour la réalisation et le bon fonctionnement du marché intérieur', *RMC* 1980, 505–18.

____, 'La libre circulation des produits alimentaires à l'intérieur de la communauté et la mise en œuvre du principe de la reconnaissance mutuelle', *European Food Law Review* 1990, 72–90.

____, 'L'article 30 du Traité CEE, la jurisprudence *Cassis de Dijon* et le principe de la reconnaissance mutuelle', *RMC* 1990, 13–71.

____, 'L'élimination des barrières techniques et la mise en œuvre de la reconnaissance mutuelle', *RMC* 1990, 80–92.

____, *Le marché unique européen: ses règles, son fonctionnement*, Paris: Jupiter, 1990.

____, 'Subsidiarité, reconnaissance mutuelle et hiérarchie des normes européennes', *RMUE* 1991, 7–10.

____, 'Les principes de "proportionnalité" et de la "reconnaissance mutuelle" dans la jurisprudence de la Cour en matière de libre circulation des personnes et des services: de l'arrêt *Thieffry* aux arrêts *Vlassopoulou*, *Mediawet* et *Dennemeyer*', *RMUE* 1992, 191–203.

____, 'L'article 30 du traité CEE, la jurisprudence *Cassis de Dijon* et le principe de la reconnaissance mutuelle. Instruments au service d'une Communauté plus respectueuse des diversités nationales', *RMUE* 1992, 13–71.

____, 'De l'arrêt *Dassonville* à l'arrêt *Keck*: l'obscure clarté d'une jurisprudence riche en principes novateurs et en contradictions', *RMUE* 1994, 117–58.

____, 'L'arrêt *Foie Gras* du 22 octobre 1998: porteur d'une nouvelle impulsion pour le perfectionnement du Marché unique européen', *RMUE* 1998, 113–24.

____, 'L'Union européenne assure le respect des identités nationales, régionales et locales, en particulier par l'application et la mise en œuvre du principe de la reconnaissance mutuelle', *RDUE* 2002, 217–39.

____, 'Le marché intérieur: une brèche dans les dures murailles des souverainetés nationales', *CML Rev.* 2002, 519–28.

____, 'La reconnaissance mutuelle: une valeur historique ancienne, un principe juridique intégrationniste, l'assise politique d'un modèle de société humaniste', *RDUE* 2009, 385–418.

____, 'L'harmonisation des législations nationales: un instrument d'intégration et de reconnaissance mutuelle', *RDUE* 2010, 679–727.

MATTHIES, H., 'Zur Anerkennung gleichwertiger Regelungen im Binnenmarkt der EG (Art. 100b EWG-Vertrag)', in *Festschrift für Ernst Steindorff zum 70. Geburtstag am 13. März 1990*, BAUR, J.F. and MAILANDER, K.P. (eds.), Berlin: De Gruyter, 1990, 1287–301.

McGEE, A. and WEATHERILL, S., 'The Evolution of the Single Market, Harmonisation or Liberalisation', *MLR* 1990, 578–603.

McMILLAN, J., 'La "certification", la reconnaissance mutuelle et le marché unique', *RMUE* 1991, 181–211.

MEEUSEN, J., 'System Shopping in European Private International Law in Family Matters', in *International Family law for the European Union*, MEEUSEN, J., PERTEGAS, M., STRAETMANS, G., and SWENNEN, F. (eds.), Antwerp: Intersentia, 2007.

MILLARG, E., 'Anmerkung zum *Cassis*-Urteil', *EuR.* 1979, 420–7.

MONTFORT, J.P., 'L'arrêt *Trichloroethylene* et la libre circulation des produits chimiques: un nouveau défi pour le marché intérieur', *C.D.E.* 2001, 313–40.

MONTI, M., *De interne markt en het Europa van morgen. Een voortgangsverslag van de Europese Commissie*, Luxemburg: Publicatiebureau Europese Gemeenschappen, 1997.

____, *A New Strategy for the Single Market –at the Service of Europe's Economy and Society. Report to the President of the European Commission, José Manuel Barroso*, 2010, retrievable at: <http://ec.europa.eu/bepa/pdf/monti_report_final_10_05_2010_en.pdf>.

MOORE, S., 'Quantitative Restrictions and Measures Having Equivalent Effect: Re-visiting the Limits of Article 30 EEC', *E.L. Rev.* 1994, 195–201.

MORIJN, J., 'Balancing Fundamental Rights and Common Market Freedoms in Union Law: *Schmidberger* and *Omega* in the Light of the European Constitution', *E.L.J.* 2005, 15–40.

MORTELMANS, K.J.M., 'Article 30 of the EEC Treaty and Legislation Relating to Market Circumstances; Time to Consider a New Definition?', *CML Rev.* 1991, 115–36.

____, 'De interne markt en het facettenbeleid na het Keck-arrest: nationaal beleid, vrij verkeer en harmonisatie', *SEW* 1994, 236–50.

____, 'The Relationship between the Treaty Rules and Community Measures for the Establishment and Functioning of the Internal Market—towards a Concordance Rule', *CML Rev.* 2002, 1346–2002.

____, 'Botsende algemene belangen en de werking van de interne markt', *SEW* 2004, 241–8.

____, 'De interne markt en de gezondheidsexcepties', *SEW* 2005, 400–10.

____, 'De *Keck* check', *NTER* 2005, 247–61.

MUIR WATT, H., 'Aspects économiques du droit international privé (réflexions sur l'impact de la globalisation économique sur les fondements des conflits de lois et de juridictions)', *Rec. Cours* 2004, 25–382.

MUÑOZ, R., 'The Development of the Ex-ante Control Mechanism Regarding Implementation of the Internal Market', in *EU Law for the 21st Century: Rethinking the New Legal Order*, TRIDIMAS, T. and NEBBIA, P. (eds.), Oxford: Hart Publishing, 2004, 103–19.

____, 'Le principe de reconnaissance mutuelle et le règlement 764/2008. Chronique d'une future révolution?', *RDUE* 2009, 513–46.

NEVILLE BROWN, L. and KENNEDY, T., *The Court of Justice of the European Communities*, London: Sweet and Maxwell, 2000.

NICOLAÏDIS, K., 'Mutual Recognition of Regulatory Regimes: Some Lessons and Prospects', in *Regulatory Reform and International Market Openness*, Paris: OECD Publications, 1996.

____, 'Managed Mutual Recognition: The New Approach to the Liberalization of Professional Services', in *Liberalization of Trade in Professional Services,* Paris: OECD Publications, 1997.

____, 'Trusting the Poles? Constructing Europe through Mutual Recognition', *JEPP* 2007, 682–98.

____ and SCHMIDT, S., 'Mutual Recognition "on Trial": the Long Road to Services Liberalization', *JEPP* 2007, 717–34.

____ and SHAFFER, G., 'Transnational Mutual Recognition Regimes: Governance without Global Government', *Law and Contem. Probs.* 2004–05, 263–317.

NIELSEN, R., 'Free Movement and Fundamental Rights', *European Labour Law Journal* 2010, 19–32.

O'LEARY, S., 'The ECJ as a Reluctant Constitutional Adjudicator: An Examination of the Abortion Information Case', *E.L. Rev.* 1992, 138–57.

OLIVER, P., 'Some Further Reflections on the Scope of Articles 28–30 (ex 30-36) EC', *CML Rev.* 1999, 783–806.

____and JARVIS, M., *Free Movement of Goods in the European Community under Articles 28 to 30 of the EC Treaty,* London: Sweet and Maxwell, 2003.

____ and ROTH, W.-H., 'The Internal Market and the Four Freedoms', *CML Rev.* 2004, 407–41.

PADOA SCHIOPPA, F.K., (ed.), *The Principle of Mutual Recognition in the European Integration Process*, New York: Palgrave Macmillan, 2005.

____, 'Dominant Losers: a Comment on the Services Directive from an Economic Perspective', *JEPP* 2007, 735–42.

PAPADOPOULOU, *Principes généraux du droit et droit communautaire. Origine et Concrétisation*, Athens: Sakkoulas, 1996.

PELKMANS, J., *European Integration. Methods and Economic Analysis*, London: Pearson, 2006.

____, 'Mutual Recognition in Goods. On Promises and Disillusions', *JEPP* 2007, 699–717.

____, 'Mutual Recognition: Economic and Regulatory Logic in Goods and Services. Bruges European Economic Research Papers 24/2012', 2012, retrievable at: <http://www.coleurope.eu/sites/default/files/research-paper/beer24.pdf>.

——, VOS, E., and DI MAURO, L., 'Reforming Product Regulation in the EU: A Painstaking, Iterative, Two-Level Game', in *Regulatory Reform and Competitiveness in Europe, I. Horizontal Issues*, Cheltenham: Edward Elgar, 2003, 272–81.

PELLEGRINO, P., 'Réflexions autour du principe du pays d'origine', *RDUE* 2010, 550–68.

PERTEK, J., 'The Europe of Universities', *Y.E.L.* 1991, 257–71.

____, *Diplôme et professions en Europe*, Brussels: Bruylant, 2008.

PESCATORE, P., 'Observations critiques sur l'Acte unique européen', in *L'Acte unique européen : journée d'études Bruxelles, 1er mars 1986*, Brussels : Institut d'Etudes Européennes, 1986, 39–66.

PHELAN, D.R., 'Right to Life of The Unborn v. Promotion of Trade in Services: The European Court of Justice and the Normative Shaping of the European Union', *MLR* 1992, 670–89.

PICOD, F., 'L'appréciation de la proportionnalité des restrictions des jeux de hasard. Rien ne va plus à la Cour de Justice?', *La Semaine Juridique.- Edition Générale* 2009, No 46, 12–14.

PIRIS, J.-C., *The Lisbon Treaty. A Legal and Political Analysis*, Cambridge: Cambridge University Press, 2010.

PLANZER, S., '*Liga Portuguesa*—the ECJ and its Mysterious Ways of Reasoning', *E.L.R.* 2009, 368–74.

POIARES MADURO, M., 'The Saga of Article 30 EC Treaty: To Be Continued', *MJ* 1998, 298–317.

____, *We The Court—The European Court of Justice and the European Economic Constitution*, Oxford: Hart Publishing, 1998.

____, 'So Close and Yet So Far: the Paradoxes of Mutual Recognition', *JEPP* 2007, 814–25.

____ and AZOULAI, L. (eds.), *The Past and Future of EU Law. The Classics of EU Law Revisited on the 50th Anniversary of the Rome Treaty*, Oxford: Oxford University Press, 2010.

PRECHAL, S., 'Annotatie *Hedley Lomas*', *SEW* 1998, 67–9.

____, 'Free Movement and Procedural Requirements: Proportionality Reconsidered', *LIEI* 2008, 201–16.

RADAELLI, C., 'The Puzzle of Regulatory Competition', *JPP* 2004, 1–23.

RADEIDEH, M., *Fair Trading in EC Law. Information and Consumer Choice in the Internal Market*, Groningen: Europa law Publishing, 2005.

RAEVENS, B., 'Le règlement 764/2008: vers une consolidation de la reconnaissance mutuelle des produits', *J.D.E.*, 2009, 131–3.

RASMUSSEN, H., *On Law and Policy in the European Court of Justice*, Dordrecht: Martinus Nijhoff, 1986.

REICH, N., 'Competition between Legal Orders: a New Paradigm of EC Law?', *CML Rev.* 1992, 861–96.

____, 'Rechtsprobleme grenzüberschreitender irreführender Werbung im Binnenmarkt', *RabelsZ.* 1992, 491–6.

____, 'The November Revolution of the European Court of Justice: *Keck, Meng* and *Audi* revisited', *CML Rev.* 1994, 459–92.

____, *Understanding EU Law*, Antwerp: Intersentia, 2005.

____, 'Gemeinschaftliche Verkehrsfreiheiten versus Nationales Arbeitskampfrecht', *EuZW* 2007, 391–6.

____, 'AGM-COS.MET or: Who is Protected by EC Safety Regulation', *E.L. Rev.* 2008, 85–100.

____, 'Wie vollständig ist die geplante Vollständige Harmonisierung im Verbrauchersrecht', *EuZW* 2008, 5–6.

RIGAUX, F., 'La diffusion d'informations relatives aux interruptions médicales de grossesse, une liberté économique selon le droit communautaire', *RTDH* 1992, 63–71.

RIVEL, G., 'Le principe de reconnaissance mutuelle dans le marché unique du XXème siècle', *RMCUE* 2007, 518–25.

RODRIGUES, S., 'La proposition de directive relative aux services dans le marché intérieur. Entre mythes et réalité', *Etudes européennes* 2005, retrievable at: <http://www.etudes-europeennes.fr/>.

ROMERO MELCHOR, S., 'La sentencia *Red Bul* de 5 de febrero de 2004: un cambio de orientación jurisprudencial sobre la necesidad de incluir cláusulas de reconocimiento mutuo en las normativas de los Estados miembros?', *U.E.A.* 2004, 13–22.

ROTH, W.-H., 'Case Note *Commission v Germany*', *CML Rev.* 1998, 459–79.

SCHAMMO, P., 'Arbitrage and Abuse of Rights in the EC Legal System', *E.L.J.* 2008, 351–76.

SCHMIDT, S., 'Mutual Recognition as a New Mode of Governance', *JEPP* 2007, 667–81.

SCHORKOPF, F., 'Beweislast im Recht des freien Warenverkehrs. Die erneuerte *Cassis*-Formel als Schnittmenge von Binnenmarktrecht und GATT', *EuR* 2009, 645–59.

SCHRAUWEN, A. (ed.), *Rule of Reason. Rethinking another Classic of European Legal Doctrine*, Groningen: Europa Law Publishing, 2005.

SCHWARZE, J., *Discretionary Powers of the Member States in the Field of Economic Policies and their Limits under the EEC Treaty*, Baden-Baden: Nomos, 1988.

____, *EU-Kommentar*, Baden Baden: Nomos, 2009.

____, GOVAERE, I., HELIN, F., and VAN DEN BOSSCHE, P., *The 1992 Challenge at National Level*, Baden-Baden: Nomos, 1990.

SEIDEL, M., 'Die sogenannte *Cassis de Dijon*-Rechtsprechung des Europäischen Gerichtshofs und der Schutz von Herkunftsabgaben in der Europäischen Gemeinschaft', *G.R.U.R. Int.* 1984, 80–9.

SEMMELMANN, C, 'The European Union's Economic Constitution under the Lisbon Treaty: Soul-Searching Shifts the Focus to Procedure', *E.L. Rev.* 2010, 516–41.

SER, 'Advies 99/10. Oneerlijke handel in de interne markt', retrievable at: <http://www.ser.nl/nl/publicaties/adviezen/1990-1999/1999/b17810.aspx>.

____, 'Advisory Report. The Directive on Services in the Internal Market', 2005, retrievable at: <http://www.ser.nl/~/media/Files/Internet/Talen/Engels/2005/2005_07_volledig%20pdf.ashx>.

____, 'Advies 2004/06. Oneerlijke handelspraktijken op consumententerrein in de EU', retrievable at: <http://www.ser.nl/nl/publicaties/adviezen/2000-2007/2004/b22670.aspx>.

SEVENSTER, H.G., *Eco-imperialisme binnen de Europese Unie; een juridisch probleem?*, Deventer: WEJ Tjeenk Willink, 1998.

SHUIBHNE, N.N., 'The Free Movement of Goods and Article 28 EC: an Evolving Framework', *E.L. Rev.* 2002, 408–25.

____, 'Margins of Appreciation: National Values, Fundamental Rights and EC Free Movement Law', *E.L. Rev.* 2009, 230–56.

SIBONY, A.L. and DEFOSSEZ, A., 'Libre circulation des marchandises (janvier 2007–septembre 2008)', *RTD. Eur.* 2008, 885–925.

____ and DEFOSSEZ, A., 'Marché intérieur (marchandises, capitaux, établissement, services et capitaux)', *RTD Eur.* 2010, 129–58.

SKOURIS, V., 'Fundamental Rights and Fundamental Freedoms: The Challenge of Striking a Delicate Balance', *E.B.L.R.* 2006, 225–39.

——, 'Commentaar op een opmerkelijke brief', *SEW* 1981, 174–84.

____, 'Harmonization', *E.L. Rev.* 1996, 378–97.

____, BARENTS, R., LAWSON, R.A., and MEEUSEN, J., *Inleiding Europees recht*, Groningen: Noordhoff Uitgevers, 2008.

____ and STRAETMANS, G., 'Harmonisatie van wetgeving in de EG', *Tijdschrift Privaat Recht* 2003, 691–837.

SNELL, J., *Goods and Services in EC Law*, Oxford: Oxford University Press, 2002.

____, 'Who's Got the Power? Free Movement and Allocation of Competences in EC Law', *Y.E.L.* 2003, 323–51.

SØNDERGÅRD BIRKMOSE, H., 'A Race to the Bottom in the EU?', *MJ* 2006, 35–80.

____, 'Regulatory Competition and the European Harmonisation Process', *E.B.L.R.* 2006, 1079–97.

SPAVENTA, E., 'On Discrimination and the Theory of Mandatory Requirements', *CYELS* 2000, 457–78.

____, 'From *Gebhard* to *Carpenter*: Towards a (non-) economic European Constitution', *CML Rev.* 2004, 743–73.

____, 'Leaving Keck behind? The Free Movement of Goods after the Rulings in *Commission v Italy* and *Mickelsson and Roos*', *E.L. Rev.* 2009, 914–32.

STEINER, J., 'Drawing the Line: Uses and Abuses of Article 30 EEC', *CML Rev.* 1992, 749–74.

STOFFEL VALLOTON, N., *La prohibición de restricciones a la libre circulación de mercancías en la Comunidad Europea*, Madrid: Dykinson, 2000.

STONE SWEET, A., *The Judicial Construction of Europe*, Oxford: Oxford University Press, 2004.

STRAETMANS, G., 'Case Note *Alpine Investments*', *Col. J. Eur. L.* 1995–96, 154–64.

____, *Consument en markt*, Antwerp: Kluwer, 1998.

____, 'Case Note *Läärä* and *Zenatti*', *CML Rev.* 2000, 991–1005.

____, 'Case Note *Gourmet*', *CML Rev.* 2002, 1407–21.

STUYCK, J., 'L'arrêt *Keck et Mithouard* (vente à perte) et ses conséquences sur la libre circulation des marchandises', *C.D.E.* 1994, 435–58.

____, 'Case Note *De Agostini*', *CML Rev.* 1997, 1445–68.

____, 'Case Note *Bacardi France*', *CML Rev.* 2005, 783–801.

SYKES, A., *Product Standards for Internationally Integrated Goods Markets*, Washington DC: The Brookings Institution, 1995.

SYRPIS, P. (ed.), *The Judiciary, the Legislature and the EU Internal Market*, Cambridge: Cambridge University Press, 2012.

TEGEDER, J., 'Applying the *Cassis De Dijon* Doctrine to Goods Originating in Third Countries', *E.L. Rev.* 1994, 86–94.

TEMPLE LANG, J., 'The Duties of Cooperation of National Authorities and Courts under Article 10 EC: Two More Reflections', *E.L. Rev.* 2001, 84–93.

____, 'The Principle of Legal Cooperation and the Role of the National Judge in Community, Union and EEA Law', *ERA Forum* 2006, 476–501.

TESAURO, G., 'The Community's Internal Market in the Light of the Recent Case Law of the Court of Justice', *Y.E.L.* 1995, 1–16.

TIMMERMAN, P., 'Legislating amidst Public Controversy: the Services Directive', Egmont Paper 32, October 2009, retrievable at: <http://aei.pitt.edu/11870/>.

TISON, M., *De interne markt voor bank- en beleggingsdiensten: een rechtsvergelijkende juridische analyse van de wederzijdse erkenning als techniek van marktunificatie in de Europese interne markt*, Antwerp: Intersentia, 1999.

____, 'De Richtlijn Elektronische Handel en financiële diensten: een brug te ver?', in *Liber amicorum Yvette Merchiers*, Bruges: Die Keure, 2001.

TODINO, M. and LUDER, T., 'La jurisprudence *Keck* en matière de publicité: vers un marché unique inachevé?', *RMUE* 1995, 171–93.

TONER, H., 'Non-Discriminatory Obstacles to the Exercise of Treaty Rights—Articles 39, 43, 49 and 18 EC', *Y.E.L.* 2004, 275–302.

TRACHTMAN, J.P., 'Embedding Mutual Recognition at the WTO', *JEPP* 2007, 780–99.

TRIDIMAS, T., *The General Principles of EU Law*, Oxford: Oxford University Press, 2009.

TROJAN, C.G., TIMMERMANS, C.W.A., BARENTS, R. et al. (eds.), *Ondernemen in Europa. Bedrijfskundige opstellen over de Europese eenwording na 1992*, Zwolle: Tjeenk Willink, 1989.

TRYFONIDOU, A., 'Further Steps on the Road to Convergence among the Market Freedoms', *E.L. Rev.* 2010, 36–56.

USHER, J., 'The Evolution of the Free Movement of Capital', *Fordh. Int. L. J.* 2007–08, 1533–70.

UYEN DO, T., 'La proposition de directive relative aux services dans le marché intérieur... définitivement hors service?', *RDUE* 2006, 111–30.

VAN DAM, C.C., 'De gemiddelde Euroconsument—een pluriform fenomeen over de Richtlijn oneerlijke handelspraktijken en de rechtspraak van het Hof van Justitie', *SEW* 2009, 3–11.

VAN DER ESCH, B., 'De voltooiing van de interne markt voor goederen en diensten volgens art. 8A EEG en het Witboek van 1985. Enkele juridische kanttekeningen', *SEW* 1989, 559–79.

VAN GERVEN, W., 'Les principes de subsidiarité, proportionnalité et coopération en droit communautaire européen', in *Hacia un nuevo orden internacional y europeo. Estudios en homenaje al Profesor Don Manuel Díez de Velasco*, Madrid: Tecnos, 1993, 1281–92.

VAN MARISSING, J., 'Vier rapporten inzake de kwaliteit van EG-regelgeving. Molitor, Koopmans, Deregulation Now en het Rapport Public. Oude wijn in nieuwe zakken?', *SEW* 1996, 124–34.

VAN RAEPENBUSCH, S., *Droit institutionnel de l'Union et des Communautés européennes*, Paris: De Boeck, 1998.

VERHOEVEN, A. and VAN DEN OOSTERKAMP, J.S., 'Naar een betere toepassing van het gemeenschapsrecht. Nieuwe voorstellen van de Europese Commissie', *SEW* 2008, 279–88.

VERLOREN VAN THEMAAT, P., 'La libre circulation des marchandises après l'arrêt *Cassis de Dijon*', *C.D.E.* 1981, 123–35.

VERSCHUEREN, H., 'Sociale zekerheid en detachering binnen de Europese Unie. De zaak *Herbosch Kiere*: een gemiste kans in de strijd tegen grensoverschrijdende sociale dumping en sociale fraude', *B.T.S.Z.* 2006, 403–53.

VIGNES, D., 'The Harmonisation of National Legislation and the EEC', *E.L. Rev.* 1990, 358–75.

____, 'Le rapprochement des législations mérite-t-il encore son nom?', in *L'Europe et le droit. Mélanges en hommage à Jean Boulouis*, Paris: Ed. Dalloz, 1991, 533–46.

VOGEL, D., *Trading up. Consumer and Environmental Regulation in a Global Economy*, Cambridge-Massachusetts: Harvard University Press, 1995.

VON BOGDANDY, A., 'Doctrine of principles', Jean Monnet Program Working Paper 2003, retrievable at: <http://centers.law.nyu.edu/jeanmonnet/archive/papers/03/030901.html>

VON HEYDEBRAND U.D. LASA, H.C., 'Free Movement of Foodstuffs, Consumer Protection and Food Standards in the European Community: Has the Court of Justice Got it Wrong?', *E.L. Rev.* 1991, 391–415.

WAELBROECK, D., 'L'harmonisation des règles et normes techniques dans la CEE', *C.D.E.* 1988, 243–75.

WAGNER, G., 'The Economics of Harmonization: the Case of Contract Law', *CML Rev.* 2002, 995–1023.

WATSON, J.S., 'Wederzijdse erkenning binnen de interne markt: een nieuwe impuls', *NTER* 2000, 41–8.

WEATHERILL, S., 'After Keck: Some Thoughts On how to Clarify the Clarification', *CML Rev.* 1996, 885–906.

____, 'Recent Case law Concerning the Free Movement of Goods: Mapping the Frontiers of Market Deregulation', *CML Rev.* 1999, 51–85.

____, *EU Consumer Law and Policy*, Cheltenham: Edgar Elgar Publishing Limited, 2005.

____, *Cases and Materials on EU Law*, Oxford: Oxford University Press, 2010.

WHITE, E., 'In Search of the Limits to Article 30 of the EEC Treaty', *CML Rev.* 1989, 235–80.

WILS, W., 'The Search for the Rule in Article 30 EEC: Much Ado About Nothing', *E.L. Rev.* 1993, 475–92.
WOODS, L., *Free Movement of Goods and Services within the European Community*, Aldershot: Ashgate, 2004.
WOUTERS, J., *Het Europees vestigingsrecht voor ondernemingen herbekeken. Een onderzoek naar de grondslagen, draagwijdte en begrenzing van de vrijheid van vestiging van ondernemingen in de Europese Unie*, Leuven: Katholieke Universiteit Leuven, Faculteit der Rechtsgeleerdheid, 1996.
____, 'The Community Legislature's Role Regarding the Freedom of Establishment and the Freedom to Provide Services: Theory and Practice', *Euredia* 1999, 241–5.
WYATT, D., 'National Safety Checks on Imported Goods Must not Duplicate Identical Checks in Country of Origin—*Denkavit* Followed', *E.L. Rev.* 1982, 201–4.

PUBLICATIONS RELATED TO JUDICIAL COOPERATION IN CRIMINAL MATTERS (AND THE AREA OF FREEDOM, SECURITY, AND JUSTICE)

ADAM, M., 'Die Wirkung von EU-Rahmenbeschlüssen im mitgliedstaatlichen Recht', *EuZW* 2005, 558–61.
AGUADO, A., ARMATI, S., LAI, M., and MATTERA, P., 'Les dossiers européens: actualités en bref. Espace de liberté, de sécurité et de justice. Le bilan du programme de Tampere et les futures orientations', *RDUE* 2004, 275–7.
AHLBRECHT, H., 'European Supervision Orders: a Matter of Vision', *JECL* 2007, 53–9.
ALBRECHT, P. and BRAUN, S., 'Deficiencies in the Development of European Criminal Law', *E.L.J.* 1999, 293–310.
ALEGRE, S., 'Human Rights and the Future of Extradition in the European Union: Implications of Recent Case Law in the United Kingdom, France and Spain', *ERA Forum* 2004, 63–9.
____ and LEAF, M., *European Arrest Warrant: A Solution Ahead of its Time?*, London: Justice, 2003.
____ and LEAF, M., 'Mutual Recognition in European Judicial Cooperation: A Step Too Far Too Soon? Case Study—the European Arrest Warrant', *E.L.J.* 2004, 200–17.
ALEJANDRO ALVAREZ, E. et al. (eds.), *Mireille Delmas-Marty et les années UMR*, Paris: Société de Législation Comparée, 2005.
ALEXY, R., 'On Balancing and Subsumption. A Structural Comparison', *Ratio Juris* 2003, No 4, 433–49.
ALSTON, P., *The EU and Human Rights*, Oxford: Oxford University Press, 1999.
ÁLVAREZ GARCÍA, F.J., *La adecuación del derecho penal español al ordenamiento de la Unión Europea. La política criminal europea*, Valencia: tirant lo blanch, 2009.
ÁLVAREZ GONZÁLEZ, S., 'Orden público y reconocimiento de resoluciones extranjeras: límites a la valoración del juez nacional y orden publico comunitario', *La Ley* 2000, No 5, 2005–09.
AMBOS, K., 'Is the Development of a Common Substantive Criminal Law for Europe possible? Some Preliminary Reflections', *MJ* 2005, 173–91.
ANDERSON, M. and APAP, J., *Striking a Balance between Freedom, Security and Justice in an Enlarged European Union*, Brussels: CEPS, 2002.
APAP, J. (ed.), *Justice and Home affairs in the EU. Liberty and Security Issues after Enlargement*, Northampton: Edward Elgar Publishing, 2004.
____ and CARRERA, S., 'Judicial Cooperation in Criminal Matters. European Arrest Warrant. A Good Testing case for Mutual Recognition in the Enlarged EU?', *CEPS* Policy Brief No 46, 2004, retrievable at: <http://www.ceps.be>.
____ and CARRERA, S., 'Progress and Obstacles in the Area of Justice and Home Affairs in an Enlarged European Union', CEPS Working Paper 2004, available at: <http://www.ceps.be>.

ARANGUENA FANEGO, C. (ed.), *Cooperación Judicial Penal en la Unión Europea: La Orden Europea de Detención y Entrega*, Valladolid: Lex Nova, 2005.

____, 'La situación actual de la orden europea de detención y entrega: dificultades y progresos de su aplicación en el espacio judicial europeo', *R.D.P.* 2007, 11–87.

____ (ed.), *Procedural Safeguards in Criminal Proceedings throughout the European Union*, Valladolid: Lex Nova, 2007.

ARROYO ZAPATERO, L. and NIETO MARTÍN, A. (eds.), *La orden de detención y entrega europea*, Cuenca: Ediciones de la Universidad de Castilla-La Mancha, 2006.

____ and NIETO MARTÍN, A. (eds.), *El derecho penal de la Unión Europea. Situación actual y perspectivas de futuro*, Cuenca: Ediciones de la Universidad de Castilla-La Mancha, 2007.

ASP, P., 'Harmonisation and Cooperation within the Third Pillar—Built in Risks', *CYELS* 2001, 15–23.

____, 'Basic Models of a European Penal Law: Mutual Recognition, Cooperation, Harmonisation', in *4th European Jurists' Forum*, Vienna: Mansche Verlags- und Universität sbuchhandlung, 2008, 256–73.

____ and VON HIRSH, A., 'Double Criminality and Transnational Investigative Measures in EU Criminal Proceedings: Some Issues of Principle', *Zeitschrift für Internationale Strafrechtsdogmatik* 2006, 512–20.

AZARIA, D., 'Part II. Minimum Standards—Protecting Individuals Involved in Transnational Criminal Proceedings', in *Extradition. European Standards. Explanatory Notes on the Council of Europe Convention and Protocols and Minimum Standards Protecting Persons subject to Transnational Criminal Proceedings*, Strasbourg: Council of Europe, 2006, retrievable at: <http://www.coe.int/t/dghl/standardsetting/pc-oc/978-92-8716076-8.pdf>.

BACIGALUPO, E., 'Bemerkungen zu strafrechtlichen Fragen des Verfassungsentwurfs', *ZStW* 2004, 326–31.

BAJO FERNÁNDEZ, M., BACIGALUPO, S. and GÓMEZ-JARA DÍEZ, C. (eds.), *Constitución europea y derecho penal económico. Mesas redondas derecho y economía*, Madrid: Centro de estudios Ramón Areces, 2006.

BAKER, E., 'Taking European Criminal Law Seriously', *C.L.R.* 1998, 361–80.

____, 'Criminal Jurisdiction, the Public Dimension to "Effective Protection" and the Construction of Community-Citizen Relations', *CYELS* 2001, 25–46.

____ and HARDING, C., 'From Past Imperfect to Future Perfect? A Longitudinal Study on the Third Pillar', *E.L. Rev.* 2009, 25–55.

BANTEKAS, I., 'The Principle of Mutual Recognition in EU Criminal Law', *E.L. Rev.* 2007, 365–85.

BARBE, E., *Justice et affaires intérieures dans l'Union européenne. Un espace de liberté, de sécurité et de justice*, Paris: La documentation française, 2002.

BARENTS, R., 'Annotatie *Pupino*', *SEW* 2006, 75–8.

____, 'De denationalisering van het strafrecht', *SEW* 2006, 358–74.

BATTJES, H., BROUWER, E., DE MORREE, P., and OUWERKERK, J., *The Principle of Mutual Trust in European Asylum, Migration and Criminal Law. Reconciling Trust and Fundamental Rights*, Utrecht: Forum, 2011.

BEAUVAIS, P., 'Droit pénal de l'Union européenne', *RTD Eur.* 2010, 721–43.

BEKAERT, P., 'Europees aanhoudingsbevel is knoeiwerk op alle niveaus', *De Juristenkrant* 2005, No. 117, 3.

BELFIORI, R., 'Movement of Evidence in the EU: The Present Scenario and Possible Future Developments', *Eur. Journ. Crime Cr.L.Cr.J.* 2009, 1–22.

BERNARDI, A., 'Europe sans frontières et droit pénal', *Rev. Sc. Crim.*, 2002, 1–13.

BIEBER, R. and MONAR, J. (eds.), *Justice and Home Affairs in the European Union: the Development of the Third Pillar*, Brussels: European University Press, 1995.

BLACKSTOCK, J., 'Briefing on the European Investigation Order for Council and Parliament. Partial General Approach', July 2011, retrievable at: <http://www.statewatch.org/news/2010/aug/eu-justice-briefing-eio.pdf>.

BLEXTOON, R., 'Haastige spoed is zelden goed (of het Europees aanhoudingsbevel "EAB")', *NTER* 2004, 23–9.

____ and VAN BALLEGOOIJ (eds.), *Handbook on the European Arrest Warrant*, The Hague: TMC Asser Press, 2005.

BOERWINKEL, A.M.C. and VAN DER GRINTEN, P.M.M., 'Wederzijdse erkenning van rechterlijke beslissingen', *Justitiële verkenningen* 2004, 51–65.

BÖHM, K.M., 'Das Europäische Haftbefehlsgesetz und seine rechtsstaatlichen Mängel', *Neue Juristische Wochenschrift* 2005, 2588–90.

BONN, M., 'Tendency and Trends in European Criminal Policy', in *4th European Jurists' Forum*, Vienna: Mansche Verlags- und Universitätsbuchhandlung, 2008, 243–56.

BORGERS, M., 'De implementatie van het Europese bevriezingsbevel en de systematiek van rechtsbescherming en rechtseenheid', *NJb* 2005, 1455–9.

____, 'Mutual Recognition and the European Court of Justice: The Meaning of Consistent Interpretation and Autonomous and Uniform Interpretation of Union Law for the Development of the Principle of Mutual Recognition in Criminal Matters', *Eur. Journ. Crime Cr.L. Cr.J.* 2010, 99–114.

BOSCH, M.K.M., 'De flagrante schending van artikel 6 EVRM anno 2010', *DD* 2010, 716–41.

BÖSE, M., 'Das Prinzip der gegenseitigen Anerkennung in der transnationalen Strafrechtspflege in der EU', in *Fragmentarisches Strafrecht*, MOMSEN, C., BLOY, R., and RACKOW, P. (eds.), Frankfurt am Main: Peter Lang, 2003, 233–50.

BOYTHA, D., 'La libre circulation des jugements dans l'espace judiciaire européen en matière civile et commerciale', *RDUE* 2006, 619–33.

BRAMMER, S., 'Case Note *Bourquain*', *CML Rev.* 2009, 1685–96.

BRANTS, C., 'Het Tampere principe van wederzijdse erkenning: problemen van strafrechtelijke rechtsbescherming in de Europese Unie', in *Het plezier van de rechtsvergelijking*, BOELE-WOELKI, K., BRANTS, C.H., and STEENHOFF, G.J.W.(eds.), Deventer: Kluwer, 2003, 103–22.

BRAUM, S. and WEYEMBERGH, A. (eds.), *Le contrôle juridictionnel dans l'espace pénal européen*, Brussels: IEE, 2009.

BRIBOSIA, H., 'Liberté, sécurité et justice: l'imbroglio d'un nouvel espace', *RMUE* 1998, 27–53.

BURUMA, Y., 'Federaal Europa en het strafrecht', *DD* 2002, 657–72.

____, 'Radikale Toleranz. Auf dem Weg zu einem zweidimensionalen Raum der Freiheit, der Sicherheit und des Rechts', *ZStW* 2004, 424–35.

CALAZA LÓPEZ, S., *El procedimiento europeo de detención y entrega*, Madrid: Iustel, 2005.

CALDERONI, F., 'A Definition that Could not Work: the EU Framework Decision on the Fight against Organised Crime', *Eur. Journ. Crime Cr.L. Cr.J.* 2008, 265–82.

CALLEWAERT, J. 'Het EVRM en de Europese Unie: van Bosphorus naar Lissabon', *NTER* 2010, 101–7.

CARBALLO PIÑEIRO, L., 'Orden jurídico comunitario, derechos fundamentales e interpretación del artículo 27.1 del Convenio de Bruselas', *La Ley* 2000, No 3, 1748–53.

CHALTIEL, F., 'Une nouvelle avancée de l'idée de souveraineté européenne: la souveraineté pénale en devenir', *RMCUE* 2006, 24–8.

CHIAVARO, M and MOORE, A., *Police and Judicial Co-operation in the EU. FIDE 2004 National Reports*, Cambridge: Cambridge University Press, 2004.

CHRISTOU, T. A. (ed.), *European Cross Border Justice: A Case Study of the EAW*, London: The Aire Centre, 2010.

CORSTENS, G.J.M, 'Het einde van het nationale strafrecht?', *NJb* 2003, 1429–30.

____, *Europeanisering van het Nederlands recht*, Deventer: Kluwer, 2004.

____, 'Europeanisering van het strafrecht en de steun van de bevolking', in *De wet voorbij. Liber amicorum Luc Huybrechts*, DERUYCK, F., DE SWAEF, M., ROZIE, J., ROZIE, M., TRAEST, P., and VERSTRAETEN, R. (eds.), Antwerp: Intersentia, 2010, 21–32.

CORTHAUT, T., 'Plus ça change, plus ç'est la même chose? A comparison with the Constitutional Treaty', *MJ* 2009, 21–34.

CRAMER, P., 'Reflections on the Roles of Mutual Trust in EU Law', in *50 Years of the European Treaties. Looking back and Thinking Forward*, Oxford: Hart Publishing, 2009, 43–61.

CULLEN, P. (ed.), *Dealing with European Evidence in Criminal Proceedings: National Practice and European Union Policy*, Trier: ERA, 2005.

____ and JUND, S., *Criminal Justice Cooperation in the European Union after Tampere*, Trier: ERA, 2002.

CUNIBERTI, G., 'The Recognition of Foreign Judgments Lacking Reasons in Europe: Access to Justice, Foreign Court Avoidance, and Efficiency', *ICLQ* 2008, 25–52.

CURTIN, D., 'Case Note *Grogan*', *CML Rev.* 1992, 583–603.

____ and POUW, J.F.M., 'La coopération dans le domaine de la justice et des affaires intérieures au sein de l'Union européenne: une nostalgie d'avant Maastricht?', *RMUE* 1995, 13–34.

____, SMITS, J.M., KLIP, A., and McCAHERY, J.A., *European Integration and Law*, Antwerp: Intersentia, 2006.

DAVIDSON, R., 'A Sledgehammer to Crack a Nut? Should there be a Bar of Triviality in European Arrest Warrant Cases?', *C.L.R.* 2009, 31–6.

DE BAERE, G., 'N.S. v. Secretary of State for the Home Department', *American Journal of International Law* 2012, 616–24.

DE BIOLLEY, S. and WEYEMBERGH, A., 'Chronique de jurisprudence consacrée à l'espace de liberté, de sécurité et de justice. Jurisprudence de la Cour de Justice relative au 3ème pilier du traité sur l'UE (2006–2009)', *C.D.E.* 2010, 165–210.

DEEN-RACSMÁNY, Z. and BLEXTOON, R., 'The Decline of the Nationality Exception in European Extradition?', *Eur. Journ. Crime Cr.L.Cr.J.* 2005, 317–63.

____ and BLEXTOON, R., 'The European Arrest Warrant and the Surrender of Nationals Revisited: The Lessons of Constitutional Challenges', *Eur. Journ. Crime Cr.L.Cr.J.* 2006, 271–306.

DE HERT, P., 'Het einde van de Europese rechtshulp', *Justitiële verkenningen* 2004, 96–116.

____, WEIS, K. and CLOOSEN, N., 'The Framework Decision of 18 December 2008 on the EEW for the Purpose of obtaining Objects, Documents and Data for Use in Proceedings in Criminal Matters—A Critical Assessment', *NJECL* 2009, 55–78.

DE HOYOS SANCHO, M., 'El principio de reconocimiento mutuo de resoluciones penales en la Unión europea: "asimilación automática o coresponsabilidad?"', *RDCE* 2005, 807–42.

____ (ed.), *Criminal proceedings in the European Union: essential safeguards—El proceso penal en la Unión Europea: garantías esenciales*, Valladolid: Lex Nova, 2008.

DEITERS, M., 'Gegenseitige Anerkennung von Strafgesetzen in Europa', *ZRP* 2003, 359–62.

DE KERCHOVE, G. and WEYEMBERGH, A. (eds.), *Vers un espace judiciaire pénal européen*, Brussels: IEE, 2000.

____ and —— (eds.), *La reconnaissance mutuelle des décisions judiciaires pénales dans l'Union européenne*, Brussels: IEE, 2001.

____ and ——, (eds.), *L'espace pénal européen: enjeux et perspectives*, Brussels: IEE, 2002.

____ and ——, (eds.), *Quelle réforme pour l'espace pénal européen?*, Brussels: IEE, 2003.

____ and ——, (eds.), *Sécurité et justice: enjeu de la politique extérieure de l'Union européenne*, Brussels: IEE, 2003.

____ and ——, (eds.), *La confiance mutuelle dans l'espace pénal européen/Mutual trust in the European Criminal Area*, Brussels: IEE, 2005.

DE LA CUESTA, J.-L., 'Concurrent National and International Criminal Jurisdiction and the Principle *ne bis in idem*. General Report', *IRPL* 2002, 707–36.

DE LA OLIVA SANTOS, A., ARMENTA DEU, T., and CALDERON CUADRADO, M.P. (eds.), *Garantías fundamentales del proceso penal en el espacio judicial europeo*, Madrid: Colex, 2007.

DELGADO, L., 'Droits fondamentaux et reconnaissance mutuelle: une jurisprudence troublante ou simplement prudente?', February 2013, retrievable at: <http://www.gdr-elsj.eu/>.

DELMAS-MARTY, M. (ed.), *Quelle politique pénale pour l'Europe*, Paris: Economia, 1993.

____ (ed.), *Procédures pénales d'Europe*, Paris: Presses universitaires de France, 1995.

____ (ed.), *The Criminal Process and Human Rights*, Dordrecht: Martinus Nijhoff Publishers, 1995.

____, 'The European Union and Penal Law', *E.L.J.* 1998, 87–115.

____ (ed.), *Corpus Juris houdende strafbepalingen ter bescherming van de financiële belangen van de Europese Unie*, Antwerp: Intersentia, 1998.

____ (ed.), *L'harmonisation des sanctions pénales en Europe*, Paris: Société de législation comparée, 2003.

____, PIETH, M., and SIEBER, U (eds.), *Los caminos de la armonización penal*, Valencia: tirant lo blanch, 2009.

DEL POZO PÉREZ, M., 'La orden europea de detención y entrega: un avance en el principio de reconocimiento mutuo de resoluciones judiciales entre los Estados de la Unión Europea', *La Ley* 2005, No 1, 1551–68.

DEN BOER, M. (ed.), *Schengen's Final Days? The incorporation of Schengen into the new TEU, External Borders and Information Systems*, Maastricht: European Institute of Public Administration, 1998.

____, 'Crime and the Constitution: a Brief Chronology of Choices and Circumventions', *MJ* 2004, 143–58.

DEN HEIJER, M., 'Case Note *N.S. and M.E.*', *CML Rev.* 2012, 1735–53.

DENZA, E., *The Intergovernmental Pillars of the European Union*, Oxford: Oxford University Press, 2002.

____, 'The 2000 Convention on mutual assistance in criminal matters', *CML Rev.* 2003, 1047–74.

DESCAMPS, M.-H., ' La reconnaissance mutuelle des décisions judiciaires pénales', *Actualités de droit pénal européen* 2003, 85–109.

DE SCHUTTER, 'The Two Europes of Human Rights: the Emerging Division of Tasks between the Council of Europe and the European Union in Promoting Human Rights in Europe', *Col. J. Eur. L.* 2008, 509–61.

DE WITTE, B., 'Setting the Scene: How did Services get to Bolkestein and Why', EUI Working Paper Law 2007, retrievable at: <http://cadmus.iue.it/dspace/bitstream/1814/6929/1/LAW_2007_20.pdf>.

____, 'The European Judiciary after Lisbon', *MJ* 2008, 43–54.

DE ZWAAN, J.W. and BULTENA, A.J., *Ruimte van vrijheid, veiligheid en rechtvaardigheid*, The Hague: Sdu, 2002.

____ and GOUDAPPEL, F.A.N.J., *Freedom, Security and Justice in the European Union. Implementation of the Hague Programme*, The Hague: TMC Asser Press, 2006.

DONNELLY, B., 'Justice and Home Affairs in the Lisbon Treaty: A Constitutionalising Clarification?', *Eipascope* 2008, 19–23.

DOUGLAS-SCOTT, S., 'The Rule of Law in the European Union—Putting the Security into the Area of Freedom, Security and Justice', *E.L. Rev.* 2004, 219–42.

____, 'A Tale of Two Courts: Luxembourg, Strasbourg and the Growing European Human Rights Acquis', *CML.Rev.* 2006, 629–65.

DUNKEL, F., PADFIELD, N., and VAN ZYL SMIT, D., *Release from Prison: European Policy and Practice*, Cullompton: Wilan Publishing, 2010.

DUTHEIL DE LA ROCHERE, J., 'La Charte des droits fondamentaux de l'Union européenne', *RMCUE* 2000, 674–80.

DUTTA, A., 'Die Pflicht der Mitgliedstaaten zur gegenseitigen Durchsetzung ihrer öffentlich-rechtlichen Forderungen', *EuR* 2007, 744–67.

ECKES, C. and KONSTADINIDES, T. (eds.), *Crime within the Area of Freedom, Security and Justice. A European Public Order*, Cambridge: Cambridge University Press, 2011.

ELHOLM, T., 'Does EU Criminal Cooperation Necessarily Mean Increased Repression?', *Eur. Journ. Crime Cr.L.Cr.J.* 2009, 191–226.

ELSEN, C., 'L'esprit et les ambitions de Tampere. Une ère nouvelle pour la coopération dans le domaine de la justice et des affaires intérieures?', *RMCUE* 1999, 659–63.

____, 'From Maastricht to The Hague: the Politics of Judicial and Police Cooperation', *ERA Forum* 2007, 13–26.

EPP, H., 'Eurowarrant: European Extradition in the 21st Century. Overcoming Constitutional Barriers—The Public Law Challenges for the EAW in National Constitutional Courts', 2003, retrievable at: <http://www.justice.org.uk/images/pdfs/eurepp.pdf>.

ESER, A., 'Entwicklung des Strafverfahrensrechts in Europa. Orientierung an polizeilicher Effektivität oder an rechtsstaatlichen Grundsätzen?' *ZStW* 1996, 86–127.

____, 'Rahmenbedingungen des Europäischen Union für das Strafverfahrensrecht in Europa', *ZeuS* 2004, 289–312.

FAHEY, E., 'How to be a Third Pillar Guardian of Fundamental Rights? The Irish Supreme Court and the European Arrest Warrant', *E. L. Rev.* 2008, 563–76.

FENNELL, P., HARDING, C., JORG, N., and SWART, B. (eds.), *Criminal Justice in Europe. A Comparative Study*, Oxford: Clarendon Press, 1995.

FENNELLY, N., 'The Area of "Freedom, Security and Justice" and the European Court of Justice. A personal view', *ICLQ* 2000, 1–14.

FICHERA, M., 'The European Arrest Warrant and the Sovereign State: A Marriage of Convenience?', *E.L.J.* 2009, 70–97.

____, *The Implementation of the European Arrest Warrant in the European Union: law, policy and practice*, Antwerp: Intersentia, 2011.

____ and JANSSENS, C., 'Mutual Recognition of Judicial Decisions in Criminal Matters and the Role of the National Judge', *ERA Forum* 2007, 177–202.

FIJNAUT, C., 'Strafrecht in de Europese Unie: een grote sprong voorwaarts of slechts een klein stapje?', *SEW* 2004, 202–11.

____, 'Een Copernicaanse revolutie in de Europese Unie', *NJb* 2008, 335–6.

____ and OUWERKERK, J., *The Future of Police and Judicial Cooperation in the European Union*, Leiden: Martinus Nijhoff Publishers, 2010.

FLETCHER, M., 'Some Developments to the *ne bis in idem* Principle in the European Union: Criminal Proceedings against *Hüseyn Gözütok and Klaus Brügge*', *MLR* 2003, 769–80.

____, 'The Problem of Multiple Criminal Prosecutions: Building an Effective EU Response', *Y.E.L.* 2007 33–56.

____, LOOF, R., and GILMORE, B., *EU Criminal Law and Justice*, Cheltenham: Edward Elgar, 2008.

FLORE, D., 'Une justice pénale après Amsterdam', *JT Dr Eur.* 1999, 121–9.

____, 'Le mandat d'arrêt européen: première mise en œuvre d'un nouveau paradigme de la justice pénale européenne', *JT Dr Eur.* 2002, 273–81.

____, 'Des organes juridictionnelles en matière pénale pour l'Union européenne', *C.D.E.* 2006, 597–637.

____, *Droit pénal européen. Les enjeux d'une justice pénale européenne*, Brussels: Larcier, 2009.

____, BOSLY, S., BRULIN, H., CLAISSE, S., de BIOLLEY, S., DESCAMPS, M.-H., JAMART, J.-S., and VAN RAVENSTEIN, M., *Actualités de droit pénal européen*, Brussels: la charte, 2003.

____, ____, HONHON, A., MAGGIO, J. (eds.), *Probation measures and alternative sanctions in the European Union*, Antwerp: Intersentia, 2012.

FONSECA MORILLO, F.J., 'La orden de detención y entrega europea', *RDCE* 2003, 69–95.

FRANCE, R. and DASSONVILLE, L., 'Les acteurs de l'espace européen de liberté, de sécurité et de justice', *JT. Dr Eur.* 2006, 65–73.

FRANSSEN, V., 'Het Europees aanhoudingsbevel gered, hoera?', *R. W.* 2008, 1138–44.

FUCHS, H., 'Bemerkungen zur gegenseitigen Anerkennung justizieller Entscheidungen', *ZStW* 2004, 368–71.

____, 'Auf dem Weg zu einem Europäischen Strafrecht: Generalbericht', in *4th European Jurists' Forum*, Vienna: Mansche Verlags- und Universitätsbuchhandlung, 2008, 317–25.

GARCIA-JOURDAN, S., *L'émergence d'un espace de liberté, de sécurité et de justice*, Brussels: Bruylant, 2005.

GENDERS, E. 'Legitimacy, Accountability and Private Prisons', *Punishment and Society* 2002, No 4, 285–303.

GEYER, F., 'European Arrest Warrant. Court of Justice, Judgment of 3 May 2007, *Advocaten voor de Wereld*', *EuConst*, 2008, 149–61.

GIBBINS, B., 'The European Arrest Warrant—Championship Contender?', *ERA Forum* 2003, 38–46.

GILMORE, B., 'The Twin Towers and the Third Pillar: Some Security Agenda Developments', EUI Working Paper Law 2003, retrievable at: <http://cadmus.iue.it/dspace/bitstream/1814/202/1/law03-7.pdf>.

GIUDICELLI-DELAGE, G. and MANACORDA, S., *L'intégration pénale indirecte. Interactions entre droit pénal et coopération judiciaire au sein de l'Union européenne*, Paris: Société de législation comparée, 2005.

GLERUM, V. and ROZEMOND, K., 'Overlevering van Nederlanders: copernicaanse revolutie of uitlevering in overgang?', *DD* 2008, 816–48.

____ and ——, 'Het *Wolzenburg* arrest, de interpretatie van het Kaderbesluit betreffende het EAB en de gevolgen voor de Nederlandse overleveringspraktijk', *DD* 2010, 271–302.

GLESZ, S., 'Zum Prinzip der gegenseitigen Anerkennung', *ZStW* 2004, 353–67.

____, 'Eine akademische Kritik des "EU-Acquis" zur grenzüberschreitende Beweissammlung', *ERA Forum: Special Issue on European Evidence* 2005, 42–52.

GÓMEZ-JARA DÍEZ, C., 'European Arrest Warrant and the Principle of Mutual Recognition', *Eucrim* 2006, 23–5.

GONZÁLEZ GONZÁLEZ, R., 'Límites a la construcción de un "orden público europeo" en materia de derechos fundamentales', *RDCE* 2000, 593–617.

GRIEF, N., 'EU Law and Security', *E.L. Rev.* 2007, 752–65.

GRIJPINK, J., 'Criminal Records in the European Union. The Challenge of Large-scale Information Exchange', *Eur. J. Crime Cr.L.Cr.J.* 2006, 1–19.

GRIMM, D., 'Comments on the German Constitutional Court's Decision on the Lisbon Treaty. Defending Sovereign Statehood against Transforming the European Union into a State', *EuConst* 2009, 365–7.

____, *Souveränität. Herkunft und Zukunft eines Schlüsselbegriffs*, Berlin: Berlin University Press, 2009.

GRÖNING, L., 'A Criminal Justice System or a System Deficit? Notes on the System Structure of the EU Criminal Law', *Eur. Journ. Crime Cr.L.Cr.J.* 2010, 115–37.

GUILD, E., 'Crime and the EU's Constitutional Future in an Area of Freedom, Security and Justice', *E.L.J.* 2004, 218–35.

____, *Constitutional Challenges to the European Arrest Warrant*, Nijmegen: Wolf Legal Publishers, 2006.

____ and CARRERA, S., 'No Constitutional Treaty? Implications for the Area of Freedom, Security and Justice', CEPS Working Document 2005, retrievable at: <http://aei.pitt.edu/ 6675/>.

____, ____, and FAURE ATGER, A., 'Challenges and Prospects for the EU's Area of Freedom, Security and Justice: Recommendations to the European Commission for the Stockholm Programme', CEPS Working document 2009, retrievable at <http://aei.pitt.edu/10762/>.

____ and GEYER, F., 'Getting Local: Schengen, Prüm and the Dancing Procession of Echternach. Three Paces Forward and Two Back for EU Police and Judicial Cooperation in Criminal Matters', *JECL* 2006, 61–6.

____ and —— (eds.), *Security versus Justice? Police and Judicial Cooperation in the European Union*, Hampshire: Ashgate, 2008.

GUZMÁN ZAPATER, M., 'Un elemento federalizador para Europa: el reconocimiento mutuo en el ámbito del reconocimiento de decisiones judiciales', *RDCE* 2001, 405–38.

HATZOPOULOS, V., 'With or Without You... Judging Politically in the Field of Area of Freedom, Security and Justice', *E.L. Rev.* 2008, 44–65.

____, 'The Third Wave of Third Pillar Law', *E.L. Rev.* 2009, 523–60.

HEARD, C. and MANSELL, D., 'The European Investigation Order: Changing the face of Evidence-gathering in EU Cross-border Cases', retrievable at: <http://www.google.be/url?sa=t&rct=j&q=&esrc=s&frm=1&source=web&cd=1&ved=0CCwQFjAA&url=http%3A%2F%2Fwww.fairtrials.net%2Fdocuments%2FNJECL_article_on_EIO.pdf&ei=buStUeCfMOnQ0QXhuIGwDg&usg=AFQjCNErttvXlyANBbbGcyyo4SCzTO6OuA&sig2=GgHCxwMrKZxxUQ2qucQfEQ&bvm=bv.47244034,d.d2k>.

HERLIN-KARNELL, E., 'Waiting for Lisbon... Constitutional Reflections on the Embryonic General Part of EU Criminal Law', *Eur. Journ. Crime Cr.L.Cr.J.* 2009, 227–42.

____, 'What Principles Drive (or Should Drive) European Criminal Law?', *German Law Journal* 2010, 1115–29.

____, 'European Arrest Warrant Cases and the Principles of Non-discrimination and EU Citizenship', *MLR* 2010, 824–35.

HIJMANS, H., 'De derde pijler in de praktijk: leven met gebreken. Over de uitwisseling van informatie tussen de lidstaten', *SEW* 2006, 375–91.

HILDEBRANDT, M., 'European Criminal law and European Identity', *Criminal Law and Philosophy* 2007, 57–78.

HINAREJOS, A., 'The Lisbon Treaty versus Standing Still: A View from the Third Pillar', *Eu Const* 2009, 99–116.

HOET, P., 'Ne bis in idem—nationaal en internationaal. De rechtspraak van het Hof van Justitie en van het Hof van de Rechten van de Mens getoetst aan de nationale rechtspraak', *CABG* 2008, 1–81.

HUSABO, E.J. and STRANDBAKKEN, A., *Harmonization of Criminal Law in Europe*, Antwerp: Intersentia, 2005.

IMPALA, F., 'The European Arrest Warrant in the Italian Legal System. Between Mutual Recognition and Mutual Fear within the European Area of Freedom, Security and Justice', *Utrecht Law Review* 2005, 56–78.

JACKSON, J.D., 'The Effect of Human Rights on Criminal Evidentiary Process: Towards Convergence, Divergence or Realignment?', *MLR* 2005, 737–64.

JACOBS, J.B. and BLITSA, D., 'Sharing Criminal Records: The United States, the European Union and Interpol Compared', *Loy. L.A. Int'l and Comp. L. Rev.* 2008, 125–214.

____ and ——, 'Major "Minor" Progress under the Third Pillar: EU Institutions Building in the Sharing of Criminal Record Information', retrievable at: <http://www.kentlaw.edu/jicl/articles/spring2008/jacobs_major_progress_2008.pdf>.

JANSSENS, C., 'Het Europees aanhoudingsbevel onder vuur: hebben de nationale (grondwettelijke) hoven het laatste woord?', *R.W.* 2006–07, 415–18.

____, 'De burger, de Unie en het Europees aanhoudingsbevel: op zoek naar het juiste evenwicht tussen vrijheid, veiligheid en rechtvaardigheid' in: *Politiële en justitiële strafrechtelijke samenwerking in de Europese Unie: welk evenwicht tussen vrijheid, veiligheid en rechtvaardigheid?*, MEEUSEN, J. and STRAETMANS, G. (eds.), Antwerp: Intersentia, 2007, 1–77.

____, 'Case Note *Advocaten voor de Wereld*', *Col. J. Eur. L.* 2007–08, 169–87.

____, 'Conferentieverslag: Mutual recognition of judicial decisions in criminal matters and the role of the national judge (Third Annual Forum)', *Panopticon* 2009, 72–4.

____, 'Europees strafrecht en het Verdrag van Lissabon: een verhaal van déjà vu's, dwarsliggers en compromissen', *Nullum Crimen* 2009, 14–28.

____, 'Case Note *Wolzenburg*', *CML Rev.* 2010, 831–43.

____, 'Annotatie *Magatte Gueye and Valentín Salmerón Sánchez*', *SEW* 2012, 159–63.

JAULT-SESEKE, F., LELIER, J., and PIGACHE, C. (eds.), *L'espace judiciaire européen civil et pénal: regards croisés*, Paris: Dalloz, 2009.

JEGOUZO, I., 'Le mandat d'arrêt européen: premiers pas d'un espace judiciaire européen en matière pénale', *R.A.E.* 2003–04, 347–59.

____, 'Le mandat d'arrêt européen ou la première concrétisation de l'espace judiciaire européen', *Gazette du Palais* 2004, 2311–13.

JIMENO-BULNES, M., 'After September 11th: the Fight against Terrorism in National and European Law. Substantive and Procedural Rules: Some Examples', *E.L.J.* 2004, 235–53.

____, *La cooperación judicial civil y penal en el ámbito de la Unión Europeo: instrumentos procesales*, Burgos: Bosch, 2007.

____, 'The Enforcement of the European Arrest Warrant: a Comparison between Spain and the UK', *Eur. Journ. Crime Cr.L.Cr.J.* 2007, 263–307.

KADRIC, M. and SCHEIBER, O., 'Ausgangspunkt Tampere: Unterwegs zum europäischen Strafprozess. Gedanken zum Vorschlag der Kommission für einen Rahmenbeschluss über bestimmte Verfahrensrechte in Strafverfahren innerhalb der Europäischen Union', *Juridikum* 2004, 207.

KAIAFA-GBANDI, M., 'The Development towards Harmonization within Criminal Law in the European Union – a Citizen's Perspective', *Eur. Journ. Crime Cr.L.Cr.J.* 2001, 239–63.

____, 'The Treaty Establishing a Constitution for Europe and Challenges for Criminal Law at the Commencement of 21st Century', *Eur. Journ. Crime Cr.L.Cr.J.* 2005, 483–514.

____, 'Gemeinsame Grundsätze des Strafprozessrechts als Basis einer grenzüberschreitenden Strafverfolgung', in *4th European Jurists' Forum*, Vienna: Mansche Verlags- und Universitäts buchhandlung, 2008, 275–315.

KAUNERT, C., 'The Area of Freedom, Security and Justice: The Contribution of a European Public Order', *European Security* 2005, 459–83.

KEIJZER, N. and VAN SLIEDREGT, E. (eds.), *The European Arrest Warrant in Practice*, The Hague: TMC Asser Press, 2009.

KLIP, A., 'Uniestrafrecht is op hol geslagen', *NJb* 1997, 663–70.

____, 'Amsterdams Uniestrafrecht. Beschouwingen over de internationaal strafrechtelijke samenwerking na het Verdrag van Amsterdam', *NJb* 1998, 811–16.

____, 'Harmonisierung des Strafrechts—eine fixe Idee?', *Neue Zeitschrift für Strafrecht* 2000, 626–30.

____, 'Grensoverschrijdende bescherming na voldoen transactie?', *SEW* 2004, 92.

____, 'Noot bij HR 25 mei 2004', *NJ* 2005, 243.

____, 'Recente rechtspraak strafrecht en Europese Unie', *DD* 2006, 1052–70.

____, 'Wederzijdse erkenning', *DD* 2008, 671–84.

____, 'Noot onder *Turansky* en *Bourquain*', *NJ* 2009, Afl. 45, 511.

____, 'Noot onder *Leymann* and *Pustovarov*', *NJ* 2009, 3920–2.

____, 'Overleveringsperikelen', *DD* 2010, 532–60.

____, *European Criminal Law. An Integrative Approach*, Antwerp: Intersentia, 2012.

____ and DANE, M., 'Improving Mutual Trust amongst European Union Member States in the areas of Police and Judicial Cooperation in Criminal Matters. Lessons from the Operation of Monitoring, Evaluation and Inventory Mechanisms in the First and Third Pillars of the European Union', Maastricht: WODC, 2009.

KNÖFEL, O.L., 'Judizielle Loyalität in der Europaïschen Union. Zur Rechts- und Beweishilfe im Verhältnis der Unionsgerichtbarkeit zu den Gerichten der Mitgliedstaaten', *EuR* 2010, 618–53.

KOMAREK, J., 'European Constitutionalism and the European Arrest Warrant: Contrapunctual Principles in Disharmony', Jean Monnet Working Paper 2006, retrievable at: <http://centers.law.nyu.edu/jeanmonnet/archive/papers/05/051001.pdf>.

KONSTADINIDES, T., 'The Perils of the "Europeanisation" of Extradition Procedures in the EU. Mutuality, Fundamental Rights and Constitutional Guarantees', *MJ* 2007, 179–201.

KOOIJMANS, T. and OUWERKERK, J.W., 'Het ontwerp-kaderbesluit betreffende het Europees surveillancebevel, de Nederlandse regeling van de voorlopige hechtenis en de overleveringsprocedure', *DD* 2008, 942–65.

KOUTRAKOS, P., 'Speeding up the Preliminary Reference Procedure—Fast but not too Fast', *E.L. Rev.* 2008, 617–18.

KOWALIK-BANEZYK, K., 'Should we Polish it Up? The Polish Constitutional Tribunal and the Idea of Supremacy of EU Law', 2005, retrievable at: <http://www.germanlawjournal.com>.

KRANIOTIS, T., 'Na uitlevering overgeleverd? Hoe dient de overleveringsrechter mensenrechtenverweren te beoordelen?', *AA* 2005, 344–51.

KURTOVIC, E. and LANGBROEK, P., 'Uitgeleverd aan overlevering? De Nederlandse overleveringspraktijk beschreven, gevolgd door een discussie over de effectuering van fundamentele rechten van verdachten en veroordeelden', *DD* 2010, 831–57.

LABAYLE, H., 'Entre désir et réalité: quelle voie pour une répression pénale des violations du droit communautaire?', *RMCUE* 2003, 293–303.

____, 'Le bilan du mandat de Tampere et l'espace de liberté, sécurité et justice de l'Union européenne', *C.D.E.* 2004, 595–656.

____, 'Architecte ou spectatrice? La Cour de justice de l'Union dans l'espace de liberté, sécurité et justice', *RTD. Eur.* 2006, 1–46.

____, 'Le juge de l'espace de liberté, sécurité et justice de l'Union européenne', in *Le dialogue des juges: mélanges en l'honneur du président Bruno Genevois*, Paris, Dalloz, 2009, 591–615.

____, 'Mandat d'arrêt européen et degré de protection des droits fondamentaux, quand la confiance se fait aveugle', March 2013, retrievable at: <http://www.gdr-elsj.eu/>.

LADENBURGER, C., 'Police and Criminal Law in the Treaty of Lisbon. A New Dimension for the Community Method', *EuConst* 2008, 20–40.

LAVENEX, S., 'Mutual Recognition and the Monopoly of Force: Limits of the Single Market Analogy', *JEPP* 2007, 762–79.

LECZYKIEWICK, D., 'Effective Judicial Protection of Human Rights After Lisbon: Should National Courts be Empowered to Review EU Secondary Law?', *E.L. Rev.* 2010, 326–48.

LENAERTS, K., 'The Contribution of the European Court of Justice to the Area of Freedom, Security and Justice', *ICLQ* 2010, 255–301.

____ and CORTHAUT, T., 'Of Birds and Hedges: the Role of Primacy in Invoking Norms of EU Law', *E.L. Rev.* 2006, 287–315.

____ and DE SMIJTER, E., 'The Charter and the Role of the European Courts', *MJ* 2001, 90–101.

LEURQUIN, X., BELLIS, J.-F., FAVART, M. and WEYEMBERGH, A. (eds.), *Actualités en droit européen et rappel de quelques principes*, Brussels: Bruylant, 2006.

LINDAHL, H., 'Finding a Place for Freedom, Security and Justice: the European Union's Claim to Territorial Unity', *E.L. Rev.* 2004, 461–84.

LJUNGQUIST, T., 'Mutual Recognition of Non-custodial Pre-trial Supervision Measures in the European Union', *International Review of Penal Law. The European Union Criminal Law* 2006, 169–77.

LÖÖF, R., '54 CISA and the Principles of ne bis in idem', *Eur. J. Crime Cr. L. Cr. J.* 2007, 309–34.

LÓPEZ ESCUDERO, M., 'El reconocimiento mutuo de sanciones pecuniarias en la Unión Europea', *Rev. Gen. Der. Eur.* 2006, No 10, 1–33.

LOZANO MANEIRO, A., 'Hacia una política penal común: posibilidades y obstáculos', *RDCE* 2001, 515–43.

LUCHTMAN, M., 'Choice of Forum in an Area of Freedom, Security and Justice', *Utrecht Law Review* 2011, 74–101.

MACKAREL, M., 'The European Arrest Warrant—The Early Years: Implementing and Using the Warrant', *Eur. Journ. Crime Cr.L.Cr.J.* 2007, 37–65.

MANACORDA, S., 'Judicial activism dans le cadre de l'Espace de liberté, de justice et de sécurité de l'Union européenne', *Revue de science criminelle et de droit pénal comparé* 2005, 940–51.

____, 'Le mandat d'arrêt européen et les décisions des Courts constitutionnelles', *Revue de science criminelle et de droit pénal comparé* 2005, 948–951.

____, 'L'exception à la double incrimination dans le mandat d'arrêt européen et le principe de légalité', *C.D.E.* 2007, 149–77.

MARCOS FRANCISCO, D., *Orden europea de detención y entrega*, Valencia: tirant lo blanch, 2008.

MARGUERY, T., 'La citoyenneté européenne joue -t- elle un rôle dans l'espace de liberté, de sécurité et de justice?', *C.D.E.* 2010, 387–423.

MARIN, L., 'The European Arrest Warrant and Domestic Legal Orders. Tensions between Mutual Recognition and Fundamental Rights: the Italian Case', *MJ* 2009, 473–92.

MARTIN, M. (ed.), *Crime, Rights and the EU: the Future of Police and Judicial Cooperation*, London: Justice, 2008.

MEEUSEN, J. and STRAETMANS, G. (eds.), *Politiële en justitiële strafrechtelijke samenwerking in de Europese Unie. Welk evenwicht tussen vrijheid, veiligheid en rechtvaardigheid?*, Antwerp: Intersentia, 2007.

MICHALKE, R., 'EU-Vertragskonformität des Rahmenbeschlusses über Europäischen Haftbefehl', *EuZW* 2007, 373–8.

MILITELLO, V., 'Der Alternativ-Entwurf Europäische Strafverfolgung: ein Januskopf', *ZStW* 2004, 436–44.

MITSILEGAS, V., 'Defining Organised Crime in the EU: the Limits of European Criminal Law in an Area of Freedom, Security and Justice', *E.L. Rev.* 2001, 565–81.

____, 'The Constitutional Implications of Mutual Recognition in Criminal Matters in the EU', *CML Rev.* 2006, 1277–311.

____, 'The Transformation of Criminal Law in the Area of Freedom, Security and Justice', *Y.E.L.* 2007, 2–31.

____, 'The Third Wave of Third Pillar Law: which Direction for EU Criminal Justice?', *E.L. Rev.* 2009, 523–60.

____, *EU Criminal Law*, Oxford: Hart Publishing, 2009.

____, 'The Limits of Mutual Trust in Europe's Area of Freedom, Security and Justice: From Automatic Inter-State Cooperation to the Slow Emergence of the Individual', *Y.E.L.* 2012, 319–72.

MONAR, J., 'Enlarging the Area of Freedom, Security and Justice. Problems of Diversity and EU Instruments and Strategies', *CYELS* 2001, 301–26.

____, 'La mise en œuvre de l'espace de liberté, de sécurité et de justice: un défi pour l'Union Européenne et pour les Etats membres', *Revue française d'administration publique* 2009, 15–34.

MONJAL, P.-Y., *Le mandat d'arrêt européen ou la confluence des droits*, Aix Marseille: Presses Universitaires, 2006.

MONVILLE, P., 'Le mandat d'arrêt européen: remise en cause du mécanisme de la simple remise', *JT Dr Eur.* 2003, 168–72.

MOREILLON, L. and WILLI-JAYET, A., *Coopération judiciaire pénale dans l'Union européenne*, Brussels: Bruylant, 2005.

MORENO CATENA, V. and ARROYO ZAPATERO, L. (eds.), *La prueba en el Espacio Europeo de Libertad, Seguridad y Justicia Penal*, Navarre: Aranzada, 2006.

MOS, M.R.B., 'Is het kaderbesluit betreffende het Europees bewijsverkrijgingsbevel doeltreffend?' *NTER* 2005, 191–6.

MÖSTL, M., 'Preconditions and Limits of Mutual Recognition', *CML Rev.* 2010, 405–36.

NALEWAJKO, P., *Grundsatz der gegenseitigen Anerkennung. Eckstein der justiziellen Zusammenarbeit in Strafsachen in der Europäischen Union?*, Berlin: Duncker & Humblot, 2010.

NARCISO DA CUNHA RODRIGUEZ, J., 'A propos du principe *ne bis in idem*—Un regard sur la jurisprudence de la Cour de justice des Communautés européennes', in *Une communauté de droit. Festschrift für Gil Carlos Rodriguez Iglesias*, Berlin: Berliner Wissenschaftsverlag, 2003, 165–77.

NESTLER, C., 'Europäisches Strafprozessrecht', *ZStW* 2004, 331–52.

NICHOLLS, C., MONTGOMERY, C., and KNOWLES, J.B., *The Law of Extradition and Mutual Assistance*, Oxford: Oxford University Press, 2007.

NILSSON, H., 'From Classical Judicial Cooperation to Mutual Recognition', *Revue Internationale de Droit Pénal. Le droit Pénal de l'Union Européenne* 2006, 53–8.

NUOTIO, K., 'Criminal Law of a Transnational Polity' in *Festschrift für Heike Jung zum 65. Geburtstag*, Baden-Baden: Nomos, 2007, 685–98.

O'KEEFFE, D., 'The Schengen Convention: A Suitable Model for European Integration?', *Y.E.L.* 1991, 185–219.

ORDOÑEZ SOLIS, D., 'El espacio judicial de libertad, seguridad y justicia en la Unión Europea', *R.E.P.* 2003, 447–83.

O'REILLY, P., 'The EEW Proposal: Keystone of Mutual Trust and Confidence or Treacherous Trojan Horse?', *JECL* 2006, 53–61.

____, 'The Exit of the Elephant from the European Arrest Warrant Parlour', *JECL* 2007, 23–30.

ORMAZABAL SÁNCHEZ, G., *Espacio penal y mutuo reconocimiento. Perspectiva alemana y española*, Madrid: Marcial Pons, 2006.

OUWERKERK, J., *Quid Pro Quo? A Comparative Law Perspective on the Mutual Recognition of Judicial Decisions in Criminal Matters*, Antwerp: Intersentia, 2011.

____, 'Case Note *Mantello*', *CML Rev.* 2011, 1687–702.

PACHE, E. (ed.), *Die Europäische Union: Ein Raum der Freiheit, Sicherheit und des Rechts?*, Baden-Baden: Nomos, 2005.

PATERSON, N. and VERMEULEN, G., 'Materiële detentiecondities en strafuitvoeringsrecht. Waarom resolute actie van de EU nu nodig is', *Panopticon* 2010, 47–52.

PEERS, S., 'Who's Judging the Watchmen? The Judicial System of the Area of Freedom, Security and Justice', *Y.E.L.* 1998, 337–414.

____, 'Criminal Suspects' Rights and EU Law', *ERA Forum* 2004, 520–33.

____, 'Mutual Recognition and Criminal Law in the European Union: Has the Council got it Wrong?', *CML Rev.* 2004, 5–36.

____, 'EU Criminal Law and the Treaty of Lisbon', *E.L. Rev.* 2008, 507–29.

____, *EU Justice and Home Affairs Law*, 3rd edn, Oxford: Oxford University Press, 2011.

____, 'Analysis Court of Justice: The *NS* and *ME* Opinions—The Death of "Mutual Trust"?', 2011, retrievable at: <http://www.statewatch.org/analyses/no-148-dublin-mutual-trust.pdf>.

____ and WARD, A. (eds.), *The European Union Charter of Fundamental Rights*, Oxford: Hart Publishing, 2004.

PEITEADO MARISCAL, P., *El reconocimiento mutuo de resoluciones penales definitivas en la Unión Europea*, Madrid: Colex, 2006.

PERRON, W., 'Sind die nationalen Grenzen des Strafrechts überwindbar?', *ZStW* 1997, 281–301.

PLACHTA, M., 'European Arrest Warrant: Revolution in Extradition?', *Eur.Journ. Crime Cr.L Cr.J.* 2003, 178–94.

PRADEL, J., CORSTENS, G.J.M. and VERMEULEN, G., *Droit pénal européen*, Paris: Dalloz, 2009.

PRECHAL, S., *Juridisch cement voor de Europese Unie*, Groningen: Europa Law Publishing, 2006.

PREVET, Ph., 'L'application du mandat d'arrêt européen', *C.D.E.* 2007, 695–731.

REESTMANS, J.H. and GOUDAPPEL, F.A.N.J., 'Het Verdrag van Lissabon en de Ruimte van Vrijheid, Veiligheid en Recht', *SEW* 2008, 441–5.

RIJKEN, C., 'Aftakeling van de derde pijler; reanimatie middels het Verdrag van Lissabon? Gevolgen voor harmonisatie van het materiële strafrecht binnen de EU', *SEW* 2008, 377–88.

____, 'Rebalancing Security and Justice: Protection of Fundamental Rights in Police and Judicial Cooperation in Criminal Matters', *CML Rev.* 2010, 1455–92.

ROHLFF, D., *Der Europäische Haftbefehl*, Frankfurt am Main: Peter Lang, 2003.

RÜBENSTAHL, M., '*Ne bis in idem*—einmal ist nicht zweimal', *E.L.R.* 2005, 221–7.

RYNGAERT, C., 'De niet-uitlevering van eigen onderdanen en het kaderbesluit betreffende het Europees aanhoudingsbevel: Belgische, Nederlandse en Duitse rechtspraak vergeleken', *R.W.* 2006, 886–91.

SAFFERLING, C., 'Europe as Transnational Law—A Criminal Law for Europe: Between National Heritage and Transnational Necessities', *German Law Journal* 2009, 1383–97.

SANFRUTOS CANO, 'Coopération policière et judiciaire en matière pénale. *Advocaten voor de Wereld*', *RDUE* 2007, 787–94.

____, 'Coopération policière et judiciaire en matière pénale. *Bourquain*', *RDUE* 2009, 122–6.

____, 'La jurisprudence de la Cour de justice et du Tribunal de première instance. Chronique des arrêts. Arrêt *Wolzenburg*', *RDUE* 2009, 787–94.

SARMIENTO, D., 'European Union: The European Arrest Warrant and the Quest for Constitutional Coherence', *IJCL* 2008, 171–83.

SATZGER, H., 'The Future of European Criminal Law between Harmonization, Mutual Recognition and Alternative Solutions', *JECL* 2006, 27–39.

____, 'Trends und Perspektiven einer europäischen Strafrechtspolitik', in *4th European Jurists' Forum*, Vienna: Mansche Verlags- und Universitätsbuchhandlung, 2008, 207–41.

SCHÜNEMANN, B., 'Europäischer Haftbefehl und EU-Verfassungsentwurf auf schiebener Ebene', *ZRP* 2003, 185–9.

____, 'Fortschritte und Fehltritte in der Strafrechtspflege der EU', *G.A.* 2004, 193–209.

____, 'Grundzüge eines Alternativ-Entwurfs zur europäischen Strafverfolgung', *ZStW* 2004, 376–99.

SHARPSTON, E and FERNANDEZ MARTIN, J.-M., 'Some Reflections on Schengen Free Movement Rights and the Principle of ne bis in *idem*', *CYELS* 2007–08, 413–48.

SIBONY, A.-L, 'Les avancées du traité de Lisbonne en matière de coopération judiciaire', *Revue de la Faculté de droit de l'Université de Liège* 2008, 249–63.

SIEBER, U., 'Die Zukunft des Europäischen Strafrechts', *ZStW* 2009, 1–67.

SKOURIS, V., 'Rechtsschutz im Raum der Freiheit, der Sicherheit und des Rechts', in *4th European Jurists' Forum*, Vienna: Mansche Verlags- und Universitätsbuchhandlung, 2008, 404–19.

SMEULERS, A. and DE VRIES, J., 'Het Europees aanhoudingsbevel: gerechtvaardigd vertrouwen?', *N.J.C.M. Bull.* 2003, 428–60.

SMITH, R., 'Old Wine in New Bottles: Human Rights, Legal Aid and the New Europe', *Justice Journal* 2005, <http://www.eurowarrant.net/documents/cms_eaw_id821_1_04%20Smith%20Old%20Wine%20in%20New%20Bottles.doc>.

SNACKEN, S. and VAN ZYL SMIT, D. (eds.), *Principles of European Prison Law and Policy*, Oxford: Oxford University Press, 2009.

SPAVENTA, E., 'Remembrance of Principles Lost: On Fundamental Rights, the Third Pillar and the Scope of Union Law', *YEL* 2006, 153–76.

SPENCER, J., 'The European Arrest Warrant', *CYELS* 2003–04, 201–17.

____, 'An Academic Critique of the EU Acquis in Relation to Trans-Border Evidence Gathering', *ERA Forum: Special Issue on European Evidence* 2005, 28–40.

____, 'Implementing the European Arrest Warrant: a Tale of How Not to Do it', *SLR* 2009, 184–202.

SPRONKEN, T., VERMEULEN, G., DE VOCHT, D., and VAN PUYENBROECK, L., *EU Procedural Rights in Criminal Proceedings*, Antwerp: Maklu, 2009.

STEIN, S., 'Ein Meilenstein für das europäische *ne bis in idem*', *NjW* 2003, 1162–4.

STESSENS, G., 'Het Europese aanhoudingsbevel', in *Internationale aspecten in de verschillende takken van het recht*, Brussels: Larcier, 2005, 337–89.

____, 'Het Europees aanhoudingsbevel en het wederzijds vertrouwen', in *De wet voorbij. Liber amicorum Luc Huybrechts*, DERUYCK, F., DE SWAEF, M., ROZIE, J., ROZIE, M., TRAEST, P., en VERSTRAETEN, R. (eds.), Antwerp: Intersentia, 2010, 369–98.

SULLIVAN, G., 'The European Arrest Warrant: Abuse of Process as a Bar to Extradition', *NJECL* 2009, 37–53.

SUOMINEN, A., *The Principle of Mutual Recognition in Cooperation in Criminal Matters. A Study of the Principle in Four Framework Decisions and in the Implementation Legislation in the Nordic Member States*, Antwerp: Intersentia, 2011.

SWART, A.H.J., 'Politie en justitie in de Europese unie', *Ars Aequi* 2001, 109–18.

____, *Een ware Europese rechtsruimte*, Deventer: Gouda Quint, 2001.

TOMBOY, C., 'Vers une meilleure connaissance des antécédents pénaux des personnes. Le casier judiciaire', *International Review of Penal Law. The European Union Criminal Law* 2006, 177–83.

TOSATO, G.L., 'Some Remarks on the Limits to Mutual Recognition of Judicial Decisions in Civil and Criminal Matters within the European Union', *Rivista di diritto internazionale privato e prozessale* 2003, 869–78.

TOWNSEND, A., 'Can the EU Deliver the Area of Freedom, Security and Justice?', retrievable at: <http://aei.pitt.edu/archive/00001804/01/EPIN_WP9.pdf>.

TRIANTAFYLLOU, D., 'The European Charter of Fundamental Rights and the "Rule of law": Restricting Fundamental Rights by Reference', *CML Rev.* 2002, 53–64.

TULKENS, F. and BOSLY, H.-D. (eds.), *La justice pénale et l'Europe*, Brussels: Bruylant, 1996, 540.

VAN BOCKEL, W.B., 'Coming of age: de ontwikkeling van het *ne bis in idem*-beginsel in de EU-rechtsorde', *NTER* 2010, 66–72.

____, *The ne bis in idem principle in EU Law*, AH Alphen aan den Rijn: Kluwer Law International, 2010.

VAN DEN WYNGAERT, C., 'L'espace judiciaire européen: Vers une fissure au sein du Conseil de l'Europe?', *Revue de droit pénal et de criminologie* 1981, 511–43.

____, 'Applying the European Convention on Human Rights to Extradition: Opening Pandora's Box?', *ICLQ* 1990, 757–79.

____ and STESSENS, G., 'The International *non bis in idem* Principle: Resolving some of the Unanswered Questions', *ICLQ* 1999, 779–804.

VANDER BEKEN, T., *Forumkeuze in het internationaal strafrecht. Verdeling van misdrijven met aanknopingspunten in meerdere staten*, Ghent: RUG, 1998–9.

VAN DER WILT, H., 'Harmonisatie van strafrecht in Europa: gewogen en te licht bevonden', *NJb.* 2002, 747–52.

VAN HOEK, A.A.H. and LUCHTMAN, MJJ.P., 'Transnational Cooperation in Criminal Matters and the Safeguarding of Human Rights', *Utrecht Law Review* 2005, 1–39.

VAN SLIEDREGT, E., SJÖCRONA, J.M., and ORIE, A.M.M. (eds.), *Handboek Internationaal Strafrecht. Schets van het Europese en Internationale Strafrecht*, Deventer: Kluwer, 2008.

VELDT-FOGLIA, M.I., 'Ruime uitleg van het ne bis in idem-beginsel in artikel 54 SUO. Geen tweede vervolging mogelijk indien verdachte met OM transactie is aangegaan', *NTER* 2003, 127–33.

VENNEMANN, N., 'The European Arrest Warrant and its Human Rights Implications', *ZaöRV* 2003, 103–21.

VERBRUGGEN, F., '(On)voorwaardelijke liefde? Strafrechtsstudie à *la bolognaise* in het Europa van de wederzijdse erkenning in strafzaken', *Lustrumboek 40 jaar Jura Falconis* 2005, 249–68.

VERMEULEN, G., 'Van Tampere tot Laken. Meer veiligheid ten koste van vrijheid en rechtvaardigheid?', *Panopticon* 2002, 1–6.

____, 'U vraagt, wij draaien... Europees aanhoudingsbevel leidt tot blinde overlevering verdachten en veroordeelden', *De Juristenkrant* 2003, No. 57, 3–4.

____, 'Over de toekomst van de Europese ruimte van vrijheid, veiligheid en rechtvaardigheid', *Panopticon* 2003, 200–12.

____, 'Het Europees bewijsverkrijgingsbevel en verder. Naar wederzijdse erkenning van onderzoeksmaatregelen en vrij verkeer van bewijs in de EU?', *Expertise en recht* 2010, 113–23.

____ and DE BONDT, W., *EULocs. The EU Level Offence Classification System*, Antwerp: Maklu, 2009.

____, ____, and VAN DAMME, Y., *EU Cross-border Gathering and Use of Evidence in Criminal Matters. Towards Mutual Recognition of Investigative Measures and Free Movement of Evidence?* Antwerp: Maklu, 2010.

____, VAN KALMTHOUT, A., PATERSON, N., KNAPEN, M., VERBEKE, P., and DE BONDT, W., *Cross-border Execution of Judgements Involving Deprivation of Liberty in the EU: Overcoming Legal and Practical Problems through Fanking Measures*, Antwerp: Maklu, 2011.

VERNIMMEN-VAN TIGGELEN, G., SURANO, L., and WEYEMBERGH, A. (eds.), *The Future of Mutual Recognition in Criminal Matters in the European Union*, Brussels: IEE, 2009.

VERVAELE, J. (ed.), *Compliance and Enforcement of European Community Law*, The Hague: Kluwer, 1999.

____, 'The Europeanization of Criminal Law and the Criminal Law Dimension of European Integration', 2005, retrievable at: <http://www.coleurop.be/content/studyprogrammes/law/studyprog/pdf/ResearchPaper_3_2005_Vervaele.pdf>.

____ (ed.), *European Evidence Warrant. Transnational Judicial Inquiries in the EU*, Antwerp: Intersentia, 2005.

____, 'European Criminal Law and General Principles of Union Law', 2005, retrievable at: <http://www.coleurop.be/content/studyprogrammes/law/studyprog/pdf/ResearchPaper_5_2005_Vervaele.pdf>.

____, 'The Transnational *ne bis in idem* Principle in the EU. Mutual Recognition and Equivalent Protection of Human Rights', *Utrecht Law Review* 2005, 100–18.

VITORINO, A., 'La Chartre des droits fondamentaux de l'Union européenne', *RDUE* 2001, 27–64.

VOGEL, J. (ed.), *Unifier le droit: le rêve impossible?*, Paris: Editions Panthéon Assas, 2001.

____, 'Abschaffung der Auslieferung?', *Juristenzeitung* 2001, 937–43.

____, 'Licht und Schatten im Alternativ-Entwurf Europäische Strafverfolgung', *ZStW* 2004, 400–23.

____, 'The European Integrated Criminal Justice System and its Constitutional Framework', *MJ* 2005, 125–47.

____ and SPENCER, J.R., 'Proportionality and the European Arrest Warrant', *C.L.R.* 2010, 474–82.

VON BOGDANDY, A., 'The European Union as a Human Rights Organization? Human Rights and the Core of the European Union', *CML Rev.* 2000, 1307–38

VON BUBNOFF, E., 'Aktuelle Fragen der Verfahrensabwicklung und Vereinfachung im Europäischen Auslieferungsverkehr aus deutsch-italienischer Sicht', *ZeuS* 1999, 393–413.

____, 'Schwerpunkte strafrechtlicher Harmonisierung in Europa unter Berücksichtigung der Orientierungsvorgaben aus der Grundrechtscharta 2000', *ZeuS* 2001, 167–93.

____, 'Institutionelle Kriminalitätsbekämpfung in der EU. Schritte auf dem Weg zu einem europäischen Ermittlungs- und Strafverfolgungsraum', *ZeuS* 2002, 185–236.

WALKER, N. (ed.), *Sovereignty in Transition*, Oxford: Hart Publishing, 2003.

____ (ed.), *Europe's Area of Freedom, Security and Justice*, Oxford: Oxford University Press, 2004.

WASMEISER, M., 'Stand und Perspektiven des EU-Strafrechts', *ZStW* 2004, 320–5.

____, 'The Principle of *ne bis in idem*', *Revue Internationale de Droit Pénal. Le droit pénal de l'Union européenne* 2006, 121–30.

WEIGEND, T., 'Strafrecht durch internationalen Vereinbarungen—Verlust an nationaler Strafrechtskultur?', *ZStW* 1993, 774–802.

____, 'Der Entwurf einer Europäischen Verfassung und das Strafrecht', *ZSt W* 2004, 275–303.

WERNER, I., *Grenzen und Möglichkeiten europäischer Strafrechtspflege*, Aachen: Shaker Verlage, 2002.

WEYEMBERGH, A., 'La coopération européenne en matière de justice et d'affaires européennes: vers un rééquilibrage du couple liberté-sécurité?', *RBDI* 2000, 612–639.

____, 'Droit pénal et reconnaissance mutuelle', *JT Dr Eur.* 2001, 193–201.

____, 'La coopération pénale européenne face au terrorisme: rupture ou continuité?', in *Le droit international face au terrorisme*, BANNELIER, K. CHRISTAKIS, T. CORTEN, O. and DELCOURT, B. (eds.), Paris: Editions Pedone, 2002, 279–95.

____, 'Le principe *ne bis in idem*: pierre d'achoppement de l'espace pénal européen?', *C.D.E.* 2004, 337–75.

____, *L'harmonisation des législations: condition de l'espace pénal européen et révélateur de ses tensions*, Brussels: IEE, 2004.

____, 'The Functions of Approximation of Penal Legislation within the European Union', *MJ* 2005, 149–71.

____, 'Approximation of Criminal Laws, the Constitutional Treaty and The Hague Programme', *CML Rev* 2005, 1567–97.

____, 'Deux ans de pratique du mandat d'arrêt européen', *JT Dr Eur.* 2006, 225–32.

____, 'Arrêts *IB* et *Mantello*: le mandat d'arrêt européen', *J.D.E.* 2011, 71–3.

____ and DE BIOLLEY, S. (eds.), *Comment évaluer le droit pénal européen?* Brussels: Editions de l'Université de Bruxelles, 2006.

WILLIAMS, C., 'The European Evidence Warrant: the Proposal of the European Commission', *ERA Forum: Special Issue on European Evidence* 2005, 17–27.

____, 'The European Evidence Warrant', *International Review of Penal Law. The European Union Criminal Law* 2006, 155–63.

WOUTERS, J. and NAERT, F., 'Of Arrest Warrants, Terrorist Offences and Extradition Deals: an Appraisal of the EU's Main Criminal Law Measures against Terrorism after 11 September', *CML Rev.* 2004, 909–35.

YBARRA BORES, A., 'La implantación del principio de reconocimiento mutuo en el ámbito de las sanciones', 2006, retrievable at: <http://www.reei.org>.

ZIMMERMANN, F., 'Judicial Assistance and Equality of Arms—to what Extent can European Cooperation in Penal Matters Serve as a Model for the Reviewed Rome Statute?', in *The Review Conference and the Future of the international Criminal Court*, BURCHARD, C., TREIFFTERER, O., and VOGEL, J. (eds.), The Hague: Wolters Kluwer, 2010, 287–308.

Index